That THEIR WORDS May Be Used AGAINST THEM

Quotes from Evolutionists Useful for Creationists

COMPILED BY

Henry M. Morris

Institute for Creation Research
San Diego, CA
1997

First printing: December 1997

That Their Words May Be Used Against Them

Henry M. Morris
Copyright © 1997

Institute for Creation Research
P.O. Box 2667
El Cajon, California 92021

Master Books
P.O. Box 727
Green Forest, AR 72638

Library of Congress Catalog Card Number 97-75947
ISBN 0-89051-228-0

Cataloging in Publication Data

Morris, Henry Madison, 1918-
       That Their Words May Be Used Against Them

Printed in the United States of America

Foreword

One of the reasons why I became a creationist many years ago was the fact that I began reading books and articles written by evolutionists. Before that I had been what might be called a "Christian evolutionist," although I now agree with the humanists that that particular term is an oxymoron. Since Jesus Christ was certainly a creationist (in fact He was the *Creator*!), and since a Christian is presumably one who believes in the person, work and teachings of Christ, it now seems anomalous to try to believe in evolution while professing to be a follower of Christ.

Anyway, while serving as a young engineering instructor on the faculty of a secular university, and also trying to be a faculty advisor to a Christian student club on campus, it soon became obvious that the Bible, if taken literally, contradicted my rather naive acceptance of the evolutionism I had been taught in high school and college. This conflict became especially apparent when I tried to answer questions by students we were trying to reach for Christ. This was during World War II, and most of the students were naval trainees sent by the Navy to study science and engineering.

Accordingly, I began an intensive study of both the Bible and the literature on evolution in the university library—of which there was an abundance. Two important conclusions resulted from this study.

First, a verse-by-verse study of the entire Bible made it crystal clear that there was no way the Bible could legitimately be harmonized with evolutionary theory. Conversely, the Bible yielded numerous evidences of its own divine inspiration, and spoke accurately whenever it touched on real science, even containing many scientific insights that were not confirmed by actual scientific studies until thousands of years later.

Secondly, my reading in the evolutionary books and articles convinced me that evolutionism was nothing but a philosophical belief with no scientific proof whatever. The types of speculative evidences cited in this literature were in no way commensurate with the scientific data required in engineering design, for example. The "scientific method" so often mentioned in the scientific engineering literature stressed the necessity of actual study and measurement of observable systems and processes, with further replication and confirmation.

But evolutionism offered none of this. No real evolution from one kind to a different kind had ever been observed in all known history, and the supposed prehistoric record in the fossils yielded no true macro-evolutionary transitional series whatever—only a few questionable mosaics such as the oft-cited *Archaeopteryx*.

As much as anything, therefore, the evolutionary literature convinced me of the necessary truth of primeval special creation. This, of course, was also what I had found the Bible to teach.

That was over fifty years ago. Since that time I have continued to read very extensively the writings by evolutionists, and have also continued to study the Bible daily. And everything I have ever read, in both fields, continues to confirm ever more strongly the fact that the evolutionary philosophy is completely false. The universe and all its systems, particularly the many kinds of organisms on Earth, were supernaturally created by God.

In my subsequent writing and speaking on this seminal subject of origins, I have found it most useful to refer frequently to writings by evolutionists in showing the evidence for creation as opposed to evolution. Many of my books, as well as my lectures and debates, have been punctuated with rather extensive documentation from the statements of evolutionists.

Over these past fifty years, therefore, I have collected numerous quotes from evolutionists that were useful for this purpose. My son and successor, Dr. John Morris, along with various others, have been suggesting for some time now that others could find this collection useful too.

Whether or not such a compilation is a good idea remains to be seen, but I have finally done that in this volume, and am submitting it for whatever use other creationist writers and speakers might be able to make of it. The format consists of fifteen chapters, each divided into three sections, corresponding to a total of forty-five general topics covered by the quotations. Each of these sections begins with a brief description and summary of the significance of that particular topic to the creation/evolution issue. Then the quotes in each section are arranged alphabetically by authors.

Since the quotes cover a wide range of years, as well as subjects, they are not all up to date. However, the reader should find even the older ones fascinating and useful. To some degree, they illustrate the changes in evolutionary thought over the past fifty years or so. The great majority, of course, are fairly recent.

Almost all are quotes by evolutionists, and these people certainly were not writing with the intention of supporting creationism. This fact may elicit charges that some quotes are taken out of context, but I don't think any of them misrepresent in any way the intent of the writers when they wrote what they did. In any case, the reference is given, so readers can check it out for themselves if they wish.

All quotes are relatively brief, but I believe all are relevant to the creation/evolution question. We have tried to check the accuracy of them whenever possible, but with so many quotes (about 3,500), there may still be some inaccuracies. I hope—and believe—that these are few and inconsequential. I would appreciate it, of course, if anyone does find an error, if he would let me know, so it can be corrected in possible future printings.

Although most quotes are from evolutionists, I have included a few from creationists when they were particularly relevant to the subject. I believe the context will alert readers whenever this is the case.

Finally, I must acknowledge with real appreciation the valuable work of my daughter and secretary, Mrs. Mary Ruth Smith, who not only typed and organized the whole manuscript from my collection of quotes on index cards, but also checked their accuracy in so far as possible, spending much time in libraries for this purpose. Even though this is an unusual sort of book, we trust it will be of interest and value to at least a few key people.

Henry M. Morris

Table of Contents

Chapter 1

Origin and History of the Universe

A. Cosmic Evolution

The theory currently in vogue on the origin of the universe is the so-called "Big Bang" theory, according to which the cosmos suddenly came into existence, sometime between 8 and 20 billion years ago by a primordial explosion of an infinitesimal particle of "space/time," which then evolved into everything else. However, many evolutionary astronomers and cosmologists are now raising serious doubts about this theory, as indicated by the sampling of quotes shown below from their writings.

Alfvén, Hannes and Asoka Mendis, "Interpretation of Observed Cosmic Microwave Background Radiation," *Nature*, vol. 266 (April 21, 1977), pp. 698-699. At the time of writing these authors were in the Department of Physics at the University of California at San Diego.

p. 698   "The observed cosmic microwave background radiation, which has a high degree of spatial isopropy and which closely fits a 2.7K black body spectrum, is generally claimed to be the strongest piece of evidence in support of hot big bang cosmologies by its proponents."

p. 698   "The claim that this radiation lends strong support to hot big bang cosmologies is without foundation."

Anonymous, "Maybe They Are Faster than Light," *Science News*, vol. 112 (August 20, 1977), p. 120.

"One of the astrophysical conundrums that will not go away concerns the objects that appear to be expanding or splitting faster than the speed of light. . . . There are now four such objects, three quasars and a galaxy. They include nearly half of the strong, compact, very distant radio sources. That one is a galaxy precludes explaining away the apparent superluminal velocities as due to misinterpretation of the objects' distances."

Anonymous, "Cosmological Anomaly: A Trip You Can't Miss," *Science News*, vol. 116 (December 22/29, 1979), p. 421.

p. 421   "Proponents of big-bang theories of the origin of the universe have usually worked from the assumption that the universe at the moment of origin was isotropic and homogeneous. . . .

"The latest results of one of several groups of observers working on the question lead them to suggest a negative answer. Furthermore, they propose that there is a supercluster of galaxies in the constellation Virgo containing 30 to 40 percent more galaxies than might be expected to be in the volume of space they occupy, which stretches across 2 billion light years of the observable universe's total diameter of about 10 billion light years or one percent of the visible volume."

p. 421   ". . . there has not been enough time since the beginning for such an agglomeration to gather together out of an originally homogeneous universe.

Therefore the clump must have been present at the beginning, a lump in the leaven, so to speak."

p. 421 "If the evidence gets too strong that the beginning of the universe was more like chicken soup with dumplings than a smooth gruel, it could be disturbing to most cosmologists."

Anonymous, "Cosmological Stretch Marks," *Science News*, vol. 119 (May 1981), p. 254.

p. 254 "Cosmologists would like to believe that the universe is homogeneous and isotropic, that is, relatively smooth over-all and the same in all directions."

p. 254 "Our evidence for isotropy is the microwave radio radiation, the so-called 3K blackbody, that pervades space and seems to be a relic of the very beginning of time. It used to seem to be the same in all directions.

"Not any more. Five or six years ago we began to hear of a possible dipole anisotrophy. Then at the beginning of 1980 came hints of a quadrupole anisotropy. . . .

"A dipole anisotropy can be attributed to motion of the observer along a certain line. The background radiation is Doppler shifted before and behind and looks different there. A quadrupole anisotropy (difference in four directions at right angles to each other) has to belong to the substance of the radiation or the universe itself."

Anonymous, "The Smoothness of the Universe," *Science News*, vol. 125 (March 24, 1984), p. 187.

"The ordinary simple theory of the beginnings of the universe predicts a very smooth distribution of matter at the start. To provide for galaxies, however, it may be necessary to amend the simple theory and say that tiny fluctuations in the density of matter were present from the very beginning.

". . . Evidence of such density fluctuations would show up as small-scale fluctuations in the temperature of the blackbody.

". . . Maybe the theory will have to be amended some other way."

Anonymous, "Big-Bang Bias," *Scientific American*, vol. 254 (June 1986), pp. 66-67.

p. 66 "The big-bang theory of the universe holds that all galaxies are rushing uniformly away from one another as the result of a primordial explosion that took place 15 to 20 billion years ago. A group of American and British astronomers has suggested that the expansion may not be so uniform after all."

p. 67 "They found that galaxies in one hemisphere of the 350-million-light-year spherical volume are receding more slowly than galaxies in the other hemisphere. . . . In other words, the uniform expansion caused by the big bang is skewed by a net drift velocity of 700 kilometers per second."

Arp, H. C., G. Burbidge, F. Hoyle, J. V. Narlikar, and N. C. Wickramasinghe, "The Extragalactic Universe: An Alternative View," *Nature*, vol. 346 (August 30, 1990), pp. 807-812.

p. 809 "The microwave background has no imprints to mark the occurrence of such events, contradicting the theoretical expectations of a decade ago and causing theoreticians in recent years to search for variants of the Big Bang that avoid a confrontation with observation on this point. Our opinion is that avoiding confrontation with observation is not the hallmark of a good theory.

"The Big Bang model offers a Universe created in a smooth featureless condition, out of which a highly structured Universe is nevertheless supposed to have evolved. Numerous attempts have been made to explain how this miracle is supposed to have happened. They have two features in common, one a retreat into the highest flights of physics and the other an unsatisfactory absence of the immense detail that would be required to support them in a proper manner, from which we suspect the attempts to be little more than ingenious handwaving. Perhaps this is why they are called 'scenarios.'

"The root of the matter, it seems to us, is one of time-ordering. In the Big Bang model, the microwave background came first and the galaxies second, whereas the observations suggest (almost to the point of compelling) the opposite."

p. 810   "The commonsense inference from the planckian nature of the spectrum of the microwave background and from the smoothness of the background is that, so far as microwaves are concerned, we are living in a fog and that the fog is relatively local. A man who falls asleep on the top of a mountain and who wakes in a fog does not think he is looking at the origin of the Universe. He thinks he is in a fog."

p. 810   "We conclude this section by emphasizing that each of these arguments which was used in the debate some twenty years ago concerning the viability of the steady-state cosmology is still with us and on balance the steady-state model is favoured."

p. 810   "The above discussion clearly indicates that the present evidence does not warrant an implicit belief in the standard hot Big Bang picture."

p. 811   "It is commonly supposed that the so-called primordial abundances of D, ^{3}He, ^{4}He and ^{7}Li provide strong evidence for Big Bang cosmology. But a particular value for the baryon-to-photon ratio needs to be assumed *ad hoc* to obtain the required abundances. A theory in which results are obtained only through *ad hoc* assumptions can hardly be considered to acquire much merit thereby."

p. 812   "The conventional critic may argue that from the standpoint of economy of postulates the idea of 'many' creation events is a lot worse than the notion of the single creation (The Big Bang). We disagree. The 'many' events in our alternative theory are potentially observable and satisfy the repeatability criterion of physical theories. The Big Bang satisfies neither of these requirements, and hence as a scientific hypothesis fails to compete with the alternative proposed here.

"Cosmology is unique in science in that it is a very large intellectual edifice based on a very few facts."

Asimov, Isaac, "What is Beyond the Universe?" *Science Digest*, vol. 69 (April 1974), pp. 69-70.

p. 69   "Where did the substance of the universe come from? What is beyond the edge of the universe?

p. 69   "If 0 = (+ 1) + (- 1), then something which is 0 might just as well become +1 and -1. Perhaps in an infinite sea of nothingness, globs of positive and negative energy in equal-sized pairs are constantly forming, and after passing through evolutionary changes, combining once more and vanishing. We are in one of these globs in the period of time between nothing and nothing, and wondering about it."

Bludman, S. A., "Thermodynamics and the End of a Closed Universe," *Nature*, vol. 308 (March 22, 1984), pp. 319-322 Bludman was in the Department of Physics, University of Pennsylvania.

p. 319   "We show that, so far as present observations are concerned, the Universe may be open or closed, monotonically expanding or reversing. We then show . . . that even if the present expansion were to reverse, the Universe cannot bounce in the future, but must end in a 'final crunch.' . . . Finally, we show that if space is closed and the Universe began with low entropy, then it had to begin, not with a big bang, but with a non-singular tepid little bang."

p. 322   "We now appreciate that, because of the huge entropy generated in our Universe, far from oscillating, a closed universe can only go through one cycle of expansion and contraction. Whether closed or open, reversing or monotonically expanding, the severely irreversible phase transitions transpiring give the Universe a definite beginning, middle and end."

Burbidge, Geoffrey, "Why Only One Big Bang?" *Scientific American* (February 1992), p. 120.

p. 120   "Big Bang cosmology is probably as widely believed as has been any theory of the universe in the history of Western civilization. It rests, however, on many untested, and in some cases untestable, assumptions. Indeed, big bang cosmology has become a bandwagon of thought that reflects faith as much as objective truth."

p. 120   "This situation is particularly worrisome because there are good reasons to think the big bang model is seriously flawed."

p. 120   "Why then has the big bang become so deeply entrenched in modern thought? Everything evolves as a function of time except for the laws of physics. Hence, there are two immutables: the act of creation and the laws of physics, which spring forth fully fashioned from that act. The big bang ultimately reflects some cosmologists' search for creation and for a beginning. That search properly lies in the realm of metaphysics, not science."

Burbidge, Geoffrey, and Adelaide Hewitt, "A Catalog of Quasars Near and Far," *Sky and Telescope* (December 1994), pp. 32-34. Burbidge is Professor of Physics, UCSD.

p. 32   "Either QSOs come in an extremely wide range of intrinsic luminosities, as most people believe, or their redshifts do not indicate distance."

p. 33   "Thus for us the only conclusion that can be drawn is that at least some QSOs are relatively nearby, and that a large fraction of their redshift is due to something other than the expansion of the universe."

[QSO = Quasi-stellar object, or quasar]

Cherry, David, "Redshifts and the Spirit of Scientific Inquiry," *21st Century* (May/June 1989), pp. 34-43.

p. 35   "The central figure in the Redshift Controversy is Halton Arp, one of the world's finest astronomical observers, who was a staff astronomer at Palomar Observatory for many years and president of the Astronomical Society of the Pacific in the early 1980's."

p. 43   "Whatever else may be said about the impossible Big Bang cosmology, it would not be directly disproven by the existence of non-distance-related redshifts, since the phenomenon is compatible with an expanding universe; expansion itself does not imply Big Bang cosmology. What is at stake in the controversy is the limit of validity of the Hubble Law that relates an object's redshift and its distance.

"There is, however, a deeper reason for the rejection of Arp by the science establishment: his very method of work. He has been prepared to entertain hypotheses that were not merely deductions from currently accepted premises, hypotheses that might not be provable or disprovable within a short time.

"In 1983, Arp's observing time at Palomar Observatory was cut off, and a year later, his access to the Carnegie Institution telescope at Las Campanas, Chile, was cut off."

p. 44   "In a recent paper, Arp discussed his philosophical outlook. What if the overall functioning of the universe were more nearly biological in nature? he asks. Then our physical and our astronomical concepts would be very primitive.

"In the breadth and depth of his vision, Arp is far ahead of most scientists. It is the quality of thought embodied in work like his that is necessary to overturn the abomination of the Big Bang theory, a theory that denies God's continuing creation by defining the universe as dying. The entire future of science—and all that implies—depends on those who are humble enough to question the foundations of our knowledge and strong enough to propagate that questioning."

Chown, Marcus, "Giant Structure Spells Trouble for Cosmology," *New Scientist*, vol. 129 (February 23, 1991), p. 24.

p. 24   "The discovery of the largest known structure in the Universe could plunge cosmology into crisis. Theorists are going to find it extremely difficult to explain how a long band of quasars stretching hundreds of millions of light years across space could have formed so early in the life of the Universe."

p. 24   "'By rights,' he says, 'quasars should not cluster at all, but be spread quite randomly across the sky.'

Clowes says the discovery of the quasar band is 'another nail in the coffin of cold dark matter.'"

p. 24   "Cold dark matter seems unable to explain the structures astronomers observe on the largest scales in the Universe. Hot dark matter, the alternative, has already been ruled out by astronomers. Theorists would seem to have some serious thinking to do to resolve the problem."

Cowen, Ron, "Searching for Cosmology's Holy Grail," *Science News*, vol. 146 (October 8, 1994), pp. 232-234.

p. 232   "How old is the universe?

                 "After years of fractious debate, astronomers still don't know the answer. Some believe the universe is 10 billion years old, others argue that it's closer to 20 billion. At the center of the controversy lies a number that has obsessed astronomers for decades—the Hubble constant."

p. 232   "The trouble is, no one can agree on the size of this constant. At best, astronomers have pinned the number down to within a factor of 2. Based on conflicting sets of observations and personal prejudices, two camps have sprung up since the 1970s. Several groups of researchers, using different measurement methods, favor a high value for the Hubble constant. This suggests a relatively small, young universe—one that began its expansion about 10 billion years ago. Others argue for a low Hubble constant, implying a cosmos about twice as old."

p. 234   "That would make many theorists happy, because such an age doesn't conflict with the estimated age of globular clusters—dense groupings of stars in the Milky Way and other galaxies that appear to be about 16 billion years old."

Croswell, Ken, "The Constant Hubble War," *New Scientist*, vol. 137 (February 13, 1993), pp. 22-23.

p. 22   "The Hubble constant has a direct bearing on the age of the Universe because the faster it is expanding, the less time it must have taken to reach its present size since the big bang, and so the younger it must be. A high value—about 70—suggests the Universe is younger than its oldest stars, a logical contradiction that would destroy the big bang theory."

p. 22   "In the past five years, however, many younger and formerly uncommitted astronomers, using new techniques, have swung towards the 'high' side, supporting de Vaucouleurs."

pp. 22-23   "But how can both sides use 'reliable methods' to reach such widely different conclusions? And what constitutes a 'reliable method'? The Canadian astronomer Sidney van den Bergh frequently writes reviews that try to sort out the mess, and is aligned with neither side. One that he wrote last year began with a quote from Mark Twain: 'The researches of many commentators have already thrown much darkness on this subject, and it is probable that, if they continue, we shall soon know nothing at all about it.'"

Croswell, Ken, "Popular Theory of Cosmology is in Trouble," *New Scientist*, vol. 142 (April 16, 1994), p. 18.

p. 18   "The Universe probably has only a fraction of the mass needed to halt and reverse its expansion, say two astronomers in the U.S. Their finding strikes a blow at the popular inflation theory, which holds that the Universe will neither collapse nor expand forever but instead lies poised on the knife edge between the two."

p. 18   "'It seems to us that no successful MDM [mixed dark matter] model can or will be found,' they write. 'It may be that the observations are pushing us firmly towards a serious consideration of open models,' in which the Universe expands forever. If so, the Universe has less mass than inflation theory predicts, and the theory is wrong."

Crowe, Richard A. "Is Quantum Cosmology Science?" *Skeptical Inquirer* (March/April 1995), pp. 53-54. Crowe is Chairman of Physics and Astronomy, University of Hawaii.

p. 54   "What about the more speculative quantum genesis, which would have preceded the inflationary era? Let me start by saying that many people believe that everything in nature has to have a causal explanation. Although this may be true at the macroscopic level, it is not necessarily the case at the microscopic level, as quantum physics has demonstrated. Transitions, decays, and nuclear reactions do sometimes occur spontaneously without apparent cause. Similarly, the universe itself does not require a cause."

Darling, David, "On Creating Something from Nothing," *New Scientist*, vol. 151 (September 14, 1996).

p. 49   "What is a big deal—the biggest deal of all—is how you get something out of nothing.

     "Don't let the cosmologists try to kid you on this one. They have not got a clue either—despite the fact that they are doing a pretty good job of convincing themselves and others that this is really not a problem. 'In the beginning,' they will say, 'there was nothing—no time, space, matter or energy. Then there was a quantum fluctuation from which . . .' Whoa! Stop right there. You see what I mean? First there is nothing, then there is something. And the cosmologists try to bridge the two with a quantum flutter, a tremor of uncertainty that sparks it all off. Then they are away and before you know it, they have pulled a hundred billion galaxies out of their quantum hats."

p. 49   "You cannot fudge this by appealing to quantum mechanics. Either there is nothing to begin with, in which case there is no quantum vacuum, no pre-geometric dust, no time in which anything can happen, no physical laws that can effect a change from nothingness into somethingness; or there is something, in which case that needs explaining."

Davies, Paul C., "Universe in Reverse: Can Time Run Backwards?" *Second Look* (London: King's College, September 1979), pp. 26-28.

p. 27   "The greatest puzzle is where all the order in the universe came from originally. How did the cosmos get wound up, if the second law of thermodynamics predicts asymmetric unwinding towards disorder?"

p. 27   "There is good evidence that the primeval universe was not ordered, but highly chaotic: A relic of the primordial chaos survives in a curious radiation from space, believed to be the last fading remnant of the primeval heat, and the characteristics of its spectrum reveal that in the earliest moments of the universe the cosmological material was completely unstructured.

"To discover the cosmic winding mechanism, one has to investigate the processes that occurred between about one second and ten minutes after the bang. Unfortunately, the expansion is now too sluggish to have much invigorating effect, so the universe seems doomed to steadily unwind again until all organized activity ceases; the interesting and varied world of our experience will be systematically destroyed."

p. 27   "So far it has been supposed that the shuffling process . . . is *random*. But how do we know that the universe which emerged from the big bang was truly chaotic so that subsequent collisions between atoms and interactions between subatomic particles are overwhelmingly likely to disintegrate any order which may appear? If the miracle of the big bang included miraculously organized subatomic arrangements too, then random shuffling would have to be replaced by *organized* rearrangement.

"Such an idea might be called a cosmic conspiracy in which vast numbers of particles will some time in the future operate in concert to rearrange the world back to its former more ordered conditions, thereby causing time to run backwards."

Davies, Paul C., "What Hath COBE Wrought?" *Sky and Telescope* (January 1993), pp. 4-5.

p. 4   "When the Big Bang theory became popular in the 1950s many people used it to support the belief that the universe was created by God at some specific moment in the past. And some still regard the Big Bang as 'the creation'—a divine act to be left beyond the scope of science."

p. 4   "However, this sort of armchair theology is wide of the mark. The popular idea of a God who sets the universe going like a clockwork toy and then sits back to watch was ditched by the Church in the last century."

p. 4   "Quantum events do not need well-defined prior causes; they can be regarded as spontaneous fluctuations. It is then possible to imagine the universe coming into being from nothing entirely spontaneously, without violating any laws.

"Although quantum cosmology must be regarded as highly speculative, it does make some predictions. Remarkably, the data gleaned from COBE bear the hallmark of a quantum origin for the cosmos. It is therefore scientifically plausible to consider a universe with no need for an external creator in the traditional sense."

Davies, Paul C., *The Last Three Minutes* (London: Orion Books, 1994), 162 pp.

p. 45   "Life-giving carbon and oxygen, the gold in our banks, the lead sheeting on our roofs, the uranium fuel rods of our nuclear reactors—all owe their terrestrial presence to the death throes of stars that vanished well before our sun existed. It is an arresting thought that the very stuff of our bodies is composed of the nuclear ash of long-dead stars."

p. 118   "In this chapter and the last, I have tried to provide a glimpse of a universe slowing down but perhaps never quite running out of steam completely, of bizarre science-fiction creatures eking out an existence against odds that become stacked forever higher against them, testing their ingenuity against the inexorable logic of the second law of thermodynamics. The image of their desperate but not necessarily futile struggle for survival may exhilarate some readers and depress others. My own feelings are mixed."

p. 155   "If there is a purpose to the universe, and it achieves that purpose, then the universe must end, for its continued existence would be gratuitous and pointless. Conversely, if the universe endures forever, it is hard to imagine that there is any ultimate purpose to the universe at all. So cosmic death may be the price that has to be paid for cosmic success. Perhaps the most that we can hope for is that the purpose of the universe becomes known to our descendants before the end of the last three minutes."

de Vaucouleurs, G., "The Case for a Hierarchical Cosmology," *Science*, vol. 167 (February 27, 1970), pp. 1203-1213.

p. 1203   "Less than 50 years after the birth of what we are pleased to call 'modern cosmology,' when so few empirical facts are passably well established, when so many different over-simplified models of the universe are still competing for attention, is it, may we ask, really credible to claim, or even reasonable to hope, that we are presently close to a definitive solution of the cosmological problem?"

p. 1212   "It seems safe to conclude that a unique solution of the cosmological problem may still elude us for quite some time."

Dingle, Herbert, "Science and Modern Cosmology," *Science*, vol. 120 (October 1, 1954), pp. 513-521.

p. 515   "We are told that matter is being continually created, but in such a way that the process is imperceptible—that is, the statement cannot be disproved. When we ask why we should believe this, the answer is that the 'perfect cosmological principle' requires it. And when we ask why we should accept this 'principle,' the answer is that the fundamental axiom of science requires it. This we have seen to be false, and the only other answer that one can gather is that the 'principle' must be true because it seems fitting to the people who assert it. With all respect, I find this inadequate."

p. 519   "So far as I can judge, the authors of this new cosmology are primarily concerned about the great difficulty which must face all systems that contemplate a changing universe—namely, how can we conceive it to have begun? They are not content to leave this question unanswered until further knowledge comes; all problems must be solved now. Nor, for some reason, are they content to suppose that at some period in the distant past something happened that does not continually happen now. It seems to them better to suppose that there was no beginning and will be no ending to the material universe, and therefore, tacitly assuming that the universe must conform to their tastes, they declare that this must have been the case."

Dingle, Herbert, *Science at the Crossroads* (London: Martin, Brian and O'Keefe, 1972).

pp. 31-32   "In the language of mathematics we can tell lies as well as truths, and within the scope of mathematics itself there is no possible way of telling one from the other. We can distinguish them only by experience or by reasoning outside the mathematics, applied to the possible relation between the mathematical solution and its supposed physical correlate."

Dirac, P. A. M., "The Evolution of the Physicist's Picture of Nature," *Scientific American*, vol. 208 (May 1963), pp. 45-53. Dirac was Lucasian Professor of Mathematics at the University of Cambridge.

p. 53   "There is one other line along which one can still proceed by theoretical means. It seems to be one of the fundamental features of nature that fundamental physical laws are described in terms of a mathematical theory of great beauty and power, needing quite a high standard of mathematics for one to understand it. You may wonder: Why is nature constructed along these lines? One can only answer that our present knowledge seems to show that nature is so constructed. We simply have to accept it. One could perhaps describe the situation by saying that God is a mathematician of a very high order, and He used very advanced mathematics in constructing the universe. Our feeble attempts at mathematics enable us to understand a bit of the universe, and as we proceed to develop higher and higher mathematics we can hope to understand the universe better."

Guth, Alan H., "Cooking Up a Cosmos," *Astronomy*, vol. 25 (September 1997), pp. 54-57.

p. 54   "Since the big bang theory implies that the entire observed universe can evolve from a tiny speck, it's tempting to ask whether a universe can in principle be created in a laboratory. Given what we know of the laws of physics, would it be possible for an extraordinarily advanced civilization to create new universes at will?"

p. 54   "So, to produce a universe by the standard big-bang description, one must start with the energy of 10 billion universes!"

p. 54   "So, in the inflationary theory the universe evolves from essentially nothing at all, which is why I frequently refer to it as the ultimate free lunch."

Guth, Alan H., and Paul J. Steinhardt, "The Inflationary Universe," *Scientific American*, vol. 250 (May 1984), p. 116-128.

p. 128   "From a historical point of view probably the most revolutionary aspect of the inflationary model is the notion that all the matter and energy in the observable universe may have emerged from almost nothing."

p. 128   "The inflationary model of the universe provides a possible mechanism by which the observed universe could have evolved from an infinitesimal region. It is then tempting to go one step further and speculate that the entire universe evolved from literally nothing."

Hawking, Stephen W., "The Edge of Spacetime," *American Scientist*, vol. 72 (July/August 1984), pp. 355-359.

p. 355   "The Greek philosophers like Plato and Aristotle, on the other hand, did not like the thought of such direct divine intervention in the affairs of the world and so mostly preferred to believe that the universe had existed and would exist forever."

p. 357   "One could still imagine the universe being created by an external agent in a state corresponding to some time after the Big Bang, but it would not have any meaning to say that it was created *before* the Big Bang."

Hawking, Stephen W., *A Brief History of Time* (New York: Bantam Books, 1988), 198 pp.

p. *vii*   "I was again fortunate in that I chose theoretical physics, because that it is all in the mind. So my disability has not been a serious handicap."

p. *x*   "Hawking embarks on a quest to answer Einstein's famous question about whether God had any choice in creating the universe. Hawking is attempting, as he explicitly states, to understand the mind of God. And this makes all the more unexpected the conclusion of the effort, at least so far: a universe with no edge in space, no beginning or end in time, and nothing for a Creator to do."

p. 37   "Stars are so far away that they appear to us to be just pinpoints of light. We cannot see their size or shape. So how can we tell different types of stars apart? For the vast majority of stars, there is only one characteristic feature that we can observe—the color of their light."

p. 42   "Now at first sight, all of this evidence that the universe looks the same whichever direction we look in might seem to suggest there is something special about our place in the universe. In particular, it might seem that if we observe all other galaxies to be moving away from us, then we must be at the center of the universe. There is, however, an alternate explanation: the universe might look the same in every direction as seen from any other galaxy, too. This, as we have seen, was Friedmann's second assumption. We have no scientific evidence for, or against, this assumption. We believe it only on grounds of modesty: it would be most remarkable if the universe looked the same in every direction around us, but not around other points in the universe!"

p. 55   "We could still imagine that there is a set of laws that determines events completely for some supernatural being, who could observe the present state of the universe without disturbing it. However, such models of the universe are not of much interest to us ordinary mortals."

p. 102   "A precise statement of this idea is known as the second law of thermodynamics. It states that the entropy of an isolated system always increases, and that when two systems are joined together, the entropy of the combined system is greater than the sum of the entropies of the individual systems."

p. 116   "At the end of the conference the participants were granted an audience with the pope. He told us that it was all right to study the evolution of the universe after the big bang, but we should not inquire into the big bang itself because that was the moment of Creation and therefore the work of God. I was glad then that he did not know the subject of the talk I had just given at the conference—the possibility that space-time was finite but had no boundary, which means that it had no beginning, no moment of Creation."

p. 140   "With the success of scientific theories in describing events, most people have come to believe that God allows the universe to evolve according to a set of laws and does not intervene in the universe to break these laws. However, the laws do not tell us what the universe should have looked like when it started—it would still be up to God to wind up the clockwork and choose how to start it off. So long as the universe had a beginning, we could suppose it had a creator. But, if the universe is really completely self-contained, having no boundary or edge, it would have neither beginning nor end: it would simply be. What place, then, for a creator?"

Horgan, John, "Big-Bang Bashers," *Scientific American*, vol. 257 (September 1987), pp. 22-24.

p. 22   "Like the theory of evolution, the big-bang model has undergone modification and refinement, but it has resisted all serious challenges.

              "Nevertheless, ever since the theory won general acceptance about 20 years ago a few scientists have persistently attacked some of its fundamental assumptions. One group of critics argues that electromagnetic forces generated by plasma have been more important than gravity in shaping the universe; another asserts that red shifts are not necessarily a relic of the big bang's continuing outward thrust."

p. 22   "The elder statesman of the plasma dissidents is Hannes Alfvén of the Royal Institute of Technology in Stockholm. Alfvén, who won the Nobel prize for physics in 1970, believes interstellar space is filled with long filaments and other structures of plasma, that is, electrons and positively charged ions. The same electromagnetic forces that push plasmas into distinctive shapes in the laboratory, Alfvén says, caused this cosmic plasma to coalesce into galaxies, stars and planetary systems."

p. 22   "Although some plasma dissidents are also red-shift dissidents, the putative dean of the latter group, Halton C. Arp of the Mount Wilson and Las Campanas Observatories, says he does not share Alfvén's 'plasma approach.'"

p. 22   "Arp says he has observed many objects with red shifts that do not conform to the Hubble relation. He maintains that quasars, for example, whose large red shifts suggest they are the most distant objects in the universe, are actually no more distant than galaxies and are probably offshoots of them."

p. 24   "Theorists are particularly disturbed, Jeremiah P. Ostriker of Princeton University notes, by the growing evidence of large scale inhomogeneity in the universe's structure, which conflicts with the uniformity of the cosmic background radiation."

Horgan, John, "Universal Truths," *Scientific American*, vol. 263 (October 1990), pp. 108-117.

p. 117   "This kind of talk concerns [Neil] Turok, the young textures advocate. He fears that as observations reveal the universe in ever greater detail, cosmologists may resort to ever more complicated, jury-rigged models—like the one that Ptolemy devised to show how the sun and planets revolve around the earth. In that event Turok says, he may abandon cosmology for another field— condensed-matter physics, perhaps. 'Maybe the problems cosmology has set for itself will turn out to be just too difficult to solve scientifically,' he says. 'After all, we've got a lot of gall to suppose that the universe can be described by some simple theory.'"

p. 117   "[James] Peebles views the ongoing surge in observations as a source of joy, not despair. The observations may eliminate many theories, but eventually, given the abundance of talent and creativity in cosmology, they will spawn new theories with far more explanatory power. In the mean time cosmologists—and the rest of us—may have to forgo attempts at understanding the universe and simply marvel at its infinite complexity and strangeness."

Hoyle, Sir Fred, "The Big Bang under Attack," *Science Digest*, vol. 92 (May 1984), p. 84.

p. 84   "Was there ever really a big bang? Even as greater and greater numbers of people have come to believe that the universe began with one great eruption, others have seen a persistent weakness in the theory—a weakness that is becoming ever harder to overlook."

p. 84   "But in a single big bang there are no targets at all, because the whole universe takes part in the explosion. There is nothing for the expanding universe to hit against, and after sufficient expansion, the whole affair should go dead. However, we actually have a universe of continuing activity instead of one that is uniform and inert."

p. 84   "As a result of all this, the main efforts of investigators have been in papering over holes in the big bang theory, to build up an idea that has become ever more complex and cumbersome. . . .

"I have little hesitation in saying that a sickly pall now hangs over the big-bang theory. When a pattern of facts becomes set against a theory, experience shows that the theory rarely recovers."

Jeans, James, *The Universe Around Us* (New York: Cambridge University Press, 1969), 297 pp.

p. 56   "Even the nearest Capheids are so remote that it is difficult to determine their absolute distances with any great accuracy. . . .

"All large distances . . . in astronomical literature . . . subject to an error of perhaps 10 per cent, from this cause alone."

p. 61   "We now know that faintness arises from two causes [distance and absorbing matter in space], and it is not generally possible to apportion it accurately between the two."

p. 280   "Short of postulating some sort of action from outside the universe, whatever this may mean, the energy of the universe must continually lose availability. . . . Change can occur only in the one direction . . . With universes as with mortals, the only possible life is progress to the grave."

p. 283-4   "At the best, life must be limited to a tiny fraction of the universe."

Lerner, Eric J., "The Big Bang Never Happened," *Discover*, vol. 9 (June 1988), pp. 70-79.

p. 72   "In the past few years astronomers have discovered still larger clumps: huge aggregates of matter that span a billion light-years or more, stretching across a substantial fraction of the observable universe.

             "These observations conflict with all current versions of the Big Bang theory, which do not explain how a smooth explosion could have produced clumps of such size. Moreover, if such clumps exist, Einstein's equations do not require the universe to have once been confined to the head of a pin."

p. 72   "But there *is* an alternative to the Big Bang, one that isn't well known. It is an entirely different view of the nature and evolution of the universe. It is not based on general relativity because, unlike conventional astrophysics it does not see gravity as the dominant force in the cosmos. Starting from the observed fact that the universe, stars and all, is 99 percent plasma—ionized gas that can conduct electricity—the alternative cosmology holds that the universe is criss-crossed and sculpted by titanic electric currents and vast magnetic fields. In this electrically engineered plasma universe, the Big Bang never happened; instead the universe has existed for infinite time, without a beginning and with no end in sight.

             "The plasma universe is a vision created not by cosmologists or astrophysicists but by plasma physicists. Its intellectual progenitor is Hannes Alfvén, an 80-year old Swedish Nobel laureate."

p. 72   "Hannes Alfvén, a perennial iconoclast, has heard that sort of talk before. Underlying his dispute with Big Bang theorists, he points out, is a radical difference in scientific approach. 'I have always believed that astrophysics should be the extrapolation of laboratory physics,' he says. In contrast, astrophysicists try to derive their models mathematically from the laws of physics."

p. 76   "There is not enough visible matter in the universe to have generated the gravity needed to do the clumping in the 10 billion to 20 billion years since the Big Bang."

p. 76   "If the megaclumps are real—and the evidence suggests they are—there is a growing consensus that, as Silk put it, 'all the conventional dark-matter theories are in deep trouble.'"

p. 78   "But if there was no Big Bang, how and when did the universe begin? 'There is no rational reason to doubt that the universe has existed indefinitely, for an infinite time,' Alfvén replies. 'It is only a myth that attempts to say how the universe came into being either four thousand years ago or twenty billion years ago.'"

p. 79   "If Hannes Alfvén turns out to be right, Hutton's capsule summary of earth's history, 'No vestige of a beginning—no prospect of an end' will be an apt description of the universe itself."

Lerner, Eric J., "COBE Confounds the Cosmologists," *Aerospace America*, vol. 28 (March 1990), pp. 38-43.

p. 38   "Most cosmologists believe the universe came into being 15 or 20 billion years ago in a tremendous explosion they call the Big Bang."

p. 38   "Theorists hoped that these traces would be detected by the sensitive instruments of COBE (Cosmic Background Explorer), a satellite launched last November by NASA. To their surprise, however, the preliminary data from COBE, announced in January, show none of these hypothetical relics of past explosions. There now seems no way to reconcile the predictions of any version of the Big Bang with the reality of the universe that we observe, no way to get from the perfectly smooth Big Bang to the imperfect lumpy universe we see today. As one COBE scientist, George Smoot of the Univ. of California at Berkeley, put it, 'Using the forces we now know, you can't make the universe we now know.'"

Linde, André, "The Self-Reproducing Inflationary Universe," *Scientific American*, vol. 271 (November 1994), pp. 48-55.

p. 48   "The first, and main, problem is the very existence of the big bang. One may wonder, What came before? If space-time did not exist then, how could everything appear from nothing? What arose first: the universe or the laws determining its evolution? Explaining this initial singularity—where and when it all began—still remains the most intractable problem of modern cosmology."

p. 51   "The main difference between inflationary theory and the old cosmology becomes clear when one calculates the size of the universe at the end of inflation. Even if the universe at the beginning of inflation was as small as 10^{-33} centimeter, after 10^{-35} second of inflation this domain acquires an unbelievable size. According to some inflationary models, this size in centimeters can equal $10^{10^{12}}$—that is, a 1 followed by a trillion zeros. These numbers depend on the models used, but in most versions this size is many orders of magnitude greater than the size of the observable universe, or 10^{28} centimeters."

p. 54   "The inflationary theory itself changes as particle physics theory rapidly evolves. The list of new models includes extended inflation, natural inflation, hybrid inflation and many others. Each model has unique features that can be tested through observation or experiment. Most, however, are based on the idea of chaotic inflation."

p. 55   "From this perspective, inflation is not a part of the big bang theory, as we thought 15 years ago. On the contrary, the big bang is a part of the inflationary model."

p. 55   "The evolution of inflationary theory has given rise to a completely new cosmological paradigm, which differs considerably from the old big bang theory and even from the first versions of the inflationary scenario. In it the universe appears to be both chaotic and homogeneous, expanding and stationary. Our cosmic home grows, fluctuates and eternally reproduces itself in all possible forms, as if adjusting itself for all possible types of life that it can support."

Maddox, John, "Down with the Big Bang," *Nature*, vol. 340 (August 10, 1989), p. 425.

p. 425 "In all respects save that of convenience, this view of the origin of the Universe is thoroughly unsatisfactory."

p. 425 "It is unthinkable that the launch of the Hubble Space Telescope can be long delayed, and it is exceedingly improbable that the succeeding decade will allow the persistence of present views of how the Universe is constructed. The Big Bang itself is the pinnacle of a chain of inference which provides no explanation at present for quasars and the source of the known hidden mass in the Universe. It will be a surprise if it somehow survives the Hubble telescope."

Marshak, Robert E., "The Nuclear Force," *Scientific American*, vol. 202 (March 1960), pp. 99-114.

p. 99 "What holds the nucleus together? The problem remains one of the most challenging in physics, as it has been ever since Lord Rutherford discovered that the atom has a nucleus. Discussing the question in *Scientific American* six years ago [September 1953], Hans A. Bethe guessed that it had consumer 'more man-hours than have been given to any other scientific question in the history of mankind.' Since then the man-hours have continued to pile up, and considerable progress has been made."

McCrea, W. H., "Cosmology after Half a Century," *Science*, vol. 160 (June 21, 1968), p. 1295-1299.

p. 1298 "In 1873, J. C. Maxwell wrote: 'In the heavens we discover by their light . . . stars so distant that no material thing can ever have passed from one to another; and yet this light . . . tells us that each of them is built up of molecules of the same kinds that we find on earth. . . .

"No theory of evolution can be formed to account for the similarity of the molecules. . . . On the other hand, the exact equality of each molecule to all others of the same kind gives it . . . the essential character of its being eternal and self-existent.'

p. 1298 "So far as we know, the result is still the same as Maxwell inferred: all electrons are everywhere the same, all protons are the same, and so on. We should expect a sufficiently sophisticated theory to tell us why this is so."

Moon, Parry, and Domina Eberle Spencer, "Binary Stars and the Velocity of Light," *Journal of the Optical Society of America*, vol. 43, no. 8 (August 1953), pp. 635-641. Moon was at MIT, and Spencer was at the University of Connecticut.

p. 635 "*Abstract.* The acceptance of Riemannian space allows us to reject Einstein's relativity and to keep all the ordinary ideas of time and all the ideas of Euclidean space out to a distance of a few light years. Astronomical space remains Euclidean for material bodies, but light is considered to travel in Riemannian space. In this way the time required for light to reach us from the most distant stars is only 15 years."

p. 635 "The principle hypothesis of special relativity is that in free space the velocity of light is constant *with respect to the observer*, independent of motion of source or observer. This assumption is contrary to all human experience, and it can be included in the theory only by abolishing ordinary ideas and time.

"The alternative assumption is that the velocity of light is constant *with respect to the source*, as advocated in the 'emission theory' of Ritz. Apparently the only evidence in favor of the Einstein hypothesis is given by the behavior of binary stars. If the velocity of light is independent of the velocity of the stellar source, then the observed motion of the star in its orbit will be the true motion, except for the constant time interval required for light to travel from star to earth. On the other hand, if the velocity of the star and the velocity of light are additive, the apparent orbit will be distorted and the apparent stellar magnitude will vary."

p. 638   "We conclude, therefore, that the *data on visual binaries prove absolutely nothing about the constancy of the velocity of light.* Contrary to the statements of Bergmann and others, the Ritz hypothesis leads to no multiple images of visual binaries, nor does it predict multiple spectral lines for these stars."

p. 639   "In essence, therefore, the method of this paper leaves astronomical space unchanged but reduces the time required for light to travel from a star to the earth."

p. 641   "Since there is no reason for assuming that the velocity of light behaves like an ordinary velocity, the foregoing explanation seems to offer a simple and reasonable world picture that allows all of our ordinary ideas of local space and time to remain unchanged. Einstein's relativity is abandoned. Velocity of light in free space is always c with respect to the source, and has a value for the observer which depends on the relative velocity of source and observer. True Galilean relativity is preserved, as in Newtonian gravitation."

Narlikar, Jayant, "Was There a Big Bang?" *New Scientist*, vol. 91 (July 2, 1981), pp. 19-21.

p. 21   "These arguments should indicate to the uncommitted that the big-bang picture is not as soundly established, either theoretically or observationally, as it is usually claimed to be."

p. 21   "Astrophysicists of today who hold the view that 'the ultimate cosmological problem' has been more or less solved may well be in for a few surprises before this century runs out."

p. 21   "But the actual measured temperature of 3K is itself something of a mystery. . . .

"To astrophysicists, however, the observed energy density of the background radiation suggests other coincidences. This energy density is not too different to the energy densities observed in other astrophysical phenomena in the Universe, such as starlight, cosmic rays, galactic magnetic fields and so on. Does this mean that the microwave radiation also is of astrophysical origin and is not a relic of the big-bang?"

Narlikar, Jayant, "Challenge for the Big Bang," *New Scientist*, vol. 138 (June 19, 1993), pp. 27-30.

p. 27   "Questions of origin have always been the most difficult ones to answer. But perhaps the most fundamental of all questions concerns the origin of the Universe. Many astronomers and physicists today feel they have found the answer. They believe that the Universe was created at one instant in a hot explosion, called the big bang, and that the basic structure of matter was decided in the first billion-billion-billion-billionth part of a second (10^{-36} seconds). But this hypothesis has serious deficiencies, which the results from the satellite COBE have only served to highlight."

p. 28-29   "There are three major problems with the big bang model. First, as a theory of physics, it breaks a cardinal rule by violating the law of conservation of matter and energy. At the instant of the big bang the entire Universe is created in what is known as a singular event, or 'singularity.' Physics is believed to apply only after this instant. Secondly, the microwave background is believed to be the strongest evidence for the big bang. Yet such a fundamental feature of the radiation as its temperature cannot be deduced from any calculations of the early Universe. Its value is assumed.

"The third problem is that big bang cosmology is supposed to explain the origin of most light nuclei. But although it can with some success explain the formation of helium and deuterium, it runs into problems with other nuclei such as lithium, beryllium and boron. Even with deuterium it places such stringent upper limits on how much baryonic matter ('ordinary' matter, in the form of neutrons and protons) is allowed in the Universe that it forces astronomers to suggest that the 'dark' matter thought to make up most of the mass is in some exotic form. Furthermore, the most popular version of the big bang model, that involving inflation, implies a total age for the Universe that is uncomfortably small compared with the ages of our Galaxy of globular clusters and other galaxies.

"The knots into which big bang theorists have tied themselves in the post-COBE era convinced Fred Hoyle, Geoffrey Burbidge and myself that we should seriously explore an alternative theoretical framework for cosmology. In this framework, which we call 'quasi-steady state cosmology' (QSSC), matter and energy are created by routine methods of theoretical physics. Using the model, we can estimate correctly the present temperature of the microwave background, explain the formation of light nuclei in the right quantities without requiring non-baryonic dark matter, and avoid the 'age difficulty.'"

Oldershaw, Robert L., "The Continuing Case for a Hierarchical Cosmology," *Astrophysics and Space Science*, vol. 92 (May 1983), pp. 347-358 Oldershaw was at Dartmouth College.

p. 354   "Both the 'Big Bang' model and the theoretical side of elementary particle physics rely on numerous highly speculative assumptions. Extrapolating back and forth between the present state of the observable universe and an ultimate cosmological singularity involves an incredible amount of faith in the completeness of our physical knowledge."

p. 356   "The deviations from a simple black-body spectrum, the indications of anisotropy and the fact that the energy density of the microwave background is suspiciously close to that of other non-cosmological phenomena (such as the energy densities of starlight, cosmic ray particles and galactic magnetic fields) all serve to strengthen the hypothesis that this radiation also has a non-primordial astrophysical origin."

Oldershaw, Robert L., "What's Wrong with the New Physics?" *New Scientist*, vol. 128 (December 22/29, 1990), pp. 56-59.

p. 56   "During the past decade or so, two worrying trends have emerged in the two areas of physics that claim to explain the nature of everything—particle physics and cosmology. The first trend is that physicists are increasingly devising mathematically elegant hypotheses, which they say are 'compelling' but which nevertheless cannot be verified by experiments or observations. The second trend is that theorists are becoming reluctant to give up their elegant notions, preferring to modify the theory rather than discard it even when observations do not support it."

p. 57   "A lot of effort has been diverted into string theory yet it has not led to a single prediction.

"In addition to these well-known theories, there are many other hypotheses of the 'new physics' that suffer from a lack of testable predictions. Some that come to mind are the existence of 'hidden dimensions,' 'shadow matter,' 'wormholes' in space-time and the 'many worlds' interpretation of quantum mechanics."

p. 58   "The big bang cosmological model has several serious problems and the inflation hypothesis, which I mentioned before, was brought in to rescue it. When the original inflation model ran into contradictions, it was replaced by a modification called the 'new inflation.' When further problems arose, theorists postulated yet another version called 'extended inflation.' Some have even advocated adding a second inflationary period—'double inflation.'"

p. 59   "First, the big bang is treated as an unexplainable event without a cause. Secondly, the big bang could not explain convincingly how matter got organized into lumps (galaxies and clusters of galaxies). And thirdly, it did not predict that for the Universe to be held together in the way it is, more than 90 per cent of the Universe would have to be in the form of some strange, unknown dark form of matter."

p. 59   "Theorists also invented the concepts of inflation and cold dark matter to augment the big bang paradigm and keep it viable, but they too have come into increasing conflict with observations. In the light of all these problems, it is astounding that the big bang hypothesis is the only cosmological model that physicists have taken seriously."

Peratt, Anthony L., "Not with a Bang," *The Sciences* (January/February 1990), pp. 24-32. Peratt is a physicist at Los Alamos National Laboratory, New Mexico.

p. 24   "Cosmology has become much more sophisticated since the sixteenth century, but the medieval dodge still applies; by adding enough epicycles—or their modern *ad hoc* counterparts—it is always possible to 'force reality to take the shape of [the] model.'"

pp. 26-7   "By the end of the 1960s the big bang had become almost universally accepted, and it has now penetrated the popular consciousness so deeply that at times one forgets it is still just a theory.

"In spite of their many successes, proponents of the big bang have lately been forced to acknowledge a growing number of inconvenient observations, and older but still nagging difficulties with the model have refused to go away. In the past twenty years, for instance, astronomers have noticed numerous cosmological objects whose enormous red shifts may be intrinsic properties of the objects themselves; if the red shift is no longer a reliable demonstration of an expanding universe, the big bang model is left without the phenomenon it was invented to explain. Perhaps more important, some of the most prominent aftereffects of the explosion have been difficult to reconcile with the observation. For example, the motions and shapes of galaxies and clusters of galaxies cannot be explained by the action of gravity alone, as the big bang model seems to require. To save the basic gravitational mechanism of the big bang itself, astronomers have postulated a variety of exotic but invisible subatomic particles that could fill the interstellar and intergalactic voids with dark but massive amounts of matter."

p. 27   "Even this *ad hoc* dark matter, however, cannot account for the enormous superclusters of galaxies astronomers have charted in recent years. West German and American astronomers recently discovered a super supercluster nearly two and a half billion light-years long; to grow to such a scale under the force of gravity alone would have taken more than 100 billion years, five times longer than the big bang model allows. Furthermore, if the universe turns out to be clumpy on this scale, where is the large-scale uniformity presumed by the big bang? Even the smooth background of cosmic microwave radiation, whose detection was once taken as proof of the big bang, does not presuppose an explosive beginning."

pp. 31-2   "One criticism of the big bang, delivered from outside the plasma physics community, challenges the idea that the observed pattern of red shifts is evidence for the expansion of the universe. If the universe is expanding, a high red shift should indicate a greater distance from the Earth. But Halton C. Arp of the Max Planck Institute for Astrophysics in Garching, West Germany, has noted numerous objects in the past two decades whose red shifts do not seem to correlate with distance.

"Quasars, for instance, have such large red shifts that they would seem to be the most distant objects in the universe. But Arp and an independent observer, Jack W. Sulentic of the University of Alabama, have found that some quasars appear in the vicinity of nearby galaxies with much smaller red shifts. If quasars and the nearby galaxies are connected, the two objects could not be moving at greatly different speeds; more likely their red shifts—and possibly all red shifts—result from something other than a rapid retreat from the Earth. One possibility is that the quasars are shrinking; red shifts can be caused not only by receding objects but also by contracting or pinched ones. A third mechanism, proposed in 1987 by Emil Wolf of the University of Rochester and confirmed in laboratory experiments, is that certain forms of coherent light can shift as the light propagates through space."

Peterson, Ivars, "State of the Universe: If not with a Big Bang, Then What?" *Science News*, vol. 139 (April 13, 1991), pp. 232-235.

p. 232　　　　"This type of uniform expansion looks much the same from our own or any other galaxy. Although other galaxies are moving away from the Milky Way, they are also moving away from each other. That makes it practically impossible to define a center from which all motion emanates or to establish an edge beyond which the universe doesn't exist."

p. 235　　　　"The standard, hot Big Bang has many rivals: plasma cosmology, a steady-state universe, a cold Big Bang, chronometric theory, a universe modeled on fractal geometry. But none of these has inspired the degree of support now accorded the Big Bang."

Powell, Corey S., and Madhusree Mukerjee, "Cosmic Puffery," *Scientific American*, vol. 275 (September 1996), pp. 20, 22.

p. 20　　　　"When the *Cosmic Background Explorer* (COBE) satellite produced its first detailed measurements of the cosmic microwave background—the so-called echo of creation—cosmologists cheered. It was a proud moment in the age-old effort to understand our origins, taken as confirmation of the prevailing model of the big bang. Four years later, however, the pages of the *Astrophysical Journal* look much as they did before, full of contentious debate over the age of the universe, the nature of 'dark matter' and the ways that mysterious physical laws may have shaped the world around us."

p. 22　　　　"Such obliging flexibility engenders a disturbing sense that cosmological theory resembles an endlessly nested set of Matryoshka dolls. Each refinement of the big bang delves deeper into abstruse theory, which grows progressively harder to prove or disprove."

Puthoff, Harold, "Everything for Nothing," *New Scientist*, vol. 127 (July 28, 1990), pp. 52-55. Puthoff is a theoretical physicist at the Institute for Advanced Studies at Austin, Texas.

p. 55　　　　"And now to the biggest question of all, where did the Universe come from? Or, in modern terminology, what started the big bang? Could quantum fluctuations of empty space have something to do with this as well? Edward Tyron of the City University of New York thought so in 1973 when he proposed that our Universe may have originated as a fluctuation of the vacuum on a large scale, as 'simply one of those things which happen from time to time.' This idea was later refined and updated within the context of inflationary cosmology by Alexander Vilenkin of Tufts University, who proposed that the universe is created by quantum tunneling from literally nothing into the something we call the Universe. Although highly speculative, these models indicate that physicists find themselves turning again to the void and fluctuations therein for their answers."

Schilling, Govert, "Quasar Pairs: A Redshift Puzzle?" *Science*, vol. 274 (November 22, 1996), p. 1305.

　　　　"Halton Arp of the Max Planck Institute for Astrophysics in Garching, Germany, has spent more than 25 years asserting that quasars, objects most astronomers believe are at the far edges of the universe, are actually the companions of relatively nearby galaxies. If he is right, the implications would be as revolutionary as those of Galileo's claim, which supported the idea that the Earth orbits the sun just as Jupiter's moons orbit the planet. The astronomical ruler, called redshift, that places the quasars and the galaxies at very different distances would be in jeopardy—and so would many of cosmologists' basic beliefs about the universe. Astronomers have largely rejected Arp's claims, but now he is presenting his most systematic study of quasar-galaxy pairings yet."

Smith, Quentin, "Did the Big Bang Have a Cause?" *British Journal for the Philosophy of Science*, vol. 45 (June 1994), pp. 649-668.

p. 666   "Thus we reach a general conclusion: there is no *philosophy of big bang cosmology* that makes it reasonable to reject the fundamental thesis of *big bang cosmology*: that the universe began to exist without a cause."

Stenger, Victor L., "Was the Universe Created?" *Free Inquiry* (Summer 1987), pp. 26-30.

p. 26   "Only fundamentalist Christians who insist on a literal interpretation of the Bible refuse to accept the biological evidence for evolution. Most other churches, including the often dogmatic Catholic church, have by now quietly accepted the notion of evolution as a scientific fact. . . .

"But what will these churchmen and their flock say about the latest conclusion of physical cosmology, that *the universe is probably the result of a random quantum fluctuation in a spaceless, timeless void?* In other words, physicists are now claiming that the hundreds of billions of stars and galaxies, including the earth and humanity, are not conscious creations but an accident. There is no Creator, because *there was no creation.*

". . . But it is fair to say that *there is not a single shred of evidence that demands that we hypothesize that the universe was created,* and we can now at least provisionally understand how all we are and all we know could have come about *by chance.*"

p. 29   "So what had to happen to start the universe was the formation of an empty bubble of highly curved space-time. How did this bubble form? What *caused* it? Not everything requires a cause. It could have just happened spontaneously as one of the many linear combinations of universe that has the quantum numbers of the void."

p. 30   "Our universe is a very unlikely one, but it is the only one we have. And this unlikeliness of our universe is no argument for its having been planned.

". . . Much is still in the speculative stage, and I must admit that there are yet no known empirical or observational tests that can be used to test the idea of an accidental origin. . . . The burden of proof that there was and is a Grand Design rests with those seeking to demonstrate it.

". . . And when that happens, I doubt very much that this new picture of the creation will resemble the primitive mythological image of the Creation that has been carried down by the Judeo-Christian tradition."

Thomsen, Dietrick E., "Cosmology against the Grain," *Science News*, vol. 114 (August 26, 1978), pp. 138-141.

pp. 138-9   "Coincidence of prediction and observation made the big bang seem the most plausible of cosmological theories. From plausible it became predominant and then virtually an orthodoxy, . . . But now its decade of total dominance may be starting to close. Suddenly it seems new cosmological theories and new twists on old ones are coming up all over the place. All the ideas that the big bang seemed to have put to rest are back."

Thomsen, Dietrick E., "A Closed Universe May Be Axionomatic," *Science News*, vol. 125 (June 23, 1984), pp. 396-397.

p. 396   "Neutrinos used to be a prime candidate for the dark, unseen matter that is supposed to pervade the universe and decisively affect its shape and ultimate fate. But now, neutrinos won't do."

p. 396   "So for philosophical reasons [UCSB cosmologist Simon] White and others would like the universe to be marginally closed—slightly curved back on itself. (If it were strongly closed, sharply curved back on itself, we would know it, or we would never have arisen to see it). This condition also requires more matter than we see."

p. 396   "So it's back to the drawing board and a consideration of cold matter; axions, gravitons, photinos, maybe magnetic monopoles. These things are called cold because they do not follow the customary thermodynamics."

p. 397   "To get the cold matter to follow the distribution of the galaxies, one is driven to an over-all density that predicts an open universe. This, as White contends, is philosophically undesirable. So he raises the question whether the dark matter necessarily has to follow the distribution of galaxies. That question is also being raised by people who study the distribution of galaxies, and who find serious deviations, not just slight ones, from random and homogeneous distribution. The dark matter represents the overwhelming majority of the universe's mass (if the universe is marginally closed). Why should it necessarily follow the distribution of the small portion that glows in the dark?"

Thomsen, Dietrick E., "The Quantum Universe: A Zero-Point Fluctuation?" *Science News*, vol. 128 (August 3, 1985), pp. 72-74.

p. 72   "All this means that the universe could be a 'quantum mechanical fluctuation.' In quantum mechanics zero does not always remain zero. In a balanced situation, as this kind of thinking postulates for the universe, the positives and negatives can separate enough for some physical processes to occur for a fleeting time. Quantum mechanical fluctuations generally last for so short a time that measuring instruments cannot be sure they existed at all. If the universe is one, and we are living in the middle of it, it is a very interesting and paradoxical place to be. The fluctuation may last eons for us who are inside it, but hardly any time at all from an outside point of view, about which we know nothing."

p. 73   "Physics restricts itself to material causes and material effects. However, the Loyola discussion dealt with what could be the very first material cause and the very last material effects, and the participants had something of a difficult time keeping God out of it. 'Why is the universe so large?' asked Don N. Page of the Institute for Advanced Study in Princeton, N.J. 'To say that God created it is outside of physics.' In the next breath Page went on to quote the Bible about the initial condition of the universe: 'without form, and void.'"

Trefil, James, "The Accidental Universe," *Science Digest*, vol. 92 (June 1984), pp. 53-55, 100-101.

p. 54   "Our present understanding now leads us to the belief that sometime around 10^{-35} second the rate of expansion underwent a dramatic, albeit temporary, increase, to which we apply the term *inflation*. The physical processes that took place during the unification of the strong force with the others caused the universe to expand from a size much smaller than a single proton to something approximately the size of a grapefruit in about 10^{-35} second."

p. 101   "In this picture, the universe came into existence as a fluctuation in the quantum-mechanical vacuum. Such a hypothesis leads to a view of creation in which the entire universe is an accident. In Tyron's words, 'Our universe is simply one of those things which happen from time to time.'"

Tyron, Edward P., "What Made the World?" *New Scientist*, vol. 101 (March 8, 1984), pp. 14-16. Tyron is a Professor of Physics, Hunter College and CUNY.

p. 14   "In 1973, I proposed that our Universe had been created spontaneously from nothing (*ex nihilo*), as a result of established principles of physics. This proposal variously struck people as preposterous, enchanting, or both."

p. 15   "So my proposal of creation *ex nihilo* was accompanied by a prediction that our Universe is finite and hence 'closed.'"

p. 15   "So I conjectured that our Universe had its physical origin as a quantum fluctuation of some pre-existing true vacuum, or state of nothingness."

p. 16   "If cosmic inflation occurred, the questions posed earlier as challenges to creation *ex nihilo* find ready answers. The 'unnecessarily large size' of our Universe is a result of that early inflation. The original quantum fluctuation created only a 'microscopic universe' which, without inflation, would never have reached macroscopic (let alone cosmic) proportions. Inflation gave rise to the rapid expansion, and converted the initial microcosm into a cosmos. . . .

            "In this scenario, the 'hot big bang' was preceded by a 'cold big whoosh.'"

Waldrop, M. Mitchell, "Do-It-Yourself Universes," *Science*, vol. 235 (February 20, 1987), pp. 845-846.

p. 845   "And while their results suggest that creating a universe in the basement may be impossible, even in principle, they also suggest that spontaneous quantum dynamics on a microscopic scale may be doing what technology cannot; creating new universes all around us.

            "The analysis of universe formation starts from the idea of cosmic inflation, which was first proposed by Guth in 1980. According to modern grand unified theories of particle physics, he explains, the dynamics of certain quantum fields may have forced the universe to undergo a period of exponentially fast expansion within the first microsecond after the Big Bang. This hypothesis turns out to be an elegant way of explaining a number of cosmological observations, such as the remarkable homogeneity of the universe, and as a general outline, it is now widely accepted among cosmologists."

p. 846   "In other words, says Guth, new universes may be constantly coming into existence all around us, spontaneously and invisibly. And conversely, since quantum fluctuations are not restricted by Einstein's equations in the same way black holes are, it is entirely possible that our own universe came into existence this way."

Weisskopf, Victor F., "The Origin of the Universe," *American Scientist*, vol. 71 (September/October 1983), pp. 473-480. Weisskopf is Professor Emeritus & Former Head, Physics, MIT.

p. 474   "It should be emphasized that all discussions of the development of the cosmos are rather hypothetical, because it is very hard to make empirical observations regarding the totality of the universe, and therefore we do not know whether we have caught the real facts. No existing view of the development of the cosmos is completely satisfactory, and this includes the standard model, which leads to certain fundamental questions and problems."

p. 480   "If the density were exactly the critical one, the expansion would go on and on but would slow down asymptotically to zero without ever turning around. It seems that the actual density is very near to this critical value."

p. 480   "The theory of the inflationary universe is still beset with a number of difficulties."

p. 480   "The hypothesis of the periodic universe is not without its own problems. . . . It could well be that the entropy of the universe increases each time, in which case one again arrives at the problem of a real beginning: the first Primal Bang."

p. 480   "Indeed, the Judeo-Christian tradition describes the beginning of the world in a way that is surprisingly similar to the scientific model. Previously it seemed scientifically unsound to have light created before the sun. The present scientific view does indeed assume the early universe to be filled with various kinds of radiation long before the sun was created. The Bible says about the beginning: 'And God said, Let there be light, and there was light. And God saw the light, that it was good.'"

B. Origin of Stars and Galaxies

Students are often led to believe that there is a known evolutionary progression of the different varieties of stars and galaxies. This is nothing but mathematical computerized metaphysics, however, since the stars and galaxies have always looked the same as they do now, as far as human observation is concerned. The only exception is that of disintegrating stars (e.g., supernovas, meteorites), but seeing them breaking up tells us nothing about how they began. The supposed evolution of stars and galaxies is entirely hypothetical, and is never observed.

Anonymous, "The Supernova that Wasn't," *Science News*, vol. 146 (October 22, 1994), p. 265.

"Some 1,800 years ago, Chinese astronomers witnessed the sudden appearance of a brilliant 'guest star.' Scientists now widely regard this celestial event, carefully noted in an official history at the time, as the oldest supernova ever recorded. . . .

"But a new analysis of the historical record suggests the ancient Chinese didn't see a supernova explosion after all. Instead, two radioastronomers now argue, the December 7, 185, discovery was in fact a comet.

"Yi-Nan Chin of the University of Bonn in Germany and Yi-Long Huang of National Tsing Hua University in Hsinchu, Taiwan, base their assertion on a reinterpretation of a key passage in the *Houhanshu*, the official history of the Later Han dynasty. Their translation, detailed in the Sept. 29 *Nature*, differs significantly from that of several other scientists."

Burbidge, Geoffrey, and Adelaide Hewitt, "A Catalog of Quasars Near and Far," *Sky and Telescope* (December 1994), pp. 32-34.

p. 32   "This was an early sign that redshifts reliably indicate the distances of galaxies. For QSOs ['QSO' = 'Quasi-Stellar Object' = 'Quasar'], however, the diagram shows a wide scatter in apparent brightness at every redshift. In fact, there is little correlation of brightness to redshift at all! Either QSOs come in an extremely wide range of intrinsic luminosities, as most people believe, or their redshifts do not indicate distance."

p. 33   "Quite a number of bright QSOs lie close to relatively bright, nearby galaxies (nearer than several hundred million light-years) that have much lower redshifts. This statistical evidence, and signs of optical or radio connections between galaxy and QSO, lead us to conclude that they are physically associated. . . . Contrary to what you are often told, the statistical evidence for association is well documented and has held up since the first proper analysis of QSOs in the 3C catalog was made in 1971."

p. 33   "Thus for us the only conclusion that can be drawn is that at least some QSOs are relatively nearby, and that a large fraction of their redshift is due to something other than the expansion of the universe."

p. 34   "Why are QSOs so bright, and where does their energy come from? Even before the discovery of QSOs it had become clear that the energy released in known active galaxies cannot come from the normal slow, evolutionary process of hydrogen burning in stars."

p. 34   "In the 1960s astronomers concluded that the energy must be gravitational in origin—due to the falling together of matter—or else it must be created somehow *in situ*. Because the latter suggestion requires a modification of the general theory of relativity, almost everyone argued that the gravitational model should be explored in every detail before any consideration is given to what is called 'new physics.'

"Thus the gravitational-energy model has been developed into what is known as the black-hole accretion disk paradigm. It is believed that in the center of a galaxy a supermassive black hole is formed by evolutionary processes."

p. 34   "Recently there has been a revival of the old idea that violent stellar activity, such as cascades of supernovae, can explain at least the optical spectra."

Carr, Bernard, "Where is Population III," *Nature*, vol. 326 (April 30, 1987), pp. 829-830.

p. 829   "A recent paper by Cayrel adds an interesting twist to speculation on the whereabouts of those most elusive of astronomical objects, Population III stars. These are the stars of zero metallicity which must have formed before the Population I stars in galactic disks and Population II stars in galactic halos. The existence of such stars is inevitable because metals can be made only by stars themselves (unlike some of the lighter elements, such as helium and deuterium, which are produced through cosmological nucleosynthesis in the Big Bang). Thus, the first stars must have contained no metals at all. One might expect Population III stars to have the same sort of distribution of masses as stars forming today, in which case some should be small enough (smaller than 0.8 M. where M. is the mass of the Sun) still to be burning their nuclear fuel. The problem is that despite extensive searches, nobody has ever found a zero-metallicity star."

Frenk, Carlos, and Simon White, "More Missing Matter Mystery," *Nature*, vol. 317 (October 24, 1985), pp. 670-671.

p. 670   "The missing mass and galaxy formation were the subjects of two major conferences this summer. It may seem remarkable that a five-day symposium could be devoted to objects that have never been seen and whose mass is uncertain by 76 orders of magnitude."

p. 670   "Planet-like objects are not excluded, but . . . no good candidates have been found so far."

p. 671   "The realization that we still do not know what makes up most of the Universe has thrown astronomy off the track of normal science and into a crisis."

Gallagher, Jay and Jean Keppel, "Seven Mysteries of Galaxies," *Astronomy*, vol. 22 (March 1994), pp. 39-45.

p. 39   "Edwin Hubble discovered the basic nature of galaxies about 70 years ago. Now, in the 1990s we can still say that we are only on the verge of understanding how galaxies are born, how they work, and what roles they play in the universe at large."

p. 40   "A few billion years later, quasi-stellar objects, or QSOs had already formed. We see them today as the earliest sign-posts of galaxy-sized objects. But what happened in the time between the appearance of the cosmic background radiation and the first quasars? So far astronomers have no observations of this lengthy period."

p. 41   "The process by which galaxies clump together poses a significant mystery for astronomers."

p. 43   "Two main forms of galaxies exist—spherical balls of stars and spirals. (The much-dimmer dwarf galaxies exist in these forms too.) Astronomers have yet to explain this dichotomy between spherical and spiral structures."

p. 44   "Proving the existence of black holes continues to be one of the hot areas of astronomical research."

Gilmore, Gerry, "Radio-Dating the Galaxy," *Nature*, vol. 328 (July 9, 1987), p. 111.

p. 111   "The determination of the age of the Universe is one of the most important, but most difficult, problems in modern astronomy. In standard models, the age of the Universe depends primarily on the present rate of expansion (measured as the Hubble constant) and deceleration rate, which is determined by the total mass in the Universe."

p. 111   "At face value, Butcher's excellent data show no decay at all in the Th/Nd relative abundance. This implies a short age scale, with the oldest stars being no more than 12 Gyr, rather than 18 Gyr old. The absence of *any* change in the ratio is surprising, and suggests that careful consideration of the relative production histories of r- and s- process elements is necessary. If the conclusion is correct, however, the implications are profound. Not only is the currently accepted physics of stellar evolution incomplete, but the Universe may be substantially younger than presently believed."

Glanz, James, "Precocious Structures Found," *Science*, vol. 272 (June 14, 1996), p. 1590.

p. 1590   "To astronomers, the story of how structures formed in the universe is like a movie with most of the frames missing. They can view at least some of the first scene, 15 billion years ago, in the cosmic microwave background, which retains an imprint of the universe's primordial fluctuations in density. And they know the denouement in today's universe: great clusters, filaments, and walls of galaxies. Because of the difficulty of surveying galaxies billions of light-years away, however, the period in between is largely a blank. Now their best look yet at the missing footage has left them more puzzled than ever."

Hecht, Jeff, "Is the Universe Made of Froth?" *New Scientist*, vol. 109 (February 13, 1986), p. 25.

               "Observations from the Harvard-Smithsonian Astrophysical Observatory indicate that bright galaxies are distributed in space like liquid in a froth of soap bubbles. Sheets containing high concentrations of galaxies surround regions where no galaxies are visible.

               "These new results cast doubt on old ideas of how galaxies formed. Margaret Geller, a theorist in the Harvard team, says there is no completely satisfactory model to explain both the origin of galaxies and their distribution pattern. In models where gravity dominates, galaxies form, but not in the observed distribution. Explosions of massive objects—perhaps a billion years after the big bang at the birth of the Universe—could explain the distribution of galaxies, but not the observed uniformity of the cosmic background radiation."

Keel, William, "Before Galaxies were Galaxies," *Astronomy*, vol. 25 (July 1997), pp. 59-63. Keel is on the astronomy faculty at the University of Alabama.

p. 59   "Galaxies cause astronomers problems. They're lumpy. And yet the earliest light we can see in the universe is smooth. So how did the universe go from smooth to lumpy, and how did galaxies form?

"It's one of the great questions of modern astrophysics and cosmology. For many astronomers, searching for the answer has been like the Quest for the Holy Grail, with potential answers constantly receding from view just as they have approached what they thought was the end."

p. 60   "The hunt for primeval galaxies, loosely defined as galaxies forming their first important generation of stars, has been a long-running quest of Arthurian proportions—and, some argue, just as embellished with myth. If most large galaxies really formed during a single short period, they would have been loaded with brilliant, short-lived blue stars, making the galaxies correspondingly powerful. If this were so, the sky would be peppered with primeval galaxies at about 20th magnitude. But these galaxies are nowhere to be found."

p. 63   "Seeing galaxies form and evolve is most important, perhaps, not for the details, but as the ultimate signal that ours is indeed an evolving universe."

Kirshner, Robert P., "The Earth's Elements," *Scientific American*, vol. 271 (October 1994), pp. 59-65.

p. 59   "Matter in the universe was born in violence. Hydrogen and helium emerged from the intense heat of the big bang some 15 billion years ago. More elaborate atoms of carbon, oxygen, calcium and iron, out of which we are made, had their origins in the burning depths of stars. Heavy elements such as uranium were synthesized in the shock waves of supernova explosions. The nuclear processes that created these ingredients of life took place in the most inhospitable of environments."

p. 59   "Even though the rug in most astronomy departments is lumpy from all the discrepancies that have been swept under it, a factor of 1,000 demands attention."

p. 65   "The composition of the earth is the natural by-product of energy generation in stars and successive waves of stellar birth and death in our galaxy. We do not know if other stars have earthlike planets where complex atoms, formed in stellar cauldrons, have organized themselves into intelligent systems."

Margon, Bruce, "The Missing Mass," *Mercury* (January/February 1975). Margon is a Research Astronomer, University of California, Berkeley.

p. 2   "Some clusters of galaxies contain over one thousand members, all in random motion with respect to each other. These random motions should have 'dispersed' the clusters long ago so that the galaxies should not be nearly as close together as we observe them to be. This dispersion is thought to be counterbalanced by the gravitational force of all the matter in the cluster. But observations indicate that only ten to twenty percent of the required mass is in the form of galaxies. The rest is unaccounted for and the understanding of this discrepancy is likely to alter some of our fundamental concepts of the universe."

p. 5   "Since the disruption time, i.e., the time for the cluster to dissipate given its known velocity dispersion, is much less than the current age of the Universe, and the cluster has not yet dissipated, this would mean that all the galaxies in the cluster must be very young.

"From everything we can see, these galaxies look old. They contain at least some stars identical to the very oldest stars in our own galaxy. Thus there seems to be no way that the Coma cluster can be younger than the Milky Way Galaxy."

p. 6   "Thus, we may wonder: does the Universe as a whole contain enough matter to gravitationally stop the overall expansion? If we total the matter we find in all observable galaxies and compare this mass with the measured expansion rate, the answer is that the Universe lacks sufficient material by a factor of about fifty to halt an apparently infinite expansion.

"Perhaps the gravitational force is not constant in time, or the redshift of spectral lines does not always indicate velocity of recession, or our understanding of stellar evolution is incorrect and the Universe abounds with young galaxies."

Parker, Barry, "Where Have all the Black Holes Gone?" *Astronomy*, vol. 22 (October 1994), pp. 36-39.

p. 39   "After three decades of study, astronomers are now relatively confident that this model is correct, but problems remain. The difficulties are in the details, not the overall model. A black hole would transform mass into energy at a rate 10 to 50 times more efficiently than a star would, but to do this the quasar, or active galaxy, would need a large supply of matter. How does it continue to pull in matter at such a tremendous rate over such a long period of time? Astronomers are not certain."

p. 39   "It is, indeed, strange that we have found so few black hole candidates. Still, Cyg X-1, LMC X-3, and A0620-00 are probably black holes, and it seems likely that some of the nearby galaxies contain black holes at their centers. The case for black holes in quasars and active galaxies seems strong and is definitely bolstered by the existence of a black hole in M87."

p. 39   "In June, Holland Ford and other astronomers using the Hubble Space Telescope found conclusive evidence for a massive black hole in the center of M87, a giant elliptical galaxy in the Virgo Cluster. The speed at which the galaxy's nuclear disk rotates, 500 km/sec, means the galaxy must have a mass of 3 billion suns in its center. The only suitable explanation for this much mass is a black hole. That brings the number of serious black hole candidates to four, the candidates for extragalactic black holes to one."

Patrusky, Ben, "Why is the Cosmos 'Lumpy'?" *Science–81* (June 1981), p. 96.

p. 96   "Few cosmologists today would dispute the view that our expanding universe began with a bang—a big, hot bang—about 18 billion years ago. Paradoxically, no cosmologist could now tell you how the Big Bang—the explosion of a superhot, superdense atom—ultimately gave rise to galaxies, stars, and other cosmic lumps.

"As one sky scientist, IBM's Philip E. Seiden, put it, 'The standard Big Bang model does not give rise to lumpiness. That model assumes the universe started out as a globally smooth, homogeneous expanding gas. If you apply the laws of physics to this model, you get a universe that is uniform, a cosmic vastness of evenly distributed atoms with no organization of any kind.'"

p. 96   "How then did the lumps get there? No one can say, at least not yet and perhaps not ever."

Peebles, P. James E., David N. Schramm, Edwin L. Turner, and Richard G. Kron, "The Evolution of the Universe," *Scientific American*, vol. 271 (October 1994), pp. 53-57.

p. 53   "Our universe may be viewed in many lights—by mystics, theologians, philosophers or scientists. In science we adopt the plodding route: we accept only what is tested by experiment or observation."

p. 57   "A pressing challenge now is to reconcile the apparent uniformity of the early universe with the lumpy distribution of galaxies in the present universe. Astronomers know that the density of the early universe did not vary by much, because they observe only slight irregularities in the cosmic background radiation."

Roth, Joshua, "Dating the Cosmos: A Progress Report," *Sky and Telescope*, vol. 94 (October 1997), pp. 42-46.

p. 44   "In principle trigonometric parallax is one of the simplest astronomical measurements, with little room for error or misinterpretation. But astronomers differ on how to correct their results for a host of effects, from the Hipparcos satellites' sensitivity limits to the reddening of starlight by intervening dust."

p. 45   "A Cepheid's pulsations are regulated in part by the opacity of its atmosphere; in turn, the opacity depends on the star's complement of heavy chemical elements, or 'metals.' As a result, two Cepheids with identical pulsation periods can have different intrinsic brightnesses, complicating their use as standard candles."

p. 46   "Nevertheless, there's no guarantee that tomorrow's three-dimensional models won't somehow change our understanding of stellar aging. Recent analyses have shaved one or two billion years from globular-cluster ages simply by modifying the way they accounted for convection in stellar atmosphere."

p. 46   "Taking stock of the universe's age, size, and speed remains very much a work in progress."

Thomsen, Dietrick E., "Astration and Galactic Evolution," *Science News*, vol. 110 (November 6, 1976), pp. 299-300.

p. 299   "So even though we cannot watch a galaxy evolve the way we watch a flower grow, the operative question is, not whether galaxies evolve, but how. How they form and how they change is one of the primary questions in astrophysics."

Thomsen, Dietrick E., "Hypersuperduper Galaxy Cluster," *Science News*, vol. 122 (December 18/25, 1982), p. 391

p. 391   "How big can an astronomical system be? Two astronomers, Riccardo Giovanelli of the Arecibo Observatory in Puerto Rico and Martha P. Haynes of the National Radio Astronomy Observatory in Green Bank, W. Va., suggest that there exists a huge supercluster of galaxies that stretches across the sky from horizon to horizon. They propose that two previously known superclusters, the Lynx-ursa Major distribution and Pisces-Perseus one, are joined to each other by a string of galaxies running across the so-called zone of avoidance, the part of the sky where visible light the sky where visible light is obscured by the dust in the plane of our own Milky Way galaxy. If they are right, the finding raises serious cosmological questions."

p. 391   "The cosmological question arises from cosmologists' habit of assuming that the universe is homogeneous. Homogeneity is known to be violated on the small scale by such things as galaxies and ordinary clusters, but cosmologists held out for a large-scale, over-all homogeneity. Now if a supercluster can extend halfway around the sky, there doesn't seem too much room left to look for homogeneity."

Waldrop, M. Mitchell, "Delving the Hole in Space," *Science*, vol. 214 (November 27, 1981), p. 1016.

p. 1016   "The recently announced 'hole in space,' a 300-million-light-year gap in the distribution of galaxies, has taken cosmologists by surprise—not because it exists but because it is so big.

"Smaller gaps are well known: when distant galaxies are plotted on a map in the sky, the result is a striking tangle of clumps and filaments and voids. Explaining how this structure arose out of the well-blended uniformity of the early universe is in fact one of the major unsolved problems of cosmology."

p. 1016   "But three [very deep core samples of the sky] in the Northern Hemisphere, lying in the general direction of the constellation Bootes, showed striking gaps in the red shift distribution. In each, the gaps extended from roughly 360 million to 540 million light-years; moreover, each showed a marked enhancement of galaxies on the inner and outer edges of the void."

p. 1016   "The largest previously known structure in the universe is the Serpens-Virgo supercluster, . . . It is about half the size of the recently found hole, and its excess of galaxies is of about the same magnitude as the apparent deficit in the hole."

Waldrop, M. Mitchell, "Are We All in the Grip of a Great Attractor?" *Science*, vol. 237 (September 11, 1987), pp. 1296-1297.

p. 1296   "In a patch of sky centered roughly on the Southern Cross, astronomers are finding increasing evidence for a 'Great Attractor,' an enormous accumulation of mass that is perturbing the motion of galaxies for hundreds of millions of light years in every direction."

p. 1297   "The uniformity of the 2.7 K microwave background radiation implies that the universe was quite homogeneous when the radiation was emitted, about 100,000 years after the Big Bang. And yet, as observers have mapped our present-day universe on larger and larger scales, they have continued to find that matter is clustered on larger and larger scales. The theorists have been having enough trouble trying to explain the formation of clusters and superclusters of galaxies. The existence of structure on the scale of the Great Attractor may only make the challenge that much tougher."

Weinberg, Steven, "Origins," *Science*, vol. 230 (October 4, 1985), pp. 15-18.

p. 15   "The brightest stars we see in the sky are close enough so that we see them now as they were only a few years ago, within our own lifetimes. Even the most distant objects that can be seen with the naked eye we see as they were a mere million years or so ago, when the universe and even Earth's inhabitants were pretty much the same as they are now."

p. 15 "It is one of the great disappointments of astrophysics that today, more than 20 years after the discovery of the remarkable properties of quasars, we still have no direct observational confirmation that the quasars actually are powered by black holes—it is just that no one can think of any equally plausible possibilities."

p. 16 "Among the most important relics are the structures we see in the sky: many stars are grouped into clusters, the clusters themselves along with loose stars like our sun are grouped into galaxies, and the galaxies themselves are grouped into clusters of galaxies. A second great disappointment of modern astrophysics has been that we still do not have a clear and detailed understanding of how these structures were formed. We do not even know whether the smaller structures formed first and then coalesced into the larger ones, or whether the larger structures formed first and then broke up into the smaller ones."

p. 16 "The theory of stellar evolution allows one to deduce the age and the initial composition of the stars in each cluster from the observed relation between these stars' colors and luminosities. The result is that these clusters are very old, much older than our own sun, indeed the oldest objects in our galaxy. In fact there seems to be a problem here—the oldest globular clusters appear to be about 15 to 20 billion years ago, older than the most popular estimates for the age of the universe, which centers on 10 billion years."

p. 16 "It is also a bit disturbing that all these estimates of the ages and compositions of the stars rest on elaborate calculations of what is going on inside them, but all that we observe is the light emitted from their surfaces."

p. 17 "For there is a scientific problem even more fundamental than the origin of the universe. We want to know the origin of the rules that have governed the universe and everything in it. Physicists, or at least some of us, believe that there is a simple set of laws of nature, of which all our complicated present physical and chemical laws are just mathematical consequences. We do not know these underlying laws, but as an act of faith if you like, we expect that eventually we will."

Windhorst, Roger A., as quoted in Corey S. Powell, "A Matter of Timing," *Scientific American* (October 1992), pp. 26-29. Windhorst is at Arizona State University.

p. 29 "Nobody really understands how star formation proceeds; it's really remarkable."

Wynn-Williams, Gareth, "The Newest Stars in Orion," *Scientific American*, vol. 245 (August 1981), pp. 46-55.

p. 46 "The more massive the star is, the faster it consumes its reserves of nuclear fuel. . . . Because of the brief lifetime Type O and Type B stars have little opportunity to stray far from their site of birth. . . .

"The constellation Orion abounds in stars of Types O and B. . . . The youngest of them, which are probably less than a million years old, lie in and around the glorious Orion Nebula, . . . The close connection between hot young stars and visible gas clouds is strong evidence for the hypothesis that new stars form by condensation out of the interstellar gas."

p. 55   "The discovery that at least some of the infrared sources once thought to be protostars are more probably very young, massive stars dramatically shedding mass has some important implications for the understanding of how new stars form. First of all, it means astronomers may have to start afresh for the precursors of typical main-sequence stars. Second, the wind from a large luminous star may have a strong influence, either positive or negative, on the creation of smaller stars, such as those resembling the sun. On the one hand, the wind could so badly disrupt the cloud surrounding it that further star formation would be impossible. On the other hand, the pressure of wind on the neighboring parts of the cloud could promote the collapse of further fragments. Third, if a strong wind is a feature of the early evolution of all stars, not just massive ones, it could adversely influence the formation of planetary systems."

Zimmerman, Robert, "Polaris, the Code-Blue Star," *Astronomy*, vol. 23 (March 1995), pp. 45-47.

p. 45   "Observers of the starry heavens have watched Cepheid variables dependably pulse in and out with exacting precision since John Goodricke first noticed the changing light of Delta Cephei in 1784. Their variability was, as Shakespeare so aptly put it, 'as constant as the northern star.' Undoubtedly, for those of us who crave dependability in our lives, Polaris has recently thrown a big monkey wrench into the predictability of Cepheid variables. As of 1994, the North Star ceased pulsating, transforming from a variable into a constant star, as constant now in light as it appears in position."

p. 46   "This cessation of a Cepheid's pulsation's, seems unique in the annals of astronomy. The only other star known to have ceased oscillating, RU Camelopardalis, did so in the middle 1960s, only to sputter back to life erratically in recent years."

p. 47   "As [Don Fernie, of the Dunlap Observatory at the University of Toronto] points out, 'There is as yet no adequate understanding of what sets the amplitude of a Cepheid.'"

C. The Impossible Solar System

There have been numerous theories in the past about the evolution of the sun, moon and planets. These have all been disproved, especially by the space program, and the best guess now is one of chaotic origins, since every planet and satellite is different from all others.

Anonymous, "Whence the Moon?" *Scientific American*, vol. 254 (June 1986), pp. 67, 69.

p. 67   "At times when close-up images of the moons of Uranus are shown on television one might think fundamental questions about the earth's own moon had been settled long ago. Far from it: it is not even clear how the moon formed. According to one theory, it is a piece of the earth's mantle that was spun off early in the planet's history; according to another, it formed in an independent orbit but was captured by the earth's gravity; still another holds that the moon and the earth accreted close together and simultaneously. Now a set of computer simulations lends support to a fourth mechanism: the impact on the earth of a planetary body a little larger than Mars."

p. 67   "Then there is the question of the moon's anomalous composition. Compared with the earth it is severely depleted in volatile chemical elements, a fact that none of the three theories accounts for well."

Bishop, Jerry E., "New Theories of Creation," *Science Digest*, vol. 72 (October 1972), pp. 40-44.

p. 41   "A. G. W. Cameron, a Goddard Institute lecturer and professor at Yeshiva University in New York, suggests that the creation of the solar system might have occurred in a matter of a few thousand years. Indeed, he suggests, it might have taken place so rapidly that the earth and some of the planets could have formed shortly before the sun did, —which, in view of traditional thought, is a revolutionary proposal."

p. 42   "To the surprise of scientists, the chemical makeup of the moon rocks is distinctly different from that of rocks on earth. This difference implies that the moon formed under different conditions, Prof. Cameron explains, and means that any theory on the origin of the planets now will have to create the moon and the earth in different ways."

Bondi, Herman, "Letters Section," *New Scientist* (August 21, 1980; quote by Karl Popper, reference to).

p. 611   "As an erstwhile cosmologist, I speak with feeling of the fact that theories of the origin of the Universe have been disproved by *present day empirical evidence*, as have various theories of the origin of the Solar System."

Boss, Alan P., "The Origin of the Moon," *Science*, vol. 231 (January 24, 1986), pp. 341-345.

p. 341   "The scientific justification for the Apollo missions to the moon was largely to determine how the moon originated. Sixteen years after the first Apollo landing, the theory of the formation of the terrestrial planets appears to have advanced sufficiently to provide an answer to the question of lunar formation. While many important details remain to be investigated, it now appears that the moon was formed after a giant impact of a roughly Mars-sized body on the protoearth. The impact injected a significant fraction of the mass of the impactor and the protoearth into geocentric orbit, where it later coagulated into the moon. Recent work has considerably strengthened the view that the older hypotheses of lunar origin (fission, capture, and binary accretion) are either physically impossible or extremely improbable."

p. 345   "Although we will never be able to state with absolute certainty that we know the origin of the moon, the giant impact hypothesis may well be the most probable one."

Drake, Michael J., "Geochemical Constraints on the Origin of the Moon," *Geochimica et Cosmochimica Acta*, vol. 47 (October 1983), pp. 1759-1767.

p. 1759   "Although it has been fourteen years since the first lunar samples were returned to Earth by the Apollo 11 Mission, the origin of the moon remains unresolved."

Gibbs, W. Wayt, and Corey S. Powell, "Bugs in the Data?" *Scientific American*, vol. 275 (October 1996), pp. 20-22.

p. 20   "Despite public enthusiasm about the conclusions, published in *Science*, many leading researchers who study meteorites and ancient life have weighed the evidence and found it unconvincing. 'There are nonbiological interpretations of McKay's data that are much more likely,' concludes Derek Sears, editor of the journal *Meteoritics and Planetary Science*."

Grady, Monica, Ian Wright, and Colin Pillinger, "Opening a Can of Worms," *Nature*, vol. 382 (August 15, 1996), pp. 575-576.

p. 575   "But each supporting thread can be regarded as weak. Even the premise that the meteorite comes from Mars is disputable."

p. 575   "Several reasons for caution on the microfossils came from William Schopf, at the NASA press conference: they are a hundred times smaller than any such fossils found on Earth, there is no measurement of the composition of the cells to show whether they are organic or not, and there is no sign of any cavities within the cells in which fluids necessary for life could reside. Some of the criteria used to identify microfossils in terrestrial rocks are present in ALH84001, but one is not: the carbonates that harbour the microfossils are found in igneous rock, rather than a sediment."

p. 576   "The leap from molecules to microfossils is an enormous one in terms of biological evolution, and there is probably not enough evidence yet for that leap's having been made on Mars."

Hecht, Jeff, "The Making of a Moon," *New Scientist*, vol. 155 (August 2, 1997), p. 8.

p. 8   "The leading theory of how the Moon formed is in trouble. A physicist announced this week that if it was born after a planet-sized body collided with the Earth in its youth, as many scientists assumed, the Earth and Moon should have far more angular momentum than they do today."

p. 8   "[Robin] Canup isn't about to abandon the giant impact theory because all the other theories 'have even more severe problems,' she says. But, she concedes, 'this does raise important questions.'"

Hughes, David W., "The Open Question in Selenology," review of *Origin of the Moon*, edited by W. K. Hartman, R. J. Phillips, and G. J. Taylor (Houston: Lunar and Planetary Institute, 1986, 781 pp.), *Nature*, vol. 327 (May 28, 1987), p. 291.

p. 291   "In astronomical terms, therefore, the Moon must be classed as a well-known object, but astronomers still have to admit shamefacedly that they have little idea as to where it came from. This is particularly embarrassing, because the solution of the mystery was billed as one of the main goals of the US lunar exploration programme."

p 291 "Twelve years after the last lunar landing was as good a time as any to hold a conference on the subject of selenology. The conference was organized by the Lunar and Planetary Sample Team and took place in Kona, Hawaii, in October 1984. Thirty three papers from the meeting are published in the volume under review, and in one way the reviewer's job is easy—the book cannot be compared with others on the subject because there are none."

p. 291 "It shows that scientific fashion wanders from theory to theory, all of which have good and bad points. At the moment co-accretion is retreating from favour and collision ejection is in the ascendent. But astronomy would be rather dull if we knew all the answers and it is clear from this book that 'Where did the Moon come from?' is still an open, exciting and challenging question."

Jeffreys, Sir Harold, *The Earth: Its Origin, History and Physical Constitution* (Cambridge, England: University Press, 1970), 525 pp. Jeffreys has long been one of the world's top planetary scientists.

p. 359 "To sum up, I think that all suggested accounts of the origin of the Solar System are subject to serious objections. The conclusion in the present state of the subject would be that the system cannot exist."

Jones, Sir Harold S., "The Origin of the Solar System," in *Physics and Chemistry of the Earth*, edited by L. H. Ahrens, Kalervo Rankana, and S. K. Runcorn (New York: McGraw-Hill, 1956).

p. 15 "The problem of formulating a satisfactory theory of the origin of the solar system is therefore still not solved."

Kerr, Richard A., "The Solar System's New Diversity," *Science*, vol. 265 (September 2, 1994), pp. 1360-1362.

p. 1360 "The solar system used to be a simple place. Before any spacecraft ventured forth from the Earth, Venus seemed likely to be a warmer, wetter version of Earth. Small, more-distant Mars seemed chillier and drier, though conceivably habitable. Little Mercury might resemble Earth's moon, only hotter. And the four giant planets—all big balls of gas—presumably were much alike, except that those farther from the sun had less energetic weather.

"But 30 years of planetary exploration have replaced that simple picture with a far more complex image. 'The most striking outcome of planetary exploration is the diversity of the planets,' says planetary physicist David Stevenson of the California Institute of Technology. Ross Taylor of the Australian National University agrees: 'If you look at all the planets and the 60 or so satellites, it's very hard to find two that are the same.'"

p. 1360 "Such discoveries are turning the field of comparative planetology on its head, as evidenced by a recent meeting where the focus was on planetary differences."

p. 1360 ". . . the challenge will be to understand how, as Stevenson puts it, 'you can start out with similar starting materials and end up with different planets.' Stevenson and others are puzzling out how subtle differences in starting conditions such as distance from the sun, along with chance events like giant impacts early in solar system history, can send planets down vastly different evolutionary paths."

Lawler, Andrew, "Finding Puts Mars Exploration on Front Burner," *Science*, vol. 273 (August 16, 1996), p. 865.

p. 865   "It is rare enough for a scientific discovery with no practical applications to draw an enthusiastic response from politicians, but it is almost unheard-of for House Speaker Newt Gingrich (R–GA) and U.S. Vice President Albert Gore to agree on the need for more government spending. The startling claim that a meteorite, consisting of a chunk of Mars rock, bears evidence of ancient life has provoked just such a reaction, however: Both political leaders told NASA Administrator Daniel Goldin separately in recent days that they are willing to find more money to beef up the agency's Mars exploration effort. If that happens, the first hints of extraterrestrial life could jump-start the struggling U.S. space science program."

Metz, William D., "Exploring the Solar System (II): Models of the Origin," *Science*, vol. 186 (November 29, 1974), pp. 814-818.

p. 814   "Speculations about the origin of the solar system have been proposed, modified, buried, and resurrected many times in the last three centuries. The best suggestion still seems to be the 'nebular hypothesis' of Laplace, who theorized that the solar system formed from the contraction of an interstellar cloud. But the laws of celestial mechanics, hydrodynamics, modern chemistry, and thermodynamics require that many steps take place before a diffuse cloud forms into a lumpy solar system with a few heavy planets."

p. 818   "Studies of the solar system seem to be at the point where, for the first time, knowledge of the compositions of various objects, particularly meteorites, can be used to put constraints on the movement of matter. Conversely, models of mass transport and accretion may soon be firm enough to put constraints on the chemistry. Judging from the diversity of assumptions, models, and predispositions among those hardy scientists who venture to try to outguess the course of evolution of the nebula that presumably predated us all, more constraint is precisely what is needed."

NASA, *Mars and Earth* (US GPO, NF-61, August 1975), 8 pp.

p. 1   "It is important to be aware that there is no one theory for the origin and subsequent evolution of the Solar System that is generally accepted. All theories represent models which fit some of the facts observed today, but not all."

p. 2   "There are striking differences among the five inner planets, and particularly between the Earth and the others."

p. 3   "Why then is the Earth so warm? The incoming sunlight is converted to infrared radiation by the Earth's surface, and because of the presence of carbon dioxide and water vapor in the Earth's atmosphere the infrared radiation is trapped in the atmosphere. The atmosphere behaves like the windows of a greenhouse, it allows the solar radiation in, but does not let the heat energy out."

p. 5   "Life might be described as an unexplained force that somehow organizes inanimate matter into a living system that perceives, reacts to, and evolves to cope with changes to the physical environment that threaten to destroy its organization."

p. 5   "We know from the Apollo program that it did not evolve on the Moon. There is no life there today, nor any trace of life having been there in the past. Mercury, too, looks most inhospitable to life, as does Venus."

p. 7   "The search for life on Mars is perhaps one of the most fascinating activities of mankind in this day and age. . . .

". . . Mankind may have to be prepared to accept a greater destiny than learning to live in harmony on its planet of birth. It may have to accept the responsibility of spreading living systems throughout the Solar System and into the cosmos.

"To search for life on Mars, it is necessary to put a lander on the Martian surface."

Taylor, Stuart Ross, "The Origin of the Moon," *American Scientist*, vol. 75 (September/October, 1987), pp. 469-477.

p. 473-4   "The major models for the origin of the moon can be grouped into five separate categories: capture from an independent orbit, fission from a rapidly rotating earth, formation with the earth as a double planet, disintegration and reaccretion of incoming planetesimals, and impact with the earth by a Mars-sized planetesimal. These are not all mutually exclusive; elements of some hypotheses occur in others."

p. 477   "Unique events are difficult to accommodate in most scientific disciplines. The solar system, however, is not uniform. All nine planets (even such apparent twins as the earth and Venus) and over 50 satellites are different in detail from one another. Bodies as massive as Mars existed during the accretional stages but have now disappeared. The planets all possess varying obliquities; the most extreme example is Uranus, lying on its side with its pole pointing toward the sun, probably the consequence of a collision with an earth-sized body. In contrast to the earth, Venus rotates slowly backward, has a low magnetic field, no oceans, a thick atmosphere mainly of carbon dioxide, and no moon. All this diversity makes the occurrence of single events more probable in the early stages of the history of the solar system. Thus a giant collision with the earth becomes a reasonable possibility for the origin of the moon."

Trimble, Virginia, "Origin of the Biologically Important Elements," *Origins of Life and Evolution of the Biosphere*, vol. 27 (June 1997), pp. 3-21. Trimble is with the Astronomy Department, University of Maryland, and with the Physics Department, University of California, Irvine.

p. 3   "Life on Earth is very complex, carbon-based chemistry. (Us reductionists would say *just* very complex, carbon based chemistry.) Would anything else do instead of carbon? Apparently not. . . ."

p. 3   "The next essential, and perhaps the limiting factor for life on any other earthlike planet, is water. That such a light substance as H_2O is a liquid at any reasonable temperature and pressure is remarkable in itself, but I will be concerned here only with the need for hydrogen and oxygen to make it. Nitrogen for proteins and DNA comes next, then perhaps phosphorus (often the least available vital element in fresh water ecologies, hence the extreme effects of phosphate-bearing detergents washed into them.)"

p. 17   "That is, no one knows how to calculate when a given gas cloud will turn into stars, how efficient the process will be, or how many stars of each mass will be formed."

pp. 19-20   "The round-trip travel time between us and the Galactic Center, 8500 parsecs away, is about 50,000 years for light and considerably longer for anything on non-zero rest mass. The problems of searching for extraterrestrial life and of establishing communication thus become very long term ones indeed. I have, of course, completely neglected the point that 'inhabited' may be a very different and less likely circumstance from 'habitable.' It is widely rumored that astronomers, physicists, and chemists are the optimists about origin of life (presumably because we do not understand the difficulties), while biologists are the pessimists. In fact, a wide divergence of opinion exists even within the life sciences community, from life as we know it as a one-shot affair to life as a cosmic imperative."

Walker, Gabrielle, "The Pegasi Planet that Never Was," *New Scientist*, vol. 153 (March 1, 1997), p. 15.

p. 15   "The hopes of planet-seekers have been dashed by a study claiming that the discovery in 1995 of a planet circling the Sun-like star 51 Pegasi was probably a false alarm.

"The 51 Pegasi planet was the first ever seen outside our Solar System. But a paper in this week's *Nature* by David Gray of the University of Western Ontario in Canada suggests that the 'planet' is really just a blip in the behavior of the parent star. 'The planet hypothesis fails for 51 Peg,' says Gray."

p. 15   "If Gray is right, several of the ten or so new planets 'discovered' since 51 Peg's could also be figments of stellar oscillations."

Chapter 2

Origin of Living Systems

A. Life from Non-Life

Evolutionists have come up with various proposals as to how life may have evolved from non-living chemicals. However, this is not happening now, and they have been utterly unable to synthesize life in the laboratory, so all such ideas are outside the scope of science. In this area, everything is speculation, and evolutionists are forced to assume that some imaginary primitive replicating molecule evolved by some unknown process in an imaginary primeval soup under assumed electrical phenomena in a non-existent ancient atmosphere. The quotes below illustrate the chaotic and controversial character of this quixotic subject.

Anonymous, "New Evidence on Evolution of Early Atmosphere and Life," *Bulletin of the American Meteorological Society*, vol. 63 (November 1982), pp. 1328-1330.

p. 1328   "Recent photochemical calculations by atmospheric researchers at Langley were presented at an international scientific conference last fall. They state that, at the time complex organic molecules (the precursors of living systems) were first formed from atmospheric gases the earth's atmosphere was not composed primarily of methane, ammonia and hydrogen as was previously supposed. Instead it was composed of carbon dioxide, nitrogen, and water vapor, all resulting from volcanic activity."

p. 1329   "Ultraviolet radiation on the earth from the young sun may have been up to 100,000 times greater than today."

p. 1329   "In the case of our calculated oxygen levels, one bit of evidence from the early geological record supports our conclusion. It was puzzling, but the geologists know from their analyses of the oldest known rocks that the oxygen level of the early atmosphere had to be much higher than previously calculated. Analyses of these rocks, estimated to be more than 3.5 billion years old, found oxidized iron in amounts that called for atmospheric oxygen levels to be at least 110 times greater and perhaps up to one billion times greater than otherwise accepted."

p. 1329   "How could life have formed and evolved in such a hostile environment? According to our calculations, there was virtually no ozone in the early atmosphere to protect against ultraviolet radiation levels that were much greater than they are today. It clearly should have affected the evolution of life on earth."

Anonymous, "Smaller Planets Began with Oxidized Atmosphere," *New Scientist* (July 10, 1980), p. 112.

"Although biologists concerned with the origin of life often quote an early atmosphere consisting of reduced gases, this stems as much from ignorance of recent advances as from active opposition to them. This important conclusion is reached by Ann Henderson-Sellers, of Liverpool University, and A. Benlow and Jack Meadows of Leicester University, after a study of how the composition of the atmosphere of the Earth and other planets may have influenced surface temperatures since the planets formed.

"... The more we have learnt about Venus and Mars the harder it is to explain how all three planets—two of them apparently lifeless—could have converted primeval reducing atmospheres into the oxidized atmospheres seen today."

p. 112   "The time has come, it seems, to accept as the new orthodoxy the idea of early oxidized atmospheres on all three terrestrial planets, and the biological primers which still tell of life on Earth starting out from a methane/ammonia atmosphere energized by electric storms and solar ultraviolet need to be rewritten."

Berry, Adrian, "Oldest Plants Breathe Chaos into Life Theory," *London Daily Telegraph* (June 2, 1990).

"The oldest plant life ever found has been discovered in the Western Australian outback. Resembling seaweed, it grew about 1,100 million years ago, compared with an age of 540 million years for the previously oldest-known plant.

"This discovery has thrown into confusion the history of how the earth's atmosphere evolved. Until the Cambrian Age began around 550 million years ago, the atmosphere was believed to have been without oxygen, a state in which only the most primitive single-celled creatures could exist.

"Dr. Chris Hill of the Natural History Museum in London, said yesterday: 'It appears from this new evidence that the build-up of oxygen in the Earth's atmosphere was a far longer process than we had previously thought.

"For such plants to have existed so long before the Cambrian Age, oxygen must have taken hundreds of millions of years to cover the planet.'"

Clemmey, Harry, and Nick Badham, "Oxygen in the Precambrian Atmosphere: An Evaluation of the Geological Evidence," *Geology*, vol. 10 (March 1982), pp. 141-146.

p. 141   "*Abstract*. Geologic evidence often presented in favor of an early anoxic atmosphere is both contentious and ambiguous. . . . Recent biological and interplanetary studies seem to favor an early oxidized atmosphere rich in CO_2 and possibly containing free molecular oxygen. The existence of early red beds, sea and groundwater sulphate, oxidized terrestrial and sea-floor weathering crusts, and the distribution of ferric iron in sedimentary rocks are geological observations and inferences compatible with the biological and planetary predictions. It is suggested that from the time of the earliest dated rocks at 3.7 b.y. ago, Earth had an oxygenic atmosphere."

p. 145   "For the past fifty years or more, speculation and experimentation have fueled the notion of an early Earth with an anoxic and possibly reducing atmosphere and coupled this to arguments concerning the origin of life. . . . General acceptance of this model has raised it to the level of dogma, and it permeates much of earth science thinking. However recent advances in many fields and new ideas on the origin of life have thrown serious doubts on the anoxic model and may have removed the need for it."

Cohen, Jon, "Getting All Turned Around Over the Origins of Life on Earth," *Science*, vol. 267 (March 3, 1995), pp. 1265-1266.

p. 1265   "Why do the sugar molecules in DNA and RNA twist to the right in all known organisms? Similarly, all of the amino acids from which proteins are formed twist to the left. The reason these molecules have such uniform handedness, or 'chirality,' is not known, but there is no shortage of theories on the subject. And, as was clear at a recent meeting on the topic in Los Angeles, there is also no shortage of passion, which is understandable, because the question of homochirality speaks to the mother of all scientific mysteries: the origin of life."

p. 1265   "The meeting participants did agree on one thing: Homochirality—the total predominance of one chiral form, or 'enantiomer'—is necessary for present-day life because the cellular machinery that has evolved to keep organisms alive and replicating, from microorganisms to humans, is built around the fact that genetic material veers right and amino acids veer left."

p. 1265   "One division came over a question that resembles the chicken-or-the-egg riddle: What came first, homochirality or life? Organic chemist William Bonner, professor emeritus at Stanford University, argued that homochirality must have preceded life."

p. 1265   "Bonner argued that homochirality is essential for life because without it, genetic material could not copy itself. Specifically, studies have shown that the two complementary strands of genetic material that make up DNA cannot bind with each other if they are in a 'racemic' mixture, a state in which there is an equilibrium of left-handed and right-handed enantiomers."

Dose, Professor Dr. Klaus, "The Origin of Life; More Questions than Answers," *Interdisciplinary Science Reviews*, vol. 13, no. 4 (1988), pp. 348-356. Dose is Director, Institute for Biochemistry, Johannes Gutenberg University, West Germany.

p. 348   "*Abstract*. More than 30 years of experimentation on the origin of life in the fields of chemical and molecular evolution have led to a better perception of the immensity of the problem of the origin of life on Earth rather than to its solution. At present all discussions on principal theories and experiments in the field either end in stalemate or in a confession of ignorance."

p. 348   "Considerable disagreements between scientists have arisen about detailed evolutionary steps. The problem is that the principal evolutionary processes from prebiotic molecules to progenotes have not been proven by experimentation and that the environmental conditions under which these processes occurred are not known. Moreover, we do not actually know where the genetic information of all living cells originates, how the first replicable polynucleotides (nucleic acids) evolved, or how the extremely complex structure-function relationships in modern cells came into existence."

p. 349   "It appears that the field has now reached a stage of stalemate, a stage in which hypothetical arguments often dominate over facts based on experimentation or observation."

p. 352   "In spite of many attempts, there have been no breakthroughs during the past 30 years to help to explain the origin of chirality in living cells."

Dyson, Freeman, "Honoring Dirac," *Science*, vol. 185 (September 27, 1974), pp. 1160-1161. Dyson was at the Institute for Advanced Study, Princeton, New Jersey.

p. 1161   "The problems of reconstructing possible pathways of prebiotic evolution in the absence of any kind of fossil evidence are indeed formidable. Successful attack on these problems will require, on the one hand, the boldness to imagine and create new concepts describing the organization of not-yet-living populations of molecules and, on the other hand, the humility to learn the hard way, by laborious experiment, which molecular pathways are consistent with the stubborn facts of chemistry. We are still at the very beginning of the quest for understanding of the origin of life. We do not yet have even a rough picture of the nature of the obstacles that prebiotic evolution has had to overcome. We do not have a well-defined set of criteria by which to judge whether any given theory of the origin of life is adequate."

Eigen, Manfred, William Gardiner, Peter Schuster, and Ruthild Winkler-Oswatitsch, "The Origin of Genetic Information," *Scientific American*, vol. 244 (April 1981), pp. 88-118.

p. 88   "It was therefore necessary for the first organizing principle to be highly selective from the start. It had to tolerate an enormous overburden of small molecules that were biologically 'wrong' but chemically possible."

pp. 88-89   "The primitive soup did face an energy crisis; early life forms needed somehow to extract chemical energy from the molecules in the soup. For the story we have to tell here it is not important how they did so; some system of energy storage and delivery based on phosphates can be assumed. Nonmetabolic replenishment of the phosphate energy reservoir . . . had to last until a mechanism evolved for fermenting some otherwise unneeded components of the soup."

p. 91   "One can safely assume that primordial routes of synthesis and differentiation provided minute concentrations of short sequences of nucleotides that would be recognized as 'correct' by the standards of today's biochemistry."

p. 91   "The primitive RNA strands that happened to have the right backbone and the right nucleotides had a second and crucial advantage. They alone were capable of stable self-replication. . . . Which came first, function or information? As we shall show, neither one could precede the other; they had to evolve together."

Gould, Stephen Jay, "An Early Start," *Natural History*, vol. 87 (February 1978), pp. 10-24.

p. 10   "Early in November, an announcement of the discovery of some fossil prokaryotes from South Africa pushed the antiquity of life back to 3.4 billion years."

p. 10   "If true monerans were alive 3.4 billion years ago, then the common ancestor of monerans and . . . 'methanogens' must be considerably more ancient. Since the oldest dated rocks, the Isua Supracrustals of West Greenland, are 3.8 billion years old, we are left with very little time between the development of suitable conditions for life on the earth's surface and the origin of life."

p. 24   "Life apparently arose about as soon as the earth became cool enough to support it."

p. 24   "Gradualism, the idea that all change must be smooth, slow, and steady, was never read from the rocks. It was primarily a prejudice of nineteenth-century liberalism facing a world in revolution. But it continues to color our supposedly objective reading of life's history."

p. 24   "The history of life, as I read it, is a series of long stable states, punctuated at rare intervals by major events that occur with great rapidity and set up the next stable era. . . . My favorite metaphor is a world of occasional pulses, driving recalcitrant systems from one stable state to the next."

Green, David E., and Robert F. Goldberger, *Molecular Insights into the Living Process* (New York: Academic Press, 1967), 420 pp.

p. 403   "The popular conception of primitive cells as the starting point for the origin of the species is really erroneous. There was nothing functionally primitive about such cells. They contained basically the same biochemical equipment as do their modern counterparts.

     "How, then, did the precursor cell arise? The only unequivocal rejoinder to this question is that we do not know."

pp. 406-7   "Although seven steps are shown, leading from atoms to ecosystems, there is one step that far outweighs the others in enormity: the step from macromolecules to cells. All the others can be accounted for on theoretical grounds—if not correctly, at least elegantly. However, the macromolecule-to-cell transition is a jump of fantastic dimensions, which lies beyond the range of testable hypothesis. In this area all is conjecture. The available facts do not provide a basis for postulating that cells arose on this planet."

Gribbin, John, "Carbon Dioxide, Ammonia—And Life," *New Scientist*, vol. 94 (May 13, 1982), pp. 413-416.

p. 413   "Pick up an encyclopedia and look up the section on the Earth's atmosphere. It will probably tell you that the primeval atmosphere of our planet was dominated by methane, and that this hydrogen-rich gas was necessary for the formation of the first complex organic molecules, the precursors of life. But an increasing number of geophysicists, biologists and climatologists would take issue with the encyclopedias on both these claims. These scientists would base their objections on modern evidence provided by other planets, by the effects of volcanic eruptions and other strands from a broad spectrum of scientific research."

p. 413   "This picture captured the popular imagination, and the story of life emerging in the seas or pools of a planet swathed in an atmosphere of methane and ammonia soon became part of the scientific folklore that 'every school child knows.'"

p. 416   "All we have to do now is rewrite all those textbooks and ensure that 'every school child knows' what the best theory of the evolution of the Earth's atmosphere and the origins of life is today: that life developed in the pools on the surface of a planet with carbon-dioxide atmosphere bearing only a trace of ammonia, perhaps itself the product of chemical reactions in the desert sands."

Haskins, Caryl P., "Advances and Challenges in Science in 1970," *American Scientist*, vol. 59 (May/June 1971), p. 298-307.

p. 305   "But the most sweeping evolutionary questions at the level of biochemical genetics are still unanswered. How the genetic code first appeared and then evolved and, earlier than that, how life itself originated on earth remain for the future to resolve, though dim and narrow pencils of illumination already play over them. The fact that in all organisms living today the processes both of replication of the DNA and of the effective translation of its code require highly precise enzymes and that, at the same time the molecular structures of those same enzymes are precisely specified by the DNA itself, poses a remarkable evolutionary mystery. . . . Did the code and the means of translating it appear simultaneously in evolution? It seems almost incredible that any such coincidence could have occurred, given the extraordinary complexities of both sides and the requirement that they be coordinated accurately for survival. By a pre-Darwinian (or a skeptic of evolution after Darwin) this puzzle would surely have been interpreted as the most powerful sort of evidence for special creation."

Hofstadter, Douglas R., *Gödel, Escher, Bach: An Eternal Golden Braid* (New York: Vintage Books, 1980), 777 pp.

p. 548   "A natural and fundamental question to ask on learning of these incredibly interlocking pieces of software and hardware is: 'How did they ever get started in the first place?' It is truly a baffling thing. One has to imagine some sort of a bootstrap process occurring, somewhat like that which is used in the development of new computer languages—but a bootstrap from simple molecules to entire cells is almost beyond one's power to imagine. There are various theories on the origin of life. They all run aground on this most central of all central questions: 'How did the Genetic Code, along with the mechanisms for its translation (ribosomes and RNA molecules), originate?' For the moment, we will have to content ourselves with a sense of wonder and awe, rather than with an answer. And perhaps, experiencing that sense of wonder and awe is more satisfying than having an answer—at least for a while."

Horgan, John, "In the Beginning," *Scientific American*, vol. 264 (February 1991), pp. 117-125.

p. 118   "None of these approaches has gained enough support to qualify as a new paradigm. On the other hand, none has been ruled out. That bothers Miller who is known as both a rigorous experimentalist and a bit of a curmudgeon. Some theories, he asserts, do not merit serious attention. He calls the organic-matter-from-space concept 'a loser,' the vent hypothesis 'garbage' and the pyrite theory 'paper chemistry.' Such work, he grumbles, perpetuates the reputation of the origin-of-life field as being on the fringe of science and not worthy of serious pursuit."

p. 119   "DNA cannot do its work, including forming more DNA, without the help of catalytic proteins, or enzymes. In short, proteins cannot form without DNA, but neither can DNA form without proteins."

p. 119   "But as researchers continue to examine the RNA-world concept closely, more problems emerge. How did RNA arise initially? RNA and its components are difficult to synthesize in a laboratory under the best of conditions, much less under plausible prebiotic ones."

p. 125   "About a decade ago Orgel and Crick managed to provoke the public and their colleagues by speculating that the seeds of life were sent to the earth in a spaceship by intelligent beings living on another planet. Orgel says the proposal, which is known as directed panspermia, was 'sort of a joke.'"

p. 125   "Miller, who after almost four decades is still in hard pursuit of life's biggest secret, agrees that the field needs a dramatic finding to constrain the rampant speculation."

p. 125   "Does he ever entertain the possibility that genesis was a miracle not reproducible by mere humans? Not at all, Miller replies. 'I think we just haven't learned the right tricks yet,' he says."

Jastrow, Robert, "What are the Chances for Life?" review of *The Biological Universe*, by Steven J. Dick (Cambridge: Cambridge University Press, 1996, 578 pp), *Sky and Telescope* (June 1997), pp. 62-63. Jastrow is Director of the Mount Wilson Institute.

pp. 62-63   "All these numbers are so small that, even when multiplied by the vast number of planets probably present in the universe, they force us to conclude that the Earth must be the only planet bearing life.

"But some astronomers argue that astrophysical findings on the cosmic distribution of the elements suggest a very different answer. They base their conclusion on the aptly named Principle of Mediocrity: The Earth is an ordinary planet, made of common materials that must be found in many solar systems. Why would the Earth alone—an undistinguished body among trillions of similar ones—be chosen by nature or the deity as the only planet on whose soil the seeds of life have taken root? They conclude that many—perhaps nearly all—Earth-like planets circling Sun-like stars bear life."

Kolata, Gina Bari, "Bacterial Genetics: Action at a Distance on DNA," *Science*, vol. 198 (October 7, 1977), pp. 41-42.

p. 42   "The apparent demonstration of action at a distance on bacterial DNA has profound implications for theories in molecular biology. . . . It indicates that mechanisms of control of gene expression may be more subtle than previously imagined. And it indicates that molecular biologists are still far from understanding how genes are regulated, even in bacteria—the simplest organisms to study."

Lawler, Andrew, "Building a Bridge between the Big Bang and Biology," *Science*, vol. 274 (November 8, 1996), p. 912.

p. 912   "In the segmented world of science, it is rare for cosmologists, planetary scientists, and microbiologists to find themselves in the same room. But last week researchers from a host of disciplines gathered in Washington to build a case for protecting and expanding work on the origins of the universe, planetary systems, and life itself. Their goal is to convince the Clinton Administration that further cuts to NASA's science budget will endanger efforts to understand how life emerged.

"The opportunity will come at a December symposium to be convened by Vice President Al Gore in the wake of a recent rash of dramatic findings, including evidence of planets circling other stars and possible fossil microbes on meteorites from Mars. The conference—which will be followed in January by a space summit between White House and congressional leaders—will give space scientists their best chance ever to escape from a severe funding squeeze."

p. 912   "For the most part, participants agreed that NASA's current priorities for space science are in tune with the search for origins."

p. 912   "For now, at least, the politicians say they are willing to listen. The unusual opportunity to make a case directly to Gore, and through him to the January space summit, flows from the August announcement of evidence of past life on Mars."

Maddox, John, "The Genesis Code by Numbers," *Nature*, vol. 367 (January 13, 1994), p. 111.

"It was already clear that the genetic code is not merely an abstraction but the embodiment of life's mechanisms; the consecutive triplets of nucleotides in DNA (called *codons*) are inherited but they also guide the construction of proteins.

"So it is disappointing that the origin of the genetic code is still as obscure as the origin of life itself."

Morowitz, Harold J., "The Six Million-Dollar Man," *Science News* (July 31, 1976), p. 73.

"High school textbooks used to make a big point about the materials that make up the human body being worth about 97 cents. Yale molecular biologist, Harold J. Morowitz . . . got out a biochemical company's catalog and added up the cost of the synthesized materials, such as hemoglobin . . . and came up with . . . a six million-dollar man ($6,000,015.44) to be exact).

"Professor Morowitz's calculations . . . drive home a more important point, however—that 'information is more expensive than matter.' What the biochemical companies offer is simply the highest 'informational' (most organized) state of materials commercially available. And even these are mostly taken from living animals; if synthesis of all the compounds offered had been done from basic elements, their cost might be as high as $6 billion.

"The logical extreme of the exercise, obviously, is that science is nowhere near getting close to synthesizing a human. Just to take the next step of organization—the organelle level—would cost perhaps $6 trillion."

Orgel, Leslie E., "Darwinism at the Very Beginning of Life," *New Scientist*, vol. 94 (April 15, 1982), pp. 149-152. Orgel is at UCSD, one of the top biochemists in the world and of special repute in origin-of-life studies.

p. 151 "We do not yet understand even the general features of the origin of the genetic code. . . . The origin of the genetic code is the most baffling aspect of the problem of the origins of life, and a major conceptual or experimental breakthrough may be needed before we can make any substantial progress."

p. 151 "Since the time of Louis Pasteur, the origin of optical activity in biological systems has attracted a great deal of attention. Two very different questions must be answered. First, why do all amino acids in proteins or all nucleotides in nucleic acids have the same handedness? Secondly, why are the animo acids all left-handed (L-) and the nucleotides all right-handed (D-)? We do not know the answer to either question, but we can make a number of plausible suggestions."

Orgel, Leslie E., "The Origin of Life on the Earth," *Scientific American*, vol. 271 (October 1994), pp. 77-83.

p. 78 "It is extremely improbable that proteins and nucleic acids, both of which are structurally complex, arose spontaneously in the same place at the same time. Yet it also seems impossible to have one without the other. And so, at first glance, one might have to conclude that life could never, in fact, have originated by chemical means."

p. 78 "We proposed that RNA might well have come first and established what is now called the RNA world. . . . This scenario could have occurred, we noted, if prebiotic RNA had two properties not evident today: a capacity to replicate without the help of proteins and an ability to catalyze every step of protein synthesis."

p. 83 "The precise events giving rise to the RNA world remain unclear. As we have seen, investigators have proposed many hypotheses, but evidence in favor of each of them is fragmentary at best. The full details of how the RNA world, and life, emerged may not be revealed in the near future."

Schmidt, Karen A., "Evolution in a Test Tube," *Science News*, vol. 144 (August 7, 1993), pp. 90-92.

p. 90 "Charles Darwin set off on a voyage in 1831 to study the exotic plants and animals of faraway places. Five years later, he returned with the discovery of a bittersweet truth about life: To leave a lasting legacy on Earth, an individual must wage a brute battle for survival and produce numerous off-spring."

p. 90 "This survival-of-the-fittest scenario takes place even at the level of molecules. On primordial Earth, chemicals with slight individual variations must have replicated themselves and competed with one another, scientists believe. The successful ones gave rise to the complex biological molecules that serve living organisms today."

p. 90 "In recent decades, researchers have hoped to harness the power of evolution to make new kinds of drugs and catalysts. Says Gerald F. Joyce, a chemist at

Scripps Research Institute in La Jolla, CA., 'People have been saying for a while, "Wouldn't it be nice to evolve our own molecules, as nature does?"'

"That dream is beginning to come true, now that scientists have developed the technological tools for staging molecular evolution in the lab."

Scott, Andrew, "Update on Genesis," *New Scientist*, vol. 106 (May 2, 1985), pp. 30-33.

p. 30   "Take some matter, heat while stirring and wait. That is the modern version of Genesis. The 'fundamental' forces of gravity, electromagnetism and the strong and weak nuclear forces are presumed to have done the rest. . . . But how much of this neat tale is firmly established, and how much remains hopeful speculation? In truth, the mechanism of almost every major step, from chemical precursors up to the first recognizable cells, is the subject of either controversy or complete bewilderment."

p. 31   "We are grappling with a classic 'chicken and egg' dilemma. Nucleic acids are required to make proteins, whereas proteins are needed to make nucleic acids and also to allow them to direct the process of protein manufacture itself."

p. 32   "The emergence of the gene-protein link, an absolutely vital stage on the way up from lifeless atoms to ourselves, is still shrouded in almost complete mystery."

p. 33   "In their more public pronouncements, researchers interested in the origin of life sometimes behave a bit like the creationist opponents they so despise— glossing over the great mysteries that remain unsolved and pretending they have firm answers that they have not really got. . . . We still know very little about how our genesis came about, and to provide a more satisfactory account than we have at present remains one of science's great challenges."

Taubes, Gary, "The Body Chaotic," *Discover*, vol. 10 (May 1989), pp. 63-67.

p. 67   "What is life: No one would accuse the new breed of mathematical biologists of setting their sights too low. They are aiming at nothing less than to understand the laws that control the behavior and organization of living organisms. Perhaps the best illustration of this ambitiousness is the research of Stuart Kauffman of the University of Pennsylvania School of Medicine."

p. 67   "The accepted theory of cell evolution says that each of the various cell types in the human body evolved through the rigors of Darwinian natural selection; that is, by conveying some competitive advantage on those of our evolutionary ancestors who had it.

"The implications of this result may be profound. If Kauffman is right, the human genome may be a self-organizing system, like his computer model: it may produce the range of human cell types on its own without benefit of natural selection. 'Organisms might have certain properties not because of selection,' he says, 'but because of the self-organizing properties of those systems on which the selection works.'"

Wald, George, in *Biological Science: An Inquiry Into Life* (Harcourt, Brace & World, Inc., 1963), 748 pp.

p. 42   "If life comes only from life, does this mean that there was *always* life on the earth? It must, yet we know that this cannot be so. We know that the world was once without life—that life appeared later. How? We think it was by spontaneous generation."

Wald, George, "Fitness in the Universe: Choices and Necessities," *Origins of Life*, vol. 5 (1974), pp. 7-27.

p. 26   "In this strange paper I have ventured to suggest that natural selection of a sort has extended even beyond the elements, to determine the properties of protons and electrons. Curious as that seems, it is a possibility worth weighing against the only alternative I can imagine, Eddington's suggestion that God is a mathematical physicist. It is the old biological problem of supernatural creation as against 'spontaneous'—i.e., natural—generation, carried back somewhat. Back of the spontaneous generation of life under other conditions than now obtained upon this planet, there occurred a spontaneous generation of elements of the kind that still goes on in the stars; and back of that I suppose a spontaneous generation of elementary particles under circumstances still to be fathomed, that ended in giving them the properties that alone make possible the universe we know."

Wald, George, "The Origin of Life," in *The Physics and Chemistry of Life* (Simon & Schuster, 1955), 270 pp.

p. 9   "One has only to contemplate the magnitude of this task to concede that the spontaneous generation of a living organism is impossible. Yet here we are—as a result, I believe, of spontaneous generation."

Yockey, Hubert P., "A Calculation of the Probability of Spontaneous Biogenesis by Information Theory," *Journal of Theoretical Biology*, vol. 67 (1977), pp. 377-398.

p. 377   "Certain old untenable ideas have served only to confuse the solution of the problem. Negentropy is not a concept because entropy cannot be negative. The role that negentropy has played in previous discussions is replaced by 'complexity' as defined in information theory."

p. 380   "Attempts to relate the idea of 'order' in a crystal with biological organization or specificity must be regarded as a play on words which cannot stand careful scrutiny."

p. 380   "An uninvited guest at any discussion of the origin of life and of evolution from the materialistic reductionist point of view, is the role of thermodynamic entropy and the 'heat death' of the universe which it predicts."

p. 396   "The 'warm little pond' scenario was invented *ad hoc* to serve as a materialistic reductionist explanation of the origin of life. It is unsupported by any other evidence and it will remain *ad hoc* until such evidence is found. . . . One must conclude that, contrary to the established and current wisdom a scenario describing the genesis of life on earth by chance and natural causes which can be accepted on the basis of fact and not faith has not yet been written."

B. Complexibility and Probability of Life

Even the simplest imaginary replicating protein molecule (actually, no such molecule exists, but life would presumably have to get started this way) would have to be so incredibly complex that it could never happen by chance. All attempts to calculate the probability of the chance origin of even the simplest form of life show it to be impossible.

Anonymous, "Hoyle on Evolution," *Nature*, vol. 294 (November 12, 1981), p. 105.

> "The essence of his argument last week was that the information content of the higher forms of life is represented by the number $10^{40,000}$—representing the specificity with which some 2000 genes, each of which might be chosen from 10^{20} nucleotide sequences of the appropriate length, might be defined. Evolutionary processes would, Hoyle said, require several Hubble times to yield such a result. The chance that higher life forms might have emerged in this way is comparable with the chance that 'a tornado sweeping through a junk-yard might assemble a Boeing 747 from the materials therein.'

> "Of adherents of biological evolution, Hoyle said he was at a loss to understand 'biologists' widespread compulsion to deny what seems to me to be obvious.'"

Capra, Fritjof, *The Web of Life* (New York: Anchor Books, 1996), 347 pp. Dr. Capra is Director of the Center for Ecoliteracy, in Berkeley, California, one of the most influential "New-Age" scientists.

p. 89   "In classical thermodynamics the dissipation of energy in heat transfer, friction, and the like was always associated with waste. Prigogine's concept of a dissipative structure introduced a radical change in this view by showing that in open systems dissipation becomes a source of order."

p. 228   "It has been estimated that those chance errors occur at a rate of about one per several hundred million cells in each generation. This frequency does not seem to be sufficient to explain the evolution of the great diversity of life forms, given the well-known fact that most mutations are harmful and only very few result in useful variations."

Crick, Francis, *Life Itself: Its Origin and Nature* (New York: Simon & Schuster, 1981) 192 pp.

p. 51-2   "If a particular amino acid sequence was selected by chance, how rare an event would this be?

> "This is an easy exercise in combinatorials. Suppose the chain is about two hundred amino acids long; this is, if anything rather less than the average length of proteins of all types. Since we have just twenty possibilities at each place, the number of possibilities is twenty multiplied by itself some two hundred times. This is conveniently written 20^{200} and is approximately equal to 10^{260}, that is, a one followed by 260 zeros.

> ". . . Moreover, we have only considered a polypeptide chain of rather modest length. Had we considered longer ones as well, the figure would have been even more immense. . . . The great majority of sequences can never have been synthesized at all, at any time."

p. 88   "An honest man, armed with all the knowledge available to us now, could only state that in some sense, the origin of life appears at the moment to be almost a miracle, so many are the conditions which would have had to have been satisfied to get it going."

Denton, Michael, *Evolution: A Theory in Crisis* (London: Burnett Books, Ltd., 1985), 368 pp.

p. 324   "Even today we have no way of rigorously estimating the probability or degree of isolation of even one functional protein. It is surely a little premature to claim that random processes could have assembled mosquitoes and elephants when we still have to determine the actual probability of the discovery by chance of one single functional protein molecule."

p. 329-30   "Altogether a typical cell contains about ten million million atoms. Suppose we choose to build an exact replica to a scale one thousand million times that of the cell so that each atom of the model would be the size of a tennis ball. Constructing such a model at the rate of one atom per minute, it would take fifty million years to finish, and the object we would end up with would be the giant factory, described above, some twenty kilometres in diameter, with a volume thousands of times that of the Great Pyramid."

p. 330   "Altogether the total number of connections in the human brain approaches 10^{15} or a thousand million million. Numbers in the order of 10^{15} are of course completely beyond comprehension. Imagine an area about half the size of the USA (one million square miles) covered in a forest of trees containing ten thousand trees per square mile. If each tree contained one hundred thousand leaves the total number of leaves in the forest would be 10^{15}, equivalent to the number of connections in the human brain."

p. 334   "The capacity of DNA to store information vastly exceeds that of any other known system; it is so efficient that all the information needed to specify an organism as complex as man weighs less than a few thousand millionths of a gram. The information necessary to specify the design of all the species of organisms which have ever existed on the planet, a number according to G. G. Simpson of approximately one thousand million, could be held in a teaspoon and there would still be room left for all the information in every book ever written."

p. 342   "It is the sheer universality of perfection, the fact that everywhere we look, to whatever depth we look, we find an elegance and ingenuity of an absolutely transcending quality, which so mitigates against the idea of chance. Is it really credible that random processes could have constructed a reality, the smallest element of which—a functional protein or gene—is complex beyond our own creative capacities, a reality which is the very antithesis of chance, which excels in every sense anything produced by the intelligence of man? Alongside the level of ingenuity and complexity exhibited by the molecular machinery of life, even our most advanced artifacts appear clumsy."

Erbrich, Paul. "On the Probability of the Emergence of a Protein with a Particular Function," *Acta Biotheoretica*, vol. 34 (1985), pp. 53-80.

p. 77　　"Why then does the scientific theory of evolution hold on to the concept of chance to the degree it does? I suspect it is the fact that there is no alternative whatsoever which could explain the fact of universal evolution, at least in principle, and be formulated within the framework of natural science. If no alternative should be forthcoming, if chance remains overtaxed, then the conclusion seems inevitable that evolution and therefore living beings cannot be grasped by natural science to the same extent as non-living things—not because organisms are so complex, but because the explaining mechanism is fundamentally inadequate."

Golay, Marcel J. E., "Reflections of a Communications Engineer," *Analytical Chemistry*, vol. 33 (June 1961), p. 23A.

"Suppose we wanted to build a machine capable of reaching into bins for all of its parts, and capable of assembling from these parts a second machine just like itself. What is the minimum amount of structure or information that should be built into the first machine? The answer came out to be of the order of 1500 bits—1500 choices between alternatives which the machine should be able to decide. This answer is very suggestive, because 1500 bits happens to be also of the order of magnitude of the amount of structure contained in the simplest large protein molecule which, immersed in a bath of nutrients, can induce the assembly of those nutrients into another large protein molecule like itself, and then separate itself from it. [Under most favorable conditions conceivable, the probability that this could have happened by chance just once in all the universe in the course of astronomic time is 2^{220}, probability against it is 2^{1500}]."

Hoyle, Sir Fred, "The Big Bang in Astronomy," *New Scientist*, vol. 92 (November 19, 1981), pp. 521-527. Sir Fred Hoyle, FRS, was an honorary research professor at Manchester University and University College, Cardiff. Twenty five years earlier he was University Lecturer in Mathematics at Cambridge University. Sir Fred Hoyle is a great British astronomer; he originated the Steady State Theory, but later repudiated both the Steady State and Big Bang theories.

pp. 526-7　　"I don't know how long it is going to be before astronomers generally recognize that the combinatorial arrangement of not even one among the many thousands of biopolymers on which life depends could have been arrived at by natural processes here on the earth. Astronomers will have a little difficulty at understanding this because they will be assured by biologists that it is not so, the biologists having been assured in their turn by others that it is not so. The 'others' are a group of persons who believe, quite openly, in mathematical miracles. They advocate the belief that tucked away in nature, outside of normal physics, there is a law which performs miracles (provided the miracles are in the aid of biology). This curious situation sits oddly on a profession that for long has been dedicated to coming up with logical explanations of biblical miracles.

". . . It is quite otherwise, however, with the modern mathematical miracle workers, who are always to be found living in the twilight fringes of thermodynamics."

p. 527   "At all events, anyone with even a nodding acquaintance with the Rubik cube will concede the near-impossibility of a solution being obtained by a blind person moving the cubic faces at random.* Now imagine 10^{50} blind persons each with a scrambled Rubik cube, and try to conceive of the chance of them all *simultaneously* arriving at the solved form. You then have the chance of arriving by random shuffling of just one of the many biopolymers on which life depends. The notion that not only the biopolymers but the operating programme of a living cell could be arrived at by chance in a primordial organic soup here on the Earth is evidently nonsense of a high order. Life must plainly be a cosmic phenomenon."

   *[There are 4×10^{19} possible scramblings of the Rubik cube (that is, ten billion billion)].

Hoyle, Sir Fred, and Chandra Wickramasinghe, "Where Microbes Boldly Went," *New Scientist*, vol. 91 (August 13, 1991), pp. 412-415.

p. 415   "Precious little in the way of biochemical evolution could have happened on the Earth. It is easy to show that the two thousand or so enzymes that span the whole of life could not have evolved on the Earth. If one counts the number of trial assemblies of amino acids that are needed to give rise to the enzymes, the probability of their discovery by random shufflings turns out to be less than 1 in $10^{40,000}$."

Hoyle, Sir Fred, and Chandra Wickramasinghe, *Evolution from Space* (New York: Simon & Schuster, 1984), 176 pp.

p. 148   "No matter how large the environment one considers, life cannot have had a random beginning. Troops of monkeys thundering away at random on typewriters could not produce the works of Shakespeare, for the practical reason that the whole observable universe is not large enough to contain the necessary monkey hordes, the necessary typewriters, and certainly not the waste paper baskets required for the deposition of wrong attempts. The same is true for living material."

   "The likelihood of the spontaneous formation of life from inanimate matter is one to a number with 40,000 noughts after it. . . . It is big enough to bury Darwin and the whole theory of evolution. There was no primeval soup, neither on this planet nor on any other, and if the beginnings of life were not random, they must therefore have been the product of purposeful intelligence."

Hoyle, Sir Fred, *The Intelligent Universe* (New York: Holt, Rinehart & Winston, 1983), 256 pp.

pp. 20-21   "If there were a basic principle of matter which somehow drove organic systems toward life, its existence should easily be demonstrable in the laboratory. One could, for instance, take a swimming bath to represent the primordial soup. Fill it with any chemicals of a non-biological nature you please. Pump any gases over it, or through it, you please, and shine any kind of radiation on it that takes your fancy. Let the experiment proceed for a year and see how many of those 2,000 enzymes [proteins produced by living cells] have appeared in the bath. I will give the answer, and so save the time and trouble and expense of actually doing the experiment. You would find nothing at all, except possibly for a tarry sludge composed of amino acids and other simple organic chemicals. How can I be so confident of this statement? Well, if it were otherwise, the experiment would long since have been done and would be well-known and famous throughout the world. The cost of it would be trivial compared to the cost of landing a man on the Moon."

p. 23   "In short there is not a shred of objective evidence to support the hypothesis that life began in an organic soup here on the Earth."

Jacobson, Homer, "Information, Reproduction and the Origin of Life," *American Scientist*, vol. 43 (January 1955), pp. 119-127.

p. 121   "Directions for the reproduction of plans, for energy and the extraction of parts from the current environment, for the growth sequence, and for the effector mechanism translating instructions into growth—*all* had to be simultaneously present at that moment. This combination of events has seemed an incredibly unlikely happenstance, and has often been ascribed to divine intervention."

Lafont, Louis, review of *Chance and Certainty: Evolution in the Light of Modern Biology* by Georges Salet, *Permanences*, no. 94 (November 1972), trans. from French by Geoffrey Lawman, *Approaches Supplement*, 12 pp.

p. 7   "In his work [Salet] draws all the consequences implicit in the law that the great mathematician Emil Borel has called '*the sole law of chance*,' since it is the basis of all the other laws of chance. It can be stated thus: a phenomenon whose probability is sufficiently weak—that is below a certain threshold—will never occur, '*never*' meaning here within the limits of space and time at our disposal, that is to say within the limits within which it is possible to repeat the trials, for as long as a world, all of whose known dimensions are finite, allows."

p. 7   "In other words, for a given event, there is a probability-limit, below which one may be certain that this event will *never* occur within a fixed time limit."

p. 8   "The number of chemical events which can have occurred on earth or which can occur in the future up to the end of the earth's existence is certainly less than 10^{80}; this is an enormous figure, but it is not infinite. 'The impossibility threshold of any chemical phenomena on earth is a probability of 10^{-100}.'"

p. 9   ". . . the geological eras in question would have to be milliards of times longer than even the most generous estimates make them . . . for the '*mutation-selection*' mechanism to have produced even a single new organ."

Mora, Peter T., "The Folly of Probability," in *The Origins of Prebiological Systems,* ed. Sydney Fox (New York: Academic Press, 1965), 482 pp.

p. 45   "I believe we developed this practice (i.e., postulating prebiological natural selection) to avoid facing the conclusion that the probability of a self-replicating state is zero. . . . When for practical purposes the concept of infinite time and matter has to be invoked, that concept of probability is annulled. By such logic we can prove anything, such as that, no matter how complex, everything will repeat itself, exactly and immeasurably."

Salisbury, Frank B., "Doubts About the Modern Synthetic Theory of Evolution," *American Biology Teacher*, vol. 33 (September 1971), pp. 335-338.

p. 336   "Now we know that the cell itself is far more complex than we had imagined. It includes thousands of functioning enzymes, each one of them a complex machine itself. Furthermore, each enzyme comes into being in response to a gene, a strand of DNA. The information content of the gene (its complexity) must be as great as that of the enzyme that it controls."

p. 336   "A medium protein might include about 300 amino acids. The DNA gene controlling this would have about 1,000 nucleotides in its chain. Since there are four kinds of nucleotides in a DNA chain, one consisting of 1,000 links could exist in $4^{1,000}$ different forms. Using a little algebra (logarithms) we can see that $4^{1,000} = 10^{600}$. Ten multiplied by itself 600 times gives the figure 1 followed by 600 zeroes! This number is completely beyond our comprehension."

p. 338   "My last doubt concerns so-called parallel evolution. In the angiosperms the same features of flower structure have apparently appeared independently several times in unrelated evolutionary lines. Indeed, the problem is so severe that no satisfactory classification scheme for flowering plants has yet been devised. Even something as complex as the eye has appeared several times; for example, in the squid, the vertebrates, and the arthropods. It's bad enough accounting for the origin of such things once, but the thought of producing them several times according to the modern synthetic theory makes my head swim."

Wald, George, "The Origin of Life," in *The Physics and Chemistry of Life* (Simon & Schuster, 1955, 270 pp.), p. 12.

p. 12   "The important point is that since the origin of life belongs in the category of at-least-once phenomena, time is on its side. However improbable we regard this event, . . given enough time it will almost certainly happen at least once. . . .

"Time is in fact the hero of the plot. The time with which we have to deal is of the order of two billion years. What we regard as impossible on the basis of human experience is meaningless here. Given so much time, the 'impossible' becomes possible, the possible probable, and the probable virtually certain. One has only to wait: time itself performs miracles."

Wickramasinghe, C., Interview in *London Daily Express* (August 14, 1981), Wickramasinghe is Professor of Applied Math & Astronomy, University College, Cardiff.

"From my earliest training as a scientist, I was very strongly brainwashed to believe that science cannot be consistent with any kind of deliberate creation. That notion has had to be painfully shed.

"Each found that the odds against the spark of life igniting accidentally on Earth were . . . '10 to the power of 40,000.'"

"They did calculations based on the size and age of the universe (15 billion years) and found that the odds against life beginning spontaneously anywhere in space were '10 to the power of 30.'"

"At the moment, I can't find any rational argument to knock down the view which argues for conversion to God. . . .

We used to have an open mind; now we realize that the only logical answer to life is creation—and not accidental random shuffling."

Yockey, Hubert P., "Self-Organization Origin of Life Scenarios and Information Theory," *Journal of Theoretical Biology*, vol. 91 (1981), pp. 13-31.

p. 26   "The calculations presented in this paper show that the origin of a rather accurate genetic code, not necessarily the modern one, is a *pons asinorum* which must be crossed to pass over the abyss which separates crystallography, high polymer chemistry and physics from biology. The information content of amino acids sequences cannot increase until a genetic code with an adaptor function has appeared. Nothing which even vaguely resembles a code exists in the physico-chemical world. One must conclude that no valid scientific explanation of the origin of life exists *at present*."

p. 27   "A practical man will not believe a scenario which appears to him to have a very small probability. . . if a tossed coin is observed to fall heads ten times consecutively, a practical man will believe it to be two-headed *without examining it* even though the sequence of all heads is exactly as probable as any other sequence" [Total No. permutations - 1024].

pp. 27-28   "Faith in the infallible and comprehensive doctrines of dialectic materialism plays a crucial role in origin of life scenarios, and especially in exobiology and its ultimate consequence the doctrine of advanced extra-terrestrial civilization. That life must exist somewhere in the solar system on 'suitable planets elsewhere' is widely and tenaciously believed in spite of lack of evidence or even abundant evidence to the contrary."

C. Exobiology

Because of the apparent impossibility of life evolving on Earth, some evolutionists have taken the extreme position that it was somehow transported to Earth from some other planet or inter-planetary source. This stratagem, of course, only transfers the impossibility to some inaccessible and unobservable location in outer space.

There is, of course, no observational evidence at all that any other planets even exist that could be capable of supporting life, let alone evolving it. Nevertheless, evolutionists continue hoping against hope, assuming some kind of strange evolutionary statistics, that life *must* have evolved elsewhere in the universe since there are so many stars. This sort of thing is science fiction, not science.

Emsley, John, "Demolisher of Myths," review of *The Relativity of Wrong*, by Isaac Asimov (Oxford University Press, 1988), 225 pp., *New Scientist*, vol. 122 (April 8, 1989), p. 60.

"Asimov also disposes of another popular myth—that one day we will journey to the stars. Here he is tampering with something that might have been better left alone. He quietly knifes the idea in the back, and thereby murders much popular culture on which today's young people are raised. Space travel is possible between the planets of the Solar System, but that is all. Whatever probe we launch from planet Earth into the cosmos will get nowhere. It will slowly come to rest between here and the next star. A manned spacecraft would suffer the same fate.

"Only if we use antimatter as a fuel can we make a return trip to the nearest star, and that form of energy is likely to remain forever beyond our grasp. In any case, the effort would never justify the visit; our intrepid voyagers, or their descendants, would not arrive back before AD 50,000.

"Because we can never visit another star, so we can never be visited by aliens from another Solar System. Another chunk of popular science folklore bites the dust. Space travel is a meaningless phrase. *Star Wars*, *Star Trek*, and a log of science fiction suddenly seems merely silly. Asimov, you're a spoilsport!"

Grady, Monica, Ian Wright, and Colin Pillinger, "Opening a Martian Can of Worms," *Nature*, vol. 382 (August 14, 1996).

p. 575   "Several reasons for caution on the micro-fossils came from William Schoff at the NASA press conference: they are a hunred times smaller than any such fossils found on Earth, there is no measurement of the composition of the cells to show whether they are organic or not, and there is no sign of any cavities within the cells in which fluids necessary for life could reside."

Horowitz, Norman H., "The Search for Life on Mars," *Scientific American*, vol. 237 (November 1977), pp. 52-61. Horowitz was Chairman of the Biology Department at California Institute of Technology.

p. 61   "Even though some ambiguities remain, there is little doubt about the meaning of the observations of the Viking landers: At least those areas on Mars examined by the two spacecraft are not habitats of life."

p. 61   "It is impossible to prove that any of the reactions detected by the Viking instruments were not biological in origin. It is equally impossible to prove from any result of the Viking experiments that the rocks seen at the landing sites are not living organisms that happen to look like rocks. Once one abandons Occam's razor the field is open to every fantasy. Centuries of human experience warn us, however, that such an approach is not the way to discover the truth."

Jastrow, Robert, "What are the Chances for Life?" *Sky and Telescope*, vol. 93 (June 1997), pp. 62-63.

pp. 62-3   "Why would the Earth alone—an undistinguished body among trillions of similar ones—be chosen by nature or the deity as the only planet on whose soil the seeds of life have taken root?"

p. 63   Confirmation of the Mars report will demonstrate that the universe is teeming with life.

Kerr, Richard A., "Martian Rocks Tell Divergent Stories," *Science*, vol. 274 (November 8, 1996), p. 918.

p. 918   "The life on Mars story took on new life of its own last week, as the international scientific community tried to fathom the meaning behind two dueling studies of meteorites from Mars. One study by a British team follows up on the original claim—that minerals deposited 3 billion years ago in a bit of Martian crust that later fell to Earth carry the hallmarks of past life (*Science*, 16 August, pp. 864 and 924). Making a bold splash in the press, the team cited strong new evidence of ancient life in both the original Martian meteorite and a second one. But another study, presented with less fanfare at an American geological meeting, suggests that both meteorites may bear the remains of Earthly contamination instead."

p. 918   "Then again, the finding may say nothing about life on Mars, if Jeffrey Bada is right about Earthly contamination of Antarctic meteorites."

p. 918   "Since both Martian meteorites spent thousands of years in Antarctic ice, Bada sees contamination problems for both. 'This looks like stuff from Earth,' he says, 'It's extremely dangerous to make these bold claims.'"

Kerr, Richard A., "Ancient Life on Mars?" *Science*, vol. 273 (August 16, 1996), pp. 864-866.

p. 865   "Meteoriticist John Kerridge of the University of California, Los Angeles . . . says, 'Decomposition could certainly produce polycyclic aromatic hydrocarbons, but there are dozens of other mechanisms for making PAHs.' They could have formed from simpler compounds on Mars that never evolved chemically to living organisms, he notes."

p. 865   "'None of this [can] distinguish between biology and chemistry,' cautions Kenneth Nealson of the University of Wisconsin at Milwaukee. Nealson, whose work on bacterial carbonate precipitation is cited by McKay and colleagues, notes that warm fluids circulating through the Martian crust might have deposited the same sequence of minerals without any help from organisms."

p. 866   "McKay and colleagues cite a paper by geologist Robert Folk of the University of Texas, Austin, reporting fossilized 'nanobacteria' in some young terrestrial rocks, but, in Folk's words, 'everybody is pretty skeptical' that his objects are fossils. The Martian look-alikes face even greater skepticism. 'The little blobs in ALH 84001 didn't convince me,' says Nealson. They aren't pollen, as in the 1960s episode, but 'I think you can form little blobs on rocks with all kinds of chemical precipitates.'

                "What's lacking is evidence other than shape that these forms were once living."

Kerr, Richard A., "Pathfinder Strikes a Rocky Bonanza," *Science*, vol. 277 (July 11, 1997).

p. 173   "But team scientists were already doing impressionistic science on images from the site, finding evidence that it was swept by one of the largest floods—or mud slides—in solar system history."

p. 173   "Golombek and his colleagues believe that the first images confirm their suspicion that billions of years ago a great flood of a billion cubic meters per second swept the region for weeks, carrying a variety of rocks from distant highlands. . . . Determining what could have unleashed the water, which was presumably stored beneath a dry surface, is one of the enduring mysteries of Mars."

McKay, David S., *et al.* (eight other co-authors), "Search for Past Life on Mars: Possible Relic Biogenic Activity in Martian Meteorite ALH84001," *Science*, vol. 273 (August 16, 1996), pp. 924-930.

p. 929   "It is possible that all of the described features in ALH84001 can be explained by inorganic processes, but these explanations appear to require restricted conditions—for example, sulfate reducing conditions in Antarctic ice sheets, which are not known to occur. Formation of the described features by organic activity in Antarctica is also possible, but such activity is only poorly understood at present."

p. 929   "In examining the martian meteorite ALH84001 we have found that the following evidence is compatible with the existence of past life on Mars: (i) an igneous Mars rock (of unknown geologic context) that was penetrated by a fluid along fractures and pore spaces, which then became the sites of secondary mineral formation and possible biogenic activity; (ii) a formation age for the carbonate globules younger than the age of the igneous rock; (iii) SEM and TEM images of carbonate globules and features resembling terrestrial microorganisms, terrestrial biogenic carbonate structures, or microfossils; (iv) magnetite and iron sulfide particles that could have resulted from oxidation and reduction reactions known to be important in terrestrial microbial systems; and (v) the presence of PAHs associated with surfaces rich in carbonate globules. None of these observations is in itself conclusive for the existence of past life. Although there are alternative explanations for each of these phenomena taken individually, when they are considered collectively, particularly in view of their spatial association, we conclude that they are evidence for primitive life on early Mars."

McSween, Harry V., Jr., "Evidence for Life in a Martian Meteorite?" *GSA Today*, vol. 7 (July 1997), pp. 1-5.

p. 5   "Even if some Martian organic matter is present, it may be impossible to disentangle its properties from the apparent overprint of terrestrial contamination."

Miller, Stanley L., and Harold C. Urey, "Organic Compound Synthesis on the Primitive Earth," *Science*, vol. 130 (July 31, 1959), pp. 245-251.

p. 251   "Surely one of the most marvelous feats of 20th-century science would be the firm proof that life exists on another planet. All the projected space flights and the high costs of such developments would be fully justified if they were able to establish the existence of life on either Mars or Venus. In that case, the thesis that life develops spontaneously when the conditions are favorable would be far more firmly established, and our whole view of the problem of the origin of life would be confirmed."

Mitton, Simon, and Roger Lewin, "Is Anyone Out There?" *New Scientist* (August 16, 1973). Mitton is Secretary of the Institute of Astronomy, Cambridge.

p. 380   "They hypothesize that thousands of millions of years ago, an intelligent civilization decided to seed other nearby planets with primitive forms of life in the hope that more advanced civilizations might develop. Crick and Orgel claim that their proposal—called Directed Panspermia—is as tenable as other theories that aim to explain the origin of life on Earth."

p. 382   "Unseen planets orbiting a star cause its position relative to very distant stars to oscillate. So far the most outstanding candidate is Barnard's star.

                "A recent dynamical analysis, carried out by David Black and Graham Suffolk of the Ames Research Center, California, attributes the behaviour of Barnard's star to the presence of two unseen companions (Icarus, vol. 19, p. 353).

                "A humble explanation of the null results of the searches for life is advanced by a Harvard student, John Ball (Icarus, vol. 19, p. 347). He steps into the realms of science fiction with a hypothesis that we on Earth are living in a galactic zoo! The idea is that a super civilization may by now have control of the whole Galaxy. Just as we have Safari parks, zoos and conservation areas, so they may have set aside the solar system as a wilderness zone. The perfect zoo keeper does not make himself known to his charges, and thus we are unaware of their presence. A version of this hypothesis is given in a best seller—the Bible."

Naeye, Robert, "OK, Where Are They?" *Astronomy*, vol. 24 (July 1996), pp. 36-43.

p. 42   "If one chooses to shun speculation and stick solely with observations, one can ask the same question that Nobel physicist Enrico Fermi put forth in 1950: If the Galaxy is teeming with intelligent life, where are they? The sobering reality is that there is no observational evidence whatsoever for the existence of other intelligent beings anywhere in the universe."

p. 43   "But until that happens, it seems prudent to conclude that we are alone in a vast cosmic ocean, that in one important sense, we ourselves are special in that we go against the Copernican grain. If so, humanity represents matter and energy evolved to its highest level; whereby a tiny part of the universe on a small rock orbiting an average star in the outskirts of an ordinary spiral galaxy has brought itself to a state of consciousness that can ponder the questions of how the universe, and life itself, began, and what it all means."

Pollard, William G., "The Prevalence of Earthlike Planets," *American Scientist*, vol. 67 (November/ December 1979), pp. 653-659.

p. 653   "It is almost certain that no other planet in our solar system now supports the phenomenon of life. The question still remains, however, as a persistent field of speculation, as to how many stars in the galaxy or the universe as a whole may support a planet like Earth."

p. 653   "Even more essential than Earthlike land masses is the presence of sizable bodies of liquid water throughout the history of the planet. A full evolutionary development of complex organelles and organisms is not conceivable apart from an ample continuous marine environment."

p. 659   "There is a deeply ingrained conviction in the great majority of mankind, to which the appeal of science fiction and fantasy bears witness, that the universe is so constituted that if an opportunity exists for life to originate, it will be actualized, and if an opportunity exists for hominids to evolve, that too will be actualized. Whatever may be the basis for such convictions, it clearly must be sought outside the domain of science."

Powell, Corey S., "Livable Planets," *Scientific American* (February 1993), pp. 18-20.

p. 20   "The researchers found that planets less than 0.95 AU from the sun would have lost their entire water supply over the 4.6-billion-year age of the solar system. Such worlds would be unsuitable for water-dependent forms of life.

"At the outer edge of the habitable zone, the main problem is one of keeping warm. A mild greenhouse effect helps the earth to maintain its comfortable temperature. Farther from the sun, a more intense greenhouse effect is needed. Kasting's calculations show that on a planet more than 1.37 AU from the sun, carbon dioxide begins to freeze in the upper parts of the atmosphere, reflecting more radiation back into space and lowering the temperature still further. This feedback would place the planet in a deep freeze.

"Kasting and his co-authors emphasize that their calculations probably underestimate the breadth of the habitable zone. They point to the example of Mars, which lies 1.52 AU from the sun. Ancient channels on the red planet's surface may indicate that nearly four billion years ago the surface was warm enough to permit large bodies of liquid water. That is all the more remarkable because, according to theories of stellar evolution, the sun was roughly 25 percent dimmer then than now. 'Early Martian climate is an unsolved problem,' Kasting says.

"Likewise, the early earth received only a paltry supply of sunlight, yet sedimentary rocks testify to the widespread presence of liquid water at least 3.8 billion years ago."

Schwartzman, David, and Lee J. Rickard, "Being Optimistic about the Search for Extraterrestrial Intelligence," *American Scientist*, vol. 76 (July/August 1988), pp. 364-369.

p. 364   "Is it still reasonable to be optimistic about the search for extraterrestrial intelligence? After all, researchers around the world have been listening for electromagnetic signals from other civilizations in the universe for more than 25 years now, using ever larger telescopes and increasingly sophisticated equipment. Tipler estimates that 120,000 hours of observing time have been spent on the search, with, of course, no positive results."

p. 364   "The basic argument for an optimistic assessment of the likelihood of intelligence elsewhere in the universe is really a reassertion of the ancient belief in the plurality of worlds, the idea that our own world must be duplicated elsewhere. In modern form, the idea assumes that, in the absence of evidence to the contrary, conditions favorable to the emergence of life and intelligence as they exist here on earth are present abundantly in the universe."

Shostak, Seth, "When E.T. Calls Us," *Astronomy*, vol. 25 (September 1997), pp. 37-41.

p. 37   "This is Project Phoenix, the most comprehensive search ever undertaken for intelligent company among the stars. Run by the SETI Institute of Mountain View, California, it is the privately funded descendant of a former NASA program. Here, at the National Radio Astronomy Observatory's 140-foot telescope in Green Bank, Project Phoenix scientists are systematically scrutinizing a thousand nearby sun-like stars for the faint signal that would betray intelligent habitation. So far, they have found nothing—not a single, extraterrestrial peep.”

Thomsen, Dietrick E., “Looking for LGM’s,” *Science News*, vol. 110 (November 20, 1976), pp. 332-333.

p. 332   “But so far, the searches that have been done have yielded negative or at least inconclusive results.”

p. 333   “Although astronomers now believe that there are unnumbered planets circling unnumbered stars, even the first man to claim evidence of planets associated with other stars (Barnard’s star and Epsilon Eridani) is cautious about any belief in widespread life. He is Peter van de Kamp of Swarthmore College, and he remarks, ‘If stars have planets, there doesn’t need to be life or life at this moment.’”

p. 333   “Verschuur’s [G. L. Verschur, professor of astronomy at University of Colorado]’s thesis is that the universe is so wasteful that there is likely only one source of life in it, and we are likely to be that.”

Wick, Gerald L., “Interstellar Molecules: Chemicals in the Sky,” *Science*, vol. 170 (October 9, 1970), pp. 149-150.

p. 149   “Although it is clear that these molecules [e.g., OH, H_2O, NH_3, H_2CO, HCN, CN, HC_3N] exist in space and that they can emit radiation, there is no clear explanation of how they are formed and why they remain stable. Their chemical bonds should be broken by the intense fluxes of ultraviolet radiation and cosmic rays. Their estimated lifetimes from ultraviolet dissociation in interstellar space is about 200 years.”

Yockey, Hubert P., “Self-Organization Origin of Life Scenarios and Information Theory,” *Journal of Theoretical Biology*, vol. 91 (1981), pp. 13-31.

p. 29   “In the absence of better knowledge of the origin of life the search now being made for little green men and their signals from planets near other stars is based on the evidence of faith and must therefore be regarded as an exercise of religious belief.”

Chapter 3

The Impossibility of Evolution

A. The Barrier of Thermodynamics

The two laws of thermodynamics are the most universally applicable and impregnably confirmed of all laws of science. In effect, they specify conservation in quantity and tendency to decline in quality, and so provide what seems to be an impregnable barrier to "upward" evolution. Although evolutionists have tried various ways of getting around this barrier, the fact remains that no case of true upward evolution has ever been observed to occur, nor has any proposed mechanism of evolution ever been found workable, and the thermodynamic barrier provides a good explanation as to why not.

Asimov, Isaac, "In the Game of Energy and Thermodynamics You Can't Even Break Even," *Smithsonian Institute Journal* (June 1970), pp. 4-10.

p. 6   "To express all this, we can say: 'Energy can be transferred from one place to another, or transformed from one form to another, but it can be neither created nor destroyed.' Or we can put it another way: 'The total quantity of energy in the universe is constant.'

". . . This law is considered the most powerful and most fundamental generalization about the universe that scientists have ever been able to make.

"No one knows *why* energy is conserved, and no one can be completely sure it is truly conserved everywhere in the universe and under all conditions. All that anyone can say is that in over a century and a quarter of careful measurement, scientists have never been able to point to a definite violation of energy conservation, either in the familiar everyday surroundings about us, or in the heavens above or in the atoms within."

p. 8   "We can say: 'No device can deliver work unless there is a difference in energy concentration within the system, no matter how much total energy is used.'

"That is one way of stating what is called the Second Law of Thermodynamics. It is one of many ways; all of them are equivalent although some very sophisticated mathematics and physics is involved in showing the equivalence."

pp. 10-11   "Another way of stating the Second Law, then, is: 'The universe is constantly getting more disorderly.'

"Viewed that way, we can see the Second Law all about us. We have to work hard to straighten a room, but left to itself, it becomes a mess again very quickly and very easily. Even if we never enter it, it becomes dusty and musty. How difficult to maintain houses, and machinery, and our own bodies in perfect working order; how easy to let them deteriorate. In fact, all we have to do is nothing, and everything deteriorates, collapses, breaks down, wears out, all by itself—and that is what the Second Law is all about.

"You can argue, of course, that the phenomenon of life may be an exception. Life on earth has steadily grown more complex, more versatile, more elaborate, more orderly, over the billions of years of the planet's existence. From no life at all, living molecules were developed, then living cells, then living conglomerates of cells, worms, vertebrates, mammals, finally Man. And in Man is a three-pound brain which, as far as we know, is the most complex and orderly arrangement of matter in the universe. How could the human brain develop out of the primeval slime? How could that vast increase in order (and therefore that vast decrease of entropy) have taken place?

"The answer is it could *not* have taken place without a tremendous source of energy constantly bathing the earth, for it is on that energy that life subsists. Remove the sun, and the human brain would not have developed—or the primeval slime, either. And in the billions of years it took for the human brain to develop, the increase in entropy that took place in the sun was far greater than the decrease that is represented by the evolution required to develop the human brain.

"But where did it all start? If the universe is running down into utter disorder, what made it orderly to begin with? Where did the order come from that it is steadily losing? What set up the extremes that are steadily being chipped away?

"Scientists are still arguing the point. Some think the universe originally had its matter and energy all smashed together into one huge 'cosmic egg'—a situation something like a tremendous deck of cards all arranged in order. The cosmic egg exploded, and ever since, for billions of years, the universe has been running down; the deck of cards is being shuffled and shuffled and shuffled.

"Others think that there is some process in the universe that spontaneously decreases entropy, some natural process that unshuffles and reorders the cards. We don't know what it can be, perhaps because it takes place under conditions we cannot observe and cannot duplicate in the laboratory—say in the center of exploding galaxies. Perhaps, in that case, as some parts of the universe run down, others build up.

"Then again, it may be that once the universe runs down, the random collisions of particles may—after some unimaginable span of years—just happen to bring about an at-least-partial unshuffling. After all, if you shuffle and reshuffle cards ceaselessly for a trillion years, you may violate the Second Law and end up with an arrangement possessing at least *some* order, just by the laws of chance.

"Once that happens, the universe begins to run down again at once. Perhaps, then, we live in a universe that was partially restored to order after a quadrillion years of having been run down. We are now running down again. After the universe is completely run down, another quadrillion years or so may see a section of it unshuffled once more.

"Stars and galaxies will then form again, and life may be established here and there, and finally some science writer will sit down and begin to wonder again where it all came from and where it will end."

Asimov, Isaac, "Can Decreasing Entropy Exist in the Universe?" *Science Digest*, vol. 73 (May 1973), pp. 76-77.

p. 76 "As far as we know, all changes are in the direction of increasing entropy, of increasing disorder, of increasing randomness, of running down. Yet the universe was once in a position from which it could run down for trillions of years. How did it get into that position?

"I can think of three possible answers, all of which are only speculations.

"1) . . . Somewhere, there may be changes under unusual conditions that we can't as yet study, . . . in the direction of decreasing entropy.

"2) . . . It may be . . . that through sheer random movement, a certain amount of energy concentration is piled into part of the universe. By random motion, a certain amount of order is produced once more."

p. 77 "3) . . . The universe may be running down as it expands and then winding up again as it contracts, and it may be doing this over and over through all eternity."

Blum, Harold F., "Perspectives in Evolution," *American Scientist*, vol. 43 (October 1955), pp. 595-610.

pp. 595-6 "A major consequence of the second law of thermodynamics is that all real processes go toward a condition of greater probability. The probability function generally used in thermodynamics is *entropy*. . . . Thus orderliness is associated with low entropy; randomness with high entropy. . . . The second law of thermodynamics says that left to itself any isolated system will go toward greater entropy, which also means toward greater randomness and greater likelihood."

Blum, Harold F., *Time's Arrow and Evolution* (Princeton University Press, 1968), 232 pp.

p. 119 "No matter how carefully we examine the energetics of living systems we find no evidence of defeat of thermodynamic principles, but we do encounter a degree of complexity not witnessed in the nonliving world."

p. 150 "Mutation, then, is not random, but may occur only within certain restricting limits and according to certain pathways determined by thermodynamic properties of the system. . . . Certainly Darwin and many who have followed him have thought of variation as completely random, and hence providing all possible variety of handles for natural selection."

Bridgman, P. W., "Reflections on Thermodynamics," *American Scientist*, vol. 41 (October 1953), pp. 549-555.

p. 549 "The two laws of thermodynamics are, I suppose, accepted by physicists as perhaps the most secure generalizations from experience that we have. The physicist does not hesitate to apply the two laws to any concrete physical situation in the confidence that nature will not let him down."

Coveney, Peter V., "The Second Law of Thermodynamics: Entropy, Irreversibility and Dynamics," *Nature*, vol. 333 (June 2, 1988), pp. 409-415.

p. 414   "Until now, many scientists have taken the view that the irreversibility observed in nature is merely illusory, and that the truth resides in the reversible dynamical laws which govern behaviour on a microscopic level (and of course is not directly observable)."

p. 414   "In short, complexity cannot be reduced to simplicity in any non-trivial manner: rather, irreversibility is seen to emerge as a necessary consequence of the instabilities present in more complicated systems."

p. 414   "Modern cosmology uses thermodynamics in discussing the irreversible, evolutionary nature of the Universe: for example, one has only to consider the importance attached to the existence of the 3K microwave black-body radiation background. Another remarkable feature of contemporary cosmology, however, is its close relation with the reversible, non-evolutionary world of particle physics, previously embodied in the Standard Model of the 1970s, and now superseded by the Inflationary Universe description."

p. 414   "From an epistemological viewpoint, the contributions of Prigogine's Brussels School are unquestionably of signal importance. The myth of a completely timeless, deterministic Universe is henceforth replaced by a world in which static affairs are enlarged to embrace the probabilistic kinetics of process; in which reversibility and irreversibility are accorded equal objectivity; and in which the notions of 'being' and 'becoming' are unified within a single conceptual framework."

Everitt, W. L., "Empathy and Entropy," *Journal of Engineering Education*, vol. 47 (April 1957), pp. 658-661, 715.

pp. 658-9   ". . . It may be inferred that entropy is a measure of randomness, confusion or lack of organization. Such a term can be applied not only in a thermodynamic sense, but also to information problems."

Feinberg, Gerald, and Maurice Goldhaber, "The Conservation Laws of Physics," *Scientific American*, vol. 209 (October 1963), pp. 36-45.

p. 36   "The physicist's confidence in the conservation principles rests on long and thoroughgoing experience. The conservation of energy, of momentum and of electric charge have been found to hold, within the limits of accuracy of measurement, in every case that has been studied. An elaborate structure of physical theory has been built on these fundamental concepts, and its predictions have been confirmed without fail."

Georgescu-Roegen, Nicholas, "Afterword," in *Entropy: A New World View* by Jeremy Rifkin (New York: Viking Press, 1980), 305 pp.

p. 263   "Because of the mysterious way the Entropy Law is usually formulated and because the great physicist A. S. Eddington hailed it as the supreme law of nature, that law has had an unusually strong appeal. The concept of entropy has also been transplanted into virtually all other domains—communications, biology, economics, sociology, psychology, political science, and even art."

p. 265 "Thermodynamics teaches what Boltzmann and, quite recently, Erwin Schrödinger said, namely, that any organism needs to continuously suck low entropy from the environment; otherwise, it would very quickly degrade entropically. But no loophole has yet been discovered in the Entropy Law to justify the impressive claim that the existence of life-bearing structures is a necessary conclusion of thermodynamic laws."

Greco, Frank A., "On the Second Law of Thermodynamics," *American Laboratory* (October 1982), pp. 80-88.

p. 88 "Being a generalization of experience, the second law could only be invalidated by an actual engine. In other words, the question, 'Can the second law of thermodynamics be circumvented?' is not well-worded and could be answered only if the model incorporated every feature of the real world. But an answer can readily be given to the question 'Has the second law of thermodynamics been circumvented?' Not yet."

Greenstein, Jesse L., "Dying Stars," *Scientific American*, vol. 200 (January 1959), pp. 46-53. Greenstein was Head of the Department of Astronomy at California Institute of Technology.

p. 46 "But the white dwarfs have a more general significance. They are a portent. They show us that the laws of thermodynamics, which circumscribe events on the minuscule scale of our planet, hold also as the inexorable plan of the life history of the stars.

"An irreverent physicist once rephrased the laws of thermodynamics to read: (1) you can't win, (2) you can't even break even, (3) things are going to get worse before they get better and (4) who says things are going to get better?

"When it is applied to stellar processes, the first law reminds us that stars do not create energy, but only convert energy from one form to an equivalent quantity of another form; that is, they convert to radiant energy the energy contained in their gravitational potential and in that fraction of their mass which is consumed in thermonuclear reactions. They can never produce more energy than they start out with. . . .

"But the second law reminds us that this cannot go on forever. A star can never recapture the energy it wastes into the sink of space; its life history is irreversible."

p. 47 "As the star enters the last phase of its existence it shrinks to the final, stable configuration of a white dwarf. The third and fourth laws of thermodynamics now assume increasing relevance to its condition. The third law says that the star will ultimately cool down to the temperature of space, and the fourth law declares that it will then no longer give forth light or heat. At this terminal point the white dwarf becomes a black dwarf."

Harris, Sydney, "Second Law of Thermodynamics," *San Francisco Examiner* (Field Enterprise), January 27, 1984.

> "There is a factor called 'entropy' in physics, indicating that the whole universe of matter is running down, and ultimately will reduce itself to uniform chaos. This follows from the Second Law of Thermodynamics, which seems about as basic and unquestionable to modern scientific minds as any truth can be.

> "At the same time that this is happening on the physical level of existence, something quite different seems to be happening on the biological level: structure and species are becoming more complex, more sophisticated, more organized, with higher degrees of performance and consciousness.

> ". . . How can the forces of biological development and the forces of physical degeneration be operating at cross purposes?

> "It would take, of course, a far greater mind than mine even to attempt to penetrate this riddle. I can only pose the question—because it seems to me the question most worth asking and working upon with all our intellectual and scientific resources. Our other quests seem trivial and time-bound compared with the fate of our species, and of all life in the universe."

Hawking, Stephen W., "The Direction of Time," *New Scientist*, vol. 115 (July 9, 1987), pp. 46-49.

p. 145   "There are at least three different arrows of time. First, there is the thermodynamic arrow of time, the direction of time in which disorder or entropy increases. Then, there is the psychological arrow of time. This is the direction in which we feel time passes, the direction in which we remember the past but not the future. Finally, there is the cosmological arrow of time. This is the direction of time in which the universe is expanding rather than contracting."

p. 47   "Why should the Universe be in a state of high order at one end of time, the end that we call the past? Why is it not in a state of complete disorder at all times? After all, this might seem more probable. And why is the direction of time in which disorder increases the same as that in which the Universe expands? One possible view is that God simply chose that the Universe should be in a smooth and ordered state at the beginning of the expansion phase. We should not try to understand why, or question His reasons because the beginning of the Universe was the work of God. But the whole history of the Universe could be said to be the work of God. It appears that the Universe evolves according to well defined laws. These laws may, or may not, be ordained by God, but it seems that we can discover and understand them. Is it therefore, unreasonable to hope that the same or similar laws may also hold at the beginning of the Universe?"

Hawking, Stephen W., *A Brief History of Time* (New York: Bantam Books, 1988), 198 pp.

p. 152   "The progress of the human race in understanding the universe has established a small corner of order in an increasingly disordered universe. If you remember every word in this book, your memory will have recorded about two million pieces of information: the order in your brain will have increased by about two million units. However, while you have been reading the book, you will have converted at least a thousand calories of ordered energy, in the form of food, into disordered energy, in the form of heat that you lose to the air around you by convection and sweat. This will increase the disorder of the universe by about twenty million million million million units—or about ten million million million times the increase in order in your brain—and that's if you remember *everything* in the book."

Klein, Martin J., "Thermodynamics in Einstein's Thought," *Science*, vol. 157 (August 4, 1967), p. 509-516.

p. 509   Citing Albert Einstein: "Classical thermodynamics . . . is the only physical theory of universal content concerning which I am convinced that, within the framework of its basic concepts, it will never be overthrown."

Layzer, David, "The Arrow of Time," *Scientific American*, vol. 233 (December 1975), pp. 56-69. Layzer was Professor of Astronomy at Harvard.

p. 56   "This law states that all natural processes generate entropy, a measure of disorder."

p. 60   "The processes that define the historical and the thermodynamic arrows of time generate information and entropy respectively."

p. 60   "Thus a gain of information is always compensated for by an equal loss of entropy."

p. 65   "[Émile] Borel showed that no finite physical system can be considered closed."

p. 66   "In the real world, then, macroscopic information decays into microscopic information, but the microscopic information is dissipated by random perturbations."

p. 66   "Moreover [the universe] seems to conform to what I shall call the strong cosmological principle, which states that no statistical property of the universe defines a preferred position or direction in space."

Lehninger, Albert L., "Energy Transformation in the Cell," *Scientific American* (May 1960), pp. 102-114.

p. 102   "From the standpoint of thermodynamics the very existence of living things, with their marvelous diversity and complexity of structure and function, is improbable. The laws of thermodynamics say that energy must run 'downhill,' as in a flame, and that all systems of atoms and molecules must ultimately and inevitably assume the most random configurations with the least energy-content. Continuous 'uphill' work is necessary to create and maintain the structure of the cell. It is the capacity to extract energy from its surroundings and to use this energy in an orderly and directed manner that distinguishes the living human organism from the few dollars' (actually $5.66 in today's inflated market) worth of common chemical elements of which it is composed."

Lindsay, R. B., "Concept of Energy in Mechanics," *Scientific Monthly*, vol. 85 (October 1957), 188-194. Lindsay was Dean of the Graduate School and Director of the Ultrasonic Laboratory at Brown University.

p. 188   "Of all unifying concepts in the whole field of physical science, that of *energy* has proved to be the most significant and useful. Not only has it played a major role in the logical development of the structure of science, but, by common consent, it is the physical concept which has had and still has the widest influence on human life in all its aspects. Under the prevailing misnomer 'power,' it is the stock-in-trade of the engineer and that which makes the wheels of the world go round. . . . The interpretation of phenomena in terms of the transfer of energy between natural systems is the most powerful single tool in the understanding of the external world."

Lipson, H. S., "A Physicist Looks at Evolution," *Physics Bulletin*, vol. 31 (May 1980), p. 138.

          "It may be thought that [crystallisation] is a simple analogue from which the principles of life may be developed. We know, however, that crystallisation occurs because entropy S is not the deciding factor, internal energy U is also important. The quantity that must be minimised is the free energy (U-TS) and U is small for a crystal because the atoms are carefully packed together. As the temperature T increases, S becomes more important, and the crystal first becomes liquid (usually) and then gaseous.

          "Therefore, if we wish to regard the birth of an animal as regulated by the principles of thermodynamics, we must believe that the developing arrangement of atoms is that of lowest internal energy. My mind boggles!

          "If living matter is not, then, caused by the interplay of atoms, natural forces and radiation, how has it come into being? . . . I think, however, that we must . . . admit that the only acceptable explanation is *creation*. I know that this is anathema to physicists, as indeed it is to me, but we must not reject a theory that we do not like if the experimental evidence supports it."

Morris, Richard, *Time's Arrow: Scientific Attitudes Toward Time* (New York: Simon and Schuster, 1984), 240 pp.

pp. 212-3   "There are other problems associated with attempts to apply the second law of thermodynamics to the universe as a whole. Presumably the universe began in a very chaotic state. A chaotic state is, by definition, a state of high entropy (when we speak of 'chaos,' we mean that there is a great deal of disorder). On the other hand, numerous kinds of structure have appeared since the universe began. For example, stars and galaxies have formed. The creation of this structure, and the fact that stars gain entropy as they burn their nuclear fuel, would seem to imply that the universe is far from a state of maximum entropy now. But how can this be, if entropy was so high at the beginning? Doesn't the second law of thermodynamics tell us that entropy always increases with time?"

p. 213   "Other physicists are not so sure. Many of them think that the universe started out in a low entropy state, and various hypotheses have been constructed that attempt to describe what this low entropy state may have been like. But it is not likely that the controversy will be settled anytime soon."

Page, Don N., "Inflation Does Not Explain Time Asymmetry," *Nature*, vol. 304 (July 7, 1983), pp. 39-41. Page is in the Physics Department at Pennsylvania State University.

p. 39   "The time asymmetry of the Universe is expressed by the second law of thermodynamics, that entropy increases with time as order is transformed into disorder. The mystery is not that an ordered state should become disordered but that the early Universe was in a highly ordered state."

p. 40   "The unexplained mystery is why all spatially separated regions were apparently uncorrelated at the beginning."

p. 40   "But even if the second law should be formulated in a weaker form than the absence of initial spatial correlations, it is clearly a strong selection principle on the state of the Universe. There is no mechanism known as yet that would allow the Universe to begin in an arbitrary state and then evolve to its present highly-ordered state."

Pippard, A. B., *Elements of Chemical Thermodynamics for Advanced Students of Physics* (Cambridge, England: Cambridge University Press, 1966). Pippard, Ph.D., F.R.S., was Professor of Physics at Cambridge.

p. 88   "As a matter of fact, the entropy law has a much wider validity than might be supposed from the foregoing discussion, from which it might have appeared likely that fluctuations lay outside the realm of the entropy law. But it seems most probable that spontaneous fluctuations cannot be used in any way to violate either the entropy law or the second law. . . ."

p. 100   "There is thus no justification for the view, often glibly repeated, that the Second Law of Thermodynamics is only statistically true, in the sense that microscopic violations repeatedly occur, but never violations of any serious magnitude. On the contrary no evidence has ever been presented that the Second Law breaks down under any circumstances, and even the entropy law appears to have an almost universal validity, except in such futile experiments as we have discussed above, the removal and reapplication of constraints."

Rifkin, Jeremy, *Entropy: A New World View* (New York: Viking Press, 1980), 305 pp.

p. 6   "Now, however, a new world view is about to emerge, one that will eventually replace the Newtonian world machine as the organizing frame of history: the Entropy Law will preside as the ruling paradigm over the next period of history. Albert Einstein said that it is the premier law of all of science; Sir Arthur Eddington referred to it as the supreme metaphysical law of the entire universe. The Entropy Law is the second law of thermodynamics. The first law states that all matter and energy in the universe is constant, that it cannot be created or destroyed. Only its form can change but never its essence. The second law, the Entropy Law, states that matter and energy can only be changed in one direction, that is, from usable to unusable, or from available to unavailable, or from ordered to disordered."

p. 8   "There will also be those who will stubbornly refuse to accept the fact that the Entropy Law reigns supreme over all physical reality in the world. They will insist that the entropy process only applies in selective instances and that any attempt to apply it more broadly to society is to engage in the use of metaphor. Quite simply, they are wrong."

p. 55   "The Entropy Law says that evolution dissipates the overall available energy for life on this planet. Our concept of evolution is the exact opposite. We believe that evolution somehow magically creates greater overall value and order on earth. Now that the environment we live in is becoming so dissipated and disordered that it is apparent to the naked eye, we are for the first time beginning to have second thoughts about our views on evolution, progress, and the creation of things of material value. More about the implications of this in later sections."

Ross, John, "2nd Law of Thermodynamics," Letter-to-the-Editor, *Chemical and Engineering News*, vol. 58 (July 7, 1980), p. 40. Ross was at Harvard University.

p. 40   ". . . there are no known violations of the second law of thermodynamics. Ordinarily the second law is stated for isolated systems, but the second law applies equally well to open systems. . . .

                ". . . There is somehow associated with the field of far-from-equilibrium phenomena the notion that the second law of thermodynamics fails for such systems. It is important to make sure that this error does not perpetuate itself."

Rothman, Tony, "The Seven Arrows of Time," *Discover*, vol. 8 (February 1987), pp. 62-77.

p. 70   "In terms of confusion-to-understanding ratio, probably no concept in physics rates higher—or has caused more headaches—than entropy."

p. 72   "Since French scientists developed thermodynamics about 150 years ago, no one has come up with a generally accepted reason for why entropy always increases.

                "The dilemma is easy to see. Take a liter of gasoline and burn it. According to thermodynamics, entropy increases irreversibly—the seventh arrow says there's no way you can run the clock backward and reconstitute your liter of gasoline. But now look at the flame under a microscope. All the molecules obey Newton's laws precisely, and so cannot be subject to an arrow of time. The microscopic events are all time-reversible, yet the macroscopic event—the burning—isn't. The two great pillars of physics, thermodynamics and mechanics, rest on totally incompatible principles. Like the Catholic Church, split since the Middle Ages into East and West, physics is divided into two domains—the reversible and the irreversible. And although many have tried, no one has succeeded in mending the schism."

p. 72   "For Prigogine, irreversibility of nature is so pervasive that it must be built in at a fundamental level."

Rush, J. H., *The Dawn of Life* (New York: Signet, 1962), 284 pp. Rush was at the National Center for Atmospheric Research, Boulder, Colorado.

p. 35 "In the complex course of its evolution, life exhibits a remarkable contrast to the tendency expressed in the Second Law of Thermodynamics. Where the Second Law expresses an irreversible progression toward increased entropy and disorder, life evolves continually higher levels of order. The still more remarkable fact is that this evolutionary drive to greater and greater order also is irreversible. Evolution does not go backward."

Smith, Charles J., "Problems with Entropy in Biology," *Biosystems*, vol. 1 (1975), pp. 259-265.

p. 259 "The thermodynamicist immediately clarifies the latter question by pointing out that the Second Law classically refers to isolated systems which exchange neither energy nor matter with the environment; biological systems are open and exchange both energy and matter.

". . . This explanation, however, is not completely satisfying, because it still leaves the problem of how or why the ordering process has arisen (an apparent lowering of the entropy), and a number of scientists have wrestled with this issue.

"Bertalanffy called the relation between irreversible thermodynamics and information theory one of the most fundamental unsolved problems in biology. I would go further and include the problem of meaning and value."

Sommerfeld, Arnold, *Thermodynamics and Statistical Mechanics,* Lectures on Theoretical Physics, vol. V (New York: Academic Press, 1956), p. 155.

$$"p\frac{\partial s}{\partial t} + div\, s = \theta \qquad \text{(eq. 10)}$$

[where θ = entropy generated locally, s = entropy flux, e = mass density, $\frac{\partial s}{\partial t}$ = time rate of entropy change.]

"Equation (10) together with the inequality $\theta =$ can be regarded as the *differential formulation of the Second Law of Thermodynamics.* The statement in integral form, namely that the entropy in an isolated system cannot decrease, can be replaced by its corollary in differential form which asserts that the quantity of entropy generated locally cannot be negative irrespective of whether the system is isolated or not, and irrespective of whether the process under consideration is irreversible or not."

Tribus, Myron, and Edward C. McIrvine, "Energy and Information," *Scientific American*, vol. 224 (September 1971), pp. 179-188.

p. 188 "Similarly, the equivalence of these concepts with the informational concept is recognized.

"It is certain that the conceptual connection between information and the second law of thermodynamics is now firmly established."

Van Wylen, Gordon J., and Richard E. Sonntag, *Fundamentals of Classical Thermodynamics* (New York: Wiley, 1986), 746 pp. Van Wylen was Dean of Engineering at the University of Michigan, now President of Hope College.

pp. 236-7   "Does the second law of thermodynamics apply to the universe as a whole? Are there processes unknown to us that occur somewhere in the universe, such as 'continual creation,' that have a decrease in entropy associated with them, and thus offset the continual increase in entropy that is associated with the natural processes that are known to us? If the second law is valid for the universe (we of course do not know if the universe can be considered as an isolated system) how did it get in the state of low entropy? On the other end of the scale, if all processes known to us have an increase in entropy associated with them, what is the future of the natural world as we know it?

    "Quite obviously, it is impossible to give conclusive answers to these questions on the basis of the second law of thermodynamics alone. However, we see the second law of thermodynamics as a description of the prior and continuing work of a creator, who also holds the answer to our future destiny and that of the universe."

B. Entropy and Probability Versus Evolution

The second law of thermodynamics is also the law of increasing entropy or increasing probability. There is always a tendency, even in open systems, for the available energy of the system to be decreased, for the organized complexity of the system to become disorganized, or for its information content to be lowered. In fact, all three of these tendencies are effectively equivalent to each other, and all are directly opposed to vertically upward evolution.

Angrist, Stanley W., "Perpetual Motion Machines," *Scientific American*, vol. 218 (January 1968), pp. 115-122.

pp. 120-1   "The fact that, on the average, entropy continually increases does not, of course, rule out the possibility that occasional local decreases of entropy take place. It is only that the odds against such an event are extraordinarily long. . . . The chemist, Henry A. Bent, has calculated the odds against a local reversal of entropy, specifically the possibility that one calorie of thermal energy could be converted completely into work. His results can be expressed in terms of a familiar statistical example: the probability that a group of monkeys hitting typewriter keys at random could produce the works of Shakespeare. According to Bent's calculations, the likelihood of such a calorie conversion is about the same as the probability that the monkeys could produce Shakespeare's works 15 quadrillion times in succession without error."

Angrist, Stanley W., and Loren G. Hepler, *Order and Chaos* (New York: Basic Books, Inc., 1967), 237 pp.

p. 159   "Every system which is left to itself will, on the average, change toward a condition of maximum probability (Sometimes paraphrased as: If you think things are mixed up now, just wait)."

p. 160 "All other variables with which science is concerned can be increased or decreased—but entropy and time always increase."

pp. 203-4 "Life, the temporary reversal of a universal trend toward maximum disorder, was brought about by the production of information mechanisms. In order for such mechanisms to first arise it was necessary to have matter capable of forming itself into a self-reproducing structure that could extract energy from the environment for its first self-assembly. Directions for the reproduction of plans, for extraction of energy and chemicals from the environment, for the growth sequence and the mechanism for translating instructions into growth *all* had to be simultaneously present at that moment. This combination of events has seemed an incredibly unlikely happenstance and often divine intervention is prescribed as the only way it could have come about."

p. 205 "We are faced with the idea that genesis was a statistically unlikely event. We are also faced with the certainty that it occurred. Was there a temporary repeal of the second law that permitted a 'fortuitous concourse of atoms'? If so, study of the Repealer and genesis is a subject properly left to theologians. Or we may hold with the more traditional scientific attitude that the origin of life is beclouded merely because we don't know enough about the composition of the atmosphere and other conditions on the earth many eons ago."

Asimov, Isaac, *In the Beginning* (New York: Crown Publishers, Inc., 1981), 234 pp.

p. 24 "The cosmic egg may be structureless (as far as we know), but it apparently represented a very orderly conglomeration of matter. Its explosion represented a vast shift in the direction of disorder, and ever since, the amount of disorder in the Universe has been increasing. . . .

"Within the vast shift toward disorder involved in the big bang and the expansion of the Universe, it is possible for there to be local shifts in the direction of order, so that the galaxies can form and within them individual stars, including our sun."

p. 24 "The existence of the cosmic egg is, however, itself something of an anomaly. If the general movement of the Universe is from order to disorder, how did the order (which presumably existed in the cosmic egg) originate? Where did it come from?"

pp. 25-26 "I have a hunch that the 'missing mass' required to raise the density to the proper figure will yet be found and that the Universe will yet be discovered to oscillate."

Capra, Fritjof, *The Web of Life* (New York: Anchor Books, 1996), 347 pp. Dr. Capra is Director of the Center for Ecoliteracy, in Berkeley, California, one of the most influential "New-Age" scientists.

p. 89 "In classical thermodynamics the dissipation of energy in heat transfer, friction, and the like was always associated with waste. Prigogine's concept of a dissipative structure introduced a radical change in this view by showing that in open systems dissipation becomes a source of order."

p. 228   "It has been estimated that those chance errors occur at a rate of about one per several hundred million cells in each generation. This frequency does not seem to be sufficient to explain the evolution of the great diversity of life forms, given the well-known fact that most mutations are harmful and only very few result in useful variations."

Darlington, P. J., Jr., *Evolution for Naturalists* (New York: John Wiley, 1980), 262 pp.

p. 15   "The outstanding evolutionary mystery now is how matter has originated and evolved, why it has taken its present form in the universe and on the earth, and why it is capable of forming itself into complex living sets of molecules. This capability is inherent in matter as we know it, in its organization and energy."

p. 234   "It is a fundamental evolutionary generalization that no external agent imposes life on matter. Matter takes the forms it does because it has the inherent capacity to do so. . . . This is one of the most remarkable and mysterious facts about our universe; that matter exists that has the capacity to form itself into the most complex patterns of life. By this I do *not* mean to suggest the existence of a vital force or entelechy or universal intelligence, but just to state an attribute of matter as represented by the atoms and molecules we know. . . . We do not solve the mystery by using our inadequate brains to invent mystic explanations."

Flam, Faye, "Could Protons be Mortal After All?" *Science*, vol. 257 (September 25, 1992), pp. 1862-1863.

p. 1862   "Perhaps the most disturbing piece of speculation to come out of theoretical physics recently is the prediction that the whole universe is in decay. Not only do living things die, species go extinct, and stars burn out, but the apparently immutable protons in the nucleus of every atom are slowly dissolving. Eventually—in more than a quadrillion quadrillion years—nothing will be left of the universe but a dead mist of electrons, photons, and neutrinos."

p. 1863   "If protons really are decaying, physicists will be elated, and that's not as cold-blooded as it sounds; for British physicist and author Freeman Dyson, there's room for hope even in a universe ruled by a grand unified theory. In his 1988 book *Infinite in All Directions*, Dyson proposes that as matter decays, humans will be able to transfer their intelligence to new media, eventually learning to live as part of the electrons and photons that are left over. 'The supreme test of life's adaptability,' he calls it."

Frautschi, Steven, "Entropy in an Expanding Universe," *Science*, vol. 217 (August 13, 1982), pp. 593-599.

p. 593   ". . . our topic is extremely speculative."

p. 594   "At present we have no idea why the early universe was so homogeneous over distance scales which were not then within each other's light horizons. But suppose we accept this as given and introduce the concept of a 'causal region,' all parts of which can influence one another causally during (say) a doubling of time of the expansion."

p. 595   "We have thus come to a conclusion which stands the closed 19th century model on its head. Far from approaching equilibrium, the expanding universe as viewed in a succession of causal regions falls further and further behind achieving equilibrium. This gives ample scope for interesting non-equilibrium structures to develop out of initial chaos, as has occurred in nature."

p. 598   "We therefore turn to black holes as the free energy source, and envision how life might attempt to maintain itself indefinitely, and even play a major role in shaping the universe. A sufficiently resourceful intelligence inhabiting a critical universe learns how to move black holes, bringing them together from increasingly widely separated locations and merging them to increase the entropy."

p. 599   "If radiant energy production continues without limit, there remains hope that life capable of using it forever can be created."

Hawking, Stephen W., "The Direction of Time," *New Scientist* (July 9, 1987), pp. 46-49.

p. 49   "If you have remembered every word in this article, your memory will have recorded about 150,000 bits of information. Thus the order in your brain will have increased by about 150,000 units. However, while you have been reading this article, you will have converted about 300,000 joules of ordered energy, in the form of food, into disordered energy, in the form of heat which you lose to the air around you by convection and sweat. This will increase the disorder of the Universe by about 3×10^{24} units, about 20 million million million times the increase in order because you remember my article."

Horgan, John, "From Complexity to Perplexity," *Scientific American*, vol. 272 (June 1995), pp. 74-99.

p. 77   "Artificial life, a major subfield of complexity studies, is 'fact-free science,' according to one critic [John Maynard Smith]. But it excels at generating computer graphics."

Huxley, Julian, *Evolution in Action* (New York: Harper and Row, 1953), 182 pp.

pp. 45-46   "A proportion of favorable mutations of one in a thousand does not sound much, but is probably generous, since so many mutations are lethal, preventing the organism living at all, and the great majority of the rest throw the machinery slightly out of gear. And a total of a million mutational steps sounds a great deal, but is probably an understatement—after all, that only means one step every two thousand years during biological time as a whole. However, let us take these figures as being reasonable estimates. With this proportion, but without any selection, we should clearly have to breed a thousand strains to get one favorable mutation; a million strains (a thousand squared) to get one containing two favorable mutations; and so on, up to a thousand to the millionth power to get one containing a million.

"Of course, this could not really happen, but it is a useful way of visualizing the fantastic odds against getting a number of favorable mutations in one strain through pure chance alone. A thousand to the millionth power, when written out, becomes the figure 1 with three million noughts after it; and that would take three large volumes of about 500 pages each, just to print! Actually, this is a meaninglessly large figure, but it shows what a degree of improbability natural selection has to surmount, and can circumvent. One with three million noughts after it is the measure of the unlikeliness of a horse—the odds against it happening at all. No one would bet on anything so improbable happening: and yet it *has* happened! It has happened, thanks to the working of natural selection and the properties of living substance which make natural selection inevitable!"

Mendelssohn, K., "Probability Enters Physics," *American Scientist*, vol. 49 (March 1961), pp. 37-49.

p. 42   "Speculations which have intrigued the philosophers more than the physicists concern the ultimate fate of the universe as a consequence of the second law of thermodynamics. There ought to exist a most probable, and therefore final, state of maximum entropy. Once this is attained, nothing more can happen and all processes, including those of life, must come to an end. This 'entropy death' seems to be as inescapable as the dissolution in a Buddhist Nirvana and equally far off. We have, at present, no evidence of any failure of the second law nor can we see how such failure could be accommodated in our physical world. However, most physicists are averse to extrapolations involving the beginning or the end of our time scale."

Potter, Van Rensselaer, "Society and Science," *Science*, vol. 146 (November 20, 1964), pp. 1018-1022.

p. 1018   "Man has long been aware that his world has a tendency to fall apart. Tools wear out, fishing nets need repair, roofs leak, iron rusts, wood decays, loved ones sicken and die, relatives quarrel, and nations make war. . . . We instinctively resent the decay of orderly systems such as the living organism and work to restore such systems to their former or even higher level of organization."

Rifkin, Jeremy, *Entropy: A New World View* (New York: Viking Press, 1980), 305 pp.

p. 6   "The Entropy Law will preside as a the ruling paradigm over the next period of history. Albert Einstein said that it is the premier law of all science; Sir Arthur Eddington referred to it as the supreme metaphysical law of the entire universe."

p. 55   "The Entropy Law says that evolution dissipates the overall available energy for life on this planet. Our concept of evolution is the exact opposite. We believe that evolution somehow magically creates greater overall value and order on earth. Now that the environment we live in is becoming so dissipated and disordered that it is apparent to the naked eye, we are for the first time beginning to have second thoughts about our views on evolution, progress, and the creation of things of material value."

p. 55   "Evolution means the creation of larger and larger islands of order at the expense of ever greater seas of disorder in the world. There is not a single biologist or physicist who can deny this central truth. Yet, who is willing to stand up in a classroom or before a public forum and admit it?"

Simpson, George Gaylord, and W. S. Beck, *Life: An Introduction to Biology*, 2nd ed. (New York: Harcourt, Brace & World, Inc., 1965).

p. 466   "We have repeatedly emphasized the fundamental problems posed for the biologist by the fact of life's complex organization. We have seen that organization requires work for its maintenance and that the universal quest for food is in part to provide the energy needed for this work. But the simple expenditure of energy is not sufficient to develop and maintain order. A bull in a china shop performs work, but he neither creates nor maintains organization. The work needed is *particular work*; it must follow specifications; it requires information on how to proceed."

p. 466   "This search led us to the nucleus and its chromosomes, which proved to be the carriers of the inherited specifications ultimately responsible for the organization of the living system."

Stravropoulos, George P., Letter-to-the-Editor, re. Weisskopf, "The Frontiers and Limits of Science," as published in July 1977 issue of *American Scientist*, vol. 65 (November-December 1977), pp. 674-676.

p. 674   "He makes it appear as though crystals and highly ordered organic molecules belong to the same class, when in fact they do not. When a crystal is broken up, the smaller crystals are physically and chemically identical to the original. This is never observed with (organic) molecules; when the original molecule is split up, lesser molecules appear, and part of the original information is lost. To ignore such fundamental differences in an effort to arrive at some general overview or law is to create a false overview, a pseudolaw.

"... To say that 'there is an obvious tendency of nature from disorder to order and organization' and to advance this idea to a 'fourth law' is to misunderstand completely and to compromise all of thermodynamics.

"... Yet, under ordinary conditions, no complex organic molecule can ever form spontaneously but will rather disintegrate, in agreement with the second law. Indeed, the more complex it is, the more unstable it is, and the more assured, sooner or later, is its disintegration. Photosynthesis and all life processes, and life itself, despite confused or deliberately confusing language, *cannot* yet be understood in terms of thermodynamics or any other exact science.

"The thrust of Dr. Weisskoff's argument that order appears in a *cooling* body ... runs against his statement that the flow of heat from the sun to the Earth resulted in photosynthesis and the development of 'highly hierarchical' forms of organic matter on earth. For one thing, why only Earth? Why has Mars failed the test? And for another, the sun cools and Earth necessarily warms up (if we consider *only* the 'sun-Earth system') and therefore it is the sun that should be drawing toward order, Earth toward disorder."

Thomas, Lewis, "The Miraculous Membrane," *Intellectual Digest*, vol. 4, no. 6 (February 1974), pp. 56-57.

p. 56   "It takes a membrane to make sense out of disorder in biology. You have to be able to catch energy and hold it, storing precisely the needed amount and releasing it in measured shares. A cell does this, and so do the organelles inside. Each unit is poised in the flow of solar energy, tapping off energy from metabolic surrogates of the sun. To stay alive, you have to be able to hold out against equilibrium, maintain imbalance, bank against entropy. In our kind of world you can only transact this business with membranes."

p. 56   "You could say that the breathing of oxygen into the atmosphere was the result of evolution, or you could turn it around and say that evolution was the result of oxygen. You can have it either way."

p. 56   "It is another illustration of our fantastic luck that oxygen filters out the very bands of ultraviolet light that are most devastating to nucleic acids and proteins, while allowing full penetration of the visible light needed for photosynthesis. If it had not been for this semipermeability, we could never have come along."

Wade, Nicholas, "Nicholas Georgescu-Roegen: Entropy the Measure of Economic Man," *Science*, vol. 190 (October 31, 1975), pp. 447-450.

p. 448   "So the entropy law is also saying that the natural state of things is to pass always from order to disorder."

p. 448   "The difference is important only to living organisms, because they exist on the slope between low entropy and high. They absorb low entropy by feeding directly or indirectly, on sunlight, and they give out high entropy in the form of waste and heat."

p. 448   "Once we recall that none of man's activities eludes the entropy law, the economic process appears in a very different light. For one thing, the process can now be recognized to be not circular and timeless, but irrevocable."

p. 448   It places paramount emphasis on the inputs to the process (energy and natural resources) and on the output (pollution)."

p. 448   "The earth's outstanding recoverable reserves of fossil fuel are estimated to be the equivalent of about two weeks sunlight."

p. 450   "Asked the reason for his critics' muteness, he replies with a Romanian proverb: ' " Don't mention the cord in the house of the hanged." ' 'I am very unpopular with economists,' he says, comparing his attack on standard economics to the action of a man who confiscates marbles from children."

Weisskopf, Victor F., "The Frontiers and Limits of Science," *American Scientist*, vol. 65 (July-August 1977), pp. 405-411. Weisskopf is former head of the Department of Physics, MIT, President of American Academy of Arts & Science.

p. 405   "Einstein considered this development to be the great miracle of science; in his words, 'the most incomprehensible fact of nature is the fact that nature is comprehensible.'"

p. 406   "The dynamics of the nucleus is dominated by the nuclear force that acts between the protons and the neutrons—the particles which are the constituents of the nucleus. This rather strong force is of non-electric character and in many ways is still a mystery to scientists."

p. 407   "Furthermore, the laws that govern radioactivity—the slow change of a neutron into a proton with the emission of an electron and a neutrino—are only superficially known, and their deeper significance is still hidden."

p. 409   "The evolutionary history of the world, from the 'big bang' to the present universe, is a series of gradual steps from the simple to the complicated, from the unordered to the organized, from the formless gas of elementary particles to the morphic atoms and molecules, and further to the still more structured liquids and solids, and finally to the sophisticated living organisms. There is an obvious tendency of nature from disorder to order and organization. Is this tendency in contradiction to the famous second law of thermodynamics, which says that disorder must increase in nature? The law says that entropy, the measure of disorder, must grow in any natural system."

p. 411   "It must be pointed out that science itself has its roots and origins outside its own rational realm of thinking. . . .

"This emotional and social embedding of science is the precondition of the quest for scientific truth."

Wicken, Jeffrey S., "The Generation of Complexity in Evolution: A Thermodynamic and Information-Theoretical Discussion," *Journal of Theoretical Biology*, vol. 77 (April 1979), pp. 349-365.

p. 349   "Evolutionary processes are *anamorphic*, or complexity-generating. The passage of evolutionary time is accompanied by the emergence of structures having progressively greater morphological and functional complexity. But the essential nature of evolutionary anamorphosis remains enigmatic."

pp. 353-4   "'Organized' systems are to be carefully distinguished from 'ordered' systems. Neither kind of system is 'random'; but whereas ordered systems are generated according to simple algorithms and therefore lack complexity, organized systems must be assembled element by element according to an external 'wiring diagram' with a high information content. Their structures are periodic without being random. Organization, then, is a functional complexity and carries functional information. It is non-random by *design* or by *selection*, rather than by the *a priori* necessity of crystallographic 'order.'"

p. 361   "The cosmological arrow generates randomness or disorder, whereas the evolutionary arrow generates complexity. A fully reductionist theory of evolution must demonstrate that the evolutionary arrow can be derived from the cosmological arrow."

C. Supposed Order from Disorder

The current efforts of evolutionists to escape the entropy barrier are mainly focused on the notion of what are called "dissipative structures," a notion proposed by Prigogine. There is also talk of self-organizing systems, of order from chaos and other such oxymorons. Wishful thinking notwithstanding, these notions remain metaphysical, not observational. The entropy barrier has not yet been scaled.

Brooks, Daniel R., and E. O. Wiley, *Evolution as Entropy* (Chicago: University of Chicago Press, 1986), 335 pp.

p. 43   "Our theory suggests that evolution is a phenomenon involving systems (species) far from equilibrium. The hierarchy results from speciation, which we will try to show exhibits entropic dynamics *analogous* to 'ordering through fluctuations' (Prigogine, Nicolis, and Babloyantz, 1972). It is important to understand that this is an analogy. Ordering through fluctuations in strictly thermodynamic systems is a direct by-product of energy flows. Ordering through fluctuations in evolution is a direct by-product of information and cohesion changes and not, we submit, energy flows."

pp. 70-1   "Why is there order and not chaos in the living world? Because living systems, organisms and species, are individualized dissipative structures (1) exhibiting finite information and cohesion, (2) maintaining themselves through irreversible dissipation of matter and energy, and (3) existing in an open energy system."

p. 72   ". . . nonequilibrium systems tend to evolve toward states of minimum entropy increase, or minimum entropy production. These states are historically emergent and can be discerned retrospectively, but cannot be predicted from initial conditions."

p. 74   "Evolution is a process that slows down the entropy decay of lineages, minimizing their entropy increases. This suggests that, as the interplay of information and cohesion, biological evolution should exhibit an intrinsic tendency toward efficiency or parsimony, which in turn should relate to the principle of minimum entropy production."

Capra, Fritjof, *The Web of Life* (New York: Anchor Books, 1996), 347 pp. Dr. Capra is Director of the Center for Ecoliteracy, in Berkeley, California, one of the most influential "New-Age" scientists.

p. 48   "According to the second law, some mechanical energy is always dissipated into heat that cannot be completely recovered. Thus the entire world machine is running down and will eventually grind to a halt.

    "This grim picture of cosmic evolution was in sharp contrast with the evolutionary thinking among nineteenth-century biologists, who observed that the living universe evolves from disorder to order, toward states of ever-increasing complexity."

p. 49   "The formulation of the new thermodynamics of open systems had to wait until the 1970s. It was the great achievement of Ilya Prigogine, who used a new mathematics to reevaluate the second law by radically rethinking traditional scientific views of order and disorder, which enabled him to resolve unambiguously the two contradictory nineteenth-century views of evolution."

p. 78   "While biologists know the precise structure of a few genes, they know very little of the ways in which genes communicate and cooperate in the development of an organism. In other words, they know the alphabet of the genetic code but have almost no idea of its syntax. It is now apparent that most of the DNA—perhaps as much as 95 percent—may be used for integrative activities about which biologists are likely to remain ignorant as long as they adhere to mechanistic models."

p. 82   "The structure of the human brain is enormously complex. It contains about 10 billion nerve cells (neurons), which are interlinked in a vast network through 1,000 billion junctions (synapses). The whole brain can be divided into subsections, or subnetworks, which communicate with each other in network fashion. All this results in intricate patterns of intertwined webs, networks nesting within larger networks."

Charlesworth, Brian, "Entropy: The Great Illusion," review of *Evolution as Entropy* by Daniel R. Brooks and E. O. Wiley (Chicago: University of Chicago Press, 1986, 335 pp.), *Evolution*, vol. 40, no. 4 (1986), pp. 879-881. Charlesworth is in the Department of Biology, University of Chicago.

p. 879   "While the structural complexity of living organisms as little violates the second law of thermodynamics (or any other law of physics) as does that of a television set or a jet engine, we need to look elsewhere for a detailed understanding of the origin of this complexity during development and evolution."

p. 879   "Their work suffers, however, from the usual faults of half-baked theorizing in biology. The worst of these is the lack of any convincing derivation of the supposed laws of change from known principles, in contrast to the program of statistical mechanics which provides the background for their ideas."

p. 880   "It should be clear that the claim for an inherent evolutionary increase in entropy and organization is based on an arbitrary model which shows signs of having been constructed simply to yield the desired result. . . . There is nothing in evolutionary or developmental biology that justifies their assumptions that a successful mutation (which seems merely to mean a selectively neutral one in their model) is always associated with an increase in some global measure of phenotype. Nor is there anything to support the assumption that new species arise as the result of single gene mutations and are initially genetically uniform. If these assumptions are removed, the whole edifice collapses."

p. 880   "Mutations with drastic phenotypic effects are overwhelmingly likely to cause disorganization of development, as a glance around a *Drosophila* lab will convince anyone."

Collier, John, "Entropy in Evolution," *Biology and Philosophy*, vol. 1, no. 1 (1986), pp. 5-24.

p. 21   "Wicken argues that dissipative structures persist by 'feeding' on the negentropy of their surroundings, but that Brooks and Wiley have developed a theory which depends only on internal factors, which he finds puzzling, and tries to trace errors in their use of equations from non-equilibrium thermodynamics. This is a misrepresentation of their views, since they assume that species are maintained by thermodynamic non-equilibrium processes, and then proceed to study how these structures evolve. Wicken has a point that there is something to be understood about the relation of species to their environment. This is a commonplace observation, however. What is really remarkable is that so much of the evolution of species can be understood without looking at the details of environmental interchanges. There is a clear sense in which species are informationally at least strongly analogous to dissipative structures in thermodynamics."

Felsenstein, Joseph, "Waiting for Post-Neo Darwin," review of *Evolutionary Theory: Paths into the Future* by E. O. Wiley (1984, 271 pp.), *Evolution*, vol. 40, no. 4 (1986), pp. 883-889. Felsenstein was at the Department of Genetics, University of Washington.

p. 887   "I was disappointed in Brooks and Wiley's discussion of entropy and evolution because it did not seem to me that they present a theory at all. It is not that their theory is wrong; it seems to be vacuous instead."

p. 888   "Brooks and Wiley have not produced a new evolutionary theory, or even a very useful redescription of existing theories, but I cannot fault them for trying. They see the importance of the task, and here they are right and my fellow population geneticists are both wrong and wrongheaded."

Lepkowski, Will, "The Social Thermodynamics of Ilya Prigogine," *Chemical and Engineering News*, vol. 57 (April 16, 1979), pp. 30-33.

p. 30   "Prigogine's work has long been of interest to systems theorists seeking to apply the logic of their fields to global problems. One such scientist is Ervin Laszlo of the United Nations. 'What I see Prigogine doing,' says Laszlo, 'is giving legitimization to the process of evolution—self-organization under conditions of change. . . . Its analogy to social systems and evolution could be very fruitful. These are the same types of equations that could be applied to social systems.'"

p. 31   "(The word entropy comes from the Greek, meaning evolution.)"

p. 31   "In fact, increased complexity leading to increased order is virtually the definition of evolution."

Lewin, Roger, "A Downward Slope to Greater Diversity," *Science*, vol. 217 (September 24, 1982), pp. 1239-1240.

p. 1239   "One problem biologists have faced is the apparent contradiction by evolution of the second law of thermodynamics. Systems should decay through time, giving less, not more, order.

                "One legitimate response to this challenge is that life on earth is an open system with respect to energy and therefore the process of evolution sidesteps the law's demand for increasing disorder with time. A different, and currently contentious, response comes from Edward Wiley and Daniel Brooks. . . . In a paper entitled 'Victims of History—a Nonequilibrium Approach to Evolution' (*Systematic Zoology* 31, 1 (1982)), they argue that evolution and the appearance of a hierarchy of life is not only compatible with the second law of thermodynamics but is also an inevitable outcome of the inescapable increase of entropy in the system."

p. 1239   "The application of nonequilibrium thermodynamics to living systems is still relatively new and controversial. . . . 'I see how you can do this with molecules,' [Prigogine] told Brooks, 'but I don't see how you can do it with species. I don't understand the extrapolation.'"

p. 1240   "What Brooks and Wiley have presented so far in their theory are heuristic formulations, not mathematical proofs. . . .

                "This quantitative analysis requires a yet to be realized ability to measure changes in information and cohesion that are reflected in a species' evolutionary change.

                "'We may postulate a theoretical amount of added information above which . . . speciation may occur,' they write. 'We would suggest that the threshold values differ between species and, that while we may examine the history of exceeding thresholds by studying the results of history, we cannot predict the future of evolution.'"

Prigogine, Ilya, Gregoire Nicolis, and Agnes Babloyantz, "Thermodynamics of Evolution," *Physics Today*, vol. 25, no. 11 (November 1972), pp. 23-28.

p. 23   "The point is that in a nonisolated system there exists a possibility for formation of ordered, low-entropy structures at sufficiently low temperatures. This ordering principle is responsible for the appearance of ordered structures such as crystals as well as for the phenomena of phase transitions.

"Unfortunately this principle cannot explain the formation of biological structures. The probability that at ordinary temperatures a macroscopic number of molecules is assembled to give rise to the highly ordered structures and to the coordinated functions characterizing living organisms is vanishingly small. The idea of spontaneous genesis of life in its present form is therefore highly improbable, even on the scale of the billions of years during which prebiotic evolution occurred."

p. 25   "In all these phenomena, a new ordering mechanism, not reducible to the equilibrium principle, appears. For reasons to be explained later, we shall refer to this principle as *order through fluctuations*. The structures are created by the continuous flow of energy and matter from the outside world; their maintenance requires a critical distance from equilibrium, that is, a minimum level of dissipation. For all these reasons we have called them *dissipative structures*."

Prigogine, Ilya, "Can Thermodynamics Explain Biological Order?" *Impact of Science on Society*, vol. 23, (July/September 1973), pp. 159-179. Prigogine was a professor on the Faculty of Sciences, Universite Libre de Belgique.

p. 162   "Entropy, in short, is the measurement of molecular disorder. The law of the irreversible increase in entropy is a law of progressive disorganization, of the complete disappearance of the initial conditions."

pp. 169-70   "It would be too simple to say that the concepts of life and dissipative structures are intermingled. In order to see where the biological structures fit, of course, it seems necessary to leave aside laws relating to equilibrium order and to keep in mind that characteristically biological phenomena occur far removed from a state of thermodynamic equilibrium. But it is not just one instability that makes it possible to cross the threshold between life and non-life; it is, rather, a succession of instabilities of which we are only now beginning to identify certain stages."

p. 170   "Moreover, we shouldn't lose sight of the fact that equilibrium structures also occur in biology. We need cite only one striking example. The virus is not a dissipative structure; it is quite simply an equilibrium structure, the laws governing the formation of which are analogous to those of crystallization. One needs to understand, however, that this equilibrium structure can be apperceived only within the framework of dissipative structures."

p. 178   "But let us have no illusions. If today we look into the situation where the analogy with the life sciences is the most striking—even if we discovered within biological systems some operations distant from the state of equilibrium—our research would still leave us quite unable to grasp the extreme complexity of the simplest of organisms."

Prigogine, Ilya, and Isabelle Stengers, *Order Out of Chaos* (New York: Bantam Books, 1984), 349 pp.

p. xxix "Our scientific heritage includes two basic questions to which till now no answer was provided. One is the relation between disorder and order. The famous law of increase of entropy describes the world as evolving from order to disorder; still, biological or social evolution shows us the complex emerging from the simple."

p. 12 "We now know that far from equilibrium, new types of structures may originate spontaneously. In far-from-equilibrium conditions we may have transformation from disorder, from thermal chaos, into order. New dynamic states of matter may originate, states that reflect the interaction of a given system with its surroundings. We have called these new structures *dissipative structures* to emphasize the constructive role of dissipative processes in their formation."

p. 129 "There is another question, which has plagued us for more than a century: What significance does the evolution of a living being have in the world described by thermodynamics, a world of ever-increasing disorder?"

p. 175 "The problem of biological order involves the transition from the molecular activity to the supermolecular order of the cell. This problem is far from being solved."

p. 176 "The early appearance of life is certainly an argument in favor of the idea that life is the result of spontaneous self-organization that occurs whenever conditions for it permit. However, we must admit that we remain far from any quantitative theory."

pp. 286-7 "We have come to one of our main conclusions: At all levels, be it the level of macroscopic physics, the level of fluctuations, or the microscopic level, *nonequilibrium is the source of order. Nonequilibrium brings 'order out of chaos.'* But as we already mentioned, the concept of order (or disorder) is more complex than was thought."

Rifkin, Jeremy, *Algeny* (New York: Viking Press, 1983), 298 pp.

pp. 211-2 "While cybernetics is largely concerned with how systems maintain themselves over time, it also makes room for the idea of evolutionary change in systems by way of positive feedback. Ilya Prigogine, a Belgian physical chemist, has devised a theory of dissipative structures to explain how cybernetic principles can incorporate the notion of evolution as well as homeostasis. According to Prigogine, all living things and many nonliving things are dissipative structures. That is, they maintain their structure by the continual flow of energy through their system. That flow of energy keeps the system in a constant state of flux. For the most part, the fluctuations are small and can be easily adjusted to by way of negative feedback. However, occasionally the fluctuations may become so great that the system is unable to adjust and positive feedback takes over. The fluctuations feed off themselves, and the amplification can easily overwhelm the entire system. When that happens, the system either collapses or reorganizes itself. If it is able to reorganize itself, the new dissipative structure will always exhibit a higher order of complexity, integration, and a greater energy flow through than its predecessor. Each successive reordering, because it is more complex than the one preceding it, is even more vulnerable to fluctuations and reordering. Thus, increased complexity creates the condition for evolutionary development."

Wald, Robert, "Particle Creation Near Black Holes," *American Scientist*, vol. 65 (September-October 1977), pp. 585-589.

p. 589   "If black holes are present in the universe, the second law of thermodynamics no longer holds in the form stated above, because matter can fall into a black hole and disappear into a spacetime singularity. When it does so, the total entropy of matter in the universe decreases. . . . However, suppose we define the total *generalized entropy S′ by*

$$S' = S + \frac{\pi}{2} \frac{KC^3}{GH} A ,$$

where S represents the total entropy of all matter in the universe *outside* black holes and A is the total surface area of all black holes. Then although S and A individually may decrease, it appears to be true that S' never decreases! . . . it appears that we have a new law of physics, the 'generalized second law of thermodynamics.'" [note, G = gravitational constant; C = speed of light, H = Planck's constant]

Chapter 4

Evolutionary Genetics

A. The Nature of Gene Mutations

Modern evolutionists have been unable to discern any biological mechanism for producing real evolutionary changes except that of gene mutations. The problem is that all mutations so far observed either in nature or the laboratory have been either neutral or harmful. The necessary "beneficial" mutations are evidently only wishful thinking. This, of course, is only to be expected in light of the universal law of entropy, as discussed in the previous chapter. Mutations are essentially random changes in highly ordered systems and the probability of a chance increase in order is vanishingly small.

Ayala, Francisco J., "The Mechanisms of Evolution," *Scientific American*, vol. 239 (September 1978), pp. 56-69.

p. 58   "A mutation can be considered an error in the replication of DNA prior to its translation into protein."

p. 59   "The forces that give rise to gene mutations operate at random in the sense that genetic mutations occur without reference to their future adaptiveness in the environment."

p. 63   "It therefore seems clear that, contrary to Darwin's conception, most of the genetic variation in populations arises not from new mutations at each generation but from the reshuffling of previously accumulated mutations by recombination. Although mutation is the ultimate source of all genetic variation, it is a relatively rare event, providing a mere trickle of new alleles into the much larger reservoir of stored genetic variation. Indeed recombination alone is sufficient to enable a population to expose its hidden variation for many generations without the need for new genetic input by mutation."

p. 64   "In any case there can be no doubt that the staggering amount of genetic variation in natural populations provides ample opportunities for evolution to occur. Hence it is not surprising that whenever a new environmental challenge materializes—a change of climate, the introduction of a new predator or competitor, man-made pollution—populations are usually able to adapt to it.

"A dramatic recent example of such adaptation is the evolution by insect species of resistance to pesticides. . . . Insect resistance to a pesticide was first reported in 1947 for the housefly (*Musca domestica*) with respect to DDT. Since then resistance to pesticides has been reported in at least 225 species of insects and other arthropods. The genetic variants required for resistance to the most diverse kinds of pesticides were apparently present in every one of the populations exposed to these man-made compounds."

Ayala, Francisco J., "Genotype, Environment and Population Numbers," *Science*, vol. 162 (December 27, 1968), pp. 1453-1459.

p. 1456   "The process of mutation ultimately furnishes the materials for adaptation to changing environments. Genetic variations which increase the reproductive fitness of a population to its environment are preserved and multiplied by natural selection. Deleterious mutations are eliminated more or less rapidly depending on the magnitude of their harmful effects. High-energy radiations, such as x-rays, increase the rate of mutations. Mutations induced by radiations are random in the sense that they arise independently of their effects on the fitness of the individuals which carry them. Randomly induced mutations are usually deleterious. In a precisely organized and coupled system like the genome of an organism, a random change will most frequently decrease, rather than increase, the orderliness or useful information of the system."

Ayala, Francisco J., "Teleological Explanations in Evolutionary Biology," *Philosophy of Science*, vol. 37 (March 1970), pp. 1-15.

p. 3   "It is probably fair to estimate the frequency of a majority of mutations in higher organisms between one in ten thousand, and one in a million per gene per generation. . . . Mutation provides the raw materials of evolution."

p. 11   "Evolution can be explained without recourse to a Creator or planning agent external to the organs themselves. . . . The evidence of the fossil record is against any necessitating force, external or immanent, leading the process toward specified goals."

Crow, James F., "Ionizing Radiation and Evolution," *Scientific American*, vol. 201 (September 1959), pp. 138-160. Crow was Chairman of Medical Genetics at the University of Wisconsin.

p. 138   "The mutation rate affects not only the evolution of the human species but also the life of the individual. Almost every mutation is harmful, and it is the individual who pays the price. Any human activity that tends to increase the mutation rate must therefore raise serious health and moral problems for man."

p. 155   "Of all the natural selection that occurs, only a small fraction leads to any progressive or directional change. Most selection is devoted to maintaining the status quo, to eliminating recurrent harmful mutations, or to adjusting to transitory changes in the environment. Thus much of the theory of natural selection must be a theory of statics rather than dynamics."

p. 156   "The process of mutation also produces ill-adapted types. The result is a lowering of the average fitness of the population, the price that asexual, as well as sexual, species pay for the privilege of evolution. Intuition tells us that the effect of mutation on fitness should be proportional to the mutation rate; Haldane has shown that the reduction in fitness is, in fact, exactly equal to the mutation rate."

p. 160   "There can be little doubt that man would be better off if he had a lower mutation-rate. I would argue, in our present ignorance, that the ideal rate for the foreseeable future would be zero."

Curtis, Howard J., "Biological Mechanisms Underlying the Aging Process," *Science*, vol. 141 (August 23, 1963), pp. 686-694.

p. 688   "Certainly the vast majority of mutations must be deleterious, so if the organs of older animals contain appreciable numbers of cells which are carrying mutations, it is a virtual certainty that the organs are functioning less efficiently than they otherwise would."

p. 694   "It is suggested that the mutation rates for somatic cells are very much higher than for gametic cells and that this circumstance insures the death of the individual and the survival of the species."

Dobzhansky, Theodosius, "On Methods of Evolutionary Biology," *American Scientist*, vol. 45 (December 1957), pp. 381-392.

p. 385   "The process of mutation is the only known source of the raw materials of genetic variability, and hence of evolution. It is subject to experimental study, and considerable progress has been accomplished in this study in recent years. An apparent paradox has been disclosed. Although the living matter becomes adapted to its environment through formation of superior genetic patterns from mutational components, the process of mutation itself is not adaptive. On the contrary, the mutants which arise are, with rare exceptions, deleterious to their carriers, at least in the environment which the species normally encounters. Some of them are deleterious apparently in all environments. Therefore the mutation process alone, not corrected and guided by natural selection, would result in degeneration and extinction."

Drake, John W., "Environmental Mutagenic Hazards," *Science*, vol. 187 (February 14, 1975), pp. 503-14. Drake was Chairman of Committee 17 of the Environmental Mutagen Society.

p. 503   "Most mutations producing effects large enough to be observed are deleterious, although other mutations may produce little or no consequence, and certain rare mutations may even be advantageous."

p. 503   "Furthermore, the wide variety of mechanisms by which radiations and chemicals induce mutations make it very unlikely that generalized schemes can be devised to protect against mutagens, except by avoiding them in the first place."

p. 504   "Mutations can arise in both somatic and germ line cells. Somatic mutation, and its probably close correlate, carcinogenesis, are already recognized as immediate toxicological problems."

p. 504   "Being an error process, mutation consists of all possible changes in the genetic material (excluding recombination and segregation)."

p. 504   "Changes in chromosome number commonly result in drastic gene imbalance, and are likely to be lethal early in development."

p. 505   "In either case, however, point mutations are likely to allow the afflicted individual to survive and reproduce, and may thus be transmitted and affect subsequent generations. In terms of human suffering, therefore, the summed effects of single gene mutations probably exceed the deleterious effects of changes in chromosome number or arrangement."

p. 512   "Human populations are now exposed to a wide variety of compounds never before encountered in the history of man. Many of these compounds are clearly mutagenic to lower organisms, and there are sound biological reasons to conclude that at least some are also mutagenic to man. Since the vast majority of detectable mutations are deleterious, an artificially increased human mutation rate would be expected to be harmful in proportion to the increase."

Glass, Bentley, "The Genetic Hazards of Nuclear Radiations," *Science*, vol. 126 (August 9, 1957), pp. 241-246. Dr. Glass was Professor of Biology at Johns Hopkins University.

p. 243   "So far, it is impossible to direct the mutation process. Radiation acts blindly, and that is why the deleterious nature of the vast majority of mutations is so important."

p. 243   "Alterations in the arrangement of the genetic material can be reversed only by an exact rearrangement to the original conditions, which the laws of probability must make exceedingly rare if the chromosomes are broken more or less at random.

"Thus, it is not surprising to find that although spontaneous mutations may undergo reversion to the original state, the radiation-induced ones have rarely, if ever, been observed to do so."

Hulse, Frederick S., *The Human Species* (New York: Random House, 1971), 524 pp.

pp. 61-2   "Mutations occur at random, not because it would be convenient to have one. Any chance alteration in the composition and properties of a highly complex operating system is not likely to improve its manner of operation, and most mutations are disadvantageous for this reason. There is a delicate balance between an organism and its environment which a mutation can easily upset. One could as well expect that altering the position of the foot brake or the gas pedal at random would improve the operation of an automobile."

Kimura, Motoo, "Population Genetics and Molecular Evolution," *Johns Hopkins Medical Journal*, vol. 138 (June 1976), pp. 253-261.

p. 260   "From the standpoint of population genetics, positive Darwinian selection represents a process whereby advantageous mutants spread through the species. Considering their great importance in evolution, it is perhaps surprising that well-established cases are so scarce; for example, industrial melanisms in moths and increases of DDT resistance in insects are constantly being cited. On the other hand, examples showing that negative selection is at work to eliminate variants produced by mutation abound . . . elimination of deviants to keep the status quo . . . is the most common type of natural selection. . . .

"At the same time, the possibility of mutational pressure directing the course of evolutionary change has been much enhanced. It appears that whenever a character becomes shielded from the direct action of natural selection, mutations start to accumulate in the population by random drift leading to degeneration in many cases."

Martin, C. P., "A Non-Geneticist Looks at Evolution," *American Scientist*, vol. 41 (January 1953), pp. 100-106. Martin was at McGill University.

p. 100   "Our first difficulty is that . . . all mutations seems to be in the nature of injuries that, to some extent, impair the fertility and viability of the affected organisms. I doubt if among the many thousands of known mutant types one can be found which is superior to the wild type in its normal environment; only very few can be named which are superior to the wild type in a strange environment."

p. 101   "The truth is that there is no clear evidence of the existence of such helpful mutations. In natural populations endless millions of small and great genic differences exist, but there is no evidence that they arose by mutation."

p. 103   "For any acceptable theory of the mechanism of evolution, a great number of fully viable hereditary variations is necessary. Mutation does produce hereditary changes, but the mass of evidence shows that all, or almost all, known mutations are unmistakably pathological and the few remaining ones are highly suspect."

Mayr, Ernst, *Populations, Species and Evolution* (Cambridge: Harvard University Press, 1970), 453 pp.

pp. 8-9   "The study of long-term evolutionary phenomena is the domain of the paleontologist. He investigates rates and trends of evolution in time and is interested in the origin of new classes, phyla, and other higher taxa. Evolution means change and yet it is only the paleontologist among all biologists who can properly study the time dimension. If the fossil record were not available, many evolutionary problems could not be solved; indeed many of them would not even be apparent."

p. 102   "It must not be forgotten that mutation is the ultimate source of all genetic variation found in natural populations and the only new material available for natural selection to work on."

p. 103   "*Recombination is by far the most important source of genetic variation, that is, of material for natural selection.*"

p. 164   "*Every character of an organism is affected by all genes and every gene affects all characters.*"

Muller, H. J., "How Radiation Changes the Genetic Constitution," *Bulletin of the Atomic Scientists*, vol. 11 (November 1955), pp. 329-338. Prepared for the Geneva Conference of the United Nations.

p. 331   "It is entirely in line with the accidental nature of natural mutations that extensive tests have agreed in showing the vast majority of them to be detrimental to the organism in its job of surviving and reproducing, just as changes accidentally introduced into any artificial mechanism are predominantly harmful to its useful operation. . . .

"It is nevertheless to be inferred that all the superbly interadapted genes of any present-day organism arose through just this process of accidental natural mutation."

p. 337   "At the same time, the dangerous mistake should not be made of considering man as a species who would himself undergo a long-term benefit from the application of radiation to his germ plasm."

Muller, H. J., "Radiation Damage to the Genetic Material," *American Scientist*, vol. 38 (January 1950), pp. 33-50, 126.

p. 35   "But mutations are found to be of a random nature, so far as their utility is concerned. Accordingly, the great majority of mutations, certainly well over 99 per cent, are harmful in some way, as is to be expected of the effects of accidental occurrences."

Simpson, George Gaylord, "Uniformitarianism: An Inquiry into Principle, Theory and Method in Geohistory and Biohistory," in *Essays in Evolution and Genetics* (New York: Appleton-Century-Crofts, 1970, 594 pp.), ed. Max K. Hecht and William C. Steere, pp. 43-96.

p. 80   "The somatic effects of mutations vary from great to barely perceptible or, quite likely, to imperceptible by usual methods of observation. The probabilities that a mutation will survive or eventually spread in the course of evolution tend to vary inversely with the extent of its somatic effects. Most mutations with large effects are lethal at an early stage for the individual in which they occur and hence have zero probability of spreading. Mutations with small effects do have some probability of spreading and as a rule the chances are better the smaller the effect. . . . Moreover, despite the fact that a mutation is a discrete, discontinuous effect at the cellular, chromosome or gene level, its effects are modified by interactions in the whole genetic system of an individual (oddly enough, there is no generally accepted term for that important concept)."

Simpson, John F., "Evolutionary Pulsations and Geomagnetic Polarity," *Bulletin, Geological Society of America*, vol. 77 (February 1966), pp. 197-203.

p. 197   "Occurring more or less at random, mutations might be expected to produce evolutionary changes at a fairly uniform rate. However, the paleontological record indicates abrupt (speaking in terms of geological time) accelerations in both the development and activation of various organisms."

p. 200   "Inasmuch as evolutionary changes are at least in part the result of genetic mutations, an increase in the flux of ionizing radiation, however small, will act to accelerate the evolutionary process."

p. 201   "It is suggested that, during these polarity reversals the strength of the earth's magnetic field dropped to zero; as the shielding effect of the magnetosphere vanished the cosmic ray flux increased worldwide to that now present only in polar regions."

Thompson, James N., Jr., and R. C. Woodruff, "Mutator Genes—Pacemakers of Evolution," *Nature*, vol. 274 (July 27, 1978), pp. 317-321.

p. 317   "Initially a genetic oddity, male recombination in *Drosophila Melanogaster* is now being viewed as a means of detecting mutator activity and chromosome breakage in hybridising populations and is causing us to reconsider the source and rate at which genetic variability may be generated in nature."

p. 318   "With frightening certainty, the history of science teaches us that the facts we observe are sometimes dictated by what we expect to observe."

p. 321   "One consequence of our hypothesis of explosive mutation events resulting from hybridisation between populations is that most current estimates of mutation rates in natural populations are probably too high. These estimates generally involve matings between wild flies and laboratory populations—an innocent act that, in itself, may generate mutations. . . .

"In summary, studies of the mutator activity associated with male recombination lines have suggested that a variety of genetic events in natural populations may be causally related—perhaps even associated with the interaction of a microorganism and the host genome. Little significant mutation may normally occur within a stable population."

Waddington, C. H., *The Nature of Life* (New York: Atheneum, 1962), 133 pp. Waddington was a prominent Edinburgh geneticist.

p. 98   "It remains true to say that we know of no way other than random mutation by which new hereditary variation comes into being, nor any process other than natural selection by which the hereditary constitution of a population changes from one generation to the next."

Warren, Shields, "Radiation and the Human Body," *Scientific Monthly* (January 1957), pp. 3-6.

p. 5   "Data on the longevity of more than 82,000 physicians indicate that the average length of life of those not known to have had contact with radiation in the period of 1930 through 1954 was 65.7 years as against an average life span of 60.5 years for the radiologists. Not only is leukemia more prevalent among those exposed, but death from causes such as heart disease and arteriosclerosis also appears to come at an earlier age. In fact, radiologists succumbed at an earlier average age to practically every type of disease, indicating that the damage done to the body is widespread in its influence."

Weaver, Warren, *et al.*, "Genetic Effects of Atomic Radiation," *Science*, vol. 123 (June 29, 1956), pp. 1157-1164. Summary report of the Committee on Genetic Effects of Atomic Radiation.

p. 1158   "Moreover, the mutant genes, in the vast majority of cases, and in all the species so far studied, lead to some kind of harmful effect. In extreme cases the harmful effect is death itself, or loss of the ability to produce offspring, or some other serious abnormality. What in a way is of even greater ultimate importance, since they affect so many more persons, are those cases that involve much smaller handicaps, which might tend to shorten life, reduce number of children, or be otherwise detrimental."

p. 1159   "Many will be puzzled about the statement that practically all known mutant genes are harmful. For mutations are a necessary part of the process of evolution. How can a good effect—evolution to higher forms of life—result from mutations practically all of which are harmful?"

p. 1159   "1) Radiations cause mutations. Mutations affect those hereditary traits which a person passes on to his children and to subsequent generations.

"2) Practically all radiation-induced mutations which have effects large enough to be detected are harmful."

p. 1160   "3) Any radiation does, however small, can induce some mutations. There is no minimum amount of radiation dose, that is, which must be exceeded before any harmful mutations occur."

p. 1160   "Like radiation-induced mutations, nearly all spontaneous mutations with detectable effects are harmful."

Wills, Christopher, "Genetic Load," *Scientific American*, vol. 222 (March 1970), pp. 98-107.

p. 98   "Some mutations are 'beneficial,' that is, the individual in whom they are expressed is better able to adapt to a given set of environmental circumstances. The large majority of mutations, however, are harmful or even lethal to the individual in whom they are expressed. Such mutations can be regarded as introducing a 'load,' or genetic burden, into the pool. The term 'genetic load' was first used by the late H. J. Muller, who recognized that the rate of mutations is increased by numerous agents man has introduced into his environment, notably ionizing radiation and mutagenic chemicals."

p. 107   "The most important actions that need to be taken, however, are in the area of minimizing the addition of new mutagens to those already present in the environment. Any increase in the mutational load is harmful, if not immediately, then certainly to future generations."

B. Molecular Homologies and Evolution

A somewhat desperate attempt to find evidence of evolution, especially because of the ubiquitous gaps in the fossil record, has centered on supposed molecular homologies between different kinds of organisms. It has even been thought that such similarities can yield an evolutionary "clock" for relative dating of evolutionary events. Initial enthusiasm for this line of evidence, however, is largely waning because of so many contradictions in its results.

Amato, Ivan, "Tics in the Tocks of Molecular Clocks," *Science News*, vol. 131 (January 31, 1987), pp. 74-75.

p. 74   "Research from a number of labs is showing that clocks based on different molecules tick at different, and often varying, rates. For instance, clocks based on a particular molecule such as ribosomal RNA sometimes run at different rates for different species. Moreover, the rates of DNA clocks based on different cellular sources of DNA can differ within the same organisms."

p. 75   "Most evolution biologists now agree that no single molecular clock is going to answer all of their questions. Ayala argues that biologists first must learn more about how and why molecular clocks vary in order to build a theory about their molecular clockworks."

Denton, Michael, *Evolution: A Theory in Crisis* (London: Burnett Books, Ltd., 1985), 368 pp. Denton is a molecular biologist and is not a creationist.

p. 289 "The really significant finding that comes to light from comparing the proteins' amino acid sequences is that it is impossible to arrange them in any sort of evolutionary series."

pp. 289-90 "Thousands of different sequences, protein and nucleic acid, have now been compared in hundreds of different species but never has any sequence been found to be in any sense the lineal descendant or ancestor of any other sequence."

pp. 290-1 "There is little doubt that if this molecular evidence had been available one century ago it would have been seized upon with devastating effect by the opponents of evolution theory like Agassiz and Owen, and the idea of organic evolution might never have been accepted."

p. 293 "In terms of their biochemistry, none of the species deemed 'intermediate,' 'ancestral,' or 'primitive' by generations of evolutionary biologists, and alluded to as evidence of sequence in nature, shows any sign of their supposed intermediate status."

p. 296 "However, as there are hundreds of different families of proteins and each family exhibits its own unique degree of interspecies variation, some greater than haemoglobin, some far less than the cytochromes, then it is necessary to propose not just two clocks but one for each of the several hundred protein families, each ticking at its own unique and highly specific rate."

p. 305 "The difficulties associated with attempting to explain how a family of homologous proteins could have evolved at constant rates has created chaos in evolutionary thought. The evolutionary community has divided into two camps— those still adhering to the selectionist position, and those rejecting it in favor of the neutralist. The devastating aspect of this controversy is that neither side can adequately account for the constancy of the rate of molecular evolution, yet each side fatally weakens the other."

Erbrich, Paul, "On the Probability of the Emergence of a Protein with a Particular Function," *Acta Biotheoretica*, vol. 34 (1985), pp. 53-80.

p. 53 "Proteins with nearly the same structure and function (homologous proteins) are found in increasing numbers in phylogenetically different, even very distinct taxa (e.g., hemoglobins in vertebrates, in some invertebrates, and even in certain plants). . . . The probability . . . of the convergent evolution of two proteins with approximately the same structure and function is too low to be plausible, even when all possible circumstances are present which seem to heighten the likelihood of such a convergence. If this is so, then the plausibility of a random evolution of two or more different but functionally related proteins seems hardly greater."

Grassé, Pierre-P., *Evolution of Living Organisms* (New York: Academic Press, 1977), 297 pp.

p. 194 "The cytochrome *c* of man differs by 14 amino acids from that of the horse, and by only 8 from that of the kangaroo. Similar facts are found in the case of hemoglobin; the β chain of this protein in man differs from that of the lemurs by

20 amino acids, by only 14 from that of the pig, and by only 1 from that of the gorilla. The situation is practically the same for other proteins."

Kolata, Gina Bari, "Evolution of DNA: Changes in Gene Regulation," *Science*, vol. 189 (August 8, 1975), pp. 446-447.

p. 446   "Since changes in genes are easier to detect than changes in regulatory DNA, most research in molecular evolution has stressed the evolution in genes. However, it has been difficult to reconcile changes in genes with changes in animal anatomy during evolution."

p. 446   "If blood proteins are a representative sample of proteins coded by structural genes, the most similar species should have the most similar blood proteins. Wilson and his colleagues found, however, that structural genes for blood proteins accumulate mutations at rates that appear independent of anatomical evolution."

p. 447   "The answer to the question of how species evolve, then, apparently involves changes in gene regulation and so awaits further studies of chromosome organization and control of gene expression in higher organisms. It thus seems evident that the old method of comparing proteins of different species may no longer be the primary tool for investigating the mechanisms underlying the evolution of organisms."

Korey, Kenneth A., "Species Number, Generation Length and the Molecular Clock," *Evolution*, vol. 35, no. 1 (1981), pp. 139-147. Korey was with the Department of Anthropology at Dartmouth College.

p. 139   "The fundamental tenet of the molecular clock hypothesis is that evolutionary rates of homologous proteins are regular, so that the interval separating living species from common ancestors is reflected in the degree of protein dissimilarity between them."

p. 139   "It is the purpose of this paper, however, to demonstrate that species numbers and generation length may be important determinants of the degree to which proteins diverge over time, and that variability in these parameters might easily lead both to the impression that molecular evolution rates are nonconstant and the systematic underestimation of species divergence times."

p. 145   "On the other hand, the results given here indicate their expression to be most pronounced in dating the separation of species with large numbers and long generation lengths, such estimates tending to be too recent. . . . Certainly the widely contested date for the separation of *Pan* and *Homo* that Sarich and Wilson suggest is subject to this bias."

p. 146.   "Coupled with complementary findings regarding the significance of species bottlenecks to protein divergence rates, these effects undermine the main premise of the clock thesis, especially as it applies to the dating of lineages not remotely separated."

Lewin, Roger, "Molecular Clocks Scrutinized," *Science* (May 3, 1985), p. 571.

p. 517   "Specifically, how accurate is the 'molecular evolutionary clock?' as Zuckerkandl and Pauling called it. . . . Two recent papers point to potential problems for would-be users of the clock."

"The very reasonable conclusion is that 'using the primary structure of a single gene or protein to time evolutionary events or to reconstruct phylogenetic relations is potentially fraught with error.'"

p. 571   "There is no such thing as *the* molecular clock: there are several, each with different attributes."

Rowe, Timothy, "New Issues for Phylogenetics," review of *Molecules and Morphology in Evolution*, edited by Colin Patterson (New York: Cambridge University Press, 1987), 229 pp., *Science*, vol. 239 (March 4, 1988), pp. 1183-1184.

p. 1183   "Morphology and molecular data are congruent in indicating that *Homo* and African apes are more closely related to each other than to the orang. The position of chimps is equivocal, however; amino acid sequencing links them with humans, morphology links them with gorillas, and DNA sequencing has produced ambiguous results."

p. 1184   "An intriguing picture develops in this volume in which molecular and morphological phylogenies sometimes agree and sometimes not. Different philosophies and methods complicate the comparison and may themselves be responsible for much of the conflict. Nevertheless, there is general agreement that both molecular and morphological phylogenetics face similar fundamental problems and that a 'touchstone' has not been found."

Schwabe, Christian, and Gregory W. Warr, "A Polyphyletic View of Evolution," *Perspectives in Biology and Medicine*, vol. 27 (Spring 1984), pp. 465-485.

p. 473   "The relaxin and insulin families do not stand alone as exceptions to the orderly interpretation of molecular evolution in conventional monophyletic terms. It is instructive to look at additional examples of purportedly anomalous protein evolution and note that the explanations permissible under the molecular clock theories cover a range of *ad hoc* explanations apparently limited only by imagination. These examples include the egg white lysozymes of goose, chicken, chachalaca, and duck."

pp. 474, 476   "This phylogenetic hopscotching of $\beta2$ microglobulin and many hormones can be taken together with amino acid sequence data for relaxins, insulins, and some other molecules, to show incompatibility with the monophyletic molecular clock models of evolution. As noted earlier, the positive selectionist neo-Darwinian views of molecular evolution are in principle unfalsifiable, but such evidence as we have presented does not strengthen the positive selectionist interpretation of the data. However, the major conclusion to which we wish to draw attention is that these findings strongly suggest that many of the genes purportedly produced by gene duplication have been present very early in the development of life. In fact, we can ask if they were not present so early that we must question whether any gene has come about by duplication or whether all have been there, from the beginning, as a potential for species development."

Schwabe, Christian, "On the Validity of Molecular Evolution," *Trends in Biochemical Sciences* (July 1986).

> "Molecular evolution is about to be accepted as a method superior to paleontology for the discovery of evolutionary relationships. As a molecular evolutionist I should be elated. Instead it seems disconcerting that many exceptions exist to the orderly progression of species as determined by molecular homologies; so many in fact that I think the exception, the quirks, may carry the more important message."

> "The early existence of some molecules of highly complex function cannot be denied and the question arises whether there are any molecules that have not already been in existence at the time of the origins of life."

> "The neo-darwinian hypothesis, in fact, allows one to interpret simple sequence differences such as to represent complex processes, namely gene duplications, mutations, deletions and insertions, without offering the slightest possibility of proof, either in practice or in principle."

> "Regrettably, there is also the pressure of creationism that seems to curb free discussions in the evolutionist's camp."

> "The quirks that will not submit to the neo-darwinian hypothesis are telling us that life had countless origins and that the chemistry of the origins of life has produced the diversity that was to become a substrate for the evolution of biological complexity."

C. Genetic Mysteries

Many geneticists are exploring the mysteries of the DNA-RNA complex and the activities of the many genes involved in molecular biology. It does seem that the whole subject becomes more complex—even more chaotic—with increasing understanding.

Boxer, Sarah, ed., "On the Rescue Gene and the Origin of Species," *Discover*, vol. 8 (August 1987), pp. 6, 7.

p. 7   "By definition, a new species arises when it splits off from a parent species. But a species is a species only if it doesn't interbreed with other species, including the one from which it arose. The critical question in species formation is how the barrier to reproduction is erected and maintained. As it turns out, the species barrier is a two-layered defense. There are pre-mating mechanisms—behavioral, ecological, and physical differences that make it difficult for two species to mate. If that line of defense fails, second-line, post-mating mechanisms ensure that the progeny of the barrier-crashers are either rendered sterile (like mules) or they die before reaching maturity."

p. 7   "The rescue gene turned out to be strange indeed. While it weakened the general health of the flies that carried it, it gave life to their hybrid progeny. However, the gene didn't completely break through the species barrier; it couldn't render the males fertile. 'The flies live,' says Hutter, 'but they're sterile.' Which raises a troublesome question: If the parents that carry it don't benefit from it, and offspring that inherit it can't pass it on, how could the gene possibly have evolved?"

de Beer, Sir Gavin, *Homology, An Unsolved Problem* (London: Oxford University Press, 1971), 16 pp.

p. 15 "What all this means is that *characters controlled by identical genes are not necessarily homologous.*"

pp. 15-16 "Therefore, *homologous structures need not be controlled by identical genes,* and *homology of phenotypes does not imply similarity of genotypes.*

"It is now clear that the pride with which it was assumed that the inheritance of homologous structures from a common ancestor explained homology was misplaced; for such inheritance cannot be ascribed to identity of genes. The attempt to find 'homologous genes,' except in closely related species, has been given up as hopeless."

p. 16 "To the question, 'Is the whole of development encoded in DNA (that is to say, in the genes)?' the answer . . . is 'No.' Whether this is applicable to 'patterns' in higher organisms, and whether homologous structures are controlled by non-DNA mechanisms awaits further research."

Jones, Steve, *The Language of Genes* (New York: Doubleday, 1993), 272 pp.

p. 84 "Biologists have an adolescent fascination with sex. Like teenagers, they are embarrassed by the subject because of their ignorance. What sex is, why it evolved and how it works are the biggest unsolved problems in biology. Sex must be important as it is so expensive. If some creatures can manage with just females, so that every individual produces copies of herself, why do so many bother with males? A female who gave them up might be able to produce twice as many daughters as before; and they would carry all her genes. Instead, a sexual female wastes time, first in finding a mate and then in producing sons who carry only half of her inheritance. We are still not certain why males exist; and why, if we must have them at all, nature needs so many. Surely, one or two would be enough to impregnate all the females but, with few exceptions, the ratio of males to females remain stubbornly equal throughout the living world."

Lewin, Roger, "Do Jumping Genes Make Evolutionary Leaps?" *Science*, vol. 213 (August 7, 1981), pp. 634-636.

p. 634 "The all-pervading message of the Cambridge meeting was that genomic DNA is a surprisingly dynamic state. . . . The notion of a fluid genome, in which there is a constant flux of sequences, is now an accepted fact."

p. 634 "The most obvious comment to make about the genomes of higher organisms is that biologists understand the function of only a tiny proportion of the DNA in them, namely, the genes that code for proteins. In the human genome, for instance, these protein-coding genes constitute marginally more than 1 percent of all the DNA. The rest of the genome is the target of much speculation, but few secure answers. . . .

". . . Some 5 percent is made up of many families (sometimes with many millions of members) of short simple repeats of nucleotide sequences known as satellite DNA. A quarter of the genome is formed of families of longer more complex repeat sequences, denoted intermediate repetitive DNA. The bulk of the genome is composed of unique sequence, or single copy DNA, that is interspersed with the intermediate repeats. The proportions of these classes, whose distinctions can often become blurred, can vary enormously between organisms.

"The longer biologists searched in vain for functions for these three classes of noncoding DNA, the stronger grew the conviction that much . . . might well be 'junk.' . . ."

p. 635   ". . . the notion that much of the noncoding DNA could be described as selfish DNA."

p. 635   "There was general agreement on the distinction between selfish and ignorant DNA."

p. 636   "'We had set out to test the junk hypothesis' said Jeffreys, 'and we were happy to rule it out provisionally in that these sequences have behaved in evolution as if they are functional.' What this function is must still be determined."

Marx, Jean L., "Aging Research (I): Cellular Theories of Senescence," *Science*, vol. 186 (December 20, 1974), pp. 1105-1107.

p. 1105   "A number of investigators, such as F. Marott Sinex of Boston University School of Medicine in Boston, Massachusetts, think that mutations may cause aging. If the damage to DNA is too subtle for the DNA repair system to detect, or if it accumulates faster than the repair system functions, the cell will gradually become defective in essential control systems or enzymes. This situation would be particularly serious for cells that do not divide after they have differentiated to their mature forms. These include brain and muscle cells. If they function poorly or die, they are not replaced. It might be less serious for dividing cells such as those of the liver or the lining of the gastrointestinal track."

p. 1106   "If mutations in somatic cells are involved in senescence, then the efficiency of DNA repair mechanisms may help to determine susceptibility to aging."

Norwak, Rachel, "Mining Treasures from 'Junk DNA'" *Science*, vol. 263 (February 4, 1994), pp. 608-610.

p. 608   "The protein-coding portions of the genes account for only about 3% of the DNA in the human genome; the other 97% encodes no proteins. Most of this enormous, silent genetic majority has long been thought to have no real function—hence its name: 'junk DNA.' But one researcher's trash is another researcher's treasure, and a growing number of scientists believe that hidden in the junk DNA are intellectual riches that will lead to a better understanding of diseases (possibly including cancer), normal genome repair and regulation, and perhaps even the evolution of multicellular organisms."

p. 610   "Enough gems have already been uncovered in the genetic midden to show that what was once thought to be waste is definitely being transmuted into scientific gold."

Ohno, Susumo, "The Significance of Gene Duplication in Immunoglobulin Evolution (Epimethean Natural Selection and Promethean Evolution)," in *Immunoglobulin*, ed. G. W. Litman and R. A. Good (New York: Plenum Medical Book Co., 1978), pp. 197-204.

p. 198   "The aforementioned nonlinkage of functionally related genes of the immune system, many of which apparently evolved from a common ancestral gene by a series of gene duplications, is fully compatible with the view that most of the gene duplication events that generated vertebrate-specific genes occurred at the stage of fish when polyploid evolution was still possible. . . .

"As vertebrates evolved beyond the amphibian stage, polyploid evolution ceased to be a factor in generating new genes from redundant copies of the old."

p. 199   "As far as I am concerned, the uniqueness of the immune system lies in its ability to cope with all sorts of previously unexperienced contingencies, thus giving an impression of having evolved in anticipation of future needs. The Darwinian concept of evolution by natural selection does not predict the development of a system that can cope with the future. It follows, then, that the immune system must have developed on the basis of a new evolutionary principle."

p. 204   "In the case of the immune system . . . almost every individual in a mammalian population appears capable of producing antibodies against all sorts of evolutionary unfamiliar molecules."

Takahata, N., "A Genetic Perspective on the Origin and History of Humans," *Annual Review of Ecology and Systematics*, vol. 26 (1995), pp. 343-372.

p. 343   "Hypotheses about the origin of *Homo sapiens*, genetic differentiation among human populations, and changes in population size are quantified. None of the hypotheses seems compatible with the observed DNA variation."

p. 344   "Even with DNA sequence data, we have no direct access to the processes of evolution, so objective reconstruction of the vanished past can be achieved only by creative imagination."

Wald, George, "Innovation in Biology," *Scientific American*, vol. 199 (September 1958), pp. 100-113.

p. 101   "When speaking for myself, I do not tend to make sentences containing the word God; but what do those persons mean who make such sentences? They mean a great many different things; indeed I would be happy to know what they mean much better than I have yet been able to discover. I have asked as opportunity offered, and intend to go on asking. What I have learned is that many educated persons now tend to equate their concept of God with their concept of the order of nature."

p. 107   "Science is dialectical, and of course materialist. Marx and Engels, recognizing this, attempted to formulate these qualities in the natural sciences so as to impress them upon philosophers, economists, sociologists and historians. To preach dialectical materialism to scientists is carrying coals to Newcastle."

Williams, George C., *Sex and Evolution* (Princeton, New Jersey: Princeton University Press, 1977), 201 pp.

p. 11   "The problem has been examined by some of the most distinguished of evolutionary theorists, but they have either failed to find any reproductive advantage in sexual reproduction, or have merely showed the formal possibility of weak advantages that would probably not be adequate to balance even modest recombinational load. Nothing remotely approaching an advantage that could balance the cost of meiosis has been suggested. The impossibility of sex being an immediate reproductive adaptation in higher organisms would seem to be as firmly established a conclusion as can be found in current evolutionary thought."

Yam, Philip, "Talking Trash," *Scientific American*, vol. 272 (March 1995), p 24.

"What's in a word? Several nucleotides, some researchers might say. By applying statistical methods developed by linguists, investigators have found that 'junk' parts of the genomes of many organisms may be expressing a language. These regions have traditionally been regarded as useless accumulations of material from millions of years of evolution. 'The feeling is,' says Boston University physicist H. Eugene Stanley, 'that there's something going on in the noncoding region.'"

"Junk DNA got its name because the nucleotides there (the fundamental pieces of DNA, combined into so-called base pairs) do not encode instructions for making proteins, the basis for life. In fact, the vast majority of genetic material in organisms from bacteria to mammals consists of noncoding DNA segments, which are interspersed with the coding parts. In humans, about 97 percent of the genome is junk."

"Over the past 10 years, biologists began to suspect that this feature is not entirely trivial."

Chapter 5

The Evolutionary Paradigm

A. The Dogmatic Evolutionists

In the post-Darwin century, evolutionism displaced creationism in the schools and colleges of practically the entire world. It now dominates all the institutions—including most of the mainline churches and seminaries—even in so-called Christendom.

Amazingly, however, it has achieved this position of intellectual eminence without one iota of real scientific proof. It has become the world view, the ruling paradigm, of every discipline of study and provides the pseudo-scientific rationale for practically every harmful philosophy and evil practice known to man. It maintains this control, not by objective scientific argument but by the anti-creationism of its leaders and spokesmen. The following quotes illustrate this religious dogmatism.

Ayala, Francisco J., "Nothing in Biology Makes Sense Except in the Light of Evolution, Theodosius Dobzhansky: 1900-1975," *Journal of Heredity*, vol. 68, (January/February 1977), pp. 3-10.

p. 3   "The place of biological evolution in human thought was, according to Dobzhansky, best expressed in a passage that he often quoted from Pierre Teilhard de Chardin: '[Evolution] is a general postulate to which all theories, all hypotheses, all systems must hence forward bow and which they must satisfy in order to be thinkable and true. Evolution is a light which illuminates all facts, a trajectory which all lines of thought must follow.'"

p. 6   "From today's perspective, Dobzhansky appears as perhaps the most eminent evolutionist of the twentieth century."

p. 9   "Dobzhansky was a religious man, although he apparently rejected fundamental beliefs of traditional religion, such as the existence of a personal God and of life beyond physical death. . . . Dobzhansky held that, in man, biological evolution has transcended itself into the realm of self-awareness and culture. He believed that somehow mankind would eventually evolve into higher levels of harmony and creativity. He was a metaphysical optimist."

Darlington, C. D., "Origin of Darwinism," *Scientific American* (May 1959), p. 60-66. Darlington was at Oxford University.

p. 60   "We owe it to [Darwin] that the world was brought to believe in evolution; . . . Here is a theory that released thinking men from the spell of a superstition, one of the most overpowering that has ever enslaved mankind."

p. 66   "We owe to the *Origin of Species* the overthrow of the myth of Creation."

de Santillana, Giorgio, and Hertha von Dechend, *Hamlet's Mill* (Boston: Gambit Inc., 1969), 505 pp.

p. 68   ". . . our ancestors of the high and far-off times were endowed with minds wholly comparable to ours, . . .

"... The simple idea of evolution, which it is no longer thought necessary to examine, spreads like a tent over all those ages that lead from primitivism into civilization. Gradually, we are told, step by step, men produced the arts and crafts, this and that, until they emerged in the light of history.

"Those soporific words 'gradually' and 'step-by-step' repeated incessantly, are aimed at covering an ignorance which is both vast and surprising. One should like to inquire: Which steps? But then one is lulled, overwhelmed and stupefied by the gradualness of it all, which is at best a platitude, only good for pacifying the mind, since no one is willing to imagine that civilization appeared in a thunderclap."

p. 70   "Animal evolution remains an over-all historical hypothesis supported by sufficient data, ... It raises an appalling number of questions to which we have no answer. Our ignorance remains vast, but it is not surprising."

p. 327   "... it was intellectual pride [on the part of cultural historians], judging from the height of Progress, which telescopes the countless centuries of the archaic past into artless primitive prattle, to be understood by analogy with the surviving 'primitives' around us. Too much of that primitiveness lies in the eye of the beholder."

Dobzhansky, Theodosius, "Evolution at Work," *Science* (May 9, 1958), pp. 1091-1098.

p. 1091   "In turn, biological evolutionism exerted ever-widening influences on the natural and social sciences, as well as on philosophy and even on politics. Not all of these extrabiological repercussions were either sound or commendable. Suffice it to mention the so-called Social Darwinism, which often sought to justify the inhumanity of man to man, and the biological racism which furnished a fraudulent scientific sanction for the atrocities committed in Hitler's Germany and elsewhere."

p. 1092   "The evidence has not satisfied quite everybody; a few people who are not ignorant of the pertinent facts are nevertheless antievolutionists."

p. 1096   "Man was not programmed in biological evolution, because evolution has no program. In one sense, man, *Drosophila*, and all other forms of life are evolutionary accidents."

Dobzhansky, Theodosius, *Genetics and the Origin of Species*, 2nd ed. (New York: Columbia University Press, 1982), 364 pp.

p. 4   "Organic diversity is an observational fact more or less familiar to everyone. ... If we assemble as many individuals living at a given time as we can, we notice at once that the observed variation does not form a single probability distribution or any other kind of continuous distribution. Instead, a multitude of separate, discrete, distributions are found. In other words, the living world is not a single array of individuals in which any two variants are connected by unbroken series of intergrades, but an array of more or less distinctly separate arrays, intermediates between which are absent or rare."

Dobzhansky, Theodosius, "Changing Man," *Science*, vol. 155, no. 3761 (January 27, 1967), pp. 409-415.

p. 409   "Evolution is a process which has produced life from non-life, which has brought forth man from an animal, and which may conceivably continue doing remarkable things in the future. In giving rise to man, the evolutionary process has, apparently for the first and only time in the history of the Cosmos, become conscious of itself."

p. 409   "Evolution comprises all the stages of the development of the universe: the cosmic, biological, and human or cultural developments. Attempts to restrict the concept of evolution to biology are gratuitous. Life is a product of the evolution of inorganic nature, and man is a product of the evolution of life."

Dubos, René, "Humanistic Biology," *American Scientist*, vol. 53 (March 1965), pp. 4-19.

p. 6   "Most enlightened persons now accept as a fact that everything in the cosmos—from heavenly bodies to human beings—has developed and continues to develop through evolutionary processes. The great religions of the West have come to accept a historical view of creation. Evolutionary concepts are applied also to social institutions and to the arts. Indeed, most political parties, as well as schools of theology, sociology, history, or arts, teach these concepts and make them the basis of their doctrines. Thus, theoretical biology now pervades all of Western culture indirectly through the concept of progressive historical change."

p. 6   "Comparative biology has revealed, furthermore, that man is linked to all living organisms through a common line of descent, and shares with them many characteristics of physicochemical constitution and of biological organization; the philosophical concept of the 'great chain of being' can thus be restated now in the form of a scientific generalization."

Goldschmidt, Richard B., "Evolution, As Viewed by One Geneticist," *American Scientist*, vol. 40 (January 1952), pp. 84-98, 135.

p. 84   "Evolution of the animal and plant world is considered by all those entitled to judgment to be a fact for which no further proof is needed. But in spite of nearly a century of work and discussion there is still no unanimity in regard to the details of the means of evolution."

p. 85   "Another type of evolutionary theory hardly deserves to be mentioned in a scientific paper. This is the mystical approach, which hides its insufficient understanding of the facts behind such empty words as creative evolution, emergent evolution, holism, and psycho-Lamarkism. It is the expression of a defeatist attitude, calling upon unknown forces when difficulties arise. This approach will always find adherents, especially outside the pale of biology. The biologist does not receive any constructive help from such ideas and is forced to ignore them."

Harper, G. W., "Alternatives to Evolutionism," *School Science Review*, vol. 61 (September 1979), pp. 15-27.

p. 16   "The conflict between evolutionism and special creationism usually boils down to the conflict between rival metaphysical beliefs, and at least in this respect evolutionism and special creationism are of comparable status."

p. 25   "A feature of Darwinism is its 'grandiosity,' by which I mean its wide coverage and the claim of many of its adherents that it is necessary for full understanding in taxonomy, paleontology, comparative anatomy, biochemistry, embryology, study of distribution, ethology—in fact, most areas of biology. In addition to this, there can be a strong hold on the imagination, so that many evolutionists simply cannot imagine any alternative way of thinking in these areas of biology. One school textbook puts it thus: 'It is impossible . . . without doing violence to the evidence, to do otherwise than accept the *fact* of evolution!' A non-evolutionist trying to imagine the state of mind in the author of that sentence may be excused for thinking that evolutionism can certainly get a tight grip on people."

p. 26   "It is frequently claimed that Darwinism is central to modern biology, on the contrary, if all references to Darwinism suddenly disappeared, biology would remain substantially unchanged. It would merely have lost a little color. Grandiose doctrines in science are like some occupants of high office; they sound very important but have in fact been promoted to a position of ineffectuality."

Harper, G. W., "Darwinism and Indoctrination," *School Science Review*, vol. 59, no. 207 (December 1977), pp. 258-268. Harper was at St. Albans School, Hertz.

p. 258   "For some time, it has seemed to me that our current methods of teaching Darwinism are suspiciously similar to indoctrination."

p. 263   "So we *cannot* have observational evidence for or against Darwin's theory, and needless to say none has ever been produced. One might have suspected the latter on other grounds, anyway, since the kind of evolution Darwin was writing about is too slow to be detected in practice."

p. 265   "There is a close similarity, for instance, between the Darwinist and the Marxist in the example quoted earlier. Both can take any relevant information whatever, true or false, and reconcile it with their theory. The Darwinist can always make a plausible reconstruction of what took place during the supposed evolution of a species. Any difficulties in reconciling a given kind of natural selection with a particular phase in evolution can be removed by the judicious choice of a correlated character. . . . Looked at in this way the teacher of Darwin's theory corresponds with the latter, since he undoubtedly is concerned to put across the conclusion that natural selection causes evolution, while he cannot be concerned to any great extent with real evidence because there isn't any."

Huxley, Julian, "Evolution and Genetics," in *What is Science?* edited by J. R. Newman (New York: Simon and Schuster, 1955), pp. 256-289.

p. 272   "The concept of evolution was soon extended into other than biological fields. Inorganic subjects such as the life-history of stars and the formation of the chemical elements on the one hand, and on the other hand subjects like linguistics, social anthropology, and comparative law and religion, began to be studied from an evolutionary angle, until today we are enabled to see evolution as a universal and all-pervading process."

p. 278   "Evolution in the extended sense can be defined as a directional and essentially irreversible process occurring in time, which in its course gives rise to an increase of variety and an increasingly high level of organization in its products. Our present knowledge indeed forces us to the view that the whole of reality *is* evolution—a single process of self-transformation."

Huxley, Julian, Associated Press Dispatch, November 27, 1959, Address at Darwin Centennial Convocation, Chicago University, see *Issues in Evolution*, edited by Sol Tax (University of Chicago Press, 1960).

p. 252   "In the evolutionary system of thought there is no longer need or room for the supernatural. The earth was not created; it evolved. So did all the animals and plants that inhabit it, including our human selves, mind and soul, as well as brain and body. So did religion.

            "Evolutionary man can no longer take refuge from his loneliness by creeping for shelter into the arms of a divinized father figure whom he himself has created, nor escape from the responsibility of making decisions by sheltering under the umbrella of divine authority, nor absolve himself from the hard task of meeting his present problems and planning his future by relying on the will of an omniscient, but unfortunately inscrutable providence."

Huxley, Julian, In *Issues in Evolution*, edited by Sol Tax (Chicago: University of Chicago, 1960).

p. 41   "The first point to make about Darwin's theory is that is it no longer a theory, but a fact. No serious scientist would deny the fact that evolution has occurred, just as he would not deny the fact that the earth goes around the sun."

p. 45   "Darwinism removed the whole idea of God as the creator of organisms from the sphere of rational discussion. Darwin pointed out that no supernatural designer was needed; since natural selection could account for any known form of life, there was no room for a supernatural agency in its evolution. . . . I think we can dismiss entirely all idea of a supernatural overriding mind being responsible for the evolutionary process."

Kerkut, G. A., *Implications of Evolution*, International Series of Monographs in Pure and Applied Biology/Zoology Division, vol. 4 (Pergamon Press, 1960). Kerkut was in the Department of Physiology and Biochemistry, University of Southampton.

p. 155   "It seems at times as if many of our modern writers on evolution have had their views by some sort of revelation and they base their opinions on the evolution of life, from the simplest form to the complex, entirely on the nature of specific and intra-specific evolution. It is possible that this type of evolution can explain many of the present-day phenomena, but it is possible and indeed probable that many as yet unknown systems remain to be discovered and it is premature, not to say arrogant, on our part if we make any dogmatic assertion as to the mode of evolution of the major branches of the animal kingdom."

Lipson, H. S., "A Physicist Looks at Evolution," *Physics Bulletin*, vol. 31 (May 1980), p. 138.

p. 138   "In fact, evolution became in a sense a scientific religion; almost all scientists have accepted it and many are prepared to 'bend' their observations to fit in with it."

p. 138   "I have always been slightly suspicious of the theory of evolution because of its ability to account for *any* property of living beings."

p. 138   "To my mind, the theory does not stand up at all."

National Association of Biology Teachers, "Statement on Teaching Evolution" (Policy adopted by NABT Board on March 15, 1995), 3 pp.

p. 1   "Whether called 'creation science,' 'scientific creationism,' 'intelligent-design theory,' 'young-earth theory' or some other synonym, creation beliefs have no place in the science classroom. Explanations employing nonnaturalistic or supernatural events, whether or not explicit reference is made to a supernatural being, are outside the realm of science and not part of a valid science curriculum. Evolutionary theory, indeed all of science, is necessarily silent on religion and neither refutes nor supports the existence of a deity or deities."

p. 2   "Evolution does not violate the second law of thermodynamics: producing order from disorder is possible with the addition of energy, such as from the sun."

p. 3   "Courts have thus restricted school districts from requiring creation science in the science curriculum and have restricted individual instructors from teaching it. All teachers and administrators should be mindful of these court cases, remembering that the law, science and NABT support them as they appropriately include the teaching of evolution in the science curriculum."

Simpson, George Gaylord, "The Nonprevalence of Humanoids," *Science*, vol. 143 (February 21, 1964), pp. 769-775.

p. 772   "The fossil record shows very clearly that there is no central line leading steadily, in a goal-directed way, from a protozoan to man. . . .

                "Neither in its over-all pattern nor in its intricate detail can that record be interpreted in any simply finalistic way. If evolution is God's plan of creation— a proposition that a scientist as such should neither affirm nor deny—then God is not a finalist."

Smith, Wolfgang, *Teilhardism and the New Religion* (Rockford, Illinois: Tan Books & Publishers, Inc., 1988), 248 pp.

p. 2   "We are told dogmatically that evolution is an established fact; but we are never told who has established it, and by what means. We are told, often enough, that the doctrine is founded upon evidence, and that indeed this evidence 'is henceforward above all verification, as well as being immune from any subsequent contradiction by experience'; but we are left entirely in the dark on the crucial question wherein, precisely, this evidence consists ."

p. 5   "And the salient fact is this: if by evolution we mean macroevolution (as we henceforth shall), then it can be said with the utmost rigor that the doctrine is totally bereft of scientific sanction. Now, to be sure, given the multitude of extravagant claims about evolution promulgated by evolutionists with an air of scientific infallibility, this may indeed sound strange. And yet the fact remains that there exists to this day not a shred of *bona fide* scientific evidence in support of the thesis that macroevolutionary transformations have ever occurred."

Teilhard de Chardin, Pierre, *The Phenomenon of Man* (New York: Harper and Row, 1965).

p. 2   "[Evolution is] above all verification, as well as being immune from any subsequent contradiction by experience."

p. 219   "Is evolution a theory, a system or a hypothesis? It is much more: it is a general condition to which all theories, all systems, all hypotheses must bow and which they must satisfy henceforward if they are to be thinkable and true. Evolution is a light illuminating all facts, a curve that all lines must follow."

Watson, D. M. S., "Adaptation," *Nature*, vol. 124 (August 10, 1929), pp. 231-234.

p. 233   "If so, it will present a parallel to the theory of evolution itself, a theory universally accepted not because it can be proved by logically coherent evidence to be true but because the only alternative, special creation, is clearly incredible."

B. The Uneasy Evolutionists

Here and there, almost apologetically, a number of evolutionists have acknowledged the unsatisfactory scientific basis of their evolutionary worldview, which their leaders keep insisting is the only legitimate scientific view. The fact is that neither evolution nor creation can be *proved* scientifically, since they deal with pre-history rather than the observable present. Evolutionists believe in evolution simply because they do not want to believe in creation. All the actual data of science fit the specifications of the creation model perfectly, but evolutionists simply want to believe in evolution.

Bowler, Peter J., "The Status of Evolutionism Examined," review of *Monad to Man* by Michael Ruse (Harvard University Press, 1996, 596 pp.), *American Scientist*, vol. 85 (May/June 1997), pp. 274-275. Bowler is on the faculty in History and Philosophy of Science, The Queen's University, Belfast.

p. 274   "Ruse is a philosopher who wants to use history as a means of assessing the theory's status as scientific knowledge. He asks why so many (and not just the creationists) remain skeptical of the theory's scientific credentials. The answer, he argues, is that evolutionism has always been linked to a nonscientific value system based on the idea of progress."

p. 275   "The biomedical sciences have flourished because they are experimental and have direct practical applications. But their success is based on a profound lack of interest in the question of how the organisms we study were formed. As long as we can fix the machines, we do not care how they were designed—and many rest content with the idea of a supernatural Designer. Evolution requires an interest in origins, and an acceptance of the different techniques needed to study them, which is simply not shared by many biologists."

Britten, Roy J., "Primate Evolution," review of *Molecular Anthropology*, edited by Morris Goodman, Richard E. Tashian and Jeanne H. Tashian, Symposium on Advances in Primatology (New York: Plenum, 1976, 466 pp), *Science*, vol. 198 (October 21, 1977), pp. 286-287.

p. 287   "The book ends with a long philosophical chapter by Zuckerkandl, full of henomenology, ideas and possibilities, that pays little heed to the matter of verification or falsification by measurement. A major idea is that 'progressive evolution' is based on the existence of only a limited number of possible variant states of the system of gene regulation. I am not sure 'progressive evolution' is a scientific concept, but I am sure we don't know the prime source of variation in evolution and don't know the mechanism or system of gene regulation, nor can we guess whether the system has few or many states that could occur as a result of frequent genome changes.

       "On the current state of theoretical evolutionary work as described in this volume I quote higher authority: the Red King acting as judge in *Alice in Wonderland* . . . If there's no meaning in it, . . . that saves a lot of trouble, you know, as we needn't try to find any."

Crick, Francis, "Lessons from Biology," *Natural History*, vol. 97 (November 1988), pp. 32-39.

p. 32   "The second property of almost all living things is their complexity and, in particular, their highly organized complexity. This so impressed our forebears that they considered it inconceivable that such intricate and well-organized mechanisms would have arisen without a designer. Had I been living 150 years ago I feel sure I would have been compelled to agree with this Argument from Design."

p. 36   "Biologists must constantly keep in mind that what they see was not designed, but rather evolved. It might be thought, therefore, that evolutionary arguments would play a large part in guiding biological research, but this is far from the case. It is difficult enough to study what is happening now. To try to figure out exactly what happened in evolution is even more difficult. Thus evolutionary arguments can usefully be used as hints to suggest possible lines of research, but it is highly dangerous to trust them too much."

Dobzhansky, Theodosius, "On Methods of Evolutionary Biology and Anthropology" (Part I—Biology), *American Scientist* (December 1957), pp. 381-392.

p. 388   "On the other hand, it is manifestly impossible to reproduce in the laboratory the evolution of man from the australopithecine, or of the modern horse from an Eohippus, or of a land vertebrate from a fish-like ancestor. These evolutionary happenings are unique, unrepeatable, and irreversible. It is as impossible to turn a land vertebrate into a fish as it is to effect the reverse transformation. The applicability of the experimental method to the study of such unique historical processes is severely restricted before all else by the time intervals involved, which far exceed the lifetime of any human experimenter. And yet, it is just such impossibility that is demanded by antievolutionists when they ask for 'proofs' of evolution which they would magnanimously accept as satisfactory. This is about as reasonable a demand as it would be to ask an astronomer to recreate the planetary system, or to ask an historian to reenact the history of the world from

Caesar to Eisenhower. Experimental evolution deals of necessity with only the simplest levels of the evolutionary process, sometimes called microevolution."

Dobzhansky, Theodosius, "Evolutionary and Population Genetics," *Science*, vol. 142 (November 29, 1963), pp. 1131-1135.

p. 1134   "It would be wrong to say that the biological theory of evolution has gained universal acceptance among biologists or even among geneticists. This is perhaps unlikely to be achieved by any theory which is so extraordinarily rich in philosophic and humanistic implications. Its acceptance is nevertheless so wide that its opponents complain of inability to get a hearing for their views."

Ehrlich, Paul R., and L. C. Birch, "Evolutionary History and Population Biology," *Nature*, vol. 214 (April 22, 1967), pp. 349-352.

p. 349   "Some biologists claim that an understanding of the evolutionary history of organisms is prerequisite to any comprehension of ecology. We believe that this notion is having the effect of sheltering large areas of population biology from the benefits of rigorous thought. . . . Indeed, since the level of speculation (rather than investigation) is inevitably high in phylogenetic of any kind, a preoccupation with the largely unknown past can be shown to be a positive hindrance to progress."

p. 351   "Indeed, we know nothing whatever of the antecedents of most species for thousands of years. Perhaps these dismal facts account for some of the strangely unsatisfying 'explanations' of the evolutionary ecologists."

p. 352   "Our theory of evolution has become . . . one which cannot be refuted by any possible observations. Every conceivable observation can be fitted into it. It is thus 'outside of empirical science' but not necessarily false. No one can think of ways in which to test it. Ideas, either without basis or based on a few laboratory experiments carried out in extremely simplified systems have attained currency far beyond their validity. They have become part of an evolutionary dogma accepted by most of us as part of our training."

Eiseley, Loren C., *The Immense Journey* (New York: Random House, 1957).

p. 199   "With the failure of these many efforts, science was left in the somewhat embarrassing position of having to postulate theories of living origins which it could not demonstrate. After having chided the theologian for his reliance on myth and miracle, science found itself in the unenviable position of having to create a mythology of its own: namely, the assumption that what, after long effort could not be proved to take place today had, in truth, taken place in the primeval past."

Futuyma, Douglas J., *Science on Trial* (New York: Pantheon Books, 1983), 251 pp.

p. 65   "He [Goldschmidt] pushed his conclusion to extremes, and theorized that each major taxonomic group had arisen as a macromutation, a 'hopeful monster' that in one jump had passed from worm to crustacean, or reptile to bird."

p. 171   "Two major kinds of argument about evolutionary theory occur within scientific circles. There are philosophical arguments about whether or not evolutionary theory qualifies as a scientific theory, and substantive arguments about the details of the theory and their adequacy to explain observed phenomena."

p. 171   "A secondary issue then arises: Is the hypothesis of natural selection falsifiable or is it a tautology? . . . The claim that natural selection is a tautology is periodically made in the scientific literature itself."

p. 197   "Creation and evolution, between them, exhaust the possible explanations for the origin of living things. Organisms either appeared on the earth fully developed or they did not. If they did not, they must have developed from preexisting species by some process of modification. If they did appear in a fully developed state, they must indeed have been created by some omnipotent intelligence."

Grassé, Pierre-P., *Evolution of Living Organisms* (New York: Academic Press, 1977), 297 pp.

p. 87   "Bacteria, the study of which has formed a great part of the foundation of genetics and molecular biology, are the organisms which, because of their huge numbers, produce the most mutants. . . . bacteria, despite their great production of intraspecific varieties, exhibit a great fidelity to their species. The bacillus *Escherichia coli*, whose mutants have been studied very carefully, is the best example. The reader will agree that it is surprising, to say the least, to want to prove evolution and to discover its mechanisms and then to choose as a material for this study a being which practically stabilized a billion years ago!"

p. 103   "The opportune appearance of mutations permitting animals and plants to meet their needs seems hard to believe. Yet the Darwinian theory is even more demanding: A single plant, a single animal would require thousands and thousands of lucky, appropriate events. Thus, miracles would become the rule: events with an infinitesimal probability could not fail to occur."

p. 103   "There is no law against daydreaming, but science must not indulge in it."

p. 107   "Directed by all-powerful selection, chance becomes a sort of providence, which, under the cover of atheism, is not named but which is secretly worshipped."

p. 130   "The fruitfly (*Drosophila melanogaster*), the favorite pet insect of the geneticists, whose geographical, biotopical, urban and rural genotypes are now known inside out, seems not to have changed since the remotest times."

p. 202   "The explanatory doctrines of biological evolution do not stand up to an objective, in-depth criticism. They prove to be either in conflict with reality or else incapable of solving the major problems involved."

Hamilton, W. D., "Ordering the Phenomena of Ecology," *Science*, vol. 167 (March 13, 1970), pp. 1478-80. Hamilton was at Imperical College, London.

p. 1479   "This criticism amounts to restating what I think is the admission of most evolutionists, that we do not yet know what natural selection maximizes.

                ". . . I feel that a great deal of complexity . . . has been rather lightly brushed aside."

Lipson, H. S., "A Physicist's View of Darwin's Theory," *Evolutionary Trends in Plants*, vol. 2, no. 1 (1988), p. 6.

p. 6   "To begin with, I have no doubt about evolution; the evidence is incontrovertible. The only question is how it came about. On reading *The Origin of Species*, I found that Darwin was much less sure himself than he is often represented to be; the chapter entitled 'Difficulties of the Theory' for example, shows considerable self-doubt. As a physicist, I was particularly intrigued by his comments on how the eye would have arisen."

p. 6   "We now know a great deal more about living matter than Darwin knew. We know how nerves work and I regard each nerve as a masterpiece of electrical engineering. And we have thousands of millions of them in our body. We know how the muscles expand and contract and we know how our hearts beat. But we do not yet know how we think. The brain has parts specifically designed for this purpose.

"'Design' is the word that springs to mind, on this subject. My biologist colleagues do not like it. They say that I should not object to a theory unless I have a better scientific one to replace it, a scientific one being a theory that can be falsified (*sensu* Popper). My unscientific theory is that we have been designed in a macromutational way by an external creator. All the evidence supports this view but, of course, it cannot be sustained scientifically."

Løvtrup, Søren, *Darwinism: The Refutation of a Myth* (New York: Croom Helm, 1987), 469 pp.

p. 422   "I suppose that nobody will deny that it is a great misfortune if an entire branch of science becomes addicted to a false theory. But this is what has happened in biology: for a long time now people discuss evolutionary problems in a peculiar 'Darwinian' vocabulary—'adaptation,' 'selection pressure,' 'natural selection,' etc.—thereby believing that they contribute to the *explanation* of natural events. They do not, and the sooner this is discovered, the sooner we shall be able to make real progress in our understanding of evolution.

"*I believe that one day the Darwinian myth will be ranked the greatest deceit in the history of science*" [Emphasis added]

Myers, Norman, "The End of the Lines," *Natural History*, vol. 94 (February 1985), pp. 2-12.

p. 2   "As in the past, new life forms will arise, but not at a fraction of the rate they are going to be lost in the coming decades and centuries. We are surely losing one or more species a day right now out of the five million (minimum figure) on Earth."

p. 2   "The average duration of a species is, roughly speaking, about 5 million years. According to Raup, there has been a crude average of 900,000 natural extinctions per one million years, or one natural extinction every one and one-ninth years. The present human-caused rate of extinction is at least 400 times higher."

Myers, Norman, "Extinction Rates Past and Present," *Bioscience*, vol. 39 (January 1989), pp. 39-41.

p. 39   "Today's rate can be estimated through various analytical techniques to be a minimum of 1000, and possibly several thousand, species per year."

p. 39   "If current land-use patterns and environment-destruction patterns persist (and many are likely to accelerate), the extinction rate could surely rise by the year 2000 to an average of 100 species per day."

p. 39   "It generally takes tens of thousands of years for a new terrestrial vertebrate or a new plant species to emerge fully, and even species with rapid turnover rates, notably insects, usually require centuries if not millennia to generate a new species."

Pesely, Gregory Alan., "The Epistemological Status of Natural Selection," *Laval Theologique et Philosophique*, vol. 38 (February 1982), pp. 61-74.

p. 74   "One of the most frequent objections against the theory of natural selection is that it is a sophisticated tautology. Most evolutionary biologists seem unconcerned about the charge and only make a token effort to explain the tautology away. The remainder, such as Professors Waddington and Simpson, will simply concede the fact. For them, natural selection is a tautology which states a heretofore unrecognized relation: the fittest—defined as those who will leave the most offspring—will leave the most offspring.

"What is most unsettling is that some evolutionary biologists have no qualms about proposing tautologies as explanations. One would immediately reject any lexicographer who tried to define a word by the same word, or a thinker who merely restated his proposition, or any other instance of gross redundancy; yet no one seems scandalized that men of science should be satisfied with a major principle which is no more than a tautology. Until there is a successful resolution to this problem, as well as most of the others already mentioned, the theory of natural selection can never be seriously scientific."

Peters, R. H., "Tautology in Evolution and Ecology," *American Naturalist*, vol. 110 (January/February 1976), pp. 1-12.

p. 1   "I argue that the 'theory of evolution' does not make predictions, so far as ecology is concerned, but is instead a logical formula which can be used only to classify empericisms and to show the relationships which such a classification implies. . . . The essence of the argument is that these 'theories' are actually tautologies and, as such, cannot make empirically testable predictions. They are not scientific theories at all."

Ridley, Mark, *The Problems of Evolution* (New York: Oxford University Press, 1985), 159 pp.

p. 13   "We have now completed a summary of the main arguments for evolution. The combination of observations of evolution on the small scale, with the principle of uniformitarianism, the nature of classification, the argument from homologies such as the universality of the genetic code, and the geological succession of organic beings, if not the evidence of observed evolution in fossils, all make up a convincing case."

pp. 71-2   "Pseudogenes provide similar evidence. A pseudogene is (probably) a molecular equivalent of the appendix in humans. It is a functionless vestige of a formerly functional gene; for instance, some pseudogenes lack one of the parts that are needed for a gene to be translated into a protein. If the gene is not translated, it must lie dormant inside its bearer. Then, according to the neutral theory, all negative selection would be removed and the genes should be free to evolve at a very high rate."

Rifkin, Jeremy, *Algeny* (New York: Viking Press, 1983), 298 pp.

p. 112   "Evolutionary theory has been enshrined as the centerpiece of our educational system, and elaborate walls have been erected around it to protect it from unnecessary abuse."

p. 125   "What the 'record' shows is nearly a century of fudging and finagling by scientists attempting to force various fossil morsels and fragments to conform with Darwin's notions, all to no avail. Today the millions of fossils stand as very visible, ever-present reminders of the paltriness of the arguments and the overall shabbiness of the theory that marches under the banner of evolution."

p. 134   "The fruit fly has long been the favorite object of mutation experiments because of its fast gestation period (twelve days). X rays have been used to increase the mutation rate in the fruit fly by 15,000 percent. All in all, scientists have been able to 'catalyze the fruit fly evolutionary process such that what has been seen to occur in *Drosophila* (fruit fly) is the equivalent of many millions of years of normal mutations and evolution.' Even with this tremendous speedup of mutations, scientists have never been able to come up with anything other than another fruit fly."

Skoog, Gerald, "Topic of Evolution in Secondary School Biology Textbooks: 1900-1977," *Science Education*, vol. 63 (October 1979), pp. 621-640.

p. 636   "Other textbooks, in a retreat from the 1960s, now have de-emphasized evolution. The de-emphasis has not been a result of a diminishing in the power of evolution to explain and make sense out of the natural world. Instead, the de-emphasis has been the result of publishers, authors, educators, and politicians responding to the strenuous efforts of antievolutionists and creationists to suppress and diminish the study of evolution. Also, citizens who do not understand evolution, the constitutional mandate that schools be neutral in matters of religious theory, doctrine, and practice, and the importance of unifying ideas to the study of a discipline, stand by and allow special interest groups to influence and dictate the content of the biology curriculum in this nation. This could result in the return of evolution to the periphery of the secondary school biology curriculum. Should this happen, evolution will remain an idea within the world and work of biologists rather than diffusing outward into the minds of all educated people."

Sokolov, B. S., "The Current Problems of Paleontology and Some Aspects of Its Future," *Paleontological Journal*, vol. 9, no. 2 (1975), pp. 135-144.

p. 137   "I know geologists who regard the whole of Darwin's theory and the present-day synthetic theory of evolution (which do in fact have weak spots) as a type of religion, but we may readily imagine the chaos that would face us in geology were the evolutionary concept to become a myth."

Thomas, Lewis, "On the Uncertainty of Science," *Key Reporter*, vol. 46 (Autumn 1980), pp. 1-3, 8.

p. 1   "Science . . . keeps changing, shifting, revising, discovering that it was wrong and then heaving itself explosively apart to redesign everything."

p. 1   "Our most spectacular biological attribute, which identifies us as our particular sort of animal, is language, and the deep nature of this gift is a mystery."

p. 2   "The culmination of a liberal arts education ought to include, among other matters, the news that we do not understand a flea, much less the making of a thought."

p. 2   "Biology needs a better word than *error* for the driving force in evolution. . . . I cannot make my peace with the randomness doctrine; I cannot abide the notion of purposelessness and blind chance in nature. And yet I do not know what to put in its place for the quieting of my mind."

Thomson, Keith Stewart, "The Meanings of Evolution," *American Scientist*, vol. 70 (September/October 1982), pp. 529-531. Thomson was Professor of Biology and Dean of the Graduate School, Yale University.

p. 529   "Twenty years ago Mayr, in his *Animal Species and Evolution* seemed to have shown that if evolution is a jigsaw puzzle, then at least all the edge pieces were in place. But today we are less confident and the whole subject is in the most exciting ferment. Evolution is both troubled from without by the nagging insistence of antiscientists and nagged from within by the troubling complexities of genetic and developmental mechanisms and new questions about the central mystery—speciation itself."

pp. 529-30   "In fact there is circularity in the approach that first assumes some sort of evolutionary relatedness and then assembles a pattern of relations from which to argue that relatedness must be true."

p. 530   "There are a number of problems with hypothetical schemes capable of producing rapid, large, coherent changes in phenotypes. Equally large immediate changes in the genotype might be needed, and any large change in genotype or phenotype must surely be sufficiently disruptive to be lethal. And where would a large change in a phenotype or genotype come from? Moreover, suppose an oddity were to be produced, how would a population be established and maintained?"

p. 531   "While we are sure that these are the principal components in mechanisms of evolutionary change, we do not yet have enough information to assemble a complete mechanistic scheme, let alone *the* scheme."

Thompson, W. R., "Introduction," *Origin of Species*, by Charles Darwin (Dutton: Everyman's Library, 1956), p. *xxii*. Dr. Thompson was Director of the Commonwealth Institute of Biological Control, Ottawa.

"It is . . . right and proper to draw the attention of the non-scientific public to the disagreements about evolution. But some recent remarks of evolutionists show that they think this unreasonable. This situation where scientific men rally to the defense of a doctrine they are unable to define scientifically, much less demonstrate with scientific rigor, attempting to maintain its credit with the public by suppression of criticism and the elimination of difficulties, is abnormal and undesirable in science."

"[The taxonomic system], whereby organisms are classified, presents an orderly arrangement of clear-cut entities, which are clear-cut because they are separated by gaps."

"Fossil evidence shows a remarkable absence of the many intermediate forms required by the theory. . . . the modern Darwinian paleontologists are obliged, just like their predecessors and like Darwin, to water down the facts with subsidiary hypotheses which, however plausible are, in the nature of things, unverifiable."

"The success of Darwinism was accompanied by a decline in scientific integrity."

"The general tendency to eliminate, by means of unverifiable speculations, the limits of the categories nature presents to us, is, the inheritance of biology from the *Origin of Species*. To establish the continuity required by theory, historical arguments are invoked, even though historical evidence is lacking. Thus are engendered those fragile towers of hypotheses based on hypotheses, where fact and fiction intermingle in an inextricable confusion."

Washburn, S. L., "Study of Evolution—More of a Game Than a Science," *Abstracts*, 71st Annual Meeting (Washington, D.C.: American Anthropological Association, 1972).

p. 121   "The behaviors that led to the origin of man are not available for study, and must be reconstructed from fragmentary fossils, the anatomy and behaviors of contemporary primates . . . but there is wide area for disagreements. Doctrines which seemed certain in one decade may crumble under the impact of new discoveries, new methods of dating, new experiments. Under these circumstances, it may be more useful to regard the study of evolution as a game rather than as a science. Uncertainties are far greater than might be thought from reading scientific papers and, in spite of the emphasis on evolutionary theory, there is no agreement on the rules of the evolutionary game."

Watson, James D., *Molecular Biology of the Gene*, 3rd ed. (New York: W. A. Benjamin, Inc., 1976), 739 pp.

p. 2   "Today, the theory of evolution is an accepted fact for everyone but a fundamentalist minority, whose objections are based not on reasoning but on doctrinaire adherence to religious principles."

Wiley, E. O., "Review of *Darwin Retried* by MacBeth," *Systematic Zoology*, vol. 24 (June 1975), pp. 269-270. Wiley was in the Department of Ichthyology, CUNY, American Museum of Natural History.

p. 269   "As such the book deserves to be read by those of us who teach our scientific theories and myths to new generations of biologists."

p. 270   "For example, he views the difference between micro and macro changes as the difference between breeding a horse of a different color and a horse with wings."

p. 270   "MacBeth suggests that we try to look at evolution with new eyes, that we admit to the public, and, if needed, to ourselves, that we have misgivings about Darwinism, and the synthetic theory, that we open debate. I think these are excellent suggestions."

C. Concern with Creationism

Not long ago evolutionists tended to ignore creationists, assuming them to be uneducated Bible-thumpers, but the situation is different now. There are now thousands of scientists who have become creationists, and evolutionists have lost several hundred formal scientific debates to creationists in the past twenty years. Even though evolutionists still hold rigid control over the schools and media, they can no longer ignore the creationists. Over fifty anti-creationist books and many hundreds of anti-creationist articles have been published in recent years. These have intimidated many evangelicals into various compromises, but creationism continues to gain adherents in significant numbers. The following quotes illustrate their concern over this development.

Anonymous, "Editorial," *Biology and Philosophy*, vol. 1, no. 1 (1986), pp. 1-3.

p. 1   "American biologists have only contempt for so-called 'Scientific Creationism,' feeling that this movement is merely a thinly veiled version of religious fundamentalism, designed only to get the Bible into schools. Yet, the Creationists have certainly forced people to go back and examine, not just the bases of their own ideas, but also their general views on the nature of proper biological education."

Azar, Larry, "Biologists, Help!" *Bioscience*, vol. 28 (November 1978), pp. 712-715. Azar was in the Department of Philosophy, Iona College.

p. 712   "Although only a philosophy teacher, I have long been fascinated by the progress of science, especially of biology. Who can doubt, for example, that the doctrine of evolution has captivated almost every area of intellectual pursuit?"

p. 713   "For a biologist to note that he is not a philosopher is indeed legitimate. However, can ignoring a philosophical question be interpreted as answering it?"

p. 713   "Is the biologist unwittingly implying that his vision of nature is so complete as to render unnecessary any consideration of nonbiological doctrines?"

p. 714   "Are the authorities maintaining, on the one hand, that evolution is documented by geology and, on the other that geology is documented by evolution? Isn't this a circular argument?"

p. 714   "I can understand the inherent difficulty in attempting to discover intermediate forms. My problem concerns the *methodology* of science: If an evolutionist accepts gaps as a prerequisite for his theory, is he not arguing from a lack of evidence? If a biologist teaches that between two existing fossils there was a non-existing third (and perhaps several others), is he not really like the man of religious faith who says: 'I believe, even though there is no evidence?'"

p. 714   "While accepting uniformitarianism in theory, biologists inevitably renege in its application. They further complicate the issue of the origin of life by insisting on a living ancestor for every organism."

Berlinski, David, "The Deniable Darwin," *Commentary*, vol. 101 (June 1996), pp. 19-29.

p. 19   "The facts in favor of evolution are often held to be incontrovertible; prominent biologists shake their heads at the obduracy of those who would dispute them. Those facts however, have been rather less forthcoming than evolutionary biologists might have hoped."

p. 28   "Biologists often affirm that as members of the scientific community they positively welcome criticism. Nonsense. Like everyone else, biologists loathe criticism and arrange their lives so as to avoid it. Criticism has nonetheless seeped into their souls, the process of doubt a curiously Darwinian one in which individual biologists entertain minor reservations about their theory without ever recognizing the degree to which these doubts mount up to a substantial deficit. Creationism, so often the target of their indignation is the least of their worries."

p. 28   "Unable to say *what* evolution has accomplished, biologists now find themselves unable to say *whether* evolution has accomplished it. This leaves evolutionary theory in the doubly damned position of having compromised the concepts needed to make sense of life—complexity, adaptation, design—while simultaneously conceding that the theory does little to explain them."

Bethell, Tom, "Agnostic Evolutionists," *Harper's*, vol. 270 (February 1985), pp. 49-61.

p. 51   "What most people do not know is that for much of this century, and especially in recent years, scientists have been fighting among themselves about Darwin and his ideas.

"Scientists are largely responsible for keeping the public in the dark about these in-house arguments. When they see themselves as beleaguered by opponents outside the citadel of science, they tend to put their differences aside and unite to defeat the heathen, the layman sees only the closed ranks."

p. 61   "No one has ever found an organism that is known not to have parents, or a parent. This is the strongest evidence on behalf of evolution." [statement to Bethell by Richard Lewontin.]

p. 61   "The theory of evolution has never been falsified. On the other hand, it is also surely true that the positive evidence for evolution is very much weaker than most laymen imagine, and that many scientists want us to imagine. Perhaps as [Colin] Patterson says, that positive evidence is missing entirely. The human mind, alas, seems on the whole to find such uncertainty intolerable. Most people want certainty in one form (Darwin) or another (the Bible). Only evolutionary agnostics like Patterson and [Gareth] Nelson and the other cladists seem willing to live with doubt. And that, surely, is the only true scientific outlook."

Broad, William J., "Creationists Limit Scope of Evolution Case," *Science*, vol. 211 (March 20, 1981), pp. 1331-1332.

p. 1331   "A rallying of the ranks would definitely be needed if creationists argued that evolution was a religion. Constitutional scholars do not scoff at the issue, one expert at Harvard recently saying it is 'far from a frivolous argument.'"

p. 1332   "For his own part, [attorney for the CSRC] Turner says his recent experience in the courtroom has whetted his desire for more. 'These scientists get up on the stand, and act as if their very lives were being attacked. They not only close ranks, but they almost deny anybody the right to know of the internal fights that go on within the evolutionary crowd. They're pompous and arrogant, just the kind of people that the First Amendment was written to protect us against."

Dawkins, Richard, "Is Science a Religion?" *The Humanist*, vol. 57 (January/February 1997), pp. 26-29.

p. 26   "I think a case can be made that *faith* is one of the world's great evils, comparable to the smallpox virus but harder to eradicate.

               "Faith, being belief that isn't based on evidence, is the principle vice of any religion."

p. 27   "Most religions offer a cosmology and a biology, a theory of life, a theory of origins, and reasons for existence. In doing so, they demonstrate that religion is, in a sense, science; it's just bad science. Don't fall for the argument that religion and science operate on separate dimensions and are concerned with quite separate sorts of questions."

p. 27   "Now, as I say, when it is put to me that science or some particular part of science, like evolutionary theory, is just a religion like any other, I usually deny it with indignation. But I've begun to wonder whether perhaps that's the wrong tactic. Perhaps the right tactic is to accept the charge gratefully and demand equal time for science in religious education classes."

p. 28   "What worries me is not the question of equal time but that, as far as I can see, children in the United Kingdom and the United States are essentially given *no* time with evolution yet are taught creationism (whether at school, in church, or at home)."

Denton, Michael, *Evolution: A Theory in Crisis* (London: Burnett Books, Ltd., 1985), 368 pp.

p. 100   "The fact that so many of the founders of modern biology, those who discovered all the basic facts of comparative morphology upon which modern evolutionary biology is based, held nature to be fundamentally a discontinuum of isolated and unique types unbridged by transitional varieties, a position absolutely at odds with evolutionary ideas, is obviously very difficult to reconcile with the popular notion that all the facts of biology irrefutably support an evolutionary interpretation."

p. 145   "The validity of the evolutionary interpretation of homology would have been greatly strengthened if embryological and genetic research could have shown that homologous structures were specified by homologous genes and followed homologous patterns of embryological development. Such homology would indeed be strongly suggestive of 'true relationship; of inheritance from a common ancestor.' But it has become clear that the principle cannot be extended in this way. Homologous structures are often specified by non-homologous genetic systems and the concept of homology can seldom be extended back into embryology."

Dobzhansky, Theodosius, "Darwinian or 'Oriented' Evolution?" *Evolution*, vol. 29 (June 1975), pp. 376-378.

p. 376   "The book of Pierre P. Grassé [*L'Évolution du vivant*, Albin Michel, Paris, 1973, 477 pp.] is a frontal attack on all kinds of 'Darwinism.' His purpose is to 'destroy the myth of evolution as a simple, understood and explained phenomenon,' and to show that evolution is a mystery about which little is, and perhaps can be, known. Now, one can disagree with Grassé but not ignore him. He is the most distinguished of French zoologists, the editor of the 28 volumes of 'Traité de Zoologie,' author of numerous original investigations, and ex-president of The Academie des Sciences. His knowledge of the living world is encyclopedic."

Eiseley, Loren C., *The Immense Journey* (New York: Random House, 1957), p. 199.

"With the failure of these many efforts, science was left in the somewhat embarrassing position of having to postulate theories of living origins which it could not demonstrate. After having chided the theologian for his reliance on myth and miracle, science found itself in the unenviable position of having to create a mythology of its own: namely, the assumption that what, after long effort could not be proved to take place today had, in truth, taken place in the primeval past."

Eldredge, Niles, *Time Frames: The Rethinking of Darwinian Evolution and the Theory of Punctuated Equilibria* (New York: Simon and Schuster, 1985), 240 pp.

p. 21   "There just is no rationale, no purpose to be served in giving different names to such virtually identical creatures just because they are separated by 3 million years of time. Yet that *is* the natural propensity of paleontologists: collections of otherwise similar, if not completely identical, fossils tend to get different names for no reason other than their supposedly significant age differences."

p. 29   "Indeed, the only competing explanation for the order we all see in the biological world, this pattern of nested similarity that links up absolutely all known forms of life, is the notion of Special Creation: that a supernatural Creator, using a sort of blueprint, simply fashioned life with its intricate skein of resemblances passing through it.

"And, of course, it was precisely this notion of divine Creation that furnished the explanation for all life—its very existence, its exuberant diversity and its apparent order—in Darwin's day."

p. 33   "And though a few of these eighteenth-century systematists had vaguely evolutionary notions, nearly all were devoutly and orthodoxly religious. They saw the order in their material, the grand pattern of similarity running through the entire organic realm, as evidence of God's plan of Creation."

p. 33   "As Ernst Mayr, one of the founders of the modern synthetic theory of evolution, pointed out in his *Systematics and the Origin of Species* (1942), Darwin never really did discuss the origin of species in his *On the Origin of Species.*"

Gould, Stephen Jay, "Darwinism and the Expansion of Evolutionary Theory," *Science*, vol. 216 (April 23, 1982), pp. 380-387.

pp. 380-1   "Darwinians cannot simply claim that natural selection operates since everyone, including Paley and the natural theologians, advocated selection as a device for removing unfit individuals at both extremes and preserving, intact and forever, the created type. The essence of Darwinism lies in a claim that natural selection is the primary directing force of evolution, in that it creates fitter phenotypes by differentially preserving, generation by generation, the best adapted organisms from a pool of random variants that supply raw material only, not direction itself. Natural selection is a creator; it builds adaptation step by step."

p. 386   "[Footnote] Failure to recognize that all creationists accepted selection in this negative role led Eiseley to conclude falsely that Darwin had 'borrowed' the principle of natural selection from his predecessor E. Blythe. The Reverend William Paley's classic work *Natural Theology*, published in 1803, also contains many references to selective elimination."

Hanson, Earl D., "Evolution/Creation Debate," Letter-to-the-Editor, *Bioscience*, vol. 30 (January 1980), pp. 4-5.

p. 4   "Why do creationists seem to be the consistent winners in public debates with evolutionists? . . . The apparent inadequacy of the performance by biologists is the problem I will comment on here."

p. 5   "We biologists are our own worst enemies in the creationist-evolutionist controversies. We must no longer duck this and other issues related to biology and human affairs, and when we do face them we must think clearly and express ourselves accordingly. We may still not be consistent winners in the creationist-evolutionist debates, but let the losses that occur be attributable to other than lapses in professional standards."

Koestler, Arthur, *Janus: A Summing Up* (New York: Vintage Books, 1978), 354 pp.

p. 170   "Once upon a time, it all looked so simple. Nature rewarded the fit with the carrot of survival and punished the unfit with the stick of extinction. The trouble only started when it came to defining 'fitness.' . . . Thus natural selection looks after the survival and reproduction of the fittest, and the fittest are those which have the highest rate of reproduction—we are caught in a circular argument which completely begs the question of what makes evolution evolve."

p. 185   "In the meantime, the educated public continues to believe that Darwin has provided all the relevant answers by the magic formula of random mutation plus natural selection—quite unaware of the fact that random mutations turned out to be irrelevant and natural selection a tautology."

p. 192   "Yet Jacques Monod was not a hypocrite. He was brilliant in his specialized field, but disarmingly naive concerning the theoretical implications of it—what his compatriots call a '*terrible generalisateur*.' This, of course, applies to many of his eminent colleagues in the neo-Darwinian establishment. Guided—perhaps unconciously—by the maxim that a bad theory is better than no theory, they are unable or unwilling to realize that the citadel they are defending lies in ruins."

pp. 249-50   "The nineteenth-century model of the universe as a mechanical clockwork is a shambles and since the concept of matter itself has been dematerialized, *materialism can no longer claim to be a scientific philosophy*."

Marshall, John C., "Everyday Tales of Ordinary Madness," review of *Why People Believe Weird Things*, by Michael Shermer (W. H. Freeman: 1997, 306 pp.), *Nature*, vol. 389 (September 4, 1997), p. 29.

p. 29   "Above all, and despite the title of his book, Shermer refuses to engage deeply with why beliefs are held (or indeed what beliefs, as opposed to scientific hypotheses, actually are). Creationists, I would divine, are lamenting the loss of a monolithic religious culture that never existed. If so, no amount of lecturing from Michael Shermer and Richard Dawkins could reconcile them to their fate, and the latter's attempts to present science as if it were a religion will only make things worse, on both sides of the divide."

p. 29   "By contrast, in the very university in which I work, there are people who claim that an occult force linking the Earth and the Moon provokes the tides to ebb and flow, and that minute creatures too small for the naked eye to see are capable of causing disease. Only this week, I heard that pink worms are dining on solid methane at the bottom of the Gulf of Mexico. And that if you send one member of a pair of simultaneously created photons to Bellevue and the other to Bernex (two villages near Geneva), each one knows what the other is doing and itself does likewise.

                "To believe in ESP and little green men seems fairly tame in comparison."

Matthews, L. Harrison (F. R. S.), "Introduction to *The Origin of Species*" (London: J. M. Dent & Sons, Ltd., 1971).

p. x   "Much of Professor Thompson's criticism of Darwin's text is unanswerable. In accepting evolution as a fact, how many biologists have paused to reflect that science is built upon theories that been proved by experiment to be correct, or remember that the theory of animal evolution has never been thus proved? . . . The fact of evolution is the backbone of biology, and biology is thus in the peculiar position of being a science founded on an unproved theory—is it then a science or a faith? Belief in the theory of evolution is thus exactly parallel to belief in special creation—both are concepts which believers know to be true but neither, up to the present, has been capable of proof."

p. *xi*   "The [Peppered Moth] experiments beautifully demonstrate natural selection—or survival of the fittest—in action, but they do not show evolution in progress, for however the populations may alter in their content of light, intermediate, or dark forms, all the moths remain from beginning to end *Bistan betularia*."

p. *xii*   "During the last fifty years genetics has unraveled many of the extremely complex phenomena of inheritance, and has shown that evolution by natural selection of random mutations, generally of small size, is a logical explanation of the origin of the immense array of organisms now and in the past living on the earth. The theory is so plausible that most biologists accept it as though it were a proven fact, although their conviction rests on circumstantial evidence; it forms a satisfactory faith on which to base our interpretation of nature."

Muggeridge, Malcolm, *The End of Christendom* (Grand Rapids: Eerdmans, 1980), 62 pp.

p. 59   "I myself am convinced that the theory of evolution, especially the extent to which it's been applied, will be one of the great jokes in the history books in the future. Posterity will marvel that so very flimsy and dubious an hypothesis could be accepted with the incredible credulity that it has. I think that I spoke to you before about this age as one of the most credulous in history, and I would include evolution as an example. I'm very happy to say I live near a place called Piltdown. I like to drive there because it gives me a special glow. You probably know that a skull was discovered there, and no less than five hundred doctoral theses were written on the subject, and then it was discovered that the skull was a practical joke by a worthy dentist in Hastings who'd hurriedly put a few bones together, not even of the same animal, and buried them and stirred up all this business. So I'm not a great man for bones."

Newell, Norman D., "Paleobiology's Golden Age," *Palaios*, vol. 2, no. 3 (1987), pp. 305-309.

p. 306   "It is sometimes suspected that comparative morphology and molecular biology of living organisms can provide a reliable record of life's history without attention to fossils. Not so! Living organisms tell little or nothing of the environmental setting or oscillations in diversity of past life—nothing about those myriads that died out without issue."

pp. 306-7   "We have not agreed on how to use the term catastrophe for geological phenomena and I would banish it from scientific use."

p. 308   "The study of fossils is associated with organic evolution, which is taboo to millions of Americans. Our profession has tended to ignore this as naive and anti-intellectual—we do not like to be tagged with religious intolerance. But we must keep in mind that it is the general public to whom we turn for approval and financial support."

p. 308   "We are at a disadvantage because, already being condemned by creationists as secular humanists (i.e., atheists), we do not like the idea of being an adversary of a religious group. Our object should be not to quarrel with the creationists, but to explain to the general public the evidence for evolution."

Patterson, Colin, "Evolution and Creationism," Speech at the American Museum of Natural History, New York (November 5, 1981). Dr. Patterson is a senior paleontologist at the British Museum of Natural History, and editor of its journal, as well as author of the book *Evolution*.

p. 1   "I'm speaking on two subjects—evolutionism and creationism—and I believe it's true to say that I know nothing whatever about either of them."

"Question is: Can you tell me anything you know about evolution, any one thing that is true? I tried that question on the geology staff at the Field Museum of Natural History and the only answer I got was silence."

". . . it does seem that the level of knowledge about evolution is remarkably shallow."

p. 2   "Then I woke up and realized that all my life I had been duped into taking evolutionism as revealed truth in some way."

"I feel that the effects of hypotheses of common ancestry in systematics has not been merely boring, not just a lack of knowledge; I think it has been positively anti-knowledge."

p. 14   "In other words, evolution may very well be true, but basing one's systematics on that belief will give bad systematics."

Thomson, Keith Stewart, "Natural Theology," *American Scientist*, vol. 85 (May/June 1997), pp. 219-21. Dr. Thomson is University Distinguished Scientist in Residence at the new School for Social Research in New York.

p. 219   "Of the various kinds of facts that one can imagine, many are really opinions in disguise."

p. 219   "The argument from design, if not exactly the last refuge of scoundrels (which is how Samuel Johnson saw patriotism), is certainly the first (and in the end, last) resort of antievolutionists."

p. 221   "God the creator of pain and suffering is never quite explainable by Malthus's arithmetic, however, and Charles Darwin himself turned away from religion as much or more because of the 'senseless' death of his 10-year-old daughter Annie than any logic."

p. 221   "*Natural Theology* gives the reader a glimpse of the philosophical debates of the day. If it did not stimulate Darwin's interest in the very subjects Paley opposed, it did introduce him to the ideas of Malthus."

p. 221   "One way or another, Paley represented the transition to modernity. If nothing else, he has passed the first test of Darwinism: He has survived."

Werthelm, Margaret, "God in the Lab," *New Scientist* (December 23/30, 1995), pp. 40-42.

p. 40   "A 1991 Gallup Poll showed that fully 47 per cent of Americans, including a quarter of college graduates, continued to believe that 'God created man pretty much in his present form at one time within the last 10,000 years.'"

p. 41   "Since the 1960's 'scientific creationism' or 'creation science' has mushroomed in the US. Instead of relying on the Bible, scientific creationists cite geological and other physical evidence as the basis for their views. Spearheading this approach is the Institute for Creation Research, an organization in El Cajon, California staffed by card-carrying PhDs such as Steve Austin, who insists that geological data reveal that life on Earth came into being just three or four thousand years ago."

Chapter 6

The Origin of Species

A. Natural Selection and Classification

Many people have the quaint notion that Darwin solved the problem of speciation with his 1859 book *The Origin of Species by Natural Selection*. Nothing could be further from the truth. Variation and recombination, within a given kind at a given level of complexity, are not evolution or even speciation.

Natural selection is now widely recognized as tautologous. That is, the "fittest" are merely those that survive, and the reason they survive is because of their fitness. Actually, natural selection is conservative, not creative. It weeds out the misfits that appear as mutated varieties, thus tending to conserve the status quo in a population.

Darwinism still has many defenders, but the trend among evolutionary biologists and paleontologists today is to abandon the idea of slow change through mutation (especially when it sinks in that truly "beneficial" mutations are still utterly hypothetical, never demonstrable) and natural selection, in favor of a mysterious "quantum-leap" type of speciation.

Ayala, Francisco J., "Biology as an Autonomous Science," *American Scientist*, vol. 56, no. 3 (Autumn, 1968), pp. 207-221.

p. 213   "Biological evolution can however be explained without recourse to a Creator or a planning agent external to the organisms themselves. There is no evidence either of any vital force or immanent energy directing the evolutionary process toward the production of specified kinds of organisms. The evidence of the fossils record is against any directing force, external or immanent, leading the evolutionary process toward specified goals. Teleology in the stated sense is, then, appropriately rejected in biology as a category of explanation."

p. 213   "One of [Darwin's] greatest accomplishments was to bring the teleological aspects of nature into the realm of science. He substituted a scientific teleology for a theological one. The teleology of nature could now be explained, at least in principle, as the result of natural laws manifested in natural processes, without recourse to an external Creator or to spiritual or nonmaterial forces. At that point biology came into maturity as a science."

Ayala, Francisco J., "Biological Evolution: Natural Selection or Random Walk?" *American Scientist*, vol. 62 (November/December 1974), pp. 692-701.

p. 692   "Before Darwin, the adaptations and the diversity of organisms were accepted as facts without an explanation, or, more frequently, they were attributed to the omniscient design of the Creator. God had created birds and butterflies in the air, fish and coral reefs in the oceans, trees in the forest, and most of all He had created man. God had provided man with eyes so that he might see and had given gills to fish to breathe oxygen in water. Theologians frequently argued that the functional design of organisms evinces the existence of a wise Creator."

p. 692   "Darwin accepted the facts of adaptation and then provided a natural explanation for these facts—the theory of natural selection. He brought the teleological aspects of nature into the realm of science, substituting a scientific teleology for a theological one. Therewith biology came into maturity as a scientific discipline. The origin and kinds of organisms as well as their adaptations could now be explained as the result of natural laws manifested in natural processes."

p. 700   "Science seeks to discover patterns of relations among empirical facts and to advance hypotheses or theories that explain why the facts are as observed. A hypothesis is empirical or scientific only if it can be tested by experience. . . . A hypothesis or theory which cannot be, at least in principle, falsified by empirical observations and experiments does not belong to the realm of science."

Brace, C. Loring, review of *Species, Species Concepts, and Primate Evolution*, edited by William H. Kimbel and Lawrence B. Martin (Plenum Press, 1993, 560 pp.), *American Scientist*, vol. 82 (September/October 1994), pp. 484-486.

p. 484   "Readers of *American Scientist* may not realize the extent to which a major part of the field of biology and almost all of paleontology has rejected Darwin's insights concerning organic evolution. Natural selection is dismissed as contributing nothing more than 'fine-tuning,' and adaptation is largely ignored in practice."

p. 485   "Buried in the miasma of wordy obfuscation, however, is an evident perpetuation of the opposition to Darwin voiced by Louis Agassiz in 1860 when he asserted that species are changeless entities reflecting thoughts in the mind of God."

p. 486   "In effect, the cladists are the 'creation scientists' of paleontology. Speciation events are instantaneous and unexaminable, as is the case of 'special creation' for Christian fundamentalists. The unchanging persistence of species is assumed as 'axiomatic.' Mechanism and process are simply regarded as irrelevant. And all this is maintained with a kind of unyielding fervor that rivals the dogmatism of the religious fundamentalists."

p. 486   "In reality, religious fundamentalism and cladistics owe their resemblance to the fact that both are firmly rooted in the typological essentialism of the same Medieval mindset."

Carson, Hampton L., "Chromosomes and Species Formation," review of *Models of Speciation* by M. J. D. White (San Francisco: Freeman, 1978, 454 pp.), *Evolution*, vol. 32 (December 1978,) pp. 925-927. Carson is in the Genetics Department at the University of Hawaii.

p. 925   "To a very large extent, the formation of a species is a phenomenon which has occurred in the past, so that the recognition of the events surrounding the actual division of an ancient gene pool cannot be directly observed. In all but a very small number of cases the biologist must become historian and deal with evidence for the past role of processes rather than deal with these processes in action in contemporary populations. The search for truly incipient species has been difficult and, to a considerable degree, frustrating."

Coyne, J. A., and N. H. Barton, "What Do We Know About Speciation?" *Nature*, vol. 331 (February 11, 1988), pp. 485-486.

p. 485   "Although darwinism is often declared to be dead, it refuses to lie down. Darwin did, however, mislead his audience in one way: his best-known work is much more about the origins of adaptations than of species. Since then, there has been much more progress in understanding the causes of adaptive change than of the mechanisms whereby new species are generated."

p. 486   "A combination of genetic and developmental approaches may offer the most progress in understanding the evolution of reproductive isolation. Without such knowledge, we are simply unable to evaluate the many theories of speciation."

Dawkins, Richard, "What Was all the Fuss About?" *Nature*, vol. 316 (August 22, 1985), pp. 683-684.

p. 683   "Darwin's own bulldog, Huxley, as Eldredge reminds us again, warned him against his insistent gradualism, but Darwin had good reason. His theory was largely aimed at replacing creationism as an explanation of how living complexity could arise out of simplicity. Complexity cannot spring up in a single stroke of chance: that would be like hitting upon the combination number that opens a bank vault. But a whole series of tiny chance steps, if non-randomly selected, can build up almost limitless complexity of adaptation. It is as though the vault's door were to open another chink every time the number on the dials moved a little closer to the winning number. Gradualness is of the essence. In the context of the fight against creationism, gradualism is more or less synonymous with evolution itself. If you throw out gradualness you throw out the very thing that makes evolution more plausible than creation."

Eden, Murray, "Inadequacies of Neo-Darwinian Evolution as a Scientific Theory," in *Mathematical Challenges to the Neo-Darwinian Interpretation of Evolution*, ed. P. S. Moorhead and M. M. Kaplan (Philadelphia: Wister Institute Press, 1967), pp. 109-111.

p. 109   "It is our contention that if 'random' is given a serious and crucial interpretation from a probabilistic point of view, the randomness postulate is highly implausible and that an adequate scientific theory of evolution must await the discovery and elucidation of new natural laws—physical, physico-chemical, and biological."

Gould, Stephen Jay, "Darwin's 'Big Book,'" review of *Natural Selection*, by Charles Darwin, (New York: Cambridge University Press, 1975), edited by R. C. Stauffer, *Science*, vol. 188 (May 23, 1975), pp. 824-826.

p. 825   "A Lamarckian inheritance of acquired characters is, to Haeckel, 'an indispensable foundation of the theory of evolution.' . . . Huxley doggedly maintained his belief in the saltational origin of species—anathema to Darwin, who saw gradual transition as the crucial test of natural selection."

p. 825   "The theory of natural selection did not triumph until the 1920's and 1930's when a rising science of population genetics equated small mutations with Darwinian variability and demonstrated that small selection pressures could account for evolutionary change. And the 'modern synthesis' between traditional subdisciplines of natural history and genetic theory did not begin much before Dobzhansky's 1937 work on *Genetics and the Origin of Species*."

p. 826   "But could the longer version, with its more copious documentation, have carried the day for his theory of natural selection? The answer again is clearly no; for the difficulties of natural selection in 1859 placed its vindication far beyond the power of any data then available."

Harris, C. Leon, "An Axiomatic Interpretation of the Neo-Darwinian Theory of Evolution," *Perspectives in Biology and Medicine*, vol. 18 (Winter 1975), pp. 179-184.

pp. 182-3   "First, the axiomatic nature of the neo-Darwinian theory places the debate between evolutionists and creationists in a new perspective. Evolutionists have often challenged creationists to provide experimental proof that species have been fashioned *de novo*. Creationists have often demanded that evolutionists show how chance mutations can lead to adaptability, or to explain why natural selection has favored some species but not others with special adaptations, or why natural selection allows apparently detrimental organs to persist. We may now recognize that neither challenge is fair. If the neo-Darwinian theory is axiomatic, it is not valid for creationists to demand proof of the axioms, and it is not valid for evolutionists to dismiss special creation as unproved so long as it is stated as an axiom."

p. 183   "The axiom of natural selection is so ingrained that a phrase like 'The action of natural selection is very strong' seems perfectly acceptable even though it often means simply that a lot of organisms died. Many alternatives to the neo-Darwinian axioms would be criticized not because they violate accepted facts but because they violate deeply rooted concepts."

Hull, David L., "The Ascent of Ideas in Evolution," review of *Monad to Man*, by Michael Ruse (Harvard University Press, 1997, 628 pp.), *Nature*, vol. 385 (February 6, 1997), pp. 497-498.

pp. 497-8   "Another intriguing part of Ruse's book is his extensive discussion of the efforts made by evolutionary biologists to transmute evolutionary biology into a mature discipline—mathematics and all. But did not Darwin and his immediate successors do that a long time ago? One of Ruse's insights, is that they did not, and the chief villain was, of all people, T. H. Huxley. Huxley played a central role in establishing science as a profession in Victorian England, but he did so only by excluding evolutionary biology. It was too hypothetical. In his popular presentations, Huxley was very much an evolutionist, but when he put on his professional hat he explicitly and pointedly omitted any reference to evolutionary theory."

Jukes, Thomas H., "On Sociobiology," *Nature*, vol. 270 (November 17, 1977), p. 203.

p. 203   "Sociobiology seeks to explain that human social behavior has a genetic and, therefore, an evolutionary background, which has long been obvious for other orders of animals, especially the *Hymenoptera*."

p. 203   "It seems to me that sociobiology aggravates its opponents by the ingenuity with which it produces explanations to make observations fit a theory. To a considerable extent, pan-selectionism has done the same by finding an adaptive advantage for each phenotypic trait."

p. 203   "Perhaps those who disbelieve and spurn sociobiological teachings may be responding to a genetic trait. The struggle against pre-ordained fate could in itself have a survival value. This struggle may include the rejection of theories that tell us we are in the grip of determinism imposed by our genes."

Mayr, Ernst, *Populations, Species and Evolution* (Cambridge, Mass.: Harvard University Press, 1970), 453 pp.

p. 321   "Recent studies on the integration of species-specific gene complexes have considerably changed our ideas on the nature of species differences. . . . Indeed, it is becoming increasingly evident that an approach that merely counts the number of gene differences is meaningless, if not misleading."

pp. 321-2   "Nor can species difference be expressed in terms of the genetic bits of information, the nucleotide pairs of the DNA. That would be quite as absurd as trying to express the difference between the Bible and Dante's *Divinia Commedia* in terms of the difference in frequency of the letters of the alphabet used in the two works. The meaningful level of integration is well above that of the basic code of information, the nucleotide pairs."

p. 360   "The most closely related species are combined into genera, groups of related genera into subfamilies and families, these into orders, classes, and phyla. Our delimitation of a higher taxon and its ranking in the hierarchy have a large arbitrary component."

Mayr, Ernst, "Behavior Programs and Evolutionary Strategies," *American Scientist*, vol. 62 (November/ December 1974), pp. 650-659.

p. 650   "For the devout of past centuries such perfection of adaptation seemed to provide irrefutable proof of the wisdom of the Creator. For the modern biologist it is evidence for the remarkable effectiveness of natural selection."

Patterson, Colin, "Cladistics," Interview by Brian Leek, interviewer Peter Franz, March 4, 1982, BBC.

"No one has ever produced a species by mechanisms of natural selection. No one has ever gotten near it and most of the current argument in neo-Darwinism is about this question: how can a species originate and is it there that natural selection seems to be fading out and chance mechanisms of one sort or another are being invoked. . . . all one can learn about the history of life is learned from systematics, from groupings one finds in nature. The rest of it is story-telling of one sort or another. We have access to the tips of a tree; the tree itself is theory and people who pretend to know about the tree and to describe what went on with it, how the branches came off and the twigs came off are, I think, telling stories."

Patterson, Colin, "Cladistics and Classification," *New Scientist*, vol. 94 (April 29, 1982), pp. 303-306.

p. 306   "The concept of ancestry, as part of evolutionary theory, has so captivated systematists that they are trained to think in terms of trees, of ancestry and descent. But the only clues to relationship between species are uniquely shared characters (homologies). . . . So hypotheses of ancestry must depend on some justification beyond character distribution: for instance, that the ancestor be represented by fossils occurring earlier in time than the descendant, and that the fossil record should be sufficiently complete and well-sampled for there to be no other potential ancestors. But fossils, too, present peculiar problems in analysis. . . .

"Because of all these problems, it is rare to find paleontologists offering ancestral species, or doing so with any conviction. Instead, they usually propose 'ancestral groups,' as approximations to the truth, with the claim that the true ancestor, if found, would fall within the group. . . . This raises yet another problem, for groups cannot evolve—species are the largest units capable of change. Thus cladistics calls into question much of conventional evolutionary history.

". . . Cladists recommend avoiding some of the problems with fossils by treating them in the same way as living species, as potential twigs of cladograms rather than stems of trees."

p. 306   "Cladistics calls into question traditional attitudes in [systematics, paleontology, and biogeography], and offers a new approach to comparative biology which has a coherent theoretical base that is not necessarily tied to evolutionary theory. . . . But if we are taught, as we have been, to see that pattern through the spectacles of evolutionary theory, how could the pattern ever test the theory?"

Popper, Karl R., "Science: Problems, Aims, Responsibilities," *Proceedings, Federation of American Society of Experimental Biology*, vol. 22 (1963), pp. 961-72.

p. 964   "Agreement between theory and observation should count for nothing unless the theory is a testable theory, and unless the agreement is the result of attempts to test the theory. But testing a theory means trying to find its weak spots; it means trying to refute it. And a theory is testable if it is refutable. . . .

"There is a difficulty with Darwinism. . . . It is far from clear what we should consider a possible refutation of the theory of natural selection. If, more especially, we accept that statistical definition of fitness which defines fitness by actual survival, then the survival of the fittest becomes tautological and irrefutable."

Raup, David M., "Conflicts Between Darwin and Paleontology," *Bulletin, Field Museum of Natural History*, vol. 50 (January 1979), pp. 22-29.

p. 26   "If we allow that natural selection works, as we almost have to do, the fossil record doesn't tell us whether it was responsible for 90 percent of the change we see, or 9 percent, or 0.9 percent."

p. 26   "It is certainly true that one would be most unlikely to develop a functioning flying insect, reptile, or bird by a chance collection of changes. Some sort of guidance is necessary. And in these cases, of course, natural selection is the only mechanism we know of to produce a workable combination of characteristics."

p. 29   "If the ideas turn out to be valid, it will mean that Darwin was correct in what he said but that he was explaining only a part of the total evolutionary picture. The part he missed was the simple element of chance!"

Richards, O. W., "A Guide to the Practice of Modern Taxonomy," review of *Principles of Systematic Zoology*, by Ernst Mayr (New York: McGraw-Hill, 1969, 434 pp.), *Science*, vol. 167 (March 13, 1970), pp. 1477-78. Richards was at Imperial College, England.

p. 1477   "According to the author's view, which I think nearly all biologists must share, the species is the only taxonomic category that has at least in more favorable examples a completely objective existence. Higher categories are all more or less a matter of opinion."

Vrba, Elizabeth S., and Stephen Jay Gould, "The Hierarchical Expansion of Sorting and Selection: Sorting and Selection Cannot be Equated," *Paleobiology*, vol. 12 (Spring 1986), pp. 217-228.

p. 226   "The concept of progress has been particularly vexatious throughout the history of evolutionary biology. Darwin denied it explicitly as a logical consequence of natural selection (which only produces local adaptation, not general advance), but smuggled it back obliquely because he could deny neither his culture's obsession with the idea nor the broad sweep of life's history from early prokaryotes to recent intelligence. Hierarchy may resolve the issue by explaining life's weak and impersistent vector of progress as the result of deeper structural principles more inclusive than natural selection."

pp. 226-7   "We must also acknowledge that Darwin's theory does not have the range to encompass the new kinds of data increasingly coming to light. In so stating, we are not merely pointing to the hitherto unsuspected *presence* of particular genomic parts or additional fossils. Rather, the *patterns* they form speak clearly of evolutionary laws beyond neo-Darwinism. Although we can as yet only see 'through a glass darkly' into the workings of genes, the ontogenies of organisms, and the lives of species in macroevolution, we already glimpse enough to know that the expanded hierarchy is a reality."

Wright, Sewall, "Character Change, Speciation, and the Higher Taxa," *Evolution*, vol. 36 (May 1982), pp. 427-443.

p. 440   "The reorganization required for the origin of the highest categories may seem so great that only 'hopeful monsters' will do. Here, however, we must consider the size and complexity of the organisms. Such changes would probably have been impossible except in an organism of very small size and simple anatomy. I have recorded more than 100,000 newborn guinea pigs and have seen many hundreds of monsters of diverse sorts but none were remotely 'hopeful,' all having died shortly after birth if not earlier."

p. 441   "According to the shifting balance theory the determining factor for rapid change, and the origin of a new higher taxon that usually accompanies such change, is the presence of one or more vacant ecological niches, whether from entrance of the species into relatively unexploited territory or from its survival after a catastrophe has eliminated other species occupying related niches, or from gradual attainment of an adaptation that opens up a new way of life."

B. Stasis and Punctuated Equilibrium

Primarily because of the ubiquitous gaps and lack of transitional forms between species and (even more) higher categories of plants and animals, many evolutionists are now favoring some kind of saltational transition to generate new kinds of organisms, even though such changes have never been observed to take place and there is no known genetic mechanism which would allow them.

The most popular term for this concept of speciation is "punctuated equilibrium," but others have referred to "quantum speciation" or even "hopeful monsters." It is not based on factual evidence, but on the absence of evidence. Its only rationale is the need for some evolutionary process instead of special creation to explain the gaps.

The long ages of evolutionary geology are retained in this scenario, with the assumption of great periods of evolutionary "stasis" punctuated occasionally by rapid evolutionary bursts. There is much evidence for stasis, of course, but none for the punctuations!

Alters, Brian J., and William F. McComas, "Punctuated Equilibrium: the Missing Link in Evolution Education," *American Biology Teacher*, vol. 56 (September 1994), pp. 334-340.

p. 337   "Gould and Eldredge content that: 'Phyletic gradualism was an *a priori* assertion from the start—it was never "seen" in the rocks; it expressed the culture and political bias of 19th century liberalism.' By the same token, while many feel that punctuated equilibrium postulates how speciation occurs, its occurrence is not based on empirical evidence but on the apparent lack of evidence—gaps in the fossil record. . . . Bodnar, Jones and Ellis suggested that one would not see intermediate forms in simple eukaryotes in the fossil record because there are no intermediate forms. A single mutation in a regulatory gene caused the change in one leap of evolutionary development."

Brett, Carlton E., "Stasis: Life in the Balance," *Geotimes*, vol. 40 (March 1995), pp. 18-20.

p. 18   "Did life on Earth change steadily and gradually through time? The fossil record emphatically says 'no.' For millions of years, life goes along uneventfully; then suddenly, a series of natural disasters disrupts the status quo and disturbs and restructures vast segments of existing ecosystems."

p. 18   "Episodes of rapid evolutionary change punctuate long intervals of stasis, during which little or no change takes place.

          "Eldredge and Gould also underscored the relative important of the two ways by which species change. Anagenesis refers to relatively gradual and perhaps continuous evolution within lineages, while speciation or cladogenesis involves the splitting of lineages into two species, typically as a result of geographic isolation. Most morphological change in evolution occurs during cladogenesis, according to Eldredge and Gould, and anagenesis is of relatively minor importance in evolution."

p. 18   "Long-term directional change appears rare. Hence, the notion of stasis itself has evolved from one of absolute stability to a concept of dynamic stability in which morphospecies display minor, non-progressive fluctuations around an unchanging average state over time."

p. 20   "Species tend to remain stable for intervals of several million years, implying very precise habitat tracking, or perhaps, 'ecological locking,' whereby incumbent species resist invasion and maintain nearly constant proportions, as suggested by Paul Morris (Paleontological Research Institute, Ithaca, N.Y.), and Linda Irany and Ken Schopf (Harvard University). Only when environmental perturbation is so severe or rapid that stable ecosystems are knocked out of equilibrium can new species and immigrants invade. Pulses of community reorganization may then take place until a new stable state is attained.

     "Coordinated stasis implies that relative stability is the norm throughout life history and that major morphological change and ecological restructuring occur rarely (less than 1 percent of geologic time)."

Dobzhansky, Theodosius, "Species of *Drosophila*," *Science*, vol. 177 (August 25, 1972), pp. 664-669.

p. 667   "The founder principle is 'establishment of a new population by a few original founders (in an extreme case, by a single fertilized female) that carry only a small fraction of the total genetic variation of the parental population.' Founder events are inevitably followed by inbreeding for one or several generations. The populations descended from the founders are then restructured by natural selection, which operates on a changed gene pool and usually in an altered environment. . . . Natural selection in experimental populations derived from small numbers of founders resulted in a greater variety of outcomes than in comparable populations descended from numerous founders. It should be noted that, although the genetic variability among the descendants of a single pair of founders is reduced compared to the population from which the founders came, it is by no means absent. Experiments on several species of *Drosophila* have shown that recombination of genes in a single pair of chromosomes drawn at random from a natural population can give rise to considerable genetic variability."

Eldredge, Niles, "Evolution Moves in Jumps," *Science Digest*, vol. 73 (March 1973), pp. 23-24.

p. 73   "Evolution in living things is not a series of changes constantly taking place, but one that proceeds by fits and starts."

     [This is the conclusion of Dr. Niles Eldredge of the American Museum of Natural History, reported in *Natural History* magazine. His findings are based on the study of the evolution of the eye lenses in the *Phacops rana*, a species of trilobite, an extinct marine arthropod. They seemed to indicate that a species can exist relatively unchanged for millions of years, until an evolutionary change occurs rapidly among members geographically isolated from the parent species.]

Eldredge, Niles, "Progress in Evolution?" *New Scientist*, vol. 110 (June 5, 1986), pp. 54-57.

p. 55   "Darwin, it has by now become commonplace to acknowledge, never really addressed the "origin of species" in his book of that title."

p. 55   "Palaeontologists ever since Darwin have been searching (largely in vain) for the sequences of insensibly graded series of fossils that would stand as examples of the sort of wholesale transformation of species that Darwin envisioned as the natural product of the evolutionary process. Few saw any reason to demur—though it is a startling fact that, of the half dozen reviews on the *On the Origin of Species* written by palaeontologists that I have seen, all take Darwin to task for failing to recognize that most species remain recognizably themselves, virtually unchanged throughout their occurrence in geological sediments of various ages."

Goldschmidt, Richard B., "Evolution, As Viewed by One Geneticist," *American Scientist*, vol. 40 (January 1952), pp. 84-98, 135.

p. 91   "If one tries to work out this idea in detail, one soon comes to a point where it is evident that something besides the Neo-Darwinian tenets needed to explain such macroevolutionary processes. The difficulties already encountered on the specific and generic level seem to the present writer to be insuperable at the level of families, orders, classes, and phyla."

p. 92   "It is hardly surprising that a number of zoologists, botanists, and paleontologists were not convinced that such a scheme could work. Certainly the evolutionary steps leading from a reptile to a bird should be infinitely more numerous than those leading from one kind of bird to another. But neither in this nor in any other comparable case of macroevolution has more than an indication of these series been found."

p. 94   "It is true that nobody thus far has produced a new species or genus, etc., by macromutation. It is equally true that nobody has produced even a species by the selection of micromutations. In the best-known organisms, like *Drosophila*, innumerable mutants are known. If we were able to combine a thousand or more of such mutants in a single individual, this still would have no resemblance whatsoever to any type known as a species in nature."

Gould, Stephen Jay, and Niles Eldredge, "Punctuated Equilibria: the Tempo and Mode of Evolution Reconsidered," *Paleobiology*, vol. 3 (Spring 1977), pp. 115-151.

p. 125   ". . . for most 'phylogenies' based on fossils rely on flimsy data. Rather, we wish to demonstrate that most cases presented as falsifications of punctuated equilibria are circular because they rely, . . . not upon clear evidence, but upon the gradualistic presuppositions they claim to test."

p. 147   "At the higher level of evolutionary transition between basic morphological designs, gradualism has always been in trouble, though it remains the 'official' position of most Western evolutionists. Smooth intermediates between *Baupläne* are almost impossible to construct, even in thought experiments, there is certainly no evidence for them in the fossil record (curious mosaics like *Archaeopteryx* do not count)."

Gould, Stephen Jay, "Evolution's Erratic Pace," *Natural History*, vol. 86 (May 1977), pp. 12-16.

pp. 12-14   "(Contrary to popular myths, Darwin and Lyell were not the heroes of true science, defending objectivity against the theological fantasies of such 'catastrophists' as Cuvier and Buckland. Catastrophists were as committed to science as any gradualist; in fact, they adopted the more 'objective' view that one should believe what one sees and not interpolate missing bits of a gradual record into a literal tale of rapid change.)"

p. 14   "The extreme rarity of transitional forms in the fossil record persists as the trade secret of paleontology. The evolutionary trees that adorn our textbooks have data only at the tips and nodes of their branches; the rest is inference, however reasonable, not the evidence of fossils."

p. 14   "Paleontologists have paid an exorbitant price for Darwin's argument. We fancy ourselves as the only true students of life's history, yet to preserve our favored account of evolution by natural selection we view our data as so bad that we never see the very process we profess to study."

p. 14   "The history of most fossil species includes two features particularly inconsistent with gradualism.

"1. *Stasis*. Most species exhibit no directional change during their tenure on earth. They appear in the fossil record looking much the same as when they disappear; morphological change is usually limited and directionless.

"2. *Sudden appearance*. In any local area, a species does not arise gradually by the steady transformation of its ancestors; it appears all at once and 'fully formed.'"

p. 16   "If gradualism is more a product of Western thought than a fact of nature, then we should consider alternative philosophies of change to enlarge our realm of constraining prejudices. In the Soviet Union, for example, scientists are trained with a very different philosophy of change—the so-called dialectical laws, reformulated by Engels from Hegel's philosophy. The dialectical laws are explicitly punctuational. . . . Eldredge and I were fascinated to learn that most Russian paleontologists support a model very similar to our punctuated equilibria. The connection cannot be accidental."

Gould, Stephen Jay, "The Return of Hopeful Monsters," *Natural History*, vol. 86 (June/July 1977), pp. 22-30.

p. 22   "The fossil record with its abrupt transitions offers no support for gradual change, and the principle of natural selection does not require it—selection can operate rapidly."

p. 24   "As a Darwinian, I wish to defend Goldschmidt's postulate that macroevolution is not simply microevolution extrapolated and that major structural transitions can occur rapidly without a smooth series of intermediate stages."

p. 24   "All paleontologists know that the fossil record contains precious little in the way of intermediate forms; transitions between major groups are characteristically abrupt."

p. 28   "The essence of Darwinism lies in a single phrase: natural selection is the creative force of evolutionary change. No one denies that natural selection will play a negative role in eliminating the unfit. Darwinian theories require that it create the fit as well."

Gould, Stephen Jay, "Is a New and General Theory of Evolution Emerging?" *Paleobiology*, vol. 6 (Winter 1980), pp. 119-130.

p. 122   "Ever since Darwin called his book *The Origin of Species*, evolutionists have regarded the formation of reproductively isolated units by speciation as a fundamental process of large-scale change. Yet speciation occurs at too high a level to be observed directly in nature or produced by experiment in most cases. Therefore, theories of speciation have been based on analogy, extrapolation and inference."

p. 125   "Thus, our model of 'punctuated equilibria' holds that evolution is concentrated in events of speciation and that successful speciation is an infrequent event punctuating the stasis of large populations that do not alter in fundamental ways during the millions of years that they endure."

p. 126   "Macroevolution is, as Stanley argues, decoupled from microevolution."

p. 127   "The absence of fossil evidence for intermediary stages between major transitions in organic design, indeed our inability, even in our imagination, to construct functional intermediates in many cases, has been a persistent and nagging problem for gradualistic accounts of evolution."

Gould, Stephen Jay, "Darwinism Defined: The Difference Between Fact and Theory," *Discover* (January 1987), pp. 64-70.

p. 65   "Our confidence in the fact of evolution rests upon copious data that fall, roughly, into three great classes. First, we have the direct evidence of small-scale changes in controlled laboratory experiments of the past hundred years (on bacteria, on almost every measurable property of the fruit fly *Drosophila*), or observed in nature (color changes in moth wings, development of metal tolerance in plants growing near industrial waste heaps), or produced during a few thousand years of human breeding and agriculture."

p. 68   "Second, we have direct evidence for large-scale changes, based upon sequences in the fossil record. The nature of this evidence is often misunderstood by non-professionals who view evolution as a simple ladder of progress, and therefore expect a linear array of 'missing links.' But evolution is a copiously branching bush, not a ladder. Since our fossil record is so imperfect, we can't hope to find evidence for every tiny twiglet."

p. 68   "Third, and most persuasive in its ubiquity, we have the signs of history preserved within every organism, every ecosystem, and every pattern of biogeographic distribution, by those pervasive quirks, oddities, and imperfections that record pathways of historical descent."

Gould, Stephen Jay, "Opus 200," *Natural History* (August 1991), pp. 12-18.

p. 14   "The oldest truth of paleontology proclaimed that the vast majority of species appear fully formed in the fossil record and do not change substantially during the long period of their later existence (average durations for marine invertebrate species may be as high as 5 to 10 million years). In other words, geologically abrupt appearance followed by subsequent stability."

p. 16 "When most of our colleagues defined evolution as gradual change, the stability of species counted as no data—that is, as absence of evolution. All paleontologists recognized the stability of species, but the subject never entered active research. At most, the fact of stability might be noted in the midst of a taxonomic description. Punctuated equilibrium has changed the context. Stasis has become interesting as a central prediction of our theory."

p. 16 "Stasis is now generally recognized as an intriguing puzzle by evolutionists. No definitive resolution is in sight, but geneticists and embryologists have offered their counsel, and I am tickled that our much maligned profession (dull, descriptive paleontology) has provided such a puzzle to kings of the theoretical mountain."

Gould, Stephen Jay, and Niles Eldredge, "Punctuated Equilibrium Comes of Age," *Nature*, vol. 366 (November 18, 1993), pp. 223-227.

p. 223 "Stasis, as palpable and observable in virtually all cases (whereas rapid punctuations are usually, but not always, elusive), becomes the major empirical ground for studying punctuated equilibrium."

p. 223 "Although punctuated equilibrium deals directly only with stability of species through time, the higher-level analogue of non-trending in larger clades has also graduated from an undefined non-subject to a phenomenon worth documenting. Moreover, because species often maintain stability through such intense climatic change as glacial cycling, stasis must be viewed as an active phenomenon, not a passive response to unaltered environments."

p. 226 "Prothero and Shubin conclude: 'This is contrary to the widely-held myth about horse species as gradualistically-varying parts of a continuum, with no real distinctions between species. Throughout the history of horses, the species are well-marked and static over millions of years. At high resolution, the gradualistic picture of horse evolution becomes a complex bush of overlapping, closely related species.'"

p. 227 "Nonetheless, contemporary science has massively substituted notions of indeterminacy, historical contingency, chaos and punctuation for previous convictions about gradual, progressive, predictable determinism."

Lewin, Roger, "Evolutionary Theory Under Fire," *Science*, vol. 210 (November 21, 1980), pp. 883-887.

p. 883 "An historic conference in Chicago challenges the four-decade long dominance of the Modern Synthesis. . . . one of the most important conferences on evolutionary biology for more than 30 years. A wide spectrum of researchers . . . gathered at Chicago's Field Museum of Natural History under the simple conference title: Macroevolution."

p. 883 "The central question of the Chicago conference was whether the mechanisms underlying microevolution can be extrapolated to explain the phenomena of macroevolution. At the risk of doing violence to the positions of some of the people at the meeting the answer can be given as a clear, No."

p. 884 "Species do indeed have a capacity to undergo minor modifications in their physical and other characteristics, but this is limited, and with a longer perspective it is reflected in an oscillation about a mean: to a paleontologist looking at the fossil record, this shows up as stasis."

p. 887   "Many people suggested that the meeting was a turning point in the history of evolutionary theory. . . . Will it prove to be the current equivalent of the 1946 Princeton meeting at which the capstone of the Modern Synthesis was laid?"

Lewin, Roger, "A Lopsided Look at Evolution," *Science*, vol. 241 (July 15, 1988), pp. 291-293.

p. 293   "Currently there is a multitude of possible explanations for this pattern, none of which is more compelling than any other. For now, however, the major point is as Jablonski and Bottjer state: 'In terms of the ecology of their evolutionary origins, higher taxa seem to have properties all of their own.' In fact, higher taxa may have several properties all of their own and evolutionary theory must strive to accommodate this."

Majer, Mirko, "Evolution Again," *Nature*, vol. 320 (March 6, 1986). p. 10.

"From his conviction of *permanent* and *gradual* change in nature, Darwin eventually got the required intellectual energy to accomplish his project. The orthodoxy, as is well known, advocated the fixity of species and acts of special creation—the first can be considered as an extreme form of stasis, the latter of jumps. Whereas Darwin himself hinted at the phenomenological similarity between special creation and evolutionary jumps, the implication of this similarity between stasis and the fixity of species should also be considered in the discussion of the development of his theory. Darwin's strategy then, was to propose an opposite picture of the living world rather than explain the old issues in terms of transmutation. If he had incorporated a plausible explanation of stasis into his theory, the orthodoxy would probably have used it as an argument in favour of the fixity of species."

Mayr, Ernst, "Speciation and Macroevolution," *Evolution*, vol. 36 (November 1982), pp. 1119-1132.

p. 1122   "The fundamental fact on which my theory was based is the empirical fact that when in a superspecies or species group there is a highly divergent population or taxon, it is invariably found in a peripherally isolated location."

p. 1122   "My conclusion was that any drastic reorganization of the gene pool is far more easily accomplished in a small founder population than in any other kind of population."

p. 1129   "It is ironical that the punctuational appearance of speeded up evolution during peripatric speciation, is likewise an artifact of the incompleteness of the fossil record. If all founder populations, which are exceedingly small, local, and of short duration, were preserved in the fossil record, they would surely document the gradual nature of the changes."

p. 1129   "More precisely, evidence has been steadily accumulating that, other factors being equal, rate of speciation is inversely correlated with population size. This is why speciation can be so rapid in founder populations, while widespread populous species may be totally inert evolutionarily."

Monastersky, R., "Life in the Jurassic: Stability amid Chaos," *Science News*, vol. 150 (September 28, 1996), p. 197.

p. 197   "[Carlton E.] Brett has documented that communities of organisms from this time tended to live and die as a group. Disparate species survived together through millions of years of environmental change and then disappeared *en masse* during particularly abrupt upheavals. This pattern, known as coordinated stasis, runs counter to traditional evolutionary theory, in which species evolve on their own."

p. 197   "[Carol M.] Tang and [David J.] Bottjer's observations do not support coordinated stasis. Although Jurassic species survived for long periods, each group appeared and went extinct separately, with apparently little interaction among species. 'We don't see coordination, we just see stasis,' says Bottjer."

Newell, Norman D., "Crises in the History of Life," *Scientific American*, vol. 208 (February 1963), pp. 77-92. Newell was Curator of Fossil Invertebrates, American Museum of Natural History.

p. 77   "The stream of life on earth has been continuous since it originated some three or four billion years ago. Yet the fossil record of past life is not a simple chronology of uniformly evolving organisms. The record is prevailingly one of erratic, often abrupt changes in environment, varying rates of evolution, extermination and repopulation. Dissimilar biotas replace one another in a kind of relay. Mass extinction, rapid migration and consequent disruption of biological equilibrium on both a local and a world-wide scale have accompanied continual environmental changes.

". . . The cause of these mass extinctions is still very much in doubt and constitutes a major problem of evolutionary history."

p. 77   "If we may judge from the fossil record, eventual extinction seems to be the lot of all organisms. Roughly 2,500 families of animals with an average longevity of somewhat less than 75 million years have left a fossil record. Of these, about a third are still living."

p. 80   "Quite recently, therefore, roughly three-quarters of the North American herbivores disappeared, and most of the ecological niches that were vacated have not been filled by other species."

Padian, Kevin, "The Whole Real Guts of Evolution," review of *Genetics, Paleontology and Macroevolution*, by Jeffrey S. Levinton (Cambridge University Press, 1988, 637 pp.), *Paleobiology*, vol. 15 (Winter, 1989), pp. 73-78.

p. 75   "After all, if microevolutionists had been looking all these years for a mechanism of evolution stasis, they would have been laughed at. (Why waste time trying to develop models for the *absence* of evolutionary change when the object is to model evolution?)"

p. 76   "Gould's arguments are generally far more complex and knowing than they are given credit for in this book. At times, Levinton quotes him out of context as well as any creationist has—for example, on hopeful monsters, on optimality and evolution, or on the relevance of the Modern Synthesis to evolution."

p. 76   "We as biologists in the 1980s still have much to learn about evolutionary processes, particularly with regard to the interplay of behavioral, environmental, developmental, and genetic factors. I am not sure we have most pieces of the puzzle yet. Why worry about violating the orthodoxy of the Modern Synthesis when the possibility of expanding it is so nearly endless?"

p. 77   "How do major evolutionary changes get started? Does anyone still believe that populations sit around for tens of thousands of years, waiting for favorable mutations to occur (and just how does *that* happen, by the way?), then anxiously guard them until enough accumulate for selection to push the population toward new and useful change? There you have the mathematical arguments of neodarwinism that Waddington and others rightly characterized as 'vacuous.'"

Perlas, Nicky, "Neo-Darwinism Challenged at AAAS Annual Meeting," *Towards*, vol. 2 (Spring 1982), pp. 29-31.

p. 29   "The neo-Darwinian theory of evolution is not only suffering from an identity crisis but may also be radically transformed to account for the growing number of scientific anomalies that continue to plague it. These were the underlying themes that could be inferred from presentations made by prominent scientists in the recently concluded symposium entitle, 'What Happened to Darwinism Between the Two Darwin Centennials, 1959-1982?' The symposium was convened under the auspices of the 148th Annual Meeting of the prestigious [AAAS] held from January 3, 1982 to January 8, 1982 at Washington, D.C."

p. 30   "The symposium was a disappointment to the true believers of neo-Darwinism. Implicit in their counter-offensive to stamp out creationism was the recognition that they had to contain and mend the fissures that were increasingly undermining the scientific foundation of their own neo-Darwinist position. To their dismay, the Provine symposium aggravated and deepened the fissures."

p. 30   "Mayr courageously admitted that his 1942 theory of speciation by way of geographic isolation is now uncertain because of the discovery of life forms which have not formed new species even though they were geographically isolated. . . . And in a more serious indictment against reductionism, Mayr concluded . . . that macroevolution should be decoupled from microevolution."

Richards, Eveleen, "A Political Anatomy of Monsters, Hopeful and Otherwise," *Isis*, vol. 85 (September 1994), pp. 377-411.

p. 378   "As a biological term, *hopeful monster* came to prominence in the writings of the saltationist evolutionist Richard Goldschmidt in the 1930s and 1940s, to be retrieved by Stephen Jay Gould in what Michael Ruse describes as the 'second' or 'most discontinuous' phase of the theory of punctuated equilibria in the late 1970s and early 1980s."

p. 379   "Ruse (along with others among Gould's critics) has no hesitation in assigning Gould's advocacy of punctuated equilibria theory and the support it has received in large part to politics, both internal and external to science. He identifies an internal political struggle among paleontologists and other evolutionists, especially geneticists, for cognitive standing in evolutionary theorizing."

p. 379 "Gould's advocacy of punctuated equilibria theory, Ruse claims, is connected with its congruency with the Marxist ideology of dialectical materialism."

p. 380 "It was the French transcendental anatomists, Étienne Geoffroy St. Hilaire and his disciple Étienne Serres, who during the 1820s turned the study of malformations or monsters as anatomical curiosities or *lusus naturae* into the science of teratology."

p. 380 "In essence, Geoffroy argued by analogy from the production of monsters to the origin of species."

pp. 389-90 "In brief, [Robert] Knox posited a common material origin of all life and its evolution by a process of saltatory descent. His scheme of 'generic descent' supposed the embryos of all members of the same natural family or genus to be essentially similar and to contain within themselves all the 'characters' or incipient structures of all the possible different species of that genus. New species arise through the action of the 'law of deformation,' which opposes the 'law of specialization' (Knox's laws of development were a materialistic variant of the transcendental principle of polarity) and therefore suppresses the formation of 'some parts of the organ or apparatus already existing in the generic being' or embryo. These 'deformations' or monstrosities are constantly generated. Those that are not 'viable' perish; those that are compatible with existing geographic and geologic conditions reproduce and increase in number, and so a new species is established. The human races (which Knox regarded as separate species) were the result of such monstrous change."

p. 392 "Belatedly, [Richard] Owen attempted to dissociate himself from the creationist label with which the Darwinians insisted on tagging him and to articulate and find an audience for his long-held views on organic descent— views that had been inspired by Geoffroy's teratological speculations but that he had earlier muted in response to public and professional criticism."

Ricklefs, Robert E., "Paleontologists Confronting Macroevolution," review of *Patterns of Evolution as Illustrated by the Fossil Record*, edited by A. Hallam (New York: Elesevier, 1977, 592 pp.), *Science*, vol. 199 (January 6, 1978), pp. 58-60.

p. 59 "The Eldredge-Gould concept of punctuated equilibria has gained wide acceptance among paleontologists. It attempts to account for the following paradox: Within continuously sampled lineages, one rarely finds the gradual morphological trends predicted by Darwinian evolution: rather, change occurs with the sudden appearance of new, well differentiated species."

p. 59 "Apart from the obvious sampling problems inherent to the observations that stimulated the model, and apart from its intrinsic circularity (one could argue that speciation can occur only when phyletic change is rapid, not vice versa), the model is more *ad hoc* explanation than theory, and it rests on shaky ground. Paleontologists seem to be enthralled by small populations."

p. 59 "The notion that small populations can evolve rapidly is based largely on such laboratory experiments as Dobzhansky's in which small 'founder' populations of *Drosophila* maintained widely divergent frequencies of chromosome arrangements—genetic reorganization, perhaps, but hardly macroevolution."

p. 59   "I hasten to point out that ecologists and geneticists have not elucidated macroevolutionary patterns: the gap has not been bridged from either side."

Stanley, Steven M., *Macroevolution: Pattern and Process* (San Francisco: W. H. Freeman and Co., 1979), 332 pp.

p. 36   "The punctuational idea emerged as a more visible alternative to English-speaking paleontologists with the publications of Eldredge (1971) and Eldredge and Gould (1972). It is both interesting and surprising that, unknown to Americans, this view had previously gained support in the paleontologic community of the Soviet Union."

pp. 61-2   "The field of genetics has shed little light on the nature or importance of quantum speciation, in part because the role of regulatory genes in large-scale adaptive transitions has only recently become apparent. Simple estimates of overall genetic distance between species reveal little about degrees and rates of morphologic divergence."

p. 69   ". . . the evidence is now mounting that most of the major fossil groups of the Cambrian arose by rapid evolution. . . . In the first place, fossil assemblages consisting of the imprints of softbodied creatures . . . have been found in many areas of the world, but are never older than latest Precambrian."

p. 187   "Macroevolution is decoupled from microevolution."

Wheeler, David L., "An Eclectic Biologist Argues that Humans Are Not Evolution's Most Important Result; Bacteria Are," *Chronicle of Higher Education*, vol. 43 (September 6, 1996), pp. A23-A24.

A23   "Even his critics grant that Dr. Gould is popular with lay readers, but this has also made him a favorite target of attack. In *The New York Review of Books* last year, John Maynard Smith, a prominent British evolutionistary theorist, said of him that 'the evolutionary biologists with whom I have discussed his work tend to see him as a man whose ideas are so confused as to be hardly worth bothering with, but as one who should not be publicly criticized because he is at least on our side against the creationists.'"

C. Mysteries of Adaptation and Speciation

The marvelous complexity and environmental adaptations noted in all species had long been considered as remarkable evidence of design by the Creator until Darwin claimed to show that natural selection could explain them. Now that many evolutionists are repudiating natural selection, they are still not returning to creationism but rather to pure chance and contingency, terms now popular among punctuationists.

To one not blinded by a personal aversion to creationism, however, or by pseudo-intellectual peer pressure, design is the overwhelmingly superior explanation of "nature's" marvels. Evolutionists may invent imaginative "just-so-stories" to account for them naturalistically, but it is really much more *natural* to understand them as God's creative handiwork. Not only has no one ever seen evolution working nor shown any satisfactory mechanism to make it work, the hoary circumstantial arguments for evolution (vestigial organs, embryologic recapitulation, comparative homologies, etc.) have all been abandoned.

Allee, W. C., A. E. Emerson, Orlando Park, Thomas Park, and Karl P. Schmidt, *Principles of Animal Ecology* (Philadelphia: W. B. Saunders Co., 1949), 837 pp.

p. 106   "The zoological dispersion of hibernation among mammals is not especially illuminating, since closely allied forms . . . may differ radically in this respect. Hibernation is reported for the orders Monotremata, Marsupiala, Insectivora, Chiroptera, Rodentia, and Carnivora."

p. 539.   "It was pointed out that an organism has but three choices available when exposed to adversity. It may die, adjust or migrate. Hibernation and aestivation are brood adjustments to adverse weather or climate. Migration or emigration are still different ways of avoiding unfavorable conditions."

Anonymous, "Scientists Charged Up Over Discovery of Electrical 'Sixth Sense' in Platypus," *San Diego Union Tribune* (Sunday, November 24, 1985), p. AA19.

  "The duckbilled platypus, one of the animal kingdom's most unconventional specimens, might be even stranger than zoologists had thought.

  "Australian scientists say a series of experiments has shown that the egg-laying, web-footed mammal detects electric signals to catch its fast-moving prey—mainly shrimp and frogs—in streams along Australia's east coast.

  "When flashlight batteries and dead shrimp were thrown into laboratory tanks, platypuses ignored the shrimp and headed for the batteries.

  "The platypus, which can stay under water for up to five minutes, swims with its eyes and ears closed, and scientists had long puzzled over how it found its food.

  "Chris Tidemann, curator of the Australian National University's Zoology Museum, said the discovery was confirmed in the experiments at his Canberra laboratory.

  "'It's unique, certainly in the mammals,' said Tidemann. 'The only other animals with it (electro-reception) are fish and a few amphibian larvae.'"

Anonymous, "The Battery-operated Duck-Billed Platypus," *New Scientist*, vol. 109 (February 13, 1986), p. 25.

p. 25   "That evolutionary enigma, the duck-billed platypus, has more than its egg-laying to distinguish it from other mammals. It now appears that in common with some species of fish and amphibians, it can detect weak electric fields (of a few hundred microvolts or less). Not only that, but it uses its electric sense to locate its prey, picking up the tiny electrical signals passing between nerves and muscles in the tail of a shrimp."

p. 25   "The trigeminal receptors are unlike those of any other electrosensitive species, suggesting that the idiosyncratic platypus may have evolved its electric sense quite independently."

Barr, Thomas C., "Biospéléology," review of *Biospeleologie: La Biologie des Avimaux Cavernicoles* by A. Vandel (Paris: Gauthier-Fillera, 1964, xviii & 619 pp.), *Science*, vol. 144 (June 26, 1964), pp. 1563-1564.

p. 1563 "There is abundant evidence, well presented by Vandel, which suggests that preadaptation has been historically significant in determining which groups of animals could successfully colonize caves. However, many American zoologists will take issue with Vandel's contention that the 'regressive' evolutionary changes in cave animals are the result of an orthogenetic 'phyletic senescence' (I am one of those who will protest this position). According to this view, troglodytes have not undergone 'subterranean evolution' because they live in caves, but rather, they live in caves because at their particular (senescent) evolutionary stage they are unable to survive in other habitats."

Benton, Mike, "Is a Dog More Like a Lizard or a Chicken?" *New Scientist*, vol. 103 (August 16, 1984), pp. 18-19. Benton is at the Oxford University Museum.

p. 18 "In 1982, Brian Gardiner of Queen Elizabeth College, London, presented an alternative 'cladogram' in which the Diapsida [archosaurs, lizards, snakes] and the Archosauria [crocodiles, birds, dinosaurs] were broken up. The most controversial feature of Gardiner's cladogram is the close relationship that is suggested between birds and mammals, both of which he puts into a new group called the Haemothermia."

p. 18 "However, others have gleefully accepted his view, and one French paleontologist has even published a restoration of the hypothetical common ancestor of birds and mammals—a sort of warm-blooded, hairy/feathery, climbing insect-eater!"

p. 19 "Adrian Friday and Martin Bishop of Cambridge have analyzed the available protein sequence data for tetrapods. . . . To their surprise, in nearly all cases, man (the mammal) and chicken (the bird) were paired off as closest relatives, with the crocodile as next nearest relative. . . . In particular, the reconstruction of evolutionary trees from molecular data is dependent on highly simplified models of protein evolution, and the particular mathematical treatment can also affect the tree that is obtained.

  "The controversy over the relationships of the tetrapods is significant to another aspect of molecular biology: the molecular clock hypothesis. . . . The molecular clock will now have to be reconsidered in view of the new evidence about tetrapod relationships, because the two cladograms give quite different branching dates (for example, bird-mammal: 330 or 225 million years)."

Black, Virginia S., "Excretion and Osmoregulation," in *The Physiology of Fishes*, edited by Margaret E. Brown (New York: Academic Press, Inc., 1957).

p. 164 "Paleontological and anatomical evidence indicates that fishes first evolved in fresh water, and gradually invaded the sea. . . . Since the quantity and variety of salts in both fresh and sea waters is different from that in the body fluids of fish, all fish must perform the function of osmotic regulation, i.e., fishes are homeosmatic. The physiological adjustments which are made in performing this function are truly remarkable."

p. 179   "In summary, it appears that the ability of stenohaline freshwater fishes to survive in salt solutions may depend on the histology of the gills, the extent of gill surface, rate of oxygen consumption, the tolerance of the tissues for salts, and control of permeability."

p. 193   "Many investigators have noticed that the presence of calcium salts in fresh water greatly increases the viability of marine and euryhaline animals in that medium. One reason for this effect is the well-known fact that calcium decreases cell permeability, both to salts and water."

p. 195   "Gunter (1942) found that for every freshwater fish that has been taken in sea water in North America, nine species of marine fish have been taken in fresh water. It seems to be easier for fishes to adapt themselves to excess water than to excess salt."

p. 197   "In nature, salinity changes are usually gradual and the fish has some choice in the speed of transfer. In most experimental procedures, however, fishes are submitted to stress because of fairly sharp changes in salinity, handling, etc., and those that survive our experiments are indeed hardy breeds."

Bock, Walter J., "Evolution by Orderly Law," *Science*, vol. 164 (May 9, 1969), pp. 684-685. Beck was at Columbia University.

p. 684   "Moreover, the biogenetic law has become so deeply rooted in biological thought that it cannot be weeded out in spite of its having been demonstrated to be wrong by numerous subsequent scholars."

p. 685   "Unfortunately, evolutionary development and ontogenetical development are separate and distinct time-related biological processes which have an extremely complex relationship to one another that precludes a simple understanding of evolutionary mechanisms and sequences through study of ontogenetical mechanisms."

Botkin, Daniel B., *Our Natural History* (New York: G. P. Putnam's Sons, 1995).

pp. 81-82   "A minimum viable population means the smallest number of individuals that has a reasonable chance of persisting. . . . Based on genetic factors, it has been estimated that a population should not fall below 50 breeding adults even for a short time to avoid genetic problems and to keep the chance of extinction acceptably low . . . to maintain a population for a long time, 500 or more breeding individuals are preferable. . . . This is sometimes referred to as the 50/500 rule."

Cherfas, Jeremy, "Clean Air Revives the Peppered Moth," *New Scientist*, vol. 109 (January 2, 1986), p. 17.

p. 17   "The peppered moth, *Biston betularia*, is a classic example of natural selection in action. As the dark satanic mills blackened the English landscape the predominant form of the peppered moth changed from light to dark, a case of industrial melanism. Since the Clean Air Acts came into force industrial pollution has declined. A new study by Sir Cyril Clarke and his associates shows that the light form of the peppered moth has become much more common (*Biological Journal of the Linnaean Society*, Vol. 26, p. 189)."

p. 17   "The first black specimen of *Biston betularia* was caught in Manchester in 1848. By 1895, 98 percent of the moths in the area were dark, an extremely rapid change given that the peppered moth breeds just once a year."

p. 17   "After 1975 there is a steep decline, and in 1984 only 60 percent were dark."

Cherfas, Jeremy, "The Difficulties of Darwinism," *New Scientist*, vol. 102 (May 17, 1984), pp. 28-30.

p. 29   "It may seem paradoxical to say that Darwin was opposed to adaptationism, in that adaptation seems to be the keystone of natural selection. In fact, as Darwin recognized, a perfect Creator could manufacture perfect adaptations. Everything would fit because everything was designed to fit. It is in the imperfect adaptations that natural selection is revealed, because it is those imperfections that show us that a structure has a history. If there were no imperfections, there would be no evidence of history, and therefore nothing to favor evolution by natural selection over creation."

p. 30   "Gould himself summed up his first two Tanner lectures thus: 'Our evolution is not progressively ordained, moving toward us. It is not for the best. It does not lead to perfect structure. There are important elements of accidental chance regulating the major structure of the biosphere. Evolution is not smooth and gradual.'"

de Beer, Sir Gavin, *Embryos and Ancestors* (London: Oxford University Press, 1958), 197 pp.

p. 13   "[The recapitulation theory] had . . . a regrettable influence on the progress of embryology."

pp. 170-1   "Recapitulation . . . does not take place."

de Beer, Gavin R., *Homology: An Unsolved Problem* (London: Oxford University Press, 1971).

p. 15   "It is now clear that the pride with which it was assumed that the inheritance of homologous structures from a common ancestor explained homology was misplaced; for such inheritance cannot be ascribed to identity of genes. The attempt to find 'homologous' genes, except in closely related species, has been given up as hopeless."

p. 16   "But if it is true that through the genetic code, genes code for enzymes that synthesize proteins which are responsible (in a manner still unknown in embryology) for the differentiation of the various parts in their normal manner, what mechanism can it be that results in the production of homologous organs, the same 'patterns,' in spite of their not being controlled by the same genes? I asked that question in 1938, and it has not been answered."

Diamond, Jared M., "Islands, Evolution and 'Supertramps,'" *Science News*, vol. 105 (May 25, 1974), p. 334. Diamond was a physiologist and ecologist at the University of California in Los Angeles.

"Contrary to the belief that colonization is a slow process, Diamond discovered that colonization can be extremely rapid, particularly on the coral islets. After he experimentally removed all birds from one small island, the numbers of bird species returned to original values within a few days, with initial colonization rates approximately one species per hour."

Ehrlich, Paul R., and Richard W. Holm, "Patterns and Populations," *Science*, vol. 137 (August 31, 1962), pp. 652-657.

p. 653   "This has led to the so-called phylogenetic approach to taxonomy, in which, in the absence of satisfactory fossil records, taxonomic systems often are used as the basis for constructing phylogenetic trees. Unfortunately, these trees sometimes are then employed to alter the original taxonomic system. This circular procedure produces systems with some predictive value and information content, although the process of creating these systems through repeated revision is time-consuming and relatively inefficient."

p. 655   "The term *species* should be retained only in its original, less restrictive sense of 'kind.' There seems to be no reason why quantitative methods should not be used to study phenetic relationships (those based on similarity rather than imagined phylogeny) at what we now loosely call the species level."

pp. 656-7   "It has become fashionable to regard modern evolutionary theory as the *only* possible explanation of these patterns rather than just the best explanation that has been developed so far. It is conceivable, even likely, that what one might facetiously call a non-Euclidean theory of evolution lies over the horizon. Perpetuation of today's theory as dogma will not encourage progress toward more satisfactory explanations of observed phenomena."

Fliermans, Carl B., and David L. Balkwill, "Microbial Life in Deep Terrestrial Subsurfaces," *Bioscience*, vol. 39 (June 1989), pp. 370-377.

p. 370   "This article describes the initial microbiological findings associated with three boreholes established at the Savannah River Plant (SRP) in Aiken, South Carolina, to a depth of 289 m beneath the soil surface and discusses how microorganisms may have come to live at these depths. Even more recent investigations have demonstrated the presence of diverse and abundant microbiological communities as deep as 520 m beneath the soil surface."

p. 376   "The traditional scientific concept of an abiological terrestrial subsurface is not valid. The reported investigation has demonstrated that the terrestrial deep subsurface is a habitat of great biological diversity and activity that does not decrease significantly with increasing depth."

pp. 376-7   "The Microbiology of the Deep Subsurface Program has opened new avenues for research into the interaction between the biosphere and the geosphere. The biosphere may extend a substantial distance into the geosphere and only cease when temperature and pressure become incompatible with life."

Gould, Stephen Jay, "To Be a Platypus," *Natural History*, vol. 94 (August, 1985), pp. 10-15.

p. 10   "The platypus sports an unbeatable combination for strangeness: first, an odd habitat with curiously adapted form to match; second, the real reason for its special place in zoological history—its enigmatic melange of reptilian (or birdlike), with obvious mammalian, characters."

p. 12   "The platypus looked like a perfectly good mammal in all 'standard' nonreproductive traits. It sported a full coat of hair and the defining anatomical signature of mammals—one bone, the dentary, in its lower jaw and three, the hammer, anvil, and stirrup, in its middle ear. (Reptiles have several jawbones and only one ear bone. Two reptilian jawbones became the hammer and anvil of the mammalian ear.)"

p. 13   "The presence of premammalian characters in platypuses does not brand them as inferior or inefficient."

p. 14   "If anything, this very antiquity might give the platypus more scope (that is, more time) to become what it really is, in opposition to the myth of primitivity: a superbly well-designed creature for a particular, and unusual, mode of life. The platypus is an elegant solution for mammalian life in streams—not a primitive relic of a bygone world."

p. 15   "The platypus is one honey of an adaptation."

Gould, Stephen Jay, "The Panda's Thumb of Technology," *Natural History* (January 1987), pp. 14-23.

p. 14   "By 1859, most educated people were prepared to accept evolution as the reason behind similarities and differences among organisms—thus accounting for Darwin's rapid conquest of the intellectual world."

p. 14   "Indeed, to make the statement even stronger, imperfections are the primary proofs that evolution has occurred, since optimal designs erase all signposts of history."

p. 14   "The seasamoid thumb is a clumsy, suboptimal structure, but it works."

p. 22   "Stasis is the norm for complex systems; change, when it happens at all, is usually rapid and episodic."

Gould, Stephen Jay, "Through a Lens, Darkly," *Natural History* (September 1989), pp. 16-24.

p. 24   "Evolution is strongly constrained by the conservative nature of embryological programs. Nothing in biology is more complex than the production of an adult vertebrate from a single fertilized ovum. Nothing much can be changed very radically without discombobulating the embryo. The order of life, and the persistence of nearly all basic anatomical designs throughout the entire geological history of multicellular animals, record the intricacy and resistance to change of complex development programs, not the perfection of adaptive design in local environments."

Grant, Peter R., "Speciation and the Adaptive Radiation of Darwin's Finches," *American Scientist*, vol. 69 (November/December 1981), pp. 653-663.

p. 653   "The frequent use in textbooks of these and other patterns of variation in Darwin's finches belies the complexity of the evolutionary processes they illustrate, the ambiguities of the evidence, and the differences of opinion among biologists about just how these birds evolved."

p. 661   "There is a need for further research into the affinities of Darwin's finches with Central and South American species to solve the enigma of the phylogenetic origin of the finches."

p. 655   "Evidently the evolutionary radiation took place fairly rapidly in geological time, for the Galápagos are no more than three to five million years old."

Griffin, Donald R., "A Possible Window on the Minds of Animals," *American Scientist*, vol. 64 (September/October 1976), pp. 530-535.

p. 530   "Language has generally been regarded by linguists, psychologists, and philosophers as a unique human attribute, different in kind from animal communication. But one of the major criteria on which this distinction has been based is the assumption that animals lack any conscious intent to communicate, whereas men know what they are doing. Yet the available evidence is so limited and indirect that it can just as plausibly be interpreted to support the view that there is no qualitative dichotomy, but a large quantitative difference in complexity of signals and range of intentions."

p. 534   "Likewise, paleontologists do their best to make sense out of the fossil record and sketch in evolutionary sequences or unfossilized morphologies without realistic hope of obtaining specific verification within the foreseeable future."

Kirbus, Federico B., "Trade Your Dog for a Midget Horse," *Science Digest*, vol. 73 (April 1973), pp. 64-67.

p. 64   "Starting with several pairs of normal-sized horses, he [Julio Cesar Falabella] accomplished a regressional evolution, or involution."

p. 65   "His smallest horse is an animal measuring 15 inches in height and weighing 26 pounds 4 ounces."

p. 65   "The mating takes place not only between 'enanos' but also between pigmy stallions and normal-sized mares."

p. 65   "The biggest of his giant horses is about 23 hands high and weighs 2,877 pounds. It seems, says Falabella, that it is easier to push an animal back into its original evolutionary stage than to create a super-breed."

p. 66   "Falabella's genuine 'enanos' live up to 40 years and are so full of exuberance and energy that their small size represents no disadvantage to them. They seem free of health problems and make ideal pets which need little extra care."

Leach, W. James, *Functional Anatomy—Mammalian and Comparative* (New York: McGraw-Hill Book Co., 1961).

p. 44   "But as a 'law' inscribed by nature (i.e., the biogenetic law of recapitulation—author) is perhaps more full of 'loopholes' and 'bypasses' than any law thus far inscribed by man."

Matthews, L. Harrison, "The Migration of Mammals," 1954 Report of Smithsonian Institution, *Discovery*, vol. 15, no. 5 (May 1954). Matthews was Director, London Zoological Society.

p. 284   "We know, therefore, something of the facts about the migrations of some mammals, but the means whereby migration is carried out still remain completely unknown. Many theories have been tried but none of them have been capable of experimental proof. It is all very puzzling; as far as we know the bodies of the other mammals are essentially similar to our own, and we flatter ourselves that our brains are more highly developed. And yet these animals that we classify as lower than ourselves can do something, and presumably with their brains too, that we cannot; something so far outside our own experience and abilities that we cannot even conceive how they do it."

Miller, J. A., "Sensory Surprises in Platypus, Mantis," *Science News*, vol. 129 (February 15, 1986), p. 104.

p. 104   "In the realm of the senses, animals continue to amaze scientists. No longer impressed by a dog's ability to hear high-pitched whistles or a cat's ability to see in dim light, researchers have gone on to document far more unexpected animal perceptions in such animals as the platypus and praying mantis.

"Take the bill of the duck-billed platypus. It serves as an antenna to pick up weak electrical signals, scientists report in the January 30 *Nature*. This is the first report of electroreception in mammals, say Henning Scheich of the technical University of Darmstadt, West Germany, Anna Guppy of the Australian National University in Canberra City and their colleagues."

p. 104   "The praying mantis provides another sensory surprise—a single 'ear' that is a groove in the underside of its thorax. Long thought to be deaf, the insect possesses a 'sensitive and specialized acoustic sense,' David D. Yager and Ronald R. Hoy of Cornell University report in the February 14 *Science*.

"What the mantis hears is ultrasonic frequencies, perhaps wings rubbing abdomen during courtship or the sonar signals of insect-eating bats. The sensitivity to ultrasound is shared by some other insects that detect sound with more conventional organs. But all other insects that hear have two 'ears,' widely separated on the body."

Nillson, Heribert, *Synthetische Artbildung* (Lund, Sweden: Verlag CWK Gleerup, 1953), English summary, pp. 1186-1212.

p. 1186   "The proof of the occurrence of mutations is by no means a proof of a current evolution. The most important the inescapable question, is whether the mutations are fully vital, so that they are able to survive in natural stands. . . .

A review of known facts about their ability to survive has led to no other conclusion than that they are always constitutionally weaker than their parent form or species, and in a population with free competition they are eliminated."

p. 1186   "It is therefore absolutely impossible to build a current evolution on mutations or on recombinations."

p. 1201   "And it is quite impossible to comprehend how the fossils have been deposited and preserved. The only certain thing is that these latter processes must have occurred during an epoch of revolution. We see every day that during a calm, alluvial epoch no fossils are formed. The length of such a period, thousands or millions of years, cannot change an *iota* in this respect. The incrustation of the fossils must, therefore, have happened during a revolutionary epoch."

p. 1211   "A perusal of past floras and faunas shows that they are far from forming continuous series, which gradually differentiate during the geological epochs. Instead they consist in each period of well distinguished groups of biota suddenly appearing at a given time, always including higher and lower forms, always with a complete variability. At a certain time the whole of such a group of biota is destroyed. There are no bridges between these groups of biota following one upon the other."

p. 1212   "It may, therefore, be firmly maintained that it is not even possible to make a caricature of an evolution out of paleobiological facts."

Rifkin, Jeremy, *Algeny* (New York: Viking Press, 1983), 298 pp.

p. 145   "Haeckel's argument, which is sometimes referred to as the 'biogenetic law,' is a myth. There is not a single prominent biologist in the world who is willing to extend so much as a scintilla of credence to it."

pp. 166-7   "Scientists are now beginning to suspect that living cells, like the iron filings, are somehow attracted by an invisible field and arrange themselves in a specific pattern along a line of force established by the field. Donna Jeanne Haraway, author of *Crystals, Fabrics and Fields*, points out that while there is only one kind of electromagnetic field or gravitational field, there are probably 'as many potential biological fields as there are organisms and species."

p. 172   "The thought of invisible fields capable of attracting chemical elements into a unified pattern called a living organism all but boggles the mind. Still, there is a feeling within some sectors of the scientific establishment that Burr, Goodwin, Weiss, Waddington, and the other field-theory proponents are breaking fertile new ground in search of the explanation for the origin and development of species."

Scadding, S. R., "Do 'Vestigial Organs' Provide Evidence for Evolution?" *Evolutionary Theory*, vol. 5 (May 1981), pp. 173-176. Scadding was in the Zoology Department, at the University of Guelph.

p. 173   "*Abstract*. An analysis of the difficulties in unambiguously identifying functionless structures and an analysis of the nature of the argument, leads to the conclusion that 'vestigial organs' provide no evidence for evolutionary theory."

p. 174   "Haeckel makes clear why this line of argument was of such importance to early evolutionary biologists. . . . It seemed difficult to explain functionless structures on the basis of special creation without imputing some lack of skill in design to the Creator. . . . It should be noted, however, that presented in this way, the vestigial organ argument is essentially a theological rather than a scientific argument, since it is based on the supposed nature of the Creator."

p. 174   "It is apparent that the discussion of vestigial organs in many biology textbooks owes more to Wiedersheim than to Darwin. . . . He provides a list of eighty-six vestigial organs, as well as many others that he considers to be retrogressive."

p. 175   "As our knowledge has increased the list of vestigial structures has decreased. Wiedersheim could list about 100 in humans, recent authors usually list four or five. Even the current short list of vestigial structures in humans is questionable. . . . Anatomically, the appendix shows evidence of a lymphoid function. . . .

"The coccyx serves as a point of insertion for several muscles and ligaments including the gluteus maximus. . . . The semilunar fold of the eye . . . aids in the cleansing and lubrication of the eyeball."

Schecter, Julie, "How Did Sex Come About?" *Bioscience*, vol. 34 (December 1984), pp. 680-681.

p. 680   "Sex is ubiquitous. . . . Yet sex remains a mystery to researchers, to say nothing of the rest of the population."

"Why sex? At first blush, its disadvantages seem to outweigh its benefits. After all, a parent that reproduces sexually gives only one-half its genes to its offspring, whereas an organism that reproduces by dividing passes on all its genes. Sex also takes much longer and requires more energy than simple division. Why did a process so blatantly unprofitable to its earliest practitioners become so widespread?"

p. 681   "All eukaryotes today are completely eukaryotic. There are no intermediates giving clues to the evolution of eukaryotes from prokaryotes. The delineation between prokaryotes and eukaryotes is sharp. . . . To all appearances, prokaryotic sex and eukaryotic sex have very little in common."

p. 681   "The problem, posed succinctly by Graham Bell of McGill University, is that the origin of sex can only be a theoretical question. This 'origin' cannot be observed, nor theories about it verified through experimentation."

Simpson, George Gaylord and W. S. Beck, *Life: An Introduction to Biology* (New York: Harcourt, Brace & World, 1965), 869 pp.

p. 241   "Haeckel misstated the evolutionary principle involved.

"It is now firmly established that ontogeny does *not* repeat phylogeny."

p. 241   "*Footnote.* You may well ask why we bother with principles that turned out to be wrong. . . . In the first place, belief in recapitulation became so widespread that it is still evident in some writings about biology and evolution."

Stradling, Richard, "Air Apparent: Moth Evolves amid Industrial Change," *San Diego Union Tribune* (October 16, 1996), pp. E4, E5.

p. E4   "For evolutionary biologists, the discovery has special significance: It's the first known case of two separate populations of a single species evolving to suit changes in their environments and then both evolving back when the environment changed again."

p. E5   "Clarke [Cyril Clarke, English scientist] found that the lighter version of peppered moths made a dramatic comeback after the passage of clean-air laws in England in the late 1950s. When he started collecting peppered moths in 1959, more than 90 percent were black. Today, it's about 20 percent."

p. E5 "Owen [Dennis Owen, England] found that the peppered moths of Michigan had followed the evolutionary pattern of their counterparts in England. The black form of peppered moths, almost never seen in Michigan in the 1920s, made up more than 90 percent of the moths Owen trapped between 1959 and 1961."

p. E5 "Grant [Bruce Grant, Biology professor at William & Mary] compared the coloring of the moths with air-pollution data and found a strong correlation between cleaner air and lighter-colored moths."

Tatarinov, L. P., "Current Problems in Evolutionary Paleontology," *Paleontological Journal*, vol. 10, no. 2 (1976), pp. 119-129.

p. 123 "Given the indeterminate nature of inherited variability it would be more natural to expect new characters to be unrepeatable even in the case of the adaptation of closely related organisms to similar environmental conditions."

Waddington, C. H., *Principles of Embryology* (New York: MacMillan, 1960), 510 pp.

p. 10 "The type of analogical thinking which leads to theories that development is based on the recapitulation of ancestral stages or the like no longer seems at all convincing or even very interesting to biologists."

Wootton, Robin J., "The Mechanical Design of Insect Wings," *Scientific American*, vol. 263 (November 1990), pp. 114-120. Wootton is Senior Lecturer in Biological Science, University of Exeter, England.

p. 114 "Insects include some of the most versatile and maneuverable of all flying machines. Although many show rather simple flight patterns, some insects— through a combination of low mass, sophisticated neurosensory systems and complex musculature—display astonishing aerobatic feats. Houseflies, for example, can decelerate from fast flight, hover, turn in their own length, fly upside down, loop, roll and land on a ceiling—all in a fraction of a second."

p. 116 "With their abundant cross veins, the wings recall the structural engineer's lattice girders and space frames, in which bending forces on the whole structure are converted to pure tensile or compression forces in the individual members."

p. 116 "But whether considered as beams or space frames, insect wings have two crucial—and for engineers, unusual—special characteristics."

p. 116 "Such deformable airfoils rarely occur in technology."

p. 117 "But the comparison can be taken too far. Insect wings are far more subtly constructed than sails and distinctly more interesting. Many, for example, have lines of flexion across the wing, as already described in the fossil cicadas. They also incorporate shock absorbers, counterweights, ripstop mechanisms and many other simple but brilliantly effective devices, all of which increase the wing's aerodynamic effectiveness."

p. 120 "The better we understand the functioning of insect wings, the more subtle and beautiful their designs appear. Earlier comparisons with sails now seem quite inadequate. The wings emerge as a family of flexible airfoils that are in a sense intermediate between structures and mechanisms, as these terms are understood by engineers. Structures are traditionally designed to deform as little as possible; mechanisms are designed to move component parts in predictable ways. Insect wings combine both in one, using components with a wide range of elastic properties, elegantly assembled to allow appropriate deformations in response to appropriate forces and to make the best possible use of the air. They have few if any technological parallels—yet."

Chapter 7

The Record of the Fossils

A. The Strategic Role of the Fossils

The key evidence both for and against evolution must be found in the fossil record. So far as can be observed, evolution is not taking place today, and it seems to be precluded by the very laws of science. Therefore, if it really happened in the past, the evidence would have to be in the fossil record of change preserved in the sedimentary rocks of the earth's crust.

The problem is, however, that there are no true transitional forms in the fossils either. There are many extinct forms, but extinction is not evolution. From the simplest prokaryotes to human beings, there are no evolutionary transitional forms between phyla (in fact, the phyla of today are the same as the phyla of the Cambrian), none between classes, orders or families, found anywhere. The handful of alleged transitions (e.g., *archaeopteryx*, mammal-like reptiles) are found, on closer inspection, to be mosaic forms, not transitional forms. Creation is a better explanation!

Ager, D. V., "The Nature of the Fossil Record," *Proceedings of the Geological Association*, vol. 87, no. 2 (1976), pp. 131-159. Presidential Address, March 5, 1976.

p. 132   "It must be significant that nearly all the evolutionary stories I learned as a student . . . have now been 'debunked.'"

p. 132   "We all know that many apparent evolutionary bursts are nothing more than brainstorms on the part of particular paleontologists. One splitter in a library can do far more than millions of years of genetic mutation."

p. 133   "The point emerges that, if we examine the fossil record in detail, whether at the level of orders or of species, we find—over and over again—not gradual evolution, but the sudden explosion of one group at the expense of another."

Boucot, A. J., *Evolution and Extinction Rate Controls* (Amsterdam: Elsevier Scientific Publishing Co., 1975), 427 pp.

p. 196   "Since 1859 one of the most vexing properties of the fossil record has been its obvious imperfection. For the evolutionist this imperfection is most frustrating as it precludes any real possibility for mapping out the path of organic evolution owing to an infinity of 'missing links' . . . once above the family level it becomes very difficult in most instances to find any solid paleontological evidence for morphological intergrades between one suprafamilial taxon and another. This lack has been taken advantage of classically by the opponents of organic evolution as a major defect of the theory. . . . the inability of the fossil record to produce the 'missing links' has been taken as solid evidence for disbelieving the theory."

Czarnecki, Mark, "The Revival of the Creationist Crusade," *MacLean's* (January 19, 1981).

p. 56   "A major problem in proving the theory has been the fossil record; the imprints of vanished species preserved in the Earth's geological formations. This record has never revealed traces of Darwin's hypothetical intermediate variants—instead species appear and disappear abruptly, and this anomaly has fueled the creationist argument that each species was created by God as described in the Bible."

p. 57   "On the other hand, [creationists] fervently pursue scientific studies legitimizing their own beliefs. Their Harvard is San Diego's Institute for Creation Research, which employs eight doctorate equipped scientists full time to demonstrate the feasibility of creationism."

Dunbar, Carl O., *Historical Geology*, 2nd ed. (New York: John Wiley & Sons, 1960).

p. 47   "Although the comparative study of living animals and plants may give very convincing circumstantial evidence, fossils provide the only historical, documentary evidence that life has evolved from simpler to more and more complex forms."

Eldridge, Niles, "Did Darwin Get It Wrong?" *Nova* (November 1, 1981), 22 pp.

p. 6   "It is, indeed, a very curious state of affairs, I think, that paleontologists have been insisting that their record is consistent with slow, steady, gradual evolution where I think that privately, they've known for over a hundred years that such is not the case. . . . It's the only reason why they can correlate rocks with their fossils, for instance. . . . They've ignored the question completely."

Eldredge, Niles, "Progress in Evolution?" *New Scientist*, vol. 110 (June 5, 1986), pp. 54-57.

p. 57   "But if species do not change much in the course of their existence, how do we explain large-scale, long-term change in evolution?"

p. 57   "Perhaps trends are best explained as a net production or survival of species that have a feature (such as large brains) towards one end of the spectrum of variation among a series of closely related species. There may be a higher-order culling device—analogous to natural selection but operating at a higher level— that underlies much of the macroevolutionary patterns seen in the history of life."

p. 57   "Extinctions disrupt eco-systems and reset the evolutionary clock: significant amounts of evolutionary change are positively correlated with episodes of ecological recovery following extinction. Moreover, the degree of change (as measured by the number of new taxa of relatively high rank that appear) is positively correlated with the degree of severity of the extinction, measured in the same way. . . ."

Goldschmidt, Richard B., "An Introduction to a Popularized Symposium on Evolution," *Scientific Monthly*, vol. 77 (October 1953), pp. 182-189.

p. 184   "Fortunately there is a science which is able to observe the progress of evolution through the history of our earth. Geology traces the rocky strata of our earth, deposited one upon another in the past geological epochs through hundreds of millions of years, and finds out their order and timing and reveals organisms which lived in all those periods. Paleontology, which studies the fossil remains, is thus enabled to present organic evolution as a visible fact."

Grassé, Pierre-P., *Evolution of Living Organisms* (New York: Academic Press, 1977), 297 pp. Grassé held the Chair of Evolution at the Sorbonne for 30 years, and was Editor of the 12 volume *Traite de Zoologie.*

p. 4   "Naturalists must remember that the process of evolution is revealed only through fossil forms. A knowledge of paleontology is, therefore a prerequisite; only paleontology can provide them with the evidence of evolution and reveal its course or mechanisms."

p. 8   "Today, our duty is to destroy the myth of evolution, considered as a simple, understood, and explained phenomenon which keeps rapidly unfolding before us."

p. 27   "The formation of the phyla or basic structural plans constitutes the most important and, perhaps, the essential part of evolution. Each phylum offers great novelties and its structural plan guides the destiny of the secondary lines.

"Since paleontology does not shed any light on the genesis of the phyla, one must have recourse to the data drawn from comparative anatomy and embryology."

p. 30   "We are in the dark concerning the origin of insects."

p. 70   "The genesis of the phyla stopped in the Ordovician, of the classes, in the Jurassic, of the orders, in the Paleocene/Eocene."

p. 71   "Evolution has not only slowed down, but with the aging of the biosphere; it has also decreased in scope and in extent."

p. 82   "The evolution of all zoological groups was initially highly productive, then slowed down and is now restricted to the creation of new species."

Raup, David M., "Probabilistic Models in Evolutionary Paleo-Biology," *American Scientist*, vol. 65 (January/February 1977), pp. 50-57. At the time, Raup was Professor of Geology at the University of Rochester, with a Ph.D. from Harvard, later moving to the University of Chicago, as Director of its Field Museum.

p. 50   "Out of all the paleontological work, there has developed a strong consensus on a couple of major generalizations; first, that there has been a marked and broad increase in number of species over the last 600 million years, interrupted only by a few periods of mass extinction; and second, it is generally agreed that the fossil record shows steady improvement or progressive optimization of fitness of biological structures. Optimal structures are common, but well-documented examples of the steps leading to the optima are hard to find."

p. 50   "Approximately 200,000 fossil species have been described since Linnaeus, and the vast majority are invertebrate animals, and most are marine [over 75%]. Plants and terrestrial vertebrates make up a small fraction. . . . Thus it is quite possible that the number of marine invertebrate species has been reasonably constant throughout most of the last 600 million years. Apparent diversity may just be tracking sample size."

p. 57   "The fossil record of evolution is amenable to a wide variety of models ranging from completely deterministic to completely stochastic. . . .

                 "The approaches discussed in this paper are bound to be controversial."

Raup, David M., "Evolution and the Fossil Record," *Science*, vol. 213 (July 17, 1981), p. 289

p. 289   "So, the geological time scale and the basic facts of biological change over time are totally independent of evolution theory."

p. 289   "In the years after Darwin, his advocates hoped to find predictable progressions. In general, these have not been found—yet the optimism has died hard, and some pure fantasy has crept into textbooks."

p. 289   "One of the ironies of the evolution-creation debate is that the creationists have accepted the mistaken notion that the fossil record shows a detailed and orderly progression and they have gone to great lengths to accommodate this 'fact' in their Flood geology."

Ridley, Mark, "Evolution and Gaps in the Fossil Record," *Nature*, vol. 286 (July 31, 1980), pp. 444-445.

p. 444   "If taken to an extreme the two ideas (that the fossil record is incomplete and that evolution proceeds at a fairly constant rate) can form an irrefutable system in which gradual temporal change in fossils is interpreted literally, but sudden jumps between species are attributed to gaps in the record. All the evidence is then consistent with a constant tempo of evolution."

Ridley, Mark, "Who Doubts Evolution?" *New Scientist*, vol. 90 (June 25, 1981), pp. 830-832. Ridley was in the Department of Zoology at Oxford University.

p. 831   "In any case, no real evolutionist, whether gradualist or punctuationist, uses the fossil record as evidence in favor of the theory of evolution as opposed to special creation. . . .

                 "So just what is the evidence that species have evolved? There have traditionally been three kinds of evidence, and it is these, not the 'fossil evidence,' that the critics should be thinking about. The three arguments are from the observed evolution of species, from biogeography, and from the hierarchial structure of taxonomy."

p. 832   "The evidence of biogeography and artificial evolution alone make a strong argument for evolution. The creationist can hardly suppose that all the infinitesimal geographical variants were independently created. . . .

                 "In order to make a comprehensive theory, the evolutionist also needs the principle of *uniformitarianism*."

p. 832   "The simple fact that species can be classified hierarchically into genera, families, and so on, is not an argument for evolution. It is possible to classify any set of objects into a hierarchy whether their variation is evolutionary or not."

p. 832   "If all species has been created separately, there is no reason why they should all have been created with the same genetic code. The more likely explanation is that all organisms derive their code by descent with modification from a common ancestor.

"These three are the clearest arguments for the mutability of species."

Ridley, Mark, *The Problems of Evolution* (New York: Oxford University Press, 1985), 159 pp.

p. 8   "Any set of objects, whether or not they originated in an evolutionary process, can be classified hierarchically. Chairs, for instance, are independently created; they are not generated by an evolutionary process: but any given list of chairs could be classified hierarchically, perhaps by dividing them first according to whether or not they were made of wood, and then according to their colour, by date of manufacture, and so on. The fact that life can be classified hierarchically is not, in itself, an argument for evolution."

p. 10   "The outstanding example of a universal homology is the genetic code. Bodies are built from the hereditary material, DNA, by the translation of a sequence made up of four bases, which are symbolized by the four letters, A, C, G, and T. A triplet of these bases specifies an amino acid; a sequence of triplets specifies a sequence of amino acids; a sequence of amino acids makes up a protein; and (roughly speaking) bodies are built of many different proteins. What matters here is that the code, although it is arbitrary, is known to be universal."

p. 10   "Now, if different species had been created separately, we should be very surprised if they had all been built with exactly the same genetic code. It would indeed be surprising if they all used DNA as their genetic material; but even more surprising if they had all hit on the same code."

p. 11   "The fossil record of evolutionary change within single evolutionary lineages is very poor. If evolution is true, species originate through changes of ancestral species: one might expect to be able to see this in the fossil record. In fact it can rarely be seen. In 1859 Darwin could not cite a single example."

Schaeffer, B., M. K. Hecht, and Niles Eldredge, "Phylogeny and Paleontology," in *Evolutionary Biology*, vol. 6, edit. by T. Dobzhansky, M. K. Hecht, and W. C. Steere (New York: Appleton-Century-Crofts, 1972), pp. 31-46.

p. 39   "The prime difficulty with the use of presumed ancestral-descendant sequences to express phylogeny is that biostratigraphic data are often used in conjunction with morphology in the initial evaluation of relationships, which leads to obvious circularity."

p. 39-40   "All organisms are bound to be relatively primitive in some respects, and relatively derived in others (the concept of mosaic evolution). The probability of finding a fossil taxon that is primitive in all respects to another, younger taxon, is small."

Sheehan, Peter M., "Species Diversity in the Phanerozoic," *Paleobiology*, vol. 3 (Summer 1977), pp. 325-329.

p. 327   "Data concerning the total numbers of described species do not seem to reflect meaningful estimates of original diversity. As Raup suggested, sampling effects seem to be the reason for changes in apparent diversity through the Phanerozoic. However, the sampling effects are more complex than originally thought. Apparent species diversity seems to be closely related to systematic effort, and

systematic effort per period of geologic time may have been apportioned to the
areal exposure of rocks of each period."

Simpson, George Gaylord, *The Major Features of Evolution* (Columbia University Press, 1953), 434 pp.

p. 360   "In spite of these examples, it remains true, as every paleontologist knows,
                  that *most* new species, genera, and families, and that nearly all new categories
                  above the level of families, appear in the record suddenly and are not led up to
                  by known, gradual, completely continuous transitional sequences."

Simpson, George Gaylord, *Tempo and Mode in Evolution* (New York: Columbia University Press,
       1984), 237 pp.

p. 99   "The facts are that many species and genera, indeed the majority, do appear
                  suddenly in the record, differing sharply and in many ways from any earlier
                  group, and that this appearance of discontinuity becomes more common the
                  higher the level, until it is virtually universal as regards orders and all higher
                  steps in the taxonomic hierarchy."

Simpson, George Gaylord, "Evolutionary Determinism and the Fossil Record," *Scientific Monthly*,
       vol. 71 (October 1950), pp. 262-267.

p. 264   "There is at present a clear consensus of paleontologists that orthogenesis,
                  in this sense, is not real. There is no known sequence in the fossil record that
                  requires or substantiates such a process. Many examples commonly cited, such
                  as the evolution of the horse family or of sabertooth 'tigers' can be readily shown
                  to have been unintentionally falsified and not to be really orthogenetic. All
                  supposed examples are more simply and fully interpreted as due to some other
                  cause, such as natural selection. . . .

                  "The fossil record definitely does not accord with . . . the concept of
                  orthogenesis or more broadly with overtly and covertly non-materialistic theories
                  like those of Driesch, Bergson, Osborne, Cuénot, du Noüy, or Vandel."

Smith, Peter J., "Evolution's Most Worrisome Questions," review of *Life Pulse* by Niles Eldredge
       (Fact on File, 1987, 246 pp.), *New Scientist* (November 19, 1987), p. 59.

p. 59   "Eldredge and Gould, by contrast, decided to take the record at face value.
                  On this view, there is little evidence of modification within species, or of forms
                  intermediate between species because neither generally occurred. A species forms
                  and evolves almost instantaneously (on the geological timescale) and then remains
                  virtually unchanged until it disappears, yielding its habitat to a new species."

p. 59   "Using examples from throughout the fossil record, both marine and
                  continental, Eldredge thus demonstrates convincingly that extinction is the motor
                  of species evolution, and that without it, there could be no development."

Stanley, Steven M., *Macroevolution: Pattern and Process* (San Francisco: W. H. Freeman and Co.,
       1979), 332 pp.

p. 2   "While many inferences about evolution are derived from living organisms,
                  we must look to the fossil record for the ultimate documentation of large-scale
                  change. In the absence of a fossil record, the credibility of evolutionists would

be severely weakened. We might wonder whether the doctrine of evolution would qualify as anything more than an outrageous hypothesis."

p. 35   "Schindewolf believed that a single *Grossmutation* could instantaneously yield a form representing a new family or order of animals. This view engendered such visions as the first bird hatching from a reptile egg. However, unacceptable his explanations may have seemed, Schindewolf at least confronted the failure of the fossil record to document slow intergradations between higher taxa."

p. 39   "The known fossil record fails to document a single example of phyletic evolution accomplishing a major morphologic transition and hence offers no evidence that the gradualistic model can be valid."

p. 144   "[Quantum speciation is] a form of speciation (branching) that yields a marked morphological divergence, with this divergence (1) within a small population and (2) during an interval that is brief with respect to the longevity of an average, fully established species of the higher taxon to which the new species belongs."

p. 145   "Evidence is also mounting that quantum speciation events themselves may span rather few generations.

". . . It is generally agreed that quantum speciation takes place within very small populations—some would say populations involving few than 10 individuals."

p. 159   ". . . there has recently been renewed expression of support for the importance in macroevolution of what Goldschmidt termed the hopeful monster. Goldschmidt's monster was a single animal that served as the progenitor of a new higher taxon. At least in principle, Goldschmidt accepted Schindewolf's extreme example of the first bird hatching from a reptile egg.

"The problem with Goldschmidt's radical concept is the low probability that a totally monstrous form will find a mate and produce fertile offspring."

Stanley, Stephen M., *The New Evolutionary Timetable: Fossils, Genes and the Origin of Species* (New York: Basic Books, Inc., 1981), 222 pp.

p. *xv*   "The [fossil] record now reveals that species typically survive for a hundred thousand generations, or even a million or more, without evolving very much. We seem forced to conclude that most evolution takes place rapidly, when species come into being by the evolutionary divergence of small populations from parent species. After their origins, most species undergo little evolution before becoming extinct."

Valentine, James W., and Cathryn A. Campbell, "Genetic Regulation and the Fossil Record," *American Scientist*, vol. 63 (November/December 1975), pp. 673-680.

p. 673   "The abrupt appearance of higher taxa in the fossil record has been a perennial puzzle. Not only do characteristic and distinctive remains of phyla appear suddenly, without known ancestors, but several classes of a phylum, orders of a class, and so on, commonly appear at approximately the same time without known intermediates. . . . If we read the record rather literally, it implies that organisms of new grades of complexity arose and radiated relatively rapidly."

p. 673   "While the types of proteins in the cells of animals belonging to different phyla are certainly not identical, their similarities nevertheless far outweigh their differences. Yet the morphologies of the phyla are strikingly diverse."

p. 675   "Most mutations to structural genes are deleterious, and presumably most regulatory gene mutations are deleterious as well, but occasionally a mutation may enhance regulatory activity."

Valentine, James W., and Douglas H. Erwin, "Interpreting Great Developmental Experiments: The Fossil Record," in *Development as an Evolutionary Process* (New York: Alan R. Lias, Inc., 1987), ed. Rudoff A. Raff and Elizabeth C. Raff, pp. 71-107. Valentine is in the Department of Geological Sciences at the University of California, Santa Barbara, and Erwin is at Michigan State University.

p. 84   "If ever we were to expect to find ancestors to or intermediates between higher taxa, it would be in the rocks of late Precambrian to Ordovician times, when the bulk of the world's higher animal taxa evolved. Yet transitional alliances are unknown or unconfirmed for any of the phyla or classes appearing then."

p. 96   "We conclude that the probability that species selection is a general solution to the origin of higher taxa is not great, and that neither of the contending theories of evolutionary change at the species level, phyletic gradualism or punctuated equilibrium, seem applicable to the origin of new body plans."

B. The Vital Gaps in the Record

As one looks at the arbitrarily constructed geologic column, as pictured in the textbooks, there does seem to be a superficial appearance of evolution over geologic time, from the marine invertebrates of the Cambrian period to the humans of the Pleistocene epoch.

When one looks at the details, however, the picture is one of very distinct kinds, from their first beginnings to their last-surviving descendants—most of them still living. There are no transitions from the protozoa to the metazoa, none from invertebrates to vertebrates, none from fishes to amphibians, none from amphibians to reptiles, none from reptiles to birds or mammals, none from apes to men.

This fact is illustrated in the following quotes from evolutionists. Such changes as have taken place are all either horizontal (within the original kind, at the same level of complexity) or downward (e.g., mutations, extinctions).

Anonymous, "Ancient Alga Fossil Most Complex Yet," *Science News*, vol. 108 (September 20, 1975), p. 181.

p. 181   "Both blue-green algae and bacteria fossils dating back 3.4 billion years have been found in rocks from S. Africa."

p. 181   "Even more intriguing, the pleurocapsalean algae turned out to be almost identical to modern pleurocapsalean algae at the family and possibly even at the generic level."

p. 181   "Do the Harvard paleontologists' findings shed any light on the origin of eukaryotes [cells with nuclei] from prokaryotes [cells without nuclei]: Probably not."

p. 181   "In brief, as Barghoorn puts it, 'We have no really good evidence from all of the Precambrian records . . . of a genuine eukaryotic cell."

Arnold, C. A., *An Introduction to Paleobotany* (Michigan: McGraw-Hill, 1949), 433 pp.

p. 7   "It has long been hoped that extinct plants will ultimately reveal some of the stages through which existing groups have passed during the course of their development, but it must be freely admitted that this aspiration has been fulfilled to a very slight extent, even though paleobotanical research has been in progress for more than one hundred years. As yet we have not been able to trace the phylogenetic history of a single group of modern plants from its beginning to the present."

p. 124   "Modern research has thrown little additional light on the *Stigmaria* problem and the remains are generally ignored by present-day paleobotanists. . . . On purely morphological grounds *Stigmaria* cannot be regarded as a true root, and probably not as a rhizome."

Axelrod, Daniel I., "Evolution of the Psilophyte Paleoflora," *Evolution*, vol. 13 (June 1959), pp. 264-275. Axelrod was at the University of California, Los Angeles.

p. 270   "Since vascular land plants had already attained some diversity of type by the Early Cambrian, their earlier evolution must have taken place in Precambrian time."

p. 272   "Judging from the inferred nature of Cambrian land plants, the late Proterozoic land flora may have been nearly as complex as that which has been preserved in the Late Silurian to Middle Devonian rocks. But rather than being in the low lands, it probably was in the more distant uplands of environmental diversity, areas propitious for rapid evolution."

Bengtson, Stefan, "The Solution to a Jigsaw Puzzle," *Nature*, vol. 345 (June 28, 1990), pp. 765-766. Bengtson is at the Institute of Paleontology, Uppsala University, Sweden.

p. 765   "Paleontologists are traditionally famous (or infamous) for reconstructing whole animals from the debris of death. Mostly they cheat."

p. 765   "If any event in life's history resembles man's creation myths, it is this sudden diversification of marine life when multicellular organisms took over as the dominant actors in ecology and evolution. Baffling (and embarrassing) to Darwin, this event still dazzles us and stands as a major biological revolution on a par with the invention of self-replication and the origin of the eukaryotic cell. The animal phyla emerged out of the Precambrian mists with most of the attributes of their modern descendants."

Birdsell, J. B., "What the Evolution of the Horse Really Shows: A Complex Adaptive Radiation," supplement 10 of *Human Evolution*, 2nd ed. (Chicago: Rand McNally, 1975), pp. 168-170.

p. 169   "Instead of being simple, the ascent of the horse was very complex, . . . And while marked changes occur in various structural features of the horse, nowhere do they happen at a single uniform rate."

p. 170   "In the Miocene and Pliocene no less than two genera of horses became larger than the present one, and four were smaller. . . . The evolution of the foot mechanism proceeded by rapid and abrupt changes rather than gradual ones. The transition from the form of foot shown by miniature *Eohippus* to larger consistently three-toed *Miohippus* was so abrupt that it even left no record in the fossil deposits."

Bockelie, T., and R. A. Fortey, "An Early Ordovician Vertebrate," *Nature*, vol. 260 (March 4, 1976), pp. 36-38.

p. 37   "Whereas deposits containing later heterostracans were laid down in freshwater or brackish conditions, the earliest sediments are regarded as fully marine, indicating that the vertebrates had their origin in the same medium as other major metazoan groups."

p. 38   "The fragments alone are of interest because they prove that the heterostracans were already present in the earliest part of the Ordovician (500 million years ago) and show that they were certainly Marine. . . . Our discovery may stimulate examination of acid residues of pre-Ordovician age for the remains of still earlier vertebrates."

Briggs, Derek E. G., "Conodonts: A Major Extinct Group Added to the Vertebrates," *Science*, vol. 256 (May 29, 1992), pp. 1285-86.

p. 1285   "After more than 130 years of the debate, definitive evidence has finally been discovered that allows the conodonts to be assigned to the vertebrates. The conodonts are a group of marine organisms that flourished for about 300 million years, ranging from Late Cambrian to Late Triassic."

p. 1286   "The addition of the conodonts increases the number of well-established Cambro-Ordovician vertebrate genera by a factor of 30, from 5 to nearly 150."

p. 1286   "If a relationship between true conodonts and these older taxa can be substantiated then the record of the vertebrates could be extended further back into the Cambrian, perhaps even predating the earliest chordate recognized so far, the soft-bodied *Pikaia* from the Middle Cambrian Burgess Shale. In any event the vertebrates can now be added to the list of major metazoan taxa that appeared during the Cambrian radiation."

Carroll, Lewis L., "Problems of the Origin of Reptiles," *Biological Reviews of the Cambridge Philosophical Society*, vol. 44 (1969).

p. 393   "Unfortunately not a single specimen of an appropriate reptilian ancestor is known prior to the appearance of true reptiles. The absence of such ancestral forms leaves many problems of the amphibian-reptilian transition unanswered."

Carroll, Robert L., *Vertebrate Paleontology and Evolution* (New York: W. H. Freeman and Co., 1988), 698 pp.

p. 138   "We have no intermediate fossils between rhipidistian fish and early amphibians. . . ."

pp. 181-4   "Despite these similarities, frogs, salamanders, and caecilians are very different from one another in skeletal structure and ways of life, both now and throughout their known fossil record . . . we have found no fossil evidence of any possible antecedents that possessed the specialized features common to all three modern orders. . . . In the absence of fossil evidence that frogs, salamanders, and caecilians evolved from a close common ancestor, we must consider the possibility that each of the modern orders evolved from a distinct group of Paleozoic amphibians."

p. 467   "No specific derived characters have been demonstrated as being uniquely shared between early primates and the early members of any other order."

Colbert, Edwin H., and M. Morales, *Evolution of the Vertebrates* (New York: John Wiley and Sons, 1991), 510 pp.

p. 99   "Despite these similarities, there is no evidence of any Paleozoic amphibians combining the characteristics that would be expected in a single common ancestor. The oldest known frogs, salamanders, and caecilians are very similar to their living descendants."

p. 223   "Unfortunately, the fossil history of the snakes is very fragmentary, so that it is necessary to infer much of their evolution from the comparative anatomy of modern forms."

Dawkins, Richard, *The Blind Watchmaker* (New York: W. W. Norton, 1987).

p. 229   ". . . the Cambrian strata of rocks, vintage about 600 million years [evolutionists are now dating the beginning of the Cambrian at about 530 million years], are the oldest in which we find most of the major invertebrate groups. And we find many of them already in an advanced state of evolution, the very first time they appear. It is as though they were just planted there, without any evolutionary history. Needless to say, this appearance of sudden planting has delighted creationists."

Douglas, Erwin, James W. Valentine, and David Jablonski, "The Origin of Animal Body Plans," *American Scientist*, vol. 85 (March/April 1997), pp. 126-137.

p. 126   "All of the basic architectures of animals were apparently established by the close of the Cambrian explosion; subsequent evolutionary changes, even those that allowed animals to move out of the sea onto land, involved only modifications of those basic body plans. About 37 distinct body architectures are recognized among present-day animals and from the basis of the taxonomic classification level of phyla."

p. 132   "Although the soft-bodied fossils that appear about 565 million years ago are animal-like, their classifications are hotly debated. In just the past few years these fossils have been viewed as protozoans; as lichens; as close relatives of the cnidarians; as a sister group to cnidarians plus all other animals; as representatives of more advanced, extinct phyla; and as representatives of a new kingdom entirely separate from the animals."

p. 137   "Clearly many difficult questions remain about the early radiation of animals. Why did no many unusual morphologies appear when they did, and not earlier or later? The trigger of the Cambrian explosion is still uncertain, although ideas abound. If the evolutionary trees are right and the fossil record is not deceptive, then many different lineages must have acquired complex anatomies and hard parts at about the same time."

Gensel, Patricia G., and Henry N. Andrews, "The Evolution of Early Land Plants," *American Scientist*, vol. 75 (September/October 1987), pp. 478-489.

p. 478   "It was not until the Silurian period, 400 to 450 million years ago, that plants and some animals adapted to a land environment and became well established there.

                "Vascular land plants—that is, plants with distinctive water-conducting tissues, as opposed to nonvascular plants such as mosses—became established by mid-Silurian times and diversified relatively rapidly in the early Devonian period."

p. 481   "We still lack any precise information concerning the presumed aquatic ancestors from which land plants evolved, and the search for evidence of these precursors and of probable transitional stages continues. . . . Further fossil evidence is needed to test these ideas and to determine whether the transition was sudden or gradual."

p. 487   "During the Carboniferous, some Iycophytes achieved heights well in excess of 30 m, and such specimens became a dominant element in the great Upper Carboniferous coal swamps. These types declined rapidly toward the end of the Carboniferous, while the smaller, herbaceous forms continued on to the present time."

George, T. Neville, "Fossils in Evolutionary Perspective," *Science Progress*, vol. 48 (January 1960). George was Professor of Geology at the University of Glasgow.

p. 1   "There is no need to apologize any longer for the poverty of the fossil record. In some ways it has become almost unmanageably rich, and discovery is outpacing integration."

p. 3   "The fossil record nevertheless continues to be composed mainly of gaps."

p. 5   "Granted an evolutionary origin of the main groups of animals, and not an act of special creation, the absence of any record whatsoever of a single member of any of the phyla in the Pre-Cambrian rocks remains as inexplicable on orthodox grounds as it was to Darwin."

Goldschmidt, Richard B., "Evolution, As Viewed by One Geneticist," *American Scientist*, vol. 40 (January 1952), pp. 84-98, 135.

p. 98   "In spite of the immense amount of the paleontological material and the existence of long series of intact stratigraphic sequences with perfect records for the lower categories, transitions between the higher categories are missing."

Gould, Stephen Jay, "The Interpretation of Diagrams: Is the Cambrian Explosion a Sigmoid Fraud?" *Natural History*, vol. 85 (August/September 1976), pp. 18-28.

p. 18   ". . . the Precambrian fossil record is little more . . . than 2.5 billion years of bacteria and blue-green algae. Complex life did arise with startling speed near the base of the Cambrian."

p. 28   "Could it be that the diversity of life has remained at equilibrium through all the vicissitudes of an earth in motion, all the mass extinctions, the collision of continents, the swallowing up and creation of oceans? The log phase of the Cambrian filled up all the earth's oceans. Since then, evolution has produced endless variation on a limited set of basic designs. . . . Yet, in an important sense, things have been pretty quiet since the Cambrian—and so they are likely to remain."

Gould, Stephen Jay, "A Short Way to Big Ends," *Natural History*, vol. 95 (January 1986), pp. 18-28.

p. 18   "Studies that began in the early 1950s and continue at an accelerating pace today have revealed an extensive Precambrian fossil record, but the problem of the Cambrian explosion has not receded, since our more extensive labor has still failed to identify any creature that might serve as a plausible immediate ancestor for the Cambrian faunas."

p. 18   "Where, then, are all the Precambrian ancestors—or, if they didn't exist in recognizable form, how did modern complexity get off to such a fast start?"

Gould, Stephen Jay, "Trends as Changes in Variance: A New Slant on Progress and Directionality in Evolution," *Journal of Paleontology*, vol. 62 (May 1988), pp. 319-329. Presidential Address.

p. 319   "When we think that we proceed with absolute and comprehensive objectivity, we are even more likely to be lost, for then we unconsciously cloak our own disabling biases and sally forth down a primrose path masquerading as the straight and narrow road to final truth."

p. 321   "If a clade has been markedly unsuccessful and now lies at the brink of extinction with but one surviving twig, then our anagenetic biases click in, and we often read the single extant path as an anagenetic trend. Thus we celebrate little, many-toed *eohippus* marching towards the large, noble, single-toed *Equus*. But *Equus* is the sole survivor of a tree once lush and vibrant (in an early Tertiary world with few artiodactyls and abundant perissodactyls). We speak of the anagenesis of horses only because our biases abstract bushes as ladders. And the clade of horses has been so depleted that only one lineage remains to be misread as the terminus of a trend. All our textbooks cite horses as the prototypical evolutionary trend, but there is no classical tale about the evolutionary 'trend' of antelopes, rodents, or bats—though these are the true success stories of mammalian evolution by the more appropriate criterion of increasing representation."

Gould, Stephen Jay, "In the Mind of the Beholder," *Natural History*, vol. 103 (February 1994), pp. 14-23.

p. 14   "But our ways of learning about the world are strongly influenced by the social preconceptions and biased modes of thinking that each scientist must apply to any problem. The stereotype of a fully rational and objective 'scientific method,' with individual scientists as logical (and interchangeable) robots, is self-serving mythology."

p. 17   "Thus the entire Cambrian explosion, previously allowed 30 or even 40 million years, must now fit into 5 to 10 (and almost surely nearer to lower limit), from the base of the Tommotian to the end of the Atdabanian."

p. 18   "So, intricate, and so mutually adapted, are the features of both flower and insect in many cases—special colors and odors to attract the insects, exquisitely fashioned mouthparts to extract the nectar, for example—that this pairing has become our classic example of coevolution, or promotion of adaptation and diversity by interaction among organisms during their evolution."

p. 20   "Looking at the taxonomic level of insect families, Labandeira and Sepkoski could find no evidence for any positive impact of the angiosperm radiation upon insect diversity."

p. 20   "How can this be? Doesn't Darwinism proclaim that organisms change within webs of competition and interaction toward mutually beneficial states?"

Gould, Stephen Jay, "The Evolution of Life on Earth," *Scientific American*, vol. 271 (October 1994), pp. 85-91.

p. 86   "*Homo sapiens* did not appear on the earth, just a geologic second ago, because evolutionary theory predicts such an outcome based on themes of progress and increasing neural complexity. Humans arose, rather, as a fortuitous and contingent outcome of thousands of linked events, any one of which could have occurred differently and sent history on an alternative pathway that would not have led to consciousness."

p. 87   "This is truly the 'age of bacteria'—as it was in the beginning, is now and ever shall be."

p. 87   "We cannot even imagine how anthropogenic intervention might threaten their extinction, although we worry about our impact on nearly every other form of life. The number of *Escherichia coli* cells in the gut of each human being exceeds the number of humans that has ever lived on this planet."

p. 89   ". . . so even the most cautious opinion holds that 500 million subsequent years of opportunity have not expanded the Cambrian range, achieved in just five million years. The Cambrian explosion was the most remarkable and puzzling event in the history of life."

Gould, Stephen Jay, *Wonderful Life* (New York: W. W. Norton Co., 1989), 347 pp.

p. 60   "An old paleontological in joke proclaims that mammalian evolution is a tale told by teeth mating to produce slightly altered descendant teeth. Since enamel is far more durable than ordinary bone, teeth may prevail when all else has succumbed to the whips and scorns of geological time. The majority of fossil mammals are known only by their teeth.

"Darwin wrote that our imperfect fossil record is like a book preserving just a few pages, of these pages few lines, of the lines few words, and of those words few letters. Darwin used this metaphor to describe the chances of preservation for ordinary hard parts, even for maximally durable teeth. What hope can then be offered to flesh and blood amidst the slings and arrows of such outrageous fortune? Soft parts can only be preserved, by a stroke of good luck, in an unusual geological context—insects in amber, sloth dung in desiccated caves. Otherwise, they quickly succumb to the thousand natural shocks that flesh is heir to—death, disaggregation, and decay, to name but three."

Gould, Stephen Jay, "The Evolution of Life on Earth," *Scientific American*, vol. 271 (October 1994), pp. 85-91.

p. 86   "*Homo sapiens* did not appear on the earth, just a geologic second ago, because evolutionary theory predicts such an outcome based on themes of progress and increasing neural complexity. Humans arose, rather, as a fortuitous and contingent outcome of thousands of linked events, any one of which could have occurred differently and sent history on an alternative pathway that would not have led to consciousness."

p. 87   "This is truly the 'age of bacteria'—as it was in the beginning, is now and ever shall be."

p. 87   "We cannot even imagine how anthropogenic intervention might threaten their extinction, although we worry about our impact on nearly every other form of life. The number of *Escherichia coli* cells in the gut of each human being exceeds the number of humans that has ever lived on this planet."

p. 89   ". . . so even the most cautious opinion holds that 500 million subsequent years of opportunity have not expanded the Cambrian range, achieved in just five million years. The Cambrian explosion was the most remarkable and puzzling event in the history of life."

Herbert, Wray, "Fossils Indicate Early Land Animals," *Science News*, vol. 123 (June 4, 1983), pp. 356-357.

p. 356   "Microscopic fossils extracted from rock in upstate New York . . . which include the oldest known centipede, several arachnids, a mite and perhaps the earliest known insect . . . have been analyzed by a team of paleontologists who now conclude that the diverse sample provides the best evidence anywhere for fully adapted land animals during the so-called Devonian era."

p. 357   "But some are 'remarkably similar' to modern forms, Shear says: the mite can actually be assigned to a living class of animals, indicating an amazing degree of evolutionary stability, the centipede looks very much like a modern centipede, he says, and one of the arachnids resembles the existing daddy longlegs. Another of the collaborators . . . has identified another of the fossils as a machlid, or silverfish; if it is indeed a silverfish, . . . it would be the oldest known insect every found.

"One of the most exciting things about these fossils, Shear says, is the 'exquisite detail' that has been preserved—including minute hairs and sense organs.... Of the animals so far, all except the mite were carnivores, suggesting the existence of soft-bodied land animals during the same time period."

Hopson, James A., and Leonard B. Radinsky, "Vertebrate Paleontology: New Approaches and New Insights," *Paleobiology*, vol. 6 (Summer 1980), pp. 250-270. Hopson and Radinsky were in the Anatomy Department at the University of Chicago.

p. 251   "Non-mammalian vertebrates usually have indeterminate growth and often show large size and shape changes during ontogeny (e.g., rhipidistian fishes) so that ontogenetic variation often presents severe problems in the recognition of species limits."

p. 256   "Discoveries of fragmentary phosphatic plates, interpreted as pertaining to heterostracans, from numerous localities in Late Cambrian and Early Ordovician marine limestones extend the vertebrate record back to more than 500 Myr BP. The marine occurrence of these early vertebrates supports the concept of a marine rather than fresh water origin of vertebrates. Fossil evidence of pre-vertebrate chordate evolution is still scanty and equivocal."

p. 258   "No known group of agnathans can be considered as lying close to the ancestry of jawed fishes."

p. 258   "The oldest known tetrapods, the ichthyostegid amphibians of the Late Devonian, though first reported on in 1932 and represented by numerous specimens, have never been completely described. No clearly intermediate form in the fish-tetrapod transition has been discovered...."

Jeram, Andrew J., Paul A. Selden, and Dianne Edwards, "Land Animals in the Silurian: Arachnids and Myriapods from Shropshire, England," *Science*, vol. 250 (November 2, 1990), pp. 658-661.

p. 658   "We report the discovery of terrestrial arthropod cuticles from Upper Silurian rocks of England. This substantially predates the three well-founded Devonian terrestrial faunas."

p. 659   "Numerous lines of evidence point to the trigonotarbid and centipede fossils being terrestrial animals."

p. 660   "The basal Prídolí arthropods described here now constitute the earliest known terrestrial fauna. Moreover, like the Devonian faunas, this assemblage is dominated by predators, suggesting that the arthropod occupiers of lower trophic levels remain to be discovered. Paleobotanical studies have indicated that terrestrial floras became established between late Ordovician and mid-Silurian times. The presence of predatory arthropods, on land in the late Silurian supports the idea that the main components of terrestrial ecosystems were in place substantially earlier than this, and that the arthropod invasion of the land may have been closely coupled with that of the plants, rather than lagging behind as some authors have suggested."

Kay, Marshall, and Edwin H. Colbert, *Stratigraphy and Life History* (New York: John Wiley and Sons, 1965), 736 pp.

pp. 102-3   "The introduction of a variety of organisms in the early Cambrian, including such complex forms of the arthropods as the trilobites, is surprising. . . .

"The introduction of abundant organisms in the record would not be so surprising if they were simple. Why should such complex organic forms be in rocks about six hundred million years old and be absent or unrecognized in the records of the preceding two billion years? . . . If there has been evolution of life, the absence of the requisite fossils in the rocks older than the Cambrian is puzzling."

Kerkut, G. A., *Implications of Evolution*, in International Series of Monographs in Pure and Applied Biology/Zoology Division, Vol. 4 (Pergamon Press, 1965). Kerkut was in the Department of Physiology and Biochemistry, University of Southampton.

p. 149   "One thing concerning the evolution of the horse has become clear. The story of the evolution of the horse has become more and more complex as further material is collected, and instead of a simple family tree the branches of the tree have increased in size and complexity till the shape is now more like a bush than a tree. In some ways it looks as if the pattern of horse evolution might be even as chaotic as that proposed by Osborn for the evolution of the Proboscidea, where, 'in almost no instance is any known form considered to be a descendant from any other known form; every subordinate grouping is assumed to have sprung, quite separately and usually without any known intermediate stage, from hypothetical common ancestors in the Earl Eocene or Late Cretaceous.'"

Knoll, Andrew H., "End of the Proterozoic Eon," *Scientific American*, vol. 265 (October 1991), pp. 64-73.

p. 64   "We now know that the Ediacaran radiation was indeed abrupt and that the geologic floor to the animal fossil record is both real and sharp."

p. 64   "As it turns out, Spitsbergen rocks provide an unmatched portrait of the earth and its biota as they existed just before the Ediacaran radiation."

p. 64   "According to Julian W. Green, a former student in my laboratory, who is now at the University of South Carolina at Spartanburg, many of the prokaryotes from Spitsbergen and related areas exhibit characteristics of morphology, development and behavior (as inferred from their orientations in the sediments) that render them virtually indistinguishable from cyanobacteria and other bacteria that live in comparable habitats today."

p. 65   "Some Spitsbergen eukaryotes resemble modern prasinophyte (green) algae, whereas others bear closer resemblance to the so-called chromophyte algae such as the dinoflagellates that are ubiquitous in modern oceans."

Leclercq, S., "Evidence of Vascular Plants in the Cambrian," *Evolution*, vol. 10, no. 2 (June 1956), pp. 109-114. Leclercq was in the Department of Palaeobotany, University of Liege, Belgium.

p. 111   "The conclusion to be drawn from these facts was that varied types of vascular plants existed in Early Paleozoic. However, skepticism was prevalent among scientists. It was suspected that the samples of rocks were probably contaminated by younger sediment. That is why Indian workers repeatedly checked their results, and this always with success."

pp. 112-13   "Incidentally palynology focuses attention on the need for caution in the interpretation of ecological facies of sedimentary rocks. On the basis of a megaflora, ecological associations may erroneously be considered as evolutionary stages. For instance the *Rhyniaceae*, upon which most of our information about the structure of the Lower Devonian plants is based, owe the simplicity of their structure *in part* to the peculiar environment to which they are adapted. Though primitive in features, they probably represent relic forms in a plant world composed of varied and more highly organized forms whose complexity we only are beginning to foresee."

p. 113   "In wider sense palynology and plant impressions of Cambrian raise the major question of the polyphyletism of the vascular plants. They carry back to Proterozoic the fundamental preliminary process that have prepared for the differentiation of the main races, which, later, have given rise to land flora. They indicate a more remote time for the epoch of the migration from sea to land, hitherto generally considered to have occurred during Siluro-Devonian. Moreover, the assumption that a varied flora existed in Cambrian time should adjust the flora to faunas which, in Lower Cambrian, show a burst of diverse creative activity."

p. 113   "Persistence of type with imperceptible change and, from time to time, the sudden influx of new types, correlative with favorable stable geologic conditions, are among the outstanding features of the history of evolution as shown by palaeontology."

Levinton, Jeffrey S., "The Big Bang of Animal Evolution," *Scientific American*, vol. 267 (November 1992), pp. 84-91. Levinton is Chairman, Department of Ecology and Evolution, State University of New York at Stony Brook.

p. 84   "Most of evolution's dramatic leaps occurred rather abruptly and soon after multicellular organisms first evolved, nearly 600 million years ago during a period called the Cambrian. The body plans that evolved in the Cambrian by and large served as the blueprints for those seen today. Few new major body plans have appeared since that time. Just as all automobiles are fundamentally modeled after the first four-wheel vehicles, all the evolutionary changes since the Cambrian period have been mere variations on those basic themes."

p. 84   "Even when we consider the taxonomic level below phyla—classes—it is apparent that most of the basic innovation occurred early. Richard K. Bambach of Virginia Polytechnic Institute and State University has shown that after the late Cambrian the number of new classes arising decreased precipitously. This evidence seems to confirm that there was a spectacular evolutionary radiation in the early Cambrian."

Lewin, Roger, "A Lopsided Look at Evolution," *Science*, vol. 241 (July 15, 1988), pp. 291-293.

p. 291   "Described recently as 'the most important evolutionary event during the entire history of the Metazoa,' the Cambrian explosion established virtually all the major animal body forms—*Baupläne* or phyla—that would exist thereafter, including many that were quickly 'weeded out' and became extinct. Compared with the 30 or so extant phyla, some people estimate that the Cambrian explosion may have generated as many as 100. The evolutionary innovation of the Precambrian/Cambrian boundary had clearly been extremely broad: 'unprecedented and unsurpassed' as James Valentine of the University of California, Santa Barbara, recently put it."

p. 291   "This strikingly asymmetric pattern demands explanation, not only in itself but also in what it might imply about the origin of major evolutionary innovation in general. This is especially important because, as David Jablonski, of the University of Chicago, and David Bottjer, of the University of Southern California recently observed: 'The most dramatic kinds of evolutionary novelty, major innovations, are among the least understood components of the evolutionary process.'"

McMenamin, Mark, "The Cambrian Explosion," *Palaios*, vol. 5 (April 1990), p. 1. McMenamin holds the Chair of the Geography Department, Mt. Holyoke College.

p. 1   "I have argued that this explosion represents a change in state or 'phase shift' in the nature of the biosphere, a sudden transformation from one stable paleoecological condition to a new configuration characterized by longer trophic chains. I see the Cambrian explosion as an unprecedented ecological event which allowed the emergence of 'higher' life forms, a time when sweeping changes rushed through the Proterozoic ecosystem, leading to its complete transformation."

Monastersky, R., "When Earth Tipped, Life Went Wild," *Science News*, vol. 152 (July 26, 1997), p. 52.

"Before the Cambrian period, almost all life was microscopic, except for some enigmatic soft-bodied organisms. At the start of the Cambrian, about 544 million years ago, animals burst forth in a rash of evolutionary activity never since equaled. Ocean creatures acquired the ability to grow hard shells, and a broad range of new body plans emerged within the geologically short span of 10 million years. Paleontologists have proposed many theories to explain this revolution but have agreed on none."

Nelson, Gareth V., "Origin and Diversification of Teleostean Fishes," *Annals of the New York Academy of Sciences* (1971), pp. 18-30. Nelson was in the Department of Ichthyology, American Museum of Natural History.

p. 22   "It is a mistake to believe that even one fossil species or fossil 'group' can be demonstrated to have been ancestral to another. The ancestor-descendant relationship may only be assumed to have existed in the absence of evidence indicating otherwise."

p. 23   "The history of comparative biology teaches us that the search for ancestors is doomed to ultimate failure, thus, with respect to its principal objective, this search is an exercise in futility. Increased knowledge of suggested 'ancestors' usually shows them to be too specialized to have been direct ancestors of anything else.

"... In contrast to what is usually stated, therefore, a more complete sample of the fossil record in itself would only complicate the problem of assessing the interrelationship of the fossil species."

p. 27   "That a known fossil or Recent species, or higher taxonomic group, however primitive it might appear, is an actual ancestor of some other species or group, is an assumption scientifically unjustifiable, for science never can simply assume that which it has the responsibility to demonstrate."

p. 27   "It is the burden of each of us to demonstrate the reasonableness of any hypothesis we might care to erect about ancestral conditions, keeping in mind that we have no ancestors alive today, that in all probability such ancestors have been dead for many tens or hundreds of millions of years, and that even in the fossil record they are not accessible to us."

Ommanney, F. D., *The Fishes* (New York: Time Life Nature Library, 1964), 192 pp.

p. 60   "How this earliest chordate stock evolved, what stages of development it went through to eventually give rise to truly fishlike creatures we do not know. Between the Cambrian when it probably originated, and the Ordovician when the first fossils of animals with really fishlike characteristics appeared, there is a gap of perhaps 100 million years which we will probably never be able to fill."

Palmer, Douglas, "Learning to Fly," review of *The Origin and Evolution of Birds*, by Alan Feduccia (Yale University Press, 1996), *New Scientist*, vol. 153 (March 1, 1997). p. 44. Palmer is a paleontologist based in Cambridge, and Feduccia is a paleo-ornithologist at the University of North Carolina.

p. 44   "It is fascinating to follow the arguments surrounding the evolution and function of feathers. The traditional view is that feathers are unique to birds, and Feduccia robustly defends this view against the feathered dinosaurs hypothesis. He follows the argument through in relation to the problem of the origin of winged flight: why did wings first evolve? As Feduccia says, feathers 'have an almost magical structural complexity,' which 'allows a mechanical aerodynamic refinement never achieved by other means,' making them one of the most remarkable structures in biology."

p. 44   "Remarkably, the wing feathers of the famous 150-million-year-old Late Jurassic bird, *Archaeopteryx*, are already well advanced and comparable to those of modern birds with an aerodynamic asymmetry and structural fabric that can evolve only as an adaptation for flight."

p. 44   "And for pursuers of palaeotrivia, the Guinness fossil record for the biggest bird known to science goes to the late Miocene teratorn *Argentavis magnificens*, weighing in at about 72 kilograms and with a wingspan of up to 7.5 metres."

Pojeta, John, Jr., "Ancient Clam is a Missing Link," *Science News*, vol. 103 (June 2, 1973), p. 358.

p. 358   "A 'missing link' has been found. For clams, that is.

"The fossilized clam, unearthed about 10 miles south of Albany, N.Y., is estimated to be about 570 million years old, some 70 million years older than any previously reported. Known as *Fordilla troyensis*, it 'appears to be a missing link between some extinct forms of mollusks and the 20,000 species of clams living in the world today,' says John Pojeta, Jr., of the U.S. Geological Survey. Pojeta and Bruce Runnegar, formerly of the Smithsonian Institution, report the find in the *May 25 Science*.

"The species has also been found in Newfoundland and Greenland, but not of such age."

p. 358   "An odd significance of the discovery is that *F. troyensis* had no teeth. 'Although some modern clams are able to survive without teeth,' Poleta says, 'the descendants of the toothless *Fordilla* probably developed such teeth during the next 70 million years as a means of surviving in an increasingly more competitive and complex world.' The apparent evolution and subsequent recession of teeth suggests 'that the evolutionary history of clams is even more complex than we once thought.'"

Rapetski, John E., "A Fish from the Upper Cambrian of North America," *Science*, vol. 200 (May 5, 1978), pp. 529-531.

p. 529   "Until recently, vertebrates have been known from rocks no older than the Middle Ordovician (about 450 million years ago). In 1976 and 1977 the known range of the vertebrates was extended back about 20 million years by discoveries of fish fossils in rocks of latest Early Ordovician and earliest Middle Ordovician age in Spitzbergen and Australia. This report of fish material from Upper Cambrian rocks further extends the record of the vertebrates by approximately another 40 million years."

Raup, David M., "Conflicts Between Darwin and Paleontology," *Bulletin, Field Museum of Natural History*, vol. 50 (January 1979), pp. 22-29. Raup is Curator of Geology at the Field Museum.

p. 23   "Instead of finding the gradual unfolding of life, what geologists of Darwin's time, and geologists of the present day actually find is a highly uneven or jerky record; that is, species appear in the sequence very suddenly, show little or no change during their existence in the record, then abruptly go out of the record. and it is not always clear, in fact it's rarely clear, that the descendants were actually better adapted than their predecessors. In other words, biological improvement is hard to find."

p. 24   "Thus, some pterosaurs were larger than all flying birds and even many small airplanes. They achieved this size and were still able to fly because their design was nearly optimal."

p. 24   "Thus, the trilobites 450 million years ago used an optimal design which would require a well trained and imaginative optical engineer to develop today."

p. 25   "The record of evolution is still surprisingly jerky and, ironically, we have
               even fewer examples of evolutionary transition than we had in Darwin's time.
               By this I mean that some of the classic cases of darwinian change in the fossil
               record, such as the evolution of the horse in North America, have had to be
               discarded or modified as a result of more detailed information—what appeared
               to be a nice simple progression when relatively few data were available now
               appears to be much more complex and much less gradualistic."

pp. 25-6   "So natural selection as a process is okay. We are also pretty sure that it goes
               on in nature although good examples are surprisingly rare. The best evidence
               comes from the many cases where it has been shown that biological structures
               have been optimized—that is, structures that represent optimal engineering
               solutions to the problems that an animal has of feeding or escaping predators or
               generally functioning in its environment. The superb designs of flying reptiles
               and of trilobite eyes are examples. The presence of these optimal structures does
               not, of course, prove that they developed from natural selection but it does provide
               strong circumstantial argument."

p. 29   "The dinosaurs died out at the end of the Cretaceous period. . . . Several
               other important animal groups also died out at about the same time. . . . (There is
               nothing surprising, by the way, in the fact that all these groups died out near the
               boundary of two periods in the geologic time scale because the boundary itself
               is defined on the basis of the extinctions.)"

Raup, David M., "On the Early Origins of Major Biologic Groups," *Paleobiology*, vol. 9, no. 2,
     pp. 107-115.

p. 107   "Students of evolutionary history have observed repeatedly that in an adaptive
               radiation, the major subgroups appear early and at about the same time."

p. 107   "Nearly all living phyla of marine invertebrates that have reasonably good
               fossil records have first occurrences either in the late Precambrian or early to
               middle Cambrian. At the class level there are 27 paleontologically important
               living groups and all have documented occurrences which are Silurian or older."

p. 107   "The same relative pattern can be seen in the geologic records of vertebrates
               and land plants, although origins are generally displaced in time toward the
               Recent. For example, nearly all orders of living mammals have origins during a
               fairly narrow interval between 50 and 70 Myr BP."

p. 113   "Let us generalize that 500 Myr BP is the minimum divergence time for a
               species pair drawn from any two of the classes. It may be that this is actually a
               conservative estimate because experience has shown that as more fossils are
               discovered, the first occurrences of major groups tend to be pushed back in time."

Romer, Alfred Sherwood, "Major Steps in Vertebrate Evolution," *Science*, vol. 158 (December 29,
     1967), pp. 1629-1637. Presidential Address, American Association for Advancement of Science.

pp. 1631-2   "But our present knowledge of the fossil record shows that the oldest of
               known vertebrates already had bone, at least as an external armor. As a
               consequence, most (but not all) students of the subject will agree with Stensiö's
               conclusion that bone developed at the base of the vertebrate series and that the

boneless condition in cyclostomes and sharks is a secondary, degenerate one; the prominence of cartilage in the young vertebrate is an embryonic adaptation."

p. 1632 "A persisting major gap in our paleontological record, however, is the almost complete absence of any trace of an earlier jawed fish. Although the common ancestor must have existed well before the Devonian, there is no earlier record of fish of this sort except for a few fragmentary remains of acanthodians in near-shore marine Silurian deposits."

Runnegar, Bruce, and John Pojeta, Jr., "Molluscan Phylogeny: The Paleontological Viewpoint," *Science*, vol. 186 (October 25, 1974), pp. 311-317.

p. 316 "Stasek theorized that the extant mollusks are the progeny of three separate lineages that separated before the phylum was well established. He wrote that no known intermediate forms, fossil or living, bridge the 'enormous gaps between any two of the three lineages,' and therefore treated each as a separate subphylum."

Sansom, I. J., M. P. Smith, H. A. Armstrong, and M. M. Smith, "Presence of the Earliest Vertebrate Hard Tissues in Conodonts," *Science*, vol. 256 (May 29, 1992), pp. 1308-1310.

p. 1308 "Furthermore, the identification of vertebrate hard tissues in the oral elements of conodonts extends the earliest occurrence of vertebrate hard tissues back by around 40 million years, from the Middle Ordovician (475 million years ago) to the Late Cambrian (515 million years ago)."

p. 1310 "The recognition of cellular bone in conodonts has important implications for studies of both conodont palaeobiology and early vertebrate evolution:

"1) Cellular bone is a hard tissue unique to vertebrates, and its occurrence in conodont elements is unequivocal evidence for the inclusion of conodonts within the vertebrates. The additional presence of enamel homologs and probable globular cartilage is consistent with this conclusion.

"2) The presence of cellular bone in the Late Cambrian-earliest Ordovician genus *Cordylodus* predates the earliest previously recorded occurrence of vertebrate hard tissues by around 40 million years."

p. 1310 "The presence of cellular bone and the absence of dentine in Cambrian conodonts indicates that the evolutionary history of vertebrate hard tissues must be reevaluated."

Scott, G. H., "Biometry of the Foraminiferal Shell," in *Foraminifera*, ed. R. H. Hedley and C. G. Adams (New York: Academic Press, 1974), pp. 55-151.

pp. 136-7 "Because of their stratigraphical value, unidirectional trends in shell morphology have attracted most comment, although it is not established that they are even a principal feature of foraminiferal evolution." (See also G. H. Scott, "Foraminiferal Biostratigraphy and Evolutionary Models," *Systematic Zoology*, vol. 25 (1976), pp. 78-80.)

Stanley, Steven M., "Macroevolution and the Fossil Record," *Evolution*, vol. 36 (May 1982), pp. 460-473.

p. 460 "Established species are evolving so slowly that major transitions between genera and higher taxa must be occurring within small, rapidly evolving populations that leave no legible fossil record."

p. 462   "What this means is that we can trace *nearly all* living species backward into the Pleistocene."

p. 464   "Those who in the past have contemplated the formation of the modern horse by gradual evolution, beginning with this early genus, must now contend with the fact that at least two species of *Hyracotherium* lasted for several million years without appreciable change."

p. 464   "It is notable that the evidence of great stability for species of *Hyracotherium* is complemented, at the other end of equid phylogeny, by data showing that ten species of horses lived through most or all of Pleistocene time—for at least the better part of 2 Myr."

p. 465   *"Barring extinction, a typical established species—whether a species of land plants, insects, mammals or marine invertebrates—will undergo little measurable change in form during $10^5 - 10^7$ generations."*

p. 472   "The implication of the stability of established species is that most evolutionary change occurs rapidly, in local populations. Because the direction taken by rapidly divergent speciation is variable and only weakly predictable for large segments of phylogeny, macroevolution is largely decoupled from microevolution."

Stanley, Steven M., "Resetting the Evolutionary Timetable," interview by Neil A. Campbell, *Bioscience*, vol. 36 (December 1986), pp. 722-727.

pp. 724-5   "If in a given time interval, there are dramatically new forms appearing— new genera, for example—and at the same time the species are quite stable, then we must conclude that, although there may be a little bit of evolution at the species level, the origin of new genera must come via rapid branching events. Maybe in some cases an entirely new genus forms via one event or in some cases by way of three or four events."

p. 725   "There are too many places where the fossil record is complete enough that we ought to see transitions occurring. Even in these cases we see very few good examples of higher taxa evolving by gradual change. There may be a few examples here and there, but by and large we just don't see the steps."

p. 725   "Evolution happens rapidly in small, localized populations, so we're not likely to see it in the fossil record."

p. 726   "The horse is the most famous example—the classic story of one genus turning into another, turning into another. Now it's becoming apparent that there's an overlap of these genera, and that there were many species belonging to each one. It's a very bushy sort of pattern that is, I think, much more in line with the punctuational model; there isn't just a simple, gradual transition from one horse to another. This is now becoming fairly well known."

Todd, Gerald T., "Evolution of the Lung and the Origin of Bony Fishes—A Causal Relationship?" *American Zoologist*, vol. 20, no. 4 (1980), p. 757. Todd was at the University of California, Los Angeles.

> "*Abstract*. All three subdivisions of the bony fishes first appear in the fossil record at approximately the same time. They are already widely divergent morphologically, and they are heavily armored. How did they originate? What allowed them to diverge so widely? How did they all come to have heavy armor? And why is there no trace of earlier, intermediate forms?"

Tudge, Colin, "Throw Away Your Zoology Textbooks," *New Scientist* (November 8, 1973), p. 393.

> "Once there were the Arthropoda: an extraordinary successful phylum of 'joint-foot' invertebrates (e.g., onychopora, trilobites, crustaceans, myriopods, arachnids, insects). . . . They were varied, these creatures; indeed, there were more species of arthropod than of all other kinds of animal put together. . . . They were nature's most supreme demonstration of adaptive radiation about a common theme.

> "All of which zoological folklore, is . . . a load of rubbish. . . . One of the fundamental weaknesses of the traditional view of arthropod phylogeny—that all forms arose from the polychaetes via a common stock—is that it presupposed the existence of intermediate ancestral types. But there is no fossil evidence for such types and there are no modern animals resembling those hypothetical types."

Wills, Christopher, "Reticulate Evolution," review of *Evolution in the Microbial World* (New York; Cambridge University Press, 1974), by W. K. Joklik, *Science*, vol. 186, (October 18, 1974), pp. 251-252. Wills is Professor of Biology at the University of California at San Diego, La Jolla.

p. 251   "In view of all this information on genetic exchange, perhaps the toughest nut for the evolutionist to crack is where the viruses came from. W. K. Joklik makes a game attempt, setting forth the multifarious properties of viruses and making a convincing case for the independent origin of many of the more than 30 virus groups. At one point, however, he relies on an argument that is essentially the same as one put forth by the antievolutionist Creation Research Society in its criticism of current interpretations of the fossil record. If viruses had a common origin, Joklik points out, then one would expect to see intermediates between the various morphological forms. No such intermediates have been found. The immediate reaction of this reviewer is that such reasoning is suspect!"

Zimmer, Carl, "Insects Ascendant," *Discover*, vol. 14 (November 1993), p. 30.

> "Compared with other life-forms, insects are actually slow to evolve new families—but they are even slower to go extinct. Some 84 percent of the insect families alive today were alive 100 million years ago; for land vertebrates the figure is 20 percent."

C. The Alleged Transitional Forms

If evolution had really taken place in the past, three ought to be multitudes of transitional forms preserved in the rocks. Instead, evolutionists have been able to cite only a handful of candidates out of the billions of known fossils. These are mainly the lungfishes, the mammal-like reptiles, the *archaeopteryx*, the horses, and—more recently—the so-called walking whales.

When these are examined more closely, however, they don't fill the bill at all. Either they are out of place in geologic time or they are separate kinds in their own right or both.

Anonymous, "Lungfish: Ins and Outs of Evolution," *Science News*, vol. 108 (November 15, 1975), p. 310.

p. 310   "Three animal physiologists, J. P. Lumhalt, . . . K. Johansen, . . . and G. M. O. Maloiy . . . state, in the Oct. 30 *Nature*, that the first appearance of negative-pressure inhalation is credited to now-extinct amphibians. Yet, no suctional breathing has been seen in air-breathing vertebrates below reptiles. . . .

"The link, then, between water breathing and air breathing, between swimming and walking, was the strange, primitive lungfish. . . . 'When he dived into the mud,' . . . he dived into a blind alley. . . . If anything, he was worse off than before."

Anonymous, "Bone Bonanza: Early Bird and Mastodon," *Science News*, vol. 112 ((September 12, 1977), p. 198.

p. 198   "In western Colorado's Dry Mesa Quarry, Brigham Young University archaeologists have come upon the 140-million-year-old remains of what they are calling 'the oldest bird ever found.' . . .

"'It is obvious that we must now look for the ancestors of flying birds in a period of time much older than that in which the *Archaeopteryx* lived,' says Yale University's John H. Ostrom who positively, identified the specimen."

p. 198   "Meanwhile, in eastern Siberia, Soviet scientists dug out a chunk of ice containing a perfectly preserved baby mammoth, about six months old with reddish fur, big feet and small ears."

Anonymous, "Jurassic Bird Challenges Origin Theories," *Geotimes*, vol. 41 (January 1996), pp. 7-8.

p. 7   "Fossil remains of a bird which lived between 142 and 137 million years ago were recently found in the Liaoning province of northeastern China. The discovery, made by a fossil-hunting farmer and announced by a Chinese/American team of scientists, including Alan Feduccia (University of North Carolina, Chapel Hill) and Larry D. Martin (University of Kansas), provide the oldest evidence of a beaked bird on Earth yet found."

p. 7   "The Chinese bird, claim its discoverers, probably lived at the Jurassic-Cretaceous boundary—prior to the arrival of *Deinonychus* and *Mononykus*—and could not possibly be descended from them.

"But there are plenty of other reasons to refute the dinosaur-bird connection, says Feduccia. 'How do you derive birds from a heavy, earthbound, bipedal reptile that has a deep body, a heavy balancing tail, and fore-shortened forelimbs?' he asks. 'Biophysically, it's impossible.'"

Anonymous, "The Oldest Fossil Bird: A Rival for *Archaeopteryx*?" *Science*, vol. 199 (January 20, 1978), p. 284.

p. 284   "Although *Archaeopteryx* is generally considered the earliest bird on record, a recent find suggests that the creature, which lived some 130 million years ago, may not have been the only bird alive then. A new fossil found by James Jensen of Brigham Young University dates back to the same period—the Late Jurassic—and appears to be the femur (thighbone) of a bird."

"No dinosaur has a reversed first toe (hallux), but all birds do—that's their perching foot,' he adds. 'All theropod dinosaurs have serrated, saberlike teeth. *Confuciusornis* has no teeth. Even though *Archaeopteryx* does have teeth, they're not serrated, but peglike and constricted at the base. All dinosaurs have two large openings at the back of the skull. Birds have none. Point by point, there's no connection."

p. 284   "The fossil resembles the thighbone of modern birds more closely than the comparable *Archaeopteryx* bone does."

p. 284   "The hypothesis that *Archaeopteryx* represents a direct link from reptiles to birds has been generally accepted. The existence of another bird—one that was an adept flyer and thus more advanced on the evolutionary scale—would present a challenge to that hypothesis."

p. 284   "Jensen thinks that he may have found such confirmatory evidence in the form of another, more complete fossil femur excavated just a few feet away from the one in question. According to the Brigham Young investigator, this second femur is very similar to that of modern birds."

Anonymous, "Whales with Legs," *Science Digest*, vol. 88 (November/December 1980), p. 25.

p. 25   "Not far from the Khyber Pass in the arid Himalayan foothills of Pakistan, University of Michigan paleontologist Philip D. Gingerich found a skull and several teeth and came to the startling conclusion that they belonged to an ancient walking whale."

p. 25   "Clue: the teeth were almost identical with those from known primitive whale fossils found on the west coast of India."

p. 25   "Gingerich is returning to the Himalayan foothills this fall to find more fossils so he can piece together a clearer picture of the whale's evolutionary history. . . .

"Most of all, he hopes to find leg bones belonging to the whale species."

Anonymous, "Adding Flesh to Bare Therapsid Bones," *Science News*, vol. 119 (June 20, 1981), p. 389.

p. 389   "Reptiles that began to acquire mammalian characteristics arose from the Pelycosaurs and were so successful that there were eventually more than 300 genera of mammal-like reptiles, ranging from the size of a rat to the size of a rhinoceros."

p. 389   "Reproductive characteristics are a major distinction between reptiles and mammals. . . . Guillete speculates that egg guarding could lead to egg brooding, and secretions produced by a brooding parent could lead to milk. Egg brooding could also evolve into egg retention and eventually to live births."

p. 389   "If therapsids were so diverse and so successful, what became of them? As
in the case of more recent extinctions, the answer is not fully known."

Anonymous, "What's a Hoatzin?" *Scientific American*, vol. 261 (December 1989), p. 30.

"Foregut fermentation also occurs in cows, sheep, deer and a number of
other mammals. But according to one of the investigators, Stuart D. Strahl of the
New York Zoological Society's Wildlife Conservation International, the little
hoatzin (adults weigh less than two pounds) does not share an evolutionary branch
with these big ruminants; it developed its digestive system independently.

"Strahl adds that some ornithologists call the hoatzin 'primitive' because of
its *archaeopteryx*-like claws; but he prefers to think of it as 'highly specialized.'
Swans, ibis and many other birds, he notes, have wing claws; they just never
make use of them."

Brush, A. H., "On the Origin of Feathers," *Journal of Evolutionary Biology*, vol. 9 (1996), pp. 131-142.

p. 140   "At the morphological level feathers are traditionally considered homologous
with reptilian scales. However, in development, morphogenesis, gene structure,
protein shape and sequence, and filament formation and structure, feathers are
different. Clearly, feathers provide a unique and outstanding example of an
evolutionary novelty."

Charig, Alan J., Frank Greenaway, Angela C. Milner, Cyril A. Walker, and Peter J. Whybrow,
"*Archaeopteryx* Is Not a Forgery," *Science*, vol. 232 (May 2, 1986), pp. 622-626.

p. 623   "We—the present official custodians, preparator and photographer of the
holotype—reject this forgery hypothesis unequivocally. It may seem that we, in
refuting the consortium's allegations, are using a sledgehammer to crack a rather
trivial nut; yet, if we bear in mind the high esteem in which the general public
holds Professor Hoyle, together with its lack of knowledge of the facts concerning
Archaeopteryx, then it is important that such doubts be finally removed—
especially where students of zoology are concerned. More important still, we
must put the record straight because of the Creationists, who are interested in
any new ideas that, implicitly or explicitly, appear to threaten the concept of
organic evolution."

Chatterjee, Sankar, "An Ictidosaur Fossil from North America," *Science*, vol. 220 (June 10, 1983),
pp. 1151-1153.

p. 1151   "Recent mammals and reptiles are easily distinguished by the differences of
anatomical, physiological, reproductive and adaptive features, but in the reptile-
mammal transition documented by the late Triassic fossils, the distinction is not
clearcut. First, diagnostic mammalian features of soft anatomy are lacking from
fossils; second, the fossil record of early mammals is very fragmentary—many
taxa are known only from tiny teeth and jaws; third, many advanced cynodonts
already possessed a large suite of mammalian features (such as secondary palate,
enlarged dentary with coronoid process, reduced postdentary bones, complex
cheek teeth with precise occlusion and limited replacement, and double occipital
condyles) which make the class boundary more difficult. The presence of a
squamosal-dentary articulation forming part or all of the joint between the skull

and lower jaw is now used as the main practical diagnostic criterion for the class Mammalia.

"This distinction in the jaw articulation was found to be inadequate, however. At least some cynodonts, such as ictidosaurs and *Probainognathus*, have a dentary-squamosal contact, which makes them mammals, by strict application of this criterion. Yet their complex lower jaws and single auditory ossicle in the middle ear are clearly still reptilian. Opinion has long been divided as to whether ictidosaurs are reptiles or mammals."

Crompton, A. W., and Pamela Parker, "Evolution of the Mammalian Masticatory Apparatus," *American Scientist*, vol. 66 (March/April 1978), pp. 192-201.

p. 194   "In reptiles and mammal-like reptiles, such as *Thrinaxodon*, new teeth tend to erupt between older teeth, and replacement usually continues throughout the life of the individual."

p. 196   "Several workers have suggested that the mammal-like reptiles had a conventional-reptilian single-bone middle ear with a tympanic membrane situated behind the quadrate. They based this conclusion partially on the fact that in advanced mammal-like reptiles such as *Thinaxodon*, a groove in the temporal bone terminates in a lip near the stapes/quadrate contact."

p. 199   "In the discussion of the structure of the reptile jaw, it was shown that transverse flanges on the pterygoid bones and a strong jaw joint were necessary to withstand the medially directed forces caused by the jaw-closing muscles."

p. 199   "In the mammal-like reptiles such as *Thrinaxodon*, which had tearing postcanine teeth and also large pterygoid flanges to withstand medially directed forces acting on the jaw, jaw movements during feeding were essentially in a vertical plane."

p. 200   "The advanced mammal-like reptiles . . . retained a small reptilian jaw joint."

Denton, Michael, *Evolution: A Theory in Crisis* (London: Burnett Books, Ltd., 1985), 368 pp.

pp. 160-1   "Since Darwin's time the search for missing links in the fossil record has continued on an ever-increasing scale. So vast has been the expansion of paleontological activity over the past one hundred years that probably 99.9% of all paleontological work has been carried out since 1860. Only a small fraction of the hundred thousand or so fossil species known today were known to Darwin. But virtually all the new fossil species discovered since Darwin's time have either been closely related to known forms or, like the Poganophoras, strange unique types of unknown affinity."

p. 177   "The systematic status and biological affinity of a fossil organism is far more difficult to establish than in the case of a living form, and can never be established with any degree of certainty. To begin with, ninety-nine per cent of the biology of any organism resides in its soft anatomy, which is inaccessible in a fossil."

p. 180   "The possibility that the mammal-like reptiles were completely reptilian in terms of their anatomy and physiology cannot be excluded. The only evidence we have regarding their soft biology is their cranial endocasts and these suggest that, as far as their central nervous systems were concerned, they were entirely reptilian."

p. 182   "Further, there is always the possibility that groups, such as the mammal-like reptiles which have left no living representative, might have possessed features in their soft biology completely different from any known reptile or mammal which would eliminate them completely as potential mammalian ancestors, just as the discovery of the living coelacanth revealed features in its soft anatomy which were unexpected and cast doubt on the ancestral status of its rhipidistian relatives."

p. 189   "On the other hand, the fact that, when estimates are made of the percentage of living forms found as fossils, the percentage turns out to be surprisingly high, suggesting that the fossil record may not be as bad as it often maintained. Of the 329 living families of terrestrial vertebrates 261 or 79.1% have been found as fossils and, when birds (which are poorly fossilized) are excluded, the percentage rises to 87.8%."

pp. 277-8   "However, as more protein sequences began to accumulate during the 1960s, it became increasingly apparent that the molecules were not going to provide any evidence of sequential arrangements in nature, but were rather going to reaffirm the traditional view that the system of nature conforms fundamentally to a highly ordered hierarchic scheme from which all direct evidence for evolution is emphatically absent. Moreover, the divisions turned out to be more mathematically perfect than even most die-hard typologists would have predicted."

Dodson, Peter, "International *Archaeopteryx* Conference," *Journal of Vertebrate Paleontology*, vol. 5 (June 1985), pp. 177-179.

p. 177   "The International *Archaeopteryx* Conference, sponsored by the Jura Museum, was held at Eichstatt, Bavaria, September 11 to 15, 1984, and included research reports from most of the world's specialists on the earliest bird."

p. 179   "At the end of the three days of presentations, Charig orchestrated a concerted effort to summarize the ideas for which consensus exists. The general credo runs as follows: *Archaeopteryx* was a bird that could fly, but it was not necessarily the direct ancestor of modern birds. It was a bipedal cursor that was facultatively arboreal. Flight developed with the assistance of gravity (e.g., from the trees down) rather than against gravity (from the ground up). *Archaeopteryx* was probably derived from theropods. A communiqué expressing the unanimous belief of all participants in the evolutionary origin and significance of *Archaeopteryx* was adopted, in order to forestall possible misuse by creationists of apparent discord among scientists."

Dunbar, Carl O., *Historical Geology* (New York: John Wiley and Sons, 1961), 500 pp.

p. 310   [re. *Archaeopteryx*] "It would be difficult to find a more perfect 'connecting link' between two great groups of animals, or more cogent proof of the reptilian ancestry of the birds."

[Yet, in the previous sentence, he says that it is . . .] "because of its feathers distinctly to be classed as a bird."

Feduccia, Alan, and Harrison B. Tordoff, "Feathers of *Archaeopteryx*: Asymmetric Vanes Indicate Aerodynamic Function," *Science*, vol. 203 (March 9, 1979), pp. 1021-1022.

p. 1022   "The shape and general proportions of the wing and wing feathers in *Archaeopteryx* are essentially like those of modern birds. The fact that the basic pattern and proportion of the modern avian wing were present in *Archaeopteryx* and have remained essentially unchanged for approximately 150 million years (since late Jurassic time), and that the individual flight feathers showed the asymmetry characteristic of airfoils seems to show that *Archaeopteryx* had an aerodynamically designed wing and was capable of at least gliding. Any argument that *Archaeopteryx* was flightless must explain selection for asymmetry in the wing feathers in some context other than flight."

Feduccia, Alan, "Evidence from Claw Geometry Indicating Arboreal Habits of *Archaeopteryx*," *Science*, vol. 259 (February 5, 1993), pp. 790-793.

p. 792   "Other evidence suggests that *Archaeopteryx* had an advanced aerodynamic morphology. (i) It had the feathers of modern birds, unchanged in structural detail over 150 million years of evolution, including microstructure, like regular spacing of barbs throughout the feather's length and clear impressions of barbules."

p. 792   "I conclude that *Archaeopteryx* was arboreal and volant, considerably advanced aerodynamically, and probably capable of flapping, powered flight to at least some degree. *Archaeopteryx* probably cannot tell us much about the early origins of feathers and flight in true protobirds because *Archaeopteryx* was, in the modern sense, a bird."

Gibbons, Ann, "New Feathered Fossil Brings Dinosaurs and Birds Closer," *Science*, vol. 274 (November 1, 1996), pp. 720-721.

p. 720   "But confirming whether the impressions are feathers, scales, or something else may prove to be difficult."

p. 720   ". . . the Chinese fossil is too recent—121 million years old—for the dinosaur to have given rise to the 150-million-year-old Jurassic bird, *Archaeopteryx*."

p. 720   "But these ideas on the evolution of feathers are, well, for the birds, according to University of North Carolina ornithologist Alan Feduccia, the best-known critic of the theory that dinosaurs gave rise to birds. He sees no proof that the dinosaur had feathers and doubts that any will be forthcoming. Feathered wings were 'the most complex appendage produced by vertebrates,' he says; it's implausible that an animal would have developed feathers if it did not fly."

Gingerich, Philip D., Donald E. Russell, Neil A. Wells, and S. M. Ibrahim Shah, "Origin of Whales in Epicontinental Remnant Seas: New Evidence from the Early Eocene of Pakistan," *Science*, vol. 220 (April 22, 1983), pp. 403-406.

p. 403   "We report diagnostic cranial remains of whales of early Eocene age . . . found in association with a terrestrial mammalian fauna. The post-cranial skeleton of early Eocene whales is not known, but a comparative study of cranial anatomy suggests that whales were probably not yet fully aquatic in the early Eocene."

p. 405   "Consequently there is no evidence that *Pakicetus* could hear directionally under water. There is no indication of vascularization of the middle ear to maintain pressure during diving, and early Eocene whales were probably incapable of diving to any significant depth. In terms of function, the auditory mechanism of *Pakicetus* appears more similar to that of land mammals than it is to any group of extant marine mammals."

p. 405   "The dentition and cranial anatomy of *Pakicetus* indicate that it was well equipped to feed on fishes in the surface waters of shallow seas, but it lacked auditory adaptions necessary for a fully marine existence. We do not yet know anything about the postcranial anatomy of early Eocene whales."

Gould, Stephen Jay, "The Telltale Wishbone," *Natural History*, vol. 86 (November 1977), pp. 26-35.

p. 26   "A striking resolution has been suggested by several paleontologists during the past decade. Dinosaurs, they argue, were fleet, active and warm-blooded. Moreover, they have not yet gone the way of all flesh, for a branch of their lineage persists in the branches—we call them birds."

p. 26   "Terrestrial vertebrates would fit into four classes—two cold-blooded, Amphibia and Reptilia, and two warmblooded, Dinosauria and Mammalia."

p. 36   "*Archaeopteryx* was a tiny animal, weighing less than a pound. It was a full foot shorter than the smallest dinosaur."

Hopson, James A., "Synapsids and Evolution," review of *Mammal-like Reptiles and the Origin of Mammals*, by Tom S. Kemp (New York: Academic Press, 1982, 364 pp), *Science*, vol. 219 (January 7, 1983), pp. 49-50.

p. 50   "The broad pattern of synapsid history is seen by Kemp to consist of three sequential adaptive radiations—pelycosaurs, non-cynodont therapsids, and cynodonts—with the last giving rise to mammals. He perceives each radiation as following a similar course: after the mass extinction of an earlier radiation, a single surviving lineage of more progressive small carnivorous forms rapidly radiated into all of the main niches formerly occupied by the less progressive forms: some turnover at low taxonomic levels occurred, but the higher taxon persisted until it, in its turn, was removed by a mass extinction. Major evolutionary change was restricted to the short interval between the mass extinction and completion of the subsequent radiation.

". . . The rapid rates of morphologic change accompanying the subsequent radiations are attributed to mutations of 'regulator genes'—in effect, the production of 'hopeful monsters'—with natural selection playing only a minor role in the process."

Kemp, Tom S., "The Reptiles that Became Mammals," *New Scientist*, vol. 93 (March 4, 1982), pp. 581-584. Kemp is Curator of the Zoological Collections, Oxford University Museum.

p. 583   "Each species of mammal-like reptile that has been found appears suddenly in the fossil record and is not preceded by the species that is directly ancestral to it. It disappears some time later, equally abruptly, without leaving a directly descended species, although we usually find that it has been replaced by some new, related species."

Kemp, Tom S., *Mammal-like Reptiles and the Origin of Mammals* (New York: American Press, 1982), 363 pp.

p. 3   "Of course there are many gaps in the synapsid fossil record, with intermediate forms between the various known groups almost invariably unknown. However, the known groups have enough features in common that it is possible to reconstruct a hypothetical intermediate stage."

p. 319   "Gaps at a lower taxonomic level, species and genera, are practically universal in the fossil record of the mammal-like reptiles. In no single adequately documented case is it possible to trace a transition, species by species, from one genus to another."

Kermack, D. M., K. A. Kermack, and F. Mussett, *Journal of the Linnaean Society*, vol. 47 (1968).

p. 418   "It differs from the lower jaw of the contemporary *Morganucodon* in its more slender shape, lower coronoid process and absence of an angle. It resembles *Morganucodon* in having a condyle on the dentary, since specimen C shows that there can now be no doubt of the existence of this condyle. Like *Morganucodon*, *Kuehnoetherium* must have had a full complement of the reptilian bones in its lower jaw, and shows a facet for the coronoid bone, as is illustrated by specimen 'C.'"

Kitts, David B., "Search for the Holy Transformation," review of *Evolution of Living Organisms*, by Pierre-P. Grassé, *Paleobiology*, vol. 5 (Summer 1979), pp. 353-355. Kitts was Professor of History of Science, University of Oklahoma.

p. 353   "Few paleontologists have, I think ever supposed that fossils, by themselves, provide grounds for the conclusion that evolution has occurred. An examination of the work of those paleontologists who have been particularly concerned with the relationship between paleontology and evolutionary theory, for example that of G. G. Simpson and S. J. Gould, reveals a mindfulness of the fact that the record of evolution, like any other historical record, must be construed within a complex of particular and general preconceptions not the least of which is the hypothesis that evolution has occurred."

p. 354   "The fossil record doesn't even provide any evidence in support of Darwinian theory except in the weak sense that the fossil record is compatible with it, just as it is compatible with other evolutionary theories, and revolutionary theories and special creationist theories and even ahistorical theories."

Koster, John, "Creature Feature: What was the New Zealand Monster?" *Oceans* (November/December 1977), pp. 56-59.

p. 56   "To Japanese scientists who examined the available evidence left in the New Zealand monster's foul-smelling wake, the most likely candidate for identification seemed to be the plesiosaur."

p. 57   "The smell was not that of fish, but of an animal."

p. 58   "The same defiance of existing knowledge and conventional wisdom that made the New Zealand monster a sort of hero to the Japanese public made it a fearsome dragon to academics around the world, and they set out to slay it with the magic sword of academic scorn."

p. 59   "In the end, everybody's individual preconceptions won out. Those who were prepared to believe in living plesiosauri were convinced or nearly so, while those who refused to believe found nothing to change their minds. For the open-minded skeptics, or for those who were just plain curious, the New Zealand monster remains one of the most tantalizing enigmas of the sea."

Lewin, Roger, "Bones of Mammals' Ancestors Fleshed Out," *Science*, vol. 212 (June 26, 1981), p. 1492.

p. 1492   "The earliest mammal-like reptiles, of the order Pelycosauria, were distinguished from their ancestors principally in size and diet: many large species rapidly arose, some of which were specialized carnivores, while others were herbivores.

               "The pelycosaurs were hugely successful during their 50-million-year tenure but became extinct in the early Permian, some 265 million years ago. Their issue, the therapsids, . . . were equally fecund, giving rise to more than 300 genera with species ranging in size from that of rats to rhinoceroses.

               "The line of advancing mammal-like features passes through the theridonts . . . to cynodonts, from which the first true mammals evolved some 200 million years ago. . . . The last of the cynodonts were very small and were probably insect-eaters like the mammals that evolved from them."

               "The transition to the first mammal, which probably happened in just one or, at most, two lineages, is still an enigma."

Lombard, R. Eric, review of *Evolutionary Principles of the Mammalian Middle Ear*, by Gerald Fleischer (Springer-Verlag, 1978), *Evolution*, vol. 33 (December 1979), p. 1230.

               "Those general statements about the evolution of the mammalian middle ear that appear are in the nature of proclamations. No methods are described which allow the reader to arrive with Fleischer at his 'ancestral' middle ear, nor is the basis for the transformation series illustrated for the middle ear bones explained. . . .

               "The otic region of the skull has always been a major source of structural grist in studies forming hypotheses about the evolution of both extinct and extant tetrapods. Here are nearly half the cranial nerves, buttresses of the jaw suspension, attachments for some jaw, neck and pharyngeal muscles, and key vessels. More to the point, the auditory structures, proper, are often very complex and within and between taxa, highly variable. Students of tetrapod evolution who rely on the otic region for phyletic information have often been naive about the function of the ear. As a result, the otic region has been misused in the past. . . .

"Those searching for specific information useful in constructing phylogenies of mammalian taxa will be disappointed."

Milner, Angela C., "Ground Rules for Early Birds," *Nature*, vol. 362 (April 15, 1993), p. 589.

p. 589   "The new specimens, designated *Monoychus*, come from the late Upper Cretaceous of Mongolia (that is, about 75 million years ago)."

p. 589   "Feathers are rarely preserved in the fossil record. In the Lower Cretaceous their only associations with skeletal material are poorly preserved traces in *Concornis*, and the record is meagre in the Upper Cretaceous. However, it is a logical assumption that feathers were present in all birds derived with respect to *Archaeopteryx*, including *Mononychus*, for insulation, if not for flight. . . . Feathers may, therefore, have been widespread among bipedal carnivorous dinosaurs as an insulating outer layer, as well as being universal in birds."

Monastersky, R., "A Clawed Wonder Unearthed in Mongolia," *Science News*, vol. 143 (April 17, 1993), p. 245.

p. 245   "Mongolian and U.S. researchers have found a 75-million-year-old, bird-like creature with a hand so strange it has left paleontologists grasping for an explanation."

p. 245   "While other paleontologists hail the new discovery, they remain unconvinced that *Mononychus* fits in the same phylogenetic category as *Archaeopteryx* and all later birds. Paul Sereno of the University of Chicago notes that *Mononychus* had arms built much like those of digging animals. Because moles and other diggers have keeled sternums and wrists reminiscent of birds, the classification of *Mononychus* becomes difficult, he says."

Monastersky, R., "Hints of a Downy Dinosaur in China," *Science News*, vol. 150 (October 26, 1996), p. 260.

p. 260   "Chinese paleontologists have unearthed the fossilized skeleton of a small dinosaur cloaked in what appears to be a layer of short feathers."

p. 260   "The feathery impressions are only a few millimeters long and resemble down more than the extended feathers seen on avian wings, he says. They run along the perimeter of the fossil, from the top of the head down to the tip of the tail and then around the underside of the tail.

"'They look so much like the feather impressions seen in the bird fossils at the same site that you can't come to any conclusion other than the fact that you're dealing with feathers,' says Currie [P. J. Currie, Tyrall Museum of Paleontology, Alberta]. 'Now, they may not be feathers. They may be featherlike scales, they may be hair, they may be something else.'"

p. 260   "The Liaoning animal cannot be considered a direct bird ancestor because it came well after the time of *Archaeopteryx*, which lived 150 million years ago. If the bird-dinosaur theory is correct, true birds must have split off the theropod line before *Archaeopteryx*.

"For now, critics of the theory remain undaunted by the new find. Larry D. Martin of the University of Kansas in Lawrence says that the structures on the back of the Chinese dinosaur may be the frayed remnants of dermal scales, similar to the frill running down the back of an iguana."

p. 260   "Like most paleontologists, however, Martin awaits a detailed report in the new find. 'The possibility for having egg on the face is tremendous at this point,' he says. 'We generally get more hard evidence with alien abductions than we have here.'"

Monastersky, R., "Paleontologists Deplume Feathery Dinosaur," *Science News*, vol. 151 (May 3, 1997), p. 271.

p. 271   "If people can have their 15 minutes of fame, so can dinosaurs. Most recently, the international spotlight has focused on a chicken-size fossil from northeast China, its body apparently fringed with downy impressions. For paleontologists who believe that birds evolved from dinosaurs, this specimen seemed the ultimate feather in their cap.

"An international team of researchers that examined the Chinese fossil now concludes that the fibrous structures are not feathers."

Olson, Storrs L., and Alan Feduccia, "Flight Capability and the Pectoral Girdle of *Archaeopteryx*," *Nature*, vol. 278 (March 15, 1979), pp. 247-248.

p. 248   "In conclusion, the robust furcula of *Archaeopteryx* would have provided a suitable point of origin for a well developed pectoralis muscle. Furthermore, the supracoracoideus muscle, and hence an ossified sternum, is not necessary to effect the recovery stroke of the wing. Thus the main evidence for *Archaeopteryx* having been a terrestrial, cursorial predator is invalidated. There is nothing in the structure of the pectoral girdle of *Archaeopteryx* that would preclude its having been a powered flier."

Ostrom, John H., "Reply to 'Dinosaurs as Reptiles'" *Evolution*, vol. 28 (September 1974), pp. 491-493.

p. 493   "Were it not for the feather impressions, *Archaeopteryx* would never have been classed as avian, but would have been labeled dinosaurian."

p. 493   "The large number of skeletal details that are common to *Archaeopteryx* and to contemporary, or nearly contemporary, small theropods makes me wonder whether some of the latter may not have been insulated with 'feathers' also."

Ostrom, John H., "Bird Flight: How Did It Begin?" *American Scientist*, vol. 67 (January/February 1979), pp. 46-56.

p. 47   "No fossil evidence exists of any pro-avis. It is a purely hypothetical pre-bird, but one that must have existed."

Sereno, Paul C., "Ruling Reptiles and Wandering Continents: A Global Look at Dinosaur Evolution," *GSA Today*, vol. 1 (July 1991), pp. 141-145).

p. 144   "The Chinese bird was arboreal, with extremely slender recurved unguals and a fully reversed hallux for perching (Fig. 12). Other characters establish the fossil avian as the second most primitive bird next to *Archaeopteryx*, such as the presence of toothed jaws, ossified stomach ribs (gastralia), and a pelvis with a footed pubis reminiscent of the ancestral theropod condition.

          "The principal groups of living birds, such as ratites, loons, pelicans, penguins, and songbirds, to name a few, must have diverged before the end of the Mesozoic in the last great radiation of the dinosauravian clade. Most Cretaceous and Paleocene avian fossils, although usually quite fragmentary, can be aligned with extant subgroups, suggesting that the principal skeletal variation among major groups of living birds arose, perhaps during a relatively short interval, before the end of the Mesozoic.

          "The recent discovery of an articulated fossil bird about 20 to 15 m.y. younger than *Archaeopteryx*, has opened a new window on early avian evolution. The sparrow sized skeleton is preserved in the fine-grained sediment of a fresh-water lake, with associated plant, insect, and fish remains. The fossil bird documents the very early appearance of anatomical features associated with sustained powered flight and perching that are absent in *Archaeopteryx*."

Vines, Gail, "Strange Case of *Archaeopteryx* 'Fraud,'" *New Scientist*, vol. 105 (March 14, 1985), p. 3.

p. 3   "One of the world's most famous fossils may be a fake, says Sir Fred Hoyle. 'Any physicist looking at it would have worries,' he claims."

p. 3   "The driving force behind the forgery allegation is Lee Spetner, an Israeli consultant in electronic systems in Rehovot. His suspicions were aroused when he read that the two specimens with the clearest feathers—the London and Berlin fossils—came from the collection of a Bavarian doctor, Dr. Karl Haberlein. Spetner and his colleagues argue that Haberlein gouged out an area around two genuine fossils of a dinosaur-like reptile, and made a matrix with cement which he applied to the fossils. Then, Spetner claims, he pressed chicken feathers or the like to the mixture to create the feather impressions.

          ". . . [Photographs taken by Robert Watkins, of the physics department at Cardiff] show signs of the forger's work: a fine-grained substrate under the feathers, blobs that look like chewing gum that could be the remnants of the forger's cement. . . . The fossil is split into two halves: an imprint of the creature is reflected in a 'counter slab' created when the rock containing the fossil was split open, like two halves of a mould. Hoyle and his colleagues find elevated or depressed regions on one slab that are not perfectly mirrored on the other. Finally, they point to 'double-strike' impressions of feathers. In a few places the same feather has apparently left two impressions slightly displaced to one side."

White, Errol, "A Little on Lungfishes," *Proceedings of the Linnaean Society of London*, vol. 177 (January 1966), pp. 1-9.

p. 1   "We must remember that the idea that these extraordinary animals were amphibia has not entirely died out."

p. 8   "... like all the other groups of fishes their origins are masked in obscurity.
              ... But whatever ideas authorities may have on the subject, the lungfishes, like
              every other major groups of fishes that I know, have their origins firmly based in
              nothing, a matter of hot dispute among the experts, each of whom is firmly
              convinced that everyone else is wrong."

p. 8   "I have often thought how little I would like to have to prove organic evolution
              in a court of law. In my experience of fossil fishes, while one can see the general
              drift of evolution readily enough, when it comes to pin-pointing the linkages,
              whether it be at generic level or at that of a higher group, the links are invariably
              either missing altogether or faulty, that is to say, always one or more characters
              are out of phase—even the ichthyostegids, which for all their superficially
              apparent intermediate position between the rhipidistion fishes and the amphibia,
              are too advanced in respect of some characters, such as the back of the head,
              to be ancestral to the first true amphibians."

Würsig, Bernd, "Dolphins," *Scientific American*, vol. 240 (March 1979), pp. 136-148.

p. 136   "Dolphins evolved at least 50 million years ago from land mammals that may
              have resembled the even-toed ungulates of today, such as cattle, pigs, and
              buffaloes. After taking to the sea, dolphins became progressively better adapted
              to life in the water: their ancestral fur was replaced by a thick coat of blubbery
              fat, they became sleek and streamlined, they lost all but internal remnants of
              their hind limbs and grew a powerful tail, their forelimbs were modified into
              steering paddles and apparently as a further aid in steering and stabilization
              many species evolved a dorsal fin."

"Whales of the World," fold-out in *National Geographic*, vol. 150 (December 1976). Reference to
    "Exploring the Lives of Whales," by Victor B. Scheffer, *National Geographic*, vol. 50 (December
    1976), pp. 752-767. Scheffer was Chairman of the U.S. Marine Mammal Committee.

              "The Whale's ascendancy to sovereign size apparently began sixty million
              years ago when hairy, four-legged mammals, in search of food or sanctuary,
              ventured into water. As eons passed, changes slowly occurred. Hind legs
              disappeared, front legs changed into flippers, hair gave way to a thick smooth
              blanket of blubber, nostrils moved to the top of the head, the tail broadened into
              flukes, and in the buoyant water world the body became enormous."

Chapter 8

The Origin of Man

A. The Hominid Fossils

Evolutionists allege that human beings and apes (including chimpanzees, gorillas, orangutans, and gibbons) all diverged from some unknown mammalian ancestor sometime in the late Tertiary period. That is about all they agree on. The dates, locations and lineages involved in this most vital and most recent evolutionary development are all subjects of much speculative controversy among paleonanthropologists.

They have coined the term "hominoids" for extinct apes that may or may not have been components in human ancestry. "Hominids" are extinct somewhat man-like apes that are considered more closely related to man. Of these, the two most often cited as human ancestors have been *Ramapithecus* and *Australopithecus*. However, as the following quotes show, there is extreme disagreement among authorities on these matters. To the creationist, all these hominids represent nothing but extinct apes.

Anonymous, "Whose Ape Is It, Anyway?" *Science News*, vol. 125 (June 9, 1984), p. 361. Reporter's account of 1984 annual meeting of American Association for Advancement of Science, in New York.

> "One sometimes wonders whether orangutans, chimps and gorillas ever sit around the tree, contemplating which is the closest relative of man. (And, would they want to be?). Maybe they even chuckle at human scientists' machinations as they race to draw the definitive map of evolution on earth. If placed on top of one another, all these competing versions of our evolutionary highways would make the Los Angeles freeway system look like County Road 41 in Elkhart, Indiana."

Anonymous, "Ethiopia Yields Oldest Human Fossils," *Science News*, vol. 106 (November 2, 1974), p. 276.

P. 276   "When—and where—was the beginning, the cradle of early man upon the earth? A succession of increasingly ancient discoveries has led some anthropologists to the point of virtually suspending their judgment, as more and more primitive examples of genus *Homo* push further back the curtain of time. The latest addition to the growing line, announced last week in Ethiopia, shows the grounds for such conservatism, as it promises to extend human lineage as far back as four million years.

> "The finds—a complete upper jaw, half of another upper jaw, all with teeth—were found on Oct. 17 and 18 by Alemeyu Asfew of the Ethiopian Antiquities Commission, a member of the four-nation Afar Research Expedition. Working with D. Carl Johanson of Case Western Reserve University in Cleveland and Maurice Taieb of the French National Center for Scientific Research, he spotted the bones lying on the surface at a volcanic deposit on the Hadar, a tributary of the Awash River between the towns of Dessie and Assab in north-central Ethiopia.

"The bones were in a stratigraphic level some 150 feet beneath, and thus probably much older than, a volcanic layer which has been dated (by the potassium-argon method, at from 3.01 to 3.25 million years old."

P. 276   "The small size of the teeth in the jawbones, hypothesizes Johanson, may well mean that genus *Homo* was 'walking, eating meat and probably using tools, perhaps bones, to kill animals' as much as four million years ago. There is even the possibility, Johanson says, that he had 'some kind of social cooperation and some sort of communication system."

P. 276   "If *Australopithecus* lived in the same region occupied a million years before by the more highly evolved genus *Homo*, suggest Johanson and his Afar colleagues, it seems likely that the 'true man' and the 'near man' lived in the area at the same time. . . . All previous theories of the origin of the lineage which lead to modern man must now be totally revised. We must throw out many existing theories and consider the possibility that man's origins go back to well over four million years."

Anonymous, "*Australopithecus*, a Long-armed, Short-legged, Knuckle-walker, *Science News*, vol. 100 (November 27, 1971), p. 357.

"*Australopithecus* limb bone fossils have been rare finds, but Leakey now has a large sample. They portray *Australopithecus* as long-armed and short-legged. He was probably a knuckle-walker, not an erect walker, as many archaeologists presently believe."

Berg, Christine, "How Did the Australopithecines Walk? A Biomechanical Study of the Hip and Thigh of *Australopithecus Afarensis*," *Journal of Human Evolution*, vol. 26 (April 1994), pp. 259-273. Berg is at the Natural History Museum in Paris, France.

p. 271   "The present results lead to the conclusion that the bipedalism of the *Australopithecus* must have differed from that of *Homo*. Not only did *Australopithecus* have less ability to maintain hip and knee extension during the walk, but also probably moved the pelvis and lower limb differently. It seems that the australopithecine walk differed significantly from that of humans, involving a sort of waddling gait, with large rotatory movements of the pelvis and shoulders around the vertebral column. Such a walk, likely required a greater energetic cost than does human bipedalism. The stride length and frequency of australopithecines, and consequently their speed, should have differed from that of *Homo* in contrast to some recent hypotheses of dynamic similarity among hominids. A previous paper has suggested that the pelvic proportions of *Australopithecus* could provide some arguments for an arboreal locomotion. The results of the present study suggest amplification of this opinion."

Cartmill, Matt, "Four Legs Good, Two Legs Bad," *Natural History*, vol. 92 (November 1983), pp. 65-79.

p. 67   "Evolutionary theorizing was shrugged off by most biologists until 1859, when Darwin and Wallace came forth with the pleasingly mechanical theory of natural selection.

". . . As the steel magnate Andrew Carnegie put it after reading Darwin and Spencer: 'Not only had I got rid of theology and the supernatural, but I had found the truth of evolution. 'All is well since all grows better,' became my motto, my true source of comfort.'"

p. 76   "Dart's 'tools' from the australopithecine cave sites had always met with coughs and raised eyebrows from his peers. But they were not ruled out of the picture until the early 1970's, when E. S. Vrba and C. K. Brain undertook more extensive studies of the animal bones from those caves. They concluded that the australopithecines, like the baboons and antelopes from the same deposits, had been dragged into the caves and eaten by leopards and carnivores. Most and probably all of the bone tools were scraps from a cat's lunch—and so were the remains of the supposed killer apes."

p. 77   "When people turn indignantly from one sort of speculation to embrace another, there are usually good, non-scientific reasons for it."

p. 77   "A myth, says my dictionary, is a real or fictional story that embodies the cultural ideals of a people or expresses deep, commonly felt emotions. By this definition, myths are generally good things—and the origin stories that paleoanthropologists tell are necessarily myths."

Cartmill, Matt, David R. Pilbeam, and Glynn Isaac, "One Hundred Years of Paleoanthropology," *American Scientist*, vol. 74 (July/August 1986), pp. 410-420.

p. 416   "It is now known that these so-called robust australopithecines coexisted with *Homo* for over a million years. The marked anatomical differences between the two imply that they were different species with quite different adaptations. Thus, the notion of one general adaptive niche for hominids must be a mistake. Whatever explains *hominid* origins cannot also be a sufficient explanation of *human* origins, for not all hominids became human."

p. 416   "However, at present there is not thought to be any good evidence for either meat-eating or tool-using by any australopithecines, and the anatomy of their jaws and teeth implies a largely or wholly vegetarian diet."

p. 417   "Nancy Tanner and Adrienne Zihlman posit a female collective as the social and economic core of early hominid life, and see hominid females as the source of technological invention (of tools for collecting and carrying food to share with offspring) and of evolutionary progress (by means of a female preference for the most feminine, sociable males as mates). By contrast, C. Owen Lovejoy and his associates see australopithecine *males* as monogamous breadwinners provisioning their more sedentary mates and offspring."

p. 417   "A social pattern like that of lions, with females working communally to support a few big, lazy, territory-patrolling males, would fit what we know about *Australopithecus*, though it might not enhance the amour-propre of either male or female scientists."

p. 417   "The early australopithecines are known from fossilized footprints to have been bipedal; but they were surprisingly apelike in skull form, premolar dentition, limb proportions, & morphology of some joint surfaces, and they may still have been spending a significant amount of time in the trees."

Davids, Meryl, "An Evolutionary Urge to Submerge?" *New Age Journal* (January/February 1995), pp. 19-20.

pp. 19-20   "Ever wonder why we love water? Why we head for the beach at the first opportunity, stay in the shower long after we're clean, even ponder water births for our babies? According to Welsh author Elaine Morgan, this urge to submerge may have an evolutionary explanation—one that holds some surprising implications for our health today.

"Traditional evolutionary theory posits that humans separated from monkeys when our ancestors dropped from trees to hunt animals on the dry African plains. In contrast, Morgan argues that the first humans evolved in a flooded wet region of north-east Africa where they spent much of their time swimming or wading hip-deep in water."

p. 20   "While largely ignored by many mainstream anthropologists, the aquatic ape theory has been attracting increasing scientific interest. Last summer, a symposium on the subject at the California Institute of Integral Studies (CIIS) attracted researchers from around the world. When earlier published in England, *The Scars of Evolution* was positively reviewed in scientific journals."

Eckhardt, Robert B., "Population Genetics and Human Origins," *Scientific American*, vol. 226 (January 1972), pp. 94-103.

p. 101   "On the basis of these tooth-size calculations, at least, there would appear to be little evidence to suggest that several different hominoid species are represented among the Old World dryopithecine fossils of late Miocene and early Pliocene times. Neither is there compelling evidence for the existence of any distinct hominid species during this interval, unless the designation 'hominid' means simply any individual ape that happens to have small teeth and a correspondingly small face. Fossil hominoids such as *Ramapithecus* may well be ancestral to the hominid line in the sense that they were individual members of an evolving phyletic line from which the hominids later diverged. They themselves nevertheless seem to have been apes—morphologically, ecologically and behaviorally."

Gould, Stephen Jay, "A Short Way to Big Ends," *Natural History*, vol. 95 (January 1986), pp. 18-28.

p. 28   "Oxnard is our leading expert on the quantitative study of skeletons. He has used the techniques of multivariate analysis—a set of statistical tools, forming the basis of my own technical work as well, that can integrate large suites of measurements and extract general estimates of similarity and difference from all measures considered together. Oxnard has spent years studying the australopithecines, the group of African hominids considered by all experts to be our closest genealogical cousins (probably our ancestors as well). Oxnard has argued in several books and articles that australopithecines are anatomically more different from us than other experts imagine. He views them as bipedal like us, but also capable of motion with all fours (probably for climbing) in a manner 'far more sophisticated than that of which any human is capable.' In short, he sees australopithecines as uniquely different from apes and humans, not as imperfect people on the way up."

Gould, Stephen Jay, "Empire of the Apes," *Natural History*, vol. 96 (May 1987), pp. 20-25.

p. 24   "The oldest human fossils are less than 4 million years old, and we do not know which branch on the copious bush of apes budded off the twig that led to our lineage. (In fact, except for the link of Asian *Sivapithecus* to the modern orangutan, we cannot trace any fossil ape to any living species. Paleontologists have abandoned the once popular notion that *Ramapithecus* might be a source of human ancestry.) Thus, sediments between 4 and 10 million years in age are potential guardians of the Holy Grail of human evolution—the period when our lineage began its separate end run to later domination, and a time for which no fossil evidence exists at all."

Herbert, Wray, "Was Lucy a Climber? Dissenting Views of Ancient Bones," *Science News*, vol. 122 (August 21, 1982), p. 116.

p. 116   "Anthropologist Randall L. Susman and anatomist Jack Stern of the State University of New York at Stony Brook say that Lucy's bones and other fossils from the Hadar region at Ethiopia indicate that the earliest known species of hominid (called *Australopithecus afarensis*), while adapted to walking, was still spending considerable time in the trees. University of Chicago anthropologist Russell Tuttle . . . also argues, based on an analysis of the Laetoli footprints in Tanzania, that another more human species of ape-man coexisted with *A. afarensis* about 3.7 million years ago; this unnamed species, rather than *A. afarensis*, was probably the direct ancestor to *Homo sapiens*, Tuttle says."

p. 116   "In addition, Susman says, Lucy's limb proportions indicate that she had not yet developed an efficient upright gait."

p. 116   "Tuttle agrees that, based on anatomical data, *A. afarensis* must have been arboreal, but he goes even further, arguing that Lucy's pelvis shows a flare that is better suited for climbing than for walking. More importantly, he says, the Laetoli footprints do not match the foot bones found in Hadar; where the Hadar foot is ape-like, with curved toes, the footprints left in Laetoli are 'virtually human.' Tuttle concludes that the bipedal species which lived in Tanzania is a different species from *A. afarensis*—and one more closely related to humans."

Herbert, Wray, "Lucy's Uncommon Forebear," *Science News*, vol. 123 (February 5, 1983), pp. 88 89, 92.

p. 88   "In 1928, Harvard University zoologist Harold J. Coolidge . . . stumbled upon . . . the first evidence of a previously unknown species of living ape, a pygmy chimpanzee. . . ."

p. 88   "For some, the newly discovered pygmy chimpanzee, graceful and human-like, provided the perfect answer: *Pan paniscus*, Coolidge declared in 1933, offered the best model for understanding the missing common ancestor."

p. 89   "Along with [Vincent] Sarich, Zihlman (of UC Santa Cruz) and [Douglas] Cramer (of New York University) have become the champions of the bonobo model, and they have based their claims primarily on studies of the anatomy of living apes and fossilized hominids."

p. 89   "To make her point, [Adrienne] Zihlman compares the pygmy chimpanzee to 'Lucy,' one of the oldest fossil hominids known, and finds the similarities striking. They are almost identical in body size, in stature and in brain size, she notes, and the major differences (the hip and the foot) represent the younger Lucy's adaptation to bipedal walking (Lucy, officially called *Australopithecus afarensis*, has been dated at 3.6 million years, although that date has recently been challenged)."

p. 92   "Susman also discovered that pygmy chimps have a unique style of locomotion. Like modern gorillas they tend to be knuckle-walkers on the ground, yet they seem to be natural bipeds, too, frequently walking upright both on the ground and in the trees."

Herbert, Wray, "Hominids Bear Up, Become Porpoiseful," *Science News*, vol. 123 (April 16, 1983), p. 246.

p. 246   "Ancient humans are going through changes that no theory of evolution could predict. The oldest known hominoid (ancestor of apes and man) from northern Africa was recently transformed into an ancient species of dolphin, while in east Africa one of the earliest bipedal hominids, or primitive humans, has changed into something like a prehistoric dancing bear. While the changes do not fundamentally alter views of early humanity, they have sparked much discussion about anthropologists' over-zealous pursuit of human ancestry."

p. 246   "[Tim] White had dubbed the hominoid species *Flipperpithecus*."

p. 246   "According to John Hopkins University anthropologist Alan Walker, there is a long tradition of misinterpreting various bones as human clavicles; in the past, he says, skilled anthropologists have erroneously described an alligator femur and the toe of a three-toed horse as clavicles. . . .

"In another fossil reassessment, University of Chicago anthropologist Russell Tuttle has examined a set of 3.5-million-year-old hominid footprints at the Laetoli site in Tanzania and has concluded that they are not hominid at all."

p. 246   "He found that the prints of a Himalayan black bear match the Laetoli [A-trail] prints very closely."

Hopson, James A., and Leonard B. Radinsky, "Vertebrate Paleontology: New Approaches and New Insights," *Paleobiology*, vol. 6 (Summer 1980), pp. 250-270. Hopson was in the Anatomy Department at the University of Chicago.

pp. 263-4   "Interestingly, despite almost a decade of technically sophisticated analyses of australopithecine remains, there is still considerable controversy over their functional and phylogenetic significance—in particular whether they are too divergently specialized to be considered suitable ancestors for *Homo*."

Lewin, Roger, *Bones of Contention* (New York: Simon and Schuster, 1987), 348 pp.

p. 27   "It is an unfortunate truth that fossils do not emerge from the ground with labels already attached to them. And it is bad enough that much of the labeling was done in the name of egoism and a naive lack of appreciation of variation between individuals; each nuance in shape was taken to indicate a difference in type rather than natural variation within a population. This problem has in some part been eased in the half-century since Hooton made his pithy remarks. But it remains inescapably true that applying the correct label is astonishingly difficult, not least because such labels are in a sense arbitrary abstractions; and especially so when the material on which the analysis is being done is fragmentary and eroded. 'It is an incredibly difficult problem,' says Lord Zuckerman. 'It is one so difficult that I think it would be legitimate to despair that one could ever turn it into a science.'"

p. 43   "In fact, 'virtually all our theories about human origins were relatively unconstrained by fossil data,' observes David Pilbeam. 'The theories are . . . fossil-free or in some cases even fossil-proof.' This shocking statement simply means that there is and always has been far more fleshing out of the course and cause of human evolution than can fully be justified by the scrappy skeleton provided by the fossils. As a result, he continues, 'our theories have often said far more about the theorists than they have about what actually happened.'"

p. 300   "All of which suggests that it is easier to recognize bias in others than to admit it in oneself. It also probably means that some questions in paleoanthropology may well be impossible to answer with any degree of certainty—and human beings dislike uncertainty, especially when it concerns themselves. Combine these two truths and you get an inevitable result, as noted by Johanson: 'Anthropologists who deal with human fossils tend to get very emotionally involved with their bones.'"

Johanson, Donald C. *et al.*, "New Partial Skeleton of *Homo habilis* from Olduvai Gorge, Tanzania," *Nature*, vol. 327 (May 21, 1987), pp. 205-509.

pp. 208-9   "Several important conclusions about the OH 62 partial skeleton emerge from the first round of analysis. First, body size for this fully adult individual is estimated to be as small as or smaller than that of any known fossil hominid. Second, in addition to size, there are striking anatomical and proportional similarities between the OH 62 postcranial skeleton and small *Australopithecus* individuals (especially A. L. 288-1). Third, the strong morphological similarities of the OH 62 face, palate and dentition to *Homo habilis* (especially Stw. 53) warrant attribution of the Olduvai individual to this taxon. This represents the first time that limb elements have been securely assigned to *Homo habilis*."

p. 209   "On the contrary, the new OH 62 partial skeleton as well as the juvenile hand parts described as part of the holotype (OH 7) show that *Homo habilis* had a postcranium similar in many ways to mid-Pliocene *A. afarensis*."

p. 209   "The discovery of long and powerful arms in *Homo habilis* and *Australopithecus*-like aspects of pelvic and proximal femoral anatomy in early *Homo erectus* (KNM-WT 15000) emphasize the mosaic pattern of evolution in the early hominid postcranial skeleton."

p. 209   "Thus, the degree of megadontia in *Homo habilis* may, in fact, be little changed from the *Australopithecus* condition.

"The very small body size of the OH 62 individual suggests that views of human evolution positing incremental body size increase through time may be rooted in gradualistic preconceptions rather than fact."

Kelso, A. J., *Physical Anthropology* (New York: J. B. Lippincott, 1974), 355 pp.

p. 142   ". . . the transition from insectivore to primate is not documented by fossils. The basis of knowledge about the transition is by inference from living forms."

p. 151   "Clearly the fossil documentation of the emergence of the Old World monkeys could provide key insights into the general evolutionary picture of the primates, but, in fact, this record simply does not exist."

Leakey, Richard E., "Hominids in Africa," *American Scientist*, vol 64 (March/April 1976), pp. 174-178.

p. 174   "The case for *Ramapithecus* as a hominid is not substantial and the fragmentary material leaves many questions open."

p. 176   "There is an inherent problem in hominid taxonomy caused by the present lack of any precise diagnosis for fossil forms. I am reluctant to anticipate further new discoveries, but I would expect that the genus *Homo* will eventually be traced into the Pliocene at an age of between 4 and 6 million years, together with *Australopithecus*."

p. 177   "At one locality, remains of a stone structure—perhaps the base of a circular hut—were uncovered; there is an excellent date of 1.8 million years for this."

Lewin, Roger, "The Earliest 'Humans' were More like Apes," *Science*, vol. 236 (May 29, 1987), pp. 1061-1063.

p. 1062   "The new Olduvai hominid, which is code named OH 62, highlights two important aspects in these changes. First, the primitive body form that characterized the earliest hominids continued much later in human history than had been expected. And second, the extreme sexual dimorphism seen in *A. afarensis*, in which the males were twice as big as the females, continued unabated through *H. habilis* and diminished only with the advent of *H. erectus*.

           ". . . Taken together, both these insights—into locomotion and social structure—affect the way anthropologists view this first member of the *Homo* genus; it looks distinctly less 'human' than most people have assumed."

p. 1063   "The evolutionary transition between *H. habilis* and *H. erectus* appears to have occurred in the narrow window of time between 1.8 and 1.6 million years ago. 'Given the primitiveness we see in *habilis* and the advanced characteristics in *erectus*, it's clear that the transition was much more abrupt than has been appreciated,' says White."

Loewenstein, Jerald M., and Adrienne L. Zihlman, "The Invisible Ape," *New Scientist*, vol. 120 (December 3, 1988), pp. 56-59.

p. 58   "But anatomy and the fossil record cannot be relied on for defining evolutionary lineages. Yet palaeontologists persist in doing just this. They rally under the banner of a methodology called cladistics, in which family trees of living and fossil primates are constructed on the basis of 'primitive' and 'derived' traits (mostly of teeth and bones), which are either shared or not shared. Shared primitive characteristics are shared because they come from a common ancestor, unshared derived characteristics reveal separate evolutionary paths. The subjective element in this approach to building evolutionary trees, which many palaeontologists advocate with almost religious fervour, is demonstrated by the outcome: there is no single family tree on which they agree. On the contrary, almost every conceivable combination and permutation of living and extinct hominoids has been proposed by one cladist or another."

p. 58   "Chimps and gorillas could resemble each other either because they are closest kin; or because they both retain ancestral traits lost in humans; or because they started out different but grew alike because they had similar ways of life. The molecular data support the second possibility. They tend to rule out the first, and it is unlikely that chimps and gorillas independently acquired knuckle-walking, thin dental enamel, body hair, small brains and other similarities. It is much more likely that humans lost these characteristics in the course of evolution."

p. 59   "Anthropologists working at Swartkrans in South Africa, recently discovered two-million-year-old thumb bones that are essentially like our own thumbs. Tools made from bone and stone, and of the same age, were found with the thumb bones. One would hardly expect to find evidence for knuckle-walking in a hand that could already manipulate such tools."

Martin, Robert D., "Et tu, Tree Shrew," *Natural History*, vol. 91 (August 1982), pp. 26-32.

p. 28   "By 1967, tree shrews had become firmly established as the most primitive living members of the order Primates."

p. 32   "After researchers widened their comparisons to include other placental mammals and even marsupials, they found many of the features that supposedly link tree shrews to primates in other mammals as well, either because of retention from ancestral placental mammals or because of convergent evolution."

p. 32   "Thus, in less than fifteen years, we have come full circle; the consensus now is that tree shrews are not relatives of the primates."

Martin, Robert D., *Primate Origins and Evolution* (Princeton University Press, 1990), 804 pp.

p. 66   "The origins of the New World monkeys therefore remain a mystery, as the only substantial fossils are known from the late Oligocene and the Miocene, and by that stage they exhibit numerous characteristics clearly allying them with the modern forms. Indeed, without exception the substantial fossils that have been described resemble true New World monkeys (family Cebidae)."

p. 68   "Although early fossil evidence of New World monkeys may be described as disappointing, it is rich in comparison to that for Old World monkeys."

p. 69   "Overall, the fossil record can tell us very little about the early origins of Old World monkeys."

p. 82   "It should be noted at the outset that substantial fossil remains are known for all of the species listed below (a quite unusual situation with respect to the primate fossil record generally), but that there is virtually no fossil evidence relating to human evolution, other than a few fragments of dubious affinities, before about 3.8 Ma ago. The preceding period of human evolution therefore remains a complete mystery and an unfortunate major gap exists whatever view one takes of the time of divergence of hominids and great apes."

p. 710   "There is now abundant evidence that tree shrews are simply unrelated to primates."

Morgan, Elaine, and Marc Verhaegen, "In the Beginning Was the Water," *New Scientist*, vol. 109 (March 6, 1986), pp. 62-63.

p. 62   "Attempts to date the emergence of speech are handicapped by the lack of agreement as to why it happened at all. Anthropoid apes are to some extent pre-adapted to every aspect of hominid development, but not this one; all researches in communication between apes confirm that, while readily learning visual or gestural symbols, they remain dumb animals."

p. 62   "The descended larynx is a very puzzling feature. In most mammals, the larynx—a tubular structure constituting the upper end of the windpipe—connects directly with the back of the nasal passages. A channel from nostrils to lungs therefore remains open at all times, so that the animals can swallow and breathe simultaneously. But in *Homo sapiens* the larynx occupies a new position low in the throat—a development fraught with disadvantages."

Oxnard, Charles E., *The Order of Man* (New Haven: Yale University Press, 1984), 366 pp.

pp. *iii-iv*   "[in *Nota bene* section in back] Though the standard idea is that some of the australopithecines are implicated in a lineage of humanlike forms, the new possibility suggested in this book, a radiation separate from either humans or African apes, has received powerful corroboration. It is now being recognized widely that the australopithecines are not structurally closely similar to humans, that they must have been living at least in part in arboreal environments, and that many of the later specimens were contemporaneous or almost so with the earliest members of the genus *Homo*."

Oxnard, Charles E., "The Place of the Australopithecines in Human Evolution: Grounds for Doubt?" *Nature*, vol. 258 (December 1975), pp. 389-395.

p. 389   "Although most studies emphasize the similarity of the australopithecines to modern man, and suggest, therefore, that these creatures were bipedal tool-makers at least one form of which (*Australopithecus africanus*—'*Homo habilis*,' '*Homo africanus*) was almost directly ancestral to man, a series of multivariate statistical studies of various postcranial fragments suggests other conclusions."

Oxnard, Charles E., *University of Chicago Magazine* (Winter, 1974), pp. 8-12.

p. 11   "Multivariate studies of several anatomical regions, shoulder, pelvis, ankle, foot, elbow, and hand are now available for the australopithecines. These suggest that the common view, that these fossils are similar to modern man or that on those occasions when they depart from a similarity to man they resemble the African great apes, may be incorrect. Most of the fossil fragments are in fact uniquely different from both man and man's nearest living genetic relatives, the chimpanzee and gorilla. . . . To the extent that resemblances exist with living forms, they tend to be with the orangutan."

Oxnard, Charles E., "Human Fossils: New Views of Old Bones," *American Biology Teacher*, vol. 41 (May 5, 1979), pp. 264-276. Oxnard was Dean of the Graduate School and University Professor in Biological Sciences and Anatomy, University of Southern California.

p. 264   "This is a time-honored method that can be extraordinarily powerful (for the eye and the mind are excellent computers of a kind). But we have merely to remember cases like Piltdown Man, which turned out to be a fraudulent composite of a genuine fossil skull cap and a modern ape jaw, or *Hesperopithecus*, the ape of the West, which eventually was discovered to be a peccary, or even of the completely different portraits that have been drawn for the facial features of a creature such as *Zinjanthropus* to realize that this method also has many difficulties."

p. 273   "Let us now return to our original problem: the australopithecine fossils. . . . The new investigations suggest that the fossil fragments are usually uniquely different from any living form; when they do have similarities with living species, they are as often as not reminiscent of the orangutan."

p. 274   "It is far more likely that the genus *Homo* is much older than currently believed and that the australopithecines of Olduvai and Sterkfontein represent only parallel evolutionary remnants. . . . It is really now somewhat unlikely that australopithecines . . . hailed as human ancestors can actually have had very much to do with the direct human pathway."

Pilbeam, David R., and Stephen Jay Gould, "Size and Scaling in Human Evolution," *Science*, vol. 186 (December 6, 1974), pp. 892-901. Pilbeam is Associate Professor of Anthropology, Yale University, and Gould is Professor of Geology, Harvard University.

p. 892   "Human paleontology shares a peculiar trait with such disparate subjects as theology and extraterrestrial biology: it contains more practitioners than objects for study."

pp. 899-900   "Both the australopithecine and the chimpanzee-gorilla sequence display this set of allometric consequences: larger forms are scaled-up replicas of their smaller prototypes. *Homo sapiens* provides the outstanding exception to this trend among primates, for we have evolved a relatively large brain and small face, in opposition to functional expectations at our size. We retain, as large adults, the cranial proportions that characterize juvenile or even fetal stages of other large primates; partial neoteny has probably played a major role in human evolution. *Australopithecus africanus* has a rounded braincase because it is a relatively small animal; *H. sapiens* displays this feature because we have evolved a large brain and circumvented the expectations of negative allometry. The resemblance is fortuitous; it offers no evidence of genetic similarity."

Pilbeam, David, review of *Origins*, by Richard E. Leakey and Roger Lewin (Dutton, 1977, 264 pp.), *American Scientist*, vol. 66 (May/June 1978), pp. 378-379. Pilbeam is in the Department of Anthropology, and is Curator of the Peabody Museum of Natural History, Yale.

pp. 378-9   "My reservations concern not so much this book but the whole subject and methodology of paleoanthropology. But introductory books—or book reviews—are hardly the place to argue that perhaps generations of students of human evolution, including myself, have been flailing about in the dark; that our data base is too sparse, too slippery, for it to be able to mold our theories. Rather, the theories are more statements about us and ideology than about the past. Paleoanthropology reveals more about how humans view themselves than it does about how humans came about."

Pilbeam, David, "Rearranging our Family Tree," *Human Nature* (June 1978), pp. 39-45.

p. 42   "As I now realize, extinct hominoids were not particularly modern. They were not like either living apes or human beings, but instead were unique, distinct animal species."

p. 43   "It is quite possible that one or more of the dryopithecids gave rise to the living forest apes. Unfortunately, the fossil record of pongids is nonexistent, making a glaring deficiency in the whole story."

p. 44   "All this makes a much more complex picture of hominoid evolution than we once imagined. It no longer resembles a ladder but is, instead, more like a bush."

p. 44   "Hominids evolved, as did many other mammal groups, with diverse and overlapping radiations. There is no clear-cut and inexorable pathway from ape to human being."

p. 45   "In the course of rethinking my ideas about human evolution, I have changed somewhat as a scientist. I am aware of the prevalence of implicit assumptions and try harder to dig them out of my own thinking. I am also aware that there are many assumptions I will get at only later, when today's thoughts turn into yesterday's misconceptions. I know that, at least in paleoanthropology, data are still so sparse that theory heavily influences interpretations. Theories have, in the past, clearly reflected our current ideologies instead of the actual data."

Potts, Richard, "Home Bases and Early Hominids," *American Scientist*, vol. 72 (July/August 1984), pp. 338-347.

p. 341   "Bones, as well as sediments, can be deposited by water, each element responding differently to the energy of the flow. Although the movement of bones in water is affected by a complex array of factors, rapidly flowing water tends to sort skeletal elements according to their hydrodynamic properties."

p. 344   "It is even more difficult to reconcile a home base interpretation with other characteristics of the fossil assemblages."

p. 344   "Olduvai hominids lived, evidently, without fire or domesticated dogs."

Rak, Yoel, "Ear Ossicle of *Australopithecus Robustus*," *Nature*, vol. 279 (May 3, 1979), pp. 62-63. Rak is in the Department of Anthropology, UCLA.

p. 62   "We report here the discovery of the first ear ossicle, an incus, of a Plio-Pleistocene hominid. It is substantially different from that of a modern man, and the dissimilarity exceeds that between the ear bones of *Homo sapiens* and of the African apes. The new incus is of interest particularly in view of the unique advantages the ear ossicles have for taxonomic and phylogenetic studies. The only other fossil hominid ear ossicles are from Qafseh and are indistinguishable from those of modern man."

p. 62   "Although the incus is tiny, its importance should not be overlooked. Furthermore, this is one of the most complete and undistorted bones of *Australopithecus robustus* yet discovered."

p. 63   "The solid appearance of the SK 848 incus and of its articular surface suggests that its shape is not the result of some pathological process. Its unusual morphology is far beyond the range of normal variation characteristic of the incudes of modern man and the great apes."

Shipman, Pat, "Where Have all the Primates Gone?" *New Scientist*, vol. 134 (June 13, 1992), p. 16.

"Interpreting the rich record of Miocene hominoids is fraught with problems because there are so few surviving examples. Today there are only three genera and four species of great apes, and these are confined to fast-vanishing tropical rainforest or woodland habitats. But there are about a dozen genera and even more species of larger-bodied hominoids known from the Miocene. This means that anthropologists are confronted with many ancient apes with no known living counterparts. Adding to the confusion are more smaller-bodied genera and species from the Miocene that appear to be related to monkeys, lesser apes, or have no apparent living relatives."

Stringer, Christopher B., "The Legacy of *Homo Sapiens*," review of *Origins Reconsidered: In Search of What Makes Us Human*, by Richard E. Leakey and Roger Lewin (Doubleday, 1992), *Scientific American*, vol. 268 (May 1993), pp. 138-141. Stringer is in the Human Origins Group of the Natural History Museum in London.

p. 138   "The study of human origins seems to be a field in which each discovery raises the debate to a more sophisticated level of uncertainty. . . . Such discussions have made the field fascinatingly contentious, and they have probably won it more newsprint than it might otherwise have received."

pp. 140-1   "Leakey and Lewin are occasionally somewhat wise after the event. Readers would probably be better served if the authors were more frank about how they (like many of us) have had to change position on a number of important issues in paleoanthropology."

Tattersall, Ian, "Out of Africa Again . . . and Again?" *Scientific American*, vol. 276 (April 1997), pp. 60-67. Tattersall is Chairman of the Anthropology Department, American Museum of Natural History.

p. 60   "Recent discoveries in Kenya of fossils attributed to the new species *Australopithecus anamensis* have now pushed back the record of upright-walking hominids to about 4.2 to 3.9 million years (Myr) ago. More dubious finds in Ethiopia, dubbed *Ardipithecus ramidus*, may extend this to 4.4 Myr ago or so."

p. 60   "Together with their ape-size brains and large, protruding faces, these characteristics have led many to call such creatures 'bipedal chimpanzees.'"

p. 61   "Exactly how many species of early hominids there were, which of them made the tools, and how they walked, remains one of the major conundrums of human evolution."

p. 63   "Thus, Swisher and his colleagues have very recently reported dates for the Ngandong *H. erectus* site in Java that center on only about 40 Kyr ago. These dates, though very carefully obtained, have aroused considerable skepticism; but, if accurate, they have considerable implications for the overall pattern of human evolution. For they are so recent as to suggest that the long-lived *H. erectus* might even have suffered a fate similar to that experienced by the Neanderthals in Europe: extinction at the hands of late-arriving *H. sapiens*."

p. 66   "The first of these models holds that the highly archaic *H. erectus* (including *H. ergaster*) is nothing more than an ancient variant of *H. sapiens* and that for the past two million years the history of our lineage has been one of a braided stream of evolving populations of this species in all areas of the Old World, each adapting to local conditions, yet all consistently linked by gene exchange. The variation we see today among the major geographic populations of humans is, by this reckoning, simply the latest permutation of this lengthy process."

Templeton, Alan R., "Phylogenetic Inference from Restriction Endonuclease Cleavage Site Maps with Particular Reference to the Evolution of Humans and Apes," *Evolution*, vol. 37 (March 1983), pp. 221-244.

p. 221   "Recombinant DNA technology provides evolutionary biologists with another tool for making phylogenetic inference through contrasts of restriction endonuclease site maps or DNA sequences between homologous DNA segments found in different groups."

p. 238   "Hence, for the gorilla-chimp-human portion of the phylogeny, there is a strong rejection of the molecular clock hypothesis."

p. 241   "Recent studies on hominid bipedalism and comparative studies with the other apes support the idea that bipedalism may have preceded the Hominidae and that a knuckle-walker, or even a brachiater, is a very poor model for a hominid ancestor. Therefore, these studies imply . . . that humans did not evolve from knuckle-walking ancestors; rather knuckle-walking is far more likely to have evolved from partial bipedality."

p. 242 "Although previous analyses of these data led to the speculation that ten times more information would be required to resolve the evolutionary relationships between man with chimps and gorillas, this algorithm resolved these relationships at the 5% level of significance. Moreover, the molecular clock hypothesis was rejected at the 1% level."

Tudge, Colin, "Human Origins: A Family Feud," *New Scientist*, vol. 146 (May 20, 1995), pp. 24-28.

p. 24 "All that palaeoanthropologists have to show for more than 100 years of digging are remains from fewer than 2000 of our ancestors. They have used this assortment of jawbones, teeth and fossilized scraps, together with molecular evidence from living species, to piece together a line of human descent going back 5 to 8 million years of time when humans and chimpanzees diverged from a common ancestor."

Zihlman, Adrienne L., "Pygmy Chimps, People and the Pundits," *New Scientist*, vol. 104 (November 15, 1984), pp. 39-40.

p. 39 "It has been said that the reception of any successful new scientific hypothesis goes through three predictable phases before being accepted.

"First, it is criticized for being untrue.

"Secondly, after supporting evidence accumulates, it is stated that it may be true, but it is not particularly relevant.

"Thirdly, after it has clearly influenced the field, it is admitted to be true and relevant, but the same critics assert that the idea was not original."

p. 39 "Except for having small rather than large teeth, and a quadrupedal rather than a bipedal pelvis, pygmy chimpanzees are remarkably like early gracile australopethecines in their skeletal dimensions."

Zihlman, Adrienne L., and Jerold M. Loewenstein, "False Start of the Human Parade," *Natural History*, vol. 88 (August/September 1979), pp. 86-91.

p. 86 "Human nature abhors a vacuum, particularly a genealogical one. There have always been gaps in the fossil record of human evolution but never a shortage of speculative 'missing links.'"

p. 89 "There are still no skulls, no pelvic or limb bones unequivocally associated with the teeth to show whether *Ramapithecus* had a brain like a hominid, swung through trees like an ape, or walked upright like a human."

p. 89 "A famous example of the unexpected is the chalicothere, an animal with teeth and skull like a horse's, but with claws instead of hoofs. For a long time, its teeth and claws were thoughts to be from two different species, until the discovery of an entire skeleton."

p. 89 "The pelvis is probably the most diagnostic bone of the human line. . . . Yet an entire *Ramapithecus*, walking upright, has been 'reconstructed' from only jaws and teeth. . . . The prince's ape latched onto the position by his teeth and has been hanging on ever since, his legitimacy sanctified by millions of textbooks and Time-Life volumes on human evolution."

p. 91   "What, finally, can we say about the position of *Ramapithecus* in primate evolution? One of several kinds of apes that lived during the Miocene, it may have fed in open country, developing jaws and teeth for chewing tough roots and fibers."

p. 91   "The case for *Ramapithecus* as an ancestral human has been weak from the start and has not strengthened with the passage of time. Now that the molecular data are in, the mythical prince's ape, who would be man, has faded until nothing is left but his smile."

Zuckerman, Solly, *Beyond the Ivory Tower* (New York: Taplinger Publishing Company, 1971), 244 pp.

p. 19   ". . . the interpretation of man's fossil history, where to the faithful anything is possible—and where the ardent believer is sometimes able to believe several contradictory things at the same time."

p. 64   ". . . no scientist could logically dispute the proposition that man . . . evolved from some ape-like creature . . . without leaving any fossil traces of the steps of the transformation."

B. The Genus *Homo*

There have been many candidates for ancient ape-like men (as distinct from man-like apes), but no true ape-men or man-apes. Many of former promise are now generally forgotten—Java man, Peking man, Piltdown man, etc. However, these are all generally lumped together with other more recent discoveries under the name *Homo erectus*. Most creationists believe these are simply extinct, somewhat degenerate, tribes of post-Flood men. There also are others accepted even by all evolutionists as true men—Neanderthal man, Cro-Magnon man, etc.

Except for the latter, however, the fossil evidence is still very fragmentary and equivocal, leading to many varied interpretations. All of these have cranial capacities within the range of modern man, and certainly do not prove human evolution from ape-like ancestors. The field of paleoanthropology has also been plagued by hoaxers as well as interpretive blunders. If evolution were really true, this supposedly most recent stage of evolution should be the best documented, but the evidence—such as it is—is almost entirely against these evolutionary assumptions.

Anonymous, "Puzzling out Man's Ascent," *Time* (November 7, 1977), pp. 64-78.

p. 77   "Still, doubts about the sequence of man's emergence remain. Scientists concede that even their most cherished theories are based on embarrassingly few fossil fragments, and that huge gaps exist in the fossil record. Anthropologists, ruefully says Alan Mann of the University of Pennsylvania, 'are like the blind men looking at the elephant, each sampling only a small part of the total reality.' His colleagues agree that the picture of man's origin is far from complete."

Anonymous, "Age of the Oldest European Doesn't Add Up," *New Scientist*, vol. 91 (August 13, 1981), p. 405.

p. 405   "Controversy continues over the age of the remarkably complete Petralona skull, whose discovery in a Greek cave in 1960 was reenacted in the BBC television series *The Making of Mankind*. . . .

"The Greek archaeologist Aris N. Poulianos, who has excavated at the cave since 1968, . . . firmly believes that the hominid, which he calls *Archanthropus europaeus petraloniensis*, 'died more than 700,000 years ago' and is the 'most ancient European yet known.'"

p. 405   "The dating of the skull and its classification have been contentious for several reasons. The calcite-embedded cranium was never photographed before its removal and there is considerable uncertainty about the sequence of sedimentary events in the cave. Then, anatomically, the skull presents a confusing mixture of primitive and modern features, some characteristic of *Homo erectus* and some that could be ascribed to early *Homo sapiens*."

Anonymous, "Evolution Revolution," *Science News*, vol. 109 (March 13, 1976), p. 164.

p. 164   "*Homo erectus* has generally been dated about 500,000 to 700,000 years old. Now this species will have to be dated at more than twice that age. Richard E. Leakey announced this week the discovery of a complete *Homo erectus* skull that has been reliably dated at 1.5 to 1.8 million years."

p. 164   "'This is a very, very exciting development for us,' says Leakey, 'particularly because it is uncontroversially *Homo* and it is from deposits that have also yielded uncontroversial evidence of *Australopithecus*.'"

p. 164   "Another piece of evidence suggesting that a true *Homo* existed almost 3 million years ago was also found. . . . It is an almost complete right pelvic bone that shows modern characteristics and comes from deposits that are older than 2 million years."

p. 164   "From a collection of more than 30 hand bones, for instance, a composite hand has been formed, 'Our preliminary observations,' says Johanson, 'suggest to us that there is nothing in the anatomy or morphology of the bones which would preclude the kinds of movements that we are capable of with our own hands today.'"

Anonymous, "The Shrinking Tooth," *Science News*, vol. 108 (December 13, 1975), p. 375.

"It has long been suspected that as human populations grew in technological elaboration they shrank in tooth dimension. . . . C. Loring Brace of Michigan University has applied the theory to populations in Australia and found that it holds true, with the largest teeth being those of Australian aborigines. Differential reduction of chewing surface gradually led to the varying facial forms of living populations."

Anonymous, "Last Adam," *Scientific American*, vol. 227 (October 1972), p. 48.

"Skulls that were buried a scant 10,000 years ago now suggest that at a time when elsewhere in the Old World the successor species *Homo sapiens* was turning from hunting and gathering to agriculture, some *Homo erectus* genes lingered on in Australia."

Anonymous, "Explorers Find Skeleton Dating 400,000 years," *Chicago Tribune* (June 6, 1976).

    <u>"Salonica, Greece (Reuters)</u> Anthropologists have discovered the skeleton of a young man believed to date back 400,000 years—the oldest human remains ever found in Europe.

    "The skeleton was found preserved in a stalagmite during an exploration of the Petralona Cave in the Chalkidiki Peninsula in southern Greece, said Dr. Aris Poulianos, President of the Greek Anthropological Society, Friday.

    "The discovery proves that the cave, which also contained primitive tools and cooked food, was inhabited by ape-age men who made intelligent use of fire. 'We discovered the cooked meat of rhinoceros, bear and deer, which proves men who lived in the cave made logical use of fire,' Poulianos said.

    "There are no plans at present to extract the skeleton from the stalagmite.

    "The cave was discovered in 1952."

Anonymous, "Calaveras Man," in *Handbook of American Indians*, bulletin 30, part I (Bureau of American Ethnology, Smithsonian Institute, September 1912).

p. 188   "The evidences of great antiquity, in many cases apparently almost conclusive, were accepted as satisfactory by J. D. Whitney, formerly state geologist of California; but the lack of expert observation or of actual record of the various finds reported makes extreme caution advisable, especially since the acceptance of the evidence necessitates conclusions widely at variance with the usual conception of the history of man, not only in America but throughout the world. The need of conservatism in dealing with this evidence is further emphasized by the fact that the human crania of the auriferous gravels are practically identical with the crania of the present California Indians, and it is also observed that the artifacts—the mortars and pestles, the implements and ornaments—found in the same connection correspond closely with those of the historic inhabitants of the Pacific slope. . . . But few are ready to accept the conclusion, made necessary if the California testimony is fully sustained, that man had then reached the stage of culture characterized by the use of implements and ornaments of polished stone. . . . Notwithstanding the well-fortified statements of early writers to the effect that this relic came from the gravels of Bald Mtn. at a depth of about 130 feet, there are good reasons for suspecting that it may have been derived from one of the limestone caves so numerous in the Calaveras region."

Anonymous, "Neandertal Noisemaker," *Science News*, vol. 150 (November 23, 1996), p. 328.

p. 328   "Amid stone implements typical of European Neandertals excavated last year in a Slovenian cave, researchers found a piece of a juvenile bear's thighbone that contains four artificial holes and resembles a flute."

p. 328   "'This bone could have been used to make noise or, possibly, music,' contends geologist Bonnie Blackwell of the City University of New York's Queens College in Flushing, N.Y. 'It would not surprise me if this was a Neandertal's musical instrument.'"

p. 328   "The Slovenian bone closely resembles several hole-bearing bones that were likely to have been used as musical instruments by humans at later European sites, according to archaeologist Randall K. White of New York University. White hopes to construct a model of the Divje Babe I bone artifact in order to explore the range of sounds that could have been produced by blowing into it.

"'Neandertals were apparently quite similar to *Homo sapiens* in their behavior and cognitive capacities,' Blackwell asserts. 'In both groups, musical traditions probably extend back very far into prehistory.'"

Anonymous, "Living Human Fossils in Outer Mongolia?" *New Scientist*, vol. 93 (March 25, 1982), p. 778.

p. 778   "Is Neanderthal man alive and living in Outer Mongolia? Myra Shackley tentatively posed this question in 1980 in her semipopular book *Neanderthal Man* (Duckworth). Probably to the surprise of many (but not all) archaeologists, she repeats it in the latest issue of the much-respected archaeology journal *Antiquity* (vol. LVI p 31)."

p. 778   "The sightings of 'wild men' with the physical appearance of Neanderthals together with the tool finds represent to Myra Shackley 'an impressive body of material which it is difficult to disregard.'"

Arnold, Dean, "Who Was Adam?" *Pascal Center Notebook*, vol. 2 (Spring 1992), pp. 2-6. Arnold is Professor of Anthropology at Wheaton College.

p. 2   "Who was Adam? Can we place Adam, as identified by the Bible, within any era of human pre-history, as identified by anthropology? That is the question I want to explore with you."

p. 3   "To answer that question, we must first ask, 'Who are humans?' If Adam was the first human, what was there about him that distinguished him from the rest of creation?"

p. 4   "Where does the biblical account of Adam fit into this outline of hominid pre-history? Can any of these forms be identified as the beginning of the human race? Based purely on biological factors, this is a difficult question to answer."

p. 5   "Who then, was Adam? Where does he fit in the schema derived from anthropology? Was he an *Australopithecus*? Early *Homo*? *Homo erectus*? Neanderthal? The first anatomically modern human? Or the first farmer?"

Birdsell, J. B., *Human Evolution* (Chicago: Rand McNally, 1975), 546 pp.

p. 294   "Once thought to represent a giant stage in the evolution of man, a gigantic fragmentary mandible from the Djetis bed, *Meganthropus*, can be matched in the lower jaw of the more robust australopithecines in Africa."

p. 294   "Virtually all of the pithecanthropine relics from these (Trinil) beds have been washed out and found by native collectors. Not only is their original location in the beds uncertain, but there is a possibility that they reached the Trinil beds by being redeposited from earlier ones."

p. 294   "Most of the Trinil crania have lost their basal portions in such a fashion as to suggest that they were murdered, and then their brains eaten."

p. 295   "In the last two years an absolute date has been obtained for (the Ngandong beds, above the Trinil beds), and it has the very interesting value of 300,000 years plus or minus 300,000 years."

Bower, Bruce, "A Walk Back through Evolution," *Science News*, vol. 135 (April 22, 1989), p. 251.

p. 251   "Three hominids made some remarkable impressions 3.5 million years ago. They walked across damp volcanic ash that later hardened and preserved their footprints at the Tanzanian site of Laetoli."

p. 251   "But the first detailed study of the gaits and footprints of modern people who walk barefooted indicates the Laetoli prints are much like those of *Homo sapiens* and were probably not produced by Lucy's relatives, reports Russell H. Tuttle of the University of Chicago."

p. 251   "The few toe bones found at Hadar curve downward in an ape-like manner. Hominids with curved toes could not have made the Laetoli footprints, he maintains."

Bower, Bruce, "Neandertals' Disappearing Act," *Science News*, vol. 139 (June 8, 1991), pp. 360-363.

p. 360   "In fact, these scientists contended, modern humans apparently evolved simultaneously in several parts of the world beginning as many as 1 million years ago."

p. 361   "Both Neandertals and early modern humans buried their dead, left behind similar types of tools and engaged in comparable animal-butchery practices, showing striking cultural parallels for different hominid species."

p. 361   "For the time being, 'you can classify an individual fossil in the Israeli caves any way you want,' he notes."

p. 361   "For instance, 10,000-year-old stone hand axes made by modern humans in Baja Mexico look virtually identical to 250,000-year-old stone hand axes produced in Africa by a direct human ancestor, *H. erectus*, yet no one lumps the two groups into one species."

Bower, Bruce, "Human Origins Recede in Australia," *Science News*, vol. 150 (September 28, 1996), p. 196.

p. 196   "Humans may have traveled over water from Southeast Asia to Australia when an ice age lowered sea levels and narrowed the gap between those land masses, prior to 135,000 years ago, asserts archaeologist Richard L. K. Fullagar of the Australian Museum in Sydney and his colleagues."

p. 196   "Those who argue that *H. sapiens* arose independently in several parts of the world over at least the past 2 million years welcome the new evidence."

p. 196   "Australian fossil evidence suggests that the region's earliest inhabitants resembled archaic *H. sapiens* in Indonesia, whose fossils date to at least 100,000 years ago, Wolpoff holds. Combined with Fullagar's results, he proposes, this indicates that art, language, and other cognitive achievements usually attributed only to modern humans could have emerged in geographically dispersed groups, each with distinctive skeletal variations on an *H. sapiens* theme."

Bower, Bruce, "*Homo erectus* Shows Staying Power in Java," *Science News*, vol. 150 (December 14, 1996), p. 373.

> "*H. erectus*, now estimated to have inhabited the Indonesian island of Java until sometime between 27,000 and 53,000 years ago, died out as *H. sapiens* more successfully exploited local Stone Age environments, assert Carl C. Swisher III of Berkeley (Calif.) Geochronology Center and his colleagues. Many researchers have argued that a similar scenario played out in Europe and the Middle East, where Neandertals lived at the same time as *H. sapiens* before going extinct around 35,000 years ago.

> "'It looks like independent [*H*] *erectus* and [*H*] *sapiens* lineages evolved in Southeast Asia,' holds study participant Susan C. Antón, an anthropologist at the University of Florida in Gainesville. 'It wouldn't have taken a huge technological or intellectual advantage for one species to have replaced another over a number of generations.'"

Bunney, Sarah, "The Puzzle of Indo-European Origins," review of *Archaeology & Language*, by Colin Renfrew (Jonathan Cape, 346 pp.), *New Scientist*, vol. 117 (January 28, 1988), pp. 64-65.

p. 64   "So, what is unusual about the book? Basically it is Renfrew's attack on a major school of thought that places the origin of the Indo-European languages, and thus modern European peoples, in the south Russian steppes in the forth millennium."

pp. 64-65   "To Renfrew, the spread of Indo-European languages was altogether more peaceful and more gradual than past theories have suggested, and began in the Neolithic rather than in the later Bronze Age.

> "The solution to the Indo-European puzzle, he suggests, lies in Anatolia in Turkey. Here, around 7000 BC, he surmises that early farmers, with a mixed economy based on a few domesticated plants and animals, spoke a prototype Indo-European language."

Bunney, Sarah, "Neanderthals Weren't So Dumb After All," *New Scientist*, vol. 123 (July 1, 1989), p. 43.

p. 43   "Paleontologists in Israel have discovered a fossil bone which shows that Neanderthals may have been just as capable of speech as modern humans. The bone, known as the hyoid, is from a Neanderthal who lived between 50,000 and 60,000 years ago. The hyoid, a small U-shaped bone, is a key part of the vocal apparatus in modern human beings."

p. 43   "According to B. Arensberg and Yoel Rak of Tel Aviv University and their colleagues, the fossil hyoid, in size and shape, is just like a modern human's. The positions of the muscle attachments are also similar. The researchers believe that, despite their heavy jawbones, Neanderthals spoke a language."

Falk, Dean, "The Petrified Brain," *Natural History*, vol. 93 (September 1984), pp. 36-39. Falk is at the Caribbean Primate Research Center, University of Puerto Rico.

p. 36   "Since the outside portion of the brain, known as the cerebral cortex, is responsible for higher thought processes, I believe that the evidence from endocasts should be given special weight in assessing the evolutionary relationships of hominids."

p. 36   "In any case, brain size varies considerably in modern humans without appearing to affect intelligence. For example, there is a record of an apparently normal human adult with a cranial capacity of 790 cc."

p. 38   "I expected the australopithecine natural endocasts to appear like miniature replicas of human brains because that had been the prevalent view in the scientific literature since 1925.

               ". . . My analysis of the seven known australopithecine endocasts shows Radinsky's hunch was right: all of the convolutions that they preserve were apelike."

p. 38   "An endocast from the Kenya National Museums, a *Homo habilis* specimen known as ER 1470, reproduces a humanlike frontal lobe, including what appears to be Broca's area. . . . ER 1470's capacity has been estimated at more than 750 cc."

p. 39   "Apes occasionally . . . hunt, make tools, and fight, but they never engage in spoken language as we know it. . . . If we wish to identify one prime mover of human brain evolution, the endocast from ER 1470 (*Homo habilis*), with its humanlike frontal lobes that contain what appears to be Broca's speech area in the left hemisphere, confirms what is suggested by comparing the behavior of apes and humans: it is language. Human technology and social achievements required conscious thought, which is, and probably was, dependent on language. In other words, until they acquired language, our early ancestors may not have been truly human."

Gibbons, Ann, "*Homo erectus* in Java: A 250,000 Year Anachronism," *Science*, vol. 274 (December 13, 1996), pp. 1841-1842.

p. 1841   "The story of human evolution has lately become as complicated as a Tolstoy novel."

p. 1841   "But lately, this tale has become thick with new subplots and characters. The recent recognition of several different species of early *Homo* living in Africa about 2 million years ago, and various forms of *Australopithecus* before that, has made it clear that there were far more lineages in the early history of the human family than previously believed. Now, it seems that later chapters may also have to be rewritten to include at least one more character: a relative who makes a surprise reappearance long after it was presumed dead.

               ". . . an interdisciplinary team of scientists suggests that one relative, *H. erectus*, was still alive in Java, Indonesia, as recently as 27,000 to 53,000 years ago—at least 250,000 years after it was thought to have gone extinct in

Asia. If so, this remnant population of *H. erectus*, a species that first appeared in the fossil record about 2 million years ago, would have been alive when modern humans and Neandertals roamed the earth."

Gibbons, Ann, "Neandertal Language Debate: Tongues Wag Anew," *Science*, vol. 256 (April 3, 1992), pp. 33-34.

p. 33   "In February, at the annual meeting of the American Association for the Advancement of Science, University of Kansas paleoanthropologist David Frayer presented a survey of accumulating data, including the discovery of the hyoid bone and a new reconstruction of an old Neandertal skull, in launching a new attack on the idea that Neandertals couldn't speak. 'It is now time to reject the notion,' Frayer said boldly, 'that Neandertals lacked the capacity for modern speech.'"

p. 33   "But in 1989 a Neandertal hyoid (throat) bone was found in Kebara cave near Mount Carmel in Israel in an excavation directed by Baruch Arensburg of Tel Aviv University. When the Arensburg group published their results in *Nature* in 1990, they argued that the hyoid was virtually indistinguishable from those of modern humans in size and shape. Neandertals 'appear to be an anatomically capable of speech as modern humans,' the authors wrote."

p. 34   "In the end, this controversy underscores a central problem in paleoanthropology: how difficult it is to reconstruct behavior (including linguistic behavior) from the remains in the fossil record."

Gribbin, John, and Jeremy Cherfas, "Descent of Man—or Ascent of Ape?" *New Scientist*, vol. 91 (September 3, 1981), pp. 592-595.

p. 592   "So the anatomical similarities of man and apes could have come about because they share a common ancestor, or they could be the result of so-called parallel evolution. The problem, for the paleontologists, is that they lack the evidence to decide."

p. 594   "To translate our suggestion in to that form of speech, we think that the chimp is descended from man, that the common ancestor of the two was much more man-like than ape-like."

p. 594   "Certainly we would not want to defend it to the death, but the very fact that it is entirely within the confines of the evidence that we have points up the frailty of the conventional history of man and the apes."

p. 595   "We do not say dogmatically that the modern chimpanzee and gorilla are the descendants of the two *Australopithecus* lines; we do suggest that this possibility resolves so many aspects of the evolutionary puzzle that it should at least be taken seriously and not dismissed out of hand by the experts."

Ivanhoe, Francis, "Neanderthals had Rickets," *Science Digest*, vol. 69 (February 1971), pp. 35-36.

p. 35   "Neanderthal man may have looked like he did not because he was closely related to the great apes, but because he had rickets, an article in the British publication *Nature* suggests."

p. 35   "The diet of Neanderthal man was definitely lacking in Vitamin D during the 35,000 years he spent on earth."

Jones, J. S., "A Thousand and One Eves," review of *The Search for Eve*, by Michael H. Brown (Harper & Row, 1990, 357 pp.), *Nature*, vol. 345 (May 31, 1990), pp. 395-396.

p. 395   "Palaeoanthropologists seem to make up for a lack of fossils with an excess of fury, and this must now be the only science in which it is still possible to become famous just by having an opinion. As one cynic says, in human palaeontology the consensus depends on who shouts loudest."

p. 395   "But although genetics can tell us a lot about the patterns of relatedness of living populations, it can do little more than speculate about the time and place when they split. What comes out of a genetic model often depends on what assumptions go in: to take an unusually rigorous view of molecular evolution— that of the creationist Duane Gish—the fact that man and watermelon are both 97 per cent water does not necessarily mean that they have a recent ancestor in common."

Kappelman, John, "They Might be Giants," *Nature*, vol. 387 (May 8, 1997), pp. 126-127. Kappelman is with the Department of Anthropology, University of Texas, Austin.

p. 126   "Body mass then seems to have increased through time, with late archaic *Homo sapiens*—dating from just 75,000-36,000 yr BP and often collectively called 'Neanderthals'—being about 30% larger than the living worldwide human average (or about 24% larger than living high-latitude humans). But modern humans (dating in this study from 90,000 yr to the present, and overlapping in time with archaic *Homo sapiens*) show a decrease in body mass."

p. 126   "Other data show that archaic *Homo* had a more strongly constructed skeleton than all but the very earliest modern humans, and the pronounced muscle markings on the bones are believed to indicate great strength."

Kaufman, Leslie, "Did a Third Human Species Live Among Us?" *Newsweek* (December 23, 1996), p. 52.

p. 52   "A geologist at the Berkeley Geochronology Center, [Carl] Swisher uses the most advanced techniques to date human fossils. Last spring he was re-evaluating *Homo erectus* skulls found in Java in the 1930s by testing the sediment found with them. A hominid species assumed to be an ancestor of *Homo sapiens*, erectus was thought to have vanished some 250,000 years ago. But even though he used two different dating methods, Swisher kept making the same startling find: the bones were 53,000 years old at most and possibly no more than 27,000 years— a stretch of time contemporaneous with modern humans."

p. 52   "Our species, *Homo sapiens*, is thought to have evolved about 200,000 years ago. It's already known that it walked the Earth at the same time as its heavy-browed cousins, the Neanderthals, who became extinct about 30,000 years ago. Now Swisher's find implies that all three hominid species were contemporaneous. Says Swisher: 'It looks like today is unique in that there is only one single species of humans.'"

Morgan, Elaine, *The Scars of Evolution* (New York: Oxford University Press, 1994), 196 pp.

p. 3   "The essential point is that evolution takes place in response to things which *have happened*, not things which are predestined to happen. Man is no more an evolutionary pinnacle than a tree is, or a termite or an octopus. His emergence was no more inevitable than that of any other species."

p. 5   "Four of the most outstanding mysteries about humans are: (1) why do they walk on two legs? (2) why have they lost their fur? (3) why have they developed such large brains? (4) why did they learn to speak?

"The orthodox answers to these questions are? (1) 'We do not yet know'; (2) 'We do not yet know'; (3) 'We do not yet know'; (4) 'We do not yet know'. The list of questions could be considerably lengthened without affecting the monotony of the answers."

p. 6   "In short, the chief mystery does not lie in any one of these anomalies, not even the wonderful brain or the dexterous hands or the miracle of speech. It lies in the sheer number and variety of the ways in which we differ from our closest relatives in the animal kingdom."

p. 22-23   "The story of the bones tells us much about the origins of man and it also tells us a few things about scientists. With few exceptions, when confronted with a maverick idea, they are confident they can identify whether or not it is preposterous by the gut instinct they have about it. Most of them feel that this absolves them of any obligation to examine it in detail or to give their reasons for rejecting it."

Pilbeam, David R., "Evolutionary Anthropology," review of *The Brain in Hominid Evolution*, by Phillip V. Tobias (New York: Columbia University Press, 1971, 170 pp.), *Science*, vol. 175 (March 10, 1972), p. 1101. Pilbeam is in the Department of Anthropology, Yale.

p. 1101   "Tobias emphasizes that paleoanthropologists concentrate on brain size only because that is all they can measure. In fact, increasing brain volume of itself tells us little, since it merely reflects changes in internal brain organization at a variety of levels."

p. 1101   "There is more to human cultural behavior than the ability simply to learn, or to chip flint. Our behavior differs from the learned behavior of all other animals, including chimpanzees, in such important ways as to render descriptions of nonhuman primate learned behavior as examples of 'crude and primitive culture' potentially highly misleading."

Rensberger, Boyce, "Human Fossil is Unearthed," *Washington Post*, October 19, 1984, pp. A1, A11.

p. A1   "The most complete skeleton of an early human ancestor ever found has been dug up in Kenya. The bones are those of a surprisingly tall 12-year-old boy of the *Homo erectus* species who died about 1.6 million years ago."

p. A1   "The new find reveals that these ancient people had bodies virtually indistinguishable from our own. . . . The skeleton showed that the boy stood 5 feet 6 inches, taller than many of today's 12-year olds."

p. A11   "From the neck down, the bones are remarkably modern in shape. . . .

"The skull and jawbone, by contrast, are more primitive in appearance. . . . The brain size of the new specimen has not been measured, but [Alan] Walker estimated it between 700 and 800 cms."

p. A11   "'When I put the mandible onto the skull,' Walker recalled, 'Richard [Leakey] and I both laughed because it looked so much like a Neanderthal.'

"The age of the skeleton at death was estimated on the basis of its teeth. It had the combination of baby teeth and permanent teeth appropriate to a 12-year-old of today. Its antiquity was determined from its location, sandwiched between layers of volcanic ash that can be dated by measuring the products of radioactive decay."

Shipman, Pat, "On the Trail of the Piltdown Fraudsters," *New Scientist*, vol. 128 (October 6, 1990), pp. 52-54.

p. 52   "[Frank] Spencer's cogent, fairminded, thorough and perceptive review of the evidence is presented in two companion volumes, *Piltdown: A Scientific Forgery* and *the Piltdown Papers 1908-1955*, just published by the Natural History Museum in London and Oxford University Press.

"The Piltdown fossils, whose discovery was first announced in 1912, fooled many of the greatest minds in palaeoanthropology until 1953, when the remains were revealed as planted, altered,—a forgery."

p. 52   "New evidence has come to light that the hoax was a plot carried out by Sir Arthur Keith, one of the most eminent anatomists of the early 20th century, and Charles Dawson, the amateur antiquarian who found the remains."

Tattersall, Ian, "Out of Africa Again . . . and Again?" *Scientific American*, vol. 276 (April 1997), pp. 60-67. Tattersall is Chairman of the Anthropology Department, American Museum of Natural History.

p. 67   "Most important, the new dates from eastern Asia show that human population mobility dates right back to the very origins of effectively modern bodily form."

p. 67   "As ever, though, new evidence of the remote human past has served principally to underline the complexity of events in our evolution."

Thomson, Keith Stewart, "Piltdown Man: The Great English Mystery Story," *American Scientist*, vol. 79 (May/June 1991), pp. 194-201.

p. 194   "The Piltdown man forgery of 1912 was one of the most successful and wicked of all scientific frauds. Although the discovery of the supposedly primitive British 'dawn man'—scientifically christened *Eoanthropus dawsoni*—was announced almost 80 years ago, the forgery continues to attract attention because it has never been satisfactorily resolved."

p. 200   "I believe the most plausible answer to all this has been sitting around for about 10 years—unappreciated perhaps because everyone else has been pursuing their own pet theories. Back in 1980, Leonard Harrison Matthews devised a devilishly ingenious scheme that explains nearly all of the anomalies and motives. Matthews scheme can be modified and woven into an account of the whole affair, making the perfect English crime.

"Once the extent to which he carefully prepared his story is appreciated, Dawson has to be seen as the sole instigator of the fraud."

p. 201   "While we can only deplore Dawson's wicked forgery, it has to be admitted that it would not have succeeded without the headlong acceptance of shoddy evidence by scientists who should have known better. As the W. C. Fields movie observes: 'You can't cheat an honest man.' Perhaps Dawson had the last laugh after all."

Tuttle, Russell H., "The Pitted Pattern of Laetoli Feet," *Natural History*, vol. 99 (March 1990), pp. 61-65.

p. 61   "The first bipedal trail, consisting of five footprints in sequence, was discovered in 1977 at Laetoli site A. In a preliminary report, Mary Leakey noted that these prints, although short and very broad, appeared to be hominid."

p. 61   "The contrast between these prints and the more distinctly human-shaped footprints from Laetoli site G, which were uncovered in 1978 and 1979, prompted me to question the initial interpretation. The two sites are only a mile apart and are virtually contemporaneous."

p. 62   "In brief, a small bear walking bipedally (a cub looking for mama bear?) could have produced the Laetoli A trail."

p. 63   "In preliminary reports by several paleoanthropologists, the trail at site G were portrayed as remarkably human. Yet they were presumed to have been created by *Australopithecus afarensis*, the same species as the 3-million-year-old skeletons of Lucy and other individuals discovered considerably to the north at Hadar, Ethiopia. My problem in accepting this was that the Hadar beasts had apelike features (notably, down-curved toes) that I just didn't detect in the G prints."

p. 63   "The humanness of the plantar (sole) anatomy exhibited by the G prints is underscored by observing the feet and footprints of habitually barefoot people. . . . The footprints of both the Machiguenga and the Laetoli G bipeds exhibit strong heel, ball, and first toe impressions and a well-developed medial longitudinal arch, which is the hallmark of human feet."

p. 64   "In sum, the 3.5-million-year-old footprint trails at Laetoli site G resemble those of habitually unshod modern humans. None of their features suggest that the Laetoli hominids were less capable bipeds than we are. If the G footprints were not known to be so old, we would readily conclude that they were made by a member of our genus, *Homo*. . . . In any case, we should shelve the loose assumption that the Laetoli footprints were made by Lucy's kind, *Australopithecus afarensis*. The Laetoli footprints hint that at least one other hominid roamed Africa at about the same time."

Watson, Lyall, "The Water People," *Science Digest*, vol. 90 (May 1982), p. 44.

p. 44   "The fossils that decorate our family tree are so scarce that there are still more scientists than specimens. The remarkable fact is that all the physical evidence we have for human evolution can still be placed, with room to spare, inside a single coffin.

"Not surprisingly, despite the diligent research done in East Africa by paleontologists Richard Leakey and Donald Johanson, there are gaping holes in the evolutionary record, some of them extending for 4 to 6 million years. Modern apes, for instance, seem to have sprung out of nowhere. They have no yesterday, no fossil record. And the true origin of modern humans—of upright, naked, toolmaking, big-brained beings—is, if we are to be honest with ourselves, an equally mysterious matter."

White, Tim, F. H. Busse, and K. E. Heikes, "Evolutionary Implications of Pliocene Hominid Footprints," *Science*, vol. 208 (April 11, 1980), pp. 175-176.

p. 175   "Vertebrate fossils and tracks from the Laetoli Beds are radiometrically dated to between 3.6 and 3.8 million years."

p. 175   "Excavations at site G in 1978 and 1979 revealed trails of at least two hominid individuals. . . . The uneroded footprints show a total morphological pattern like that seen in modern humans. . . Spatial relationships of the footprints are strikingly human in pattern. . . . The Laetoli hominid trails at site G do not differ substantially from modern human trails made on a similar substrate."

Wolpoff, Milford, and Alan Thorne, "The Case Against Eve," *New Scientist*, vol. 130 (June 22, 1991), pp. 37-41.

p. 37   "What made the Eve theory revolutionary was not so much the idea of a single place of origin, but that modern humans (wherever they evolved) replaced, rather than mixed with, indigenous archaic humans."

p. 38   "The Eve theory makes a number of predictions, which biologists can test by consulting the fossil record. According to the theory, Eve must have lived in Africa at the beginning of the Upper Pleistocene, between 100,000 and 200,000 years ago."

p. 38   "Crucially, there should be no continuity over time in the anatomical characteristics of humans living in any one region. By stark contrast, if modern people evolved locally in many different places, then each population ought to resemble its own antecedents. In this case regional continuity in the features of human fossils should be the norm."

p. 39   "In conflict with the Eve theory, our measurements show that modern Chinese, Australasians and Europeans each resemble their local predecessors much more than they resemble archaic Africans. But that is not all. In each region of the world, we have uncovered links that tie living populations to their own local antecedents, whose remains are preserved in the fossil record for the area."

p. 41   "So, if not in Africa, where did we originate? The fossils point to several places rather than just one. The era of the modern human began with a smooth transition rather than an abrupt invasion. Humans may be unique, but the signs are that we are not a new species."

C. Origin of Civilization

Once within the realm of real human history, rather than evolutionary speculation, the archaeological, linguistic and demographic evidence is quite consistent with the Biblical accounts of ancient history. It is certainly strange, if evolution is true, that modern man has been evolving within the past million years or so (the so-called Old Stone Age, or Paleolithic period) whereas records of true civilization—including written records—only date within the past few thousand years.

Albright, William F., *Recent Discoveries in Bible Lands* (appended to Young's *Analytical Concordance to the Bible* (New York: Funk and Wagnalls, 1955), pp. 5-51. Dr. Albright, at Johns Hopkins, was probably the greatest of all modern archaeologists.

p. 5　　　"When Adam Clarke published his famous *Commentary on the Holy Scriptures* (1810-26) in which he gathered together all available material for the elucidation of the Bible, nothing whatever was known about the world in which the Bible arose except what could be extracted from extant Greek and Latin authors. . . . Since most of the fragmentary data on the ancient Orient in classical sources was erroneous, the picture then drawn of it was not only very dim and full of great blank spaces, the vague outlines of it were so badly distorted as to be almost unrecognizable to us today. From the chaos of prehistory, the Bible projected as though it were a monstrous fossil, with no contemporary evidence to demonstrate its authenticity and its origin in a human world like ours."

p. 30　　　[Regarding Genesis 10] "It stands absolutely alone in ancient literature, without a remote parallel, even among the Greeks, where we find the closest approach to a distribution of peoples in genealogical framework. . . .

　　　". . . The Table of Nations remains an astonishingly accurate document."

p. 51　　　"Of first importance is the fact that the history and culture of Israel now form part of the organic continuity of Western civilization, which originated in the ancient Orient, spread westward in the Mediterranean basin, and then flowered in Europe. No philosopher of history can henceforth disassociate the Bible from the historical evolution of our own race and culture. There are innumerable points of contact between the details of Hebrew history, life, and literature, and the world around it."

p. 51　　　"As research and discovery continue [the Bible] will become greater and greater in the widening perspective which they will give to our children."

Anonymous, "Neanderthal Man, Victim of Malnutrition," *Prevention* (October 1971), pp. 115-121.

pp. 116-7　　　"Now at long last, thanks to the investigations of Dr. Francis Ivanhoe of London, who published his findings in the August 8, 1970, issue of *Nature*, the Neanderthal puzzle may have been solved. His review of the currently available anthropological and medical evidence shows that Neanderthal man was evidently the victim of his decision to move too far north at the wrong time, the onset of a glacial age. In doing so, contends Dr. Ivanhoe, he lost sufficient contact with the ultra-violet rays of the sun and because his diet did not provide the missing nutrient, he contracted rickets, the vitamin D deficiency disease, which was to deform him for thousands of years to follow."

p. 117   "He had a brain with a capacity sometimes larger than that of modern man. He was a talented toolmaker and successful hunter, even dabbled in art and most importantly from a cultural standpoint, developed a rudimentary social and religious consciousness."

Anonymous, "Use of Symbols Antedates Neanderthal Man," *Science Digest*, vol. 73 (March 1973), pp. 22-23.

p. 22   "Communication with inscribed symbols may go back as far as 135,000 years in man's history, antedating the 50,000-year-old Neanderthal man.

                "Alexander Marshack of Harvard's Peabody Museum made this pronouncement recently after extensive microscopic analysis of a 135,000-year-old ox rib covered with symbolic engravings."

p. 22   "The results of his findings are that it is a sample of 'pre-writing,' that there is a distinct similarity in cognitive style between it and those 75,000 years later, and, according to Mr. Marshack, 'it establishes a tradition of carving that stretches over thousands of years.'"

pp. 22-3   "The implication of such a tradition is that there had to be some form of language and social continuity to carry on the tradition of carving. This bone, Marshack feels, is an indirect indicator that Neanderthal man must have talked and could well have communicated in a reasonably sophisticated manner."

Bower, Bruce, "Early Culture Found in New Guinea," *Science News*, vol. 130 (December 13, 1986), p. 374.

                "Investigators have uncovered evidence of the earliest known human occupation of the island of New Guinea, at least 40,000 years ago. This provides the first archaeological support for the suggestion that New Guinea was inhabited at an early stage in the settlement of Australia by people from Indonesia and Indochina; at the time, New Guinea and Australia were connected by a land bridge.

                "Anthropologist Les Groube of the University of Papua new Guinea in Port Moresby and his colleagues uncovered more than 100 'waisted' stone axes at the north coast site. These axes are notched on both sides, giving the appearance of a waist, and are similar to tools found at Australian sites dated at 35,000 to 40,000 years old."

Brower, Bruce, "Talking Back in Time," *Science News*, vol. 145 (June 11, 1994), pp. 376-377.

p. 376   "Johanna Nichols, a linguist at the University of California Berkeley . . . presented evidence that the common ancestor of the world's modern languages arose at least 1,000,000 years ago, suggesting ancient roots of premodern types of vocal communication. She obtained this estimate by calculating the time necessary to achieve current world-wide linguistic diversity."

p. 376   "Until now, comparative linguistics revolved around studying corresponding use of sounds in a few languages at a time. This approach traces language roots back some 8,000 years at most."

p. 377   "Remarks Leslie C. Aiello of University College, London: 'The problem of linguistic and cognitive evolution in the later hominids is far from solved.'"

Chomsky, Noam, *Language and Mind* (New York: Harcourt Brace Jovanovich, Inc., 1972). Chomsky is Professor of Linguistics, MIT, said by Dr. John Oller, Chairman of Linguistics, New Mexico University, to be the "world's foremost linguist."

p. 67   "Human language appears to be a unique phenomenon, without significant analogue in the animal world."

p. 68   "There is no reason to suppose that the 'gaps' are bridgeable. There is no more of a basis for assuming an evolutionary development of 'higher' from 'lower' stages, in this case, than there is for assuming an evolutionary development from breathing to walking."

Coale, Ansley J., "The History of the Human Population," *Scientific American*, vol. 231 (September 1974), pp. 41-51. Coale was Director, Office of Population Research, Princeton.

p. 41   "Any numerical description of the development of the human population cannot avoid conjecture, simply because there has never been a census of all the people in the world."

p. 41   "A conspicuous source of uncertainty in the population of the world today is the poorly known size of the population of China, where the most recent enumeration was made in 1953 and was of untested accuracy."

p. 41   "The earliest date for which the global population can be calculated with an uncertainty of only, say, 20 percent is the middle of the 18th century. The next-earliest time for which useful data are available is the beginning of the Christian era, when Rome collected information bearing on the number of people in various parts of the empire. . . .

"For still earlier periods the population must be estimated indirectly from calculations of the number of people who could subsist under the social and technological institutions presumed to prevail at the time. Anthropologists and historians have estimated, for example, that before the introduction of agriculture the world could have supported a hunting-and-gathering culture of between five and 10 million people."

p. 43   "Thus whatever the size of the initial human population, the rate of growth during man's first 990,000 years (about 99 percent of his history) was exceedingly small. Even if one assumed that in the beginning the population was two—Adam and Eve—the annual rate of increase during this first long interval was only about 15 additional persons per million of population.

". . . The eight million of 8000 B.C. became by A.D. 1 about 300 million (the midpoint of a range of informed guesses of about 200 million to 400 million).

". . . From A.D. 1 to 1750 the population increased by about 500 million to some 800 million (the median of a range estimated by John D. Durand of the University of Pennsylvania)."

p. 43   "Even if we again assume that humanity began with a hypothetical Adam and Eve, the population has doubled only 31 times, or an average of about once every 30,000 years."

Cole, Glen, "Of Land Bridges, Ice-Free Corridors, and Early Man in the Americas," *Bulletin, Field Museum of Natural History*, vol. 50 (January 1979), pp. 15-21. Cole is Curator of Prehistory.

p. 18   "On occasions when sea level had dropped by 150 feet, enough of the floor of the Bering and Chukchi Seas emerged to form a land connection between Siberia and Alaska. . . . So much water was locked up in ice during the maximum extent of the late Wisconsin glaciation that sea level was lowered by more than 300 feet, exposing a land bridge over 1,000 miles wide."

p. 18   ". . . but it is now known that man with the aid of boats or other means of crossing appreciable stretches of open water reached Australia as much as 40,000 years ago."

p. 18   "By 10,000 B.P. evidence of Paleo-Indian occupation is widespread in the Americas, extending from the tip of South America to Alaska."

Dayton, Leigh, "The Incredible Shrinking Aborigines," *New Scientist*, vol. 142 (April 2, 1994), p. 13.

p. 13   "Aborigines in eastern Australia shrank dramatically in stature after the last ice age, according to scientists who have examined human remains unearthed there. This challenges the popular assumption that humans gradually increased in size as they learnt to master fire and exploit the environment.

               "Peter Brown, a physical anthropologist at the University of New England in Armidale, has documented the change in human fossils found in early 'cemeteries' at Coobool Creek and Kow Swamp, on the Murray and Darling rivers. He discovered that, between 10,000 and 6000 years ago, people's average height fell by roughly one-fifth."

p. 13   "David Frayer of the University of Kansas has reported that between 25,000 and 5000 years ago, the size of European hunters declined along with the size of their prey. He concludes that men declined in stature by about 5.5 per cent and women by 3.4 per cent."

Falk, Bertil, "For Six Days Shalt Thou Labour," *New Scientist*, vol. 125 (March 31, 1990), pp. 68-69.

p. 68   "The seven-day week is an ancient institution. And it is a marvelous one. Its divine origin is established in the Bible, where God spent six days creating the world. The seventh day became a day of rest, meditation and worship, the day when people recovered their strength after having worked by the sweat of their brows for six long days."

p. 68   "God may have decreed that the day of rest should be holy, but he never stated that the day of rest had to be a Sunday. He did not even proclaim that the seventh day of Margaret Thatcher must be on exactly the same day as the seventh day of Yitzhak Samir or the seventh day of Yasser Arafat."

pp. 68-69   "The day of rest can be different for different people. What is important is to rest after six (or even fewer) days of work. It is thanks to ancient wisdom that this psychological understanding of physical needs are met."

Freedman, Ronald, and Bernard Berelson, "The Human Population," *Scientific American*, vol. 231, (September 1974), pp. 31-39. Freedman was Professor of Sociology, Chicago, and Berelson was President of the Population Council, Chicago.

p. 31   "In the 1970's the rate of increase has slightly exceeded 2 percent per year. That means a doubling time of less than 35 years, and the number currently being doubled is a very large one. Projection of such growth for very long into the future produces a world population larger that the most optimistic estimates of the planet's carrying capacity. In the long run near-zero growth will have to be restored—either by lower birth rates or by higher death rates."

Glueck, Nelson, *Rivers in the Desert* (New York: Farrar, Straus and Cudahy, 1968), 302 pp. Glueck was President of Hebrew Union College, Jewish Institute of Religion.

p. 11   "Centuries earlier, another civilization of high achievement had flourished between the twenty-first and nineteenth centuries B.C. till it was savagely liquidated by the Kings of the East. According to the Biblical statements which have been borne out by archaeological evidence, they gutted every city and village at the end of that period from Ashtaroth-Karnaim in southern Syria through all of Trans-Jordan and the Negev to Kadesh(-barnea) in Sinai (Gen. 14:1-7)."

p. 31   "As a matter of fact, however, it may be stated categorically that no archaeological discovery has ever controverted a Biblical reference. Scores of archaeological findings have been made which confirm in clear outline or in exact detail historical statements in the Bible. And, by the same token, proper evaluation of Biblical descriptions has often led to amazing discoveries. They form tesserae in the vast mosaic of the Bible's almost incredibly correct historical memory."

pp. 72-3   "The rebellion of the small kings of the cities on the east side of the Dead Sea against what must have been the extortionate rule of absentee suzerains was brutally crushed. . . . From southern Syria to central Sinai their fury raged. . . . I found that every village in their path had been plundered and left in ruins, and the countryside laid waste. The population had been wiped out and led away into captivity. For hundreds of years thereafter, the entire area was like an abandoned cemetery. . . ."

Kildare, Paul, "Monkey Business," *Christian Order*, vol. 23 (December 1982), pp. 588-598. This is a British Roman Catholic periodical.

p. 591   "[Darwin's] aim was 'to show that there is no fundamental difference between man and the higher mammals (monkeys) in their mental faculties.' [In his *Voyage of the Beagle*, describing 'the miserable inhabitants of Tierra del Fuego.']

"Darwin hardly saw an Indian at all and could not speak one word of their language, yet his description of the Fuegians is still quoted as authoritative over a century later in countless so-called scientific works. . . . But these superficial comments of a passing tourist in 1832 were entirely without foundation. They were completely demolished by the findings of two missionary priests, both highly qualified scientists . . . on the staffs of American and European universities. . . . Darwin had no scientific qualifications at all."

p. 592   "The Fuegian Indians were not cannibals; they believed in one Supreme Being, to whom they prayed with confidence; they had 'high principles of morality' and they rightly regarded the white people who exploited them as morally inferior to themselves."

p. 594   "His friend Lyell, after reading *Origin*, suggested that in a future edition he should 'here and there insert an actual case to relieve the vast number of abstract propositions.' It is, of course, the absence of *actual* cases that has always been the main difficulty with Darwin's evolution. There are no actual cases."

Krantz, Grover S., "The Populating of Western North America," *Society for California Archaeology Occasional Papers in Method and Theory in California Archaeology*, no. 1 (December 1977), pp. 1-63.

p. 1   "It is assumed here that ancestral derivations of people are best reflected in linguistic distributions rather than in other cultural items or even in anatomical traits. Material culture and anatomy respond to environmental pressures, but 'genetic' relationships among languages are not so affected."

p. 5   "Successful migrations are made possible only when the movers have the military capacity or its equivalent to overcome any real or passive resistance. When two agriculturally based peoples engage in a dispute over territory, the one with the greater resources will prevail. When an agriculturally based people disputes with a hunting and gathering group, the agriculturalists will ordinarily prevail for obvious reasons. . . .

              "When two hunting groups contest a piece of territory, neither side has any of these advantages. If they do fight, both sides have the same minimal capacities, with one major exception. The group defending its own land will know the territory and its resources, thus giving them a significant edge. When all else is equal, the defender should always prevail."

p. 5   "In general, the rule is that if hunting peoples expand their area, it is only into essentially empty territories, and never at the expense of previously settled inhabitants. The obvious application of this rule is to the initial occupation of a continent like North America, which must have been a single event and not a series of waves of immigration."

Lewin, Roger, "Rise and Fall of Big People," *New Scientist*, vol. 146 (April 22, 1995), pp. 30-33.

p. 30   "The growth spurt we are seeing in affluent parts of the world is fueled by better nutrition. Until this effect kicked in, humans were smaller than at any point in our history or that of our ancestors, stretching back some two million years. Virtually all anthropologists agree that we are shorter, lighter and less robust than our forebears. And our brains are the smallest they have been for 200,000 years."

Linton, Ralph, *The Tree of Culture* (New York: Alfred A. Knopf, 1955), 692 pp.

p. 9   "The so-called primitive languages can throw no light on language origins, since most of them are actually more complicated in grammar than the tongues spoken by civilized peoples."

Matthews, Stephen, Bernard Comrie, and Marcia Polinsky, eds., *Atlas of Languages: The Origin and Development of Languages throughout the World* (New York: Facts on File, Inc., 1996), 224 pp.

p. 7   "Any human can potentially learn any language. An English baby adopted by Quechuan or Turkish speaking parents would grow up speaking fluent Quechuan or Turkish with no difficulty. Language, we now realize, is an intrinsic part of being human, and is biologically programmed into the species.

"This powerful communication system emerged around 100,000 years ago, probably in the east of Africa, according to current majority opinion. Humans moved northward into Asia Minor maybe 50,000 years ago, then spread around the world. As humans travelled, languages split and proliferated. There are now around 5,000 languages, according to most counts. They can be grouped into around a dozen major clusters, and a number of minor ones.

"No languageless community has ever been found."

p. 10   "Language is perhaps the most important single characteristic that distinguishes human beings from other animal species."

p. 10   "Because of the different structure of the vocal apparatus in humans and chimpanzees, it is not possible for chimpanzees to imitate the sounds of human language, so they have been taught to use gestures or tokens in place of sounds. The successes that have been achieved over the last few decades by dedicated researchers on chimpanzees' linguistic abilities have certainly gone beyond what most linguists would have predicted, but chimpanzees never attain a level of linguistic complexity beyond the approximate level of a two-year-old child."

pp. 11-12   "It would seem likely that further light could be thrown on the evolution of human language by studying more and less complex human languages spoken today. However, while it is possible to find parts of one language that are simpler than the corresponding parts of another language, no evidence has ever been produced that would suggest that one particular language as spoken by modern humans is more or less complex than any other."

p. 13   "It is a mistake to assume that a language will have a simpler structure because it is spoken in a culture that has simpler political structures or a less advanced technology. Linguists are continually surprised by the distinctions that are made in languages outside the mainstream of more familiar languages."

p. 13   "In the last decade of the twentieth century, it is estimated that over 6,000 languages are spoken in the world."

Molnar, Stephen, *Human Variation: Races, Types and Ethnic Groups* (Englewood Cliffs, N.J.: Prentice-Hall, 1975), 253 pp.

pp. 65-6   "In modern populations . . . there is a wide range in variation, however. The lower end of the range is well below the capacity for certain fossil hominids, yet there is no evidence that these individuals are any less intelligent than persons with larger cranial vaults. . . . Variation of plus or minus 100 cc about the mean is evident in most European populations. These individuals with larger or smaller cranial capacities are normally functioning and intellectually competent individuals, in fact, there are many such persons with 700 to 800 cc capacities."

Pei, Mario, *The Story of Language* (Philadelphia: J. P. Lippincott & Co., 1965), 491 pp.

p. 22   "Leibnitz, at the dawn of the eighteenth century, first advanced the theory that all languages come not from a historically recorded source but from a protospeech. In some respects he was a precursor of the Italian twentieth-century linguist Trombetti, who boldly asserted that the Biblical account of the Tower of Babel is at least figuratively true, and that all languages have a common origin."

Renfrew, Colin, "The Origins of Indo-European Languages," *Scientific American*, vol. 261 (October 1989), pp. 106-114. Renfrew is Professor of Archaeology, Cambridge University.

p. 113   "The archaeological evidence makes it clear that Anatolia was not the only region in which early domestication took place. The zone of origination of agriculture had at least two other lobes, more or less self-contained regions within the larger zone. These were the Levant, a strip some 50 to 100 kilometers wide on the Mediterranean coast of what is now Jordan, Lebanon, Syria and Israel, and the Zagros region of Iraq and Iran."

p. 113   "This somewhat expanded version of the wave-of-advance model has the effect of situating the ancestral languages of the Indo-European, Afro-Asiatic and Dravidian groups quite close together in the Near East about 10,000 years ago. Although still hypothetical, this picture finds remarkable support from recent work in linguistics and genetics."

Schiller, Ronald, "New Findings on the Origin of Man," *Reader's Digest* (August 1973), pp. 86-90.

p. 86   "In the last couple of years, two phenomenal discoveries have been made in Africa that . . . challenge the validity of long-cherished theories concerning the origin and evolution of the human race. One was the finding in Kenya of a human skull and bones below a layer dated about 2.8 million years. The second was the discovery that a cave in southern Africa on the border between Swaziland and Natal was inhabited by men of modern type quite possibly as long as 100,000 years ago."

p. 87   "The Border Cave dwellers had already learned the art of mining. They manufactured a variety of sophisticated tools, including agate knives with edges still sharp enough to slice paper. They could count and kept primitive records on fragments of bone. They also held religious convictions and believed in the afterlife."

pp. 89-90   "The descent of man is no longer regarded as a chain with some links missing, but rather as a tangled vine whose tendrils loop back and forth as species interbred to create new varieties, most of which died out."

p. 90   "It may be that we did not evolve from any of the previously known human types, but descended in a direct line of our own."

Schmidt, Peter, and Donald H. Avery, "Complex Iron Smelting and Prehistoric Cultures in Tanzania," *Science*, vol. 201 (September 22, 1978), pp. 1085-1089.

p. 1089   "We find in traditional Africa an Iron Age technological process that was exceedingly complex and, in historical and relative terms, also advanced."

p. 1089   "One of the more profound implications of the West Lake discoveries is that we are now able to say that a technologically superior iron-smelting process developed in Africa more than 1500 years ago. This knowledge will help to change scholarly and popular ideas that technological sophistication developed in Europe but not in Africa. In that respect, the ramifications are significant for the history of Africa and her people."

Stent, Gunther S., "Limits to the Scientific Understanding of Man," *Science*, vol. 187 (March 21, 1975), pp. 1052-1057. Stent was Professor of Molecular Biology, University of California, Berkeley.

p. 1054   "Chomsky holds that the grammar of a language is a system of transformational rules that determines a certain pairing of sound and meaning. It consists of a syntactic component, a semantic component, and a phonological component. The surface structure contains the information relevant to the phonological component, whereas the deep structure contains the information relevant to the semantic component, and the syntactic component pairs surface and deep structures. Hence, it is merely the phonological component of grammar that has become greatly differentiated during the course of human history, or at least since the construction of the Tower of Babel. The semantic component has remained invariant and is, therefore, the 'universal' aspect of the universal grammar, which all natural languages embody."

p. 1057   "No matter how deeply we probe into the visual pathway, in the end we need to posit an 'inner man' who transforms the visual image into a precept. And, as far as linguistics is concerned, the analysis of language appears to be heading for the same conceptual impasse as does the analysis of vision. . . . It is significant that Chomsky . . . has encountered difficulty with the postulated semantic component. Thus far, it has not been possible to spell out how the semantic component manages to extract meaning from the informational content of the deep structure. . . . That is to say, for man the concept of 'meaning' can be fathomed only in relation to the self, which is both ultimate source and ultimate destination of semantic signals."

Thomas, Lewis, M.D., "On Science and Uncertainty," *Discover*, vol. 1 (October 1980), pp. 58-59. Dr. Thomas was Chancellor, Memorial Sloan Kettering Cancer Center, Manhattan.

p. 59   "We know a lot about the structure and function of the cells and fibers of the human brain, but we haven't the ghost of an idea about how this extraordinary organ works to produce awareness; the nature of consciousness is a scientific problem, but still an unapproachable one."

p. 59   ". . . but we do not understand language itself. Indeed, language is so incomprehensible a problem that the language we use for discussing the matter is itself becoming incomprehensible."

p. 59   "We do not understand the process of dying, nor can we say anything clear,
for sure, about what happens to human thought after death."

Chapter 9

The Geologic Column and Its Fossils

A. Fossils and Geologic Dating

It is widely believed that geologists know how to determine the age of rocks and can pinpoint the particular geologic period in which each rock system was formed. It is not widely understood, however, how subjective such decisions are, and how utterly dependent they are on the prior assumption of a long, long evolutionary history of the earth and its inhabitants.

As illustrated in the following quotes, such geologic dating is squarely based on the fossils and their assumed evolutionary history. The resulting geologic column (or geologic time scale) is then taken as the proof of evolution. This is purely circular reasoning. It is not uncommon under this system to find many rock systems "out-of-place" in the column—that is, "old" rocks overlying "young" rocks, fossils from different "ages" together, entire ages missing, etc. When such anomalies are encountered, imaginary earth movements or other geologic phenomena must be postulated to account for them. All of this creative thinking is necessary under the false assumption that the evolutionary ages of geologic history really existed at all.

Ager, Derek V., "Fossil Frustrations," *New Scientist*, vol. 100 (November 10, 1983), p. 425.

> "No paleontologist worthy of the name would ever date his fossils by the strata in which they are found. It is almost the first thing I teach my first-year students. Ever since William Smith at the beginning of the 19th century, fossils have been and still are the best and most accurate method of dating and correlating the rocks in which they occur.

> "Apart from very 'modern' examples, which are really archaeology, I can think of no cases of radioactive decay being used to date fossils."

Allan, Robin S., "Geological Correlation and Paleoecology," *Bulletin, Geological Society of America*, vol. 59 (January 1948), pp. 1-10.

p. 2   "Because of the sterility of its concepts, historical geology, which includes paleontology and stratigraphy, has become static and unproductive. Current methods of delimiting intervals of time, which are the fundamental units of historical geology, and of establishing chronology are of dubious validity. Worse than that, the criteria of correlation—the attempt to equate in time, or synchronize, the geological history of one area with that of another—are logically vulnerable. The findings of historical geology are suspect because the principles upon which they are based are either inadequate, in which case they should be reformulated, or false, in which case they should be discarded. Most of us refuse to discard or reformulate, and the result is the present deplorable state of our discipline."

Anonymous, "Fossil Changes: 'Normal Evolution,'" *Science News*, vol. 102, (September 2, 1972) p. 152. From the 24th International Geological Congress at Montreal.

> "The boundaries between eras, periods and epochs on the geological time scale generally denote sudden and significant changes in the character of fossil remains. For example, the boundary between the Triassic and Jurassic periods of the Mesozoic era (about 180 million years ago) was supposedly marked by spontaneous appearance of new species. Researchers have sometimes come up with drastic explanations for these changes such as an increase in mutation rates due to cosmic rays.

> "A reassessment of the data by Jost Wiedmann of the University of Tübingen in the Federal Republic of Germany gives a clearer picture of evolution at the boundaries of the Mesozoic (225 million to 70 million years ago). He concludes that there were no worldwide extinctions of species or spontaneous appearances of new species at the boundaries. Instead, there was a continuous disappearance of 'old' fauna, a continuous and gradual appearance of 'new' fauna, and sudden diversification of species that had appeared previously. These changes can be explained by 'normal' evolutionary processes, he says; worldwide ecology may simply have warranted greater diversity of species."

Berry, W. B. N., *Growth of a Prehistoric Time Scale* (San Francisco: W. H. Freeman & Co., 1968), 158 pp.

pp. *iii-iv*   "This book tells of the search that led to the development of a method for dividing prehistoric time based on the evolutionary development of organisms whose fossil record has been left in the rocks of the earth's crust."

Cook, Frederick A., Larry D. Brown, and Jack E. Oliver, "The Southern Appalachians and the Growth of Continents," *Scientific American*, vol. 243 (October 1980), pp. 156-168.

p. 156   "The most spectacular finding was made in the southern Appalachians. The profiles revealed that the mountains are underlain to a depth of at least 18 kilometers by horizontal layers of material that is sedimentary or once was. . . .

          "Most of the rocks at the surface in the southern Appalachians are highly deformed metamorphic ones. Furthermore, they are older than or contemporaneous with the horizontal sedimentary strata that were discovered under them. . . . The discovery confirms the hypothesis that horizontal or near-horizontal thrusting can carry large volumes of crustal material great distances, and it suggests that a continent could grow and evolve by the emplacement of thin horizontal slices of material at the continental margins."

p. 161   "The only explanation for the buried strata is that the overlying crystalline rocks were emplaced along a major subhorizontal thrust fault (a horizontal fault below the surface)."

Cutler, Alan H., and Karl W. Plessa, "Fossils out of Sequence: Computer Simulations and Strategies for Dealing with Stratigraphic Disorder," *Palaios*, vol. 5 (June 1990), pp. 227-235. Cutler is in the Department of Geoscience at the University of Arizona.

p. 227   "We define stratigraphic disorder as the departure from perfect chronological order of fossils in a stratigraphic sequence. Any sequence in which an older fossil occurs above a younger one is stratigraphically disordered. Scales of stratigraphic disorder may be from millimeters to many meters. Stratigraphic disorder is produced by the physical or biogenic mixing of fossiliferous sediments, and the reworking of older, previously deposited hard parts into younger sediments. Since these processes occur to an extent in virtually all sedimentary systems, stratigraphic disorder at some scale is probably a common feature of the fossil record."

p. 234   "Stratigraphic disorder can result from mixing of sediments by physical and biological processes as well as from the introduction of older, reworked hard parts into younger sediments. The extent of disorder in modern and ancient sequences is not well documented; however, the widespread occurrence of anomalies in dated sections suggest that disorder should be taken seriously by paleobiologists and stratigraphers working at fine stratigraphic scales."

Davis, D. Dwight, "Comparative Anatomy and the Evolution of Vetebrates," in *Genetics, Paleontology and Evolution*, edited by Glenn Jepsen, Ernst Mayr, and G. G. Simpson (Princeton University Press, 1949). Davis was Curator, Division of Vertebrate Anatomy, Chicago Natural History Museum.

p. 74   "The sudden emergence of major adaptive types as seen in the abrupt appearance in the fossil record of families and orders, continued to give trouble. The phenomenon lay in the genetical no man's land beyond the limits of experimentation. A few paleontologists even today cling to the idea that these gaps will be closed by further collecting, . . . but most regard the observed discontinuity as real and have sought an explanation."

p. 77   "But the facts of paleontology conform equally well with other interpretations that have been discredited by neobiological work, e.g., divine creation, etc., and paleontology by itself can neither prove nor refute such ideas."

Eldredge, Niles, *Time Frames: The Rethinking of Darwinian Evolution and the Theory of Punctuated Equilibria* (New York: Simon and Schuster, 1985), 240 pp.

p. 45   "This hierarchy of life—the pattern of inter-nested resemblances interlinking all organisms—was perhaps Darwin's best argument of all that life has in fact evolved."

p. 46-47   "Popper was describing the logical structure of the way things ought to be. In the real world, in the competitive fray that is science, data forging, plagiarism and all manner of base and venal but utterly human failings make a mockery of the counterimage of detached objectivity. Such pure, dispassionate, cold logic is rare—though more common, one assumes, than the cheating of its opposite extreme."

p. 51   "Paleontologists cannot operate this way. There is no way simply to look at a fossil and say how old it is unless you know the age of the rocks it comes from."

p. 52   "And this poses something of a problem: if we date the rocks by their fossils, how can we then turn around and talk about patterns of evolutionary change through time in the fossil record?"

p. 75   "Neo-Darwinian gradualists would predict a time gap between ancestor and descendent, and, of course, they'd be right. Score one for convention. Saltationists, however, justly point to the prodigious stability they see in the ancestors, and ask an interesting question: if gradualism is the rule, why don't we see any hint of change? We might not be faced with a perfect record, but *if* gradualism is the rule, our sporadic sampling up and down cliff faces should give us some hints, some directional drifting, from the primitive state of the ancestor on over toward the condition we eventually find in the descendant. Why is *all* the gradual change going on in those very gaps?"

Fischer, Alfred G., and David J. Bottjer, "Pattern and Process in Paleontology and Stratigraphy," review of *Sedimentary and Evolutionary Cycles*, edited by U. Bayer and A. Seilacher (New York: Springer-Verlag, 1985), *Paleobiology*, vol. 12 (Spring 1986), pp. 229-232.

p. 230   "Phylogeny can be viewed not only as a 'succession of forms' but a 'succession of ecologies,' and evolution as not only an 'unfolding of forms' but an 'unfolding of ecologies.'"

p. 231   "The interpretation of process, however, has varied widely, from Hilgendorf's Darwinian explanation to the anti-evolutionist view that these are simply ecophenotypes developed in response to a transient geothermal heating (now geochemically disproved), and to Lamarckian interpretations."

pp. 231-2   "This book points the way to the future: much of what we have 'learned' about Earth and life history has been read through glasses colored by simplistic paradigms. The story is to be found in the rocks. Organisms and their habitats evolved together, and must be studied in concert, with all the new methods coming into use (including the chemical approaches, not much stressed in this book). What are the relative roles of stochastic versus deterministic processes? Major discoveries about Earth's history and the fundamentals of evolution are only now coming into reach."

Gould, Stephen Jay, "The Ediacaran Experiment," *Natural History*, vol. 93 (February 1984), pp. 14-23.

p. 16   "[Dolf] Seilacher now argues, . . . The entire Ediacaran fauna . . . represents a unique and extinct experiment in the basic construction of living things. Our planet's first fauna was replaced after a mass extinction, not simply improved and expanded."

p. 22   "As we survey the history of life since the inception of multicellular complexity in Ediacaran times, one feature stands out as most puzzling—the lack of clear order and progress through time among marine invertebrate faunas. We can tell tales of improvement for some groups, but in honest moments we must admit that the history of complex life is more a story of multifarious variation about a set of basic designs than a saga of accumulating excellence. The eyes of early trilobites, for example, have never been exceeded for complexity or acuity by later arthropods. Why do we fail to find this expected order?"

p. 23   "I regard the failure to find a clear 'vector of progress' in life's history as the most puzzling fact of the fossil record."

p. 23   "Heretofore, we have thrown up our hands in frustration at the lack of expected pattern in life's history—or we have sought to impose a pattern that we hoped to find on a world that does not really display it. . . . If we can develop a general theory of mass extinction, we may finally understand why life has thwarted our expectations—and we may even extract an unexpected kind of pattern from apparent chaos."

Gretener, P. E., "On the Character of Thrust Faults with Particular Reference to the Basal Tongues," *Bulletin, Canadian Petroleum Geologists*, vol. 25 (1977).

p. 110   "The following observations (about 'overthrusts') seem to have universal validity: 1. The contact is usually sharp and unimpressive in view of the great amount of displacement. 2. Structures which have been named 'tongues' appear to be common. They are features where material from the overridden sequence is seemingly injected as a tongue into the base of the overthrust plate. 3. Secondary (splay) thrusts are common. 4. Coalescence of tongues may produce pseudo-boudins. 5. Minor folding and faulting can usually be observed in both the thrust plate and the underlying rocks. The intensity of such deformations is normally comparatively weak, at least in view of the large displacements these thrust plates have undergone. . . . 6. Late deformations, particularly by normal faulting, are present in many thrust plates. They should be recognized for what they are: post-thrusting features completely unrelated to the emplacement of the thrust plates."

p. 111   "Different lithological units, usually with stratigraphic separation measured in kilometers, are in juxtaposition along a sharp contact, often no more impressive than a mere bedding plane."

Guth, Peter L., Kip V. Hodges, and James H. Willemin, "Limitations on the Role of Pore Pressure in Gravity Gliding," *Bulletin, Geological Society of America*, vol. 93 (July 1982), pp. 606-612. Guth was in the Department of Earth and Planetary Sciences, Massachusetts Institute of Technology.

p. 607   "In the absence of further data on the state of stress at depth for various lithologies in different tectonic environments, we can only emphasize, first, the apparent importance of weak beds in inhibiting hydrofractures and, second, the importance of horizontal tectonic stress in allowing high pore pressures to build up in competent terrane."

p. 610   "On the basis of the limited *in situ* data presently available, only shales and evaporites appear to have effective permeabilities low enough to qualify as possible cap rocks in a gravity-gliding scenario. If effective permeabilities prove to be higher due to fractures present on a regional scale, only incredible fluid production rates could maintain sufficient pore pressure for gravity gliding."

p. 611   "We suspect that over the areas of large thrust sheets such as those in the Appalachians or the western Cordillera, effective permeabilities would have been too large to allow gravity gliding, even with shale or evaporite cap rocks."

p. 611   "Simple gravity gliding under the influence of elevated pore pressures cannot explain the Heart Mountain fault. . . .

"Pierce has suggested a catastrophic genesis for the Heart Mountain allochthon. . . . Castrophic processes are beyond the scope of this analysis; . . ."

p. 611   "Our findings suggest that extreme caution should be exercised in erecting gravity-glide models for faults not incorporating shales or evaporites as a decollément horizon. Furthermore, we have not considered a number of additional factors which might argue against gravity gliding in a given case; ramp and toe effects, dilatancy effects, and the often ignored need for a suitably denuded source region."

Harris, Leonard D., Anita G. Harris, Wallace DeWitt, Jr., and Kenneth C. Bayer, "Evaluation of Southern Eastern Overthrust Belt beneath Blue Ridge-Piedmont Thrust," *Bulletin, American Association of Petroleum Geologists*, vol. 65 (December 1981), pp. 2497-2505.

p. 2497   "A growing body of subsurface data from different parts of the Appalachian orogen necessitates a reevaluation of long-held concepts concerning the probable distribution of sedimentary, metamorphic and igneous rocks within this mountain system. A summary of subsurface data available from the southern Appalachians to the Quebec lowlands of eastern Canada reveals that the entire orogen from the Appalachian Plateau to the Piedmont is probably underlain by an eastward-dipping low-angle thrust system."

p. 2497   "That survey clearly showed approximately 20,000 ft. (6,100 m) of Paleozoic sedimentary rocks of the Valley and Ridge projecting eastward beneath allochthonous metamorphic and igneous rocks of the Blue Ridge."

p. 2500   "The detached sequence in our southern Appalachian seismic reflection profile contains a few great thrust faults with miles of displacement and numerous minor thrusts with lesser amounts of displacement. . . . Each thrust sheet is enormously complex, containing a related group of small and large thrust faults."

Hedberg, Hollis D., "The Stratigraphic Panorama," *Bulletin, Geological Society of America*, vol. 72 (April 1961), pp. 499-518.

p. 503   "That our present-day knowledge of the sequence of strata in the earth's crust is in major part due to the evidence supplied by fossils is a truism. Merely in their role as distinctive rock constituents, fossils have furnished, . . . through their record of the evolution of life on this planet, an amazingly effective key to the relative positioning of strata in widely separated regions and from continent to continent."

Hirschfeld, Sue Ellen, "Earth—History of the Earth," *World Book Encyclopedia*, vol. 6 (1996), p. 26. Compare with definitions by Samuel Paul Welles in the *World Book Encyclopedia*.

"Fossils help geologists figure out the ages of rock strata and the times at which animals and plants lived."

Hubbert, M. King, and W. W. Rubey, "Role of Fluid Pressure in the Mechanics of Overthrust Faulting," *Bulletin, Geological Society of America*, vol. 70 (February 1959), pp. 115-166.

p. 122   "Since their earliest recognition, the existence of large overthrusts has presented a mechanical paradox that has never been satisfactorily resolved."

pp. 126-7   "Consequently, for the conditions assumed, the pushing of a thrust block, whose length is of the order of 30 km or more, along a horizontal surface appears to be a mechanical impossibility."

Jeletzky, J. A., "Paleontology, Basis of Practical Geochronology," *Bulletin, American Association of Petroleum Geologists*, vol. 40 (April 1956), pp. 679-706.

p. 684   "The more than amply proved and almost universally recognized impossibility of establishing any practically useful broadly regional or world-wide geologic time scale based on the physical-stratigraphical criteria alone for the vast expanse of pre-Cambrian time supplies conclusive proof that these phenomena are devoid of any generally recognizable geologic time significance."

p. 685   "It is, indeed, a well-established fact that the [physical-stratigraphic] rock units and their boundaries often transgress geologic time planes in most irregular fashion even within the shortest distances."

Jeletzky, J. A., "Is it Possible to Quantify Biochronological Correlation?" *Journal of Paleontology*, vol. 39 (January 1965), pp. 135-140. Jeletzky was with the Geological Survey of Canada.

p. 138   "The best example of how *qualitative* and *non-statistical* paleontological correlation is, is provided by the already-mentioned fact that only a minority of fossils of most faunas (and this often amounts to the minority of one fossil species or genus only!) are reliable time indices or index fossils. The great majority of fossils are conversely either inferior (parachronological) time indices or have little or no practical biochronological value (ecostratigraphical indices). Any single, readily identifiable specimen or fragment of a known diagnostic ammonite, belemite, planktonic foaminifer, graptolite, trilobite, etc., is, therefore, often more significant for the dating and correlation of the rock units concerned than all the rest of their faunas taken together."

Kemp, Tom S., "A Fresh Look at the Fossil Record," *New Scientist*, vol. 108 (December 5, 1985), pp. 66-67. Kemp is Curator, University Museum, Oxford University.

p. 66   "In other words, when the assumed evolutionary processes did not match the pattern of fossils that they were supposed to have generated, the pattern was judged to be 'wrong.' A circular argument arises: interpret the fossil record in terms of a particular theory of evolution, inspect the interpretation, and note that it confirms the theory. Well, it would, wouldn't it?"

p. 66   "As is now well known, most fossil species appear instantaneously in the record, persist for some millions of years virtually unchanged, only to disappear abruptly—the 'punctuated equilibrium' pattern of Eldredge and Gould."

Kitts, David B., "Paleontology and Evolutionary Theory," *Evolution*, vol. 28 (September 1974), pp. 458-472. Kitts was Professor of Geology, University of Oklahoma.

p. 466   "Evolution, at least in the sense that Darwin speaks of it, cannot be detected within the lifetime of a single observer. Darwinian theory, however, is supposed to have, in addition to evolution, other less sweeping consequences which are more amenable to observational test."

p. 466   "But the danger of circularity is still present. For most biologists the strongest reason for accepting the evolutionary hypothesis is their acceptance of some theory that entails it. There is another difficulty. The temporal ordering of biological events beyond the local section may critically involve paleontological correlation, which necessarily presupposes the non-repeatability of organic events in geologic history. There are various justifications for this assumption but for almost all contemporary paleontologists it rests upon the acceptance of the evolutionary hypothesis."

p. 467   "Despite the bright promise that paleontology provides a means of 'seeing' evolution, it has presented some nasty difficulties for evolutionists the most notorious of which is the presence of 'gaps' in the fossil record. Evolution requires intermediate forms between species and paleontology does not provide them. The gaps must therefore be a contingent feature of the record. Darwin was concerned enough about this problem to devote a chapter of the 'Origin' to it. He accounts for 'the imperfections of the geological record' largely on the basis of the lack of continuous deposition of sediments."

Krassilov, V., "Causal Biostratigraphy," *Lethaia*, vol. 7, no. 3 (1974), pp. 173-179.

p. 174   "It is worth mentioning that continuous 'evolutionary' series derived from the fossil record can in most cases be simulated by chronoclines—successions of a geographical cline population imposed by the changes of some environmental gradients."

Miller, T. G., "Time in Stratigraphy," *Paleontology*, vol. 8 (February 1965).

p. 119   "Thus it appears that the only presently available rational geochronological indices are biostratigraphically based—i.e., *biochronologic*."

p. 128   "Physico-geometrical data (apart from radio-metric) can do no more than provide a crude local relative chronology or circumstantial evidence in support of a biochronologic framework."

Miller, William J., *An Introduction to Historical Geology* (Van Nostrand, 1952).

p. 12   "Comparatively few remains of organisms now inhabiting the earth are being deposited under conditions favorable for their preservation as fossils. . . . It is nevertheless remarkable that so vast a number of fossils are embedded in the rocks."

p. 16   "Footprints of animals, made in moderately soft mud or sandy mud which soon hardens and becomes covered with more sediment, are especially favorable for preservation. Thousands of examples of tracks of great extinct reptiles have been found in the red sandstone of the Connecticut River Valley alone."

O'Rourke, J. E., "Pragmatism versus Materialism in Stratigraphy," *American Journal of Science*, vol. 276 (January 1976), pp. 47-55.

p. 51   "The theory of dialectic materialism postulates matter as the ultimate reality, not to be questioned. All matter is in motion, which is its mode of existence. Motion involves not only a change of place but also a change of quality, an ascending development. Evolution is more than a useful biologic concept: it is a natural law controlling the history of all phenomena. . . ."

pp. 51-2   "These principles have been applied in *Feinstratigraphie*, which starts from a chronology of index fossils, abstracts time units from it, and imposes them on the rocks. Each taxon represents a definite time unit and so provides an accurate even 'infallible' date. If you doubt it, bring in a suite of good index fossils, and the specialist, without asking where or in what order they were collected, will lay them out on the table in chronological order."

p. 52   "Correlation is said to derive a guarantee from the irreversibility of evolution. Each fossil was a unique event; each taxon, an interval of time in a cumulative sequence. A taxon, once extinct, cannot reappear."

p. 53   "The rocks do date the fossils, but the fossils date the rocks more accurately. Stratigraphy cannot avoid this kind of reasoning, if it insists on using only temporal concepts, because circularity is inherent in the derivation of time scales."

p. 54   "Structure, metamorphism, sedimentary reworking, and other complications have to be considered. Radiometric dating would not have been feasible if the geologic column had not been erected first."

p. 54   "The axiom that no process can measure itself means that there is no absolute time, but this relic of the traditional mechanics persists in the common distinction between 'relative' and 'absolute' age."

pp. 54-55   "The charge of circular reasoning in stratigraphy can be handled in several ways. It can be *ignored*, as not the proper concern of the public. It can be *denied*, by calling down the Law of Evolution. Fossils date rocks, not vice-versa, and that's that. It can be *admitted*, as a common practice. The time scales of physics and astronomy are obtained by comparing one process with another. They can also be compared with the geologic processes of sedimentation, organic evolution, and radioactivity. Or it can be *avoided*, by pragmatic reasoning.

"The first step is to explain what is done in the field in simple terms that can be tested directly. The field man records his sense perceptions on isomorphic maps and sections, abstracts the more diagnostic rock features, and arranges them according to their vertical order. He compares this local sequence to the global column obtained from a great many man-years of work by his predecessors. As long as this cognitive process is acknowledged as the pragmatic basis of stratigraphy, both local and global sections can be treated as chronologiea without reproach."

Pierce, William G., "Role of Fluid Pressure in Mechanics of Overthrust Faulting: Discussion," *Bulletin, Geological Society of America*, vol. 77 (May 1966), pp. 565-568.

p. 568   "In summary, the arguments cited by Rubey and Hubbert to support the fluid pressure concept as a mechanism for the emplacement of the Heart Mountain fault masses seem unlikely to me on the basis of clear and abundant field evidence."

Platt, Lucian B., "Fluid Pressure in Thrust Faulting, a Corollary," *American Journal of Science*, vol. 260 (February 1962), pp. 107-114.

p. 107   "Obviously an important factor is the quality of the seal that forms in the clay or shale. No matter how small the permeability in the relatively impermeable layer that effectively seals the connate water beneath the thick sequence, some leakage does occur. . . . Hence, if fluid support is to be available to 'float' the rocks, the thrust movement must occur soon (geologically) after the deposition of the final weight of the thick sediments. If the delay is sufficient, the seal of shale becomes very good, but there is no fluid left to seal off."

Prothero, D. R., *Interpreting the Stratigraphic Record* (New York: Freeman, 1990).

p. 230   "The evolution of organisms is the enabling factor, providing the progressive changes in species through time that makes biostratigraphy possible. Unlike any other means of correlation, biostratigraphy is based on the unique, sequential, nonrepeating appearance of fossils through time. The presence of a single fossil can often be used to determine the age of a rock very accurately. This is not true of the lithology of the rock, its magnetic polarity, its seismic velocity, or its isotopic composition; none of these are unique an dcannot be used alone."

Ransom, Jay E., *Fossils in America* (New York: Harper and Row, 1964), 402 pp.

p. 43   "In each sedimentary stratum certain fossils seem to be characteristically abundant: these fossils are known as *index fossils*. If in a strange formation an index fossil is found, it is easy to date that particular layer of rock and to correlate it with other exposures in distant regions containing the same species."

p. 43   "Once it was understood that each fossil represents a biologic entity, instead of a special divinely created life form, it became quite obvious that the plants and animals of each stratigraphic division had simply evolved from those of the preceding epoch through gradual adaptation. They were, in turn, ancestral to those that followed."

Rastall, R. H., "Geology," *Encyclopedia Brittanica*, vol. 10 (1949). Rastall was a lecturer in Economic Geology, University of London.

p. 168   "It cannot be denied that from a strictly philosophical standpoint geologists are here arguing in a circle. The succession of organisms has been determined by a study of their remains embedded in the rocks, and the relative ages of the rocks are determined by the remains of organisms that they contain."

Raup, David M., "Geology and Creationism," *Bulletin, Field Museum of Natural History*, vol. 54 (March 1983), pp. 16-25.

p. 16   "I doubt if there is any single individual within the scientific community who could cope with the full range of [creationist] arguments without the help of an army of consultants in special fields."

p. 21   "A great deal has changed, however, and contemporary geologists and paleontologists now generally accept catastrophe as a 'way of life' although they may avoid the word catastrophe. In fact, many geologists now see rare, short-lived events as being the principal contributors to geologic sequences. . . . The periods of relative quiet contribute only a small part of the record."

p. 21   "The charge that the construction of the geologic scale involves circularity has a certain amount of validity. . . . Thus, the procedure is far from ideal and the geologic ranges of fossils are constantly being revised (usually extended) as new occurrences are found. In spite of this problem, the system does work! The best evidence for this is that the mineral and petroleum industries around the world depend upon the use of fossils in dating. . . . I think it quite unlikely that the major mineral and petroleum companies of the world could be fooled."

p. 25   "But we are not sure whether we can extrapolate this process of *microevolution* to explain the larger scale events of *macroevolution*. Even if it turns out that the classical Darwinian model does not explain some aspect of evolution, we will not be obliged to shift to a creation model. The literature of evolutionary biology and paleobiology contains a host of alternative *biological* models and these are being evaluated and tested in many separate research projects. Thus, the scientific creationists are totally wrong in their so-called two-model approach: the claim that if the Darwinian model is discredited, the only alternative is the creation model."

Ryan, B. F., "Mountain-building in the Mediterranean," *Science News*, vol. 98 (October 17, 1970), p. 316.

p. 316   "Early studies of mountain geology revealed that mountains are sites of tremendous folding and thrusting of the earth's crust. In many places the oceanic sediments of which mountains are composed are inverted, with the older sediments lying on top of the younger. Terranes of Jurassic and Cretaceous limestone several hundred feet thick are commonly found displaced by several miles from their original locations."

p. 316   "At a trench in the eastern Mediterranean, one oceanic plate is sliding beneath another. Sediments from the subsiding plate, says Dr. Ryan, scrape off against the upper plate and pile up. This accumulation, he explains, constitutes an embryonic mountain.

"It had been known for years that mountains are composed of ocean sediments. . . .

". . . In one location, they found limestones 120 million years old directly above oozes only 5 million to 10 million years in age."

Schindewolf, O. H., "Comments on Some Stratigraphic Terms," *American Journal of Science*, vol. 255 (June 1957), pp. 394-399.

p. 394   "The sedimentary rocks, by themselves, however, do not yield any specific time marks, setting aside the old law of superposition, which can provide relative age indication only in a restricted manner, and which is unfit for age correlations. Moreover, it may be misleading in some cases: the beds in a section may be overturned or, owing to a hidden thrust plane, older beds may overlie younger ones."

p. 395   "The only chronometric scale applicable in geologic history for the stratigraphic classification of rocks and for dating geologic events exactly is furnished by the fossils. Owing to the irreversibility of evolution, they offer an unambiguous timescale for relative age determinations and for world-wide correlations of rocks."

Schuchert, Charles, and Carl O. Dunbar, *Outlines of Historical Geology* (New York: Wiley, 1943).

p. 5   "Of course, there are many places where the succession has been locally inverted by folding or interrupted by faulting, but such exceptions will betray themselves in the evidences of disturbance and in the unnatural succession of the fossils."

Spieker, E. M., "Mountain-Building Chronology and Nature of Geologic Time Scale," *Bulletin, American Association of Petroleum Geologists* (August 1956), pp. 1769-1815. Spieker was at Ohio State University.

p. 1803   "Does our time-scale then partake of natural law? No. . . .

                "I wonder how many of us realize that the time scale was frozen in essentially its present form by 1840? . . . How much world geology was known in 1840? A bit of western Europe, none too well, and a lesser fringe of eastern North America. All of Asia, Africa, South America, and most of North America were virtually unknown. How dared the pioneers assume that their scale would fit the rocks in these vast areas, by far most of the world. Only in dogmatic assumption—a mere extension of the kind of reasoning developed by Werner from the facts in his little district of Saxony. And in many parts of the world, notably India and South America, it does not fit. But even there it is applied! The followers of the founding fathers went forth across the earth and in Procrustean fashion made it fit the sections they found, even in places where the actual evidence literally proclaimed denial. So flexible and accommodating are the 'facts' of geology."

p. 1805   "Further, how many geologists have pondered the fact that lying on the crystalline basement are found from place to place not merely Cambrian, but rocks of all ages?"

p. 1806   "And what, essentially, is this actual time-scale?—on what criteria does it rest? When all is winnowed out and the grain reclaimed from the chaff, it is certain that the grain in the product is mainly the paleontologic record and highly likely that the physical evidence is the chaff."

Stanley, Steven M., Warron O. Addicott, and Kiyotaka Chinzei, "Lyellian Curves in Paleontology: Possibilities and Limitations," *Geology*, vol. 8 (September 1980), pp. 422-426.

p. 422   "In about 1830, Charles Lyell, Paul Deshayes, and Heinrich Georg Bronn independently developed a biostratigraphic technique for dating Cenozoic deposits based on relative proportions of living and extinct species of fossil mollusks. . . . Strangely, little effort has been made to test this assumption. This failure leaves the method vulnerable to circularity. When Lyellian percentages alone are used for dating, it remains possible that enormous errors will result from spatial variation in the temporal pattern of extinction."

p. 424   "One source of error for Lyellian data that may, in general, bias estimates of extinction rates is a failure to recognize living representatives of some fossil species."

p. 425   "One might imagine that our well-documented Lyellian curves would lend precision to the traditional technique of using Lyellian percentages to date Cenozoic deposits. Unfortunately, this possibility is not realized. . . . Thus, our analysis casts doubt on the universal utility of the Lyellian dating method, even for faunas of a single province."

Stubblefield, Cyril James, "Evolution in Trilobites," Presidential Address, *Quarterly Journal Geological Society of London*, vol. 115, no. 458 (December 1959).

p. 158   "Trilobite history, in general, seems to indicate that most of the larger taxonomic units appeared cryptogenetically and diversified themselves within certain limits. . . . In fact, most of the trilobite superfamilies appear to be cryptogenetic. Cryptogenesis in trilobites is as frustrating to paleontologists concerned with evolution as in any other biological class."

p. 146   "The classification of trilobites has attracted much attention, with far from conclusive results. . . . A well-authenticated phylogeny of the trilobite class is still elusive."

p. 145   "Nevertheless, little or nothing is yet known about pre-Cambrian animal life."

von Englen, O. D., and K. E. Caster, *Geology* (McGraw-Hill, 1952).

p. 25   "Lyell strongly opposed any appeal, in explanation of geologic phenomena, to violent 'revolutions,' i.e., catastrophes and deluges with periods of repose between. As a result of his observations, he was imbued with a conviction that present causes solely have operated in the past. More than that, he insisted that they have always acted at the same rate."

p. 417   "If a pile were to be made by using the greatest thicknesses of sedimentary beds of each geologic age, it would be at least 100 miles high. . . . It is of course impossible to have even a considerable fraction of this at one place. . . . By application of the principle of superposition, lithologic identification, recognition of unconformities, and reference to fossil successions, both the thick and the thin masses are correlated with other beds at other sites. Thus there is established in detail the stratigraphic succession for all the geologic ages."

p. 423   "Historic geology relies chiefly on paleontology, the study of fossil organisms.
                . . . The geologist utilizes knowledge of organic evolution, as preserved in the
                fossil record, to identify and correlate the lithic records of ancient time."

Welles, Samuel Paul, "Fossils," *World Book Encyclopedia*, vol. 7 (1978), p. 364. Welles was Research
     Associate, Museum of Paleontology, University of California, Berkeley.

                "Scientists determine when fossils were formed by finding out the age of the
                rocks in which they lie."

Welles, Samuel Paul, "Paleontology," *World Book Encyclopedia*, vol. 15 (1978), p. 85.

                "Paleontology (the study of fossils) is important in the study of geology. The
                age of rocks may be determined by the fossils found in them."

West, Ronald R., "Paleontology and Uniformitarianism," *Compass*, vol. 45, no. 4 (May 1968),
     pp. 212-218.

p. 216   "Contrary to what most scientists write, the fossil record does not support
                the Darwinian theory of evolution because it is this theory (there are several)
                which we use to interpret the fossil record. By doing so, we are guilty of circular
                reasoning if we then say the fossil record supports this theory."

White, E. I., "Original Environment of the Craniates," in *Studies on Fossil Vertebrates*, ed. by
     T. S. Westoll (London: University of London, the Athlone Press, 1958).

                "Paleogeography is anything but an exact science, largely owing to our limited
                knowledge but also to subjective interpretation, and moreover, there is also the
                danger of circular argument, since the geography of these early times is based at
                least in part on the distribution and supposed habitat of the very fossils with
                which we are dealing. There are, however, important points of agreement among
                authors."

Willemin, J. H., P. L. Guth, and K. V. Hodges, "Comment and Reply on 'High Fluid Pressure, Isothermal
     Surfaces, and the Initiation of Nappe Movement,'" *Geology*, vol. 8 (September 1980), pp. 405-406.

p. 405   "At high enough pressures and temperatures, plastic flow will certainly reduce
                pore space inter-connectivity. To be effective mechanically, pore fluids must be
                in interconnected pore space; it is not clear that this is always the case during
                metamorphism."

pp. 405-6   "Our preliminary results suggest that the effective permeability of the upper
                plate must be on the order of 10^{-3} mD or less for gravity gliding to be feasible.
                Otherwise, the fluid will leak away from the zone of decollement before pore
                pressure can reach the levels needed for gravity gliding. Although *in situ* rock
                permeabilities are poorly known, the few existing measurements suggest that
                effective permeabilities as low as 10^{-3} mD are rare in the geologic column and
                may be restricted to argillaceous rocks and evaporites. Upper plate permeability
                is certainly one of the most important perameters in the gravitational stability of
                a potential nappe; it is, for example, far more important than slope."

p. 406   "If we assume that rocks have no tensile strength (or at most a few
                megapascals), then when the pore fluid pressure exceeds the least compressive
                stress, fractures will form normal to that stress direction. These fractures limit

pore pressure not only by increasing pore volume but also by increasing the effective permeability of the upper plate. If the least compressive stress is horizontal (as is the case in most proposed gravity gliding scenarios), we suggest that pore pressure may never get high enough to allow gravity gliding as envisaged by Hubbert and Rubey and Ayrton; the rocks might fail in vertical hydrofracture first."

B. Problems in Fossil Geochronology

The use of fossils in geologic dating has many problems. For example, many fossil organisms are found in many different "ages"—often still living today. This problem requires use of so-called "index fossils," usually marine organisms which presumably lived only during one certain geologic age. Even many of these have been found still extant today, in which case they are called "living fossils."

There is even considerable evidence that dinosaurs supposedly survived into recent times, being called "dragons" by ancient, even medieval, peoples. A similar problem arises when human remains or artifacts (or other recent creatures) are found in coal beds or other supposedly early geologic formations.

Evolutionists can always explain these away by various assumptions such as reworking of strata—or by simply ignoring them. Such phenomena do exist, however, and do cast further doubt on the entire evolutionary geologic-age system.

Anderson, Ian, "Dinosaurs Breathed Air Rich in Oxygen," *New Scientist*, vol. 116 (November 5, 1987), p. 25.

p. 25   "The Earth's atmosphere 80 million years ago contained 50 per cent more oxygen than it does now, according to an analysis of microscopic air bubbles trapped in fossilized tree resin. The implications of the discovery—if confirmed by more experiments—are enormous."

p. 25   "One implication is that the atmospheric pressure of the Earth would have been much greater during the Cretaceous era, when the bubbles formed in the resin."

p. 25   "A dense atmosphere could also explain how the ungainly pterosaur, with its stubby body and wing span of up to 11 metres, could have stayed airborne, he said.

     "The spread of angiosperms, flowering plants, during the Cretaceous era could have caused the high oxygen levels reported by Berner and Landis, scientists said last week."

Anonymous, "Ancient 'Dubiofossils' of Wyoming," *Science News*, vol. 110 (November 27, 1976), p. 346.

p. 346   "A diverse array of tubelike structures found in Precambrian rock on a mountain in southern Wyoming has the scientists studying them in a quandary. The series of curving indentations of various configurations look like the fossil traces of wormlike metazoan animals. There is only one problem: They are a billion years older than any previous proven metazoan fossil. And that seems way too old to be possible."

p. 346   "Kauffman reports no fewer than seven lines of evidence for biological origin, including the fact that all the forms have Cambrian and younger counterparts to be biogenic."

Anonymous, "Thin View of Appalachian Formation," *Science News*, vol. 115 (June 2, 1979), p. 374.

p. 374   "The Appalachians, which run from Newfoundland to Alabama, were probably formed not by upward thrusting, as previously believed, but by a thick conglomerate of oceanic and continental rock that was shoved horizontally at least 250 kilometers over existing sediments, according to researchers from Cornell University and Florida State Universities."

p. 374   "The Tennessee-Georgia profile shows, as expected, that the upper 6 to 10 km of the crust is made of fragments of ocean floor, parts of island arcs and continental rock. But beneath that jumble of rock, says Cook [Fred A. Cook, Cornell], lies a younger, flat, thin (1-5 km thick) layer of sediments that 'no one thought existed.' The unbroken, wide extent of the layer—researchers estimate it covers 150,000 km^2 from near the coastal plain to the western edge of the Blue Ridge—and its similarity to sediments found on the East Coast indicate that the mountains 'couldn't have been pushed up.'"

Anonymous, "Bushmen's Paintings Baffling to Scientists," Evening News, January 1, 1970, London Express Service, printed in *Los Angeles Herald-Examiner*, January 7, 1970.

"A fantastic mystery has developed over a set of cave paintings found in the Gorozomzi Hills, 25 miles from Salisbury. For the paintings include a brontosaurus—the 67-foot, 30-ton-like creature scientists believed became extinct millions of years before man appeared on earth.

"Yet the bushmen who did the paintings ruled Rhodesia from only 1500 B.C. until a couple of hundred years ago. And the experts agree that the bushmen always painted from life.

"This belief is borne out by other Gorozomzi Hills cave paintings—accurate representations of the elephant, hippo, buck and giraffe.

"The mysterious pictures were found by Bevan Parkes, who owns the land the caves are on.

"Adding to the puzzle of the rock paintings found by Parkes is a drawing of a dancing bear. As far as scientists know, bears have never lived in Africa."

Anonymous, "Serpent-Bird of the Mayans," *Science Digest*, vol. 64 (November 1968), p. 1.

"An ancient Mayan relief sculpture of a peculiar bird with reptilian characteristics has been discovered in Totonacapan, in northeastern section of Veracruz, Mexico.

"José Diaz-Bolio, a Mexican archaeologist-journalist responsible for the discovery, says there is evidence that the serpent-bird sculpture, located in the ruins of Tajín, is not merely the product of Mayan flights of fancy, but a realistic representation of an animal that lived during the period of the ancient Mayans— 1,000 to 5,000 years ago.

"If indeed such serpent-birds *were* contemporary with the ancient Mayan culture, the relief sculpture represents a startling evolutionary oddity. Animals with such characteristics are believed to have disappeared 130 million years ago. The *archaeornic* and the *archaeopteryx*, to which the sculpture bears a vague resemblance, were flying reptiles that became extinct during the Mesazoic age of dinosaurs."

Anonymous, "Dinosaur Found in NT Harbor," *Darwin News*, Australia (February 2, 1980).

"A species of aquatic dinosaur thought to have become extinct 70 million years ago is believed to be using the water of Bynoe Harbor near Darwin as a hatchery. Bynoe Harbor resident, Mr. Burge Brown, had seen up to three large, shiny black reptiles with serpentine necks in the area over the past seven years he has been living there.

"Naturalist and authority on strange animals, Mr. Rex Gilroy, director of the Mount York Natural History Museum, Katoomba, said the creatures are Plesiosaurus, related to the alleged Loch Ness Monster.

"Mr. Brown said although not many whites knew about the monsters the local Aborigines knew of their existence.

"Mr. Gilroy said they had been depicted in Aborigine cave paintings in the north."

Anonymous, "Living Dinosaurs," *Science–80*, vol. 1 (November 1980), pp. 6, 7.

p. 6 "In the swampy jungles of western Africa, reports persist of an elephant-sized creature with smooth, brownish-gray skin, a long, flexible neck, a very long tail as powerful as a crocodile's, and three-clawed feet the size of frying pans. Over the past three centuries, native Pygmies and Western explorers have told how the animals feed on the nutlike fruit of a riverbank plant and keep to the deep pools and subsurface caves of waters in this largely unexplored region.

"After a recent expedition there, two American researchers conclude that these stories refer to a real animal, not a myth. Fantastic as it seems, Roy Mackal and James Powell believe that this creature, called 'Mokele-Mbembe' by the natives, may actually be a dinosaur, perhaps one resembling brontosaurus, which is thought to have died out 70 million years ago."

p. 7 "There are precedents. No one believed that the prehistoric coelacanth could still be living until one was fished up off the African coast in 1939. The paleotragus, a giraffe-like creature that lived 20 million years ago, was thought to be extinct until one turned up in the Congolese rain forests at the turn of the century."

Barnes, F. A., "Mine Operation Uncovers Puzzling Remains of Ancient Man," *Moab, Utah, Times-Independent*, June 3, 1971.

"Lin Ottinger, Moab back-country tour guide and amateur geologist and archaeologist, made a find early last week that could possibly upset all current theories concerning the age of mankind on this planet. While searching for mineral specimens south of Moab, Ottinger found traces of human remains in a geological stratum that is approximately 100 million years old. . . . He carefully uncovered enough of what later proved to be the parts of two human skeletons.

"Dr. Marwitt [J. P., Prof. of Anthropology, Utah University] pronounced the discovery 'highly interesting and unusual' for several reasons. As the bones were uncovered, it soon became obvious that they were 'in place' and had not washed in or fallen down from higher strata. . . . The rock and soil that had been above the remains had been continuous before the dozer work, with no caves or major faults or crevices visible. Thus, before the mine exploration work, the human remains had been completely covered by about fifteen (15) feet of material, including five or six feet of solid rock. . . . Due to some local shifting and faulting, it was uncertain, without further investigation, whether the find is in the lower Dakota, or still older upper Morrison formation.

"Of course, despite evidence that these human remains are 'in place' in a formation 100 million years old, the probability is very low that they are actually that old. The bones appeared to be relatively modern in configuration, that is, of *Homo sapien* rather than one of his ancient, semi-animal predecessors."

Barnes, F. A., "The Case of the Bones in Stone," *Desert* (February 1975), pp. 36-39.

pp. 38-9   "The bones were obviously human and '*in situ*,' that is, in place and not washed or fallen into the stratum where they rested from higher, younger strata. The portions of the two skeletons that were exposed were still articulated indicating that the bodies were still intact when buried or covered.

". . . In addition, the dark organic stains found around the bones indicated that the bones had been complete bodies when deposited in the ancient sandstone.

". . . Mine metallurgist Keith Barrett of the Big Indian Copper Mine that owned the discovery site, recalled that the rock and sandy soil that had been removed by dozer from above the bones had been solid with no visible caves or crevices. He also remembered that at least 15 feet of material had been removed, including five or six feet of solid rock. This provided strong, but not conclusive, evidence that the remains were as old as the stratum in which they were found.

"And that stratum was at least 100 million years old. Due to considerable local faulting and shifting, the site could either be in the lower Dakota or the still older upper Morrison formation."

p. 39   "Somehow, the university scientists never got around to age-dating the mystery bones. Dr. Marwitt seemed to lose interest in the matter, then transferred to an eastern university. No one else took over the investigation. . . .

"We may never know exactly how human bones came to be in place in rock formations more than 100 million years old. It is highly probable that the bones are, indeed, this old. Yet, who knows? . . .

"Part of the mystery, of course, is why the University of Utah scientists chose not to age-date the mystery bones and clear up at least the question of their actual age."

Battersby, Stephen, "Prehistoric Monsters," *Nature*, vol. 387 (May 29, 1997), p. 451.

p. 451   "In France, the bohemian tradition goes back a long way. Palaeolithic cave artists of the Lot valley in southwestern France not only experimented with surrealism, they may also have found inspiration in hallucinogenic drugs. So say Michel Lorblanchet and Ann Sieveking, in an analysis of engravings in the innermost room (IV) of the cave of Pergouset.

"Room IV is hard to reach; the passage is narrow, mud-choked and steep. Once there, the explorer faces a sloping ceiling on which a fantastic bestiary is engraved. Part of it is transcribed here, showing a long-necked creature with a horse-like head, and next to it a 'monstrous head' that is harder to categorize. Elsewhere there are both less and more peculiar creatures, including one that vaguely resembles a fox's head on two narrow legs.

Edwards, Frank, *Stranger than Science* (New York: Bantom Books, 1959).

p. 77   "Two giant human molars found in Eagle Coal Mine at Bear Creek, Montana, 1926.

"Entire human skeleton in anthracite mine in Italy, 1958."

Forest, Jacques, and Michèle de Saint Laurent, "*Neoglyphea Inopinata*: A Crustacean 'Living Fossil' from the Philippines," *Science*, vol. 192 (May 28, 1976), p. 884.

p. 884   "A crustacean 11.5 cm long that remained unidentified in the collections of the Smithsonian Institute for more than half a century has finally been recognized as a member of the Glypheidae, a family with an extensive fossil record but one that was presumed to lack living representatives."

p. 884   "Only then will it be possible to conduct a thorough comparative study of the internal anatomy and, it is to be hoped, the ethnology and life history of this relict of a phylogenetically important group of animals that was believed to have reached its heyday more than 150 million years ago and to have died out little more than 100 million years later."

Galston, Arthur W., "A Living Fossil," *Natural History*, vol. 87 (February 1978), pp. 42-44.

p. 42   "Since the rocks in which Barghoorn's forms appeared [i.e., fossil microorganisms found in chert in Kakabek, Ontario] dated from the middle Precambrian period, about two billion years ago, the microorganisms were among the oldest of all plantlike fossils. Siegel's discovery of a living relative of Barghoorn's fossils established a remarkable thread of biological history."

Gould, Stephen Jay, "The Ediacaran Experiment," *Natural History*, vol. 93 (February 1984), pp. 14-23).

p. 23   "Whatever accumulates by punctuated equilibrium in normal times can be broken up, dismantled, reset, and dispersed by mass extinction.

"If punctuated equilibrium upset traditional expectations, mass extinction is even worse.

"Heretofore, we have thrown up our hands in frustration at the lack of expected pattern in life's history—or we have sought to impose a pattern that we hoped to find on a world that does not really display it. . . . If we can develop a general theory of mass extinction, we may finally understand why life has thwarted our expectations—and we may even extract an unexpected kind of pattern from apparent chaos."

Herbert, Wray, "Fossils Indicate Early Land Animals," *Science News*, vol. 123 (June 4, 1983), pp. 356-357.

p. 356   "Microscopic fossils extracted from rock in upstate New York have provided the earliest known evidence for the evolution of land animals in the Americas, suggesting that aquatic animals may have come ashore much earlier than previously thought."

p. 357   "All of the fossils represent animals that are now extinct, probably for more than 200 million years, according to Shear. But some are 'remarkably similar' to modern forms, Shear says: the mite can actually be assigned to a living class of animals, indicating an amazing degree of evolutionary stability, the centipede looks very much like a modern centipede, he says, and one of the arachnids resembles the existing daddy longlegs. Another of the collaborators, Edward L. Smith of the California Academy of Sciences, has identified another of the fossils as a machlid, or silverfish; if it is indeed a silverfish (others on the team are less sure), it would be the oldest known insect ever found.

          "One of the most exciting things about these fossils, Shear says, is the 'exquisite detail' that has been reserved—including minute hairs and sense organs."

Hutchinson, G. Evelyn, "Living Fossils," *American Scientist*, vol. 58 (September/October 1970) pp. 528-535.

p. 534   "Among single-celled organisms, the discovery, during the past decade, of survivors from a very remote past has been equally remarkable, though here it is partly a matter of finding essentially modern forms as Precambrian fossils. The most remarkable of these and also one extraordinary form first known as a fossil and then discovered living today, came from the Gunflint Iron Formation of Southern Ontario, which is about 1.9×10^9 years old."

Ingalls, Albert G., "The Carboniferous Mystery," *Scientific American*, vol. 162 (January 1940), p. 14.

p. 14   "On sites reaching from Virginia and Pennsylvania, through Kentucky, Illinois, Missouri and westward toward the Rocky Mountains, prints similar to those shown above, and from 5 to 10 inches long, have from time to time been found on the surface of exposed rocks, and more and more keep turning up as the years go by. What made these prints? As yet the answer is unknown to science. They look like human footprints and it often has been said, though not by scientists, that they really are human footprints made in the soft mud before it became rock.

          "If man made these prints in this manner, then man's antiquity is no matter of a mere million years or so, as scientists think, but a quarter of a billion years, for they are found in rocks of the Carboniferous Period and those rocks were laid down about 250,000,000 years ago."

p. 14   "If man, or even his ape ancestor, or even that ape ancestor's early mammalian ancestor, existed as far back as in the Carboniferous Period in any shape, then the whole science of geology is so completely wrong that all the geologists will resign their jobs and take up truck driving. Hence, for the present at least, science rejects the attractive explanation that man made these mysterious prints in the mud of the Carboniferous Period with his feet."

Kruzhilin, Yu, and V. Ovcharov, "A Horse from the Dinosaur Epoch?" *Moskovskaya Pravda* ("*Moscow Truth*"), trans. A. James Melnick (February 5, 1984).

"Soviet paleontologists have discovered the fossilized tracks of an unknown species of perissodactyles (odd-toed animals) in the spurs of the Gissar Mountains in southern Uzbekistan near the village of Baysun. . . . An analysis of the rocks, which were taken to Tashkent, indicated that their age was about 90 million years old!

"The paleontologists on the expedition immediately thought of comparing the 86 horseshoe-shaped tracks with equine imprints of hoofs. In any case, one could talk about animals very much resembling the horse.

"A TASS correspondent turned to the famous Soviet paleontologist, Academician B. Sokolov, Secretary of the Department of Geology, Geophysics and Geochemistry of the USSR Academy of Sciences, for an answer to this question. . . . the scientist said, '. . . there is not the slightest doubt concerning the accuracy of the determination of the geologic age of the "Baysun tracks." They are of the Creataceous period. . . . The tracks of any reptiles similar to these tracks are unknown to science at the present time. It is difficult to place them with confidence with any known group of mammals—the horse which they are now compared with, indisputably, appeared much later. Most likely, we are talking about the discovery of some whole new group of mammals.'"

Langenheim, R. L., Jr., "Recent Developments in Paleontology," *Journal of Geological Education*, vol. 7 (Spring 1959). Langenheim was at the Museum of Paleontology, University of California.

p. 7   "Inasmuch as fossil foraminifera are of preeminent economic importance, the work of Arnold with *Allogromia laticollaris* has special interest to paleontologists. Arnold has made a complete study of the life history of this living foraminifer and has discovered, among other things, great morphologic variation within laboratory cultures. . . . Inasmuch as these forms mimic most of the basic plans of foraminiferan test morphology, it may be deduced that specific and generic concepts based on shell shape—which includes all fossil foraminifera—are based on insecure biologic criteria. . . . Any given body form or chamber arrangement apparently must be potentially derivative from almost any ancestral type. This, of course, is of fundamental importance and indicates that a critical reevaluation of foraminiferan micropaleontology is in order."

Leary, Warren E., "Dinosaurs May Inhabit Remote Jungle," *San Diego Union Tribune*, October 18, 1980, (Washington Date Line).

"Persistent reports of strange creatures in remote, swampy jungles of western Africa has led two scientists to believe that dinosaurs still may walk the Earth.

Both historical reports from Westerners and firsthand accounts from natives indicate dinosaur-like creatures may exist today in a virtually unexplored jungle in the People's Republic of the Congo, the researchers said yesterday. Dr. Roy Mackal, a research associate at the University of Chicago, said he believes the animals may be elephant-sized dinosaurs. . . .

"In an article in *Science-80* magazine, published by the American Association for the Advancement of Science, the researchers say natives call the creature 'Mokele-Mbembe.'

"The researchers say they believe it actually may be a dinosaur that looks like a smaller version of the brontosaurus, a giant plant-eater that died out 70 million years ago. Natives shown pictures of many kinds of animals picked illustrations of the brontosaurus as most closely resembling the creatures they say they saw, Mackal said."

Lindall, Carl, "Dragon," *World Book Encyclopedia*, vol. 5 (1996), pp. 265-266.

p. 265   "Dragon was the name given to the most terrible monsters of the ancient world. Dragons did not really exist, but most people believed in them. They were huge fire-breathing serpents with wings like those of a great bat, and they could swallow ships and men at one gulp. Maps of early times represent unknown parts of the world as being the homes of these mythical creatures. The dragons of legend are strangely like actual creatures that have lived in the past. They are much like the great reptiles which inhabited the earth long before man is supposed to have appeared on earth."

pp. 265-6   "Dragons were generally evil and destructive. Every country had them in its mythology. In Greece dragons were slain by Hercules, Appollo, and Perseus. Sigurd, Siegfried, and Beowulf killed them in Norse, German, and early English legend."

Monastersky, R., "Old Pseudoscorpion Has Modern Features," *Science News*, vol. 136 (October 21, 1989), p. 263.

p. 263   "Scientists digging in upstate New York have discovered 380-million-year-old fossils of a tiny land-dwelling animal called a pseudoscorpion, pushing the history of this creature back to Earth's Devonian period, when animal communities were beginning to develop on land."

p. 263   "Before the new finds established the great antiquity of these animals, the pseudoscorpion fossil record went back only 35 million years."

p. 263   "The first land animals appear in the fossil record at the end of the Silurian period and the beginning of the Devonian period, roughly 400 million years ago. But many of these earliest fossils, including the newly found pseudoscorpions, show highly evolved features, including evidence of well-developed sensory hairs. Shear says this indicates either that early land creatures evolved rapidly after leaving an aquatic environment or that animals established themselves on land long before they appeared in the fossil record—a distinct possibility because of the rarity of fossils from that time."

Radforth, N. W., and D. C. McGregor, "Some Plant Microfossils Important to Pre-Carboniferous Stratigraphy and Contributing to Our Knowledge of the Early Floras," *Canadian Journal of Science*, vol. 32 (1954), pp. 601-621.

p. 601   "Fifty-six recently discovered spores and sporelike microfossils from Canadian non-coaly Middle and Upper Devonian age are described and classified. . . . Relative to the history of plants, the microfossils convey evidence of a more complex and more highly evolved Devonian flora than has been apparent from the macrofossil record. In addition, preliminary examination has disclosed spores of comparable abundance and of only slightly less complexity in rocks of Lower Devonian and Silurian age."

p. 608   "Its occurrence is unique, since angiosperm pollens have not been previously reported from strata older than Jurassic."

p. 613   "On the basis of the present evidence the land flora of the Devonian period was extensive and varied. This is contrary to the common interpretation."

p. 614   "This work has shown that complexity of pattern and form in microfossils came into existence in a marked degree long before it could have been assumed from any previous evidence."

p. 619   "The apparent early complexity reflected in the microfossil evidence presented lends support for the concept of polyphylogeny."

Rigby, Sue, "Graptolites Come to Life," *Nature*, vol. 362 (March 18, 1993), pp. 209-210. Rigby is in the Department of Geology, University of Leicester.

p. 209   "All palaeontologists dream of finding a 'living fossil.' Noel Dilly, it seems has done so and an account of the discovery appears in a recent issue of the *Journal of Zoology*. A trawl from deep water off New Caledonia, half way between Brisbane and Fiji, has brought to light an extant ptero-branch (a colony-forming hemichordate) that has an astonishing physical resemblance to graptolites, a group considered to have been extinct since the Carboniferous, 300 million years ago."

p. 209   "As graptolites are arguably the most important zone fossils of the Lower Palaeozoic (570-360 million years before present), this is far from being an esoteric issue."

Romashko, Alexander, "Tracking Dinosaurs," *Moscow News Weekly: Science and Engineering News*, no. 24 (1983), p. 10.

p. 10   "This spring, an expedition from the Institute of Geology of the Turkmen SSR Academy of Science found over 1,500 tracks left by dinosaurs in the mountains of the southeast of the Republic. Impressions resembling in shape a human footprint were discovered next to the tracks of the prehistoric animals."

p. 10   "'Science might possibly say that in the affirmative sometime in the future,' said Professor Kurban Amanniyozov, head of the expedition [answering the question about the co-existence of men and dinosaurs], corresponding member of the Turkmen SSR Academy of Sciences, Director of the Institute of Geology. 'However, at present, we don't have enough grounds to say this. We've discovered imprints resembling human footprints, but to date have failed to determine with any scientific veracity who they belong to, after all. Of course, if we could prove that they do belong to a humanoid, then it would create a revolution in the science of man. Humanity would grow older thirty-fold and its history would be at least 150 million years long.'"

Sanderson, Ivan T., *Uninvited Visitors* (New York: Cowles Education Corp., 1967), 244 pp.

pp. 195-196   "A much greater enigma is presented by the items that have been found in coal. This substance has been deposited on the surface of this earth at various times but most notably in what is called the Carboniferous (and specifically the Upper Carboniferous, so-called, or Pennsylvanian of America) which is calculated to be from 270 to 230 millions of years old; and from the Miocene of the Tertiary Era estimated to be from 26 to 12 million years of age. From it several items have appeared that confound just about everything we believe. For instance, it has been reported that in 1891 a Mrs. Culp of Morrisonville, Illinois, dropped a shovelful of coal in transferring it to her cooking range, and a large lump broke in two, disclosing a lovely little gold chain of intricate workmanship neatly coiled and embedded."

Schultz, Leonard G., "Petrology of Underclays," *Bulletin, Geological Society of America*, vol. 69, no. 4 (April 1958), pp. 363-402.

p. 391   "The relationships between underclays and coals indicate that the underclays formed before the coals were deposited. Furthermore, lack of a soil profile similar to modern soils and similarity of the mineralogy of all rock types below the coals indicate that underclay materials were essentially as they were transported into the basin."

p. 392   "The underclays were probably deposited in a loose, hydrous, flocculated state, and slickensides developed during compaction."

Smith, Grant Sackett, "Gaps in the Rock and Fossil Records and Implications for the Rate and Mode of Evolution," *Journal of Geological Education*, vol. 36 (May 1988), pp. 143-146.

p. 143   "All sedimentary sections are affected by basin stability, and subsidence and fluctuations in erosion and transport. Over a geologically significant time span all these factors will vary and directly affect the amount of time represented by sediment. Unfortunately, there is no method for restoring all that has gone unrecorded. The fraction of time recorded by rock formations is not large."

p. 144   "The discovery of living fossils such as the *Metasequoia* and the crossopterygian fish *Latimeria*, once thought to be extinct for tens of millions of years, are reminders of how much we have to discover. The fact that there is still no post-Cretaceous fossil record of *Latimeria* demonstrates how profound these gaps can be."

Stewart, Doug, "Petrified Footprints: a Puzzling Parade of Permian Beasts," *The Smithsonian*, vol. 24 (July 1992), pp. 70-79.

p. 79   "During a later prospecting trip through the nearby Doña Ana Mountains, [Jerry] MacDonald leads me up a dry arroyo and points out a long row of ancient petroglyphs. Local scholars believe they were carved by native desert dwellers about the time of Columbus. We scramble up the slope to examine a turtle, a rabbit, a deer, a hunter with a bow and arrow—all simplified but clearly identifiable and anatomically correct, opposable thumbs and all. On a single block of sandstone is a large figure MacDonald calls Godzilla. Its face is featureless except for a beaklike nose and mouth. Below its head are patterns of mountain peaks and a spiral shape that, according to local lore, has spiritual significance. Inside the spiral is a mysterious footprint.

"'Four toes,' MacDonald says. 'There's no animal around like that now.' Some of the Permian amphibians, however, had four toes."

Stutzer, Otto, *The Geology of Coal*, trans. by A. C. Noé (University of Chicago Press: 1940), 461 pp.

p. 271   "In the coal collection of the Mining Academy in Freiberg there is a puzzling human skull composed of brown coal and manganiferous and phosphatic limonite, but its source is not known. This skull was described by Karsten and Dechen in 1842."

Tilden, Paul Mason, "Mountains that Moved," *Science Digest* (June 1959), pp. 73-76.

pp. 74-5   "How can we be so sure that these great masses of rock, weighing untold millions of tons, have really been moved across the surface of the earth for distances that may range up to 25 miles?

"The answer to this question is provided by nature herself. Where ages of erosion have stripped away enough of the overlying rocks, geologists can look through the resulting erosion-openings, or 'windows,' and see the younger rocks below, with their younger fossils—a contradiction of one of the established rules of the science of geology."

Wilson, Knox, "Dragons," *Encyclopedia Britannica*, vol. 4 (Chicago: 1993), p. 209.

"Dragon, legendary monster usually conceived as a huge, bat-winged, fire-breathing, scaly lizard or snake with a barbed tail. The belief in these creatures apparently arose without the slightest knowledge on the part of the ancients of the gigantic, prehistoric, dragon-like reptiles. In Greece, the word *drakon*, from which the English word was derived, was used originally for any large serpent (*see* sea serpent), and the dragon of mythology, whatever shape it later assumed, remained essentially a snake.

"In general, in the Middle Eastern world, where snakes are large and deadly, the serpent or dragon was symbolic of the principle of evil."

C. Fossil Graveyards

A serious problem with the use of fossils for geological dating is the fact that their very existence requires rapid, permanent burial of the organism, before decay or scavengers can destroy it. This becomes especially obvious when, as is often the case, fossils are found buried together in great fossil graveyards, indicating that the animals (and/or) plants had been suddenly overwhelmed by a geologic catastrophe of some kind. This very fact argues strongly against long ages required to produce the geologic column, every fossil-bearing unit of which must have been deposited rapidly.

This becomes even more determinative in the case of so-called "trace fossils" such as footprints made in sand, worm trails, and the like. It seems very clear that these must have been buried quickly to be preserved at all.

The quotes below give examples of such rapid burial and fossilization—all over the world.

Ager, Derek V., *The New Catastrophism* (New York: Cambridge University Press, 1993), 231 pp.

p. 47   "Probably the most convincing proof of the local rapidity of terrestrial sedimentation is provided by the presence in the coal measures of trees still in position of life."

p. 49   ". . . we cannot escape the conclusion that sedimentation was at times very rapid indeed and that at other times there were long breaks in sedimentation, though it looks both uniform and continuous."

p. 52   "One of the most remarkable geological sights I have ever seen was at Mikulov in Czechoslovakia where an excavation in Danubian loess shows the remains of literally dozens of mammoths."

p. 149   "I suppose I had better mention the concept of a divine creator, but personally I do not find that particular hypothesis useful and I am tempted to ask about the cosmic accident that created Him (presumably before the 'big bangs' that started the universe). And what did He do before He created the world and mankind?"

Allison, Peter A., "Soft-bodied Animals in the Fossil Record: the Role of Decay in Fragmentation During Transport," *Geology*, vol. 14 (December 1986), pp. 979-981.

p. 979   "*Abstract.* Freshly killed, soft-bodied, and lightly skeletized animals display considerable resistance to skeletal damage during transport under experimental conditions. This resistance diminishes as decay advances. In addition a high degree of decay-induced disarticulation may occur with minimal transport when carcasses are buoyed up from the sediment-water interface by decay gases. Decay, rather than nature or duration of transport, determines the completeness of fossil soft-bodied and poorly mineralized animals."

Anonymous, "Fossil Finds," *Geotimes*, vol. 33 (May 1988), p. 27.

"He said he knew immediately what it was when he saw it: the oldest bee known, neatly preserved in amber. David Grimaldi, a curator at the American Museum of Natural History, New York, reported in December that the stingless bee's advanced features show that bees have changed little in the last 80 million years.

"The bee and many other specimens were collected years ago at Kinkora, New Jersey, near Trenton. It has been in storage at the museum with thousands of other specimens—waiting to be discovered.

"The amber comes from 80-million year-old sediments. Chemical analysis of the resin shows it came from the primitive Araucariacea family of primitive conifers, which lived in the Cretaceous.

" . . . The oldest bee known before this find is 45 million years old.

"The stingless characteristic and other features of the fossilized bee indicate that bees are far older than 80 million years."

Anonymous, "Chemistry of Still-Green Fossil Leaves," *Science News*, vol. 111 (June 18, 1977).

p. 391   "Thirty million years ago some green leaves from elm trees in Oregon were rapidly buried under volcanic ash. Some of those leaves are still a vivid green today.... So far they find the chemical profile of the prehistoric leaves surprisingly similar to that of modern leaves.

"The Oregon leaves are not the oldest leaves that have been studied: Green leaves, at least 60 million years old, were reported previously in Germany."

Anonymous, "A Fossil Bonanza in the Baja," *Science News*, vol. 106 (October 19, 1974), p. 247.

"But the highway has opened up to a team of Mexican and American paleontologists a bonanza of fossils that may prove to be one of the largest finds in recent years.

"Shelton Applegate and William Morris of the Natural History Museum of Los Angeles County reported to a meeting of the Vertebrate Paleontological Society of America in Flagstaff, Ariz., last week the discovery of more than 18 fossil sites on the peninsula. The sites dot a 350-mile stretch of rugged coastal and inland terrain from Santa Rosalia to Cabo San Lucas. Applegate told *Science News* that fossils literally cover the group for square miles in some locations where torrential rains have washed away the soil. At other sites, the team found fossil beds thousands of feet thick."

Behrensmeyer, Anna K., "Taphonomy and the Fossil Record," *American Scientist*, vol. 72 (November/December 1984), p. 558-566.

p. 560   "The chances for preservation may be enhanced by severe storms, epidemics, or changes in the temperature, availability, or chemistry of water, all of which can leave large numbers of buried and unburied dead at one time."

p. 560   "Because mass mortality or instantaneous death and burial create the optimal initial conditions for fossilization, it is possible that a significant portion of our fossil record is due to such exceptional events."

p. 560   "Once an organism dies, . . . there is usually intense competition among other organisms for the nutrients stored in its body. This combined with physical weathering and the dissolution of hard parts soon leads to destruction unless the remains are quickly buried."

p. 560   "These mechanisms contrast with the popular image of burial as a slow accumulation of sediment through long periods of time, a gentle fallout from air or water that gradually covers organic remains."

p. 561   "For remains with simple or complex taphonomic histories, burial is still the most critical step in the process of preservation, and only permanent burial will produce lasting fossils."

Brett, Carlton E., "Comparative Taphonomy and Ecology of Fossil 'Mother Lodes,'" review of *Extraordinary Fossil Biotas: Their Ecological Significance*, edited by H. B. Whittington and Conway Morris (London: Philosophical Transactions of the Royal Society, Series B, 311, 1985, 191 pp.), *Paleobiology*, vol. 14 (Spring 1988), pp. 214-220.

p. 216   "Given the evidence for weak to moderate current activity (5-25 cm per second), even on anoxic seafloors, it is unlikely that skeletons could remain intact without rapid burial even in the supposedly sapropelic settings of the Posidonia shales or other classic anoxic basin sediments. Hence, purely stagnation-type *Lagerstätten* may not exist."

p. 216   "Studies by Allison on the decay and early diagenesis of arthropods and other types of weakly skeletonized organisms demonstrate that burial in anaerobic muds leads to rapid destruction of organic matter (within a few months) by anaerobic bacteria; such tissues can only be preserved if early mineralization inhibits further decay."

p. 217   "Moreover, the very conditions that lead to preservation of fossil *Lagerstätten* are hostile to the development of normal benthic communities. Therefore, many if not most, extraordinary fossil biotas record unusual, stressed environments."

Briggs, Derek E. G., "Extraordinary Fossils," *American Scientist*, vol. 79 (March/April 1991), pp. 130-141.

p. 134   "Soft-bodied organisms must be protected from the attention of scavengers; this usually comes about through a lack of oxygen or by rapid burial. Although anaerobic conditions may eliminate scavengers, they do not prevent decay. Indeed, anaerobic decay is the norm, and can consume soft tissues in a few weeks (Allison, 1988a)."

p. 135   "In certain circumstances the organic tissues themselves can survive for geologically significant periods of time. Refractory plant cuticles have the highest preservation potential, but heavily tanned arthropod cuticles also resist decay. For example, there is a diverse assemblage of early terrestrial arthropods from mudstones near Gilboa, New York, which date from the middle Devonian. The cuticles of trigonotarbids, centipedes, mites, spiders, and possible insects are semi-translucent and appear unaltered."

p. 136   "Mineralized skeletons are not ubiquitous in the animal kingdom. Two-thirds of existing phyla lack any mineralized hard parts."

p. 137   "Extraordinary fossils are the only direct source of data on the evolutionary history of soft-bodied animals, including all animals more than about 600 million years old that predate the appearance, in the late Precambrian, of the first mineralized skeletons."

p. 137   "The discovery of Waukesha, Wisconsin, of the first significant assemblage of soft-bodied animals from the Silurian period, 400 million years ago, extends the known time range of some taxa back several millions of years."

p. 139   "Phyla are defined by their uniqueness. When an organism does not seem to fit into any existing phylum, it is thought to be a part of a phylum of its own.

During the hundreds of millions of years since the initial radiation of the metazoan phyla, intermediate forms have become extinct. Hence the morphological separation between the survivors has increased, so that the representatives of the living phyla are quite distinct."

p. 139 "One possible explanation for the vast diversity of these creatures is that each major group originated independently."

pp. 139-40 "How generally representative are these extraordinary preservations? First, they are not as rare as originally thought. From the beginning of the Cambrian the number of known sites displaying significant soft-part preservation exceeds 60 and for each of these major sites there are many minor ones."

Broadhurst, F. M., "Some Aspects of the Paleoecology of Non-Marine Faunas and Rates of Sedimentation in the Lancashire Coal Measures," *American Journal of Science*, vol. 262 (Summer 1964), pp. 858-869. Broadhurst was in the Department of Geology, University of Manchester.

p. 865 "In 1959 Broadhurst and Magraw described a fossilized tree, in position of growth, from the Coal Measures at Blackrod near Wigan in Lancashire. This tree was preserved as a cast, and the evidence available suggested that the cast was at least 38 feet in height. The original tree must have been surrounded and buried by sediment which was compacted before the bulk of the tree decomposed, so that the cavity vacated by the trunk could be occupied by new sediment which formed the cast. This implies a rapid rate of sedimentation around the original tree."

p. 866 "It is clear that trees in position of growth are far from being rare in Lancashire (Teichmuller, 1956, reaches the same conclusion for similar trees in the Rhein-Westfalen Coal Measures), and presumably in all cases there must have been a rapid rate of sedimentation."

Buchheim, H. Paul, and Ronald C. Surdam, "Fossil Catfish and the Depositional Environment of the Green River Formation, Wyoming," *Geology*, vol. 5 (April 1977), pp. 196-198.

p. 196 "The discovery of abundant fossil catfish in oil shales in the Green River formation results in a better understanding of the near-bottom conditions during part of the history of Lake Gosiute."

p. 198 "Furthermore, fossil catfish are distributed in the Green River basin over an area of 16,000 km^2."

p. 198 "The catfish range in length from 11 to 24 cm, with a mean of 18 cm. Preservation is excellent. In some specimens, even the skin and other soft parts, including the adipose fin, are well preserved."

p. 198 "The abundant and widespread occurrence of skeletons of bottom feeders, some with soft fleshy skin intact, strongly suggests that the catfish were a resident population. It is highly probable that the catfish could have been transported to their site of fossilization. Experiments and observations made on various species of fish have shown that fish decompose and disarticulate after only very short distances of transport."

Dalquest, W. W., and S. H. Mamay, "A Remarkable Concentration of Permian Amphibian Remains in Haskell County, Texas," *Journal of Geology*, vol. 71 (September 1963), pp. 641-644.

p. 641   "*Abstract.* The remains of 400 or more Permian amphibians were found in a series of siltstone channels confined to an area 50 feet square. The fossils include 90 per cent *Diplocaulus*, 8 per cent *Trimerorachis* and 2 per cent other types. The channels are thought to be the remnants of a drying watercourse in which aquatic amphibians were concentrated by drought. The absence of fish remains suggests that the fishes died at an earlier stage of the desiccation of the stream. Absence of *Eryops* and amphibians of more terrestrial habits indicates that these forms left the water for more suitable habitat. The fossils are mostly or entirely of heavy-bodied, weak-limbed forms that probably could not walk about on land."

Ekdale, A. A., "Dinosaur Tracks and Traces," review of symposium *Dinosaur Tracks and Traces*, edited by D. D. Gillette and M. G. Lockley (New York: Cambridge University Press, 1989, 454 pp.), *Palaios*, vol. 5 (April 1990), pp. 199-200.

p. 199   "Much to my surprise, the book documents literally hundreds, not just a handful, of well-exposed dinosaur tracksites spread all over the world."

p. 199   "Tracks, trackways, nests, eggs and coprolites of the reptilian masters of the Mesozoic are chronicled from all over the world, and the record is an impressive one—indeed, in terms of not only abundance and geographic distribution but also quality of preservation. Lockley and Gilette report >400 dinosaur tracksites in North and South America alone, and they especially note 12 'large' localities around the world that contain >1000 individual tracks and/or >100 different trackways each."

p. 199   "Dinosaur traces are not restricted to just one or two sedimentary facies. Lockley and Conrad report North American occurrences of dinosaur tracks in alluvial fans, fluvial flood-plains, desert dunes, interdune environments, lacustrine settings (both clastic and carbonate), deltas and marine shoreline systems. Alonso notes that some dinosaur footprints occur in association with algal stromatolites in northern Argentina. Pittman reports an interesting occurrence in Texas of theropod tracks on top of a Lower Cretaceous rudist mound, which probably lay offshore but was frequently emergent."

Feduccia, Alan, "*Presbyornis* and the Evolution of Ducks and Flamingos," *American Scientist*, vol. 66 (May/June 1978), pp. 298-304.

p. 298   "Because most bird bones are hollow or pneumatic as an adaptation for flight, they are not well preserved in the fossil record."

p. 299   "During the early to mid-1970s enormous concentrations of *Presbyornis* have been discovered in the Green River Formation."

p. 299   "*Caption.* Even with such concentrations of fossils there is no reason to assume that a catastrophe suddenly destroyed great numbers of the birds; normal attrition within a large population of the highly colonial *Presbyornis* could easily account for such a dense collection of bones in the bottom of a lake."

p. 300   "*Presbyornis* is an evolutionary mosaic, combining a strange montage of morphological characteristics of shorebirds, modern ducks and allies, and modern flamingos."

p. 302   "A search for ancestors in the fossil record is not likely to prove fruitful; organisms simply cannot make a living as generalized ancestors."

p. 302   "Likewise, *Presbyornis* illustrates many of the morphological features that one would associate with the ancestry of modern ducks and, to a lesser extent, flamingos, but it lived in the Eocene, no doubt after the actual transitions occurred."

Gretener, P. E., "Significance of the Rare Event in Geology," *Bulletin, American Association of Petroleum Geologists*, vol. 51 (November 1967), pp. 2197-2206. Gretener was in the Department of Geology, University of Calgary, Alberta.

p. 2204   "Of 50,000 mammoths, four have met death in a most peculiar way. . . .

"The fully preserved mammoth represents a rare event. The rarity of the event supports the occurrence of unusual circumstances on a local scale but at the same time refutes the occurrence of these conditions on a broad scale."

p. 2205   "Accepting the principle of the rare event as a valid concept makes it even more desirable to retire the term 'uniformitarianism.' If further investigations should prove that singular events of great importance have indeed taken place in the past, then the term 'uniformitarianism' not only becomes confusing but outright erroneous."

Grimaldi, David, "Forever in Amber," *Natural History*, vol. 102 (June 1993), pp. 59-61.

p. 61   "If one were searching for dinosaur blood, an amberized fossil insect would be an imaginative place to look for it—but then the real difficulties begin. Amplifying and cloning minuscule, undigested dinosaur DNA from the gut of a blood-sucking fly remains fiction, especially since red blood cells have very little DNA. Consider the magnitude of the current effort to sequence the human genome (which is the entirety of human DNA), for which billions of dollars, hundreds of researchers, and an almost infinite source of fresh samples are available. Reconstructing the genome of a dinosaur from base pairs of DNA would be like trying to reconstruct Tolstoy's *War and Peace* from a gigantic vat of alphabet soup."

Kerr, Richard A., "Fossils Tell of Mild Winters in an Ancient Hothouse," *Science*, vol. 261 (August 6, 1993), p. 682.

p. 682   "According to computer models of climate North Dakota and other continental interiors also had relatively harsh winters in the geologic past, even during periods like the early Eocene, about 50 million years ago, when global temperatures were the highest in the past 65 million years. But while the computers insist on harsh winters, Eocene fossils from continental interiors tell a different story: winters mild enough for crocodiles to roam through Wyoming and tree ferns to shade Montana."

p. 682   "The fossil fauna records compiled by Wing and Greenwood include abundant signs of mild Eocene winters in continental interiors: cold-sensitive land turtles too large to burrow for protection during the winter, diverse communities of tree-living mammals dependent on year-round supplies of fruit and insects, and crocodile relatives, all found as far into the continental interior as Wyoming."

p. 682   "The fossil plant data, Wing and Greenwood's specialty, also call for equable continental climate 50 million years ago. Palms cycads (resembling a cross between ferns and palms), and tree ferns extended into Wyoming and Montana in the Eocene." [Scott Wing and David Greenwood are paleobotanists at the Smithsonian, National Museum of Natural History]

Kroll, Paul, "The Day the Dinosaurs Died," *The Plain Truth Magazine* (January 1970), pp. 22-29.

p. 26   "*New Mexico*. As the layer was exposed [the workers cut a large scallop into the hillside] it revealed a most REMARKABLE DINOSAURIAN GRAVEYARD in which there were literally scores of skeletons one on top of another and INTERLACED WITH one another. It would appear that some local catastrophe had overtaken these dinosaurs, so that they all died together and were buried together (*Men and Dinosaurs*, by Edwin Colbert, p. 141).

                "They were found in the GREATEST PROFUSION, piled on top of one another, with heads and tails and feet and legs often inextricably mixed in a jackstraw puzzle of bones." [from *Men and Dinosaurs*, by Edwin Colbert, p. 143]

p. 26   "*Alberta, Canada*. There is a rich bed of fossil dinosaurs in Alberta, Canada. Here is one of the most RICHLY fossiliferous regions in the world for dinosaur bones.

                "'Innumerable bones and many fine skeletons of dinosaurs and other associated reptiles have been quarried from these badlands, particularly in the 15-mile stretch of the river to the east of Steveville, a stretch that is a veritable DINOSAURIAN GRAVEYARD'" (*The Age of Reptiles*, Edwin Colbert, p. 169).

p. 26   "*Wyoming*. [A 1934 discovery by Barnum Brown, famous dinosaur discoverer, on ranch owned by Barker Howe, who lived at the foot of the Big-Horn Mountains in Wyoming] 'The concentration of the fossils was remarkable; they were piled in LIKE LOGS IN A JAM'" (*Men and Dinosaurs*, Edwin Colbert, p. 173).

p. 26   "The Morrison formation—somewhat north of Como Bluff, Wyoming, is known as a tremendous source of dinosaur fossils throughout Western North America.

                "In the general area north of Como Bluff, on June 12, 1898, the famous Bone Cabin Quarry was located. It was named after an old sheepherder who had built a cabin out of dinosaur bones he found in the area."

p. 26   "'At this spot the fossil hunters found a hillside literally covered with large fragments of dinosaur bones that had weathered out of the sediments composing the ridge . . . the party went to work, digging down into the surface of the hill, and as they dug, more and more bones came to light. In short, it was a veritable MINE OF DINOSAUR BONES'" (*Men and Dinosaurs*, Edwin Colbert, p. 151].

p. 26   "'In the Bone Cabin Quarry . . . we came across a veritable Noah's Ark deposit, a perfect museum of all the animals of the period.'" (*Dinosaurs*, W. D. Matthew, pp. 136].''

p. 26-27   "*Tanzania.* One of the most important paleontological expeditions was the 1909-1914 one to what was then German East Africa, now Tanzania.

"'The site contained on ENORMOUS NUMBER of fossils—far more than could be carried off by one expedition. As in most of such sites, the greater parts of the remains were fragmentary . . . there was much speculation as to how the remains of so many dinosaurs came to be CONCENTRATED in beds otherwise *rather poor* in fossil remains. Some German scientists suggested that the animals had been overwhelmed by a *natural catastrophe.*'"(*The Day of the Dinosaur*, L. Sprague de Camp and Catherine Crook de Camp, p. 250).

p. 27   "*Belgium.* Back in 1878 a remarkable concentration of *Iguanodon* skeletons were discovered one thousand feet below the ground in a Belgian coal mine."

p. 27   'Thus it could be seen that the FOSSIL BONEYARD was evidently one of *gigantic proportions*, especially notable because of its vertical extension through more than a hundred feet of rock.'" (*Men and Dinosaurs*, Edwin Colbert, p. 58).

p. 28   "*Mongolia.* 'These eggs were in a GREAT DEPOSIT FULL OF DINOSAUR SKELETONS and containing, so far as we could discover, no remains of other animals or of birds . . . the deposit was unbelievably rich. Seventy-five skulls and skeletons were discovered, SOME OF THEM ABSOLUTELY PERFECT. Obviously the Flaming Cliffs were a region of *great concentration* of dinosaurs during the breeding season." (*On the Trail of Ancient Man*, Roy Chapman Andrews, pp. 228-231).

p. 28   "Another intriguing type of dinosaur fossil—if we can call it that—is the footprint.

"Such tracks are worldwide in extent. They are found in western North America and in New England.

"Dinosaur tracks are also found in South America, especially in Argentina. England also has them. And so has Basutoland, down in the southern part of Africa. In this out-of-the-way place, dinosaur tracks are quite abundant.

"The dinosaur hunters have also found tracks in such diverse places as Morocco, Portugal and Australia. Canada has not been neglected either. Dinosaur footprints are also found in British Columbia."

pp. 28-29   "And why aren't tracks and bones found together? Could intense heat have cremated the dinosaurs and preserved their footprints? Or was it because the dinosaur themselves were FLOATED and carried away by the same rising waters that preserved their tracks?"

p. 29   "'Another set of tracks, of a single individual, start off deeply impressed, as though the animal were unsupported by water, and *become less and less well marked.*'" ("Pterodactyl Tracks from the Morrison Formation," by William Lee Stokes, p. 952 in *Journal of Paleontology*, vol. 31, no. 5, September, 1957)."

Ladd, Harry S., "Ecology, Paleontology, and Stratigraphy," *Science*, vol. 129, no. 3341 (January 9, 1959), pp. 69-78.

p. 72   "In many parts of the geological record fossils are scattered sparsely through the rocks, but in other parts they are densely concentrated on one or more bedding planes. The numbers of fossils may be so great as to suggest abnormal conditions, possibly a catastrophe of some sort. Such an example was described by D. S. Jordan from the Miocene of California. Enormous numbers of the herring *Xyne grex* were found crowded on a bedding plane in the 'Monterey shale.' Jordan estimated that more than a billion fish, averaging 6 to 8 inches in length, died on 4 square miles of bay bottom. Catastrophic death in the sea on a comparable scale occurs today, due, in many instances, to the development of 'red water.' Studies of ecologic conditions in the existing seas again bear directly on paleontologic studies."

Lewin, Roger, "They Came from 40 Million B.C.," *New Scientist*, vol. 146 (May 27, 1995), p. 18.

p. 18   "From bees entombed in amber for up to 40 million years. US scientists have extracted bacterial spores and brought them back to life."

p. 18   "Cano and Borucki identified the bacterium by its shape and by the sequence of its ribosomal DNA. The sequence was similar to that of *Bacillus sphaericus* found in bees today. The differences can be explained by mutations over the past 25 to 40 million years."

p. 18   "The researchers say that their latest discovery should not arouse the same skepticism that met Cano's claim for 135-million-year-old DNA in 1993. Many scientists suspected that biological molecules could not survive that long, and that the samples had been contaminated with modern DNA. However, Cano and Borucki say that in this case the tightly controlled conditions of isolation and growth, and the DNA analysis, should convince any skeptics that the bug is genuinely ancient."

Middleton, Drew, "Fossil Lode in Gobi Reported by Soviet," *New York Times* (February 4, 1947), p. A23.

p. A23   "From this and other excavations, the expedition took seven tons of bones, which are now en route to Moscow, and the scientists expect to take scores of tons more."

p. A23   "Professor Efremov pointed out that 65,000,000 years ago, Mongolia was a fertile region, a fact proved by the discovery of fossilized tree trunks two yards across."

p. A23   "There are hundreds of dinosaur skeletons lying on or just below the surface of the red rock, . . . as well as dinosaur eggs [from 30 to 40 centimeters long]."

p. A23   "When the animals died, their bodies floated down rivers and settled in lake bottoms, where they were buried in sand and clay."

Morell, Virginia, "30-Million Year-Old DNA Boosts an Emerging Field," *Science*, vol. 257 (September 25, 1992), pp. 1860-1862.

p. 1860 "Using that method, they have now succeeded in extracting and amplifying tiny remnants of DNA from a 30-million-year-old termite fossilized in amber from the Dominican Republic."

p. 1862 "Some researchers interested in molecular evolution suspect the window could be cloudier than the enthusiasts are letting on, however. Aside from the problems of contamination, there's the fundamental question of whether enough DNA can really survive in these ancient specimens to produce meaningful results. 'Most dead DNA is degraded,' explains Rebecca Cann, a molecular geneticist at the University of Hawaii who was a collaborator of Wilson's in work on (modern) DNA sequences that led to the 'mitochondrial Eve' hypothesis. 'It's nasty, damaged stuff. We know from chemical experiments that it degrades. After 25 million years there shouldn't be any DNA left at all.'"

p. 1862 "Poinar, who says his colleagues put him 'in the crazy chair' when he announced plans to extract DNA from amber-preserved insects, concedes, however, that 'we don't understand the chemistry in detail' because 'no one has been able to imitate how resin becomes amber in the lab.'"

Newell, Norman D., "Adequacy of the Fossil Record," *Journal of Paleontology*, vol. 33 (May 1959), pp. 488-499. Newell was at the American Museum of Natural History.

p. 492 "Robert Broom, the South African paleontologist, estimated that there are eight hundred thousand million skeletons of vertebrate animals in the Karroo formation."

p. 495 "There are innumerable well-documented records of preservation of tissues of animals and plants in pre-Quaternary rocks."

p. 496 "One of the most remarkable examples of preservation of organic tissues in antiseptic swamp waters is a 'fossil graveyard' in Eocene lignite deposits of the Geiseltal in central Germany. . . . More than six thousand remains of vertebrate animals and a great number of insects, molluscs, and plants were found in these deposits. The compressed remains of soft tissues of many of these animals showed details of cellular structure and some of the specimens had undergone but little chemical modification. . . .

". . . Well-preserved bits of hair, feathers and scales probably are among the oldest known examples of essentially unmodified preservation of these structures. The stomach contents of beetles, amphibia, fishes, birds, and mammals provided direct evidence about eating habits. Bacteria of two kinds were found in the excrement of crocodiles and another was found on the trachea of a beetle. Fungi were identified on leaves, and the original plant pigments, chlorophyll and coproporphyrin, were found preserved in some of the leaves."

p. 497 "The oldest known fossils still preserve traces of amino acids after seventeen hundred million years."

Novacek, Michael J., Mark Norell, Malcolm C. McKenna, and James Clark, "Fossils of the Flaming Cliffs," *Scientific American*, vol. 271 (December 1994), pp. 60-69.

p. 60   "The Gobi Desert of Central Asia is one of the earth's desolate places."

p. 60   "Yet the Gobi is a paradise for paleontologists. Its eroding terrain exposes nearly complete skeletons of creatures hitherto known only through painstaking reconstructions from a few scattered bones. Our expeditions, jointly sponsored by the Mongolian Academy of Sciences and the American Museum of Natural History, have excavated dinosaurs, lizards and small mammals in an unprecedented state of preservation. Freshly exposed skeletons sometimes look more like the recent remains of a carcass than like an 80-million-year-old fossil."

p. 62   "Among them are 25 skeletons of theropod dinosaurs. This group of agile carnivores runs the gamut from the enormous *Tyrannosaurus* and *Allosaurus* through fast-running dromaeosaurs such as *Velociraptor* (the villainous predator of *Jurassic Park*, a title some 60 million years out-of-date) to smaller birdlike creatures such as the oviraptorids. We also gathered an unprecedentedly rich collection of small vertebrates: more than 200 skulls of mammals—many with their associated skeletons—and an even greater number of lizard skulls and skeletons."

p. 66   "The Cretaceous Gobi is unquestionably one of the world's great dinosaur hunting grounds. The fossils range from complete skeletons of *Tarbosaurus*, a fierce carnivore closely related to the North American *Tyrannosaurus*, to giant sauropods, duck-billed dinosaurs, armored ankylosaurs, frilled ceratopsian dinosaurs such as *Protoceratops* and a magnificent assemblage of smaller carnivores. Birdlike oviraptorids and dromaeosaurs such as *Velociraptor* are better represented in the stratified rocks of the Gobi than anywhere else in the world."

pp. 68-9   "In addition, Gobi rock sequences are entirely sedimentary, without even traces of volcanic rocks. Thus, geologists cannot determine the age of these strata by analyzing their proportions of radioactive isotopes."

p. 69   "In yet another ironic twist, the rocks of the Gobi appear to be missing precisely those strata that currently hold the greatest public interest: no sections found thus far include the Cretaceous-Tertiary (K-T) boundary, when the dinosaurs became extinct. Although the Gobi is richly endowed with early Tertiary mammal faunas, there seems to be a gap of at least several million years between these and the late Cretaceous dinosaur faunas. Whatever cataclysm wiped out the dinosaurs (and many other species then on the earth), its mark on Central Asia seems to have been erased."

Poiner, George O., Jr., and Roberta Hess, "Ultrastructure of 40-Million-Year-Old Insect Tissue," *Science*, vol. 215 (March 5, 1982), pp. 1241-1242.

p. 1241   "*Abstract.* Examination of the ultrastructure of preserved tissue in the abdomen of a fossil fly (*Mycetophilidae: Diptera*) entombed in Baltic amber revealed recognizable cell organelles. Structures that corresponded to muscle fibers, nuclei, ribosomes, lipid droplets, endoplasmic reticulum, and mitochondria were identified with the transmission electron microscope. . . ."

p. 1241   "Well-preserved fossilized soft tissues of animals are rare. . . . Cell ultrastructure has apparently not been studied in soft tissues more than 1 million years old.

". . . Baltic amber is believed to have originated in the late Oligocene to early Eocene, or about 40 million years ago."

p. 1242   "The ultrastructural remains of fossilized insect tissues in Baltic amber corresponded to what one would expect to find in a routine examination of present-day insects."

Raymond, Chris, "Scientists Report Finding Fossils of Dinosaurs in Antarctica's Interior," *Chronicle of Higher Education* (March 20, 1991), p. A11.

p. A11   "Scientists have reported discovering the first set of dinosaur fossils ever to be found in the interior of Antarctica.

"The fossils are said to be the remains of a plant eating dinosaur, 25 to 30 feet long, that lived about 200 million years ago in what geologists call the early Jurassic age."

p. A11   "The bones were spotted at a small section of exposed rock alongside the mountain, which lies about 400 miles from the South Pole."

Raymond, Chris, "Discovery of Leaves in Antarctica Sparks Debate over Whether Region Had Near-Temperate Climate," *Chronicle of Higher Education* (March 20, 1991).

p. A9   "The discovery of thousands of well-preserved leaves in Antarctica has sparked a debate among geologists over whether the polar region, rather than being blanketed by a massive sheet of ice for millions of years enjoyed a near-temperate climate as recently as three million years ago."

pp. A9-10   "In January, Mr. Webb—with David Harwood, an assistant professor of geology at the University of Nebraska at Lincoln, and Barrie McKelvey, a professor of geology at the University of New England in Australia—found the deposit of leaves on the side of a cliff in a desolate stretch of the Transantarctic Mountains, about 250 miles from the South Pole."

p. A10   "The leaves, compressed by subsequent layers of ice, look like fossils. But unlike fossils, which leave only mineral traces of the original organism, the leaves retain their original cellular structure and organic content."

Rhodes, F. H. T., H. S. Zim, and P. R. Shaffer, *Fossils* (New York: Golden Press, 1962), 160 pp.

p. 10   "To become fossilized, a plant or animal must usually have hard parts, such as bone, shell or wood. It must be buried quickly to prevent decay and must be undisturbed throughout the long process."

Stewart, Doug, "Petrified Footprints: A Puzzling Parade of Permian Beasts," *The Smithsonian*, vol. 24 (July 1992), pp. 70-79.

p. 78   "The fossil tracks that [Jerry] MacDonald has collected include a number of what paleontologists like to call 'problematica.' On one trackway, for example, a three-toed creature apparently took a few steps, then disappeared—as though it took off and flew. 'We don't know of any three-toed animals in the Permian,'

MacDonald pointed out. 'And there aren't supposed to be any birds.' He's got several tracks where creatures appear to be walking on their hind legs, others that look almost simian. On one pair of siltstone tablets, I notice some unusually large, deep and scary-looking footprints, each with five arched toe marks, like nails. I comment that they look just like bear tracks. 'Yeah,' MacDonald says reluctantly, 'they sure do.' Mammals evolved long after the Permian period, scientists agree, yet these tracks are clearly Permian."

Stuermer, Wilhelm, "Soft Parts of Cephalopods and Trilobites: Some Surprising Results of X-ray Examinations of Devonian Slates," *Science*, vol. 170 (December 18, 1970), p. 1300-1302.

p. 1300   "The discovery of soft parts of Paleozoic fossils is a very rare event. During an extended x-ray investigation of Devonian fossils from the famous localities of Bundenbach and Wissenbach (Lower and Middle Devonian, West Germany) many unprepared slates were found in which soft parts and extremely fine structures of the embedded fossils are preserved. These structures, consisting of a very fine-grained pyrite, are so delicate that they are normally destroyed by the usual mechanical preparation of the specimens."

Wright, Marshall B., "Mysteries of LaBrea," *The Citizen Newspapers* (June 11, 1976), p. 5.

"If the beasts of the famous tar pits did not die in the tar when coming to LaBrea to drink, as is generally held, how then did their bones get there?

"The assortment of mammals at LaBrea is not found living together today. . . . How did these various animals and birds and plants which we observe living in different environmental situations today, get mixed up together under the soil at Hancock Park? The solution may be a stream or river swollen by heavy rains flowing over a long distance which passing through different regions swept up representative animals, birds and trees eventually depositing them together at the site.

"Attempts to date the bones with accuracy by the Carbon 14 method may be unreliable if, in fact, many of these animals were swept away in a flood. This is due to the fact that water which has flowed over limestone high in dissolved dead carbon from calcium carbonate can contaminate the bones 'and make them appear older than they actually are,' says Dr. Akersten [William A. Akersten, curator at LaBrea].

"In a recent article in Los Angeles County Natural History Museum's *Terra* Magazine, Dr. Barnes [Larry Barnes, L.A. County Museum paleontologist] wrote that after these animals had proven their adaptability by surviving for thousands of years, they had become extinct in a relatively short period and suggests a combination of circumstances 'or even a major catastrophe' may have been the cause of several species disappearing at the same time."

Chapter 10

The Rapid Formation of the Geologic Column

A. Neo-Catastrophism versus Uniformitarianism

Uniformitarianism—the maxim that "the present is the key to the past" has been the governing principle in historical geology ever since the days of Hutton and Lyell, serving also as the key factor in the rise of Darwinian evolutionism. Originating as a reaction to the Biblical catastrophism implied by the global flood of Genesis, it assumed that present geologic processes acting over vast ages of time are sufficient to explain the development of all the geological features of the earth's sedimentary crust.

Modern geologists are now realizing that this approach does not work, and so they are developing what is called "neo-catastrophism," or "episodicity." This system postulates intermittent regional—or even global—catastrophes, accompanied by mass extinctions (the "punctuations" in the "stasis" of modern biologists and paleontologists), all within the standard uniformitarian framework of billions of years. They are still insistent that Biblical catastrophism must be rejected, but it is more obvious all the time that the hard facts of geology do correlate with one worldwide hydraulic cataclysm in the not-too-distant past.

Ager, Derek V., *The Nature of the Stratigraphical Record* (New York: John Wiley & Sons, 1993), 151 pp. Ager was Professor and Head of the Department of Geology and Oceanography, University College of Swansea. He had also served as president of the British Geological Association.

p. 32   "That brings me to the second most surprising feature of the fossil record. Alongside the theme of the geographical persistence of particular fossils, we have as a corollary, the abruptness of some of the major changes in the history of life.

     "It is both easy and tempting (and very much in line with the other ideas expressed in this book) to adopt a neocatastrophist attitude to the fossil record. Several very eminent living palaeontologists frequently emphasize the abruptness of some of the major changes that have occurred, and seek for an external cause. This is a heady wine and has intoxicated palaeontologists since the days when they could blame it all on Noah's flood. In fact, books are still being published by the lunatic fringe with the same explanation. In case this book should be read by some fundamentalist searching for straws to prop up his prejudices, let me state categorically that all my experience (such as it is) has led me to an unqualified acceptance of evolution by natural selection as a sufficient explanation for what I have seen in the fossil record. I find divine creation, or several such creations, a completely unnecessary hypothesis. Nevertheless this is not to deny that there are some very curious features about the fossil record."

pp. 68, 69   "Uniformitarianism triumphed because it provided a general theory that was at once logical and seemingly 'scientific.' Catastrophism became a joke and no geologist would dare postulate anything that might be termed a 'catastrophe' for fear of being laughed at or (in recent years) linked with a lunatic fringe of

Velikovsky and Californian fundamentalists. But I would like to suggest that, in the first half of the last century, the 'catastrophists' were better geologists than the 'uniformitarians.'"

p. 70   "Lyell himself was an excellent man on principles and processes, but he did not take very much interest in rocks. . . . So it was—as Steve Gould put it—that Charles Lyell 'managed to convince future generations of geologists that their science had begun with him.'"

p. 80   "The hurricane, the flood or the tsunami may do more in an hour or a day than the ordinary processes of nature have achieved in a thousand years. Given all the millennia we have to play with in the stratigraphical record, we can expect our periodic catastrophes to do all the work we want of them."

p. 98   "It is a problem not easily solved by the classic methods of stratigraphical paleontology, as obviously we will land ourselves immediately in an impossible circular argument if we say, firstly that a particular lithology is synchronous on the evidence of its fossils, and secondly that the fossils are synchronous on the evidence of the lithology."

p. 132   "I am coming more and more to the view that the evolution of life, like the evolution of continents and of the stratigraphical column in general, has been a very episodic affair, with short 'happenings' interrupting long ages of nothing much in particular."

p. 141   "In other words, the history of any one part of the earth, like the life of a soldier, consists of long period of boredom and short periods of terror."

Ager, Derek V., *The New Catastrophism* (Cambridge, U.K.: Cambridge University Press, 1993), 231 pp.

p. xi   "On that side, too, were the obviously untenable views of bible-oriented fanatics, obsessed with myths such as Noah's flood, and of classicists thinking of Nemesis. That is why I think it necessary to include the following 'disclaimer': **in view of the misuse that my words have been put to in the past, I wish to say that nothing in this book should be taken out of context and thought in any way to support the views of the 'creationists' (who I refuse to call 'scientific').**"

p. xii   "My thesis is that in all branches of geology there has been a return to ideas of rare violent happenings and episodicity. So the past, as now interpreted by many geologists, is not what it used to be. It has certainly changed a great deal from what I learned about it in those far-off days when I was a student."

p. xvi   "I must emphasize that I am concerned with the whole history of the earth and its life and in particular with the dangerous doctrine of uniformitarianism."

p. xix   "This is not the old-fashioned catastrophism of Noah's flood and huge conflagrations. I do not think the bible-oriented fundamentalists are worth honouring with an answer to their nonsense. No scientist could be content with one very ancient reference of doubtful authorship."

p. 163   "So there was never anything gradual or continuous about igneous activity, either volcanic or plutonic and here surely, I am entitled to use the term 'catastrophism.' In modern times it has certainly always been catastrophic for those people living in the vicinity."

p. 180   "I am sorry if I appear to be neurotic about this, especially as Velikovsky seems to be on the side of the catastrophists, but I do not want to be associated in any way with such nonsense. This, together with the writings of the Californian 'creationists' are the reason for my disclaimer at the beginning of this book."

p. 186   "Always it comes back to the extinction of the dinosaurs. I must admit to being a little tired of those stupid great beasts, though they are the best recruiting sergeants for our subject among young people (including myself). Their importance, in my view, is grossly exaggerated."

Ager, Derek V., "The Stratigraphic Code and What It Implies," in *Catastrophes and Earth History*, W. A. Berggren and John A. Van Couvering, eds. (Princeton University Press, 1984), 464 pp.

p. 93   "To me, the whole record is catastrophic, not in the old-fashioned apocalyptic sense of Baron Cuvier and the others, but in the sense that only the episodic events—the occasional ones—are preserved for us."

p. 96   "If the history of the earth in physical terms—either global or local—will not serve us, then can we not surely say that the evolution of organic life, as still our best method of correlation, will ultimately provide the synchronous events that will solve all our problems? Now that we know so much more about almost every major group in the organic world throughout the greater part of its history, is this not true? What do we do to piece together those evolutionary lineages that we feel so certain really exist? (I include the last phrase to protect myself from California fundamentalists who have already clasped to their bosoms a most-unwilling me!)."

Allmon, Warren D., "Post-Gradualism," review of *The New Catastrophism*, by Derek V. Ager (New York: Cambridge University Press, 1993, 231 pp.), *Science*, vol. 262 (October 1, 1993), pp. 122-123. Allmon is at the Paleontological Research Institution, Ithaca, New York.

p. 122   "Indeed geology appears at last to have outgrown Lyell. In an intellectual shift that may well rival that which accompanied the widespread acceptance of plate tectonics, the last 30 years have witnessed an increasing acceptance of rapid, rare, episodic, and 'catastrophic' events.

          "Two aspects of this shift are noteworthy. First, it represents a powerful response to creationists who often argue for wholesale rejection of all of historical geology whenever they find any indication of rapid geological phenomena."

p. 122   "The volume is the summation of a lifetime of global geological work by one of the most influential startigrapher-paleontologists of his generation, a highly eclectic compilation of the author's geological observations from around the world in support of the general view that the geological record is dominated not by slow, gradual change but by episodic rare events causing local disasters."

pp. 122-3   "Yet by the eminence of its author and the straightforwardness of its tone this volume may mark the arrival of catastrophism at the status quo."

Alvarez, Walter, and Frank Asaro, "What Caused the Mass Extinction? An Extraterrestrial Impact," *Scientific American*, vol. 263 (October 1990), pp. 76-84.

p. 84   "Catastrophes have an important role to play in evolutionary thinking as well. If a chance impact 65 million years ago wiped out half the life on the earth, then survival of the fittest is not the only factor that drives evolution. Species must not only be well adapted, they must also be lucky.

"If chance disaster occasionally wipes out whole arrays of well-adapted organisms, then the history of life is not pre-ordained. There is no inevitable progress leading inexorably to intelligent life—to human beings."

p. 84   "And with the removal of the huge reptiles from the scene, mammals began an explosive phase of evolution that eventually produced human intelligence. As detectives attempting to unravel this 65-million-year-old mystery, we find ourselves pausing from time to time and reflecting that we owe our very existence as thinking beings to the impact that destroyed the dinosaurs."

Arkell, W. J., *Jurassic Geology of the World* (New York: Hafner Publishing Co., 1956) 806 pp.

p. 615   "However, nothing can seriously detract from the fact that during some part of the Jurassic a fairly rich flora of temperate facies flourished within or near both the Arctic and Antarctic Circles, in East Greenland and Grahamland."

p. 617   "All things considered, therefore, the most probable explanation of the warm temperature of the Jurassic is that which depends on receipt of more solar radiation."

p. 618   "The infrequency of glacial episodes and especially the rarity of fossil tills in Arctic regions indicate that if, in fact, the poles have always been approximately where they are now, the warm state of the earth in the Jurassic was normal and our present condition, with polar ice caps, is exceptional."

Bak, Per, *How Nature Works* (New York: Springer, Verlag, 1996), 212 pp.

pp. 18-19   "Lyell's uniformitarian view appears perfectly logical. The laws of physics are generally expressed as smooth, continuous equations. Since these laws should describe everything, it is natural to expect that the phenomena that we observe should also vary in a smooth and gradual manner. An opposing philosophy, catastrophism, claims that changes take place mostly through sudden cataclysmic events. Since catastrophism smacks of creationism, it has been largely rejected by the scientific community, despite the fact that catastrophes actually take place."

p. 29   "The concept of punctuated equilibrium turns out to be at the heart of the dynamics of complex systems. Large intermittent bursts have no place in equilibrium systems, but are ubiquitous in history, biology, and economics."

p. 31   "In the popular literature, one finds the subjects of chaos and fractal geometry linked together again and again, despite the fact that they have little to do with each other."

p. 31   "In short, chaos theory cannot explain complexity."

p. 31   "Self-organized critical systems evolve to the complex critical state without interference from any outside agent. The process of self-organization takes place over a very long transient period. Complex behavior, whether in geophysics or biology, is always created by a long process of evolution. It cannot be understood by studying the systems within a time frame that is short compared with this evolutionary process."

p. 32   "Self-organized criticality can be viewed as the theoretical justification for catastrophism."

Benton, Michael J., "Large-scale Replacements in the History of Life," *Nature*, vol. 302 (March 3, 1983), pp. 16-17. Benton was in the Department of Zoology, Oxford University.

p. 16   "There is increasing evidence that major physical changes have caused more large-scale evolutionary changes than has competition. At the same time, computer simulations suggest that the apparent pattern in disappearances of whole groups may sometimes be the result of a purely random summing of events at a lower level."

p. 17   "Many hundreds of pages have been written about how the dinosaurs became extinct without our being any the wiser."

p. 17   "Competition may increase the probability of extinction of a particular lineage, but it will rarely be the sole cause, whereas it could be postulated that a catastrophic change in the physical environment is sufficient on its own."

Brown, Bahngrell W., "Induction, Deduction, and Irrationality in Geologic Reasoning," *Geology*, vol. 2, no. 9 (September 1974), p. 456.

p. 456   "The inferential perspective of the founding geologists was a unique one in the overall development of science and constituted a revolution against a scholastic system in which orthodox principles (global flood, for example) were rigorously maintained. But what of today? What is the essential difference between a statement beginning 'Because the continents drifted 2.5 cm per year. . .' and one that might have begun 'Because the flood of Noah drifted the icebergs. . .'? I fail to see any difference; both are deductive arguments, arguing the specific from the general. Both arguments begin with conceptual principles. One could challenge this statement by remarking that there is 'scientific' data in support of the first principle but not the second. But one could equally argue that within the *framework of the respective principles involved* there is as much support for one as the other; fundamentalists certainly find that to be the case."

p. 456   "Of late there has been a serious rejuvenation of catastrophism in geologic thought. This defies logic; three is no science of singularities. If catastrophe is not a uniform process, there is no rational basis for understanding the past. For those who would return us to our Babylonian heritage of 'science' by revelation and possibility, we must insist that the only justifiable key to the past is probability and the orderliness of natural process; if uniformity is not the key, there is no key in the rational sense, and we should pack up our boots and go home."

Courtillot, Vincent E., "What Caused the Mass Extinction? A Volcanic Eruption," *Scientific American*, vol. 263 (October 1990), pp. 76-77, 85-92.

p. 92   "Both the asteroid impact and volcanic hypotheses imply that short-term catastrophes are of great importance in shaping the evolution of life. This view would seem to contradict the concept of uniformitarianism, a guiding principle of geology that holds that the present state of the world can be explained by invoking currently occurring geologic processes over long intervals. On a qualitative level, volcanic eruptions and meteorite impacts happen all the time and are not unusual. On a quantitative level, however, the event witnessed by the dinosaurs is unlike any other of at least the past 250 million years.

                "Magnetic reversals in the earth's core and eruptions of large plumes in the mantle may be manifestations of the fact that the earth is a chaotic system. Variations in the frequency of magnetic reversals and breakup of continents over the past few hundred million years hint that the system may be quasi-periodic: catastrophic volcanic episodes seem to occur at intervals of 200 million years, with lesser events spaced some 30 million years apart."

Davies, Gordon L. H., "Bangs Replace Whimpers," review of *The New Catastrophism*, by Derek Ager (Cambridge University Press, 1993, 231 pp.), *Nature*, vol. 365 (September 9, 1993), p. 115.

p. 115   "Now all is changed. We are rewriting geohistory. Where once we saw a smooth conveyor belt, we now see a stepped escalator. Upon that escalator the treads are long periods of relative quiescence when little happens. The risers are episodes of relatively sudden change when the landscape and its inhabitants are translated into some fresh state. Even the most staid of modern geologists are invoking sedimentary surges, explosive phases of organic evolution, volcanic blackouts, continental collisions and terrifying meteoroid impacts. We live in an age of neocatastrophism."

p. 115   "As a vastly experienced field-observer (at the time of his writing he had plied his hammer to the face of 57 countries) he takes us from a Norwegian landslip to pillow-lavas in New Zealand and from Arizona's meteor crater to the flysch of Hokkaido. And everywhere the message is the same. We are on an escalator, not a conveyor belt."

Dott, Robert H., "Episodic View Now Replacing Catastrophism," *Geotimes*, vol. 27 (November 1982), pp. 16-17. Report of Presidential Address to Society of Economic Paleontologists and Mineralogists (June 1982).

p. 16   "What do I mean by 'episodic sedimentation?' Episodic was chosen carefully over other possible terms. 'Catastrophic' has become popular recently because of its dramatic effect, but it should be purged from our vocabulary because it feeds the neo-catastrophist-creation cause."

p. 16   "I hope I have convinced you that the sedimentary record is largely a record of episodic events rather than being uniformly continuous. My message is that episodicity is the rule, not the exception."

Dott, Robert H., and Roger L. Batten, *Evolution of the Earth* (New York: McGraw-Hill, 1971), 649 pp.

p. 227   "It has long been assumed that preserved sedimentary rocks record primarily normal or average conditions for past epochs, but this uniformitarian assumption must be challenged."

p. 298   "It has long been felt that the average climate of the earth through time has been milder and more homogeneous than it is today. If so, the present certainly is *not* a very good key to the past in terms of climate."

p. 417   "A uniquely satisfactory theory of mountain-building still eludes us."

Dunbar, Carl O., *Historical Geology*, 2nd ed. (New York: Wiley, 1960), 500 pp.

p. 18   "The uprooting of such fantastic beliefs [that is, those of the catastrophists] began with the Scottish geologist, James Hutton, whose *Theory of the Earth*, published in 1785, maintained that the **present is the key to the past** and that, given sufficient time, processes now at work could account for all the geologic features of the Globe. This philosophy, which came to be known as the **doctrine of uniformitarianism** demands an immensity of time; it has now gained universal acceptance among intelligent and informed people."

Gould, Stephen Jay, "Is Uniformitarianism Necessary?" *American Journal of Science*, vol. 263 (March 1965), pp. 223-228.

p. 223   "*Abstract.* Uniformitarianism is a dual concept. Substantive uniformitarianism (a testable theory of geologic change postulating uniformity of rates of material conditions) is false and stifling to hypothesis formation. Methodological uniformitarianism (a procedural principle asserting spatial and temporal invariance of natural laws) belongs to the definition of science and is not unique to geology."

p. 226   "Substantive uniformitarianism as a descriptive theory has not withstood the test of new data and can no longer be maintained in any strict manner."

p. 227   "As a special term, methodological uniformitarianism was useful only when science was debating the status of the supernatural in its realm; for if God intervenes, then laws are not invariant and induction becomes invalid. . . . The term today is an anachronism: for we need no longer take special pains to affirm the scientific nature of our discipline."

Gould, Stephen Jay, "Is Uniformitarianism Useful?" *Journal of Geological Education*, vol. 15 (October 1967).

p. 150   "Often, I am afraid, the subject is taught superficially with Geikie's maxim 'the present is the key to the past' used as a catechism and the imposing term 'uniformitarianism' as a smokescreen to hide confusion both of student and teacher."

Gould, Stephen Jay, reply to criticism by C. R. Longwell, *American Journal of Science*, vol. 263 (December 1965), pp. 919-921.

pp. 919-20 "*The only observable processes are present processes*. Of the operation of processes in past times, we have only fossilized results. Any inference as to the mode of action of past processes can be made only by comparing ancient results with modern ones formed by processes we can directly observe."

Gould, Stephen Jay, "The Ediacaran Experiment," *Natural History*, vol. 93 (February 1984), pp. 14-23.

p. 14   "I was in Indianapolis to attend the annual meeting of the Geological Society of America. There . . . a group of my colleagues in paleontology began to dismantle an old order of thinking about old objects—and to construct a new and striking approach to a major history of life's history on earth: mass extinctions."

p. 14   "Mass extinctions have been more frequent, more unusual, more intense (in numbers eliminated), and more different (in effect versus the patterns of normal times) than we had ever suspected."

p. 14   "About 570 million years ago, our modern fossil record began with the greatest of geological bangs—the Cambrian explosion. . . . In rocks just preceding the Cambrian explosion, we find a moderately diverse assemblage of medium to large (up to a meter in length), soft-bodied, shallow-water marine invertebrates."

p. 15   "[Dolf] Seilacher now argues, . . . The entire Ediacaran fauna . . . represents a unique and extinct experiment in the basic construction of living things. Our planet's first fauna was replaced after a mass extinction, not simply improved and expanded."

p. 22   "As we survey the history of life since the inception of multicellular complexity in Ediacaran times, one feature stands out as most puzzling—the lack of clear order and progress through time among marine invertebrate faunas."

Grayson, Donald K., "Death by Natural Causes," *Natural History*, vol. 96 (May 1987), pp. 8-13.

p. 8   "All in all, the North American mammal fauna at the end of the Pleistocene constituted a diverse set of often very large land animals. Why all these mammals became extinct and why the extinctions apparently occurred at about the same time are questions that have exercised scientists for nearly two centuries."

p. 12   "Of all genera of mammals that became extinct in North America during the entire Pleistocene (1.6 million to 10,000 years ago), nearly half disappeared at the epoch's end. Similarly, of all bird genera that became extinct in North America during the Pleistocene, 45 percent (ten genera) were lost at the end of it."

p. 12   "All take note that at the end of the Ice Age some North American mammals retained their geographic ranges unaltered, the distribution of others changed drastically, while still others became extinct. Those whose ranges changed were primarily small, while those that became extinct were primarily large."

Greensmith, John T., "The Status and Nomenclature of Stratified Evaporites," *American Journal of Science*, vol. 255 (October 1957), pp. 593-595.

p. 593   "As more fundamental data on stratified evaporites accumulate in current literature, it becomes demonstrably more apparent that their status as sediments is declining. Whereas they could once be grouped in their entirety as rocks formed by sedimentary processes, there is little doubt that some, if not the majority, could now be quite logically grouped as resulting from metamorphism."

Heylmun, Edgar B., "Should We Teach Uniformitarianism?" *Journal of Geological Education*, vol. 19, no. 1 (January 1971), pp. 35-37.

p. 35 "It is hereby submitted that most scientists are guilty of an overly-zealous interpretation of the doctrine of uniformitarianism. Many instructors dismiss the possibilities of global catastrophes altogether, whereas others ridicule and scoff at the early ideas. These same instructors will implore their students to think scientifically and to develop the principles of multiple-working hypotheses. The fact is, the doctrine of uniformitarianism is no more 'proved' than some of the early ideas of world-wide cataclysms have been disproved."

p. 36 "There are many other reasons why we should not blindly accept the doctrine of uniformitarianism, without at least qualifying the concept. For example, there is little evidence that climatic belts existed in the earlier history of the earth, yet climatic zonation, both latitudinal and vertical, is clearly apparent in all parts of the earth today. This anomalous situation is difficult to explain. It is impossible to reconstruct a super-continent which could lie entirely within one climatic regime. Any rotating planet, orbiting the Sun on an inclined axis of rotation, must have climatic zonation. It is obvious, therefore, that climatic conditions in the past were significantly different from those in evidence today.

"We find certain rock types in the geologic column that are not being seen to form, at least in quantity, anywhere on earth today. Where can granite be observed forming? Where can dolomite or siliceous iron formations be seen to form in quantity? Yet we have thousands of cubic miles of these rock types in the crust of the earth. The Paleozoic Era was marked by carbonate rock deposition, yet carbonate types are quite subordinate in modern sequences of sediments. Herz attributes the formation of anorthosite to the 'anorthosite event,' which was possibly a great cataclysm in the Precambrian history of the earth. It is possible that other rock types were created during and following catastrophic events on earth."

Hsü, Kenneth J., and Judith A. McKenzie, "Rare Events in Geology Discussed at Meeting," *Geotimes*, vol. 31 (March 1986), pp. 11-12.

p. 11 "Catastrophism is enjoying a renaissance in geology. For the last 180 years, geologists have applied consistently a uniformitarian approach to their studies that has stressed slow gradual changes as defined by Lamarck, Lyell, and Darwin. Now, many of us are accepting that unusual catastrophic events have occurred repeatedly during the course of Earth's history. The events were significant, since they caused sudden drastic environmental disturbances as well as mass extinctions.

"Two international projects on this theme began in 1980. Project 199 of the International Geological Correlation Program is aimed at cooperation and information exchanges among researchers of rare geologic events. Working Group 7 of the International Lithosphere Program coordinates international investigations of ocean history. The 2 groups joined forces May 20-22, 1985, at Gwatt, Switzerland, in a workshop, Rare Events in Geology and Biotic Crisis in the Oceans."

Hsü, Kenneth J., "Darwin's Three Mistakes," *Geology*, vol. 14 (June 1986), pp. 532-534.

p. 532   "We learned evolution in school, along with aphorisms about the struggle for existence, natural selection, adaptation, and survival of the fittest. Few of us have found it necessary to check the scientific basis of the Darwinian theory."

p. 532   "Mass extinction is not an artifact of imperfect geologic records. Mass extinction is a reality and has to be explained by a theory on the history of life. Darwin erred when he ignored this most important phenomenon in the history of life."

p. 533   "Darwin's view of killing the competition reflected the philosophy of his time. The motto of our age is peaceful coexistence and symbiosis."

p. 534   "Specialists on extinction have found little evidence that biotic competition had ever led to extinction until *Homo sapiens* came onto the scene."

p. 534   "But many of us now think that the history of the real world is different from that imagined by the nineteenth-century scientists. Conditions could have vanished suddenly and catastrophic extinctions ensued."

p. 309   "Lyell set up, however, a straw man to defeat his opponent, when he implied that Cuvier's alternative to his substantive uniformitarianism was to invoke the supernatural. In fact, Cuvier was not a creationist and never did invoke the supernatural as a cause."

p. 309   "But the working hypothesis of the last century has been turned into a dogma of today. Substantive uniformitarianism has been adopted as an article of faith, and catastrophists have been labeled fellow travelers of creationists."

Hsü, Kenneth J., "Actualistic Catastrophism and Global Change," *Paleogeography, Paleoclimatology, Paleoecology (Global and Planetary Change Section)*, vol. 89 (1990), pp. 309-313.

p. 310   "In my presidential address to the International Association of Sedimentologists, I pointed out the fallacy of the Lyellian dogma and coined the term actualistic catastrophism. Statistics have shown that frequency of occurrence of natural processes is inversely related to their magnitude."

Kauffman, Erle G., "The Uniformitarian Albatross," *Palaios*, vol. 2, no. 6 (1987), p. 531.

p. 531   "Our science is too encumbered with uniformitarian concepts that project the modern Earth/Life system as the primary model for interpretation of evolution and extinction patterns in ancient ecosystems. Detailed paleoenvironmental data tell us that the past is the key to the present, not vice versa. Today's Earth is still strongly influenced by the Pleistocene Ice Age. . . .

"In marked contrast, the typical Phanerozoic Earth lacked permanent ice, cold climatic zones, and glacioeustatic effects. Base eustatic sealevel stood considerably higher and was greatly amplified during tectoneustatic rise to 300+ meters above present stand, drowning up to 85% of the Earth. Warm, equable, maritime climates dominated, reducing seasonality and both latitudinal and vertical temperature gradients; deep marine circulation slowed, enhancing the establishment of widespread dysaerobic anoxic intervals. . . .

"... Abrupt, even catastrophic, regional to global mass mortalities and extinctions (bioevents) are predictable and commonly observed in Phanerozoic strata. ..."

Kauffman, Erle G., and Douglas H. Erwin, "Surviving Mass Extinctions," *Geotimes*, vol. 40 (March 1995), pp. 14-17. Kauffman is in the Department of Geological Sciences, Colorado University, and Erwin is in the Paleobiology Department at the Smithsonian.

p. 14 "In contrast to our views of a decade ago, we now recognize that all well-studied mass extinctions are complex, multicausal phenomena, not single catastrophes; however, a biological catastrophe related to a giant impact (such as end-Cretaceous) may primarily determine the timing and scale of a mass extinction."

p. 16 "Lazarus Taxa are species that disappear from the fossil record during mass extinctions for significant time intervals; they return, relatively unchanged, to become important components of recovery biotas. The lairs of Lazarus Taxa during mass extinctions are enigmatic, raising many questions."

p. 16 "During recovery intervals, which rarely last more than 1-2 My, both new and surviving lineages, diversity significantly. Early phases of recovery are characterized by fluctuating diversity, punctuated evolution during early radiations, and minor short-term extinction events."

Kennedy, George C., "The Origin of Continents, Mountain Ranges, and Ocean Basins," *American Scientist*, vol. 47 (December 1959), pp. 491-504. Kennedy held a full professorship at UCLA. This paper was from a National Sigma Xi lectureship.

p. 491 "Ocean basins are not merely the low lying parts of the Earth's surface flooded by salt water but are great, relatively steep-sided, structural depressions. In fact, there is too much water for the size of the ocean basins, and parts of the edges of the continents are now flooded and probably have been flooded through a great deal of the geologic past."

Krynine, P. D., "Uniformitarianism Is A Dangerous Doctrine," *Paleontology*, vol. 30 (1956). Krynine was a member of the Geology Faculty, Pennsylvania State University.

p. 1004 "Conventional uniformitarianism, or 'gradualism,' i.e., the doctrine of unchanging change, is verily contradicted by all post-Cambrian sedimentary data and the geotectonic histories of which these sediments are the record. Thus, quantitative interpretations of the *Ordovician* from the *Recent* are meaningless."

Lewin, Roger, "Extinctions and the History of Life," *Science*, vol. 221 (September 2, 1983), pp. 935-937.

p. 935 "'It is a great philosophical breakthrough for geologists to accept catastrophism as a normal part of Earth history.' This comment, made by Erle Kauffman at a meeting on the dynamics of extinction held recently at Northern Arizona University, Flagstaff, identifies a currently important, perhaps revolutionary, shift in collective professional perspectives among paleontologists as well as geologists."

p. 935 "The new catastrophism, if such an emotive phase can be permitted, for many would disavow the designation, merely allows for asteroid impact as one of many agents that from time to time profoundly perturb global conditions important to life, including atmospheric and oceanic circulation, temperature gradient, and sea level."

p. 935   "Each mass extinction in a sense resets the evolutionary clock and so makes the history of life strikingly spasmodic and governed by a greater element of chance than is palatable in strict uniformitarianism."

p. 935   "The notorious paucity of the fossil record combines with a greatly varying sedimentation rate to make time resolution of faunal changes little short of a nightmare."

McLaren, Digby J., "Bolides and Biostratigraphy," Presidential Address, *Bulletin, Geological Society of America*, vol. 94 (March 1983), pp. 313-324.

p. 314   "Robert Dott, in his Presidential Address to the SEPM in June of this year, has drawn attention to the importance of recognizing the need to adopt an episodic view of the sedimentary record. . . . recognizing that the sedimentary record is largely one of episodic events rather than being uniformly continuous."

p. 314   "A new uniformitarianism has moved to embrace at least a modified form of catastrophism. It may be that biostratigraphy for a time has lagged."

p. 317   "Arthur Boucot, in his presidential address to the Paleontological Society last year, evaluated diversity changes through geological time for level-bottom marine benthic organisms, and has divided the whole Phanerozoic fossil record into twelve ecologic-evolutionary units. Within each unit, the varied community groups of organisms maintain their generic integrity from beginning to end of the time interval; each unit appears abruptly and becomes extinct relatively abruptly. The causes for each extinction are not necessarily the same, if they can be determined at all."

p. 317   "All evidence points to the fact that geological time is punctuated by physical and biological events of many kinds. Increasingly, we are forced to the conclusion that the driving force of evolution operates at highly variable levels. . . . From examination of the major extinctions in the record, however, disappearance of the dominant biomass on a vast scale is perhaps the most potent driving force in evolutionary innovation."

p. 318   "Extinctions commonly, although not always, coincide approximately with System boundaries. This is hardly surprising, in view of the fact that the stratigraphic column was largely built up by using fossil evidence."

Shea, James H., "Twelve Fallacies of Uniformitarianism," *Geology*, vol. 10 (September 1982), pp. 455-460.

p. 456   "Furthermore, much of Lyell's uniformitarianism, specifically his ideas on identity of ancient and modern causes, gradualism, and constancy of rate, has been explicitly refuted by the definitive modern sources, as well as by an overwhelming preponderance of evidence that, as substantive theories, his ideas on these matters were simply wrong."

p. 457 "The idea that the rates or intensities of geologic processes have been constant is so obviously contrary to the evidence that one can only wonder at its persistence."

p. 457 "Modern uniformitarianism . . . asserts nothing about the age of Earth or about anything else."

p. 458 "The most serious problem with this concept grows out of the fact that it uses a metaphor, the *laws that govern or control* nature. Unfortunately, geologists have not recognized the metaphorical character of the expression and have accepted it at face value. We seem to believe that there literally *are* such laws. The concept is anachronistic in that it originated at a time when the Almighty was thought to have established the laws of nature and to have decreed that nature must obey them."

p. 458 **"Uniformitarianism must be viewed as telling us how to behave as scientists and not as telling nature how it must behave."**

Shea, James H., "Creationism, Uniformitarianism, Geology and Science," *Journal of Geological Education*, vol. 31, no. 2 (1985), pp. 105-110.

p. 105 "If the creationists could mount a successful attack on the validity of uniformitarianism, they would succeed in their effort to discredit modern geology."

p. 107 "Furthermore, modern uniformitarianism says nothing about the age of the earth and it makes no claim about theories of orogeny or anything else."

p. 107 "Before we castigate the creationists too heavily for committing egregious errors with respect to uniformitarianism, however, it must be acknowledged that they can (and do) support their concept of uniformitarianism by extensive quotations from recent geological literature. . . .

"In fact, as I have shown elsewhere, the geological literature . . . is replete with fallacious and misleading discussions of uniformitarianism.

"Indeed, they are extremely common in the geological literature and this clearly creates a problem for anyone who tries to show that the creationist concept of uniformitarianism is not the concept actually followed by geologists."

p. 109 "Morris apparently does not recognize that inference, extrapolation, induction, and even speculation are all essential parts of science."

Thornbury, William D., *Principles of Geomorphology* (New York: Wiley, 1954), 618 pp.

pp. 16-17 "This is the great underlying principle of modern geology and is known as the principle of *uniformitarianism*. . . . Without the principle of uniformitarianism there could hardly be a science of geology that was more than pure description."

Toon, Owen B., and Kevin Zahnle, "All Impacts Great and Small," *Geotimes*, vol. 40 (March 1995), pp. 21-23. Toon and Zahnle are scientists at NASA Ames Research Center, California.

p. 21 "The idea that comets or asteroids colliding with Earth might create the markers that subdivide geologic time is quite old. Yet it was largely dismissed as unduly catastrophic until Louis and Walter Alvarex and their coworkers discovered that the clay layer marking the Cretaceous-Tertiary (K-T) boundary was created in just such a manner."

p. 21   "In 1908, a massive explosion occurred over the Tunguska area of Siberia. Its origin is one of the great mysteries of this century. Without warning, an energy release of about 10 Mt between 5 km and 10 km above the surface flattened and partially burned about 2,000 square kilometers of forest."

p. 22   "It is now clear that the Tunguska event was a high-energy representation of the typical fate of small impactors. And astronomers are not crying wolf about those two nuclear-size explosions which should occur each year. In fact, such high-energy explosions are routinely witnessed by Department of Defense satellites, which monitor explosions in the atmosphere. As they explode, the objects disintegrate in the atmosphere, leaving only small pieces of debris. The vast majority are small enough and weak enough to disintegrate at very high altitudes, thus failing to produce a blast wave that reaches Earth's surface. The Tunguska object, probably a stony asteroid, is at the upper end of the energy range of small objects since its explosion caused surface damage."

p. 22   "Imagine the effects of 10^{20} shooting stars suddenly entering the atmosphere and ablating at an altitude above 60 km! The sky would turn from its normal transparent blue to a brilliant red sheet of glowing lava. During the following hour or so, the red sky would cool, plunging the world into total darkness as the shooting star remnants blot out the sun. Vast billows of smoke would fill the sky from the continental-scale fires. Pity the poor dinosaurs."

Valentine, James W., "The Present is the Key to the Present," *Journal of Geological Education*, vol. 14 (May 1966), pp. 59-60. Valentine is at the University of California, Davis.

p. 59   "The doctrine of uniformitarianism has been vigorously disputed in recent years. A number of writers, although approaching the subject from different directions, have agreed that this doctrine is composed partly of meaningless and erroneous components and some have suggested that it be discarded as a formal assumption of geological science."

p. 60   "Frequently the doctrine of uniformitarianism is used fruitfully to explain the anti-catastrophist viewpoint of history and to illuminate the practical working method of consulting nature for clues to natural history."

p. 60   "It seems unfortunate that uniformitarianism, a doctrine which has so important a place in the history of geology, should continue to be misrepresented in introductory texts and courses by 'the present is the key to the past,' a maxim without much credit."

van Andel, Tjeerd H., "Consider the Incompleteness of the Geological Record," *Nature*, vol. 294 (December 3, 1981), pp. 397-398.

p. 397   "Thus it appears that indeed the geological record is exceedingly incomplete, and that the incompleteness is greater the shorter the time span at which we look."

p. 397   "If erosion and other ravages of time are the cause of the missing record, one should expect the incompleteness to increase with age. This, however, is not the case and the explanation cannot be so simple."

p. 398   "The geological record may thus be a record of rare events separated on any time scale by numerous and long gaps."

p. 398   "Among the many ideas fermenting today in the study of evolution there is one, frequently heard, that ascribes the major evolutionary steps to a jump advance, a concentration of major change in a very brief interval of time. There seems to be no good reason why such pulses of evolutionary change should coincide with the major rare events that built the sedimentary sequence in which the record of evolution is contained. Thus, the new 'catastrophist' view of the sedimentary record implies that key elements of the evolutionary record may be forever out of reach."

Zumberge, James H., *Elements of Geology*, 2nd. ed. (1963).

p. 200   "Opposed to this line of thinking was Sir Charles Lyell (1797-1875), a contemporary of Cuvier, who held that earth changes were gradual, taking place at the same uniform slowness that they are today. Lyell is thus credited with the propagation of the premise that more or less has guided geological thought ever since, namely, that *the present is the key to the past*. In essence, Lyell's *doctrine of uniformitarianism* stated that past geological processes operated in the same manner and at the same rate they do today."

p. 201   "From a purely scientific point of view, it is unwise to accept uniformitarianism as unalterable dogma. As pointed out in chapter one, man's experience with geological processes is restricted to only a minute fraction of the total span of earth history. He should never close his mind to the possibility that conditions in past geological time were different than today, and that the doctrine of uniformitarianism may not apply in every case where the reconstruction of some segment of earth history is involved."

B. Rapid Processes Everywhere

It is remarkable that geologic processes acting slowly as at present are no longer deemed able to account for the corresponding geologic structures produced in the past. This applies not only to ordinary layered sedimentary rocks—which can now best be understood in terms of rapid depositional processes— but also to those formations which used to be explained in terms of supposed modern analogues (e.g., salt deposits, coral reefs, coal beds, stalactites, river valleys, and other such features).

The quotes in this section illustrate this trend. Even fossil fuels can be formed rapidly. Furthermore, significant climatic changes can generate global warm climates or ice ages. Even extra-terrestrial impacts are now being invoked to account for various phenomena. Although coming closer all the time to the Biblical explanation—and, no doubt, influenced in part by the creationist revival of the past half-century—all the establishment journals and schools still seem firmly committed to evolutionism and the geologic ages.

Ager, Derek V., *The Nature of the Stratigraphical Record* (New York: John Wiley & Sons, 1993), 151 pp. Ager was Professor and Head, Department of Geology and Oceanography, University College of Swansea.

p. 33   "I am now very much of the opinion that most evolution proceeds by sudden short steps of *quanta* as brilliantly expressed by S. J. Gould and Niles Eldredge who suggested that new species arise, not in the main center of its ancestors, but in peripheral, somewhat isolated populations. As Gould expressed it: 'The history of evolution is not one of stately unfolding, but a story of homeostatic equilibria, rarely disturbed by rapid events of speciation.'"

p. 41   "At the end of the Miocene, the Mediterranean became a deep, desiccated basin with evaporites and lacustrine diatomites. At the beginning of the Pliocene, the Strait of Gibraltar opened again, according to Hsü, as a fantastic cataract through which a catastrophic deluge refilled the Mediterranean."

p. 52   "But I maintain that a far more accurate picture of the stratigraphical record is of one long gap with only very occasional sedimentation."

p. 64   "Although at the surface there are only flat green fields, underneath a pillar of chalk was found pushing up some 200 feet through the Tertiary, like an igneous intrusion. The most surprising fossil find of the study was an 18th century clay pipe, more than 20 feet down."

p. 64   "It is well known that Roman remains are found at considerable depth in the lower Thames Valley and that the 'Roman snail' they introduced to Britain is found far down in hill wash and similar deposits."

p. 65   "The point I am trying to make all the time is that erosion and deposition have frequently in the past been very short-term phenomena."

p. 65   "In the late Carboniferous Coal Measures of Lancashire, a fossil tree has been found, 38 feet high and still standing in its living position. Sedimentation must therefore have been fast enough to bury the tree and solidify before the tree had time to rot. Similarly, at Gilboa in New York State, within the deposits of the Devonian Catskill delta, a flashflood (itself an example of a modern catastrophic event) uncovered a whole forest of *in situ* Devonian trees up to 40 feet high."

p. 75   "Similarly, it has been shown that tsunami, or 'tidal waves' as they were for long mis-named, have an immense effect on shorelines, both in erosion and in the shifting of great quantities of sediment. To quote a recent author on the subject: '. . . the action of tsunamis is short and extremely violent. . . .' It has been suggested that sea-floor sediments as deep as 1000 metres may be disturbed. Waves up to 40 metres high have been recorded rushing inland, carving out valleys, stripping off deltas and wiping out hills. The resultant mass of land, beach and shallow water sediments is just as violently carried out to sea and dumped."

p. 80   "One of the most spectacular sights ever seen by man must have been the mile-high fiery cascade when a lava flow poured into the Grand Canyon in Arizona. Earlier lava flows, before the coming of man, date back a million years, but since that time the Colorado River has only cut down about 50 feet. The canyon itself cannot have started more than 10 million years ago, so here too three must have been some very rapid erosion at some time."

Anderson, Larry L., "Oil Made from Garbage," *Science Digest*, vol. 74 (July 1973), pp. 76-77.

p. 77   "[There is] great promise in a system being developed by government scientists that coverts organic material to oil and gas by treating it with carbon monoxide and water at high temperature and pressure."

p. 77   "By using the waste-to-oil process, 1.1 billion barrels of oil could be gleaned from the 880 million tons of organic wastes suitable for conversion (each year)."

Anonymous, "Striking Oil in the Laboratory," *Science News*, vol. 125 (March 24, 1984), p. 187.

"For six years, two Australian researchers patiently watched over a set of 1-gram samples of organic materials sealed inside stainless steel 'bombs.' the samples were derived from brown coal and a type of oil shale called torbanite. Each week, the temperature of the samples was increased by 1° C, gradually heating the material from 100° to 400° C. . . .

"The researchers found that after four years a product 'indistinguishable from a paraffinic crude oil' was generated from the torbanite-derived samples, while brown coal produced a 'wet natural gas.'"

Anonymous, "Basic Coal Studies Refute Current Theories of Formation," *Research and Development*, vol. 26 (February 1984), p. 92.

p. 92   "A group at Argonne National Laboratory near Chicago, Illinois, recently uncovered some clues as to the origin of coal. The studies indicate that currently accepted theories of the development of coal probably are wrong.

"'We made simple coals by duplicating conditions that are known to occur in nature,' explained Randall Winans, who headed the research team. 'But we started with material that was less decomposed than the material nature is thought to have used.'"

p. 92   "The group heated undecomposed lignin, the substance that holds plant cells together, in the presence of montmorillite, or illite clay. The process led to simple coals, whose rank depended on the length of exposure to the 300-F temperature."

p. 92   "Although the experiments did not fully reproduce conditions in nature, they do suggest how natural coal could have formed. 'It appears that the clay acts as a catalyst to form coal from lignin,' explained Winans. Backing that speculation is the fact that montmorillite and illite clays are often found in natural coal."

Berthault, Guy, "Experiments on Laminations of Sediments, Resulting from a Periodic Graded-bedding Subsequent to Deposit: A Contribution to the Explanation of Lamination of Various Sediments and Sedimentary Rocks," *C. R. Academic des Sciences Paris*, vol. 303, series 2, no. 17 (1986), pp. 1569-1574.

p. 1574   "The continuous deposit of a heterogranular sediment in still water was studied. 1. It was noted that the deposited material organized itself immediately after deposition into periodic graded laminae giving the appearance of successive beds. 2. One of the more striking features of these laminae formed in the sediment itself was their regular periodicity. 3. The thickness of the laminae is measured in millimetres. It is independent of the speed of sedimentation and varies according to the extreme difference in the size of the mixed particles. 4. When deposition took place in a water flow, the lamination phenomenon was also observed. The geometry of lamination was modified by the water flow, but the latter was not the cause of the modification. 5. The periodic graded laminae were similar to the laminae or varves observed in nature which are interpreted as a superposition of seasonal or annual beds. Their origin, however, was quite different arising from periodic structuring after deposit. 6. The question now is to study a number of laminated or varved formations in relation to this mechanism for physical structuring obtained from experimentation."

Blatt, H., G. Middleton, and R. Murray, *Origin of Sedimentary Rocks* (Englewood Cliffs, New Jersey: Prentice-Hall, 1972), 634 pp.

pp. 410-11   "Closer inspection of many of these ancient carbonate 'reefs' reveals that they are composed largely of carbonate mud with the larger skeletal particles 'floating' within the mud matrix. Conclusive evidence for a rigid organic framework does not exist in most of the ancient carbonate mounds. In this sense they are remarkably different from modern coral reefs."

Braithwaite, C. J. R., "Reefs: Just a Problem of Semantics?" *Bulletin, The American Association of Petroleum Geologists*, vol. 57, no. 6 (June 1973), pp. 1100-1116. Braithwaite was Professor of Geology, The University, Dundee.

p. 1100   "For many authors, the recognition of reefs in the geologic column has presented no problem, but it seems fair to say that this has been less often a result of their clarity of thought than of their use of some quite personal definition."

p. 1104   "Growth is not necessary to provide the morphology nor, conversely, is the morphology necessary to support the growth; it simply provides a convenient substrate. This may at first seem unconvincing, but in the Seychelles, as noted above, there are both 'reefs' without corals and areas of prolific coral growth which are not associated with reefs."

p. 1104   "Newell and Rigby suggested that the Florida reefs are probably a thin skeletal veneer overlying the Key Largo limestone, and Tracey *et al.* believed that the reefs of Bikini were growing on an older surface. Even in Yucatan, the main reefs are localized in inorganic banks."

p. 1105   "Among the best documented examples are the classic syntheses of the Permian Guadalupe Mountains complex. . . .

"There is little doubt that this 'reef' had real topographic expression and that it controlled the distribution and character of sediments and organisms in the region. What does seem questionable is that this was an organic reef in which bioconstruction determined the feature."

p. 1105   "Dunham stated that the structure was in fact largely the product of inorganic binding, and that organisms, although present, did not provide a rigid framework."

p. 1108   "MacNeil put forward the idea that much of the morphology of modern reefs is explicable in terms of growth of corals on a preexisting base, the shape of which was largely responsible for the form which the reef later took."

p. 1108   "In summary, present reefs commonly are bedded structures. This is borne out by excavations in recent sediments in the Seychelles, observation of the Pleistocene of Aldabra and of the East African coast, and examination of the boreholes listed earlier. Coral frames commonly represent only a small part of the volume."

Breger, Irving A., "Geochemistry of Coal," *Economic Geology*, vol. 53 (November 1958), pp. 823-841. Breger was a member of the U.S. Geological Survey.

p. 823   "Based on a review of the literature, the consensus is that coal was formed predominantly from lignin. The potential contributed from cellulose or its degradation produces is, however, difficult to evaluate. Consideration of sources of energy for the metamorphic processes that convert plant residues into high-rank coals leads to the conclusion that neither bacteria, hydrostatic head, nor localized high temperatures were the geologically active agencies. The application of shear force may provide the energy necessary, but the effectiveness of low-grade thermal activation over long periods of time cannot be overlooked."

Butler, Elizabeth J., and Sir Fred Hoyle, "On the Effect of a Sudden Change in the Albedo of the Earth," *Astrophysics and Space Science*, vol. 60 (February 1979), pp. 505-511.

p. 505   "Acquisition by the upper atmosphere of some 10^{14} gm. of cometary dust would have major implications on the Earth's climate. Pluvial activity would increase dramatically as temperature differences between sea and land widened. Global distribution of precipitation would be controlled by the density of the dust in the atmosphere; for a partially reflective blanket, a fraction of solar energy would still reach ground level creating new climatic zones. The totally undecomposed state of the interiors of Siberian Mammoths and the state of the interiors of Siberian Mammoths and the curious distribution, often uphill, of erratic boulders point to unbelievably sudden and severe conditions at the onset and possibly end of a glacial period. We suggest that a reflective blanket of particles could promote such conditions."

p. 508   "Streams and rivers would flow for a while in enormous abundance, and inland lakes would fill to exceptionally high levels, as in fact they did. The concurrence of pluvial conditions with ice ages is another challenge to 'small cause' theories, since a slow cooling together of oceans and lands over a time-scale of approximately 10^4 years would decrease evaporation and precipitation, which the known pluvial conditions clearly show to be wrong."

p. 508   "The mammoths became extinct during the last ice-age. . . . But if the ice came slowly, over a time-span of approximately 10^4 years, a slow migration to the south would not only be possible, but we think inevitable."

Clube, Victor, and Bill Napier, "Close Encounters with a Million Comets," *New Scientist*, vol. 95 (July 15, 1982), pp. 148-151. Authors of *The Cosmic Serpent: A Catastrophist View of Earth History* (Faber, 1982), at the Royal Observatory, Edinburgh.

p. 150   "The current overabundance of interplanetary particles, fireball activity and meteor streams in Apollo orbits all seem to bear witness to a sky that must have been exceedingly active within the past few thousand years."

p. 151   "One catastrophic inundation may well have been responsible for worldwide stories of the Flood, another for the later events leading up the Exodus."

p. 151   "Charles Lyell and Charles Darwin, for example, were allowed to imagine evolution without the devastating influence of comets. . . . Indeed, it is likely that large comets and Apollos correspond to the punctuation marks, those short spells of dramatic change, in evolutionary history that separate periods of 'punctuated equilibrium.'"

Coffin, Harold G., "Orientation of Trees in the Yellowstone Petrified Forests," *Journal of Paleontology*, vol. 50, no. 3 (May 1976), pp. 539-543.

p. 539   "*Abstract*. The orientation of prostrate trees and the long axes of cross sections of non-round upright trees are in general agreement for Yellowstone petrified forests. The only factor normally operating on a level growing forest that might cause such an alignment of both downed and standing trees is a dominant direction of prevailing strong winds. Examination of living forests on flat terrain (similar to the Yellowstone petrified forests) failed to show consistent orientation of upright and prostrate trees. The whole sequence of petrified forests is intercalated between volcanic breccia deposits (lahars). This suggests that the upright trees also may have been moved and oriented (erect stance generally unchanged by these coarse flows)."

pp. 542-3   "In view of the fact that the prone petrified logs are often split and fractured, almost always devoid of limbs and bark, and lie well above the root levels of the erect petrified stumps in volcanic breccia showing both normal and reverse grading, the orientation of the horizontal trees is clearly the result of transport by volcanic mud flows (lahars). It is probable that the same lahars removed, transported and deposited the upright stumps (vertical stance generally little disturbed). The major roots which usually control the asymmetry of the lower tree bole are acted upon by moving mud. Thus both prone and erect trees are deposited with long axes in the same general direction."

Corliss, W. A., "Living Stalactites," *Science Frontiers*, no. 57 (May/June 1988), p. 3.

Translation of the introduction of an article from *Science et Vie*:

"One has always held that the calcareous concretions in caves are the work of water and the chemical constituents of the rock. Surprise! The true workers in the kingdom of darkness are living organisms.

"It's all true. All the references we have state unequivocally that stalactites and stalagmites are created by dripping water that is charged with minerals, calcium carbonate in particular.

"That stalactites contain crystals of calcite is not denied in the *Science et Vie* article. Indeed, an electron microscope photograph shows them clearly; but it also shows that a web of mineralized bacteria is also an integral part of the stalactite's structure. Laboratory simulations have shown that micro-organisms take an active role in the process of mineralization.

"Besides being a surprising adjustment of our ideas about stalactite growth, the recognition that microorganisms may play an active role in the subterranean world stimulates two new questions: (1) Can we believe any longer that stalactite size is a measure of age, as is often claimed? (2) Is the immense network of known caves (some as long as 500 kilometers) the consequence *only* of chemical action?"

Davies, Paul, *The Last Three Minutes* (New York: Basic Books, 1994), 162 pp.

p. 3   "Estimates suggest that 10,000 objects half a kilometer or more in diameter move on Earth-intersecting orbits. . . . Many of these objects are capable of causing more damage than all the world's nuclear weapons put together. It is only a matter of time before one strikes."

p. 123   "The 'big crunch,' as far as we understand it, is not just the end of matter. It is the end of everything . . . time itself ceases at the big crunch."

p. 155   "If there is a purpose to the universe, and it achieves that purpose, then the universe must end, for its continuing existence would be gratuitous and pointless. Conversely, if the universe endures forever, it is hard to imagine that there is any ultimate purpose to the universe at all. So cosmic death may be the price that has to be paid for cosmic success. Perhaps the most that we can hope for is that the purpose of the universe becomes known to our descendants before the end of the last three minutes."

Dietz, Robert S., and Mitchell Woodhouse, "Mediterranean Theory May Be All Wet," *Geotimes*, vol. 33 (May 1988), p. 4.

p. 4   "We have been disturbed lately by the repeated media promotion accorded the deep-dry-basin model developed by Kenneth J. Hsü (ETII, Zurich, Switzerland) and William B. F. Ryan (Lamont-Doherty Geological Observatory). Their model supposedly explains the 'giant salt' (1-km-plus-thick evaporites) beneath the Mediterranean Basin."

p. 4   "In referring to 'evaporite' of the evaporitic facies, the term begs the question as it implies desiccation. For clarity, geology needs a new term; namely 'precipitite,' rock created by precipitation. Hence, rocks of the evaporitic facies could be evaporites resulting from evaporation of precipitites, deposited by precipitation from a supersaturated solution. Our view is that the sub-Mediterranean salts are precipitites."

Dott, Robert H., Jr., "Dynamics of Subaqueous Gravity Depositional Processes," *Bulletin, American Association of Petroleum Geologists*, vol. 47 (January 1963), pp. 104-128.

p. 107   "Certain colloids tend to aggregate very quickly; even in minutes. For example, polymerization of silica occurs most rapidly and produces an extremely powerful, irreversible cohesion. . . . Such effects are very important in sediments, particularly the clays. . . .”

Dury, G. H., “Contribution to a General Theory of Meandering Valleys,” *American Journal of Science*, vol. 252, no. 4 (April 1954), pp. 193-224.

p. 215   “As has already been stated, the bed widths of the filled channels are some ten times those of the present channels in the same localities. . . . The whole of the present annual precipitation, with no loss to percolation or to evaporation, could similarly have been run off in no more than five days. It is therefore necessary to postulate a former precipitation greater, and probably considerably greater, than that which is now recorded.”

Fox, Sir Cyril S., *Water*, (Philosophical Library, 1952). Fox was Director, Geological Surveyor of India.

p. 30   “If the continental lands were leveled down to a uniform sea floor, the mean depth of a completely covering ocean would be roughly 9,000 feet, and its surface would stand at a height about 600 feet about our present sea level. . . . There would be no mountain chains to precipitate rain or snow, and it is probable that a uniform climate would prevail over the face of this earth ocean.”

pp. 70-71   “P. D. Oldham has given a brief description of the carrying power of flood streams in the Cherrapunji (Assam) region, which is subject to heavy rain. He wrote: ‘The water had risen only 13 feet above the level at which it had stood a few days previously; the rush was tremendous . . . hugh blocks of rock measuring some feet across were rolled along with an awful crashing, almost as easily as pebbles in an ordinary stream. In one night, a block of granite, which I calculated to weigh upwards of 350 tons, was moved for more than a 100 yards; while the current was actually turbid with pebbles of some inches size, suspended almost like mud in the rushing stream.”

p. 111   “From the above description it is clear that when the Colorado River was in flood it was acting on the solid rock of its bed down to a depth of over 120 feet from the top of the floor water, but that as the current subsided it first filled up the inner and deep canyon and then covered the rock platform, thus giving no idea of the violence of its action in depth, where it could flush with great force more than 115 feet of sand-filled cuttings.”

Fritz, William J., “Reinterpretation of the Depositional Environment of the Yellowstone Fossil Forest,” *Geology*, vol. 8 (July 1980), pp. 309-313.

p. 309   “If these identifications are correct, the mixture of temperate and tropical plant remains is extreme, even for a Paleogene flora. . . . Although common for transported Paleogene floras, this mixture seems out of place for ‘forests’ interpreted as having been buried in place with little or no transportation.”

p. 312   “Besides vertical stumps, logs that are parallel and diagonal to the bedding also occur in abundance. . . . In some areas, . . . all trees are horizontal and most of the logs are oriented in a particular direction, as in log jams. . . . The vertical stumps are shorter than horizontal logs and were broken above the root level before burial. Only in a few locations are branches and small roots present, both generally having been broken off during transport before deposition at present sites."

p. 313   "Due to the complex alluvial system responsible for deposition of the Lamar River formation fossil wood deposits, it is not possible to determine the exact number of 'layers' or 'forests.' I do not think that entire Eocene forests were preserved *in situ* even though some upright trees were apparently preserved where they grew. It is also difficult to determine how many times nearby volcanoes erupted."

Fritz, William J., "Stumps Transported and Deposited Upright by Mount St. Helens Mud Flows," *Geology*, vol. 8 (December 1980), pp. 586-588.

p. 586   "During several visits to Mount St. Helens, Washington, from July to September 1980, I observed numerous stumps that had been deposited upright after being transported many kilometres by streams and mudflows resulting from the May 18, 1980, eruption. These observations support the conclusion that mud flows and streams of the same variety transported and deposited stumps that are preserved in a vertical position in the Eocene Lamar River Formation."

p. 588   "Deposits of recent mud flows on Mount St. Helens demonstrate conclusively that stumps can be transported and deposited upright. These observations support conclusions that some vertical trees in the Yellowstone 'fossil forests' were transported in a geologic situation directly comparable to that of Mount St. Helens."

Froelich, Warren, "Deep-Sea Vents May be Making Oil," *Copley News Service*, in *The Daily Tribune* (January 30, 1982).

"Oceanic hot springs, the site of strange colonies of marine life, may also be a breeding ground for new sources of oil and gas, according to new findings from a research mission in the Gulf of California.

"Scientists say that the discovery, in the Guaymas basin off Baja California, indicates that petroleum may be rapidly produced in nature under the pressure-cooker environment of these deep-sea springs—in thousands of years, rather than millions."

Hoffmeister, J. E., and H. G. Multer, "Growth-Rate Estimates of a Pleistocene Coral Reef of Florida," *Bulletin, Geological Society of America*, vol. 75 (April 1964), pp. 353-358.

pp. 354-5   "After a study which lasted nearly 3 years, it was determined that the average upward growth of these specimens amounted to 10.7 mm a year. . . . An upward growth of one foot would take about 28.5 years."

p. 356   "If there is any merit in this estimate, one of the most significant results is the realization of the rapidity at which coral reef material can accumulate."

Hsü, Kenneth J., "Actualistic Catastrophism and Global Change," *Paleogeography, Paleoclimatology, Paleoecology (Global and Planetary Change Section)*, vol. 89 (1990), pp. 309-313.

p. 310   "The statistics relating the magnitude and frequency of earthquakes, river discharges, volcanic eruptions, and meteorite impacts have been given in numerous publications . . . although we did not know that the empirical relations is a manifestation of the fractal geometry of Nature."

p. 310   "Fractal relations imply that the interval elapsed between two events of the same magnitude is proportional to the magnitude of the events."

Hutchinson, G. Evelyn, *A Treatise on Limnology*, vol. I (New York: Wiley, 1957), 1015 pp.

p. 238   "Almost all the drainage basins of the closed lakes of the world bear, above the modern lake level, raised beaches which clearly testify to high lake levels at a previous time; Bonneville and Lahontan are only two of the more dramatic examples."

p. 16   "Lake Lahontan at its height had an area of 21,860 km^2 and a maximum depth of 270 m. . . .

                "Bonneville had an area of 51,300 km^2 at its maximum extent, and a maximum depth of 320 m."

p. 17   "In addition to the two immense lakes, about seventy other Pleistocene lakes of much smaller size, nearly all of tectonic origin, are known in the basin-and-range area."

Jopling, Alan V., "Some Principles and Techniques Used in Reconstructing the Hydraulic Parometers of a Paleo-Flow Regime," *Journal of Sedimentary Petrology*, vol. 36 (March 1966), pp. 5-49.

p. 6   "Many problems confront the hydraulician concerned with the study of sediment transport in either a flume or a natural river system. In environmental studies, however, the geologist labors under an even greater disadvantage than the hydraulician because of the fragmentary evidence that he is required to work with. Much of his work is therefore inferential and deductive."

p. 34   "It may be considered therefore that the time required for the deposition of the entire delta deposit amounted to several days. . . Based on the computed rate of delta advance and the thickness of individual laminae, the average time for the deposition of a lamina must have been several minutes."

p. 46   "A straightforward and readily interpretable field deposit was analyzed in this paper. [*However, nine major sources of error are listed.*] As a general rule, however, there are many unknowns to contend with in the interpretation and synthesis of paleo-flow regimes. Field relationships are often complex, exposures are poor, and the sedimentologic record is incomplete. Last, but not least, environmental reconstruction falls short of its avowed objectives because of the limited techniques presently available."

Lasemi, Z., and P. A. Sandberg, "Transformation of Aragonite-dominated Lime Muds to Microcrystalline Limestones," *Geology*, vol. 12 (July 1984), pp. 420-423.

p. 420   "Micritic limestones, composed essentially of calcite, have textures quite different from those of the aragonite-dominated modern lime muds that have long been regarded as their precursors."

Martinez, Joseph D., "Salt Domes," *American Scientist*, vol. 79 (September/October 1991), pp. 420-431.

p. 420   "Many salt domes of the Gulf Coast would tower above Mount Everest if they were above ground. Some reach as much as eight miles above the bed of salt that formed them. At their caps the domes average two miles in diameter, and they are still broader at greater depth. From east Texas through Louisiana and Mississippi to Alabama, and offshore under the Gulf itself, more than 500 salt domes have been identified."

Moore, E. S., *Coal*, 2nd ed. (New York: Wiley, 1940), 473 pp.

pp. 143-4   ". . . though a peat-bog may serve to demonstrate how vegetal matter accumulates in considerable quantities, it is in no way comparable in extent to the great bodies of vegetation which must have given rise to our important coal seams."

p. 177   "From all available evidence it would appear that coal may form in a very short time, geologically speaking, if conditions are favorable."

Murray, Grover E., "Salt Structures of Gulf of Mexico Basin—A Review," *Bulletin, American Association of Petroleum Geologists*, vol. 50 (March 1966), pp. 439-478. Murray was Vice President at Louisiana State University.

pp. 467-8   "If a single, continuous salt bed is the source of all salt structures in the northern Gulf region, it has an areal extent in excess of 200,000 square miles. . . .

"Current knowledge indicates that the mother bed of salt must be several thousand feet thick for diapirs to form. . . . If the thickness averaged 5000 feet, it would have had an original volume in the order of 200,000 cubic miles.

"Precipitation of such a great volume of sodium chloride poses numerous problems. It would require the evaporation of immense quantities of sea water, presumably in some sort of isolated basin or basins which would receive fresh supplies of saline water from time to time. Furthermore, it is necessary to account for the apparent absence of sulfate and carbonate in quantities commensurable with the volumes which should have existed in the vast quantities of sea water needed to produce so much sodium chloride."

Newell, Norman D., "Supposed Permian Tillites in Northern Mexico are Submarine Slide Deposits," *Bulletin, Geological Society of America*, vol. 68, no. 11 (November 1957), pp. 1569-1576. Newell was at the Museum of Natural History and is an outstanding authority on Permian stratigraphy.

p. 1569   "The succession in which the conglomerates lie is noteworthy as one of the most fully representative and best-documented sequences of Permian rocks in North America."

p. 1572   "These Mexican boulder beds and volcanic rocks most probably are submarine slide deposits that accumulated in a stagnant basin adjacent to active volcanoes fringed by growing reefs. . . . Submarine slide deposits are much more abundant in the stratigraphic record than are tillites, and stratigraphers are becoming increasingly alert to their significance."

Newell, N. D., J. K. Rigby, A. G. Fischer, A. J. Whiteman, J. E. Hickox, J. S. Bradley, *The Permian Reef Complex of the Guadelupe Mountain Region, Texas and New Mexico* (San Francisco: W. H. Freeman & Co., 1953), 236 pp.

p. 6   "The area contains one of the most complete representations of the Permian system known."

p. 9   "The greatest of the reefs, the Capitan reef, forms a conspicuous but narrow rim around the Delaware Basin for a distance of about 350-400 miles; probably it is the most extensive fossil reef on record."

p. 38   "The Capitan reef ranges in thickness, roughly between 400 and 1,200 feet."

p. 38   "The reef talus over which the reef was built ranges in vertical thickness from perhaps 1,000 to about 1,500 feet."

p. 51   "Rocks of the Delaware Basin are characteristically stratified in very thin and uniform laminations marked by slight differences in texture and color. . . . Udden, Lang, and others have noted the resemblance between the laminations and glacial varves."

p. 54   "Turbidity currents originating in storms may have provided one of the means by which the fine sand was spread widely over the basin, and they may have been responsible for the abruptness of the textural differences between adjacent laminae. Kuenen has advanced cogent arguments to show that turbidity currents might play an important role in the formation of even typical glacial varves."

O'Brien, Neal R., "Origin of Pennsylvanian Underclays in the Illinois Basin," *Bulletin, Geological Society of America*, vol. 75 (September 1964), pp. 823-832.

p. 829   "The author suggests that underclays in the Illinois Basin formed during a period of very slow sedimentation of flocculated clay particles. . . . This writer has observed that underclays also commonly grade into underlying shales. It seems reasonable that the gradation of shale or sandstone upward into an underclay may simply represent conditions of transitional sedimentation from coarse to fine particle sizes. It appears that this evidence also may be used to explain the detrital origin of underclay."

Paine, Roland D., "NOAA-sponsored Undersea Study of Coral Reefs Opens New Prospects for Oil Exploration," *U.S. Department of Commerce News* (March 27, 1973).

p. 1   "Carbon 14 dating of rock samples taken from the reefs has shown the rock to be only 5000 to 10,000 years old. During this time, the living coral died, fell down the reef front, became infilled with other calcium deposits from marine plants, and hardened into limestone."

Pennisi, Elizabeth, "Water, Water Everywhere," *Science News*, vol. 143 (February 20, 1993), pp. 121-125.

p. 124   "To understand this process better, the Exxon group collected samples of oil shale from different parts of the world. The samples included a series from oil shale under the North Sea, where rocks in different locations exhibit different degrees of transformation. Siskin then placed the samples into a pressurized reaction vessel and heated them individually to temperatures ranging from 570°

C to 750° C. These hotter-than-natural conditions sped up the transformation from a geologic time frame of millions of years to one measured in days and hours."

p. 124   "As early as 1979 [Michael] Lewan, (of U.S. G.S., Denver) then working with an oil company, and his colleagues had demonstrated that they could stimulate oil formation in the laboratory, but only if they added water to their system."

p. 125   "They discovered that high temperatures cause an organic molecule to break into fragments—and so does water and brine, sometimes more effectively."

p. 125   "The results indicate that hot water becomes a catalyst for a series of ionic reactions—creating a second pathway for the cascade of molecular transformations that leads to oil. The acidic and basic nature of hot water—rather than heat—drives this cascade."

Plummer, P. S., and V. A. Gostin, "Shrinkage Cracks: Desiccation or Synaeresis?" *Journal of Sedimentary Petrology*, vol. 51 (December 1981), pp. 1147-1156.

p. 1147   "*Abstract.* Casts of shrinkage cracks found within sedimentary sequence are frequently cited as being diagnostic of depositional environments periodically subjected to subaerial exposure. The term *shrinkage cracks*, however, encompasses a broad suite of sedimentary structures having various origins. Shrinkage cracks can form not only at the sediment-air interface by desiccation processes but also at the sediment-water interface or substratally by synaeresis processes.

". . . Unfortunately, because of the complex interplay of these factors, no single feature of any shrinkage crack is necessarily useful in differentiating between a desiccation or synaeresis origin." [*synaeresis* = "coming together"]

Porfir'ev, V. B., "Inorganic Origin of Petroleum," *Bulletin, American Association of Petroleum Geologists*, vol. 58 (January 1974), pp. 3-33.

p. 22   "My analysis of the literature concerning the time of petroleum accumulation quite unexpectedly showed that all oil fields on the earth were formed by vertical migration between early Miocene and early Quaternary times. Before and after this period of time, no petroleum accumulations formed. In any case, I have not found in the literature any geologic proof for the existence of oil fields in Mesozoic, Paleozoic and Precambrian time."

p. 23   "Mud volcanism provides a valuable clue, because it is related to oil deposits, and mud volcanism was most intense from late Tertiary time to the present. . . . Before the beginning of the Tertiary period, mud volcanoes did not exist on the earth."

p. 27   "Petroleum hydrocarbons which constitute the substance called 'natural petroleum' are one of the several natural fluid mixtures. Its components—petroleum, gas and juvenile water formed under the thermodynamic conditions of the upper mantle—ascended under great pressure along plutonic faults close to the earth's surface where, depending on pressure and temperature, the fluid mixture separated into independent phases."

Porfir'ev, V. B., review of *Geology and Genesis of Salt Formations*, by V. I. Sozansky (Kiev, Izd. Naukova Dumka, 1973, 200 pp.), *Bulletin, American Association of Petroleum Geologists*, vol. 58 (December 1974), pp. 2543-2544.

p. 2543   "In Sozansky's book, new data on the geology of world saliferous basins are compiled and summarized and result in the conclusion that, contrary to the classic conception of evaporitic origin, salt arises along faults as juvenile hot brines from the mantle."

p. 2544   "Sozansky comes to the conclusion that basins of salt accumulation were in active tectonic relation to depressions of block structure in which volcanic eruptions were common. Salt is not an evaporitic formation or a derivative from volcanic rock, it is a product of degasification of the earth's interior. The salt precipitated from juvenile hot water which emerged along deep faults into a basin as a result of change in thermodynamic conditions."

Raup, Omer B., "Brine Mixing: An Additional Mechanism for Formation of Basin Evaporites," *Bulletin, American Association of Petroleum Geologists*, vol. 54 (December 1970), pp. 2246-2259.

p. 2258   "The following conclusions are based on the results of three brine experiments and their relations to a geologic model.

          "1. Salt precipitation can occur in a marine evaporite basin by mixing brines of different composition and specific gravity.

          "2. Precipitation occurs without further loss by evaporation.

          "3. Precipitation can occur from brines that were undersaturated before mixing."

Raymond, Chris, "Discovery of Leaves in Antarctica Sparks Debate over Whether Region had Near-Temperature Climate," *Chronicle of Higher Education* (March 20, 1991), pp. A9, A11.

p. A9   "The discovery of thousands of well-preserved leaves in Antarctica has sparked a debate among geologists over whether the polar region, rather than being blanketed by a massive sheet of ice for millions of years, enjoyed a near-temperate climate as recently as three million years ago."

p. A11   "The leaves compressed by subsequent layers of ice, look like fossils. But unlike fossils, which leave only mineral traces of the original organism, the leaves retain their original cellular structure and organic content."

Seilacher, Adolf, "Paleotological Studies in Turbidite Sedimentation and Erosion," *Journal of Geology*, vol. 70 (March 1962), pp. 227-234. Seilacher was with the Geologisches Institut, University of Frankfurt, Germany.

p. 227   "*Abstract.* The post-depositional sole trails of Flysch psammites occur only in thinner beds up to a thickness particular to each species. This proves instantaneous deposition of the individual beds, as postulated by the turbidity-current theory. The majority of the sole trails are pre-depositional mud burrows washed out and sand cast by turbidity currents. The erosion of an unusual type must have preceded every turbidite sedimentation."

Sozansky, V. I., "Geological Notes. Origin of Salt Deposits in Deep-Water Basins of Atlantic Ocean," *Bulletin, American Association of Petroleum Geologists*, vol. 57, no. 3 (March 1973), pp. 589-595.

p. 589   "The presence of volcanic rocks in halogenic formations attests to the manifestation of volcanism during the time the salt was accumulating. This in turn contradicts the classical views regarding the formation of salt-bearing sections in lagoons or epicontinental seas."

pp. 589-90   "It is well known that salts are chemically pure formations which are void of the remains of marine organisms. . . . If salt-bearing sections were formed in lagoons or marginal seas by the evaporation of seawater, then organic matter, chiefly plankton, would have to enter the salt-forming basin together with the waters. As a result, the bottom sediments would be rich in organic matter. The analysis of data from modern salt-forming lagoons such as the Gulf of Kara-Bogaz and Sivashi shows that large quantities of organic matter enter the lagoons."

p. 590   "The absence of remains of marine organisms in ancient salts indicates that the formation of the salt-bearing sections was not related to the evaporation of marine water in epicontinental seas.

"Other geologic data, such as the great thickness of salt deposits, the rapid rate of formation of salt-bearing sections, the presence of ore minerals in salts and in the caprocks of salt domes do not conform with the bar hypothesis.

"The analysis of recent geologic data, including data on the diapirs found in ocean deeps, permits the conclusion that these salts are of a juvenile origin—that they emerged from great depths along faults during tectonic movements. This process is often accompanied by the discharge of basin magmas."

Sozansky, V. I., "Depositional Environment of the Green River Formation of Wyoming: Discussion," *Bulletin, Geological Society of America*, vol. 85 (July 1974), p. 1191. Sozansky is at the Institute of Geological Sciences of the Academy of Sciences of the Ukrainian S.S.R., Kiev.

     "These data contradict the evaporitic hypothesis and need a new explanation. Precipitation of salt from highly mineralized thermal brines of juvenile origin that escaped from the mantle along deep faults is the most logical explanation for the origin of salt deposits. Because halite and trona are genetically related, I believe that trona is also of juvenile origin."

Stow, Dorrik A. V., and Anthony J. Bowen, "Origin of Lamination in Deep Sea, Fine-grained Sediments," *Nature*, vol. 274 (July 27, 1978), pp. 324-328.

p. 324   "Silt laminated muds are very common marine facies and occur repeatedly in geological records. Although there have been many mechanisms suggested for their deposition, the mode of emplacement and the process of lamina formation are still not fully understood. Velocity fluctuations are, perhaps, the most commonly endorsed mechanism for the generation of lamination in marine sediments."

p. 327   "The primary mechanism for laminae formation seems to be the depositional sorting by the increased shear at the bottom of the bottom boundary layer. The destruction of the flocs lead to differential settling . . . producing a clean, silt layer. The continual accumulation of fine material during this phase eventually leads to a rapid deposition of a mud layer: the absence of the coarser silts from this layer indicates that the process is rapid. . . .

"One of the interesting features of this depositional sorting process is, therefore, the suggestion that the depositional rate from the turbidity current is proportional to the modal size of the silts, the clay flocs falling out being of equivalent settling velocity. The depositional processes as a whole are therefore much more rapid than would be anticipated using any model that views the deposition of the mud layer as a separate process, characterized by the size distribution of the mud alone."

Stutzer, Otto, *Geology of Coal*, trans. by A. C. Noé (Chicago: University of Chicago Press, 1940), 461 pp.

p. 105-6   "Petzolat describes very remarkable observations which he made during the construction of a railway bridge at Alt-Breisach near Freiburg. The wooden piles which had been rammed into the ground were compressed by overriding rocks. An examination of these compressed piles showed that in the center of the compressed piles was a black, coal-like substance. In continuous succession from center to surface was blackened, dark-brown, light-brown and finally yellow-colored wood." [The coal-like substance corresponded in its chemical composition to anthracite, and the blackened wood resembled brown coal.]

p. 277   "Numerous theories have been advanced to explain the transportation of these boulders to their position in the coal beds. Phillips' explanation that the boulders were floated in, held by the roots of floating trees, has still the greatest support among geologists."

Suykowski, Z. L., "Diagenesis," *Bulletin, American Association of Petroleum Geologists* (November 1958), pp. 2694-2697.

p. 2694   "Water is the main agent of diagenesis and organic matter is an auxiliary."

p. 2696   "Diagenesis consists of many simultaneous or consecutive processes such as the following: solution and redeposition, commonly combined with recrystallization; replacement, partial or complete; cementation; change in position of minerals; base exchange; diffusion, absorption, and others."

p. 2697   "But one thing is clear: time alone is not sufficient to produce any change."

p. 2697   "It seems, rather that diagenesis sometimes follows sedimentation so closely that it begins while the deposit is still on the sea-bottom, especially in pure calcareous sediments, as in coral reefs."

Thomsen, Dietrick E., "The Day the Dam Burst," *Science News*, vol. 106 (October 19, 1974), pp. 250-251.

p. 250   "The flood, usually called the Spokane Flood, was possibly the greatest the earth has ever seen. It did not rise slowly from the rain-soaked earth like the Biblical deluge that floated Noah's ark; it was a flashflood of supercolossal proportions. In two days time it drained a no-longer-existing lake that covered

3,000 square miles of what is now Montana and is called Lake Missoula because the site of that town was then 950 feet under its waters."

C. The Testimony of the Column

The quotes in this section deal with miscellaneous topics relevant to historical geology and the real significance of the geologic column (not as it is in the textbooks, but as it really occurs in the earth's crust). For example, the strata give abundant evidence of a global sub-tropical climate during most of the supposed geologic ages, prior to the recent Ice Age. Furthermore, despite the rapid acceptance of the new paradigm of plate tectonics and continental drift, this system still has many unresolved problems.

Most importantly, the strata indicate *no worldwide time break in sediment deposition*, even at the bottom of the Cambrian system. Since they also indicate that all individual formations have been deposited rapidly, they bear clear testimony to the formation of the entire column by a worldwide cataclysm, primarily hydraulic in nature.

Anonymous, "Were Climate Changes Global During Ice Ages," *Geotimes*, vol. 41 (January 1996), p. 7.

p. 7   "Using evidence collected in South America and New Zealand, an international team of researchers has determined that climate changes—both warming and cooling patterns—during the late Pleistocene occurred rapidly and were global in scale. As giant iceberg armadas flooded the North Atlantic, alpine glaciers were simultaneously advancing across the Chilean Andes and Southern Alps of New Zealand. Thomas Lowell, associate professor of geology at the University of Cincinnati, and his colleagues published their findings in the September 15, 1995, issues of *Science*."

p. 7   "So, what did cause the climate changes? Lowell admits that he and his colleagues have no quick and easy answers. Possibly water vapors played a role. 'A lot of water vapor in the atmosphere leads to a warmer climate,' he states. 'If there's less vapor, temperatures become colder. Amounts of water vapor can change quickly, and the geological record indicates that climate changes could be very fast."

Broecker, Wallace S., Maurice Ewing, and Bruce C. Heezen, "Evidence for an Abrupt Change in Climate Close to 11,000 Years Ago," *American Journal of Science*, vol. 258 (June 1960), pp. 429-448.

p. 429   "*Abstract*. Evidence from a number of geographically isolated systems suggests that the warming of world-wide climate which occurred at the close of Wisconsin glacial times was extremely abrupt. Surface ocean, temperatures in the Atlantic Ocean increased by several degrees centigrade and deep-sea sedimentation rates sharply decreased in the equatorial Atlantic."

p. 441   "From the evidence listed above it is clear that a major fluctuation in climate occurred close to 11,000 years ago. The primary observation that both surface ocean temperatures and deep sea sedimentation rates were abruptly altered at this time is supplemented by evidence from more local systems. The level of the Great Basin lakes fell from the highest terraces to a position close to that observed at present. The silt and clay load of the Mississippi River was suddenly retained in the alluvial valley and delta. A rapid ice retreat opened the northern drainage systems of the Great Lakes and terrestrial temperatures rose to nearly interglacial levels in Europe. In each case the transition is the most obvious feature of the entire record."

Chang, K. Hong, "Unconformity-Bounded Stratigraphic Units," *Bulletin, Geological Society of America*, vol. 86 (November 1975), pp. 1544-1552.

p. 1544　　　"*Abstract*. Many unconformity-bounded units are considered to be chronostratigraphic units in spite of the fact that unconformity surfaces inevitably cut across isochronous horizons and hence cannot be true chronostratigraphic boundaries."

p. 1545　　　"In the early history of stratigraphy, unconformities were overestimated in that they were believed to represent coeval diastrophism over areas of infinitely wide extent."

Chang, K. Hong, "Rethinking Stratigraphy," *Geotimes*, vol. 26 (March 1981), pp. 23-24. Chang was in the Department of Geology, Kyungpook National University, Daegu, Korea.

p. 23　　　"Many unconformity-bounded units have been erroneously regarded as lithostratigraphic units, even though they are characterized not by lithologic unity but by the fact of being bounded by unconformities. . . . Similarly, many unconformity-bounded units have been erroneously considered to be chronostratigraphic units, in spite of the fact that unconformity surfaces are apt to be diachronous and hence cannot constitute true chronostratigraphic boundaries."

Dietz, Robert S., "In Defense of Drift," *The Sciences*, vol. 23 (November/December 1983), pp. 22-26. Dietz was Professor of Geology, Arizona State University.

p. 26　　　"Meanwhile, since the continents drift as slowly as one's fingernails grow—from one to ten centimeters per year—even the most precise surveying methods available today have not yet detected drift."

Dott, Robert H., Jr., review of *The Earth in Decay: A History of British Geomorphology 1578-1878*, by Gordon L. Davies (New York: American Elsevier, 1970, 390 pp.), *Journal of Geology*, vol. 79 (September 1971), p. 633. Dott was at the University of Wisconsin.

"The book provides vivid, poorly known details that undercut several long-cherished and oversimplified historical dogmas. Most significant is documentation of a well-developed seventeenth-century conception of fluvial denudation. The author makes, for example, a good case for Hutton's geomorphology having been derived from Woodward's. (But he neglects the more fundamental original Huttonian conception of a dynamic solid earth.)

"Davies shows eloquently how changing world views influenced British geologic thought. Besides showing that seventeenth-century thinkers were well-aware of denudation, he argues that they were not inhibited by the Mosaic chronology. A rapidly decaying earth seemed fully consistent with a wrathful God and the general abhorrence of useless mountains piled up by the Deluge after the fall of man. By 1700, however, a retarding teleological view of nature emerged and was later adopted by deists, such as Hutton. God now was seen as 'the gracious architect of a magnificent creation' and denudation seemed counter to His Grand Design. This 'denudation dilemma,' says Davies, stalled geomorphic thought until it was satisfactorily rationalized by Hutton's perpetual balancing of decay by structural renewal. With the Mosaic chronology finally discredited and denudation again theologically respectable, nineteenth-century British geologists could return to the issue of fluvialism. Acceptance of Agissiz's glacial theory finally destroyed Diluvialism and paved the way for final establishment of the major role of fluvial processes by 1878."

Dury, G. H., "Results of Seismic Explorations of Meandering Valleys," *American Journal of Science*, vol. 260 (November 1962), pp. 691-706.

p. 691   "*Abstract.* Subsurface exploration of meandering valleys in the Driftless Area of Wisconsin, by means of a refraction seismograph, reveals large filled channels similar to those previously determined in English rivers, where the auguring technique was used. The channels are asymmetrical in cross profile and attain their greatest depths at valley bends. In cross-sectional area of probable bankfill they are some 25 times as large as the present stream channels."

Engel, A. E. J., "Time and the Earth," *American Scientist*, vol. 57 (Winter 1969), pp. 458-483. Engel was Professor of Geology, Cal Tech, and at the Scripps Institute of Oceanography.

p. 469   "A team of imaginative and clever geologists and geochronologists can extract enormous quantities of information about time and the earth from reconstructions of such age relations of rocks using index fossils, the time stratigraphic units such as S5, and dating each of the several igneous and metamorphic events by radiometric methods."

p. 474   "Thus the evolution of the more complicated animal phyla seems to have occurred during times when as yet there are few datable rocks and innumerable degrees of freedom. These are optimal conditions for the imaginative megathinker and *ad hoc* hypothecator."

p. 475   "Large convective cells in the earth's mantle caused by terrestrial reheating have been invoked to move the continents, make the mountains, spread the ocean's floor, and create the tremendous secular changes that we see manifest in the surficial complexity of the earth's crust. The mechanism of large convective cells as agents of these several major dynamic events in the earth's crust is a most functional, if untestable hypothesis. Belief in cells is akin to belief in an orthodox God. Few earth scientists, I suspect, really believe in either completely; yet none is clever enough to invent working hypotheses less testable, more tantalizing, self-sufficing, and all-encompassing as God or the convective cell."

Hall, J. M., and P. T. Robinson, "Deep Crustal Drilling in the North Atlantic Ocean," *Science*, vol. 204 (May 11, 1979), pp. 573-586.

p. 578   "An unexpected result of drilling is the almost complete lack of lateral lithologic and stratigraphic continuity in the crust. . . . This lack of stratigraphic continuity suggests that eruptions onto the sea floor are very local, building accumulations directly over the vent."

p. 578   "It is clear that the simple model of uniformly magnetized crustal blocks of alternating polarity does not represent reality. Clear reversals of polarity with depth are observed in a number of the deeper holes. In addition, inclinations often deviate systematically over long core intervals from expected dipole values by more than normal secular variation. Lateral magnetic heterogeneity is evident from marked differences in magnetization (including reversals) where adjacent basement holes have been drilled a few hundred meters apart."

p. 579   "Because the magnetic structure of the upper oceanic basement in the North Atlantic differs so markedly from the predicted model, a comparison with the magnetic structure of Tertiary and younger subaerial flood basalts is useful. In both environments, magnetic reversals are common in vertical sections of flows and those help to define thick magnetic-lithologic units. Dikes often have polarities opposite from those of the host rocks, and many rocks exhibit overprinting of stable remanence by later viscous components acquired in the present field."

p. 585   "Where and what is the source of the linear magnetic anomalies on the sea floor? Drilling has shown convincingly that the source of the anomalies does not lie in the upper 600 m of oceanic crust as previously thought."

p. 586   "It is apparent that crustal drilling to date has shown that the processes of generation and modification of oceanic crust are much more complex than originally thought."

Hallam, A., "Basic Tectonics," *Nature*, vol. 253 (February 6, 1975), pp. 396-398.

p. 396   "The widespread indications of marginal downwarping of continents such as seaward descent of erosion surfaces and warping of marine terraces, seaward dip and thickening of Cretaceous and Tertiary sediments, palaeo-geographical evidence of foundered offshore land areas and, more controversially, submarine canyons, led many geologists to agree with Kuenan's judgment of a quarter century ago that it was 'difficult to avoid the conclusion that marginal areas have subsided to form part of the present deep sea floor.'

          "Drilling on the Orphan Knoll seamount had located Middle Jurassic continental coal measure deposits, which points indubitably to over 2000 m. of subsidence since that time. Ruffman and van Hinte argue for a much more extensive subsidence, of as much as 3,500 m, of a vast area of deep sea floor to the south and west of Orphan Knoll."

p. 398   "Can the underlying phenomena be readily reconciled with our present geophysical concepts, which lean heavily on plate tectonics, or are other mysterious forces at work?

          "My dear Watson, it's not so elementary!"

Hollingsworth, S. E., "The Climatic Factor in the Geological Record," *Quarterly Journal, Geological Society of London*, vol. 118 (March 1902), pp. 1-21. Hollingsworth was President of the Geological Society of London.

p. 13 "In the case of the Permo-Carboniferous of India, the Barakar Series of the Damuda System, overlying the Talchir Boulder Bed, includes numerous coal seams, some up to 100 feet thick, occurring in a well-developed and oft-repeated cycle of sandstone, shale, coal. . . .

"The environment was a subsiding lacustrine one, in general without marine intercalations, and evidence of base-level control by changes in sea-level is lacking.

"The vegetation is considered to be drift accumulation.

"The concept of periodic epirogeny is a reasonable one, but a more or less complete cessation of clastic sedimentation in the lacustrine basin during coal accumulation is difficult to account for on a wholly diastrophic origin. As an explanation for the fifty to sixty cycles of the Damuda system, it has a element of unreality."

Kerr, Richard A., "How Is New Ocean Crust Formed?" *Science*, vol. 205 (September 14, 1979), pp. 1115-1118.

p. 1115 "Somewhat to the chagrin of paleomagneticians, when they examined the rocks recovered by the Deep Sea Drilling Project from the crust of the Atlantic Ocean, the magnetic stripes were nowhere to be found. The recovered rocks not only were too weakly magnetized to account for the observed stripes, but their directions of magnetization were sometimes wrong. Instead of being constant down a drill hole, the magnetization sometimes jumped between normal and reversed or even gradually rotated with increasing depth."

Lucas, Spencer G., discussion of "A Critique (of) Chronostratigraphy," by R. A. Watson (*American Journal of Science*, vol. 283, 1983, pp. 173-177), *American Journal of Science*, vol. 285 (October 1985), pp. 764-767.

p. 764 "It is widely acknowledged that chronostratigraphic units which, by definition, have isochronous boundaries do not coincide everywhere with the diachronous boundaries of lithostratigraphic and biostratigraphic units."

p. 764 "It has never been the purpose of chronostratigraphy to construct units that correspond to diachronously bounded lithostratigraphic and biostratigraphic units."

p. 765 "*Footnote*. It should also be noted that geochronologic units are not chronostratigraphic units. They are subdivisions of geologic time, are not stratigraphic units, and have no necessary spatial component beyond the fact that they are Worldwide (or, from one point of view, Universal) in their extent."

Lyttelton, R. A., "The Earth and its Mountains," *Nature*, vol. 305 (October 20, 1983), p. 672. Lyttelton was at the Institute of Astronomy, Cambridge University.

p. 672 "I would like to comment on the diaskeuastic assessment of the relative merits of the three contending theories of mountain-building [*Nature*, 300, 681, 1982]."

p. 672   "Thermal contraction is therefore ruled out as an admissible hypothesis, and besides, where are the folded and thrusted mountains on Mars, Mercury, and the Moon?"

p. 672   "As for the vast verbal and pictorial literature of plate tectonics, with its large number of purely asseverated assumptions, it may surprise some to learn that it simply fails to qualify as a scientific theory. I am sure [Sir Harold] Jeffries fully agrees with this. Long ago, the great Poincaré explained that 'such descriptive accounts are not the role of physical theories, which should not introduce as many or more arbitrary constants (or verbal assumptions) as there are phenomena to be accounted for; they should establish connections between different experimental facts, and above all they should enable predictions to be made.'

"The real problem of orogeny is to account for over 20 major periods of mountain-building, and not just the one that produced the existing systems of folded and thrusted mountains. This the phase-change theory is able to do. . . ."

Maxwell, John C., "The New Global Tectonics," *Geotimes*, vol. 18 (January 1973), p. 31. Maxwell was at the University of Texas.

p. 31   "Why then do a few crabbed earth scientists refuse to accept some or all of the tenets of the 'new global tectonics'? . . .

"It is not possible in this short review to evaluate the numerous arguments for and against the new global tectonics. . . . It may be useful to note, however, that no satisfactory driving mechanism has yet been identified and hence the sense and velocity of plate motions cannot be predicted. Strictly speaking, then, we do not have a scientific hypothesis, but rather a pragmatic model, reshaped to include each new observation. The model is highly versatile, even able to incorporate quite easily such out-of-character behaviour as 'behind-the-arc spreading.' Obviously, this kind of model is not testable in any rigorous scientific sense."

McMenamin, Mark A. S., "The Emergence of Animals," *Scientific American*, vol. 256 (April 1987), pp. 94-102.

p. 94   "The start of the Cambrian marks the first appearance of a large number of major groups of animals. Many of these have survived until today."

p. 98   "In the 19th century the boundary between the Precambrian and the Cambrian was relatively easy to find, because the areas then under study showed major gaps or unconformities (representing an interval of time in which there was no preservation or deposition of rocks) between Precambrian and Cambrian sedimentary layers. The expanded data base available to 20th century paleontologists has actually complicated the task of locating the boundary precisely, because many regions are now known where Precambrian and Cambrian formations grade continuously into each other."

p. 100   "Perhaps the most astonishing aspect of the Cambrian faunas is that so many radically different types of animals appeared in such a short interval."

Meynen, S. V., "The Continental Drift Hypothesis in the Light of Carboniferous and Permian Paleoflora," *Geotectonics*, vol. 3 (1969), pp. 289-295.

p. 290   "Paradoxical as it appears, it is at times difficult to judge the aridity and humidity of a climate from the fossil plants. This is because the buried plants are mainly those growing near or in the basins. For example, the Kazanian flora . . . contains only mosses, ferns, and sphenopsids . . . i.e., obviously hydrophylic forms. However, the flora-bearing beds alternate in this section with rocks indicative of an arid climate (gypsums, dolomites).

"This stratigraphic pattern can be taken at face value as supporting evidence for the fact that gypsum and dolomite are not products of evaporation in arid climates."

Pratsch, J. C., "Petroleum Geologist's View of Oceanic Crust Age," *Oil and Gas Journal*, vol. 84 (July 14, 1986), pp. 112-116. Pratsch is a Consulting Geologist in Houston.

p. 114   "Similar to conditions on land, magnetic polarity changes occur also in oceanic crustal rock and sedimentary cover sequences. . . . .

"Internal polarity changes with depth in a drilled sequence of oceanic crustal rocks do not match the observed magnetic 'stripe' polarity measured on the surface."

p. 115   "No direct age determinations of any rock sequence can be made, though, merely from magnetic-stratigraphic data; direct ages have to be drawn from other sources."

p. 115   "Second, just these several vertically alternating layers of opposing magnetic polarization directions found in cored oceanic crust disproves one of the basic parameters of seafloor spreading theory, namely that the oceanic crust was magnetized entirely as it spread laterally from the magmatic center."

p. 115   "It appears today that oceanic magnetic stripes have no value for age determinations of oceanic crusts; they are originating beneath oceanic basalt levels, and they originate in linear fault or fracture systems."

p. 116   "Seafloor spreading, as was pointed out, is based on the erroneous assumptions that magnetic anomalies over oceanic areas ('oceanic magnetic stripes') indicate directly geologic ages of oceanic crustal rocks. We cannot obtain crustal age dates through such an approach, and the entire hypotheses built on such assumptions will have to be modernized or discarded."

p. 116   "Continental drift theories similarly are based largely on seafloor spreading concepts. . . . But we would be well advised to reconsider the mechanics and scales of continental drift. And we may have to take more seriously the warning signals given by the message of data that 'do not fit.' . . ."

p. 116   "However, none of the geological and geophysical data from subduction zones indicate absolute motions of oceans or adjacent continents."

Rezanov, I. A., "Paleomagnetism and Continental Drift," translated from Russian, *International Geology Review*, vol. 10 (July 1968), pp. 765-776.

p. 772   "The following relationship is becoming recognizable: the larger the number of paleomagnetic measurements for any given region, the broader becomes the scattering of the paleomagnetic poles, as determined by the rocks of some single geological epoch in one and the same continental, even in one and the same district."

p. 775   "The foregoing discoveries led the author to one conclusion only, that paleomagnetic data are still so unreliable and contradictory that they cannot be used as evidence either for or against the hypothesis of the relative drift of continents or their parts. Nor are they serviceable as proofs of an expansion of the earth."

Salvador, Amos, "Unconformity-Bounded Stratigraphic Units," *Bulletin, Geological Society of America*, vol. 98 (February 1987), pp. 232-237. Salvador was Chairman, International Subcommission on Stratigraphic Classification.

p. 232   "Bounding unconformities were the basis for establishing many of the earliest stratigraphic units recognized in western Europe. Many of the systems of the presently accepted Standard Global Chronostratigraphic Scale were originally unconformity-bounded units. This procedure has not been restricted, however, to the earliest days of stratigraphic work or to western Europe; it has been used, and continues to be used, in all parts of the world. Unconformity-bounded units became very popular at the time tectonic episodes were considered essentially synchronous world-wide, but did lose favor among geologists when synchroneity was found not to hold true."

p. 234   "Unconformity-bounded unites, therefore, are not lithostratigraphic units or biostratigraphic units, because they are not established and distinguished on the basis of their lithologic composition or fossil content. They may comprise rocks of widely varied lithology and contain different types of fossil remains. Unconformity-bounded units are not chronostratigraphic units, either, because they are not established and distinguished on the basis of their time of formation, and because their boundaries are never isochronous over more than short distances."

Shepherd, R. G., and S. A. Schumm, "Experimental Study of River Incision" (Sinuous Channel Incision, Stabilized Alluvial Channel Incision), *Bulletin, Geological Society of America*, vol. 85 (February 1974, pp. 257-268. Shepherd and Schumm were in the Department of Earth Resources, Colorado State University, Ft. Collins.

p. 257   "*Abstract.* The results also suggest that incised meanders superimposed from an earlier pattern on a peneplain should rarely occur in nature, if epeirogenic tilting caused the incision."

p. 263   "The results of this experiment indicate that incision due to a regional slope increase will result in lateral erosion and destruction of the initial alluvial-stream pattern. From these observations, it is difficult to accept the hypothesis that symmetrical incised meanders in nature inherited their patterns from an alluvial channel superimposed from an uplifted peneplain."

Simon, Cheryl, "In with the Older," *Science News*, vol. 123 (May 7, 1983), pp. 300-301.

p. 300   "Even the most enthusiastic traveler might be daunted by the logistics of visiting the banks of the Aldan and Lena Rivers in eastern Siberia . . . for a first-hand look at what may be the vest sequences of rocks spanning the boundary, about 570 million years old, between the Cambrian and Precambrian geological periods."

p. 300   "*Caption.* These rocks along the Aldan River in Siberia span the boundary with little or no disruption, and clearly log the evolution of shelled animals and their soft-bodied antecedents."

p. 301   "It is only in the last 30 years that scientists have found imprints of soft-bodied Precambrian animals. The trace fossils first were recognized in the Ediacara Hills in southwestern Australia. One of the benefits of the efforts to set a boundary has been the collection of bountiful information about the diversity and extent of Precambrian marine life. Since the early 1960's nearly 20 deposits bearing traces of animals such as shell-less segmented worms, soft corals, and jellyfish have been found."

Starke, George W., and Arthur D. Howard, "Polygenetic Origin of Monterey Submarine Canyon," *Bulletin, Geological Society of America*, vol. 79 (July 1968), pp. 813-826.

p. 813   "*Abstract.* Monterey Submarine Canyon, one of the world's largest and deepest, heads immediately offshore on the central California coast. Starke reported the presence of a deep buried canyon inland from, and aligned with, the head of the submarine canyon. Cumulative well records, gravity surveys, and field investigations strongly suggest that the buried ancestral canyon was eroded by fluvial processes, and that the present submarine canyon originated, at least in part, by the fluming out of the ancestral canyon by dominantly submarine processes. Other submarine canyons off unstable coasts may be polygenetic in origin."

Stehli, Francis G., "Possible Permian Climatic Zonation and Its Implications," *American Journal of Science*, vol. 255 (November 1957), pp. 607-618.

p. 607   "Attention has focused primarily on the climatic conditions responsible for 'Permo-Carboniferous' glaciation in the southern hemisphere. The causes of glaciation are imperfectly understood, however, and the climatic implications of an ancient glacial interval cannot yet be adequately interpreted."

p. 617   "The faunal boundary parallels the earth's present equator and, if truly caused by temperature, precludes the possibility of changes in the position of the poles with respect to the major land masses of the northern hemisphere. Also precluded is the possibility that the crust or mantle has shifted its position relative to the core."

Thomsen, Dietrick E., "Mark III Interferometer Measures Earth, Sky and Gravity's Lens," *Science News*, vol. 123 (January 8, 1983), pp. 20-21.

p. 20   "Interferometry is a technique for combining signals received simultaneously from a given astronomical source at two or more different telescopes. . . . The latest thing in radio interferometry . . . is a data recording and processing system called Mark III."

p. 20   "It provides about six times the sensitivity of previous systems. It has been used by Rogers *et al.* to plot the distances . . . between locations of telescopes on earth in an intercontinental array to within five (5) centimeters."

p. 20   "Rogers *et al.* used Mark III on six telescopes, one each at Owens Valley, California; Fort Davis, Texas; the Haystack Observatory in Massachusetts; Onsala, Sweden; Effelsberg, Germany; and Chilbolton, England. They have done geodetic and astronometric measurements since 1979 and in that time have noticed no significant changes in the distances between the telescopes. Theories of continental drift and gravity theories in which the earth expands over time would expect changes."

Weisburd, Stefi, "Rooting for Continental Roots," *Science News*, vol. 130 (December 13, 1986), pp. 380-382.

p. 380   "But plate tectonics, too, has its faults. While the theory is very successful at explaining how oceans and oceanic crust form, in many ways it leaves the continents high and dry. In the case of the India-Asia collision, for instance, it doesn't explain why the oldest part of the Indian plate has survived the collision intact while sections of Asia have been violently deformed.

            "Plate tectonics also assumes that plates are no thicker than about 100 kilometers and that the structure of the lithosphere and athenosphere beneath the continents is essentially the same as that underlying oceanic crust. Over the last several years, however, many scientists have come to think that the plates under cratons—the oldest continental cores which have remained undeformed for more than a billion years—are much thicker than 100 km and may indeed have temperature and chemical profiles that differ from plates under oceans."

p. 382   "Continental roots may not represent another geosciences revolution in the making, but they certainly demonstrate that the conventional plate tectonics theory is not gospel."

Wheeler, H. E., and E. M. Beesley, "Critique of the Time-Stratigraphic Concept," *Bulletin, Geological Society of America*, vol. 59 (1948), pp. 75-86.

p. 84   "The employment of unconformities as time-stratigraphic boundaries should be abandoned.

            "Because of the failure of unconformities as time indices, time-stratigraphic boundaries of Paleozoic and later age must be defined by time,—hence by faunas."

Wilson, J. Tuzo, "Geophysics and Continental Growth," *American Scientist*, vol. 47 (March 1959), pp. 1-24.

p. 1   "When one considers that in a country so well mapped as Switzerland, the competent Swiss geologists have often been unable to predict in advance the precise arrangement of the strata to be found in railway tunnels a few thousand feet below the surface, one is forced to conclude that geological observations, while valid enough, are not of a type that lend themselves to extensive extrapolation."

p. 14   "The emission of lava at the present rate of 0.8 km^3/year throughout the Earth's history of 4.5×10^9 years or even for the 3×10^9 years since the oldest known rocks were formed would have poured out lava of the order of 3×10^9 km^3 on the Earth's surface. This corresponds approximately to the volume of the continents (about 30 km times 1.1×10^8 km^2). A slightly higher rate of volcanism in the early stages of the Earth would allow for the emission of the oceanic crust as well."

p. 21   "These Proterozoic rocks, although little altered, are always younger than the metamorphosed Archean rocks upon which they rest, but they may be older than Archean rocks elsewhere. Archean and Proterozoic are types of rocks and do not represent just two eras of time. Rocks of either type may be of any Precambrian age."

Chapter 11

Geochronology and Its Hidden Assumptions

A. Radiometric Dating

The dating of geologic ages and events in terms of years rather than stage of evolution) depends on a handful of radiometric techniques—especially the decay of uranium into lead. Also of importance are the potassium/argon method, the rubidium/strontium method, the fission-track method and a few others of less importance. These are widely trumpeted as proving the billion-year order of magnitude age of the earth and of the evolutionary process.

Not so widely known, however, are the many untestable assumptions in these methods (e.g., isolated system, constant decay rate, initial conditions) as well as the fact that most such measurements give inconsistent results and are never published. The bottom line is that *no* radiometrically determined date obtained by these methods is valid. Simply by changing the assumptions, all actual radiometric dates can be brought down to essentially zero. Although evolutionary geochronologists do not say much about this, occasional quotes such as the following help to point out these fallacies.

Anonymous, "Natural Plutonium," *Chemical and Engineering News*, vol. 49 (September 20, 1971), p. 29.

> "Plutonium occurs in nature. . . . Detection of this relatively short-lived isotope (80 million years) may indicate that synthesis of heavy elements was still occurring at the time of formation of the solar system." [Plutonium-224 found in bastnasite are in California.]

Armstrong, R. L., "K-Ar Dating: Late Cenozoic McMurdo Volcanic Group and Dry Valley Glacial History, Victoria Land, Antarctica," *New Zealand Journal of Geology and Geophysics*, vol. 21 (1978).

p. 692   "This is an inherent uncertainty in dating young volcanic rocks: anomalies may be detected only by stratigraphic consistency tests, independent dating techniques, and comparison with the known time scale of geomagnetic reversals during the last five million years (Cox 1969)."

Arndts, Russell, *et al.*, "Radiogenic Isotopes, Straight Lines and the Mixing Model," Paper presented at the Creation Convention, Atlanta, August 1981. Arndts is Professor of Chemistry at St. Cloud State University, Minnesota.

p. 6   "These pseudo or fictitious isochrons are readily recognized in evolutionary textbooks. In general this mechanism is used to explain ages which do not fit evolutionary philosophy.

> "Mixing often can be easily detected. The addition of more common strontium (greater dilution) means a lower $^{87}Sr/^{86}Sr$ ratio. Thus the $^{87}Sr/^{86}Sr$ is dependent on the total strontium. A formula is given by isotope geology texts to determine mixing. If one plots $^{87}Sr/^{86}Sr$ versus $^{1}/Sr$, a straight line relationship denotes the mixing phenomenon."

p. 8   "However, mixing can be the source of an isochron and *not* be detectable by this procedure." [i.e., it only detects *binary* mixing]

[Arndts determined "mixing" produced hitherto unrecognized pseudoisochrons on over 23 published ages, on samples taken randomly from the literature.]

Austin, Steven A., "Excess Argon within Mineral Concentrates from the New Dacite Lava Dome at Mount St. Helens Volcano," *Creation Ex Nihilo Technical Journal*, vol. 10, no. 3 (1996), pp. 335-344.

p. 335   "*Abstract.* The conventional K-Ar dating method was applied to the 1986 dacite flow from the new lava dome at Mount St. Helens, Washington. Porphyritic dacite which solidified on the surface of the lava dome in 1986 gives a whole rock K-Ar 'age' of 0.35 ± 0.05 million years (Ma). Mineral concentrates from this same dacite give K-Ar 'ages' from 0.35 ± 0.06 MA to 2.8 ± 0.6 Ma. These 'ages' are, of course, preposterous. The fundamental dating assumption ('no radiogenic argon was present when the rock formed') is questioned by these data. Instead data from this Mount St. Helens dacite argue that significant 'excess argon' was present when the lava solidified in 1986. . . . This study of Mount St. Helens dacite causes the more fundamental question to be asked—how accurate are K-Ar 'ages' from the many other phenocryst-containing lava flows worldwide?"

Bowring, Samuel A., and Todd Housh, response to critique of paper entitled "Sm-Nd Isotopic Data and Earth's Evolution" (*Science*, vol. 269, 1995), *Science*, vol. 273 (September 27, 1996), pp. 1878-1879.

p. 1879   "It is possible to produce linear arrays on isotope correlation diagrams (even statistically significant ones) that do not have any age significance and are best interpreted as mixing lines. The half-life of ^{147}Sm is so long that even for geologically significant periods of time (hundreds of millions of years) little change occurs in the Nd isotopic composition of rocks; thus, a number of rocks that start with slightly different initial ratios and Sm/Nd may produce linear arrays on an isotope correlation diagram with no age significance."

p. 1879   "There is a significant difference between interpreting all linear arrays on isotope correlation diagrams as having geological significance and actually documenting it."

Boyle, R. W., "Some Geochemical Considerations on Lead Isotope Dating of Lead Deposits," *Economic Geology*, vol. 54, no. 1 (January/February 1959), pp. 130-135.

p. 133   "The ratio of the lead isotopes in deposits deriving their lead from such rocks [i.e., Precambrian granites] is, therefore, neither a measure of the age of the deposits nor the age of the sedimentary host rocks but is rather a function of the complex geochemical processes through which the lead may have passed."

p. 135   "From these examples it is readily apparent that the amount of accumulated radiogenic lead contributed to a deposit is the deciding factor in age determinations and must be known before any age can be assigned to a deposit."

Brooks, C., D. E. James, and S. R. Hart, "Ancient Lithosphere: Its Role in Young Continental Volcanism," *Science*, vol. 193 (September 17, 1976), pp. 1086-1094.

p. 1093   "One serious consequence of the mantle isochron model is that crystallization ages determined on basic igneous rocks by the Rb-Sr whole-rock technique can be greater than the true age by many hundreds of millions of years. This problem of inherited age is more serious for younger rocks, and there are well-documented instances of conflicts between stratigraphic age and Rb-Sr in the literature."

Brown, P. E., and J. A. Miller, "Interpretation of Isotopic Ages in Orogenic Belts," in Kent *et al.*, "Time and Place in Orogeny," *Geological Society of London Special*, vol. 3, (1969).

p. 137   "Much still remains to be learned of the interpretation of isotopic ages and the realization that the isotopic age is not necessarily the geologic age of a rock has led to an over-sceptical attitude by some field geologists."

Carmichael, C. M., and H. C. Palmer, "Paleomagnetism of the Late Triassic North Mountain Basalt of Nova Scotia," *Journal of Geophysical Research*, vol. 73 (April 15, 1968), pp. 2811-2822.

p. 2813   "The Mississippian age for sample NS-45 cannot be correct because it is grossly inconsistent with the stratigraphic position of the lavas."

Catanzaro, E. J., and J. L. Kulp, "Discordant Zircans from the Little Belt (Montana), Beartooth (Montana) and Santa Catalina (Arizona) Mountains," *Geochimica et Cosmochimica Acta*, vol. 28 (January 1964), pp. 87-124.

p. 87   "The common occurrence of discordant results in isotopic geochronometry presents an intriguing and complicated problem. It has become obvious that many mineral samples used in age determinations have not been closed systems throughout their histories. The interpretation of isotopic ages ultimately requires knowledge of the processes which can cause alteration of the isotopic ratios."

Driscoll, Everly, "Dating of Moon Samples: Pitfalls and Paradoxes," *Science News*, vol. 101 (January 1, 1972), pp. 12-14.

p. 12   "If all of the age-dating methods (rubidium-strontium, uranium-lead and potassium-argon) had yielded the same ages, the picture would be neat. But they haven't. The lead ages, for example, have been consistently older.

     "This led Leon T. Silver of the California Institute of Technology to study the temperatures at which lead volatilizes (vaporizes) and moves out of the lunar sample. Theoretically, this could happen on the moon and this volatilized lead would become 'parentless'—separated from its uranium parent. More lead (parentless lead added to the material) would yield older ages."

Dudley, H. C., "Ether—the Fifth Element Rediscovered," *Science Digest*, vol. 77 (May 1975), pp. 57-63. Dr. Dudley was Professor of Radiation Physics, University of Illinois Medical Center, Chicago.

p. 62   "Finally, our space program efforts since 1957 have made all textbooks on astronomy published before 1965 so dated that they may as well have been written in Sanskrit for all their present usefulness.

     "Out of all this information explosion has come the realization that there is as much mass between the stars as there is contained in them and in the planets as well. In short, empty space is in fact crowded with interlocking magnetic and electric fields."

p. 62   "During the past decade there has been developing in astrophysics the concept of a generalized neutrino sea, a flux of uncharged, minute particles that arose from the myriad stars scattered throughout the universe."

p. 63   "This neutrino sea around us has already provided scientists with fresh views on:

"Causes of radioactivity and methods of increasing the rates of radioactive decay."

Dudley, H. C., "Is there an Ether?" *Industrial Research* (November 15, 1974), pp. 41-46.

p. 42   "The above discoveries and changes in viewpoint indicate that the simplistic Newtonian concept of celestial mechanics must be modified. New concepts must include the parameters of magnetic and electrostatic interactions of celestial bodies. These forces contribute to a resultant of three 'forces at a distance.'

"The electroscope and spinthrascope were used in early study of radioactive alpha-decay rates. The inherent limitations of these early instruments led to erroneous conclusions:

"That radioactive decay rates are constant.
"That these rates cannot b altered by change of the energy state of the electrons orbiting the nucleus.
"That radioactivity results from processes which involve only the atomic nucleus.

"The observed variations in the decay rates (changes in the half life) were produced by changes in pressure, temperature, chemical state, electric potential, stress of monomolecular layers, etc.

"The decay 'constant' is now considered to be a variable. The value is dependent on the energy state of the entire atom as the basic unit system, not just on the energy state of the atomic nucleus.

"Radioactivity is thus shown experimentally not to be, as described by Millikan, 'an unalterable property of the atom.' Half lives are NOT constant."

p. 44   "During the past decade there has been developing in astrophysics the concept of a generalized 'neutrino sea.' This flux of uncharged particles arises from the nuclear reactions in the myriad of nearly randomly-distributed stars.

"The 'subquantic medium' or 'neutrino sea' has been defined as an energy-rich substrate, the common denominator in all particle reactions:

"Muon neutrinos or e^o: Rest mass ~ 0.6 Mev.
"Electron neutrinos: Rest mass ~ 60 ev.
"Particle velocity range: a continuum from near zero to near c.
"Particle density: ~ $10^{12}/cm^3$.
"Energy density estimates: up to 10^{19} ev/cm^3.

"It is reasonable to conclude that populations of nuclei undergoing what is now termed 'spontaneous decay' consist of units each of which is a linear, resonant system. Parametric excitation of such units by interaction with the uncharged particles of the neutrino sea would provide a cause-effect mechanism for the phenomena of radioactivity. Thus the observed 'decay constant' (λ) is considered to be a complex variable, dependent on the energy content of the atom as a whole and the parameters defining interactions with the neutrino flux. In short, λ becomes a stability index rather than a constant."

Duncan, R. A., and W. Compston, "Sr-Isotopic Evidence for an Old Mantle Source Region for French Polynesian Volcanism," *Geology*, vol. 4 (December 1976), pp. 728-732.

p. 732   "The data from French Polynesia likewise imply that the source region from which Holocene to Miocene partial melts have been derived had previously maintained its Rb/Sr heterogeneity for a period of from 1 to 1.5 b.y."

Engels, Joan C., "Effects of Sample Purity on Discordant Mineral Ages Found in K-Ar Dating," *Journal of Geology*, vol. 79 (September 1971), pp. 609-616.

p. 609   "It is now well known that K-Ar ages obtained from different minerals in a single rock may be strikingly discordant."

p. 615   "Discordances between mineral K-Ar ages in a single rock sample are common, and if these minerals are mutual contaminants, purity levels must be carefully established in order to avoid mixed, meaningless ages."

Evernden, J. F., D. E. Savage, G. H. Curtis, and G. T. James, "Potassium-Argon Dates and the Cenozoic Mammalian Chronology of North America," *American Journal of Science*, vol. 262 (February 1964), pp. 145-198.

p. 154   "The materials used in this study were welded tuffs, extrusive flows of various lithologies, and pyroclastic non-welded vitric and crystal vitric tuffs. These materials were not used indiscriminately, however; a point that cannot be stressed too strongly. Careful evaluation of each sample and careful sample preparation is the cardinal rule."

p. 154   "Processes of rock alteration may render a volcanic rock useless for potassium-argon dating. Devitrification of glass results in a microcrystalline aggregate that is apparently too fine-grained to retain argon at low temperatures. We have analyzed several devitrified glasses of known age, and all have yielded ages that are too young. Some gave virtually zero ages although the geological evidence suggested that devitrification took place shortly after the formation of the deposit."

p. 155   "For dating purposes the sample must be virtually unaffected by weathering or post-depositional chemical alteration [applies to 'whole-rock' analyses of basic fine-grained flows]."

p. 157   Table 4—[Gives 7 'ages' of Hawaiian basalt.

Age Scatter: 0 to 3.34 (10^6). Avg. age taken at 250,000 years.]

p. 166   "Vertebrate paleontologists have relied upon 'stage-of-evolution' as the criterion for determining the chronologic relationships of faunas. Before the establishment of physical dates, evolutionary progression was the best method for dating fossiliferous strata."

Evernden, J. F., and J. R. Richards, "Potassium-Argon Ages in Eastern Australia," *Journal of the Geological Society of Australia*, vol. 9, no. 1 (1962).

p. 3   "Thus, if one believes that the derived ages in particular instances are in gross disagreement with established facts of field geology, he must conjure up geological processes that could cause anomalous or altered argon contents of the minerals."

Faure, G., and J. L. Powell, *Strontium Isotope Geology* (New York: Springer-Verlag, 1972).

p. 102   "It is readily apparent that these rocks [i.e., the Pahrump diabase from the Panamint Mountains in California] scatter widely on the isochron diagram. . . . Dates ranging from 1.09 to 34 billion years could be calculated for individual specimens. . . . Dates in excess of the age of the earth (4.6 x 10^9 years) are obviously not acceptable. A possible explanation for the scatter of points on the isochron diagram is that these rocks may have been variously enriched in radiogenic ^{87}Sr which might have been derived from the adjacent granite and gneiss during Mesozoic metamorphism. These results indicate that even total-rock systems may be open during metamorphism and may have their isotopic systems changed, making it impossible to determine their geologic age."

p. 102   "All of the above conclusions regarding the suitability for dating of rocks and minerals apply only when the rocks or their minerals have not been altered by chemical weathering at or near the surface of the Earth. Because most rocks that are used for dating are usually collected from outcrops, the effects of chemical weathering on the ^{87}Rb-^{87}Sr decay scheme may be important."

Gancarz, A. J., and G. J. Wasserburg, "Initial Pb of the Amîtsog Gneiss, West Greenland, and Implications for the Age of the Earth," *Geochimica et Cosmochimica Acta*, vol. 41 (September 1977), pp. 1283-1301.

p. 1283   "The isotopic composition of Pb in igneous rocks at the time of their formation, the initial Pb, records the U-Th-Pb fractionation history of source regions from which these rocks were derived. Studies of Pb isotopic composition in ancient igneous rocks are thus a key in deciphering the early chemical history of the earth. In principle the most ancient rocks should provide the best record of early differentiation if the initial Pb isotopic abundances have survived unaltered. Ancient cratonic blocks, however, typically have polymetamorphic histories and the rocks usually show evidence of significant modification of their primary isotopic abundances."

p. 1283   "The initial Pb is the Pb common to all phases of a rock at the time of isotopic homogenization."

pp. 1283-4   "Because of the mobility of U, Th, and Pb, most terrestrial rocks do not behave as simple systems and few isochrons have been determined. However, in typical igneous and metamorphic rocks, feldspars are very strongly enriched in Pb relative to U and Th which, therefore, may be close to the initial Pb. 'Initial'

Pb isotopic abundances in terrestrial rocks most frequently have been determined this way."

p. 1296 "There are two basic mechanisms by which a planet can consistently yield a 'young' model age. One mechanism is that the planet actually formed at a young time with concomitant enrichment of U relative to Pb. This would imply that the earth aggregated at a late stage from older material and lost Pb during the process. We note that the planet cannot be formed simply by late accumulation of older debris in a process which does not fractionate U and Pb in the debris. The other mechanism is that the planet accreted at a time earlier than the model age and then differentiated forming reservoirs with different μ values."

p. 1300 "Finally, if the 'young' model age of the earth is not due to planetary differentiation, then we must conclude that the earth really is 'young' and that planets must have been formed by the accumulation of older debris on a 10^8 yr time scale."

Gentry, Robert V., *et al.*, "Radiohalos in Coalified Wood: New Evidence Relating to the Time of Uranium Introduction and Coalification," *Science*, vol. 194 (October 15, 1976), pp. 315-318.

p. 315 "*Abstract.* The discovery of embryonic halos around uranium-rich sites that exhibit very high $^{238}U/^{206}Pb$ ratios suggests that uranium introduction may have occurred far more recently than previously supposed. The discovery of ^{210}PO Halos derived from uranium daughters, some elliptical in shape, further suggests that uranium-daughter infiltration occurred prior to coalification when the radionuclide transport rate was relatively high and the matrix still plastically deformable."

pp. 316-17 "Such extraordinary values admit the possibility that both the initial U infiltration and coalification could possibly have occurred with the past several thousand years."

p. 317 "Since it seems clear that the U radiocenters formed during the initial introduction of U and if this were as long ago as the Triassic or Jurassic are generally thought to be, then there should be evident not only fully developed, but overexposed U halos as well."

p. 317 "If remobilization is not the explanation, then these ratios raise some crucial questions about the validity of present concepts regarding the antiquity of these geological formations and about the time required for coalification."

Hayatsu, A., "K-Ar Isochron Age of the North Mountain Basalt, Nova Scotia," *Canadian Journal of Earth Sciences*, vol. 16 (April 1979), pp. 973-975.

p. 974 "In conventional interpretation of K-Ar age data, it is common to discard ages which are substantially too high or too low compared with the rest of the group or with other available data such as the geological time scale. The discrepancies between the rejected and the accepted are arbitrarily attributed to excess or loss of argon."

Jager, E., and J. C. Hunziker, ed., *Lectures in Isotope Geology* (New York: Springer-Verlag, 1979) 329 pp.

p. 36   "[Negative sloped isochrons] are obviously the result of mixing since isochrons always have positive slopes."

p. 59   "The coincidence of K-Ar whole-rock ages on slates with the age of sedimentation can be explained as the result of a mixture of 2Ml older ages and 1Md younger ages in the right proportions."

pp. 115-7   "As an explanation for discordia curves $\left(\frac{Pb206}{U238} \text{ vs } \frac{Pb207}{U235} \right)$ which yield geologically unacceptable dates: A linear data array can be produced by mixing old zircons with those which crystallized much later. . . . Sometimes it might be possible to distinguish the two types. . . . In a similar way a discordia trajectory can be produced by a mixed zircon population formed in an igneous rock by the assimilation of country rocks. . . . However, even within a single zircon crystal more than one age might occur."

Jueneman, Frederic B., "Secular Catastrophism," *Industrial Research and Development* (June 1982), p. 21.

"The age of our globe is presently thought to be some 4.5 billion years, based on radiodecay rates of uranium and thorium. Such 'confirmation' may be short-lived, as nature is not to be discovered quite so easily. There has been in recent years the horrible realization that radiodecay rates are not as constant as previously thought, nor are they immune to environmental influences. And this could mean that the atomic clocks are reset during some global disaster, and events which brought the Mesozoic to a close may not be 65 million years ago but, rather, within the age and memory of man.

"The mechanism for resetting such nuclear clocks is not clear, but knowledge has never really stood in our way in the quest for ignorance. Meanwhile, such prehistoric 'creatures' as Nessie from Loch Ness or Champ from Lake Champlain, as well as others, may not be avatars at all, but survivors from the last catastrophe.

"Even as we."

Macdougall, J. D., "Fission-Track Dating," *Scientific American*, vol. 235 (December 1976), pp. 114-122. Macdougall was Associate Professor of Geological Research, Scripps Institute, UCSD.

p. 115   "Uranium 238 is the only significant producer of tracks in terrestrial rocks and in natural and man-made glasses."

p. 118   "The fourth assumption presupposes that the concentration of uranium in any specimen has remained constant over the specimen's lifetime. . . . A combination of elevated temperatures and ground-water percolation can leach away a proportion of the uranium present in rock crystals. The mobility of the uranium is such that as one part of a rock formation is being impoverished another part can become abnormally enriched. Such changes can also take place at relatively low temperatures."

p. 119 "The spontaneous-track densities in the calcite crystals [growing in the marrow cavities of old bones, among them the fossil bones of the genus *Australopithecus* unearthed in the limestone caves of South Africa] proved to be much lower than we had expected, suggesting that the fossil bones were by no means as old as other evidence indicated. . . . It appears that exposure to ambient temperatures over a period of a million years or so is enough to anneal existing fission tracks in calcite and thereby give rise to anomalously young age determinations."

Mauger, R. L, "K-Ar Ages of Biotites from Tuffs in Eocene Rocks of the Green River, Washakie, and Uinta Basins, Utah, Wyoming, and Colorado," (University of Wyoming) *Contributions to Geology*, vol.. 15, no. 1 (Winter 1977), pp. 17-41.

p. 37 "In general, dates in the 'correct ball park' are assumed to be correct and are published, but those in disagreement with other data are seldom published nor are discrepancies fully explained."

Noble, C. S., and J. J. Naughton, "Deep Ocean Basalts: Inert Gas Content and Uncertainties in Age Dating," *Science*, vol. 162 (October 11, 1968), pp. 265-266.

p. 265 "*Abstract.* The radiogenic argon and helium contents of three basalts erupted into the deep ocean from an active volcano (Kilauea) have been measured. Ages calculated from these measurements increase with sample depth up to 22 million years for lavas deduced to be recent. Caution is urged in applying dates from deep-ocean basalts in studies on ocean-floor spreading."

p. 265 ". . . it is possible to deduce that these lavas are very young, probably less than 200 years old. The samples may, in fact, be very recent, as judged by their fresh appearance and the extreme thinness of the palagonite and manganese oxide layers on the surfaces."

Rancitelli, L. A., and D. E. Fisher, "Potassium-Argon Ages of Iron Meteorites," *Planetary Sciences Abstracts*, 48th Annual Meeting, p. 167.

"The potassium-argon ages of the meteorites investigated ranged from 5×10^9 years to 15.6×10^9 years. In particular, the potassium-argon age of the iron meteorite Weekeroo Station is found to disagree with the previously determined strontium-rubidium age of the silicate inclusions in this meteorite. The spatial distribution of potassium in several iron meteorites indicate it is highly concentrated in grain boundaries and inclusions. As much as 80% of the potassium in a small sample of an iron meteorite can be removed by distilled water in 4.5 hours."

Seidemann, David E., "Effects of Submarine Alteration on K-Ar Dating of Deep-Sea Igneous Rocks," *Bulletin, Geological Society of America*, vol. 88 (November 1977), pp. 1660-1666.

p. 1660 "*Abstract.* In an attempt to establish criteria for obtaining reliable K-Ar dates, conventional K-Ar studies of several Deep Sea Drilling Project sites were undertaken. K-Ar dates of these rocks may be subject to inaccuracies as the result of sea-water alteration. Inaccuracies may also result from the presence of excess radiogenic ^{40}Ar trapped in rapidly cooled rocks at the time of their formation. . . . Because of the problems involved, caution must be used in interpreting the meaning of conventional K-Ar dates for deep-sea rocks."

p. 1666   "Strong indications of the reliability of a conventional K-Ar date, such as its concordance with the dates of coexisting minerals, must exist before geologic significance can be attributed to it."

Spanglet, Mark, Hannes R. Brueckner, and Ronald G. Senechal, "Old Rb-Sr Whole-Rock Isochron Apparent Ages from Lower Cambrian Psammites and Metapsammites, Southeastern New York," *Bulletin, Geological Society of America*, vol. 89 (May 1978), pp. 783-790.

p. 789   "These data suggest that great caution must be used when applying the Rb-Sr whole-rock technique to metamorphic rocks. This and other studies show that metasedimentary rocks can yield linear arrays of points on isochron diagrams, but that the age can have a variety of geological meanings and need not define the date of deposition or metamorphism of the sediment. Thus, the application of the Rb-Sr whole-rock method to time-stratigraphic correlation of metamorphic rocks is in doubt except where it can be demonstrated the rock has had an igneous origin."

Stansfield, William D., *The Science of Evolution* (New York: Macmillan, 1977), 614 pp. Stansfield was at the University of California, Santa Barbara.

p. 80   "Several methods have been devised for estimating the age of the earth and its layers of rocks. These methods rely heavily on the assumption of uniformitarianism, i.e., natural processes have proceeded at relatively constant rates throughout the earth's history."

p. 84   "It is obvious that radiometric techniques may not be the absolute dating methods that they are claimed to be. Age estimates on a given geological stratum by different radiometric methods are often quite different (sometimes by hundreds of millions of years). There is no absolutely reliable long-term radiological 'clock.'"

Stanton, R. L., and R. D. Russell, "Anomalous Leads and the Emplacement of Lead Sulfide Ores," *Economic Geology*, vol. 54 (June/July 1959), pp. 588-607.

p. 606   "Variations in the isotope ratios lead to the recognition of lead of two types— ordinary leads and anomalous leads, and different galenas are characterized by one or the other of these. True ordinary leads are probably derived from below the crust, and anomalous leads are derived in turn from these by variable radiogenic contamination in the crust. Thus ordinary and anomalous leads form a series rather than two distinct groups. It is likely, furthermore, that no absolutely ordinary leads occur on the earth's surface, as all have probably received at least minute radiogenic contamination in coming from the mantle."

Stieff, L. R., T. W. Stern, and R. N. Eichler, "Algebraic and Graphic Methods for Evaluating Discordant Lead-Isotope Ages," *United States Geological Survey Professional Paper 414-E* (1963), p. E1.

"The most reasonable age can be selected only after careful consideration of independent geochronologic data as well as field, stratigraphic and paleontologic evidence, and the petrographic and paragenetic relations.

> "In an effort to evaluate a discordant age sequence, therefore, the data are adjusted in one of several ways . . . until the lead-uranium and lead-lead ages are in agreement."

Talbot, Stephen L., "Mystery of the Radiohalos," *Research Communications Network*, newsletter #2 (February 10, 1977), pp. 3-6.

p. 3   "Gentry's studies have led to the following conclusions. (1) Some halos ('polonium' halos) imply a nearly instantaneous crystallization of Earth's primordial rocks, and this crystallization must have occurred simultaneously with the synthesis/creation of certain elements."

p. 4   "In this report we will discuss only those researches leading to conclusion (1)."

p. 4-5 "The last three alpha decay steps in the Uranium 238 decay series involve the successive decay of polonium-218, polonium-214, and polonium 210. In contrast to the decay of the parent uranium, these steps occur very quickly; the half-lives of the three forms of polonium are 3.05 minutes, 164 microseconds, and 140 days respectively. Polonium, therefore, is not thought to be observed in nature except as a daughter product of uranium and thorium decay.

"That is where the enigma begins. For Gentry has analyzed numerous polonium halos possessing, in some cases, the rings for all three polonium isotopes; in other cases the rings for ^{214}Po and ^{210}Po; and in other cases the ring for ^{210}Po alone—*but none of these halos exhibit rings for the earlier uranium-238 daughters*. These halos are evidence for parentless polonium, not derived from uranium.

". . . They require nearly instantaneous crystallization of the rocks, simultaneously with the synthesis or creation of the polonium atoms."

Wanless, R. K., R. D. Stevens, G. R. Lachance, and R. N. Delabio, "Age Determinations and Geological Studies: K-Ar Isotopic Ages, Report 9," *Geological Survey of Canada Paper*, vol. 69, no. 2A (1970).

p. 24   "No stratigraphic evidence is available to confirm or deny this age."

Weaver, Charles E., and J. M. Wampler, "K, Ar, Illite Burial," *Bulletin, Geological Society of America*, vol. 81 (November 1979), pp. 3423-3430.

p. 3423   "*Abstract*. K, Ar, and mineral analyses of montmorillonite mud samples 4233 feet to 16,450 feet deep from a well in the Mississippi Delta area show that, with depth, the apparent K-Ar ages of the bulk samples decrease 100 m.y."

p. 3423   "The side-wall core samples range in age from Pliocene to upper Miocene."

Whitney, P. R., and P. M. Hurley, "The Problem of Inherited Radiogenic Strontium in Sedimentary Age Determinations," *Geochimica et Cosmochimica Acta*, vol. 28 (April 1964), pp. 425-436.

p. 425   "*Abstract*. The major source of error in Rb/Sr age determinations on whole-rock samples of shale is the presence of inherited radiogenic strontium in the detrital minerals."

p. 433   "Application of the whole-rock Rb/Sr age measurement technique to argillaceous sediments yields results in excess of the true age of sedimentation due to the presence of inherited radiogenic strontium in the elastic compounds of the sediment. The magnitude of this effect depends upon the provenance of the detritus and the degree to which it has been altered during weathering, transportation, and sedimentation."

Williams, I. S., W. Compston, B. W. Chapell, and T. Shirahase, "Rubidium-Strontium Age Determinations on Micas from a Geologically Controlled Composite Batholith," *Journal of the Geological Society of Australia*, vol. 22, no. 4 (1975).

p. 502   "The internal consistency demonstrated above is not a sufficient test of the accuracy of the age determinations; they must also be consistent within any age constraints placed on intrusion by fossils in the country rocks."

B. Other Methods of Geochronometry

There actually are a great many worldwide natural processes that can be used to estimate the age of the earth—such processes as the decay of the earth's magnetic field, the buildup of helium and radiocarbon in its atmosphere, the influx of sodium and other substances into the ocean, and many others. All of these will yield much younger ages than the billion-year estimates of the handful of radiologic methods. The problem is that these ages are too small for evolution to be feasible, and so are rejected arbitrarily.

They all may be wrong, of course, since they must be based on the same untestable assumptions as the radiometric methods. However, there are many more of them, and the assumptions are more reasonable, so the great weight of scientific evidence favors a young earth. The only *true* chronologies are those based on reliable historical records, and these are all in terms of thousands of years—not millions or billions.

Anonymous, "Magsat Down, Magnetic Field Declining," *Science News*, vol. 117 (June 28, 1980), p. 407.

p. 407   "Preliminary results from the just-downed Magsat—for Magnetic Field Satellite—confirm a previously detected decrease in the intensity of the earth's magnetic field, NASA scientists said, last week."

p. 407   "Measurements of the main field . . . show that the overall intensity of the field is declining at a rate of 26 nanoteslas per year."

p. 407   "If the rate of decline were to continue steadily . . . the field strength would reach zero in 1,200 years. In that event, according to current theory, the magnetic field would be likely to rebuild with a polarity opposite to that of the present, so that compass needles that now point north would point south. . . . Moreover, little is known about what may cause the field—which is created by churning in the earth's molten core—to decline in strength."

Anonymous, "The Disappearing U.S.," *Scientific American*, vol. 211 (October 1964), p. 58.

"The question of how fast the U.S. land mass is being washed into the sea has been given a new answer by two Princeton University geologists, Sheldon Judson and Dale F. Ritter. They calculate that solid and dissolved material carried by the rivers of the U.S. is sufficient to lower the average land surface by 2.4 inches in 1,000 years, a rate about twice as high as previous estimates.

"To reach this conclusion, reported in *Journal of Geophysical Research* [vol. 72, April 15, 1967, pp. 3395-3401], Judson and Ritter examined the annual records of suspended sediment in the country's major rivers compiled by the U.S. Geological Survey and the Army Corps of Engineers. The highest erosion rate, 6.5 inches per 1,000 years, is found in the Colorado River basin. The next highest rate, 3.6 inches, is recorded for the rivers draining California. The largest river basin, that of the Mississippi, is eroding at the rate of two inches per 1,000 years. The lowest rate is for the Columbia River basin, 1.5 inches.

"The authors conclude: 'Taking the average height of the United States above sea level as 2,300 feet and assuming that the rates of erosion reported here are representative, we find that it would take 11 to 12 million years to move to the oceans a volume equivalent to that of the United States lying above sea level. At this rate there has been enough time since the Cretaceous to destroy such a landmass six times.'"

Behrman, Daniel, *The New World of the Oceans* (Boston: Little, Brown & Co., 1973), 436 pp.

p. 209   "The theories of continental drift and sea-floor spreading are highly conjectural, but it is hard to stop anything as big as the floor of the ocean once it has been put into motion."

p. 259   "We know that the intensity of the magnetic field has dropped from 0.8 to 0.5 gauss over the last 2500 years in Western Europe. In Japan, it was 0.7 gauss in A.D. 300 and it is now 0.55 gauss. We also know that reversals of the magnetic field are not random. Its behavior is cyclical; it goes through zero and comes out the other side. Intensity drops before reversals. They occur on an average of every half a million years." [Quoting Dr. Neil Vroyke of Lamont]

Bloch, Salman, "Some Factors Controlling the Concentration of Uranium in the World Ocean," *Geochimica et Cosmochimica Acta*, vol. 44 (February 1980), pp. 373-377.

p. 373   "The oceans contain over 4 billion tons of dissolved U, at a concentration of 3.3 ppb, and recovery of this element from sea water is presently being considered by a number of countries.

"A detailed mass-balance calculation for U has shown that only about 10% (0.2×10^{10} g/yr) of the present-day river input of dissolved U can be removed by known sinks."

p. 373   "The mean U concentration in world rivers is about 0.6 ppb. This value multiplied by the total river flux of water of 0.32×10^{20} g/yr gives 1.92×10^{10} g/yr as the total riverine influx of dissolved U."

p. 376   "Low- and high-temperature alteration of basalts, organic-rich sediments and coexisting phosphorites on continental margins, metalliferous sediments, carbonate sediments, and sediments in anoxic basins deeper than 220 m remove about three-fourths of the present-day riverine supply to the ocean."

[Mass in Ocean $= 4(10)^9 \left(\frac{1000}{2.2} \right) = \frac{40}{11}(10^{15}) = 3.64(10^{15})$ gm.

River Influx $= 1.92(10^{10})$ gms/yr.

Sinks $= \left(\frac{1}{10} + \frac{3}{4} \right)(1.92)(10^{10})$ gms/yr.

Net Increment to Ocean Mass $= 0.15(1.92)(10^{10})$ gms/yr.

Age of Ocean $= \frac{3.64}{0.15(1.92)}(10^5) = \frac{364}{28.8}(10^5) = \frac{52}{4.1}(10^5) = 1,250,00$ years.

Calculations by HMM]

Bloxham, Jeremy and David Gubbins, "The Evolution of the Earth's Magnetic Field," *Scientific American*, vol. 261 (December 1989), pp. 68-75.

p. 71   "The dipole component of the earth's field was considerably stronger 2,000 years ago than it is today. (Dipole decay is evident in Roman ceramic artifacts, which contain iron particles that are magnetized to a greater extent than are those in modern products.) In the next two millennia, if the present rate of decay is sustained, the dipole component of the field should reach zero."

p. 74   "Evidence is mounting that the present dramatic fall in the dipole component of the field is caused by the growth and propagation of the reverse-flux features beneath Africa and the Atlantic Ocean."

p. 75   "Curiously, the historical record shows that reverse-flux features have formed and intensified but that none has decayed. Evidence suggests, however, that these features do decay during periods of dipole growth. During the past 10 million years the earth's magnetic field has reversed polarity once every 500,000 years or so. Yet the dipole field decays on a much shorter time scale. These facts suggest that the field does not reverse polarity after every period of dipole decay."

Blumer, Max, *Science*, vol. 176, p. 1257, summarized in *New Scientist*, vol. 54 (June 29, 1972), p. 726.

          "Making a liberal estimate [Blumer] claims that offshore oil resources—the source of the proposed seepage—do not amount to more than some 100-billion tons in total. Between one and ten million tons of oil probably enter the oceans annually, when all sources are included. If, says Blumer, submarine seepage accounts for as much as five million tons of this pollution, this loss alone would have completely depleted the existing reserves in a mere 20,000 years."

Bower, Bruce, "Siberian Site Cedes Stone-Age Surprise," *Science News*, vol. 145 (February 5, 1994), p. 84.

p. 84   "Preliminary soil analysis by two U.S. geologists indicates that stone tools found at the Siberian location, known as Diring, date to around 500,000 years ago. However, Russian investigators date the artifacts to at least 2 million years ago, argued excavation director Yui A. Mochanov last week in a talk at the Smithsonian Institution in Washington D.C."

p. 84   "Only East African stone tools that date to between 1.8 million and 2.5 million years old resemble the Diring artifacts."

p. 84   "Measurements of magnetic reversals and radioactivity in Diring soil—the latter relying on a technique unknown to Western scientists—place the finds at 2 million to 3 million years old, Mochanov maintains."

p. 84   "In fact, thermoluminescence dates for two soil samples collected at Diring last summer by Michael Waters, a geologist at Texas A & M University in College Station, place the stone tools at about 500,000 years old."

Burroughs, W. J., *Weather Cycles: Real or Imaginary*.

p. 74   "There is one further example of cyclic behavior in geological records which needs to be taken on its own. This is what appeared to be the most stunning evidence of solar influence on the weather. It came from the work of George Williams in South Australia. He became intrigued in 1979 by the laminated sandstones and siltstones in the Elatina formation in South Australia which appeared to reveal the Sun's influence on the climate in the Precambrian era."

p. 74   "The geological explanation of the Elatina formation was that the layers were standard varves which were produced from the sediment when turbid glacial meltwater filled a lake each summer.

"The laminations studied occupied a 10-m thick unit in the 60-m thick formation. This contained roughly 19,000 laminations which contained 1580 cycles."

p. 76   "All of this bore an uncanny resemblance to the observed variations in sunspot number which have occurred since 1700. This led to two fascinating hypotheses. First, that the behavior of the Sun had remained relatively unchanged for 700 million years. Second, that for all this time, solar activity had been modulating the weather. But subsequent analysis of this record and others from Australia suggests that the explanation may be lunar rather than solar. The new explanation is that the laminations record the variations in sediment laid down by daily tides. So the 19,000 laminations studied would have been deposited in just 56 years rather than the 19,000 'years' originally assumed."

Cook, Melvin A., "Where is the Earth's Radiogenic Helium?" *Nature*, vol. 179 (January 26, 1957), p. 213.

p. 213   "At the estimated 2×10^{20} gm. uranium and 5×10^{20} gm. thorium in the lithosphere, helium should be generated radiogenically at a rate of about 3×10^9 gm./year. Moreover, the (secondary) cosmic-ray source of helium has been estimated to be of comparable magnitude. Apparently nearly all the helium from sedimentary rocks and, according to Keevil and Hurley, about 0.8 of the radiogenic helium from igneous rocks, have been released into the atmosphere during geological times (currently taken to be about 5×10^9 year). Hence more than 10^{20} gm. of helium should have passed into the atmosphere since the 'beginning.' Because the atmosphere contains only 3.5×10^{15} gm. helium-4, the common assumption is therefore that about 10^{20} gm. of helium-4 must also have passed out through the exosphere, and that its present rate of loss through the exosphere balances the rate of exudation from the lithosphere."

p. 213   "This leads to an 'anomalous' atmospheric chronometry which is, on the other hand, in approximate agreement with the chronometry one obtains from the annual uranium flux in river water (10^{10} - 10^{11} gm./yr.) compared with the total uranium present in the oceans (about 10^{15} gm.)."

Engel, A. E. J., "Time and the Earth," *American Scientist*, vol. 57 (Winter 1969), pp. 458-483.

p. 461   "The fact that the calculated age of the earth has increased by a factor of roughly 100 between the year 1900 and today—as the accepted 'age' of the earth has increased from about 50 million years in 1900 to at least 4.6 aeons today—certainly suggests we clothe our current conclusions regarding time and the earth with humility."

p. 462   "Paradoxically, contemporary studies also show that pyroxenes tend to scavenge and hold excessive argon, the decay product of potassium 40. This extra argon would suggest, incorrectly, a much greater age for the host mineral and rock."

p. 462   "No more than one percent or so of the history of the earth is decipherable. But that one percent is dispersed through a series of events, or episodes, extending back through geologic time. By imaginative manipulation of the evolving data we can reconstruct a magnificent and awesome history of the earth and its life."

p. 463   "We will speculate a lot about the first aeon or more of earth's history (prior to 3.5×10^9 years) in the next few years; but in the foreseeable future it will be mostly speculation—essentially geopoetry."

p. 480   "Earth scientists are now in their own special rococo phase. The current majority have a method involving a beautiful 'black box,' and are in search of money, a sample, and, too often, an idea. There is evolving, however, a much more sophisticated group. They much prefer to calculate than to be right. From time to time these several types intercommunicate and learn more of time and the earth."

p. 480   "The most honest concede freely we know almost nothing of the earth or its processes."

Ewing, Maurice, J. I. Ewing, and Manik Talwani, "Sediment Distribution in the Oceans: The Mid-Atlantic Ridge," *Bulletin, Geological Society of America*, vol. 75 (January 1964), pp. 17-36.

p. 24   "According to such theories [i.e., general crustal stability] the sediments found on the ocean floor should represent the accumulations of perhaps billions of years."

p. 24   "According to the theories of drift, the sediments on the floors of these oceans represent accumulations of the order of 100 million years (or less if the drift is still going on) in the younger parts and perhaps 150 million years in the older parts."

p. 33   "The thickness of sediment on the Mid-Atlantic Ridge is small. It averages 1–200m in the carbonate zone (< 2500 fm), except in the immediate vicinity of the crest, where it is almost zero. The bordering areas, with depths of 2500 fm or greater, now receive red clay. The clay has a total thickness of less than 50 m, and is generally draped over rough basement topography, except where the basin sediments have encroached upon and buried the basement rocks. The basin sediments are known, from studies still in progress, to range in thickness from zero up to several kilometers. Strong evidence . . . indicates that they are terrigeneous, very homogeneous, and have been deposited in extensive beds that remained almost level during the process, filling the basin and burying the rough basement topography. . . .

". . . The uniformity of this distribution denies the possibility that an appreciable amount of downhill sediment transport has occurred. . . . The fact that a 75-mile wide zone at the crest is bare of sediment would point to either extreme youth or recent burial of sediments by volcanic rocks."

p. 34   "The accepted rate of sedimentation for *Globigerina* ooze on the Mid-Atlantic Ridge in depths < about 2500 fm is about 2-4 cm/1000 years. If one assumes that this rate has been constant, the total time for accumulating the observed carbonate sediments is calculated at about 2-5 million years, except for a younger zone very near the crest. . . . The time computed from accepted sedimentation rates is unacceptably small."

Games, Ken, "The Earth's Magnetism—in Bricks," *New Scientist*, vol. 90 (June 11, 1981), pp. 678-681. Games was in the Department of Geophysics, University of Liverpool.

p. 678   "So we have measured directly the strength of the Earth's magnetic field for less than 150 years. . . . Nevertheless, these direct measurements are helpful, and they show that even over this short period the geomagnetic field has been growing weaker by an average of 5 per cent per century. At this rate, the geomagnetic field would disappear in about 3000 years."

p. 679   "Clearly the geomagnetic field in Egypt has varied rapidly and by large amounts. The greatest rate of change, which occurred around the maximum at about 1400 BC, was about 140 nanoteslas/year, and lasted about 300 years either side of the maximum. For the rest of the time the rate of change was only about 40 nT/year.

p. 680-1   "In fact, as already stated, the dipole field has been decreasing on average at 5 per cent per century during the past 150 years—corresponding to about 20 nt/yr. in Egypt given the present value of the field in that country.

"We can explain the periods of rapid rates of change in the magnetic field in Egypt in two ways. They could have been caused by non-dipole centers, localized around Egypt. Such centers would have to have been about as big as the largest recorded by observatories over the past century, and would have had to have persisted for longer than we have been able to observe since records began. Alternatively, these changes could have been caused by changes in the dipole field. . . . The problem with the second explanation is that although the dipole field could easily produce the amplitude of the changes seen in Egypt, the *rate* of change of the dipole field would need to be much greater than has ever been observed since direct measurements were first made. So we have to conclude that in ancient Egypt either the non-dipole centers persisted for longer than they do now, or that the dipole field changed more rapidly than it does at present."

Gribbin, John, "The Inconstant Sun," in *Death of the Sun* (New York: Delacorte Press, 1980), 195 pp.

pp. 119-20   "We can surely take it for granted that the Astronomer Royal was *looking* for sunspots in the intervening eight years! But, in this modern age, astronomers have been curiously reluctant to accept Spörer's and Maunder's accounts. There is still too much of an arrogant tendency to dismiss nineteenth-century scientists as bunglers, even though our present scientific knowledge builds from their work. So it was necessary for Eddy to silence those doubting Thomases by going back to the original sources, repeating and improving on the studies of his two pioneering predecessors, and publishing his results in the journal *Science* in 1976, a respectable journal and a modern date to bring the evidence to the attention of late-twentieth-century science.

"His research is impeccable and his results unquestionable. The Maunder Minimum is real; sunspot activity really did almost switch off between 1645 & 1715."

p. 120 "So the Maunder Minimum is real and we have proof that the Sun can vary in a way which directly affects the Earth (certainly through carbon-14, perhaps by affecting the climate) for periods of tens or hundreds of years.*"

"*Quotations in this section are as reported by Eddy, *Science*, 192 (1976): 1200."

p. 121 "With the new carbon-14 tool proved as a good guide to solar activity, John Eddy has been able to use the technique to push back the story of solar variability to the Bronze Age. During the past 5,000 years, he finds, there have been times when the Sun was much more active than it is today, and also times when it was much less active."

Gribbin, John, "The Curious Case of the Shrinking Sun," *New Scientist*, vol. 97 (March 3, 1983), pp. 592-595.

p. 592 "Astronomers were startled, and laymen amazed, when in 1979 Jack Eddy, of the High Altitude Observatory in Boulder, Colorado, claimed that the sun was shrinking, at such rate that, if the decline did not reverse, our local star would disappear within a hundred thousand years. . . . Together they [with A. Boornazian] found evidence of a decline in solar angular diameter of two seconds of arc—equivalent to 0.1 percent—per century."

p. 593 "Even if the sun is shrinking at a rate of merely 0.01 percent per century it would totally disappear in a million years; and it would be twice its present size a million years ago."

p. 594 "The breakthrough came from one of Eddy's colleagues, Ronald Gilliland, . . . His first conclusion, from a battery of statistical tests, was that the over-all decline in solar diameter of about 0.1 seconds of arc per century since the early 1700s is real. And when standard statistical tests aimed at revealing small, regular changes in the pattern of variability were turned on the data from the meridian circle they showed an unambiguously clear trace of a periodic variation with a repeating rhythm of 76 years."

p. 594 "As for the longer-term decline in solar diameter, the discovery that started the whole ball rolling, Gilliland was cautious in his claims. 'Given the many problems with the data sets,' he said, 'one is not inexorably led to the conclusion that a negative secular solar radius trend has existed since A.D. 1700, but the preponderance of current evidence indicates that such is likely to be the case.'"

Hendrix, Charles E., *The Cave Book* (Revere, Massachusetts: Earth Science Publishing Co., 1950).

p. 26 "How long does it take for a stalactite to grow? Many people, impressed by repeated statements of the extreme duration of geologic time, have made statements to the effect that it takes dripstone practically forever to grow appreciably. However there is more than a little evidence that growth is considerably rapid. First of all, stalactites are found in man-made tunnels that are only a few years old. . . . Second, certain conditions are so favorable to dripstone growth that as much as several cubic inches a year may be deposited in a single stalactite. . . . Third, there are many examples of large stalagmites growing on blocks of stone that have fallen from cave ceilings."

Hoyle, Sir Fred, "Stars as Thermonuclear Reactors," in *Astronomy* (New York: Doubleday, 1962), pp. 232-251.

p. 232 "In the nineteenth century the scientists Kelvin and Helmholtz offered an explanation of how the Sun might go on producing its colossal output of energy for a period much greater than a mere two thousand years. Their explanation depended on gravity, and we can best begin to understand it by noting what happens when a stone drops from a high tower."

p. 234 "This then, was the theory that Helmholtz and Kelvin put forward and it would certainly suffice to explain how the Sun could go on emitting vast quantities of energy for many thousands of years. Calculation shows that, on this theory, a reduction in the diameter of the Sun of only some fifty yards a year would be sufficient to account for its known output of energy."

p. 234 "Nevertheless, if the theory of Helmholtz and Kelvin were correct, the diameter of the Sun would have diminished markedly over periods of several million years. But we know from geological evidence that it has not done so. From fossil evidence it is known that some genera of animals—brachiopods, the tuatara and some lizards, for example—have persisted relatively unchanged for upward of a hundred million years. This is convincing evidence of a constancy of physical environment on the Earth that would be impossible if the Sun had changed its diameter a very great deal during that period. In fact, we know from fossil records that the Sun must have been shining pretty much as it is now for at least a thousand million years. Thus the idea that a slow shrinkage of the Sun accounts for the energy it radiates into space is simply not tenable.

"In brief, the ideas of Kelvin and Helmholtz could explain a source of energy 10,000 times more potent than any form of chemical combustion; but in view of what the fossil record reveals, we must seek for an explanation that will account for a potency 10,000 times as great again."

Kazmann, Raphael G., "It's About Time: 4.5 Billion Years," *Geotimes*, vol. 23 (September 1978), pp. 18-20. Taken from a symposium, April 13, 1978, at Louisiana State University.

p. 18 John Eddy: "Time, Trees and Solar Change"

"I suspect . . . that the Sun is 4.5 billion years old. However, . . . I suspect that we could live with Bishop Ussher's value for the age of the Earth and Sun. I don't think we have much in the way of observational evidence in astronomy to conflict with that."

p. 18   Melvin S. Freedman: "The Solar Neutrino Dilemma"

"After 15 years of experimentation (and successfully answering all criticisms of the experimental procedure) they have concluded that they have, indeed, recorded the arrival of neutrinos, but at a rate of only about 1/3 the number predicted by the standard solar model."

p. 19   Stephen P. Maran, "The Sirius Mystery: Unsolved Problems of Stellar Evolution"

"Some people have suggested that in historic time Sirius B was a red giant and it was so observed by the ancient astronomers. It takes, by modern calculation, at least 100,000 years for a red giant to collapse to a white dwarf. But Arab astronomers catalogued Sirius in the 11th century as a white star and listed the five other stars in the original group as 'red.' This might imply that we have a historical observational record that the transformation from red giant to white dwarf occurred in a thousand years or less, in grave disagreement with modern astrophysics. This, in essence, is the mystery."

p. 20   "Kazmann pointed out that his impression from the papers and discussion is that cosmochronology and geochronology are far from reliable in yielding ages. . . . Therefore, as an engineer, he concluded that many engineering structures or designs that were based on such determinations, whether for the containment of rad-waste or evaluation of activities of faults would be questionable if not downright hazardous."

Kennedy, George C., "The Origin of Continents, Mountain Ranges, and Ocean Basins," *American Scientist*, vol. 47 (December 1959), pp. 491-504. Kennedy held a full professorship at UCLA. This paper was from a National Sigma Xi lectureship.

p. 498   "At this rate, all the land masses of the world would be eroded to sea level in something of the order of 10-25 million years. This is particularly surprising in view of the fossil record. Land animals and plants have been known on the surface of the Earth for well over 300 million years, and the sedimentary record indicates high land masses extending back at least two billion years. Much geological evidence indicates that the ancient continents were in approximately the same place as the present continents and that continents have existed more or less as they are today and for a period of at least two billion years. . . .

". . . the rates of erosion along the slopes of steep mountains are many times those of lower lying continental land masses. The lifetime of mountains, therefore, must be far less than the 25 million years estimated for continents. In contrast to this reasoning, however, is the geologic record which strongly suggests that the Appalachian Mountain Range has existed more or less where it is today and, as far as we know, with reasonably similar relief for the last 200 million years, shedding sediments both to interior valleys and coastward."

Kerr, Richard A., "The Sun is Fading," *Science*, vol. 231 (January 24, 1986), p. 339.

p. 339   "Three independent measures of the brightness of the sun as seen from Earth now show the same 0.02 percent per year decrease during at least the past 5 years. Thus, as suspected in the early years of these observations, the sun does seem to be fading. But it is fading too fast for it to be part of a long-term change, so the decrease is presumably linked to some well-known solar cycle, such as the 11-year sunspot cycle or more probably the 22-year magnetic cycle. Over a decade or two, such changes could affect climate."

p. 339   "The solar irradiance decrease seems real enough, but what known solar behavior is associated with it remains uncertain, so that predictions of the direction of future irradiance changes and any climatic effects remain uncertain as well."

Lambert, André, and K. J. Hsü, "Non-annual Cycles of Varve-like Sedimentation in Walensee, Switzerland," *Sedimentology*, vol. 26 (June 1979), pp. 453-461.

p. 456   "The number deposited in the years between 1811-1971 is not 160 as predicted by the assumption of annual cyclicity, but ranges from 300 to 360. We also counted some seventy coarse silt laminae for a 30-year interval since the deposition of the 1944 flood-deposit. The sedimentary record thus indicates that more than two laminated silts, on the average, were deposited annually."

pp. 459-60   "Both the sedimentological and hydrological records of the Walensee show unmistakably that graded laminae of silt and clay are not necessarily deposits of annual cycles. . . . As a consequence, a vertical succession of laminae may have been deposited from underflows of different origin. Thus the number of laminae deposited annually at any given spot depends not only upon the floodstage of any particular stream, but also upon that of adjacent streams, which may issue turbidity underflows that travel long distances."

Maddox, John, "Halley's Comet is Quite Young," *Nature*, vol. 339 (May 11, 1989), p. 95.

p. 95   "In this accepted view of the appearance of comets, the existence of the Oort cloud itself is not a firm reality, but is inferred, essentially from calculations of the chance that such an object will be captured into the inner Solar System and from the number of known comets. In the circumstances, many people would be happier if there were more objective evidence for the reality of the Oort cloud."

p. 95   "Indeed the rate at which comets such as Halley lose material near perihelion is so great that they cannot have been in their present orbits for very long, either."

p. 95   "Their conclusion is that the time Halley's comet has spent in the Inner Solar System is a mere 23,000 years, perhaps enough for fewer than 300 revolutions of the orbit."

Merritt, Richard S., and Ernest H. Muller, "Depth of Leaching in Relation to Carbonate Content of Till in Central New York State," *American Journal of Science*, vol. 257 (Summer 1959), pp. 465-480.

p. 478   "Within soils of till of comparable age, density and texture on similar slopes in central New York, depth of leaching is primarily a function of original carbonate content."

p. 478   "Under the control of initial carbonate content, depth of leaching varies as much within a single drift as it does across a drift border.

"Depth of leaching alone, without knowledge of variation of carbonate content, may prove an unreliable criterion of relative age of drift sheets."

Monastersky, R., "Earth's Magnetic Follies Revealed," *Science News*, vol. 147 (April 22, 1995), p. 244.

p. 244   "Boy Scouts would have gotten horribly lost 16 million years ago. So, too, pilots, ship navigators, and anyone else who tried to rely on the geomagnetic field to find their way. Earth's field was shifting direction so rapidly back then that compasses would have lost all utility, according to new evidence gleaned from ancient lava flows in Oregon.

"Over an 8-day span, the orientation of the ancient field rotated at the astounding rate of 6° a day, report Robert S. Coe of the University of California, Santa Cruz, and Michel Prévot and Pierre Camps of the University of Montpellier in France. If that happened today, compass needles would swing from magnetic north toward Mexico City in little over a week. Such a change is 1,000 times faster than the slow magnetic wanderings currently measured."

p. 224   "In their present study, Coe, Prévot, and Camps analyze a different lava flow in detail and then consider five possible alternative explanations. They conclude that the flow did not become remagnetized. In fact, the field changed faster than they had originally thought. They suggest that full reversals take thousands of years but that the field can display brief bursts during a reversal."

Narlikar, Jayant V., "What if the Big Bang Didn't Happen?" *New Scientist*, vol. 129 (March 2, 1991), pp. 48-51.

p. 49   "The trouble starts right here. There is no unambiguous way of estimating the distance of a galaxy."

p. 50   "There are even more serious difficulties concerning the cosmic microwave background. The problem is that it is much too smooth. Observations have shown that matter in the Universe is in the form of galaxies grouped into clusters and superclusters with long filamentary stretches and giant voids in between. When these structures formed in the early Universe, they should have left an imprint on the microwave background, in the same way holiday-makers leave behind footprints on the beach. So far, COBE, the satellite currently investigating the microwave background, has found no evidence for any unevenness in the radiation. These latest observations pose a serious problem for cosmologists dedicated to the big bang. Indeed, a considerable amount of theoretical ingenuity is being devoted towards scenarios that would leave imprints below the observable threshold. Avoiding confrontation with observations is scarcely the hallmark of a good theory."

Peterson, I., "Counting Neutrinos from an Artificial Sun," *Science News*, vol. 147 (January 7, 1995), p. 6.

p. 6   "Over the last few years, however, several Earth-based neutrino detectors have found fewer solar neutrinos than scientists had expected, based on theorectical models of how the sun generates energy. That deficit has proved an enduring puzzle."

p. 6 "Preliminary results indicate that the GALLEX detector picks up essentially all of the available neutrinos. Submitted for publication to *Physics Letters B*, this finding helps rule out the possibility that detector inefficiency accounts for the solar neutrino deficit. It confirms that about 40 percent of the expected neutrinos are missing and focuses renewed attention on possible explanations for the conflict between theory and experiment."

p. 6 "'Solar neutrino science is entering a new phase,' comments R. S. Raghavan of AT&T Bell Laboratories in Murray Hill, N.J., in the Jan. 6 *Science*. 'The solar neutrino puzzle is deepening into a paradox that refutes the basic logic of the reaction chain that powers the sun by the fusion of protons into heavy elements.'"

Pettersson, Hans, "Cosmic Spherules and Meteoritic Dust," *Scientific American*, vol. 202 (February 1960), pp. 123-132. Pettersson was Director of the Oceanographic Institute of the University of Göttenborg in Sweden.

p. 125 "Just how much extraterrestrial material the meteor-falls contribute to the earth cannot be estimated with certainty from purely astronomical data. The atmosphere so effectively reduces this substantial quantity of matter to impalpable dust that only a tiny fraction of it, represented by the larger meteorites, has been available for scientific study. The meteoritic dust, especially that of the stony meteorites, cannot be easily distinguished from terrestrial dust. Even the larger meteorites become lost in the turnover of material on the earth's surface; there are no 'fossil' meteorites, that is none more than 25,000 years old.

"During the past 13 years I have been engaged in efforts to secure direct measurements of the meteoritic fallout. My samples of meteoritic dust and cosmic spherules have come from the tops of high mountains remote from industrial civilization, and from the bottom of the ocean. Though the study is by no means complete, the data now show that meteoritic material comes down to earth in much larger quantity (about five million tons per year) than earlier estimates, based on astronomical information, had indicated."

pp. 128-30 "In general the cosmic spherules from the ocean floor indicate a higher rate of meteor-fall in recent times. The divergence of the count in different parts of the ocean, however, does not yet permit the computation of dependable averages that would fix the variation over time. . . . Judging from the visible effects of cosmic bombardment on the face of the moon, there may be an extremely large number of cosmic spherules and other meteor fragments in the very deepest and oldest layers of ocean sediments."

pp. 130-2 "From such a study one group of workers in the U. S. has estimated that several million metric tons of spherules fall annually on the earth. This estimate, however, seems improbably high, Their samples may have been contaminated with man-made spherules originating in industrial centers; pellets from welding plants, for example, can be carried by winds over great distances."

p. 132   "If meteoritic dust descends at the same rate as the dust created by the explosion of the Indonesian volcano Krakatoa in 1883, then my data indicate that the amount of meteoritic dust landing on the earth every year is 14 million tons. From the observed frequency of meteors and from other data Watson calculates the total weight of meteoritic matter reaching the earth to be between 365,000 and 3,650,000 tons a year. His higher estimate is thus about a fourth of my estimate, based upon the Hawaiian studies. To be on the safe side, especially in view of the uncertainty as to how long it takes meteoritic dust to descend, I am inclined to find five million tons per year plausible.

        "The five-million-ton estimate also squares nicely with the nickel content of deep-ocean sediments. . . .

        "If five million tons of meteoritic dust fall to the earth each year, of which 2.5 per cent is nickel, the amount of nickel added to each square centimeter of ocean bottom would be .000000025 gram per year, or .017 per cent of the total red-clay sediment deposited in a year. This is well within the .044-per-cent nickel content of the deep-sea sediments and makes the five-million-ton figure seem conservative."

Pratsch, J. C., "Petroleum Geologist's View of Oceanic Crust Age," *Oil and Gas Journal*, vol. 84 (July 14, 1986), pp. 112-116.

p. 112   "The basic questions here are not different from those on land, yet the approaches are quite different, . . . The reason for these differences, of course, lie in the lack of deep crustal data in the oceans, although this lack of data has prevented only few in the last 30 years from developing new globe girdling theories."

p. 113   "Current radiometric age determinations of oceanic crustal rocks simply do not furnish the absolute data we need."

p. 114   "In summary, stratigraphic methods are not suitable for determining the age of oceanic crust. . . ."

p. 114   "It is interesting, though, to state that there is no accepted explanation of the origin and physical significance of earth magnetic polarity changes."

Ray, Louis L., "Pleistocene Research," Part 9: "Problems of Pleistocene Stratigraphy," *Bulletin, Geological Society of America*, vol. 60 (September 1949), pp. 1463-1474.

p. 1468   "[Quoting Sigurd Hansen, (Danmarks Geology), 1940] Many of the varves measured by DeGeer 'cannot be taken to be annual deposits or varves; they are sub-sections of annual deposits, registering shorter periods of change in the force of the water movement or in the quantity of the mud carried. . . . all distant or telecorrelations between Danish and Scanian varve localities mutually and between Scanodanian on the one hand and North American on the other, must be regarded as fallacious.'"

Richter, Frank M., "Kelvin and the Age of the Earth," *Journal of Geology*, vol. 94 (May 1986), pp. 395-401.

p. 395   "The purpose of this paper is to restate Kelvin's (1863) problem for the thermal evolution of the earth in terms of having to reconcile the present thermal state of the earth with its great age. It will be seen that, despite conventional wisdom, the addition of a reasonable amount of heat producing radioactive elements does not itself suffice to effect such a reconciliation."

p. 397   "The general conclusion is that, even if Kelvin had included a reasonable radiogenic heat production in his thermal evolution models, he would still have found grounds for arguing that the age of the earth was of the order of 10^8 years. The essential missing process is not really radiogenic heating at all but thermal convection, which allows the surface flux to exploit the entire internal heat of the earth as opposed to simply that of a shallow conductive boundary layer."

p. 400   "A more complete discussion of thermal evolution must include secular cooling, convective transport of heat, conduction, and radiogenic heat production."

p. 401   "The original problem was to determine the age of the earth from a thermal model. . . . The modern problem is almost the reverse of the original: given the great age of the earth one seeks a thermal and dynamical model that can account for the present thermal state. Such a model must take account of not only radiogenic heat but also the role of mantle convection as a means of exploiting the entire heat content of the earth."

Schoff, Thomas J. M., "Paleontological Clocks," review of *Growth Rhythms and the History of the Earth's Rotation*, ed. G. D. Rosenberg and S. K. Runcorn (New York: Wiley-Interscience, 1975, 560 pp.), *Science*, vol. 191 (January 30, 1976), pp. 375-376.

p. 375   "As J. W. Evans remarks: 'The trouble is that counting growth lines is not easy, as anyone who has tried can testify. It is constantly necessary to make subjective decisions about whether a line is really a line or where an annual or monthly series begins or ends. As a result it is not surprising to find that counts often come out close to the hypothesized values."

p. 375   "Assuming that daily growth bands were in fact rigorously identified, and that they have been correctly partitioned into lunar and solar months, the main paleontological conclusion is that through the Phanerozoic the number of hours per day has decreased, and correspondingly the number of days per year has increased.' . . . Indeed, paleontological data indicate that for a 100-million-year interval in the Mesozoic the earth's rotation accelerated. This, of course, cannot possibly be accounted for by the dissipative mechanism of tidal friction, and demands that the paleontologic data be as firmly established as possible."

p. 376   ". . . all the astronomical observations from 13 B.C. onward . . . conclude that for 3000 years the acceleration rate in day length due to all causes (both tidal and nontidal components) has been a constant 2.5 milliseconds per century."

Sonka, L. J., "Origins of Planetary Mechanisms," *American Geophysical Union*, Report on conference at the Lunar & Planetary Institute, Houston, November 8-11, 1978, pp. 185-186.

p. 185   "It is now generally accepted that planetary magnetic fields are generated by dynamo action resulting from convection in a rotating, electrically conducting fluid core. However, major uncertainties still exist in our understanding of such processes some 30 years after the core dynamo concept was introduced by E. C. Bullard, W. M. Elsasser, and others. The surprising discovery of lunar magnetism as a result of the Apollo program and the growing body of data which show high paleofield values in meteorites have raised the possibility that some planetary magnetic fields may be due primarily to permanent magnetization acquired early in the body's development."

Sutton, Christine, "Where Have all the Solar Neutrinos Gone?" *New Scientist*, vol. 127 (August 18, 1990), p. 24.

p. 24   "Solar neutrinos appear to be in short supply. In fact, the latest experiment, carried out by a joint team of physicists from the Soviet Union and the US has found none at all. The results, announced at the Neutrino '90 conference, held at CERN, the European laboratory for particle physics near Geneva, confirm those of a 20-year experiment deep in a gold mine in the US which also found far fewer neutrinos than predicted by theory."

p. 24   "Davis has consistently detected about one-third fewer neutrinos than predicted by theories of the solar interior. And this result has been confirmed recently by a detector in Japan that works in an entirely different way from Davis's."

p. 24   "The results so far are a surprise. SAGE began operation last year, and since then the team has seen no sign of any radioactivity that it can definitely attribute to the absorption of neutrinos."

Turekian, Karl K., "The Fate of Metals in the Oceans," *Geochimica et Cosmochimica Acta*, vol. 41 (August 1977), pp. 1139-1144.

p. 1139   "The startling conclusion . . . is that most trace metals are at extremely low concentrations in the oceans and have rather unspectacular variations in their concentrations. The calculated theoretical concentrations of copper, nickel, silver, gold, lead and other metals in the oceans are many orders of magnitude higher than the best currently measured values.

          "Why are the oceans so depleted of these trace metals? Certainly it is not for the lack of availability from rock weathering or because of constraints imposed by the solubility of any unique compound of these elements. . . .

          "I believe that the secret lies in the role particles play as the sequestering agents for reactive elements during every step of the transport process from continent to ocean floor."

Vallentyne, J. R., "A Laboratory Study of the Formation of Sediment Bands," *American Journal of Science*, vol. 253, no. 9 (September 1955), pp. 540-552.

p. 550   "It has been shown above that periodic red bands are formed in reduced lake sediments rich in iron, if those sediments are exposed to air at room temperature in the laboratory."

p. 551   "If the bands do form in lake sediments *in situ*, then there is of course the possibility that they may be confused with some types of varves."

Weisburd, Stefi, "The Earth's Magnetic Hiccup," *Science News*, vol. 128 (October 5, 1985), pp. 218-220.

p. 218   "In all the thousands of years that people have lived in the aura of the earth's magnetic field, no one has ever discovered why it exists. . . . It took until the middle of this century for geophysicists to arrive at the idea that the swirling dance of the earth's liquid iron core somehow generates the magnetic field. But the detailed choreography of this motion, what energy sources drive it and how it gives rise to the field, remain stubbornly out of reach.

"There are all sorts of sources outside the earth—ionospheric currents and magnetic storms, for example—that induce currents to flow in the mantle, setting up magnetic fields that merge with that generated by the core."

Weisburd, Stefi, "Atmospheric Footprints of Icy Meteors," *Science News*, vol. 128 (December 21/28, 1985), p. 391.

"On the basis of radar measurements, scientists have come to think of the meteors that rain on the earth as small pebble-like objects plunging through the atmosphere. But recent satellite images of the sunlit side of the atmosphere imply another picture, in which a meteor starts as a much more massive clump of material, possibly a dirty-snowball-type piece of a comet, which sheds gases in the upper atmosphere before releasing the pebbles that are tracked by radar.

"This means 'there has to be 1,000 to 10,000 times more material coming in and being added to the earth's atmosphere than we would have guessed with radar measurements,' says Louis Frank."

p. 391   "Thus far, from the sizes of the holes created by the vaporized meteor material, the researchers conclude that the mass of each meteor is probably around 10 kilograms—much greater than the pebbles, each weighing less than a gram. And in order to deposit most of that material into the atmosphere, a meteor must be mostly like a fluffy snowball and contain a relatively small amount of the denser pebbles that fall to the earth."

Wood, A. E., "Multiple Banding of Sediments Deposited During a Single Season," *Bulletin, Geological Society of America*, vol. 57 (December 1946), p. 1245. Wood was in the Department of Biology, Amherst College.

"*Abstract.* The Arkport Flood Control Reservoir near Hornell, N.Y., held water for the first time during the spring of 1940. This flood had 3 peaks over a period of 2 weeks. The sediments deposited during this period form what appear to be three typical varves. . . . A series of varvelike bands, not readily distinguishable from varves, may be deposited in a very short time and may by no means indicate the number of years required for the formation of a given deposit." [From article in *American Journal of Science*, vol. 245 (May 1947), pp. 304-312]

C. Dating of Recent Events

There are a few methods in geochronology that have been used to "date" events in human history—especially radiocarbon decay and dendrochronology. These also involve a number of assumptions, but they can be tested and corrected by known historical dates, back to about 3000 BC.

For dates much older than this, on the other hand, there are few adequate written records to serve as controls, and the assumptions become increasingly questionable with increasing age. However, once again, by simply changing the assumptions a bit, they can be reduced to dates much more compatible with what is known about human history.

Antevs, Ernst, "Geological Tests of the Varve and Radiocarbon Chronologies," *Journal of Geology*, vol. 65 (March 1957), pp. 125-148.

p. 129   "There are only a few radiocarbon dates that unquestionably and exactly apply to important geological stages or events. . . . All too often there is doubt about the exact source of the material or about the true relationship of the source bed to an outstanding stage, feature, or event. Most applied ^{14}C dates are inferred or generalized."

pp. 129-30   "In appraising ^{14}C dates, it is essential always to discriminate between the C^{14} age and the actual age of the sample. . . . A date does not become correct simply because several tests agree. . . .

     "Therefore, each ^{14}C date needs a thorough, independent checking, and those of geological bearing should be evaluated in relation to our geological knowledge."

Bartlett, H. H., "Radiocarbon Datability of Peat, Marl, Caliche, and Archaeological Materials," *Science*, vol. 114 (July 20, 1951), pp. 55-56.

p. 56   "The object of this article is to put enthusiasts for the radiocarbon dating of postglacial and prehistorical events on their guard against assuming that the method will have no gross sources of error. . . . Except under thoroughly understood conditions, marl cannot be considered datable. Neither can *caliche*. Even peat found in close association with marl or calcareous tufa is somewhat doubtful. . . . Precautions must be taken to detect possibilities, not only of materials having had their carbon radioactivity diminished by entry of 'dead' carbon, but also of having been enriched in radiocarbon content by physical and chemical processes that are constantly taking place."

Fairhall, A. W., and J. A. Young, "Radiocarbon in the Environment," *Advances in Chemistry*, vol. 93 (1970), pp. 401-418.

p. 402   "We note in passing that the total natural ^{14}C inventory of 2.16 x 10^{30} atoms . . . corresponds to a ^{14}C decay rate of 1.63 disintegrations/sec./cm.^{2} of the earth, considerably below the estimated production rate of ^{14}C atoms averaged over the last 10 solar cycles (111 years) of 2.5 ± 0.5 atoms/sec./cm.^{2} From a geophysical point of view, it would be very surprising if the decay rate and the production rate of ^{14}C were out of balance as seriously as the difference between the above two numbers would suggest. It is difficult to reconcile this discrepancy by errors in computing the ^{14}C inventory since the bulk of the ^{14}C is in the sea, where the ^{14}C concentration relative to the terrestrial biosphere is known fairly well. . . . The source of the discrepancy is therefore unknown unless the present-day production rate is indeed significantly higher than the average production rate over the last 8000 years, the mean life of ^{14}C."

Gladwin, Harold S., "Dendrochronology, Radiocarbon, and Bristlecones," *Anthropological Journal of Canada*, vol. 14, no. 4 (1976), pp. 2-7.

p. 4   "For those who are neither radiocarbon physicists nor 'dendrochronologists,' it is essential to know that *all* trees are not of equal value for tree-ring dating. It probably would be safe to say that the great majority of deciduous trees are of little or no value, because of the difficulty in deciphering rings."

p. 5   "Among the conifers, junipers are unsatisfactory to the point of being actually misleading, chiefly because many species are partly dead and consequently undependable; the living parts of the tree either grow no annual rings at all or very often grow multiple rings in the same year. . . . Among the pines, *Pinus aristata* (i.e., the bristlecone pine) is, if anything, even more undependable than the junipers, principally because of the size of the tree, so much of which is dead.

"We have many cores at the Santa Barbara Botanic Garden that were collected from Bristlecones growing in the White Mountains of California east of the Sierra Nevada, at altitudes of 10,000 feet, where the rainfall is low and erratic. There are also a number of cores from Bristlecones growing at high altitudes in southwestern Utah and on the San Francisco Peaks at Flagstone, Arizona. Comparison of charts of measured rings show no similarity whatever."

Goodfriend, Glenn A., and Jerry J. Stipp, "Limestone and the Problem of Radiocarbon Dating of Land-Snail Shell Carbonate," *Geology*, vol. 11 (October 1983), pp. 575-577.

p. 575   "Numerous studies have shown that ^{14}C analyses of land-snail shell carbonate often produce anomalously old ages. . . . It has been hypothesized that ingestion of ^{14}C-free limestone (older than ca. 50,000 yr) and its subsequent incorporation into the shell are responsible for such anomalies. . . . No association between age anomaly and substrate (limestone vs. non-limestone) has been demonstrated. Because in many paleontological and archaeological studies land-snail shells are the only material available for radiocarbon dating, it is of considerable interest to know whether land snails can be relied on for accurate dates and, if so, under what circumstances."

p. 577   "In limestone areas, no land-snail has been shown to be free of ^{14}C anomaly. . . . Because of the variability of ^{14}C content of land-snail shells from limestone areas, no standard factor can be applied to correct for ^{14}C depletion due to incorporation of limestone carbon."

p. 577   "The maximum age anomaly observed in land-snail shell carbonate is that reported here of 3,120 years."

Hunt, Charles B., "Radiocarbon Dating in the Light of Stratigraphy and Weathering Processes," *Scientific Monthly*, vol. 81 (November 1955), pp. 240-247.

p. 240   "The published radiocarbon dates are numerous. When considered stratigraphically, they are sufficiently scattered and erratic to provide some determinations that will support almost any supposed correlation."

p. 240   "No one seriously proposes that all the determined dates are without error, but we do not know how many of them are in error—25 percent? 50 percent? 75 percent? And we do not know which dates are in error, or by what amounts, or why."

Jueneman, Frederic B., "Scientific Speculation by Jueneman," *Industrial Research* (September 1972), p. 15. Jueneman is Director of Research, Innovative Concepts Association.

          "Being so close, the anisotropic neutrino flux of the superexplosion must have had the peculiar characteristic of resetting all our atomic clocks. This would knock our carbon-14, potassium-argon, and uranium-lead dating measurements into a cocked hat! The age of prehistoric artifacts, the age of the earth, and that of the universe would be thrown into doubt."

Krantz, Grover S., "The Populating of Western North America," *Society for California Archaeology Occasional Papers in Method and Theory in California Archaeology*, no. 1 (December 1977), pp. 1-63.

pp. 7-8   "There are also many sites which have yielded carbon 14 dates that are clearly too recent to be correct. Often these spuriously young dates are not published, though every archaeologist is aware of some examples. Those that are published rarely receive the special attention they deserve. The significance of these inexplicably recent dates is that they also are often quite secure and no flaw can be found in their determination."

p. 55   "Archaeological confirmation is more difficult. Dating the initial occupation of each area would be crucial, but this effort is often clouded by the headline-hunting tendencies of many workers who want to find dates older than anyone else's."

Lee, Robert E., "Radiocarbon, Ages in Error," *Anthropological Journal of Canada*, vol. 19, no. 3 (1981), pp. 9-29.

p. 9   "The troubles of the radiocarbon dating method are undeniably deep and serious. Despite 35 years of technological refinement and better understanding, the underlying *assumptions* have been strongly challenged, and warnings are out that radiocarbon may soon find itself in a crisis situation. Continuing use of the method depends on a 'fix-it-as-we-go' approach, allowing for contamination here, fractionation there, and calibration whenever possible. It should be no surprise, then, that fully half of the dates are rejected. The wonder is, surely, that the remaining half come to be *accepted*."

p. 27   "Ultimately, we must question the reliability of radiocarbon dating—even for use as a *relative* chronology. For one thing, we are trying to compare dates obtained on *different* materials, some of which are more prone to contamination than others. Even where the material is of only one kind, as in the case of peat, dates from just above an impermeable zone will date younger than the more recent deposits nearer the surface, because modern-carbon contaminants *accumulate* in just such places."

p. 29   "No matter how 'useful' it is, though, the radiocarbon method is still not capable of yielding accurate and reliable results. There are *gross* discrepancies, the chronology is *uneven* and *relative*, and the accepted dates are actually *selected* dates."

Lingenfelter, Richard E., "Production of Carbon-14 by Cosmic Ray Neutrons," *Reviews of Geophysics*, vol. 1, no. 1 (February 1963), p. 51.

"There is strong indication, despite the large errors, that the present natural production rate exceeds the natural decay rate by as much as 25%. . . . It appears that equilibrium in the production and decay of Carbon-14 *may not be maintained* in detail."

Ralph, Elizabeth K., and Henry N. Michael, "Twenty-five Years of Radiocarbon Dating," *American Scientist*, vol. 62 (September/October 1974), pp. 553-560. Ralph and Michael were Professors of Archaeology and Radiocarbon, University of Pennsylvania.

p. 553   "We have now learned that one of the basic implicit assumptions of the method—namely, the constancy of the atmospheric inventory of $C^{14}O_2$—is not strictly correct."

p. 555   "We now know that the assumption that the biospheric inventory of C^{14} has remained constant over the past 50,000 years or so is not true."

p. 556   "The validity of the bristlecone pine-sequoia time scale has been questioned for a number of reasons. To us, the most serious concern is that for periods earlier than 3,000 years ago, it is based entirely on one species of tree that grows, or grew, under rather atypical conditions—namely, at elevations of 10,000 to 11,000 feet. That the extension of the dendro-time scale during the past fifteen years has been done in a single laboratory and mostly by one person we consider to be a minor point, because of the reputation of the Laboratory of Tree-Ring Research at the University of Arizona and of the extreme care which C. Wesley Ferguson has exercised in building this chronology."

Renfrew, Colin, *Before Civilization* (New York: Alfred A. Knopf, 1975), 292 pp.

pp. 21-2   "Nor was this belief restricted to the credulous or the excessively devout. No less a thinker than Sir Isaac Newton accepted it implicitly, and in his detailed study of the whole question of dating, *The Chronology of Ancient Kingdoms Amended*, took the ancient Egyptian severely to task, since they had set the origins of the monarchy before 5000 B.C., and 'anciently boasted of a very great Empire under their kings . . . reaching eastward to the Indies, and westward to the Atlantic Ocean; and out of vanity have made this monarchy some thousands of years older than the world.'[4] This criticism was meant literally; for an educated man in the seventeenth or even the eighteenth century, any suggestion that the human past extended back further than 6,000 years was a vain and foolish speculation."

p. 25   "Until the discovery of radiocarbon dating, therefore, there was really only one reliable way of dating events in European prehistory after the end of the last glaciation around 8000 B.C.—only one way, that is, to date the neolithic, bronze age and iron age periods. This was by the early records of the great civilizations, which extended in some cases as far back as 3000 B.C. The records of the Greeks did not go back before the first millinium B.C., but in Mesopotamia the Assyrians and their predecessors the Sumerians left records of kings and dynasties extending back well before 2000 B.C. The Egyptian king lists go back to the First Dynasty of Egypt, a little before 3000 B.C. Before that, there were no written records anywhere."

p. 28   "The date in question corresponds to 1872 B.C., so that the reign of Sesostris III is now set with some confidence from 1878 B.C. to 1843 B.C.

"This is, in fact, the earliest fixed calendrical date in human history. And while some uncertainties of detail makes possible an error of a decade or so, it is a date which Egyptologists accept with considerable confidence. Using the information from the annals, the end of the Eighth dynasty, with which the so-called 'Old Kingdom' of Egypt terminated, may be set at 2160 B.C. As we have seen, the Turin Royal Canon reports a total duration for the Old Kingdom of 955 years. Some scholars think this may be inaccurate by a couple of centuries or so, but if the figure is accepted, the beginning of the Old Kingdom of Egypt—the founding of Egypt's first historic dynasty—can be set close to 3100 B.C.

". . . The Mesopotamian chronology is less reliable than the Egyptian, and it does not go back so far.

"This date of 3100 B.C. thus sets the limit of recorded history. No earlier dates can be obtained by calendrical means, and indeed the dates cannot be regarded as reliable before 2000 B.C. There is thus a theoretical limit beyond which the traditional chronology for Europe, based, as it was, ultimately on Egypt, simply could not go. Any dates before 3000 B.C. could be little more than guesswork, however persuasive the arguments and the evidence after that period."

p. 52   "Radiocarbon dating is not only subject to errors; like all scientific procedures, it depends on definite assumptions, and these must be understood if the method is to be used properly.

"Firstly, it is assumed that the radioactive decay of radiocarbon will take place in a regular way, quite unaffected by physical or chemical conditions such as temperature or contact with the air, and also that the decay rate is known. This is a fundamental principle of modern physics.

"Secondly it is assumed that the samples to be dated have not been contaminated since their death, so that the proportion of carbon-14 to carbon-12 has not been changed, other than by the steady process of radioactive decay. This depends on the careful collection of samples by the archaeologist in the field.

"The third assumption is that the small proportion of radiocarbon in all living things at a given time is, in fact, a constant, and that it does not vary from place to place, or among different species. This too is found in practice to be broadly justified.

"And finally it is assumed that the concentration of radiocarbon in the earth's atmosphere has remained constant through time. If this is so, by measuring the proportion of radiocarbon present in living things today we can obtain a valid value for the proportion that the sample contained when it was alive."

p. 74   "The oldest living tree yet discovered has been alive for 4,900 years—the earth's oldest living thing."

p. 74   "Professor Charles Wesley Ferguson, who took over after Schulman's death, has succeeded in building up a continuous tree-ring sequence, which at present extends back nearly 8,200 years, using the wood from many trees both living and long dead."

p. 75   "The other common pitfall of tree-ring dating, the existence of several tree-rings for a single year, is less important: in this species multiple growth-rings are rare."

Suess, Hans E., "Secular Variations of the Cosmic-Ray-Produced Carbon-14 in the Atmosphere and Their Interpretations," *Journal of Geophysical Research*, vol. 70, no. 23 (December 1, 1965), pp. 5937-5952.

p. 5947   "It seems probable that the present-day inventory of natural C^{14} *does not correspond* to the equilibrium value, but is increasing."

Tang, Tong B., "Did Sirius Change Colour?" *Nature*, vol. 352 (July 4, 1991), p. 25.

p. 25   "Schlosser and Bergmann claim that Babylonian and early mediaeval authors saw Sirius as red, which if true would represent an anomaly in current evolutionary theories of white dwarfs. But van Gent and I independently suggested that it might be a case of mistaken identity, and that, on evidence from Chinese sources, the brightest star in our sky has been white all along."

p. 25   "Support for a gradual variation in Sirius's colour comes from a Chinese work of the first century BC."

p. 25   "I maintain that the fact that Sirius looked white was not contradicted in any of the other dynastic histories compiled at later times."

Taylor, R. E., *et al.*, "Major Revisions in the Pleistocene Age Assignments for North American Human Skeletons by C-14 Accelerator Mass Spectrometry: None Older than 11,000 C-14 years B.P.," *American Antiquity*, vol. 50, no. 1 (January 1985), pp. 136-140.

p. 136   "*Abstract.* Radiocarbon analyses by accelerator mass spectrometric (AMS) techniques on organic fractions of human bone from various North American localities previously assigned ages ranging from about 70,000 to 15,000 years B.P. now suggest that none of these skeletons is older than 11,000 C-14 years B.P."

p. 136   "An important part of the data that has been presented to support the assertion that human populations arrived in North America prior to 11,000-11,500 years B.P. (Clovis Culture) has been C-14, amino acid racemization (AAR)-, and uranium series (U-series)-deduced age estimates obtained directly on *Homo sapiens* skeletal materials. These age estimates and particularly the AAR determinations have been employed by some as part of the data used to argue that *Homo sapiens* has been in the Western Hemisphere in excess of several tens of thousands, if not several hundreds of thousands of years."

pp. 138-9   "Our C-14 data support views previously expressed that, in a significant number of situations, there is no clear relationship between the C-14 age and the extent of aspartic acid racemization in bone samples."

Twain, Mark, *The Damned Human Race*, quoted by Robert L. Bates, "The Geologic Column," *Geotimes*, vol. 29 (June 1984), p. 54.

p. 54   "If the Eiffel Tower were now representing the world's age, the skin of paint on the pinnacle-knob at its summit would represent man's share of that edge, and anybody would perceive that that skin was what the tower was built for. I reckon they would. I dunno."

Wilford, John N., "Chemist Queries an Atomic Theory," *New York Times*, March 30, 1971, p. A6.

p. A6   "A fundamental assumption of nuclear physics—the predictable decay rates of radioactive materials—has been opened to question on the basis of research reported here today at the national meeting of the American Chemical Society."

p. A6   Dr. John Anderson, a Tennessee chemist, described experimental observations with radioactive carbon-14 that he said 'do not fit the accepted theory.'"

p. A6   "For some 70 years, scientists have operated on the assumption, based on accepted laws of atomic forces, that radioactive materials decay at precisely known rates."

p. A6   "Dr. Anderson said that his observations indicated that the decay rates might not be as constant as assumed. Other forces, perhaps from adjacent atoms, could alter the process."

Chapter 12

History of Evolutionary Thought

A. America and its Creationist Beginnings

With creationism banned today in America's public schools and under frequent sarcastic attack by practically all the news media, it is both sad and salutary to recall that the American nation and all its colonies had a solid background of Biblical creationist beginnings. The following quotes from a number of our founding fathers, as well as others, point up this truth.

Boudinot, Dr. Elias, Independence Day Address on July 4, 1783, New Jersey Society of the Cincinnati. Boudinot was President of the Continental Congress in 1783 and first President of the American Bible Society.

> "The history of the world, as well sacred as profane, bears witness to the use and importance of setting apart a day as a memorial of great events, whether of a religious or a political nature.

> "No sooner had the great Creator of the heavens and the earth finished his almighty work, and pronounced all very good, but he set apart (not an anniversary, or one day in a year, but) one day in seven, for the commemoration of his inimitable power in producing all things out of nothing.

> "The deliverance of the children of Israel from a state of bondage to an unreasonable tyrant was perpetuated by the Paschal Lamb, and enjoining it on their posterity as an annual festival forever, with a 'remembrance this day, in which ye came out of Egypt, out of the house of bondage.' The resurrection of the Saviour of mankind is commemorated by keeping the first day of the week, not only as a certain memorial of his first coming in a state of humiliation but the positive evidence of his future coming in glory. Let us then, my friends and fellow citizens, unite all our endeavors this day to remember with reverential gratitude to our supreme Benefactor, all the wonderful things He has done for us, in our miraculous deliverance from a second Egypt—another house of bondage."

Brewer, David J., "America—A Christian Nation," a Supreme Court Opinion by Justice Brewer, who served on the Court from 1890 to 1910, reprinted in *The Forerunner* (July 1986).

> "This republic is classified among the Christian nations of the world. It was so formally declared by the Supreme Court of the United States. In the case of the Holy Trinity Church vs. United States, 143 U.S. 471, that Court, after mentioning various circumstances, added, 'these and many other matters which might be noticed, add a volume of unofficial declarations to the mass of organic utterances that this is a Christian nation' (Unanimous opinion, February 29, 1892).

> "Its use has had from the early settlements on our shores and still has an official foundation. It is only about three centuries since the beginning of civilized

life within the limits of these United States. And those beginnings were in a marked and marvelous degree identified with Christianity. . . .

"It is not an exaggeration to say that Christianity in some of its creeds was the principle cause of the settlement of many of the colonies, and cooperated with business hopes and purposes in the settlement of the others. Beginning in this way and under these influences it is not strange that the colonial life had an emphatic Christian tone. . . .

"In short, there is no charter or constitution that is either infidel, agnostic or anti-Christian. Wherever there is a declaration in favor of any religion it is of the Christian. In view of the multitude of expressions in its favor, the avowed separation of church and state is a most satisfactory testimonial that it is the religion of this country, for a peculiar thought of Christianity is of a personal relation between man and his Maker, uncontrolled by and independent of human government.

"Think of the vast number of academies, colleges and universities scattered through the land. Some of them, it is true, are under secular control, but there is yet to be established in this country one of those institutions founded on the religions of Confucius, Buddha or Mohammed, while an overwhelming majority are under special direction and control of Christian teachers. . . ."

Edwords, Frederick, "The Religious Character of American Patriotism," *The Humanist*, vol. 47 (November/December 1987), pp. 20-24, 36. Edwords is Executive Director of the American Humanist Association, a member of the Board of Directors of the National Center for Science Education, and Editor of *Creation/Evolution* Journal.

pp. 20-1   "The United States is indeed a religious nation, but its unifying religion is not Christianity or any other world faith—not even 'the religion of secular humanism,' as has been claimed of late. It is instead a unique national belief system best called Americanism."

p. 21   "Conspicuously absent from the writings of many of the nation's founders and first presidents are indications of belief in Christ, hell, and Original Sin. But they all mentioned God—and not merely the clockwork God of deism but a god actively involved in history. Their 'public religion' clearly was not Christianity, though it could include Christians and others within its embrace. In some ways it harked back to the Old Testament with its view of America as 'the promised land.' This was prevalent in many writings of the time."

Eidsmoe, John, "Creation, Evolution and Constitutional Interpretation," *Concerned Women*, vol. 9 (September 20/27, 1987), pp. 7-8.

p. 7   "Underlying the disagreement over interpretation of the Constitution is a major confrontation between the two world views—the creationist, absolutist, Newtonian views of the Framers, versus the evolutionist, relativist, Darwinian views of most legal scholars today."

pp. 7, 8   "Thus the debate over constitutional interpretation is no mere academic or legal matter. Rather it is a major battle between two conflicting philosophies, two conflicting religions and two conflicting world views. Justice Brennan acknowledged this in his Georgetown address, declaring that our society must continue its upward progress unbounded by the fetters of original intent, or the literal words of the Constitution, through an '*evolutionary process (that) is inevitable and, indeed, it is the true* interpretive genius of the text.'"

Foster, Marshall, "Christian Offensive or Secular Check-Mate?" *Mayflower Institute Journal*, vol. 1 (July/August 1983), pp. 1-3.

p. 1   "On February 13, 1833, a Rev. Jasper Adams preached a sermon in St. Michael's Church in Charleston, South Carolina, entitled 'The Relation of Christianity to Civil Government in the United States.' But then men were beginning to leverage God out of society, and Rev. Adams determined to speak to this issue. . . . 'The originators and early promoters of the discovery and settlement of this continent had the propagation of Christianity before their eyes, as one of the principal objects of their undertaking.' Then, Rev. Adams goes on to say in his sermon: 'In perusing the twenty-four [state] constitutions of the United States, we find all of them recognized Christianity as the well-known and well-established religion of the communities whose legal, civil and political foundations these constitutions are.'"

p. 2   "How many of our pastors know . . . that, during the Revolutionary War, Congress resolved to import 20,000 Bibles from neutral nations like Holland and Scotland. The reason? It was because 'the use of the Bible is so universal and its importance so great.' How many pastors know that on September 12, 1782, Congress also passed a resolution recommending to the inhabitants of the United States the first Bible in English to be published in America? . . . Although the Supreme Court in recent years has frequently flouted Biblical law, the Ten Commandments are still engraved in marble behind the seat of the Chief Justice and remain a model for courts of the future who will remember our roots if we, the American people, will remember them."

Franklin, Benjamin, quoted in *The Writings of Benjamin Franklin*, vol. 10 (New York: Macmillan Co., 1905-1907).

p. 84   "Here is my creed. I believe in one God, the Creator of the universe. That he governs it by His Providence. That he ought to be worshipped. That the most acceptable Service we render to him is in doing good to his other Children. That the soul of Man is immortal, and will be treated with Justice in another Life respecting its conduct in this. These I take to be the fundamental principles in all sound religion."

Jefferson, Thomas, miscellaneous writings as inscribed on the walls of Jefferson Memorial, Washington, D.C.

     "We hold these truths to be self-evident: that all men are created equal, that they are endowed by their Creator with certain inalienable rights, among these are life, liberty, and the pursuit of happiness, that to secure these rights governments are instituted among men."

"Almighty God hath created the mind free. All attempts to influence it by temporal punishments or burthens . . . are a departure from the plan of the Holy Author of our religion. . . ."

"God who gave us life gave us liberty. Can the liberties of a nation be secure when we have removed a conviction that these liberties are the gift of God? Indeed I tremble for my country when I reflect that God is just, that his justice cannot sleep forever."

Ostrander, Gilman M., *The Evolutionary Outlook, 1875-1900* (Clio, Michigan: Marston Press, 1971), 81 pp.

p. 1   "The American nation had been founded by intellectuals who had accepted a world view that was based upon biblical authority as well as Newtonian science. They had assumed that God created the earth and all life upon it at the time of creation and had continued without change thereafter. Adam and Eve were God's final creations, and all of mankind had descended from them. When Jefferson, in his old age, was confronted with the newly developing science of geology, he rejected its evolutionary concept of the creation of the earth on the grounds that no all-wise and all-powerful Creator would have gone about the job in such a slow and inefficient way."

p. 2   "In a nation that was undergoing a tremendous urban, industrial and technological revolution, the evolutionary concept presented itself to intellectuals as the key to knowledge. . . . In general the concept of education from kindergarten to graduate school was reoriented from the teaching of a fixed body of knowledge to the teaching of methods of inquiry to be applied to the continually changing facts of existence."

p. 39   "Darwinian evolutionary science presented little or no challenge to [Henry Ward] Beecher's doctrinal beliefs, for Beecher's Christianity was already far removed from Biblical literalism into a vague poetic emotional realm of edifying thoughts, elevated feelings and joyful noises unto the Lord."

Robbins, L. Edward, "Evolution and the Law," *The Constitution* (May/June 1988).

p. 17   "Why was Dean Langdell so anxious to divert the attention of his students from Blackstone? The answer is that Langdell was an evolutionist."

               [Dean Christopher Columbus Langdell, who introduced "case study" into
               law practice, became Dean of the Harvard Law School in 1870. He and
               his successor, Roscoe Pound, were founders of "legal positivism."]

Swanson, Mary-Elaine, "An Education for Greatness," *Mayflower Institute Journal*, vol. 1 (January/ February 1985), pp. 1-4.

p. 1   "Parents who opt for home teaching are in good company. Many of our most distinguished leaders in the early days of our nation were educated primarily at home."

p. 2   "George Washington's education began in the home at his mother's knee with lessons from the Bible and the Anglican Prayer Book which are said to have been her constant companions.

"In addition to his studies at home, Washington also attended a small school run by the sexton of the local church. . . . At about 20 years of age, he produced a notebook of prayers . . . which reflect a devout faith in Jesus Christ as Lord and Savior, and a desire to live in accord with the Will of God.

"Abraham Lincoln's education, too, began at a godly mother's knee and was carried on later with the help of a devout stepmother. Like Washington's education, Lincoln's was rooted in the Bible and in a firm belief in Divine Providence. . . . Young Abe also learned to educate himself in the law and other subjects through extensive reading of his own."

Swanson, Mary-Elaine, "Teaching Children the Bible," *Mayflower Institute Journal*, vol. 1 (July/August 1983), p. 5.

"In colonial times, the Bible was the primary tool in the educational process. In fact, according to Columbia University professor Dr. Lawrence A. Cremin, the Bible was 'the single most primary source for the intellectual history of colonial America.' From their knowledge of the Bible, a highly literate, creative people emerged. Their wise system of education was later replaced by a man-centered system which has caused a steady decline in literacy and creativity. Children have become the docile computers processing whatever knowledge their educators have chosen to pump into them."

Tobey, Ronald C., "New Ideas in America," review of *Creation by Natural Law*, by Ronald L. Numbers (Seattle: University of Washington Press, 1977, 184 pp.), *Science*, vol. 197 (September 2, 1977), p. 977.

p. 977   "In *Creation by Natural Law*, Ronald Numbers demonstrates that the scientific and religious establishments had accepted a naturalistic theory of the origin of the solar system decades before the *Origin of Species*."

p. 977   "Acceptance of the nebular hypothesis had become sufficiently entrenched that Asa Gray, appealing for Darwinian evolution in the 1860's pointed to the hypothesis as an analogy in organic development for the organic development of species."

p. 977   "Yet Numbers is unable to establish the direct link between a scientist's espousal of the nebular hypothesis at one time and Darwinism at another. It is more probable as Numbers hints, that the nebular hypothesis was one element in a growing scientific culture in which secular naturalism broadly prepared the way for Darwinism."

Washington, George, quoted in *Maxims of Washington*, edited by John F. Schroeder (Mt. Vernon, Virginia: Mt. Vernon Ladies Association, 1942), 348 pp.

p. 275   "It is impossible to account for the creation of the universe, without the agency of a Supreme Being.

"It is impossible to govern the universe without the aid of a Supreme Being. It is impossible to reason without arriving at a Supreme Being. Religion is as necessary to reason, as reason is to religion. The one cannot exist without the other. A reasoning being would lose his reason, in attempting to account for the great phenomena of nature, had he not a Supreme Being to refer to; and well has it been said, that if there had been no God, mankind would have been obliged to imagine one.

B. Darwin and His Predecessors

Charles Darwin was not the originator of the theory of evolution, or even of what he called "my" theory of natural selection. There were many who came before him, but none more vital than Alfred Russel Wallace, a self-taught naturalist and leader in the reviving spiritist movement of the day. Other pagan and occult concepts and cults had kept evolutionism alive during the Middle Ages and Renaissance periods, though it was largely an underground movement until about the end of the 18th century.

During these same years, the founding fathers of modern science (Newton, Boyle, Faraday, etc.) were practically all Bible-believing creationists. One of the most enigmatic developments in history was the sudden transformation of a creation-based science establishment into one returning to ancient pagan evolutionism. Darwin, despite his very ordinary scientific abilities, was mysteriously used to anchor this sad transmutation.

Baggott, Jim, "The Myth of Michael Faraday," *New Scientist*, vol. 131 (September 21, 1991), pp. 43-46.

pp. 44-5   "However Faraday's belief in an underlying unity is not so surprising. He was a devout member of the Sandemanian Church, a fundamentalist Christian order that demanded total faith and total commitment. Sandemanians organized their daily lives through their literal interpretation of the Bible. Both Faraday's father and grandfather had been Sandemanians and, when he married Sarah Bernard in 1821, he married into a leading Sandemanian family.

"Faraday found no conflict between his religious beliefs and his activities as a scientist and philosopher. He viewed his discoveries of nature's laws as part of the continual process of 'reading the book of nature,' no different in principle from the process of reading the Bible to discover God's laws. A strong sense of the unity of God and nature pervaded Faraday's life and work."

p. 46   "But Faraday laid down the conceptual framework of modern physics, later to be expressed in elegant mathematical form by Maxwell and others. So let us respect his work and remember him, not only as an experimental physicist and chemist, but also as a philosopher and the grandfather of field theory."

Barzun, Jacques, *Darwin, Marx, Wagner*, 2nd ed. (Garden City, New York: Doubleday and Co., 1959), 373 pp.

p. 69   "Clearly, both believers and unbelievers in Natural Selection agreed that Darwinism had succeeded as an orthodoxy, as a rallying point for innumerable scientific, philosophical, and social movements. Darwin had been the oracle and the *Origin of Species*, the 'fixed point with which Evolution moved the world.'"

p. 84   "Darwin was not a thinker and he did not originate the ideas that he used. He vacillated, added, retracted, and confused his own traces. As soon as he crossed the dividing line between the realm of events and the realm of theory he became 'metaphysical' in the bad sense. His power of drawing out the implications of his theories was at no time very remarkable, but when it came to the moral order it disappeared altogether, as that penetrating Evolutionist, Nietzsche, observed with some disdain."

Darlington, C. D., "The Origin of Darwinism," *Scientific American*, vol. 200 (May 1959), pp. 60-66.

pp. 61-2   "In favor of the evolution of animals from 'one living filament' Erasmus Darwin [who died before Charles was born] assembled the evidence of embryology, comparative anatomy, systematics, geographical distribution and, so far as man is concerned, the facts of history and medicine. . . . These arguments about the fact of transformation were all of them already familiar. As to the means of transformation, however, Erasmus Darwin originated almost every important idea that has ever appeared in evolutionary theory."

Darlington, C. D., *Darwin's Place in History* (London, 1959).

pp. 60, 62   "Darwin was slippery, . . . [using] a flexible strategy which is not to be reconciled with even average intellectual integrity. . . . He began more and more to grudge praise to those who had in fact paved the way for him. . . . Darwin damned Lamarck and also his grandfather for being very ill-dressed fellows at the same moment he was engaged in stealing their clothes."

Darwin, Charles, "Autobiography," reprinted in *The Voyage of Charles Darwin*, edited by Christopher Rawlings (BBC, 1978), "A Scientist's Thoughts on Religion," *New Scientist*, vol. 104 (December 20/27, 1984), p. 75.

p. 75   "On 7 March 1837 I took lodgings in Great Marlborough Street in London and remained there for nearly two years until I was married. . . .

"During these two years I was led to think much about religion. . . . But I had gradually come, by this time, to see that the Old Testament, from its manifestly false history of the world . . . was no more to be trusted than the sacred books of the Hindus, or the beliefs of any barbarian."

p. 75   "Thus disbelief crept over me at a very slow rate, but was at last complete. The rate was so slow that I felt no distress, and have never since doubted even for a single second that my conclusion was correct. I can indeed hardly see how anyone ought to wish Christianity to be true, for if so the plain language of the text seems to show that the men who do not believe, and this would include my father, brother and almost all my best friends, will be everlastingly punished. And this is a damnable doctrine."

Eiseley, Loren C., "Alfred Russel Wallace," *Scientific American*, vol. 200 (February 1959), pp. 70-84.

p. 80   "Suddenly it occurred to the feverish naturalist in a lightning flash of insight that Malthus' checks to human increase . . . must, in similar or analogous ways, operate in the natural world as well."

p. 80   "It was Darwin's unpublished conception down to the last detail, independently duplicated by a man sitting in a hut at the world's end."

p. 81   "A man pursuing birds of paradise in a remote jungle did not yet know that he had forced the world's most reluctant author to disgorge his hoarded volume, or that the whole of Western thought was about to be swung into a new channel because a man in a fever had felt a moment of strange radiance."

Eiseley, Loren C., "Charles Lyell," *Scientific American*, vol. 201 (August 1959), pp. 98-106.

p. 106   "Darwin and Wallace were Lyell's intellectual children. Both would have
              failed to be what they were without the *Principles of Geology* to guide them."

Fowles, John, "Where Evolution Breaks into Fiction," review of *Darwin's Plots*, by Gillian Beer
    (Routledge, 1983, 303 pp.), *New Scientist*, vol. 100 (December 1, 1983), p. 676.

              "As a child, Darwin was a determined fibber, or reality-improver—he would
              claim he had seen unusual birds, that he could change the colour of crocuses,
              and so on. He admits that these imaginative lies gave him acute but two-edged
              pleasure—'pleasure like a tragedy.' Some such childish guilt at pure invention
              finally came to rule his adult life. He felt he had to amass observations, and
              establish his great 'plot.'"

Gillispie, Charles Coulston, "Lamarck and Darwin in the History of Science," *American Scientist*,
    vol. 46 (December 1958), pp. 388-409. Gillespie was Professor of History of Science, Princeton
    University.

p. 409   "For the continuum as the program of nature goes back to that aspect of
              classical philosophy which was a prolongation of cosmogony, back through the
              Stoics and Heraclitos to fire and the world as flux and process. But it is cosmology,
              the opposite of this, from which science derives, rather from the contemplation
              of being in the light of reason than of becoming in the light of process. And this
              resolves, perhaps another apparent paradox: i.e., that providentialism and belief
              in fixity and divine design have in effect been more conducive to positive scientific
              work—in Newton, for example, in Linnaeus, or in Cuvier—than has belief in
              process. For though ultimately untenable, providentialism establishes a reason
              in things for science to find. It posits the existence of specific entities which may
              serve as the term of analysis. But in becoming everything blends into everything
              and nothing may ever be defined."

Glasson, Francis, "Darwin and the Church," *New Scientist*, vol. 99 (September 1, 1983), pp. 638-639.

p. 638   "Darwin expected that his book would arouse violent criticism from the
              scientific world, and it certainly came from that quarter. According to his own
              account, most of the leading scientists of the day believed in the ummutability
              of species."

p. 638   "On the other hand, many Christian leaders took a very different line, even
              from the early stages; and Kingsley was representative of a very large number."
              [Canon Kingsley, novelist and social reformer]

p. 639   "Owen Chadwick, Regius professor of modern history at Cambridge, wrote
              after extensive research: 'At first much of the opposition to Darwin's theory
              came from scientists on grounds of evidence, not from theologians on grounds
              of scripture."

p. 639   "Despite abundant evidence to the contrary, it is widely believed that the
              Church was a bitter opponent of evolution. . . .

              "[The Huxley-Wilberforce] encounter in a highly dramatized form with
              invented speeches has been broadcast so often on radio and television that the

impression given is that Samuel Wilberforce spoke for the Church and that this was the official Christian response!"

Goodfield, June, "Humanity in Science," *Key Reporter* (Summer 1957), pp. 2-4, 8. Address given by Dr. Goodfield (a scientific historian) at joint meeting of AAAS and Phi Beta Kappa, February 24, 1977.

p. 2 "In spite of the [British] association's very genuine attempts to improve public understanding of science, what in fact emerged was an indiscriminate mixture of science, technology, pomposity and vanity."

p. 3 "Somehow science manages to extract the warmth and beauty from the world and also to drain the humanity from the personalities of the practitioners of science. Consequently, insofar as they are scientific, our solutions to society's problems inevitably become inhumane and cold, too."

p. 3 "In the effort to humanize ourselves, to enhance our ethical and moral sensibilities, people have often appealed to the humanities to do it for us, almost as to an ideology. The redemptive power of the humanities to produce an enlarged consciousness, to make us aware of the reality of the human predicament, and to enlarge our sympathies has been an important theme in Wordsworth, in Shelley and in many twentieth-century writers. I am skeptical about this assumption. People can be extraordinarily sensitive to music and poetry and not necessarily apply this sensitivity to their daily lives. George Steiner . . . has reminded us that people returned from a day's work as guards in the concentration camps and then put Mozart on their gramophones. . . . The people who went to the Globe Theatre and saw [Shakespeare's] marvelous dramas, with their rich poetry and their human understanding, would at the same place, in the same afternoon, watch a monkey tied to the back of a horse being chased by dogs who slowly bit it to death. . . . I think, too, that we must not delude ourselves into believing that words and university courses are a substitute for human hearts and human action."

p. 4 "Judged by scientists and others, much philosophy of science has been downright irrelevant, at best a series of brilliant axiomatic games, more often pretentious nonsense."

p. 8 "I think we are reasonably entitled to ask the scientific profession to assess the problems of contemporary society, and where scientific solutions are called for, to give them their first priority. It would be most rewarding if, instead of being on the defensive vis-a-vis society, as they have been in recent years, scientists, actively extended their notion of accountability in this way. With their example before us, we might then go on to deal with the problem of accountability in other groups—in industry and in the media for example, and thus help to create a climate where all professional groups recognize their debt and responsibility to society at large. Now is very much the right time—is it not—where we may use old-fashioned words such as 'morality' and 'honor' without fear of being sneered at."

Gould, Stephen Jay, "First Man of the Earth," *Nature*, vol. 352 (August 15, 1991), pp. 577-578.

p. 577   "Lyell certainly understood his enterprise as a battle for an unconventional point of view. In a private letter, he wrote about his intent in *Principles*: 'I am grappling not with the ordinary arm of flesh, but with principalities and powers, with Sedgwick, Whewell and others, for my rules of philosophising, as contra-distinguished from them, and I must put on all my armour.' When we recall that, in the full citation (Ephesians 6:12-13), Paul includes among the enemies 'rulers of the darkness' and 'spiritual wickedness in high places,' and that he donned his armour to 'be able to withstand in the evil day' we get a better sense of Lyell's self-perceived mission."

p. 577   "*Quote*: My work . . . will not pretend to give even an abstract of all that is known in geology, but it will endeavour to establish the principles of reasoning in the science . . . which, as you know, are neither more nor less than that no causes whatever have from the earliest time to which we can look back, to the present, ever acted, but those now acting; and that they never acted with different degrees of energy from that which they now exert." [Letter from Lyell to Murchison]

Gould, Stephen Jay, "Fall in the House of Ussher," *Natural History*, vol. 100 (November 1991), pp. 12-21.

p. 15   "To this day, one can scarcely find a textbook in introductory geology that does not take a swipe at Ussher's date as the opening comment in an obligatory page or two on older concepts of the earth's age (before radioactive dating allowed us to get it right)."

p. 16   "Ussher represented the best of scholarship in his time. He was part of a substantial research tradition, a large community of intellectuals working toward a common goal under an accepted methodology—Ussher's shared 'house' if you will pardon my irresistible title pun. Today we rightly reject a cardinal premise of that methodology—belief in biblical inerrance—and we recognize that this false assumption allowed such a great error in estimating the age of the earth."

p. 16   "Moreover, within assumptions of the methodology, this research tradition had considerable success. Even the extreme values were not very discordant—ranging from a minimum, for the creation of the earth, of 3761 B.C. in the Jewish calendar (still in use) to a maximum of just over 5500 B.C. for the Septuagint. Most calculators had reached a figure very close to Ussher's 4004. The Venerable Bede had estimated 3952 B.C., several centuries before, while J. J. Scaliger, the greatest scholar of the generation just before Ussher, had placed creation at 3950 B.C. Thus, Ussher's 4004 was neither idiosyncratic nor at all unusual; it was, in fact, a fairly conventional estimate developed within a large and active community of scholars."

p. 16   "James Barr explains the problems and complexities in an excellent article, 'Why the World was Created in 4004 B.C.: Archbishop Ussher and Biblical Chronology,' (*Bulletin, John Rylands University Library of Manchester*, vol. 67, pp. 575-608)."

Grant, Edward, "Science and Theology in the Middle Ages," in *God and Nature: Historical Essays on the Encounter between Christianity and Science*, edited by David C. Lindberg and Ronald L. Numbers (Berkeley: University of California Press, 1986), pp. 49-75. Dr. Grant is Distinguished Professor of History and Philosophy of Science at Indiana University.

p. 51   "By the twelfth century, significant changes were under way that would eventually challenge theology's interpretation of the cosmos and the God who created it. The threat to theology and the church did not derive from astrology or magic, which, though potentially dangerous, were successfully contained in the Middle Ages. It came from Greek natural philosophy and science, initially in its benign Platonic and Neoplatonic forms in the twelfth century and then in its powerful and truly menacing Aristotelian form in the thirteenth century."

Harper, G. W., "Darwinism and Indoctrination," *School Science Review*, vol. 59, no. 207 (December 1977), pp. 258-268.

p. 267   "Perhaps the most intangible but far-reaching influence of evolution theory is to keep alive the notion of the *scala naturae*. This was an important idea before 1860, and involved the ordering of plant and animal species along a scale from the lowest to the highest. It was given a new lease on life by Darwinism, since the scale could now be seen as the sequence of stages through which the higher, complex and advanced species might have evolved from the lower, simple and primitive species."

Hoyle, Sir Fred, and N. C. Wickramasinghe, *Evolution from Space* (New York: Simon and Schuster, 1981).

p. 96   "In 1835 and 1837 Edward Blyth published two papers in which he considered the effects of natural selection. He argued that once species were adapted to their environment, natural selection would prevent them become disadapted."

pp. 96-7   "What Darwin, and also Alfred Russel Wallace, did nearly a quarter of a century after Blyth was to assert that natural selection could indeed get the adaptation there in the first place, a position which Blyth had considered and rejected. The assertion was without proof, although the scientific world has been persuaded into thinking that exhaustive proofs were given in *The Origin of Species* (1859). What we are actually given in Darwin's book are very many changes of adaptation by already adapted species, of which there had never been any real cause for argument since Blyth's papers in 1835 and 1837. The key issue, namely that origins from scratch cannot be explained in the same way, is not dealt with at all.

     "The speculations of *The Origin of Species* turned out to be wrong, as we have seen in this chapter. It is ironic that the scientific facts throw Darwin out, but leave William Paley, a figure of fun to the scientific world for more than a century, still in the tournament with a chance of being the ultimate winner. We shall see how the argument goes in the remaining chapters."

Løvtrup, Søren, *Darwinism: The Refutation of a Myth* (London: Croom Helm, 1987), 469 pp.

pp. 44, 46   "*The Scala Naturae,* the *Ladder of Nature,* the *Chain of Being, l'Ehcelle des Êtres*, is a notion traceable back to Plato Aristotle and the Neo-Platonians, which experienced a resurgence in the eighteenth century."

p. 67   "The idea of ontogenetic recapitulation dates back to a speech given by Kidmayer in Tubingen, 1793. . . .

                   "The succession of organisms mentioned here may be taken to represent the 'Chain of Being', and Kielmayer thus states that individual organisms during their development follow this sequence."

Mayr, Ernst, "Darwin and Natural Selection," *American Scientist*, vol. 65 (May/June, 1977), pp. 321-327.

p. 323   "It is apparent that Darwin lost his faith in the years 1836-39, much of it clearly prior to the reading of Malthus. In order not to hurt the feelings of his friends and of his wife, Darwin often used deistic language in his publications, but much in his Notebooks indicates that by this time he had become a 'materialist' (more or less = atheist)."

p. 324   "Nevertheless, it is highly probable that Darwin had been gradually conditioned by his reading to a far less benign interpretation of the struggle for existence than that held by the natural theologians. . . . By necessity, accepting evolutionary thinking undermined a continued adherence to a belief in a harmonious universe."

p. 327   "One of these shifts has been rather consistently sidestepped by all those who have occupied themselves with the history of the theory of natural selection. It is the question of the extent that Darwin's loss of Christian faith affected the conceptual framework on which the theory of natural selection rests. . . . Adopting natural selection rather than the hand of God as the active factor responsible for all that was formerly considered evidence for design was, of course, the last step. However, even the acceptance of evolution was already a fatal undermining of natural theology."

Oldroyd, D. R., *Darwinian Impacts* (Atlantic Highlands, New Jersey: Humanities Press, 1983), 348 pp.

pp. 9-11   "Neo-Platonism has for long exerted a powerful influence on the Christian West, particularly in the Florentine period of the Renaissance. And it might be said that the doctrine of the Great Chain of Being formed part of the general mental furniture of most educated men from the Renaissance until almost the end of the eighteenth century. . . . References to the Great Chain of Being abound in Spenser, Henry More and Milton. One finds it in the philosophical writings of Leibniz, Spinoza and Locke in the seventeenth century, and in the eighteenth century it was one of the standard ways of conceptualizing nature. . . .

                   "The doctrine of the Great Chain of Being probably had its last resting place (at least among biologists) among the German Nature Philosophers of the nineteenth century, immediately before Darwin's time."

Patterson, Colin, "Cladistics and Classification," *New Scientist*, vol. 94 (April 29, 1982), pp. 303-306. Patterson is Head of Paleontology at the British Museum of Natural History.

p. 303   "Linnaeus and his successors recognized genera, families and other categories on the basis of similarities in structure, and believed that each group had a set of features which were its essence, or ideal plan, corresponding to something in the mind of the Creator. Comparative anatomy developed as a means of searching out these ideal plans."

Polkinghorne, John, "Religion's Private Hold on Faraday," review of *Michael Faraday: Sandemanian and Scientist*, by Geoffrey Cantor (Macmillan, 359 pp.), *New Scientist*, vol. 130 (June 1, 1991), p. 46.

p. 46   "The sect sought to follow the teaching of the Bible, interpreted with a simple literalism and used as the sole guide."

p. 46   "Almost all the great figures of British physical science in the 19th century, such as Clerk Maxwell, Kelvin and Stokes, were men of deep religious conviction. They seemed untroubled by the evolutionary storms that raged around them."

p. 46   "Faraday was a man of modesty and integrity, a scientist of great distinction and a religious believer of deep conviction and surprising simple-mindedness."

Powicke, F. M., *Modern Historians and the Study of History, Essays and Papers* (London, 1955), 256 pp.

p. 228   "Sometimes people talk as though the 'higher criticism' of texts in recent times has had more influence upon the human mind than the higher criticism of nature. This seems to me to be nonsense. The higher criticism has been simply an application of an awakened critical faculty to a particular kind of material, and was encouraged by the achievement of this faculty to form its bold conclusions. If the biologists, the geologists, the astronomers, the physicists, the anthropologists had not been at work, I venture to think that the higher critics would have been either non-existent or a tiny minority in a world of fundamentalists."

Rifkin, Jeremy, *Algeny* (New York: Viking Press, 1983), 298 pp.

p. 86   "Darwin borrowed heavily from the popular economic thinking of the day. While by Darwin's own admission, Malthus's economic writings were a key influence in the development of his theory, Darwin was equally influenced by one of the other great economic philosophers of the eighteenth century, Adam Smith. An examination of Smith's and Darwin's writings shows how deeply indebted the latter was to the thoughts Smith penned in *The Wealth of Nations*, published in 1776."

p. 89   "The bourgeoisie was in need of a 'proper' justification for the new factory system with its dehumanizing process of division of labor. By claiming that a similar process was at work in nature, Darwin provided an ideal rationale for those capitalists hell-bent on holding the line against any fundamental challenge to the economic hierarchy they managed and profited from."

Wallace, Alfred Russel, *The Wonderful Century: its Successes and its Failures* (New York,:1898).

p. 139   "I was then [February 1858] living at Ternate in the Moluccas, and was suffering from a rather severe attack of intermittent fever, which prostrated me every day during the cold and succeeding hot fits. During one of these fits, while again considering the problem of the origin of species, something led me to think of Malthus' Essay on Population."

p. 140   "The whole method of species modification became clear to me, and in the two hours of my fit I had thought out the main points of the theory. That same evening I sketched out the draft of a paper; and in the two succeeding evenings I wrote it out, and sent it by the next post to Mr. Darwin."

p. 362   "Then it suddenly flashed upon me that this self-acting process would necessarily improve the race, because in every generation the inferior would inevitably be killed off and the superior would remain—that is, the fittest would survive. Then at once I seemed to see the whole effect of this."

C. The Ancient Evolutionists

Before the rise and spread of Christianity, either pantheistic or atheistic evolutionism was practically universal in ancient religions and philosophies. The Graeco/Roman religious philosophies, with their nature-centered polytheism—whether called Gnostics, Stoics, Epicureans or what—all denied true creationism and a true beginning of the space-time cosmos.

The pre-Socratic Greek Milesian philosophers evidently received their concepts of evolutionary cosmogony from the even more ancient religious leaders of Egypt and Babylonia or Sumeria. The basic unity of all ancient religions in a pantheistic, polytheistic, astrological, spiritist, evolutionary cosmology is one of the most remarkable features of the ancient world. Thus, evolution is not in any way a modern "scientific" discovery, but rather a modern revival of the primeval anti-God world religion.

Abel, Ernest L., *Ancient Views on the Origin of Life* (Farleigh: Dickinson University Press, 1973), 93 pp.

p. 15   "Although it is customary to credit the inception of this theory to Charles Darwin and his immediate predecessors, a rudimentary form of this notion can be traced back to the beginnings of written history itself. In fact, the belief that life had its origins in a single basic substance is so wide-spread among the various peoples of the world, primitive or civilized, that it can be considered one of the few universal themes in the history of ideas."

p. 15   "In general, myth conveys the impression of a story invented *ex nihilo*, a story describing the irascible and typically irresponsible actions of various divine malcontents. But these deities are not simply malevolent gods capriciously toying with mankind. They are actually personifications of Nature, and their activities, predictable and unpredictable, determine what life will be like on earth."

p. 23   "For instance, when the Babylonian priests turned their attention to natural phenomena such as the stars, it was for the purpose of knowing better the will of the gods whose actions were believed to be intimately linked with the movements of these heavenly bodies."

p. 24   "In the end, observation and introspection caused him [Thales] to conclude that all of the variations in Nature could in fact be accounted for in terms of a single substance—water."

Allegro, John M., "Divine Discontent," *American Atheist*, vol. 28 (September 1986), pp. 25-30. Allegro was a member of the Dead Sea Scrolls editing team.

p. 30   "Historically, the cult of the Earth Mother, the ancient religion of the witches, has probably come nearest to fulfilling this role, and being sexually oriented has been especially concerned with this most disturbing and potentially disruptive element in man's biological constitution."

Budge, E. A. Wallis, *The Gods of the Egyptians*, vol. 1 (New York: Dover, 1969), 595 pp.

pp. 293-4   "Be this as it may, our present interest in the papyrus centers in the fact that it contains two copies of the story of the Creation which are of the greatest interest. . . . Each copy is entitled, 'The Book of knowing the Evolutions of R~, and of overthrowing Apepi.' The word here rendered by 'Evolutions' is *kheperu*, being derived from the root *kheper*, which means 'to make, to fashion, to produce, to form, to become,' and in a derived sense 'to roll,' . . . In the text, the words are placed in the mouth of the god Neb-er-tcher, the lord of the universe and a form of the sun-god R~, who says, 'I am he who came into being in the form of the god Kheperá [Evolution], and I was the creator of that which came into being, . . .'"

p. 302   "Returning to our narrative we find that the god continues. 'I came into being from primeval matter, and I appeared under the form of multitudes of things from the beginning. Nothing existed at that time, and it was I who made whatsoever was made. . . . I made all the forms under which I appeared by means (or, out of) the god-soul which I raised up out of Nu [i.e., the primeval inactive abyss of water].'"

Concord, F. M., "Pattern of Ionian Cosmogony," in *Theories of the Universe*, edited by Milton K. Munitz (New York: The Free Press, 1965), pp. 21-31.

p. 21   "The Milesian system pushed back to the very beginning of things the operation of processes as familiar and ordinary as a shower of rain. It made the formation of the world no longer a supernatural, but a natural event. Thanks to the Ionians, and to no one else, this has become the universal premise of all modern science."

p. 22   "[They believed that] the order arose by differentiation out of a simple state of things, at first conceived as a single living substance, later by the pluralists, as a primitive confusion in which 'all things,' now separate, 'were together.'"

Denton, Michael, *Evolution: A Theory in Crisis* (London: Burnett Books, Ltd., 1985), 368 pp.

p. 37   "Even some primitive mythologies express the idea that life in all its diverse manifestations is not the creation of the gods but a purely natural phenomenon being the result of normal flux of the world. The ancient Norse, for example, held that the first living beings, the giant Ymir and the primordial cow Audumla, were formed gradually from the ice melted by the action of a warm wind which blew from a southern land Muspellsheim, the land of fire.

"The majority of the old pre-Socratic philosophers were strikingly materialistic in their interpretation of nature. To them life was a natural phenomenon, the result of processes no less natural than those which moulded the forms of rocks or rivers, no less inevitable than the turn of the tides, the phases of the moon. Life was for them part of a continuum with the soil and sea."

p. 53   "Although Darwin had nearly all the key ideas of the *Origin* clear in his mind as early as 1838, he deliberated for twenty years before committing himself publicly to evolution. A number of factors were probably responsible for this delay. One may have been its controversial and anti-religious character. We know that his wife, with whom he was very close, found his views disturbing as they seemed to her to 'be putting God further and further off.'"

Dreyer, J. L. E., "Medieval Cosmology," in *Theories of the Universe*, edited by Milton K. Munitz (New York: The Free Press, 1965). pp. 115-138.

p. 117   "This desire to find allegories in Scripture was carried to excess by Origen (185-254), who was likewise associated with Alexandrian thought, and he managed thereby to get rid of anything which could not be harmonized with pagan learning, such as the separation of the waters above the firmament from those below it, mentioned in Genesis, which he takes to mean that we should separate our spirits from the darkness of the abyss, where the Adversary and his angels dwell."

Hamilton, Edith, *Mythology* (Boston: Little, Brown and Co., 1942), 497 pp. Miss Hamilton is here paraphrasing Hesiod's great poem *Theogony*.

p. 77   "Long before the gods appeared, in the dim past, uncounted ages ago, there was only the formless confusion of Chaos brooded over by unbroken darkness. At last, but how no one ever tried to explain, two children were born to this shapeless nothingness."

p. 78   "What took place next was the creation of the earth, but this, too, no one ever tried to explain. It just happened. . . . The poet Hesiod, the first Greek who tried to explain how things began, wrote,

> 'Earth, the beautiful, rose up,
>
> Broad-bosomed, she that is the steadfast base
>
> of all things. And fair Earth first bore
>
> the starry Heaven, equal to herself,
>
> To cover her on all sides and to be
>
> a home forever for the blessed gods.'"

Jacobsen, Thorkild, "Enuma Elish—the Babylonian Genesis," in *Theories of the Universe*, edited by Milton K. Munitz (New York: The Free Press, 1965), pp. 8-20.

p. 9   "[Specifically, *Enuma Elish* assumes that all things have evolved out of water.] 'This description presents the earliest stage of the universe as one of watery chaos. The chaos consisted of three intermingled elements: Apsu, who represents the sweet waters; Ti'amat, who represents the sea; and Mumnu who cannot as yet be identified with certainty but may represent cloud banks and mist. These three types of water were mingled in a large undefined mass. . . .

"Then, in the midst of this watery chaos two gods came into existence,— Lahmu and Lahamu.'"

Jaki, Stanley L., "Science: Western or What?" *Intercollegiate Review*, vol. 26 (Fall 1990), pp. 3-12. Jaki is Distinguished Professor at Seton Hall University, with doctorates in theology and physics, and has written 32 books.

p. 8   "All of those ancient cultures were pagan. The essence of paganism, old and new, is that the universe is eternal, that its motions are without beginning and without end.

"Belief in creation out of nothing and in time is the very opposite of paganism."

p. 8   "Insofar as that broad credal or theological consensus is the work of Christianity, science is not Western, but Christian."

p. 9   "All ancient cultures were pantheistic. By contrast, the Christian concept of God has for its essence the belief that He is truly a Creator, that is, a being absolutely transcendental to the world. He exists whether He creates a universe or not."

p. 9   "Such a fact was the belief of medieval Christians, or of genuine Christians in any age for that matter, in a personal transcendental Creator. Moreover, for those Christians the transcendental Creator was substantially identical with the Incarnate Logos, or Reason Incarnate. They also believed that He could only create a fully logical or rational universe. It may sound most surprising that the first unambiguous declarations about the unrestricted rationality of the universe are found not in Greek philosophical writings, but in the writings of Saint Athanasius, the great defender of the divinity of the Logos against the Arians."

Lindsay, Arthur Ward, *Principles of Organic Evolution* (St. Louis: The C. V. Mosby Co., 1952), p. 21.

"During this period it is significant that several of the church fathers expressed ideas of organic evolution even though the trend of ecclesiastical thought led more readily into other lines of reasoning. St. Gregory of Nyssa (331-396 A.D.), St. Basil (331-379 A.D.), St. Augustine (353-430 A.D.), and St. Thomas Aquinas (1225-1274 A.D.) expressed belief in the symbolical nature of the Biblical story of creation and in their comments made statements clearly related to the concept of evolution."

Lucretius, *The Nature of the Universe*, trans. R. E. Lathan (New York: Penguin Books, 1951), p. 58, also cited in *Theories of the Universe*, ed. Milton K. Munitz (Glencoe, Illinois: The Free Press, 1957, 437 pp), p. 53. Lucretius lived from 96 to 55 B.C.

"Certainly the atoms did not post themselves purposefully in due order by an act of intelligence, nor did they stipulate what movements each should perform. As they have been rushing everlastingly throughout all space in their myriads, undergoing myriad changes under the disturbing impact of collisions, they have experienced every variety of movement and conjunction till they have fallen into the particular pattern by which this world of ours is constituted. This world has persisted many a long year, having once been set going in the appropriate motions. From these everything else follows."

More, Louis Trenchard, *The Dogma of Evolution* (Princeton University Press, 1925), 386 pp. This book was a series of lectures given by Dr. More at Princeton University in January 1925.

p. 66   "After Aristotle's death, Greek thought gradually divided into the two schools of the Stoics and the Epicureans. . . . As these two schools held the world of thought in allegiance well into the Roman Empire and exerted much influence on Christian writers, their ideas of science and evolution are very important."

p. 67   "'The Epicureans were materialistic monists without any reservations. . . .

              "The Stoics were also materialistic monists but of a less thorough going type.'"

Munitz, Milton K., *Space, Time and Creation* (Glencoe, Illinois: The Free Press, 1957), 182 pp. Munitz was Professor of Philosophy at New York University.

p. 8   "The fact is that primitive mythology lingers on in one form or another in the early career of science and, in the case of the efforts made in cosmologic speculation, determines the very pattern, in a broad sense, which these proto-scientific schemes exhibit."

pp. 8-9   "One evidence of the influence of myth upon these earliest instances of 'scientific' thought is to be found in the interest in formulating a complete cosmogony which would show how from some primordial state an ordered world arose and underwent successive differentiations of an astronomic, geographic, and meteorologic kind, culminating ultimately, in the emergence of living things and human society."

p. 13   "That the ordered world as we know it is not everlasting but arose in some fashion from an earlier primordial state, is for Anaximander a belief which is not questioned but rather taken over from mythology. . . . Anaximander reinterprets, while at the same time retaining, basically the same pattern of cosmogonical development that is to be found in the Babylonian myth as this had already been partly transformed in the Greek version of Hesiod's *Theogony*."

Munitz, Milton K., *Theories of the Universe* (New York: The Free Press, 1965), 438 pp.

p. 6   "The type of thinking initiated by the Milesian school of pre-Socratic thinkers—Thales, Anaximander, and Anaximenes—in the sixth century B.C. was carried forward in many directions. One of the most remarkable outcomes of such speculations, representing a culmination of their materialistic thought, was to be found in the Atomist school. Originally worked out in its main features by Leucippus and Democritus in the fifth century B.C., the teachings of atomism were later adopted as a basis for the primarily ethical philosophy of Epicureanism. . . . It elaborates the conception of a universe whose order arises out of a blind interplay of atoms rather than as a product of deliberate design; of a universe boundless in spatial extent, infinite in its duration and containing unnumerable worlds in various stages of development or decay. . . . It was the same conception, however, which once more came into the foreground of attention at the dawn of modern thought and has remained up to the present time an inspiration for those modes of scientific thinking that renounce any appeal to teleology in the interpretation of physical phenomena."

pp. 63-64   "Like his master Plato, Aristotle insists there is but one world, that is a central body like the earth surrounded by a finite number of planets and stars. This one world, of course, which makes up the entire universe, contains all existent matter. . . . Aristotle argues that the one world or universe we know is eternal, without beginning and without end."

Osborn, Henry Fairfield, *From the Greeks to Darwin* (New York: Charles Scribner's Sons, 1929), p. 48.

"Aristotle believed in a complete gradation in Nature, a progressive development corresponding with the progressive life of the soul. . . . He put his facts together into an Evolution system which had the teaching of Plato and Socrates for its primary philosophical basis."

Ruse, Michael, "The Long March of Darwin," review of *China and Charles Darwin*, by James R. Pusey (Harvard University Press, 1983, 544 pp.), *New Scientist*, vol. 103 (August 16, 1984), p.35.

p. 35   "[Darwin's] ideas took root at once, for China did not have the innate intellectual and religious barriers to evolution that often existed in the West. Indeed, in some respects Darwin seemed almost Chinese! . . . Taoist and neo-Confucian thought had always stressed the 'thingness' of humans. Our being at one with the animals was no great shock.

". . . As with American industrialists, what made Darwinism attractive were the notions of struggle, and survival, and (most particularly) of success."

p. 35   "Today, the official philosophy is Marxist-Leninism (of a kind). But without the secular, materialist approach of Darwinism (meaning now the broad social philosophy), the ground would not have been tilled for Mao and his revolutionaries to sow their seed and reap their crop."

Topoff, Howard, "A Charles Darwin (187th) Birthday Quiz," *American Scientist*, vol. 85 (March/April 1997), pp. 104-107.

p. 106   "2 (c) Darwin's first use of the word 'evolution' was in his second major book, *The Descent of Man*, published in 1871. The following year, it was added to the sixth edition of the *Origin*. In an important sense, the *Origin* also did not address the question suggested by its very title, namely speciation. Instead, it focused on changes within a single lineage over long periods of time. The issue of how a single group of organisms with a shared gene pool could split into two or more genetically distinct populations remained unexplained until well into the 20th century."

p. 106   "5 (a) Not only the phrase, but the terms 'ontogeny' and 'phylogeny' were coined by Ernst Haeckel, a German naturalist and contemporary of Darwin. According to his 'biogenetic law,' there is a parallelism between the stages of embryonic growth in the individual, and the succession of fossil stages in the phylogeny of the species. The embryos of all major groups of vertebrates do possess gill pouches and gill furrows, and these similarities clearly reveal Darwin's evolutionary principle of descent with modification from a common ancestor. But the embryos of different vertebrate groups diverge progressively during ontogeny, and no species passes through an adult stage of an ancestral type."

p. 106   "7 (d) Erasmus Darwin, Charles's grandfather, was one of the most celebrated personalities in England during the last decade of the 18th century. As physician, philosopher and poet, his writings on evolution utilized evidence from embryology, comparative anatomy, systematics and zoogeography. Two years after his death, the word 'Darwinian' was in common use. His book *Zoonomia* was translated into French, German and Italian. Four years after its publication, Thomas Malthus elaborated on Erasmus's ideas in his *Essays on Population*. And nine years later, Lamarck expounded a theory of evolution based on Erasmus's notion of the effects of use and disuse. Another 63 years elapsed before Charles Darwin published *On the Origin of Species*."

Veith, Ilza, "Creation and Evolution in the Far East," in *Issues in Evolution*, edited by Sol Tax (University of Chicago Press, 1960), pp. 1-17.

p. 1   "In contrast to the Western world, the Far Eastern philosophers thought of creation in evolutionary terms."

p. 2   "The striking feature of the Chinese concept of cosmogony is the fact that creation was never associated with the design or activity of a supernatural being, but rather with the interaction of impersonal forces, the powers of which persist interminably."

p. 7   "Though completely fanciful, this ladder of nature is noteworthy because it was conceived more than two millennia before the Western world began to re-examine its biblical chronology. But beyond this, the above-quoted passage contains two highly important points: first, a belief in an inherent continuity of all creation and, second, a reference to the merging of one species into another—from primordial germ to man."

Young, Davis A., *Christianity and the Age of the Earth* (Grand Rapids: Zondervan, 1982), 188 pp.

p. 25   "It cannot be denied, in spite of frequent interpretations of Genesis 1 that departed from the rigidly literal, that the almost universal view of the Christian world until the eighteenth century was that the Earth was only a few thousand years old. Not until the development of modern scientific investigation of the Earth itself would this view be called into question within the church."

Zindler, Frank R., "Religion, Hypnosis and Music: An Evolutionary Perspective," *American Atheist*, vol. 26 (October 1984), pp. 22-24. Zindler is former Chairman, Division of Science, Nursing & Technology, Fullton-Montgomery College, SUNY.

p. 22   "Take religion, for instance. If religion is all a pack of lies—a muddle of myths—why would natural selection allow religion to survive? How could natural selection allow a behavior that has nothing at all to do with the real world to develop in the first place?"

p. 22   "Whether we like it or not, there was a long time ago when religion was actually a 'good' thing. That is to say, religion increased group fitness."

p. 22   "This truly 'old time religion' developed at the end of the last Ice Age, when the tribe was the largest human grouping maintaining any degree of coherence. The religion of the *Old Testament* is a cultural fossil held over from the Pleistocene Epoch, and it reflects an atmosphere of intense intergroup competition. Petrified like the bones in a paleontologist's cabinet, the greatest ideas of the Ice Age still can be found on display between *Genesis* and *Malachi*."

p. 23   "Although we are accustomed to think of prayer as a type of cosmic begging, it is likely that this type of prayer was a later evolutionary development. The original purpose of prayer, I believe, was to induce trance and, thereby, to effect hallucinatory communication with the 'spirit world.'"

Chapter 13

The Modern War Against God

A. The Current Creation-Evolution Conflict

With their great apparent victory at the Scopes Trial of 1925, then their unilateral proclamation of victory at the 1959 Darwin Centennial, evolutionists concluded that creationism was effectively dead and could henceforth be ignored. The modern creationist revival began shortly thereafter, however, so it was first answered by sarcasm and ridicule.

It was not long before the realization sank in that creation was now being promoted by scientists rather than preachers, so the evolutionary establishment soon became concerned and angry. As a result, at least forty anti-creationist books have been published since 1970, plus hundreds of articles. The media and the courts, as well as the scientific and educational establishments, have also attacked the creationists vigorously. Nevertheless, the movement continues to grow, for truth and reality support creation, not evolution. The following quotes are mere samples of multitudes that could be cited to illustrate the bitter nature of this opposition.

Anonymous, "One Fifth of All Scientists Reject Evolution," *Bible Science Newsletter* (June 1988), p. 17.

> "Origins survey published in *Industrial Chemist*. . . . February 1988. . . . Most surprising to nearly everyone was the fact that 20.6 percent of the scientists responding *completely reject evolution*! The editors wrote, 'Remember these respondents are scientists and do not represent a typical sample of the U.S. population.' Further, the scientific community is quite split on the question of whether creationism is hurting scientific education. A surprising 37.9 percent don't think that creationism is hurting scientific education, while 46.7 think it is. Less than half the scientists polled believed that it is even possible for *man to have evolved without supernatural intervention* (48.3%)! A number of the scientists polled, 22.8 percent, believed that humans could only have evolved with supernatural intervention, while another 22.8 percent feel that human evolution is impossible under any circumstances."

Asimov, Isaac, Letter from the President, American Humanist Association (January 1986), 4 pp.

p. 2
> "Such action, coupled with a series of recent legal defeats for 'scientific creationism,' means that the AHA's participation in the creation-evolution controversy has borne fruit. For *it was the AHA, before any other organization*, that issued in 1977 its famous 'Statement Affirming Evolution as a Principle of Science' and warned the public of the dangers posed by the creationist movement. It was the AHA, and no other organization, that chose to publish *Creation/ Evolution*, a journal that continues to provide scientific rebuttals to creationist nonsense, thereby aiding those fighting at the local level. The AHA has been in this battle from the beginning and will stay with it as long as necessary."

p. 3   "If, as Humanist Manifesto II declares, the next century is to be the Humanist century, we must act now. Opportunities as good as this simply cannot be missed."

Asimov, Isaac, Fund appeal letter for ACLU (March 1982), 4 pp.

p. 1   "You and I and other scientifically minded citizens must help the ACLU fight this movement to force fundamentalist religious doctrine into the public schools. . . . We must be prepared for the long and costly battle of challenging every creationist statute in every state in which it is introduced.

                "Unbelievable as it may seem, there are millions of Americans who call themselves 'scientific creationists.' . . .

                "These religious zealots . . . are marching like an army of the night into our public schools with their Bibles held high."

p. 2   "As a fellow advocate for science, I urge you to consider giving the ACLU the most generous contribution you can possibly afford to help it wage this most important, historical legal battle."

p. 4   "Today, I am writing my personal check for $100 to help the ACLU finance this important case.

                "I urge you too to write your check today. *Your help is needed desperately, right now.* Sincerely, Isaac Asimov."

Asimov, Isaac, Fund raising letter for AHA (March 1988), 4 pp.

p. 2   "But, as we all know, the fundamentalists don't give up easily. For example, after the Supreme Court voted 7-2 against creationism last June in the Louisiana creationism case, a case in which the AHA was a plaintiff, the various creationist organizations began shifting gears. What is their newest tack? *Academic freedom*, of all things!

                "The Institute for Creation Research has begun encouraging the many existing creationist teachers in the public schools to teach creationism on their own in their science classes. Meanwhile other creationist groups are preparing test cases so they can launch a 'Scopes trial in reverse.' These organizations want one of their creationist teachers to get fired for teaching creationism so they can take that case all the way to the Supreme Court using a free speech and academic freedom line of argument."

p. 2   "To combat this new thrust by creationists, *the AHA has secured a $5,000.00 grant* to help develop a computer network of concerned local organizations nationwide."

p. 4   "*We're on a roll and you can keep us there.* The fundamentalists can't stop us now. Only a lack of support from you can bring our growth to a halt. But I'm confident you're with me. I'm sure you think it's high time the AHA realized its full potential. So let's go for it?

                "Please make out a check right now, while this is in front of you."

Barr, James, Letter to David Watson, 1984. Barr is Professor of Hebrew Bible, Vanderbilt University, and former Regius Professor of Hebrew, Oxford University, Oxford, England.

> "Probably, so far as I know, there is no professor of Hebrew or Old Testament at any world-class university who does not believe that the writer(s) of Gen. 1-11 intended to convey to their readers the ideas that (a) creation took place in a series of six days which were the same as the days of 24 hours we now experience (b) the figures contained in the Genesis genealogies provided by simple addition a chronology from the beginning of the world up to later stages in the biblical story (c) Noah's flood was understood to be world-wide and extinguish all human and animal life except for those in the ark. *Or, to put it negatively, the apologetic arguments which suppose the 'days' of creation to be long eras of time, the figures of years not to be chronological, and the flood to be a merely local Mesopotamian flood, are not taken seriously by any such professors, as far as I know.*"

Bozarth, G. Richard, "The Meaning of Evolution," *American Atheist* (February 1978), pp. 19, 30.

p. 19   "These 'creation-science' textbooks, if allowed in our schools, can only serve to increase that mental anguish by teaching that the *Genesis* gibberish is a legitimate scientific theory."

p. 19   "Christianity is—must be!—totally committed to the special creation as described in Genesis, and Christianity must fight with its full might, fair or foul, against the theory of evolution."

p. 19   "It becomes clear now that the whole justification of Jesus' life and death is predicated on the existence of Adam and the forbidden fruit he and Eve ate. Without the original sin, who needs to be redeemed? Without Adam's fall into a life of constant sin terminated by death, what purpose is there to Christianity? None."

p. 30   "What all this means is that Christianity cannot lose the *Genesis* account of creation like it could lose the doctrine of geocentrism and get along. The battle must be waged, for Christianity is fighting for its very life."

p. 30   "Atheism is science's natural ally. Atheism is the philosophy, both moral and ethical, most perfectly suited for a scientific civilization. If we work for the American Atheists today, Atheism will be ready to fill the void of Christianity's demise when science and evolution triumph.

     "Without a doubt humans and civilization are in sore need of the intellectual cleanness and mental health of atheism."

p. 30   "Christianity has fought, still fights, and will fight science to the desperate end over evolution, because evolution destroys utterly and finally the very reason Jesus' earthly life was supposedly made necessary. Destroy Adam and Eve and the original sin, and in the rubble you will find the sorry remains of the son of god. Take away the meaning of his death. If Jesus was not the redeemer who died for our sins, and this is what evolution means, then Christianity is nothing!"

Bradley, Walter L, and Roger Olsen, "The Trustworthiness of Scripture in Areas Relating to Natural Science," in *Hermeneutics, Inerrancy and the Bible*, edited by Earl D. Radmacher and Robert D. Preuss (Grand Rapids: Zondervan Publishing House, 1984), pp. 283-317.

p. 299   "The Hebrew word 'yom' and its plural form 'yamim,' are used over 1900 times in the Old Testament. . . . Outside of the Genesis 1 case in question, the two-hundred plus occurrences of 'yom' preceded by ordinals all refer to a normal twenty-four hour day. Furthermore, the seven-hundred plus appearances of 'yamim' always refer to a regular day. Thus, it is argued [by young-earth creationists] that the Exodus 20:11 reference to the six 'yamim' of creation must also refer to six regular days.

        "These arguments have a common fallacy, however. There is no other place in the Old Testament where the intent is to describe events that involve multiple and/or sequential, indefinite periods of time."

Chambers, Bette (president, ASA), Isaac Asimov, Hudson Hoagland, Chauncey D. Leake, Linus Pauling, and George Gaylord Simpson (Sponsoring Committee), "A Statement Affirming Evolution as a Principle of Science," *The Humanist*, vol. 37, no. 1 (January/February 1977), pp. 4-6 (signed by 163 others—Rogers, Skinner, LaMont, Tax, Cloud, Commoner, Mayr, etc.).

p. 4   "There are no alternative theories to the principle of evolution, with its 'tree of life' pattern, that any competent biologist of today takes seriously. . . .

        "Creationism is not scientific; it is a purely religious view held by some religious sects and persons and strongly opposed by other religious sects and persons. . . . Evolution is . . . therefore the only view that should be expounded in public-school courses on science.

        "We, the undersigned, call upon all local school boards . . . to do the following:

        "—Resist and oppose measures . . . that would require creationist views of origins be given equal treatment and emphasis. . . .

        "—Reject the concept, currently being put forth by certain religious and pressure groups, that alleges that evolution is itself a tenet of a religion of 'secular humanism,' and as such is unsuitable for inclusion in the public school science curriculum."

Chambers, Bette, "Isaac Asimov: A One-Man Renaissance," *The Humanist*, vol. 53 (March/April 1993), pp. 6-8.

p. 6   "However, Asimov's earliest involvement with the AHA dates almost a decade earlier, when in 1976 he joined with such noted scientists as Hudson Hoagland, George Gaylord Simpson, Chauncey Leake, and Linus Pauling in sponsoring a national education campaign promoted by the AHA. A *Statement Affirming Evolution As a Principle of Science*, adapted from an earlier text written by Hermann J. Muller, Nobelist and former AHA president, was sent to every major school district in the United States."

Chase, Richard, "Teaching Science," *Wheaton Alumni* (April/May 1990).

p. 4   "For at least six decades, Wheaton's faculty have supported our Statement of Faith, affirmed the truthfulness of the Genesis account (including the historicity of Adam and Eve as the first persons, created in the image of God), and have held that the 'days' of Genesis are most likely to have been extended periods of time. Further, they have also noted that the Bible does not comment on the exact origin of species as described today."

p. 4 "In summary, we boldly affirm our Statement of Faith and seek to explore and teach within the parameters of our biblical foundation. Above all, we proclaim that the Bible concerns itself primarily with the nature of God, the nature of man, and the relationship between God and man, rather than with how God created all that he did."

Cloud, Preston, "Scientific Creationism—A New Inquisition Brewing?" *The Humanist*, vol. 37, no. 1 (January/February 1977), pp. 6-15.

p. 6 "Religious bigotry is abroad again in the land. . . . It does not satisfy them that biblical creationism receives equal time with other religious accounts of origins in courses in comparative theology. They demand that creationism be presented as a 'scientific' alternative to evolution in science textbooks that deal with the origin and subsequent development of life before such textbooks can be approved for use in the public schools."

p. 7 "Although the creationists may be irrational, they are not to be dismissed as a lunatic fringe that can best be treated by being ignored. In California . . . they have proven themselves to be skillful tacticians, good organizers and uncompromising adversaries."

p. 7 "And anyone who has studied their benign manner in public debate, their tortured logic and their often scurrilous expression in books and tracts for the faithful, has little difficulty in visualizing creationist polemicists, given the opportunity, in the role of Pius V himself."

Fortas, Justice Abe, (comment in connection with ruling striking down Arkansas anti-evolution law).

"Government in our democracy . . . state and federal, must be neutral in matters of religious theory. . . . It may not aid, foster, or promote one religious theory as against another."

Frazier, Kendrick, "Competency and Controversy: Issues and Ethics on the University/Pseudoscience Battlefield," *Skeptical Inquirer*, vol. 8 (Fall 1983), pp. 2-5.

p. 2 "Every professor should have the right to fail any student in his class, no matter what the grade record indicates, [and should even have the right of] retracting grades and possibly even degrees if such gross misunderstandings are publicly espoused after passing the course or after being graduating."

Gallup Poll, "44% Believe God Created Mankind 10,000 Years Ago," *San Diego Union Tribune*, August 30, 1982, p. A-12, *New York Times Service.*

p. A12 "The American public is almost entirely divided between those who believe that God created man in his present form at one time in the last 10,000 years and those who believe in evolution or an evolutionary process involving God."

p. A12   "Of the participants in the poll, 44 percent, nearly a quarter of whom were college graduates, said they accepted the statement that 'God created man pretty much in his present form at one time within the last 10,000 years.'"

p. A12   "Nine percent agreed with the statement: 'Man has developed over millions of years from less advanced forms of life. God had no part in this process.' Thirty-eight percent said they agreed with the suggestion that 'man has developed over millions of years from less-advanced forms of life, but God guided this process, including man's creation.' Nine percent of those interviewed simply said they did not know."

Gould, Stephen Jay, "The Verdict on Creationism," *New York Times Sunday Magazine*, July 19, 1987, pp. 32, 34.

p. 32   "H. L. Mencken, who attended the Scopes 'Monkey Trial' in 1925, wrote of William Jennings Bryan, counsel for the supporters of Tennessee's anti-evolution law: 'Once he had one leg in the White House and the nation trembled under his roars. Now he is a tinpot pope in the Coca-Cola belt and a brother to the forlorn pastors who belabor half-wits in galvanized iron tabernacles behind the railroad yards.

                "Americans, like people of all cultures, I suppose have been deluged throughout history with our share of Philistines and Yahoos. We tend, as Mencken did, to treat the fundamentalist anti-evolution movement as a primary example of Know-Nothingism, an aberrant phenomenon meriting only our ridicule. But it would be a bad mistake to banish these important chapters of American history to the sidelines of humor."

Gould, Stephen Jay, "The First Unmasking of Nature," *Natural History*, vol. 102 (April 1993), pp. 14-21.

p. 19   "Since creationist-bashing is a noble and necessary pursuit these days, readers may wonder why I am praising such an invocation of God's power to create immutable entities all at once—especially since Linnaeus substituted this idea for earlier notions of looser definition and mutability. But, as I argued above, the history of science progresses in such a manner—from theory to theory along a complex surface with a slant toward greater empirical adequacy, not along a straight and narrow path, pushed by a gathering snowball of factual accumulation. The conceptual change may be enormous, but Darwin's substitution of natural selection in steps, for God all at once, did not require any major overhaul in practice. Species are real whether created by God or constructed by natural selection."

Gould, Stephen Jay, *Dinosaur in a Haystack* (New York: Harmony Books, 1995), 480 pp.

p. 327   "Humans are not the end result of predictable evolutionary progress, but rather a fortuitous cosmic afterthought, a tiny little twig on the enormously arborescent bush of life, which, if replanted from seed, would almost surely not grow this twig again, or perhaps any twig with any property that we would care to call consciousness."

p. 332   "The course of evolution is only the summation of fortuitous contingencies, not a pathway with predictable directions."

p. 423   "In later books, Linnaeus argued that new species could form by hybridization between pairs from the original creation. He even toyed with the idea that God may have created only a common source for each genus, or even for each order, and then allowed subsequent species to form as hybrids."

p. 47   "It would not be an exaggeration to say that the Darwinian revolution directly triggered this influential nineteenth-century conceptualization of Western history as a war between two taxonomic categories labeled science and religion."

Gould, Stephen Jay, "Nonoverlapping Magisteria," *Natural History*, vol. 106 (March 1997), pp. 16-22, 60-62.

p. 60   "John Paul states—and I can only say amen, and thanks for noticing—that the half century between Pius's surveying the ruins of World War II and his own pontificate heralding the dawn of a new millennium has witnessed such a growth of data, and such a refinement of theory, that evolution can no longer be doubted by people of good will:

p. 61   "In conclusion, Pius had grudgingly admitted evolution as a legitimate hypothesis that he regarded as only tentatively supported and potentially (as I suspect he hoped) untrue. John Paul, nearly fifty years later, reaffirms the legitimacy of evolution under the NOMA principle—no news here—but then adds that additional data and theory have placed the factuality of evolution beyond reasonable doubt. Sincere Christians must now accept evolution not merely as a plausible possibility but also as an effectively proven fact."

p. 62   "I dedicate this essay to his memory. Carl [Sagan] also shared my personal suspicion about the nonexistence of souls—but I cannot think of a better reason for hoping we are wrong than the prospect of spending eternity roaming the cosmos in friendship and conversation with this wonderful soul."

Gurin, Joel, "The Creationist Revival," *The Sciences* (New York Academy of Science, vol. 23 (April 1981), pp. 16-19, 34.

p. 34   "The creationists have portrayed Darwinism as a cornerstone of 'secular humanism,' a term they use to describe the belief that man, not God is the source of right and wrong. They blame humanist teaching for all sorts of modern ills—from juvenile delinquency to the high rate of abortions—and want to replace it with the teaching of Christian morality. . . .

"As the creationists' goals become clear, many scientists, realizing that they have been secular humanists all along, are beginning to marshal their forces. . . . Evolutionists are beginning to realize that, for the first time in half a century, they may have to defend themselves in court."

Hager, Dorsey, "Fifty years of Progress in Geology," *Geotimes*, vol. 1 (August 1957), pp. 6-13.

pp. 12-13   "The most important responsibilities of the geologists involve the effect of their findings on the mental and spiritual lives of mankind. Early geologists fought to free people from the myths of Biblical creation. Many millions still live in mental bondage controlled by ignorant ranters who accept the Bible as the last word in science, and accept Archbishop Ussher's claim that the earth was created 4004 B.C. Attempts to reconcile Genesis with geology lead to numerous contradictions. . . . Also the theory of evolution greatly affects modern thinking. Man's rise from simple life forms even today causes much controversy among 'fundamentalists' who cling to a literal belief in the Bible."

Holland, Earle, "Creation 'Science': A Survey of Student Attitudes," *Ohio State University Quest*, vol. 7 (Spring 1985).

p. 16   "The attitudes of college students—even those taking basic science courses— differ from those of the general public when it comes to the controversy over evolution versus creation science.

               "This was one of the conclusions surprising researchers who conducted a year-long survey of nearly 2,400 students at Ohio State University."

p. 16   "1. 'Do you believe in Darwin's theory of evolution?' 63% Yes.

               "2. 'If Darwin's theory of evolution is taught in public schools, should other views (including the divine origin of life through special creation) be taught too?' 80% Yes."

Johnston, George Sim, "The Genesis Controversy," *Crisis* (May 1989), pp. 12-18.

p. 17   "In other words, it's natural selection or a Creator. There is no middle ground. This is why prominent Darwinists like G. G. Simpson and Stephen Jay Gould, who are not secretive about their hostility to religion, cling so vehemently to natural selection. To do otherwise would be to admit the probability that there is design in nature—and hence a Designer."

Lazen, Alvin G., "Summary Report: Meeting on Creationism-Evolutionism," *National Academy of Sciences* (October 19, 1981), 6 pp. Lazen is Executive Director of the Assembly of Life Sciences, NAS.

p. 2   ". . . a communications network called Committees of Correspondence . . . to use political action at the local level."

p. 3   "It was generally agreed that debates were to be avoided. . . . However, it was recognized that debate might be unavoidable . . . and that it was necessary to find means to identify appropriate debaters and to better prepare them for their task.

               "It was suggested by several persons that an 'Institute for Evolution Research' was needed to counter the San Diego-based Institute for Creation Research."

               [Delegates to Meeting: 26]

               [Organizations Represented: (1) National Science Teachers Association; (2) American Humanist Association; (3) American Museum of National History; (4) American Institute of Biological Sciences; (5) State University of New York; (6) University of Massachusetts; (7) American Society of Biological Chemists; (8) University of California, Berkeley; (9) Smithsonian Institution; (10) Federation of American Societies for Experimental Biology; (11) American Anthropological Association; (12) Biological Sciences Curriculum Study; (13) University of California, Riverside; (14) National Association of Biology

Teachers; (15) American Association for the Advancement of Science; (16) University of Kentucky; (17) National Academy of Sciences; (18) National Cancer Institute; (19) American Geological Institute.]

Lewis, C. S., Private letter to B. Acworth (1951), father of Richard Acworth, of the Creation Science Movement, in files of latter, as reported by Ronald Numbers in *The Creationists* (New York: Adolph Knopf Co., 1992), 458 pp.

> "I wish I were younger. . . . What inclines me now to think you may be right in regarding [evolution] as *the* central and radical lie in the whole web of falsehood that now governs our lives is not so much your arguments against it as the fanatical and twisted attitudes of its defenders."

Marsden, George M., "Creation versus Evolution: No Middle Way," *Nature*, vol. 305 (October 13, 1983), pp. 571-574. Marsden was in the Department of History, Calvin College.

p. 572   "Such folk epistemology is close to that which works best for engineers, straightforward, consistent, factual, with no nonsense. In fact, there are an unusual number of engineers in the creation science movement.

"Most contemporary scientists have difficulty understanding the appeal of alleged scientific arguments of creation science to popular common sense. Evolution may have scientific experts on its side, but it strains popular common sense. It is simply difficult to believe that the amazing order of life on Earth arose spontaneously out of the original disorder of the Universe."

p. 573   "The American folk epistemology, then, is by no means anti-scientific in principle. Rather it is based on a naive realism plus popular mythology concerning proper scientific procedure and verification. These procedures are essentially Baconian, favouring simple empirical evidence."

p. 574   "In any case, creation scientists are correct in perceiving that in modern culture 'evolution' often involves far more than biology. The basic ideologies of the civilization, including its entire moral structure, are at issue. Evolution is sometimes the key mythological element in a philosophy that functions as a virtual religion. . . . Dogmatic proponents of evolutionary anti-supernaturalistic mythologies have been inviting responses in kind."

Mattill, A. J., Jr., "Three Cheers for the Creationists," *Free Inquiry*, vol. 2 (Spring 1982), pp. 17-18.

p. 17   "Cheer Number One goes to the creationists for serving rational religion by demonstrating beautifully that we must take the creation stories of Genesis at face value. . . . Creationists list twenty or more contradictions that arise between science and Scripture if the days are taken as geological eras instead of ordinary days."

p. 17   "Many Christians have taken the dishonest way of lengthening the days into millions of years, but the creationists make it clear that such an approach is nothing but a makeshift that is unacceptable biblically and scientifically."

p. 17   "And the creationists have also shown irrefutably that those liberal and neo-orthodox Christians who regard the creation stories as myths or allegories are undermining the rest of Scripture, for if there was no Adam, there was no fall;

and if there was no fall there was no hell; and if there was no hell, there was no need of Jesus as Second Adam and Incarnate Savior, crucified and risen. As a result, the whole biblical system of salvation collapses."

p. 17   "Evolution thus becomes the most potent weapon for destroying the Christian faith."

p. 18   "Creationists deserve Cheer Number Two for serving rational religion by effectively eliminating the idea of 'theistic evolution.' . . . Creationists rightly insist that evolution is inconsistent with a God of love."

p. 18   "Three cheers then, for the creationists, for they have cleared the air of all dodges, escapes, and evasions made by Christians who adopt nonliteral interpretations of Genesis and who hold that evolution is God's method of creation."

McKown, Delos B., "Close Encounters of an Ominous Kind: Science and Religion in Contemporary America," *The Humanist*, vol. 39 (January/February 1979), pp. 4-7. Dr. McKown was Head of the Philosophy Department, Auburn University.

p. 4   "But modern, scientific, progressive America witnesses, at this very moment, a resurgence of biblical literalism, fundamentalism and evangelicalism that almost defies belief. . . . But of all the recent manifestations of old-time religion, I can think of none more intellectually impertinent or socially and politically ominous than that of the Creation Research Society and its Institute of Creation Research, devoted to destroying the ideas of cosmic and organic evolution. The mischief that this organization is prepared to do to the life and earth sciences, particularly in elementary and secondary schools, staggers the scientific imagination."

Milne, David H., "How to Debate with Creationists—and 'Win,'" *American Biology Teacher*, vol. 43 (May 1981), pp. 235-245.

p. 239   "A second facet of my presentation . . . consisted of a series of 'one-liners' designed to show the audience the diversity of evidence that supports evolution and, not incidentally, to present my opponent with a barrage of examples he could not possibly hope to refute within the allotted time."

p. 244   "Finally, if you do not believe in God's existence, be tactful about it."

p. 244   "The odds are heavily in favor of the creationists. . . ."

p. 245   "My audience was profoundly interested in the debate and more concerned and attentive throughout the entire three hours than any 50-minute class in all of my 12 years of teaching experience."

Moore, John A., "Countering the Creationists," Paper at *Ad Hoc* Committee on Creationism, NAS (October 19, 1981), 6 pp.

p. 1   "The climate of the times suggests that the problem will be with us for a very long time, . . ."

p. 2   ". . . local responses might become more effective if there is a national coalition to support the local efforts. Such a national consortium might have these main functions:

"(1) network to assemble information; (2) keep scientific and educational establishments informed; (3) assemble statements . . . classroom materials; (4) maintain list of individuals . . ; (5) support travel, etc. . . ; (6) cooperation of church groups—arts and letters, social scientists; (7) collect funds . . ; (8) short courses . . ; (9) reform scientific education . . ; (10) contact lawmakers . . ; (11) speak with force—and authority."

p. 5   "Seek to have every American scientist and science teacher contribute about $10 annually for the work of the consortium."

p. 6   "If we do not resolve our problems with the creationists, we have only ourselves to blame. Let's remember, the greatest resource of all is available to us—the educational system of the nation."

National Academy of Sciences Resolution, "An Affirmation of Freedom and Inquiry and Expression" (April 1976).

"That the search for knowledge and understanding of the physical universe and of the living things that inhabit it should be conducted under conditions of intellectual freedom, without religious, political or ideological restrictions. . . . that freedom of inquiry and dissemination of ideas require that those so engaged be free to search where their inquiry leads . . . without political censorship and without fear of retribution in consequence of unpopularity of their conclusions. Those who challenge existing theories must be protected from retaliatory reactions."

Patterson, John, "Do Scientists and Educators Discriminate Unfairly against Creationists?" *Journal of the National Center for Science Education* (Fall 1984), pp. 19-20.

p. 19   "Creationists often complain that their theories and their colleagues are discriminated against by educators. . . . As a matter of fact, creationism should be discriminated against. . . . No advocate of such propaganda should be trusted to teach science classes or administer science programs anywhere or under any circumstances. Moreover, if any are now doing so, they should be dismissed. . . . I am glad this kind of discrimination is finally catching on, and I hope the practice becomes much more vigorous and widespread in the future."

Pun, Pattle P. T., "A Theory of Progressive Creationism," *Journal of the American Scientific Affiliation*, vol. 39 (March 1987), pp. 9-19. Dr. Pun is Professor of Biology, Wheaton College.

p. 14   "It is apparent that the most straightforward understanding of the Genesis record, without regard to all of the hermeneutical considerations suggested by science, is that God created heaven and earth in six solar days, that man was created in the sixth day, that death and chaos entered the world after the Fall of Adam and Eve, that all of the fossils were the result of the catastrophic universal deluge which spared only Noah's family and the animals therewith."

p. 14   "However, the Recent Creationist position has two serious flaws. First, it has denied and belittled the vast amount of scientific evidence amassed to support the theory of natural selection and the antiquity of the earth. Secondly, much Creationist writing has 'deistic' implications. Although Creationists would probably not admit that their position could suggest that the Creator only intervenes in the creation occasionally to perform creative acts and miracles, the stipulation that the varieties we see today in the biological world were present in the initial Creation implies that the Creator is no longer involved in His creation in a dynamic way."

p. 17   "Progressive Creationism can be further described briefly, as follows:

"1) It posits that God is involved in His creation in a dynamic way by shaping the variation of the biological world through mechanisms such as natural selection, thus avoiding the deistic mentality of the God-of-the-Gaps theory.

"2) It stresses the historicity of Adam and Eve and gives the creation of Adam and Eve special significance, since it was an extraordinary act of God that is not explainable by known natural causes.

"3) It focuses on the unity of God's revelation in nature as well as in Scripture and tries to maintain the historical and theological integrity of the creation account."

p. 17   "Although carnivorousness was not mentioned before the Fall, this does not eliminate the possibility of animal death. The fossil record is replete with carnivores who existed long before the appearance of man. God used natural selection to propagate those species most adapted to survive, thereby ensuring that the resources in His creation not suffer from depletion and that the population of the creatures remain under control. He has allowed natural selection to maintain a finely tuned ecological balance."

Ramsey, Pamela, Questionnaire from 125 teachers in 31 states—56 (45%) in Christian schools, 69 (55%) in public schools (Cornell University, 1983).

"96% have read some creationist literature

16% have attended an ICR seminar

50% attended a creationist presentation

93% Christian teachers, 29% public teachers use two-model approach

92% Christian teachers, 18% public teachers, believe Bible takes precedence over science interpretation.

98% Christian teachers, 18% public teachers believe in special creation of man.

74% Christian teachers, 17% public teachers believe evolution is atheistic."

Reagan, Ronald, Address at National Prayer Breakfast (1982).

"I've always believed that we were, each of us, put here for a reason. That there is a plan, somehow—a divine plan for all of us. I know now that whatever days are left of me belong to Him.

"I also believe this blessed land was set apart in a very special way. A country created by men and women who came here not in search of gold, but in search of God. They would be free people, living under the law with faith in their Maker and their future. Sometimes, it seems we've strayed from that noble beginning, from our conviction that standards of right and wrong do exist and must be lived up to. God, the source of our knowledge, has been expelled from the classroom. He gives us His greatest blessing: life—and yet many would condone the taking of innocent life. We expect Him to protect us in a crisis, but turn away from Him too often in our day-to-day living. And I wonder if He isn't waiting for us to wake up."

Scott, Eugenie C., "Monkey Business," *The Sciences* (January/February 1996), pp. 20-25. Scott is Executive Director of the National Center for Science Education, Berkeley, California, and received his Ph.D. in Anthropology, Missouri University, 1974. Past previous position, Assistant Professor, University of Colorado at Boulder, 1984-86.

p. 20   "What makes well-meaning people fight so hard to keep children from learning a basic scientific principle? From the beginning of the American antievolution movement, the driving force has been the same: a struggle for souls. Students who learn evolution, the creationists reason, will come to doubt the existence of God. Without the moral rudder that religion provides, they will become bad people doing bad things. Evolution is thus evil and a cause of evil. As Henry M. Morris, the most influential twentieth-century creationist, wrote in 1963, 'Evolution is at the foundation of communism, Fascism, Freudianism, social Darwinism, behaviorism, Kinseyism, materialism, atheism, and, in the religious world, modernism and Neo-orthodoxy.'"

p. 25   "**Avoid Debates**. If your local campus Christian fellowship asks you to 'defend evolution,' please decline. Public debates rarely change many minds; creationists stage them mainly in the hope of drawing large sympathetic audiences. Have you ever watched the Harlem Globetrotters play the Washington Federals? The Federals get off some good shots, but who remembers them? The purpose of the game is to see the Globetrotters beat the other team.

"And you probably will get beaten."

van der Lingen, Gerrit J., "Creationism," Letter-to-the-Editor, *Geotimes*, vol. 29 (October 1984), p. 4. van der Lingen is with the New Zealand Geological Survey, University of Canterbury, Christchurch.

p. 4   "It seems to be common in the defense against creationism to point out that many scientists who accept evolution are also devoutly religious. No doubt this is a useful strategy, to give evolution respectability in the eyes of non-scientists. But. . . . Trying to reconcile evolution and religion leads to doublethink. Orwell defined doublethink as 'the power of holding two contradictory beliefs in one's mind simultaneously, and accepting both of them.'"

p. 4   "Relevant also in this context is the 1981 resolution of the N.A.S. Council, mentioned in the preface of their brochure, stating that 'Religion and science are separate and mutually exclusive realms of human thought whose presentation in the same context leads to misunderstanding of both scientific and religious belief.' A very courageous resolution! However, the corollary of it is that religious scientists have to entertain 'mutually exclusive realms of human thought,' that is, to practice doublethink.

"I generally put it to my religious colleagues more bluntly: 'You can't have your cake and eat it.'"

Weinberg, Stan, "Committees Active Against Creationism," *Transactions, American Geophysical Union*, vol. 64 (August 23, 1983), p. 514. Weinberg is President, National Committees of Correspondence.

> "The Committees of Correspondence (C/C's), headquartered in Iowa, are a continent-wide communications network working at grassroots levels to defend the teaching of evolution from such creationist incursions. Founded in December 1980, the C/C's now encompass 55 committees in 48 states and 4 Canadian provinces.

> "Whether you join a committee or not, you may want to subscribe to *Memo to C/C's*, the newsletter of the C/C national office. the *Memo* comes out five to nine times a year with current news items from both sides of the creation/evolution controversy; it costs $5 per year for C/C members, $8 for non-members, payable to Committees of Correspondence, . . . 156 East Alta Vista, Ottumwa, Iowa, 52501."

Yao, Richard, and James Luce, Fund raising letter for "Fundamentalists Anonymous" (February 1987), 6 pp.

p. 1

> "The fundamentalist political agenda is extremely hazardous to American democracy. Right-wing Christian fundamentalists hope to convert our democracy into a Theocracy—an intolerant, authoritarian state in which our rulers will be true 'Christians' (i.e., fundamentalists) claiming a divine mandate.

> "If their plan should ever become a reality, it will truly be hell on earth for every self-respecting man, woman and child in the nation who cherishes individual freedom, civil rights and a pluralistic society."

B. The Agenda of Atheism and Humanism

Not all evolutionists are atheists or humanists, of course. Despite the fact that theistic evolution is an oxymoron, there are many evolutionists who believe that evolution was God's method of creation. However, all atheists and humanists are evolutionists, and evolution is essentially an atheistic concept, since it purports to explain the origin of all things without God.

Humanism professes to be more idealistic than raw atheism, but the agenda of both is to dethrone God (especially as revealed in the Bible and taught by Christians) and to enthrone man in His place, as the pinnacle of the assumed evolutionary process.

American Humanist Association, "Humanist Manifesto I," *The New Humanist*, vol. 6 (May/June 1933).

> "Humanism is a philosophical, religious and moral point of view as old as human civilization itself. It has its roots in classical China, Greece, and Rome; it is expressed in the Renaissance and the enlightenment, in the scientific revolution, and in the twentieth century. [Preface by Paul Kurtz to AHA republication of Humanist Manifestos I and II.]

> "We therefore affirm the following:

>> "*First*: Religious humanists regard the universe as self-existing and not created.

>> "*Second*: Humanism believes that man is a part of nature and that he has emerged as the result of a continuous process.

"*Third*: Holding an organic view of life, humanists find that the traditional dualism of mind and body must be rejected.

"*Fourth*: . . . *Fifth*: Humanism asserts that the nature of the universe makes unacceptable any supernatural or cosmic guarantees of human values. . . . *Tenth*: It follows that there will be no uniquely religious emotions and attitudes of the kind hitherto associated with belief in the supernatural."

American Humanist Association, "Humanist Manifesto II," *The Humanist*, vol. 33 (September/October 1973), pp. 4-9.

p. 4   "It is forty years since Humanist Manifesto I (1933) appeared. . . .

"As in 1933, humanists still believe that traditional theism, especially faith in the prayer-hearing God, assumed to love and care for persons, to hear and understand their prayers, and to be able to do something about them, is an unproved and outmoded faith."

p. 5   "As non-theists, we begin with humans, not God, nature not deity."

p. 6   "But we discover no divine purpose or providence for the human species. While there is much that we do not know, humans are responsible for what we are or will become. No deity will save us; we must save ourselves. . . .

"Promises of immortal salvation or fear of eternal damnation are both illusory and harmful."

American Humanist Association, quoted in American Humanist Association brochure.

"Humanism is the belief that man shapes his own destiny. It is a constructive philosophy, a non-theistic religion, a way of life.

"The American Humanist Association is a non-profit, tax-exempt organization, incorporated in the early 1940's in Illinois for educational and religious purposes.

"Humanist counsellors to solemnize weddings, and conduct memorial services and to assist in individual value 'counselling.'

"<u>Prominent Humanists</u>:

Julian Huxley	Eustice Hayden	Brock Chisholm
H. J. Muller	Mary Marain	Carl Rogers
Linus Pauling	Margaret Sanger	Hudson Hoagland
Erich Fromm	Richard McCarthy	A. H. Maslow
Benjamin Spock	Buckminster Fuller	John Dewey, etc."

Asimov, Isaac, Interview by Paul Kurtz: "An Interview with Isaac Asimov on Science and the Bible," *Free Inquiry*, vol. 2 (Spring 1982), pp. 6-10.

p. 9   "I am an atheist, out and out. It took me a long time to say it. I've been an atheist for years and years, but somehow I felt it was intellectually unrespectable to say one was an atheist, because it assumed knowledge that one didn't have. Somehow it was better to say one was a humanist or an agnostic. I finally decided that I'm a creature of emotion as well as of reason. Emotionally I am an atheist. I don't have the evidence to prove that God doesn't exist, but I so strongly suspect he doesn't that I don't want to waste my time."

p. 10   "Furthermore, I can't help but believe that eternal happiness would eventually be boring. I cannot grasp the notion of eternal anything. My own way of thinking is that after death there is nothingness. Nothingness is the only thing that I think is worth accepting."

Briggs, Kenneth A., "Secular Humanists Attack a Rise in Fundamentalism," *New York Times*, October 15, 1980, p. A18.

p. A18   "A group of 61 prominent scholars and writers have attacked the recent rise in Christian fundamentalism by issuing a declaration that denounces absolutist morality and calls for an emphasis on science and reason rather than religion as a means of solving human problems."

p. A18   "Called 'A Secular Humanist Declaration,' the statement warns that 'the reappearance of dogmatic authoritarian religions' threatens intellectual freedom, human rights and scientific progress."

p. A18   "Dr. Paul Kurtz, a member of the faculty at the State University of New York at Buffalo, drafted the basic document and gathered the signatures. The declaration appears in the first issue of a secular humanist magazine, *Free Inquiry*, edited by Dr. Kurtz."

p. A18   "Reflecting elements of two earlier humanist manifestos, in 1933 and 1973, the declaration depicts supernatural religion and divine revelation as enemies of the rational process that leads to progress."

          [*Signers*: Isaac Asimov, Sir Francis Crick, Albert Ellis (Executive Director, Institute for Rational-Emotive Therapy), B. F. Skinner, Sidney Hook, Kai Nielsen, Dora Russell (widow of Bertrand), Joseph Fletcher, Ernest Nagel (Professor of Philosophy, Columbia), Sir A. J. Ayer (Professor of Philosophy, Oxford), Sir Raymond Firth (Professor of Anthropology, University of London), Milovan Djilas (former vice-president, Yugoslavia), Baroness Barbara Wootton (Deputy Speaker, British House of Lords), etc.]

Buchanan, Patrick J., "The President's Biased Opposition—The Media," *Chicago Tribune-New York News Syndicate*, December 30, 1981.

          "The dilemma's expanding dimensions are newly detailed by S. Robert Lichter and Stanley Rothman in *Public Opinion* magazine. The authors spent an hour with each of 240 members of the 'media elite'—reporters, editors, columnists, bureau chiefs, news executives, T.V. correspondents, anchormen, producers, film editors. . . . Ninety-five percent are white, four of five are male. Almost all have college degrees, 55 percent attended graduate school. By 1978, 78 percent had crossed the $30,000 mark in income; one in three had a salary above $50,000. . . . Not once in four national elections did the GOP win the support of even 20 percent. . . . In the landslide of 1972, when three-fourths of white America voted for Nixon, this dominantly white male institution went 81-19 for George McGovern.

"Nowhere does the media seem more estranged from Main Street, however, than in religious belief and practice. Only 8 percent regularly attend church or synagogue; 86 percent answered 'seldom or never.' Asked their religious affiliation, half replied: None.

"Ninety percent of the media elite endorse the proposition that women have a right to an abortion. . . . Only 9 percent are convinced that homosexuality is morally wrong; 85 percent support the right of homosexuals to teach in public schools. Fifty-four percent see nothing wrong with adultery."

Chambers, Bette, "Isaac Asimov: A One-Man Renaissance," *The Humanist*, vol. 53 (March/April 1993), pp. 6-8.

p. 6   "In what may be his last book, *Asimov Laughs Again*, he answers a rhetorical question on why, as an atheist, he so enjoys telling jokes about God and religion:

"'You must not get me wrong. I am the president of the American Humanist Association, a thoroughgoing materialist and rationalist organization. If anyone asks me I will admit to being an atheist. However, in the world of jokedom, God, Satan, angels, demons, Adam and Eve, and all the paraphernalia of mythology exist, and I accept them gladly. Anything for a laugh.'

"Asimov became president of the AHA in the spring of 1985, following his election to its board of directors late in 1984."

Charles, Prince of Wales, Foreword to *Save the Earth*, ed. Jonathan Porritt (London: Kindersly Ltd., 1991), 208 pp.

p. vi   "One of the underlying factors [why Western man has] dominate[d] nature, rather than lived in harmony with it, . . . [can be] found in Genesis 1 where it records that: 'God said unto man, be fruitful and multiply, and replenish the Earth and *subdue it: and have dominion over the fish of the sea and over the fowl of the air and over every living thing that moveth upon the earth.*' [This passage] has provided Western man, accompanied by his Judaeo-Christian heritage, with an overbearing and domineering attitude towards God's creation. [This, he says, has contributed] to a feeling that the world is somehow entirely man's to dispose of—as income, rather than a capital asset which needs husbanding. By contrast, the Koran specifically mentions the fact that the natural world is loaned from God."

Dunphy, John J., "A Religion for a New Age," *The Humanist*, vol. 43 (January/February 1983), pp. 23-26.

p. 26   "I am convinced that the battle for humankind's future must be waged and won in the public school classroom by teachers who correctly perceive their role as the proselytizers of a new faith: a religion of humanity that recognizes and respects the spark of what theologians call divinity in every human being. These teachers must embody the same selfless dedication as the most rabid fundamentalist preachers, for they will be ministers of another sort, utilizing a classroom instead of a pulpit to convey humanist values in whatever subject they teach, regardless of the educational level—preschool day care or large state university. The classroom must and will become an arena of conflict between the old and the new—the rotting corpse of Christianity, together with all its adjacent evils and misery, and the new faith of humanism, resplendent in its promise of a world in which the never-realized Christian ideal of 'love thy neighbor' will finally be achieved."

Hall, Norman K., and Lucia K. B. Hall, "Is the War between Science and Religion Over?" *The Humanist*, vol. 46 (May/June 1986), pp. 26-32.

p. 26   "Let us be blunt. While it may appear open-minded, modest, and comforting to many, this conciliatory view is nonsense. Science and religion are dramatically opposed at their deepest philosophical levels. And, because the two worldviews make claims to the same intellectual territory—that of the origin of the universe and humankind's relationship to it—conflict is inevitable."

p. 27   "As evolution is the unifying theory for biology, so naturalism is the unifying theory for all of science."

Himmelfarb, Gertrude, "Revolution in the Library," reprinted from Spring 1997 edition of *The American Scholar*, *Key Reporter*, vol. 62 (Spring 1997), pp. 1-5. Dr. Himmelfarb is Professor Emeritus of History at the Graduate School of the City University of New York.

p. 4   "For the postmodernist, there is no truth, no knowledge, no objectivity, no reason, and ultimately, no reality. Nothing is fixed, nothing is permanent, nothing is transcendent. Everything is in a state of total relativity, and perennial flux. There is no correspondence between language and reality; indeed, there is no 'essential' reality. What appears to be real is illusory, deceptive, problematic, indeterminate. What appears to be true is nothing more than what the power structure, the 'hegemonic' authority in society, deems to be true.

               "To those of you who have been happily spared this latest intellectual fashion, it may seem bizarre and improbable. I can only assure you that it is all too prevalent in all fields of the humanities."

p. 4   "More important is the fact that even those who do not think of themselves as postmodernists often share the extreme relativism and subjectivism that now pervade the humanities as a whole. In the leading professional journals today, the words *truth, objectivity, reason* and *reality* generally appear with quotation marks around them, suggesting how specious these concepts are."

Hoagland, Hudson, "Science and the New Humanism," *Science*, vol. 143 (January 10, 1964), pp. 111-114. Hoagland was affiliated with the Worcester Foundation for Experimental Biology, Shrewsbury, Mass., and President of the American Academy of Arts and Sciences. This article is adapted from the fourth George Sarton Memorial meeting of the AAAS.

p. 111   "Man's unique characteristic among animals is his ability to direct and control his own evolution, and science is his most powerful tool for doing this. We are a product of two kinds of evolution, biological and cultural. We are here as a result of the same processes of natural selection that have produced all the other plants and animals.

"A second kind of evolution is psychosocial or cultural evolution. This is unique to man. Its history is very recent; it started roughly a million years ago with our hominid tool-making ancestors."

p. 113   "But man himself and his behavior are an emergent product of purely fortuitous mutations and evolution by natural selection acting upon them. Non-purposive natural selection has produced purposive human behavior, which in turn has produced purposive behavior of the computers."

Humanist Association of San Diego, "Who or What is a Humanist?" *San Diego Humanist* (April 1985), p. 7.

"Humanist Association of San Diego (HASD) desires to make contact with kindred spirits. Please look over the statements below. If you check YES to most of them, then we encourage you to get in touch with us.

"1. No deity will save us; we must save ourselves.
"2. Birth control, abortion and divorce should be available to all who desire and need it.
"3. Individuals should be free to use the full range of civil liberties.
"4. Persons should have sexual freedom in so far as they do not harm themselves or others.
"5. Human beings are the source of meaning and value.
"6. Authority must always be tested by our own reasonings and experiences.
"7. The preciousness and dignity of the individual person is a prime value.
"8. Planning and organization are indispensable to build a better world.
"9. Nature may be broader and deeper than we know; however, we do not need to call on the supernatural to explain it.
"10. A plan for dying while still healthy is the quintessence of successful self-deliverance from a terminal illness.
"11. Moral equity must be achieved by eliminating discrimination based on race, religion, sex, age, or national origin.
"12. Religions are immoral that place revelation, God, ritual, or creed above human development.
"13. There is no scientifically validated evidence demonstrating life after death."

Huxley, Julian, "The Coming New Religion of Humanism," *The Humanist*, vol. 22 (January/February 1962).

"The beliefs of this religion of evolutionary humanism are not based on revelation in the supernatural sense, but on the revelations that science and learning have given us about man and the universe. A humanist believes with full assurance that man is not alien to nature, but a part of nature, albeit a unique one. . . .His true destiny is to guide the future course of evolution on earth towards greater fulfillment, so as to realize more and higher potentialities. . . . A humanist religion will have the task of redefining the categories of good and evil in terms of fulfillment and of desirable or undesirable realizations of potentiality, and setting up new targets for its morality to aim at. . . . Humanism also differs from all supernaturalist religions in centering its long-term aims not on the next world but on this. . . . The humanist goal must therefore be . . . the Fulfillment Society."

Huxley, Julian, "A New World Vision," *The Humanist*, vol. 39 (March/April 1979), pp. 34-40 (Original framework proposed for UNESCO, by its first Director-General).

p. 35   "Accordingly, [UNESCO's] outlook must, it seems, be based on some form of humanism."

p. 35   "Finally it must be an evolutionary humanism as opposed to a static or ideal humanism. It is essential for UNESCO to adopt an evolutionary approach."

p. 35   "Thus the general philosophy of UNESCO should, it seems, be a scientific world humanism, global in extent and evolutionary in background."

p. 36   "Thus the struggle for existence that underlies natural selection is increasingly replaced by conscious selection, a struggle between ideas and values in consciousness.

             "Through these new agencies, the possible rate of evolution is now once more enormously speeded up."

p. 36   "From the evolutionary point of view, the destiny of man may be summed up very simply: it is to realize the maximum progress in the minimum time."

p. 37   "The analysis of evolutionary progress gives us certain criteria for judging the rightness or wrongness of our aims or activities and the desirability, or otherwise, of the tendencies of which UNESCO must take account."

p. 38   "The unifying of traditions into a single common pool of experience, awareness, and purpose is the necessary prerequisite for further major progress in human evolution. Accordingly, although political unification in some sort of world government will be required for the definitive attainment of this stage, unification in the things of the mind is not only necessary also, but it can pave the way for other types of unification."

Huxley, Julian, quoted in American Humanist Association brochure.

             "I use the word 'Humanist' to mean someone who believes that man is just as much a natural phenomenon as an animal or plant; that his body, mind and soul were not supernaturally created but are products of evolution, and that he is not under the control or guidance of any supernatural being or beings, but has to rely on himself and his own powers."

Lamont, Corliss, "Humanism and Civil Liberties," *The Humanist*, vol. 51 (January/February 1991), pp. 5-8. Lamont is former Professor of Philosophy, Columbia University. He was also named "Humanist of the Year" in 1977.

p. 5   "Human beings are the natural culmination of millions of years of evolution; the body and brain (or personality) are so intimately connected that, when the body dies so does the brain—and the personality dies with it. No educated man or woman can possibly believe in the Christian notion of bodily resurrection. For similar reasons, humanists cannot believe in reincarnation."

Larson, Edward J., and Larry Witham, "Scientists are Still Keeping the Faith," *Nature*, vol. 386 (April 3, 1997), pp. 435-436.

p. 435   "When Americans are asked to define 'God,' a quarter opt for something other than a conventional theistic deity. They see 'God' as higher consciousness (11 per cent), full realization of personal potential (8 per cent), many gods (3 per cent) or everyone as their own god (3 per cent) [Barna, G. *The Index of Leading Spiritual Indicators* (Dallas: Word, 1996)]."

McKown, Delos B., and Clifton B. Perry, "Religion Separation and Accommodation," *National Forum: Phi Kappa Phi Journal*, vol. 68 (Winter 1988), pp. 2-7. McKown and Perry are Professors of Philosophy, Auburn University.

p. 6   "Johnny learns many remarkable doctrines at his full-gospel school, including the recent creation of the earth and the impossibility of organic evolution due to God's curse (Genesis 3:17b), from which entropy has resulted."

p. 6   "The ideas and subjects Johnny is led to avoid are as noteworthy as the doctrines he learns. Since he learns that the fear of the Lord is the beginning of wisdom (Job 28:28; Prov. 1:7) and that he should stultify his intellect that he may truly be wise (I Cor. 1:20; 3:18-20), he does not miss at the time the critical thinking that he might have been taught."

p. 6   "How much income will he, unnecessarily, forfeit because of his educational retardation, and what of the continuing psychological trauma inflicted on him due to having been sold a bill of goods in his early schooling? How badly has his career already been blighted? In light of the foregoing, it now occurs to him that he may have been abused as a child. Has Johnny been abused and, if so, does he enjoy a remedy?

         "It might seem that he has suffered an actionable harm, i.e., one for which the law will offer a remedy."

p. 7   "Put differently, should children have a positive right to be taught the truth and nothing but the truth (in appropriate depth, of course) as it can be ascertained at any given time, or should parents have as much leeway as possible in indoctrinating their children as they please? Put in yet a third way, should it now become possible to succeed in court with wrongful education suits when the gravity of what is alleged is tantamount to child abuse?"

Midgley, Mary, *Science as Salvation: A Modern Myth and Its Meaning* (London: Routledge, 1992), 239 pp. (1990 Gifford lectures).

p. 129   "Today, it is the admission, not the denial, of belief in central Christian doctrines that can damage the reputation of an academic in Britain."

Mondale, Lester, "False Gods," *The Humanist*, vol. 44 (January/February 1984), pp. 33-34. Mondale is the brother of Walter Mondale, former vice president.

p. 33   "Humanistically committed, I share—but with one dissent—the prophet Elijah's repugnance of false gods."

p. 33   "Although I sympathize with Elijah's zeal in exposing false gods, I must observe—and herein lies my dissent—that Elijah's Yahweh is also false. In a universe of law and order, any god who reputedly sends down all-consuming fire at the behest of a prophet can't be anything but false."

p. 33   "What holds for the typical godhead Father holds also for the Son. . . . The divine Biblical Christ to whom all appeal is actually many, impossible to pin down as one."

p. 34   "There is always the philosophical possibility that someone, somewhere, might come up with God, the real thing. Meanwhile, it is incumbent on intellectually self-respecting persons to avoid at all cost being duped by any one of the innumerable false gods whom the would-be godly would foist on the nation. In any case, I feel certain that, in holding fast to the standards, values and culture by which we are driven to judge false gods as false, we are vastly closer to the moral character a real Supreme Being would be likely to exemplify were He (?) to overcome the world with an authentic First Coming."

Morain, Lloyd, and Mary Morain, in "How do Humanists Define Their Beliefs?" *The Humanist*, vol. 47 (September/October 1987), back cover. Morain was Editor of *The Humanist*.

        "Humanism does not include the idea of a God and as such is considered a philosophy rather than a religion. In a way, it is an alternative to all religions. However, whether or not one looks to humanism as a religion or as a philosophy to live by or as a way of life is, we believe, largely a matter of personal temperament and preference. Those caught up by its religious aspects know that it provides a vibrant, satisfying faith. Those who think of it as a philosophy find it both reasonable and adequate.

Muller, H. J., "Human Values in Relation to Evolution," *Science*, vol. 127 (March 21, 1958), pp. 625-629.

p. 629   "It has rightly been said that biological evolution is multi-directional and cruel and that the vast majority of lines of descent end in pitiful anticlimaxes."

p. 629   "Through the unprecedented faculty of long-range foresight, jointly serviced and exercised by us, we can, in securing and advancing our position, increasingly avoid the missteps of blind nature, circumvent its cruelties, reform our own natures, and enhance our own values."

p. 629   "The foregoing conclusions represent, I believe, an outgrowth of the thesis of modern humanism, as well as of the study of evolution, that the primary job for man is to promote his own welfare and advancement, both that of his members considered individually and that of the all-inclusive group in due awareness of the world as it is, and on the basis of a naturalistic, scientific ethic."

Müller-Hill, Benno, "Science, Truth and Other Values," *Quarterly Review of Biology*, vol. 68 (September 1993), pp. 399-407. Professor Müller-Hill is at the Institute für Genetik der Universitat zu Köln, Germany.

p. 400   "You have to get older, perhaps as old as I am, to see that self-deception plays an astonishing role in science in spite of all the scientists' worship of truth."

p. 401   "There the temptation to be first with a good experiment was overwhelming, for important discoveries may bring you fame in the media and money from industry."

p. 404   "Some people think that truth and science survive only when truth prevails under all conditions. I think this is a profound misunderstanding."

p. 405   "The German human geneticists were a prominent group of scientists who explicitly paved the way for the murderers to kill their victims during the Third Reich."

p. 406   "I do not know how many of you here and how many scientists elsewhere believe in this new bible written by scientists in four letters (A, G, C, and T). I hope that there are not too many. But I know pretty well that very few scientists read the Old Testament and know the Ten Commandments and the Mosaic Laws. Therefore the question has to be raised as to what can be said to them. I know that to say 'Read the Old Testament' or 'Respect the commandments' will result in laughter. So I have to retreat to my last line of defense and say: Listen carefully to your conscience! It is a voice that sometimes says NO. It never says YES, as Socrates has already remarked."

Nielsen, Kai, "Religiosity and Powerlessness," Part III of "The Resurgence of Fundamentalism," *The Humanist*, vol. 37 (May/June 1977), pp. 46-48. Nielsen is Professor of Philosophy, University of Calgary.

p. 46   "In cultures such as ours, religion is very often an alien form of life to intellectuals. Living, as we do, in a post-Enlightenment era, it is difficult for us to take religion seriously. The very concepts seem fantastic to us."

p. 46   "That people in our age can believe that they have had a personal encounter with God, that they could believe that they have experienced conversion through a 'mystical experience of God,' so that they are born again in the Holy Spirit, is something that attests to human irrationality and a lack of a sense of reality."

p. 47   "Many have come to believe that science and clear rational thought cannot save us and that, indeed, nothing that human beings can collectively do can save us. There is, many think, no rational hope for changing society and, indeed, we would not even know how to change it if we could."

p. 47   "The dominant new religious response is hardly a genuine one, but an ersatz religious response in which religion takes the form of the triumph of the therapeutic."

Provine, William B., review of *Trial and Error: The American Controversy over Creation and Evolution*, by Edward J. Larson (New York: Oxford University Press, 1985, 224 pp.), *Academe*, vol. 73 (January/ February 1987), pp. 50-52. Provine was Professor of History of Biology, Cornell University.

pp. 51-2   "Of course, it is still possible to believe in both modern evolutionary biology and a purposive force, even the Judaeo-Christian God. One can suppose that God started the whole universe or works through the laws of nature (or both). There is no contradiction between this or similar views of God and natural selection. But this view of God is also worthless. . . . [Such a God] has nothing to do with human morals, answers no prayers, gives no life everlasting, in fact does nothing whatsoever that is detectable. In other words, religion is compatible with modern evolutionary biology (and, indeed, all of modern science) if the religion is effectively indistinguishable from atheism.

"My observation is that the great majority of modern evolutionary biologists now are atheists or something very close to that. Yet prominent atheistic or agnostic scientists publicly deny that there is any conflict between science and religion. Rather than simple intellectual dishonesty, this position is pragmatic. In the United States, elected members of Congress all proclaim to be religious. Many scientists believe that funding for science might suffer if the atheistic implications of modern science were widely understood."

p. 51   "Modern evolutionary biology is utterly devoid of purposive mechanisms. . . .

"Compatibility between evolution and religion was a far less defensible position to evolutionary biologists in the 1960s than in the 1920s."

Provine, William B., "Progress in Evolution and Meaning in Life," in *Evolutionary Progress*, ed. Matthew H. Nitecki (University of Chicago Press, 1988), pp. 49-74.

p. 65   "Modern science directly implies that the world is organized strictly in accordance with deterministic principles or chance. There are no purposive principles whatsoever in nature. There are no gods and no designing forces that are rationally detectable. The frequently made assertion that modern biology and the assumptions of the Judaeo-Christian tradition are fully compatible is false."

p. 69   "The conflict is fundamental and goes much deeper than modern liberal theologians, religious leaders and scientists are willing to admit. Most contemporary scientists, the majority of them by far, are atheists or something very close to that. And among evolutionary biologists, I would challenge the reader to name the prominent scientists who are 'devoutly religious.' I am skeptical that one could get beyond the fingers of one hand. Indeed, I would be interested to learn of a single one."

p. 70   "A widespread theological view now exists saying that God started off the world, props it up and works through laws of nature, very subtly, so subtly that its action is undetectable. But that kind of God is effectively no different to my mind than atheism. To anyone who adopts this view I say, 'Great, we're in the same camp; now where do we get our morals if the universe just goes grinding on as it does?' This kind of God does nothing outside of the laws of nature, gives us no immortality, no foundation for morals, or any of the things that we want from a God and from religion."

Provine, William B., "Scientists, Face It! Science and Religion are Incompatible," *The Scientist* (September 5, 1988), p. 10.

p. 10   "The implications of modern science, however, are clearly inconsistent with most religious traditions. No purposive principles exist in nature. Organic evolution has occurred by various combinations of random genetic drift, natural selection, Mendelian heredity, and many other purposeless mechanisms. Humans are complex organic machines that die completely with no survival of soul or psyche."

p. 10 "No inherent moral or ethical laws exist, nor are there absolute guiding principles for human society. The universe cares nothing for us and we have no ultimate meaning in life."

Ruse, Michael, "A Few Last Words—Until the Next Time," *Zygon*, vol. 29 (March 1994), pp. 75-79. Ruse is Professor of Philosophy and Zoology, University of Guelph, Guelph Ontario, Canada N1G 2WI.

p. 78 "Either humankind is in a state of original sin or it is not. If it is, then there was reason for Jesus to die on the cross. If it is not, Calvary has as much relevance as a gladiator's death in the Coliseum."

p. 79 "Either Jesus Christ was the Son of God or He was not. If he was, other religions are false. Missionaries—Jesuits past and Evangelicals present—are right about this. If he was not, Christianity is a fraud—no salvation, no heaven, no nothing. You cannot be a Christian on Sunday and a Hindu on Monday.

"I am sorry to be so rude about this (not that sorry!), but perhaps my indignation is a good point on which to go out. Unlike George Williams, I really want to believe. I find the goodies offered by Christianity extremely attractive. But I am damned (again!) if I am going to sell my evolutionary birthright for a mess of religious pottage. We see through a glass darkly; but, thanks to Charles Darwin, it is no longer so dark as when Saint Paul was penning a few thoughts to the Corinthians."

Ruse, Michael, "From Belief to Unbelief—and Halfway Back," *Zygon*, vol. 29 (March 1994), pp. 25-35.

p. 31 "The problem of evil is the most troubling of all. Frankly the free-will defense seems to me just not to wash, logically. If God be all-powerful, why did He not simply make us to do good freely? Far worse than the logic, however, is the dreadful implication of the free-will defense. God, this all-loving father, is prepared to let small children suffer in agony to satisfy the freedom of monsters like Hitler. As one of the Brothers Karamazov says, I simply do not want salvation at that price. How can one enjoy eternity, if it be bought by the blood of innocents?

"Some of the problems of Christianity strike me as being so blatantly rational-belief-destroying that there is almost a sense of farce in seeing its devotees trying to wriggle from under them. Chief among these is the problem of explaining how somebody's death two thousand years ago can wash away my sins. When you combine this with the doctrine of the Trinity and the implication that the sacrificial lamb is God Himself (or Itself) and that this therefore makes things all right with this self-same God, the rational mind boggles."

p. 33 "And if this were not enough, I have a loathing of attempts to meld science and religion which entail the trimming of religion in such a way that it fits with science, but at the cost of gelding it of real content and mystery—attempts which include the traditional varieties of evolutionary humanism, based all too often on so-called 'noble lies' or just plain bad arguments."

Thomas, Randell, "Moral Majority: The Way of the Cross," quote on cover of *American Atheist*, vol. 24 (August 1982), illustrated by Swastika.

> "American religious fundamentalism is not only an increasingly malignant threat to human dignity, intellect, and reason, but also one of the most calculated campaigns of demagoguery, hate, cruelty, greed, ignorance, persecution, intolerance, oppression, injustice, exploitation, and pseudo-Christian barbarity that has existed within the borders of a civilized nation."

Turner, Ted, "Humanism's Fighting Chance," *The Humanist*, vol. 51 (January/February 1991), pp. 12-15, 34.

p. 13   "So, I began to lose my faith. And the more I lost it, the better I felt. I mean, it starts out with this notion that we're all horrible. We're all born with sin and we're so bad that this wonderful person . . . and I'm sure Christ *was* a wonderful person. If he was here today, the way his stuff has been twisted around, he'd probably be sick at his stomach to see it. . . . But at any rate, he had to come down here and suffer and die on the cross so that with his blood our sins would be washed away. Weird man, I'm telling you."

p. 15   "The Christian faith—the Judeo-Christian tradition—says that God gave dominion over the planet to human beings; as for animals, they don't count for anything. They don't go to heaven. That's another reason why I didn't want to go there; no trees, no animals, just these fundamentalist Christians.

Wilson, Edward O., "The Relation of Science to Theology," *Zygon* (September/December 1980). Paper presented at 1979 Star Island Conference, co-sponsored by Institute of Religion in an Age of Science and American Academy of Arts & Sciences. Dr. Wilson is a leading sociobiologist and is Curator of Entomology at the Museum of Comparative Zoology, Harvard University.

> "Bitter experience has taught us that fundamentalist religion, which in its aggressive form is one of the unmitigated evils of the world, cannot be quickly replaced by benign skepticism and a purely humanistic world view, even among educated and well-meaning people. The reasons are the immaturity of the scientific study of mankind (which is being remedied rapidly) and the power and rigidity of the epigenetic rules that tend to draw people into dogmatic religions and religion-like political ideologies. Liberal theology can serve as a buffer."

Wilson, Edward O., "Toward a Humanistic Biology," *The Humanist*, vol. 42 (September/October 1982), pp. 38-41, 56-58.

p. 40   "As were many persons from Alabama, I was a born-again Christian. When I was fifteen, I entered the Southern Baptist Church with great fervor and interest in the fundamentalist religion; I left at seventeen when I got to the University of Alabama and heard about evolutionary theory."

p. 41   "From the viewpoint of the biological sciences, sociobiology is very orthodox, because it has been based cautiously on population genetics, ecology, and evolutionary theory and is a new amalgam or body of evolutionary theory. . . . That is why sociobiology is widely accepted among biologists and other natural scientists, except by a few Marxists who consider the discipline to be inimical to their fundamental beliefs."

p. 41   "Above all, sociobiology is the scientific discipline most congenial to humanism."

p. 56   "When we understand the evolutionary sources, the adaptive meaning, and genetic history of the religious impulse, I suspect the fatal blow will have been dealt to religious dogmatism, and yet it will simultaneously disclose a human history and a set of mental phenomena so complex as to serve as a permanent source of wonder."

C. The Impact of Evolutionism on Religion

Evolutionism is opposed not only to creation and the book of Genesis, or even to Christianity in general, but also to all aspects of monotheistic religion. Its most vitriolic attacks, of course, are reserved for "Biblical fundamentalists," but its ultimate aim is to eliminate the very idea of a personal Creator God from the very consciousness of mankind.

The quotes in this section constitute a somewhat miscellaneous collection of statements regarding this conflict, including a few observations by prominent Christians.

Ager, Derek V., *The New Catastrophism* (Cambridge, UK: Cambridge University Press, 1993), 231 pp.

p. 129   "One of the most fundamental changes that have happened in recent years in our thoughts about the geological past was again one towards concepts of episodicity, this time in the evolution of life. Thus the doctrine of what is called 'punctuated equilibria' replaced that of 'phyletic gradualism,' which had been the almost subconscious presumption of palaeontologists since the days of Darwin. . . . On the other hand Engels, that remarkable capitalist who supported Karl Marx, said that 'nature is composed entirely of leaps.' I regret to say that I prefer the view of one of the founding fathers of communism to that of one of the founding fathers of evolution by natural selection."

pp. 129-30   "Since the ideas of Darwin and Wallace first burst upon the scientific world, we need no longer concern ourselves with the opposition of the 'fundamentalists' and 'creationists,' unless we live in California (see the 'Disclaimer' in the Preface of this book). The arguments about the literal truth of the Bible is one of Wordsworth's 'battles long ago' so far as I am concerned. It is quite obvious that if we do not accept evolution then the fossil record shows us quite clearly that we would have to accept many creations, not just the one of Genesis. This to me is just nonsense, so I am not going to waste time on it."

Allegro, John M., "Divine Discontent," *American Atheist*, vol. 28 (September 1986), pp. 25-30. Allegro was a member of the Dead Sea Scrolls editing team.

p. 26   "For what religious man came eventually to think of as 'conscience' is simply the faculty that enabled his hominid ancestors to inhibit their programmed responses to stimuli in the interests of some longer-term advantage. 'Guilt' is the unease that accompanies and sometimes motivates that control, and 'god' is the idealist projection of the conscience in moral terms."

p. 30   "It may be that, despite our rightly-prized rationality, religion still offers man his best chance of survival, or at least of buying himself a little more time in which to devise some more reasoned way out of his dilemma. If so, it must be a faith that offers something more than a formal assent to highly speculative dogma about the nature of a god and his divine purpose in creation; it must promise its adherents a living relationship that answers man's individual needs within a formal structure of communal worship. It has to satisfy the emotions without violating the believer's intellectual integrity, and it must avoid the tragic divisiveness of ethnic or social affiliations by finding a common reference in our biological heritage."

Baker, John R., "Fundamentalism as Anti-Intellectualism," *The Humanist*, vol. 46 (March/April 1986), pp. 26-28, 34.

p. 26   "Examples of individual irrationality are numerous in contemporary America. . . . But perhaps the best example of group irrationality is Christian fundamentalism."

p. 26   "Fundamentalism began in several U.S. Protestant denominations in the early twentieth century as a conservative protest against the liberal reinterpretation of Christianity that incorporated historical and scientific discoveries. . . . The most visible conflict between fundamentalism and science is caused by fundamentalists' literal interpretation of Genesis."

p. 34   "Fundamentalism is part of a fantasy world that many people believe or wish to be true. These people wish that the reason for human existence is an afterlife and that their lives are guided by a benevolent deity. In actuality, events in the universe may be based upon chance and physical laws that have always existed, and human existence has no other meaning than that we exist."

Bauman, Michael, *Roundtable: Conversations with European Theologies* (Grand Rapids: Baker Book House, 1990), from an interview with Thomas Torrance.

p. 115   ". . . the countries of the Far East and of the Southern Hemisphere want our science and technology, but they have no doctrine of creation. They do not realize that science and technology rest upon, indeed arise from, Christian foundations. This is true both historically and epistemologically. We must show them that it is the Creator God himself who stands behind everything, and that he provides the rational ground upon which the various sciences rest, as well as the world those sciences unlock and help to tame."

Davies, Paul C., "Law and Order in the Universe," *New Scientist*, vol. 120 (October 15, 1988), pp. 58-60. Davies was Professor of Theoretical Physics, University of Newcastle-on-Tyne.

p. 58   "The assumption that the external world has systematic features that rational inquiry can uncover and incorporate into a coherent world view, probably owes its origin more to theology than science. The Judaic, Muslim and Christian traditions all propose a rational deity who is the creator of, but distinct from, the physical Universe. This Universe carries the imprint of a rational design in its detailed workings. This belief was implicit in the work of Isaac Newton and his contemporaries during the rise of modern science in the 17th century. Although the theistic dimension has long since faded, its implications for the natural order of the physical world remain little changed."

Davies, Paul C., "What Hath COBE Wrought?" *Sky and Telescope*, vol. 85 (January 1993), pp. 4-5.

p. 5   "However, there is little real conflict between scientists and most modern theologians. The serious tension lies between these same theologians and their followers, many of whom are unaware that their naive yet cherished images of God the Creator were abandoned by their ministers long ago."

Dyson, Cindy, "Fathers, Faith and Fossils," *New Man* (July/August 1996), pp. 52-55. *New Man* is the official magazine of the "Promise Keepers" magazine, with a circulation of 300,000 subscribers.

p. 54   "Remember, however, that the debate over how God created the world—through millions of years of evolutionary work or through a few words spoken over a few days—is not the central tenet of Christianity."

p. 55   "*Inset*. Christian evolutionists' [believe that] God used his creative power in many ways, one of which was to design creatures that were capable of changing or evolving over time. For example, God created egg and sperm cells that evolve or change to become babies."

Fehlner, Fr. Peter Damian, "In the Beginning: The Church's Teaching on the Origin of Man," *Christ to the World*, vol. 33, (May/August 1988), pp. 237-248. The author is a Conventional Franciscan and has a doctorate in Sacred Theology at the Seraphicum in Rome (Pontifical Theological Faculty of St. Bonaventure). These articles all carry the "Imprimatur" of the Catholic Church.

p. 247   "The doctrine of creation, in general and in all its detail, is intimately bound up with the mystery of salvation. That is why no Catholic may call into question, any aspect of the doctrine of creation which in fact the Church believes related to the mystery of salvation without also doubting that latter mystery."

p. 248   "1) The whole world was created by God *ex nihilo* in the beginning of time.

"2) The essential structure or order of the world presupposed for any subsequent activity or development was established by God and admits of no exceptions, except those directly produced by divine intervention."

"3) The first man and first woman were made directly by God, by forming the male body out of pre-existing matter, the female body out of the body of the first man, by creating out of nothing a soul for each and then uniting soul to body as its form."

Goss, Richard J., "Biology of the Soul," *The Humanist*, vol. 54 (November/December 1994), pp. 21-25. Goss is Professor of Biology Emeritus, Brown University.

p. 23   "It is incumbent on the theologian proposing the existence of souls to explain how they may have evolved. For more fundamentalist types who do not believe in evolution, this is not a problem. But for the majority of clergy who accept scientific discoveries, including evolution, there are serious inconsistencies to be explained. Few people bother to think about these matters, but the inquiring mind cannot ignore the incompatibilities implicit in considering the phylogeny of the soul. Indeed, this is the main reason why religion and evolution cannot be reconciled, even by those religious liberals who would have us believe that evolution was itself part of the divine handiwork of the creator.

". . . There was no specific point during this transition when a pair of ape parents begat a human baby. And even if they did, the entire human race would have had to descend from that one infant. . . .

"In any case, if the biological differences between humans and beasts are genetic, then their so-called spiritual differences must also have a genetic basis. This implies that there ought to be a gene for soul in human DNA—a gene that arose by mutation at that landmark in primate evolution when the first human being made its appearance amongst a population of astonished apes. Yet even if the soul gene were dominant, it would still have taken many generations for it to have spread throughout the population. And this presupposes that it was such an advantageous adaptation that it would have been favored by natural selection. One wonders if possession of a soul might really have enhanced survival in the struggle for existence, thereby promoting greater reproduction by those with a soul over those without."

Gould, Stephen Jay, Interview in *Unitarian Universalist World*, reported in *Context* (June 15, 1982), p. 5.

"The Unitarian Universalist folk, with Rev. Peter L. Richardson as interviewer, asked superstar popular scientist Stephen Jay Gould of Harvard, 'Is there any place for God in evolution?'

"Gould: 'That's in a way a false question, because God is not part of the subject matter of science. There is no place for God in evolution because there isn't a place for God in that sense in empirical science. That doesn't mean that there isn't a God or that one shouldn't believe in one. It is just like saying there is no place for a game of baseball in an opera house. They're just different things.'"

Gould, Stephen Jay, "Fall in the House of Ussher," *Natural History*, vol. 100 (November 1991), pp. 12-21.

p. 18   "First of all, the date 4004 rests comfortably with the most important of chronological metaphors—the common comparison of the six days of God's creation with 6,000 years for the earth's potential duration. 'But, beloved, be not ignorant of this one thing, that one day is with the Lord as a thousand years and a thousand years as one day' (2 Peter 3:8). Under this widely accepted scheme, the earth was created 4,000 years before the birth of Christ and could endure as much as 2,000 years thereafter (a proposition soon to be tested empirically and, we all hope, roundly disproved!)."

p. 20   [Quoting James Barr] "'It is a great mistake, therefore, to suppose that Ussher was simply concerned with working out the date of creation: this can be supposed only by those who have never looked into its pages. . . . The Annales are an attempt at a comprehensive chronological synthesis of all known historical knowledge, biblical and classical. . . . Of its volume only perhaps one sixth or less is biblical material.'"

Gould, Stephen Jay, "Modified Grandeur," *Natural History*, vol. 102 (March 1993), pp. 14-20.

p. 20   "Many paleontologists, myself included, now view *Homo sapiens* as a tiny and unpredictable twig on a richly ramifying tree of life—a happy accident of the last geological moment, unlikely ever to appear again if we could regrow the tree from seed."

p. 20   "We first located ourselves at the center of a limited universe, but Copernicus and Galileo taught us that we inhabit a peripheral speck in a cosmos 'of a magnitude scarcely conceivable.' We then imagined that God had created us in his own image on this little speck, until Darwin 'relegated us to descent from an animal world.'"

Gould, Stephen Jay, "Nonoverlapping Magisteria," *Natural History*, vol. 106 (March 1997), pp. 16-22, 60-62.

p. 16   "At lunch, the priests called me over to their table to pose a problem that had been troubling them. What, they wanted to know, was going on in America with all this talk about 'scientific creationism'? One asked me: 'Is evolution really in some kind of trouble; and if so, what could such trouble be? I have always been taught that no doctrinal conflict exists between evolution and Catholic faith, and the evidence for evolution seems both entirely satisfactory and utterly overwhelming. Have I missed something?'"

p. 16   "We all left satisfied, but I certainly felt bemused by the anomaly of my role as a Jewish agnostic, trying to reassure a group of Catholic priests that evolution remained both true and entirely consistent with religious belief."

p. 16   "Again, I gulped hard, did my intellectual duty, and reassured him that evolution was both true and entirely compatible with Christian belief—a position I hold sincerely, but still an odd situation for a Jewish agnostic."

p. 18   "In the context of this standard position, I was enormously puzzled by a statement issued by Pope John Paul II on October 22, 1996, to the Pontifical Academy of Sciences, the same body that had sponsored by earlier trip to the Vatican. In this document, entitled 'Truth Cannot Contradict Truth,' the pope defended both the evidence for evolution and the consistency of the theory with Catholic religious doctrine."

p. 18   "The Catholic Church had never opposed evolution and had no reason to do so. Why had the pope issued such a statement at all? And why had the press responded with an orgy of worldwide, front-page coverage?"

Johnston, George Sim, "The Genesis Controversy," *Crisis* (May 1989), pp. 12-18. Johnston is a Catholic writer.

p. 14   "No one, then, has ever seen one species change into another either in the fossil record or in breeding experiments. Darwin himself was unable to come up with a single indisputable case of one animal changing into another via 'natural selection.' His case was entirely theoretical; it rested on a chain of suppositions rather than empirical observation; the 'facts' that he mustered were either made to fit the theory or were explained away."

p. 16   "The tenacity of Darwin's theory among scientists and educators can only be explained by its crude materialism. The biologist Julian Huxley, who was a kind of roving statesman for Darwinism in the 1940s and '50s, claimed that

Darwin's real achievement was to remove the idea of a Creator from intelligent discourse. Huxley's famous grandfather, T. H. Huxley, was more explicit; he claimed (wrongly, it turned out) that the great merit of evolutionary theory was its complete and irreconcilable antagonism to that vigorous and consistent enemy of the highest intellectual, moral, and social life of mankind—the Catholic Church."

Larson, Edward J., and Larry Witham, "Scientists are Still Keeping the Faith," *Nature*, vol. 386 (April 3, 1997), pp. 435-436.

p. 435   "To measure the strength of religious belief in an era of ascendant science, the eminent researcher James Leuba conducted a landmark survey in 1916. He found that 60 per cent of 1,000 randomly selected scientists did not believe in God, and predicted that such disbelief would increase as education spread [Leuba, J. H., *The Belief in God and Immortality: A Psychological, Anthropological and Statistical Study* (Boston: Sherman, French & Co., 1916)]. To test that prediction, we replicated Leuba's survey as exactly as possible. The result: about 40 per cent of scientists still believe in a personal God and an afterlife. In both surveys, roughly 45 per cent disbelieved and 15 per cent were doubters (agnostic)."

p. 435   "In the intervening years, religious belief has become more diverse. But, to the extent that both surveys are accurate readings, traditional Western theism has not lost its place among US scientists, despite their intellectual preoccupation with material reality."

p. 435   "And although biologists showed the highest rates of disbelief or doubt in Leuba's day (69.5 per cent), that ranking is now given to physicists and astronomers (77.9 per cent).

          "Higher belief among physicists in Leuba's survey might have been expected at a time when leading physicists such as Lord Kelvin, Robert Millikan and Sir Arthur Eddington publicly defended religious belief. (Brooke, J. H., *Science and Religion: Some Historical Perspectives* (Cambridge: Cambridge University Press, 1991)]."

Lewis, C. S., "Is Theology Poetry?" *Oxford Socratic Club Digest* (1944).

p. 150   "It must also be remembered that only a minority of the religions of the world have a theology. There was no systematic series of statements which the Greeks agreed in believing about Zeus."

p. 162   "The picture so often painted of Christians huddling together on an ever narrower strip of beach while the incoming tide of 'Science' mounts higher and higher, corresponds to nothing in my own experience. That grand myth which I asked you to admire a few minutes ago is not for me a hostile novelty breaking in on my traditional beliefs. On the contrary, that cosmology is what I started from. Deepening distrust and final abandonment of it long preceded my conversion to Christianity. Long before I believed Theology to be true I had already decided that the popular scientific picture at any rate was false. One absolutely central inconsistency ruins it; it is the one we touched on a fortnight ago. The whole picture professes to depend on inferences from observed facts.

Unless inference is valid, the whole picture disappears. Unless we can be sure that reality in the remotest nebula or the remotest part obeys the thought-laws of the human scientist here and now in his laboratory—in other words unless Reason is an absolute—all is in ruins. Yet those who ask me to believe this world picture also ask me to believe that Reason is simply the unforeseen and unintended by-product of mindless matter at one stage of its endless and aimless becoming. Here is flat contradiction. They ask me at the same moment to accept a conclusion and to discredit the only testimony on which that conclusion can be based."

p. 164   "Granted that Reason is prior to matter and that the light of that primal Reason illuminates finite minds, I can understand how men should come, by observation and inference, to know a lot about the universe they live in. If, on the other hand, I swallow the scientific cosmology as a whole, then not only can I not fit in Christianity, but I cannot even fit in science. If minds are wholly dependent on brains, and brains on bio-chemistry, and bio-chemistry (in the long run) on the meaningless flux of the atoms, I cannot understand how the thought of those minds should have any more significance than the sound of the wind in the trees. And this is to me the final test."

p. 165   "Christian theology can fit in science, art, morality, and the sub-Christian religions. The scientific point of view cannot fit in any of these things not even science itself. I believe in Christianity as I believe that the Sun has risen, not only because I see it but because by it I see everything else."

Machen, J. Gresham, 1912 article reprinted in *Banner of Truth*, no. 69 (June 1969).

"False ideas are the greatest obstacles to the reception of the gospel. We may preach with all the fervor of a reformer and yet succeed only in winning a straggler here and there, if we permit the whole collective thought of the nation or of the world to be controlled by ideas which, by the resistless force of logic, prevent Christianity from being regarded as anything more than a harmless delusion. Under such circumstances, what God desires us to do is to destroy the obstacle at its root.

"The great questions may easily be avoided and many Christians are avoiding them, preaching to the air. The Church is shrinking from the conflict. Driven from the spiritual realm by the current of modern thought, she is consoling herself with things about which there is no dispute. The Church is waiting for men of another type, men to fight her battles and solve her problems. They need not all be men of conspicuous attainments. But they must all be men of thought."

Marton, Alex, "What is Uniformitarianism and How Did it Get here?" *Horus*, vol. 1, no. 2 (1985), pp. 12-14.

p. 12   "In 1807, a small group of amateurs had formed the London Geological Society. . . . Of the original group of thirteen . . . Only one member had training in geology, but he did not pursue it as a livelihood."

p. 12   "In the 18th century, the winds of democracy from America and the attacks of thinkers like Locke and Rousseau, among others, questioned the Monarchy as the natural form of government. Liberalism was moving, and its method was to go after Biblical geology (specifically the Flood) in order to disarm the Monarchists."

p. 13   "Paley's doctrine was required study in the universities, and was the received wisdom in society. There was only one way to reform Parliament, and that was to destroy Paley's Natural Theology—and the only way to do that was to discredit the catastrophist notions of its religious defenders who sought to reconcile the geological evidence with the story of Genesis.

". . . If the scientific evidence denied the truth of the Bible, then it also denied any connection between God and the Monarchy, thus freeing Parliament and the people to redefine the political equations."

Mayr, Ernst, "The Nature of the Darwinian Revolution," *Science*, vol. 176 (June 2, 1972), pp. 981-989.

p. 981   "I am taking a new look at the Darwinian revolution of 1859, perhaps the most fundamental of all intellectual revolutions in the history of mankind. It not only eliminated man's anthropocentrism, but affected every metaphysical and ethical concept, if consistently applied."

p. 988   "Every anti-evolutionist prior to 1859 allowed for the intermittent, if not constant, interference by the Creator. The natural causes postulated by the evolutionists completely separated God from his creation, for all practical purposes. The new explanatory model replaced planned teleology by the haphazard process of natural selection. This required a new concept of God and a new basis for religion."

Mayr, Ernst, "Evolution," *Scientific American*, vol. 239 (September 1978), pp. 47-55.

p. 47   "Man's world view today is dominated by the knowledge that the universe, the stars, the earth and all living things have evolved through a long history that was not foreordained or programmed, a history of continual, gradual change shaped by more or less directional natural processes consistent with the laws of physics. Cosmic and biological evolution have that much in common."

p. 50   "The proponents of teleological theories, for all their efforts, have been unable to find any mechanism (except supernatural ones) that can account for their postulated finalism. The possibility that any such mechanism can exist has now been virtually ruled out by the findings of molecular biology. . . . The frequency of extinction in every geological period is another powerful argument against any finalistic trend toward perfection."

p. 52   "Deterministically inclined astronomers are convinced by statistical reasoning that what has happened on the earth must also have happened on planets of stars other than the sun. Biologists impressed by the inherent improbability of every single step that led to the evolution of man consider what Simpson called 'the prevalence of humanoids' exceedingly improbable."

Mondale, Walter, Taken from *The Siecus Circle*, by Claire Chambers (Western Islands, Massachusetts: Western Islands Publisher, 1977), p. 346.

"*Footnote.* Walter Mondale was a major participant at the Fifth Congress of the International Humanists and Ethical Union at MIT in August, 1970. In his opening remarks, he said: 'Although I have never formally joined a humanist society, I think I am a member by inheritance. My preacher father was a humanist . . . I grew up on a very rich diet of humanism from him. All of our family has been deeply influenced by this tradition including my brother Lester, a Unitarian minister, Ethical Culture leader, and Chairman of the Fellowship of Religious Humanists.'

[Walter Mondale was on the 8 member advisory council of the Institute of Society Ethics and the Life Sciences, financed by John D. Rockefeller III, the Rockefeller Foundation, and the Rockefeller Brothers Fund, along with identified humanists, including Karl Menninger.]

Morain, Lloyd, and Oliver Reiser, "Scientific Humanism: A Formulation," *The Humanist*, vol. 48 (September/October 1988), pp. 33-34, reprinted from Spring 1943 issue. Morain was editor of *The Humanist*; Reiser was Professor of Philosophy at University of Pittsburgh.

p. 33 "The scientific humanist holds that humans are natural creatures living in a natural universe. Evolved from stardust by cosmic processes, humans emerged from creatures that *adapt* themselves to nature into the self-directive agents who *re-create* that nature to serve the needs of their own progressive enlightenment. There are in this universe not gods and humans, masters and slaves, but human beings in various stages of development, all born of the Earth-womb."

p. 33 "They see, however, that there are some things in this universe we must accept as basic, brute fact. An uncreated universe—the space-time-matter trinity, or the cosmic movement continuum—is one such brute fact."

Oldroyd, D. R., *Darwinian Impacts* (Atlantic Highlands, New Jersey: Humanities Press, 1983), 398 pp.

p. 254 "It will be appreciated from this list that although most Western men and women may not choose to identify themselves explicitly as philosophical humanists or spend their time at humanist society meetings, these ten points do encapsulate many of the basic assumptions of educated, Western, liberal society. Clearly, the humanist creed represents a major component of the thinking of many of us."

Pitch, Walter M., "The Challenges to Darwinism since the last Centennial and the Impact of Molecular Studies," *Evolution*, vol. 36 (November 1982), pp. 1133-1143.

p. 1138-9 "By a metaphysical construct I mean any unproved or unprovable assumption that we all make and tend to take for granted. One example is the doctrine of uniformitarianism that asserts that the laws of nature, such as gravity and thermodynamics, have always been true in the past and will always be true in the future. It is the belief in that doctrine that permits scientists to demand repeatability in experiments. I like the word doctrine in this case because it makes clear that matters of faith are not restricted to creationists and that in the intellectual struggle for citizen enlightenment we need to be very clear just where the fundamental differences between science and theology lie. It is not, as many scientists would like to believe, in the absence of metaphysical underpinnings in science."

Provine, William B., "Influence of Darwin's Ideas on the Study of Evolution," *Bioscience*, vol. 32 (June 1982), pp. 501-506. Provine is Professor of History and Biological Sciences, Cornell University.

p. 506   "Evolutionists still disagree about the precise mechanisms of evolution in nature, but they have nevertheless given overwhelming support to Darwin's belief that design in nature results from purely mechanistic causes. As Jacques Monod, E. O. Wilson, and many other biologists have pointed out, modern evolutionary biology has shattered the hope that some kind of designing or purposive force guided human evolution and established the basis of moral rules. Instead, biology leads to a wholly mechanistic view of life, as Darwin suspected.

"Here are the implications of this mechanistic view of life as I see them. First, except for purely mechanistic ones, no organizing or purposive principles exist in the world. There are no gods and no designing forces. The frequently made assertion that modern biology and the assumptions of the Judeo-Christian tradition are fully compatible is false. Second, there exist no inherent moral or ethical laws, no absolute guiding principles for human society. Third, humans are marvelously complex machines. The individual human becomes an ethical person by two primary mechanisms: heredity and environmental influence. . . .

"Fourth, free will, as usually conceived, does not exist."

Rolston, Holmes, III, "Does Nature Need to Be Redeemed?" *Zygon*, vol. 29 (June 1994), pp. 205-229. Rolston is Distinguished Professor of Philosophy at Colorado State University.

p. 205   "Biologists believe in genesis, but if a biologist begins reading Genesis, the opening story seems incredible. The trouble is not so much the six days of creation in chapters 1 and 2, though most of the controversy is usually thought to lie there, as in chapter 3, where, spoiling the Garden Earth, the first couple fall and Earth becomes cursed. A biologist realizes that prescientific peoples expressed themselves in parables and stories. The Earth arising from a formless void, inspired by a command to bring forth swarms of creatures, generated in the seas, filling the land, multiplying and filling the Earth, eventuating in the appearance of humans, made of dust and yet remarkably special—all of this is rather congenial with the evolutionary genesis. The real problem is with the Fall when a once-paradisiacal nature becomes recalcitrant as a punishment for human sin.

"That does not fit into the biological paradigm at all. Suffering in a harsh world did not enter chronologically after sin and on account of it. There was struggle for long epochs before the human arrival, however problematic the arrival of sinful humans may also be."

p. 206   "But nature is also where the fittest survive, 'red in tooth and claw,' fierce and indifferent, a scene of hunger, disease, death. And nature is what it is regardless of human moral failings, indeed regardless of humans at all."

Russell, Colin, "Whigs and Professionals," *Nature*, vol. 308 (April 26, 1984), pp. 777-778. Russell was Professor of History of Science and Technology at the Open University.

p. 777   "Given that the history of science can only be understood in a mature way by taking into account all kinds of other influences, the subject becomes fair game for those who have an ideological axe to grind, consciously or not. Thus some

Victorian writers, intoxicated with the idea of progress and unimpressed by the filibustering of the established church in the wake of Darwinism, rewrote the history of science in terms of a conflict between science and religion, whose outcome was as inevitable as any good Whig could expect."

p. 778   "Today historical justification for that position is amazingly hard to justify. It is widely accepted on all sides that, far from undermining it, science is deeply indebted to Christianity and has been so from at least the scientific revolution. Recent historical research has uncovered many unexpected links between scientific enterprise and Biblical theology. The 'conflict' model is not just a harmless anachronism. It is truth standing on its head."

Ryrie, Charles C., *Neo-orthodoxy* (Chicago: Moody Press, 1956).

p. 18   "Out of Darwin and his so-called scientific method grew the higher criticism of the 19th century. . . . What were the results of this teaching of liberalism? There was a high and false estimate of the ability of human nature. It promoted the illusion that the Kingdom of God was capable of being fulfilled in history, for man's ability could bring this to pass. There came with it the abandonment of the distinctive and exclusive character of the message of the Gospel and the loss of the uniqueness of Christianity, and secularization of life and thought can also be traced at least in part to the teaching of liberalism in the last century."

p. 51   "Thus the Genesis account of creation and the fall is rejected as history—as most of us understand history. Science, the Barthians say, has delivered us from having to believe the Genesis stories, and through this deliverance, we are supposed to be able to see their real meaning."

Scott, Otto, "Playing God," *Chalcedon Report*, no. 247 (February 1986).

p. 1   "Founded, as are most great fallacies, upon a half-truth, Darwinism spawned many offshoots. One of these was launched by Darwin's first cousin, Francis Galton.

"Obsessed, as were many, by the implications of the 'fittest,' Galton set out in 1883 to study heredity from a mathematical viewpoint. He named his new 'science' *eugenics*, from a Greek root meaning both 'good in birth' and 'noble in heredity.' His stated goal was to improve the human race, by giving 'the more suitable races or strains of blood a better chance of prevailing speedily over the less suitable.' His unstated goal was to play God."

p. 1   "Through the years since then, the ideas of superior and inferior people and societal control inherent in eugenics have helped bring real-life horrors to the world.

"The idiot-savants engaged in eugenics studies, programs or promotion reads like a list of 20th Century Who's Who. Hitler was, of course, a very eminent convert, though seldom claimed by the Movement. Margaret Sanger, a vicious and open racist, is . . . despite her horrifying writings, lectures and activities, still publicly honored for her efforts in birth control. These led to the 'family planning' and 'birth control' clinics now rife on the landscape. And these in turn preceded and paved the way for modern abortion 'clinics' and their apologists, lobbyists, protectors and financiers."

Smith, Huston, "Two Evolutions," in *On Nature*, vol. 6, Boston University Studies in Philosophy and Religion, edited by Leroy S. Rouner (University of Notre Dame Press, 1984, 188 pp.), pp. 42-59.

p. 43   "An age comes to a close when people discover that they can no longer understand themselves by the theory their age professes. For a while its denizens will continue to think that they believe it, but they feel otherwise and cannot understand their feelings. This has now happened to us. We continue to believe Darwinism, even though it no longer feels right to us. Darwinism is in fact dying, and its death signals the close of our age."

p. 48   "Darwin saw his discovery as strongly resistant to admixture with belief in God, while Jacques Monod goes further. 'The mechanism of evolution as now understood,' he tells us, 'rules out any claim that there are final causes, or purposes being realized. [This] disposes of any philosophy or religion that believes in cosmic . . . purpose.' Realizing that this conclusion could be colored by Monod's personal philosophy, I turn to the entry on 'Evolution' in *The New Encyclopaedia Britannica* for a statement that might reflect, as well as any, consensus in the field. It tells me that 'Darwin showed that evolution's cause, natural selection, was automatic with no room for divine guidance or design.'"

Spurgeon, Charles Haddon, *Commentaries*, vol. 5. See also: *Treasury of the Bible*, New Testament, vol. 1 (Grand Rapids: Zondervan, 1968), 903 pp.

p. 498   "Philosophically the dogma of evolution is a dream, a theory without a vestige of proof. Within fifty years, children in school will read of extraordinary popular delusions, and this will be mentioned as one of the most absurd. Many a merry jest will be uttered bearing upon the follies of nineteenth century science."

p. 504   "The tendency of the times is not toward religion, but towards unbelief, materialism and sordid selfishness. A current, nay a torrent, of unbelief is roaring around the foundation of society, and our pulpits are reeling beneath its force. Many Christian people are only half believers now, they are almost smothered in the dense fog of doubt which is now around us. We have come into cloud-land and cannot see our way. Many are sinking in the slough and those of us who have our feet upon the Rock of Ages have our hands full with helping our slipping friends."

Zindler, Frank R., "Religion, Hypnosis and Music: An Evolutionary Perspective," *American Atheist*, vol. 26 (October 1984), pp. 22-24. Zindler is former Chairman, Division of Science, Nursing and Technology, Fulton-Montgomery College, SUNY.

p. 24   "Religion is like the human appendix: although it was functional in our distant ancestors, it is of no use today. Just as the appendix today is a focus of physical disease, so too religion today is a focus of social disease. Although religion was a force accelerating human evolution during the Ice Age, it is now an atavism of negative value."

Chapter 14

The Corrupt Fruits of Evolution

A. The Cruel Basis of Evolutionism

The Lord Jesus said that "a good tree cannot bring forth evil fruit, neither can an evil tree bring forth good fruit" (Matthew 7:18). A good test by which to evaluate the validity of a philosophy is to examine the fruit it produces in human society and human individual behavior.

The evolutionary philosophy dismally fails this fruit test. The very essence of evolutionism involves the survival of the fittest, the corollary of which is the elimination of the unfit. This concept led Darwin, Wallace and others to the idea of natural selection as the presumed mechanism of evolution. However, the basic cruelty of the evolutionary process, by whatever mechanism it is supposed to be achieved, is intrinsic to the very idea of evolution itself.

As the following quotes illustrate, it is not too much to conclude that evolution—if it were true—would be the most wasteful and cruel process that could ever be devised by which to arrive at its supposed goal, the production of humans. "Theistic" evolution thus becomes an oxymoron. A good and wise and powerful God would *never* stoop to invent and use such a process. Thus, while there are evolutionists who are theists, they are totally inconsistent. Evolution itself, as a process, must be atheistic.

Begley, Sharon, "Science Contra Darwin," *Newsweek* (April 8, 1985), p. 80-81.

p. 80   "Some critics go so far as to liken Darwinism to creationism because of its slipperiness: it does not make specific predictions about what sorts of organisms evolution will produce, they charge, and so is never vulnerable to disproof. Like creationism, Darwinian evolution 'can equally well explain any evolutionary history,' says ichthyologist Donn Rosen of the American Museum of Natural History in New York in a recent book. So heated is the debate that one Darwinian says there are times when he thinks about going into a field with more intellectual honesty: the used-car business."

Cudmore, Lorraine Lee Larison, "The Center of Life," *Science Digest*, vol. 82 (November 1977), pp. 41-46.

p. 46   "Evolution is a hard, inescapable mistress. There is just no room for compassion or good sportsmanship. Too many organisms are born, so, quite simply, a lot of them are going to have to die because there isn't enough food and space to go around. You can be beautiful, fat, strong, but it might not matter. The only thing that does matter is whether you leave more children carrying your genes than the next person leaves. It's true whether you're a prince, a frog, or an American elm. Evolution is a future phenomenon. Are your genes going to be in the next generation. That is all that counts."

Darwin, Charles, *Origin of Species*, last paragraph.

> "Thus, from the war of nature, from famine and death, the most exalted object which we are capable of conceiving, namely the production of the higher animals, directly follows."

Dawkins, Richard, "Creation and Natural Selection," *New Scientist*, vol. 111 (September 25, 1986), pp. 34-38. Dawkins was in the Zoology Department, Oxford University.

p. 35   "Evolution has no long-term goal. There is no long distance target, no final perfection to serve as a criterion for selection, although human vanity cherishes the absurd notion that our species is the final goal of evolution. In real life, the criterion for selection is always short-term, either simple survival or, more generally, reproductive success."

p. 37   "All these children are mutant offspring of the same parent, differing from their parents with respect to one gene each. This very high mutation rate is a distinctly unbiological feature of the computer model. In real life, the probability that a gene will mutate is often less than one in a million. The reason for building a high mutation rate into the model is for the benefit of human eyes, and humans haven't the patience to wait a million generations for a mutation."

Dawkins, Richard, "The Necessity of Darwinism," *New Scientist*, vol. 94 (April 15, 1982), pp. 130-132.

p. 130   "The more statistically improbable a thing is, the less can we believe that it just happened by blind chance. Superficially the obvious alternative to chance is an intelligent Designer."

p. 130   "I know of only two alternatives to Darwinism that have been offered as explanations of the organized and apparently purposeful complexity of life. These are God and Lamarckism. I am afraid I shall give God rather short shrift. He may have many virtues: no doubt he is invaluable as a pricker of the conscience and a comfort to the dying and bereaved, but as an explanation of organized complexity he simply will not do. It is organized complexity we are trying to explain, so it is footling to invoke in explanation a being sufficiently organized and complex to create it."

Dawkins, Richard, "God's Utility Function," *Scientific American*, vol. 273 (November 1995), pp. 80-85.

p. 85   "The total amount of suffering per year in the natural world is beyond all decent contemplation. During the minute that it takes me to compose this sentence, thousands of animals are being eaten alive, many others are running for their lives, whimpering with fear, others are being slowly devoured from within by rasping parasites, thousands of all kinds are dying of starvation, thirst and disease. It must be so. If there is ever a time of plenty, this very fact will automatically lead to an increase in population until the natural state of starvation and misery is restored.

"In a universe of electrons and selfish genes, blind physical forces and genetic replication, some people are going to get hurt, other people are going to get lucky, and you won't find any rhyme or reason in it, nor any justice. The universe that we observe has precisely the properties we should expect if there is, at bottom, no design, no purpose, no evil and no good, nothing but pitiless indifference."

Dobzhansky, Theodosius, "Ethics and Values in Biological and Cultural Evolution," *Zygon, the Journal of Religion and Science,* as reported in *Los Angeles Times,* part IV (June 16, 1974), p. 6.

"Man has evolved from ancestors that were not human. . . . The creation of God's image in man is not an event but a process, and therefore the moral law is a product of an evolutionary development.

"It is futile to look for special genes for ethics or for values,—it is the genetic endowment as a whole which makes us human.

"Natural selection can favor egotism, hedonism, cowardice instead of bravery, cheating and exploitation, while group ethics in virtually all societies tend to counteract or forbid such 'natural' behavior, and to glorify their opposites: kindness, generosity and even self-sacrifice for the good of others of one's tribe or nation and finally of mankind.

"Evolution on the cosmic, biological and human levels are parts of one grand process of universal evolution.

"Man is an ethicizing being. Ethics are human ethics. They are products of cultural evolution."

Falk, Arthur, "Reflections on Huxley's Evolution and Ethics," *The Humanist,* vol. 55 (November/December 1995), pp. 23-25.

p. 23   "Nature makes everything in vain. After all, what is evolution? A mindless process built on evil; that's what it is."

p. 24   "So natural selection seems smart to those who see only the surviving products, but as a design process it is idiotic. And the raw brutality of the process is offensive."

p. 24   "When I dispel the illusions of springtime, the horrific truth returns to mind. The mix of good and evil in evolution is diabolical."

p. 25   "In the long run, all good loses out to evil."

p. 25   "Since Huxley published the words I've quoted, the leaves have fallen a hundred times. It's about time we conceded that he was right. We can believe in evolution and yet *not condone it.* We ought to combat it."

Goodwin, Brian, "Rumbling the Replicator," *New Scientist,* vol. 117 (March 10, 1988), pp. 56-58.

p. 57   "The dualistic theory proposed by Weismann which splits organisms into an immortal essence (germ plasma, or Dawkins's replicator) and a mortal, derived soma or body, did not come from a vacuum. It is remarkably like the immortal soul and the mortal body of Christian doctrine. In itself this should not disturb us: lots of ideas in science come from theology. *The Blind Watchmaker* is particularly full of them, from the title to the last word, which happens to be 'miracle.' A little exegesis on Dawkins's books yields some fascinating insights. The major theme of *The Selfish Gene* bears a strong parallel to that of Christian fundamentalism. Dawkins argues that our essential nature, the hereditary material, is selfish, but this base inheritance (coded indeed in base pairs) can be overcome by a product of those selfish genes themselves, our thinking brains, by dint of education and social effort. There are serious contradictions in such arguments, but they cause no more confusion than other dualisms about mind and body in our culture."

Gould, Stephen Jay, "The Power of This View of Life," *Natural History*, vol. 103 (June 1994), pp. 6-8.

pp. 6, 8   "Moreover, natural selection, expressed in inappropriate human terms, is a remarkably inefficient, even cruel process. Selection carves adaptation by eliminating masses of the less fit—imposing hecatombs of death as preconditions for limited increments of change. Natural selection is a theory of 'trial and error externalism'—organisms propose via their storehouse of variation, and environments dispose of nearly all—not an efficient and human 'goal-directed internalism' (which would be fast and lovely, but nature does not know the way)."

p. 8   "This is not the 'age of man'; it is not even the 'age of insects'— a proper designation if we wish to honor multicellular animal life. As it was in the beginning, is now, and ever shall be until the sun explodes, this is the 'age of bacteria.' Bacteria began the story 3.5 billion years ago, as life arose near the lower limits of its preservable complexity. The bacterial mode has never altered; the most common and successful forms of life have been constant. Bacteria span a broader range of biochemistries and live in a wider range of environments; they cannot be nuked into oblivion; they overwhelm all else in frequency and variety; the number of *E. Coli* cells in the gut of any human exceeds the count of all humans that have lived since our African dawn."

Gould, Stephen Jay, "Darwin and Paley Meet the Invisible Hand," *Natural History*, vol. 99 (November 1990), pp. 8-16.

p. 12   "We call this third view natural selection by survival of the fittest, or Darwinism. Darwin himself commented most forcefully upon the inefficient and basically unpleasant character of his process, writing to his friend Joseph Hooker in 1856: 'What a book a devil's chaplain might write on the clumsy, wasteful, blundering, low, and horribly cruel works of nature!'"

p. 14   "You can hardly blame the divine Paley for not even imaging such a devilish mechanism."

Harris, Marvin, "Our Pound of Flesh," *Natural History*, vol. 88 (August/September 1979), pp. 30-36. Harris was in the Department of Anthropology, Columbia University.

p. 30   "According to [Michael] Harner, the Aztecs sought to overcome the depletion of faunal resources by consuming the flesh of enemy soldiers ostensibly sacrificed to appease the gods."

p. 32   "The body's need for protein rises rather sharply after it has been traumatized or debilitated by infections or wounds."

p. 32   "Both plants and animals contain the essential amino acids, but any specific animal food generally has more of them and in nutritionally better balance. . . .

Thus the preference for animal protein is not merely a matter of arbitrary cultural taste, but a fundamental biocultural adaptation that can be surrendered only at great risk to the population concerned."

p. 36   "Surely there can be no special pride in the practice of letting millions of soldiers rot on the battlefield because of a taboo against cannibalism. One can even argue that, nutritionally, the best source of protein for human beings is human flesh because the balance of amino acids is precisely that which the body requires for its own proper functioning."

p. 36   "We have thus already entered an era of continuously rising food prices in which animal flesh may soon become as much of a luxury as it was for the Aztecs. . . . But the decline in the availability of animal proteins constitutes yet another threat to the health and well-being of future generations and is certain to provoke strong and justified public reaction."

Harvey, Paul, "Revive your Interest in Biology," review of *The Rise and Fall of the Third Chimpanzee*, by Jared M. Diamond (Radius, 330 pp.), *New Scientist*, vol. 130 (June 1, 1991), p. 48.

"The theme that impresses most is the universality of internecine tribal and racial warfare, a claim hammered home by accounts of genocides in almost every civilization from historical times to the present. There were no Golden Ages. And just as people have not been at peace with their neighbours, so we have never lived in harmony with nature.

"The human story is one of continued and ever-accelerating habitat destruction. Before we moved in, each subcontinent was populated richly with large mammals or birds. Within a few centuries of the arrival of humans, the stock of species was decimated while their habitats were destroyed."

Hsü, Kenneth J., "Is Darwinism Science?" *Earthwatch* (March 1989), pp. 15-17. Hsü is Chairman of the Department of Earth Sciences, Swiss Federal Institute of Technology.

p. 15   "Though both of us survived the war, we were victims of a cruel social ideology that assumes that competition among individuals, classes, nations, or races is the natural condition of life, and that it is also natural for the superior to dispossess the inferior. For the last century and more this ideology has been thought to be a natural law of science, the mechanism of evolution which was formulated most powerfully by Charles Darwin in 1859 in his *On the Origin of Species by Means of Natural Selection, or the Preservation of Favored Races in the Struggle for Life*."

p. 16   "Very rapid change, on the other hand must increase the extinction rate way beyond the speciation rate because there is a limit to how quickly any organism can evolve to suit its evolving environment."

p. 16   "The rate of environmental change thus deserves a central position in the formula for extinction: The faster the rate of change, the greater the extinction rate. Thinking along these lines, it seems possible that something drastic happened to the environment to cause the mass extinction of all the wonderful beasts paleontologists have been digging from the earth this last century or so. Were a catastrophe to prove the explanation for this or other extinctions, the very root of Darwin's 'law' becomes suspect."

p. 17   "The law of the survival of the fittest may be, therefore, a tautology in which fitness is defined by the fact of survival, not by independent criteria that would form the basis for prediction. The 'natural law' that has given a 'scientific' basis for so much wickedness may also be falsified: If most extinctions are caused by catastrophes, then the whole course of evolution may be governed by chance, and not reflect at all the slow march from inferior to superior forms so beloved of Victorians, and so deeply embedded in Western thought."

p. 17   "The law of natural selection is not, I will maintain, science. It is an ideology, and a wicked one, and it has as much interfered with our ability to perceive the history of life with clarity as it has interfered with our ability to see one another with tolerance."

Hull, David L., "The God of the Galápagos," review of *Darwin on Trial*, by Philip Johnson (Washington, D.C.: Regnery Gateway, 1991, 195 pp.), *Nature*, vol. 352 (August 8, 1991), pp. 485-486. Hull is in the Department of Philosophy, Northwestern University.

p. 486   "What kind of God can one infer from the sort of phenomena epitomized by the species on Darwin's Galÿpagos Islands? The evolutionary process is rife with happenstance, contingency, incredible waste, death, pain and horror."

p. 486   "Whatever the God implied by evolutionary theory and the data of natural history may be like, He is not the Protestant God of waste not, want not. He is also not a loving God who cares about His productions. He is not even the awful God portrayed in the book of Job. The God of Galápagos is careless, wasteful, indifferent, almost diabolical. He is certainly not the sort of god to whom anyone would be inclined to pray."

Medawar, P. B., and J. S. Medawar, *The Life Science: Current Ideas of Biology* (New York: Harper and Row, 1977), 196 pp.

p. 11   "The attitude of biologists to teleology is like that of the pious towards a source of temptation which they are unsure of their ability to resist. This is the reason why biologists prefer to use the genteelism *teleonomy* with merely descriptive connotations to signify the goal-directed or 'as-if purposive' character of biological performances."

p. 169   "Unfortunately, the testimony of Design is only for those who, secure in their beliefs already, are in no need of confirmation. This is just as well, for there is no theological comfort in the ampliation of DNA and it is no use looking to evolution: the balance sheet of evolution has so closely written a debit column of all the blood and pain that goes into the natural process that not even the smoothest accountancy can make the transaction seem morally solvent according to any standards of morals that human beings are accustomed to."

Monod, Jacques, *Chance and Necessity* (New York: Alfred A. Knopf, 1971), 199 pp.

p. 180   "Where then shall we find the source of truth and the moral inspiration for a really *scientific* socialist humanism, if not in the sources of science itself, in the ethic upon which knowledge is founded, and which by free choice makes knowledge the supreme value—the measure and warrant for all other values? . . . It prescribes institutions dedicated to the defense, the extension, the enrichment of the transcendent kingdom of ideas, of knowledge, and of creation—a kingdom which is within man, where progressively freed both from material constraints and from the deceitful servitudes of animism, he could at last live authentically, protected by institutions which, seeing in him the subject of the kingdom and at the same time its creator, could be designed to serve him in his unique and precious essence.

". . . The ancient covenant is in pieces; man knows at last that he is alone in the universe's unfeeling immensity, out of which he emerged only by chance. His destiny is nowhere spelled out, nor is his duty. The kingdom above or the darkness below: it is for him to choose."

Monod, Jacques, "The Secret of Life," Interview with Laurie John, Australian Broadcasting Co., June 10, 1976 (shortly before his death).

"If we believe in a Creator—it is basically for moral reasons, in order to see a goal for our own lives. And why would God have to have chosen this extremely complex and difficult mechanism. When, I would say by definition He was at liberty to choose other mechanisms, why would He have to start with simple molecules? Why not create man right away, as of course classical religions believed.

"[Natural] selection is the blindest, and most cruel way of evolving new species, and more and more complex and refined organisms. . . . The struggle for life and elimination of the weakest is a horrible process, against which our whole modern ethics revolts. An ideal society is a non-selective society, one where the weak is protected; which is exactly the reverse of the so-called natural law. I am surprised that a Christian would defend the idea that this is the process which God more or less set up in order to have evolution."

Murdy, W. H., "Anthropocentrism: A Modern Version," *Science*, vol. 187 (March 28, 1975), pp. 1168-1172. Murdy was a Professor of Biology, Emory University.

p. 1169   "Before life, our ancestry extends back through billions of years of molecular change to the nuclei of former stars. Here the elements necessary for life were built up from hydrogen, the simplest and most abundant element in the universe. Beyond primordial hydrogen, our ancestral roots became lost in a profound mystery,—the beginning of things, the origin of the universe of matter, energy, space and time."

p. 1171   "The maximization of reproductive potential is, from the biological point of view, in the best interest of most species. This was true for man throughout most of his history."

p. 1172   "Unbridled self-indulgence on the part of one generation without regard to future ones is the modus operandi of biological evolution and may be regarded as rational behavior."

Ruse, Michael, and Edward O. Wilson, "Evolution & Ethics*," New Scientist*, vol. 108 (October 17, 1985), pp. 50-52.

p. 50   "Attempts to link evolution and ethics first sprang up in the middle of the last century, as people turned to alternative foundations in response to what they perceived as the collapse of Christianity. If God does not stand behind the Sermon on the Mount, then what does?"

pp. 51-2   "Morality, or more strictly our belief in morality, is merely an adaptation put in place to further our reproductive ends. Hence the basis of ethics does not lie in God's will. . . . In an important sense, ethics as we understand it is an illusion fobbed off on us by our genes to get us to cooperate."

p. 52   "Ethical codes work because they drive us to go against our selfish day-to-day impulses in favor of long-term group survival and harmony. . . . Furthermore, the way our biology forces its ends is by making us think that there is an objective higher code, to which we are all subject.

Russell, Bertrand, *Religion and Science*, (Oxford University Press, 1961), pp. 73-81.

p. 73   "Religion, in our day, has accommodated itself to the doctrine of evolution, and has even derived new arguments from it. We are told that 'through the ages one increasing purpose runs,' and that evolution is the unfolding of an idea which has been in the mind of God throughout. It appears that during those ages which so troubled Hugh Miller, when animals were torturing each other with ferocious horns and agonizing stings, Omnipotence was quietly waiting for the ultimate emergence of man, with his still more widely diffused cruelty. Why the Creator should have preferred to reach His goal by a process, instead of going straight to it, these modern theologians do not tell us. Nor do they say much to allay our doubts as to the gloriousness of the consummation. It is difficult not to feel, as the boy did after being taught the alphabet, that it was not worth going through so much to get so little. This, however, is a matter of taste.

"There is another, and a graver objection to any theology based on evolution. In the 60's and 70's, when the vogue of the doctrine was new, progress was accepted as a law of the world. Were we not growing richer year by year, and enjoying budget surpluses in spite of taxation? . . . And could anyone doubt that progress would go on indefinitely? Science and mechanical ingenuity, which had produced it, could surely be trusted to go on producing it ever more abundantly. In such a world, evolution seemed only a generalization of everyday life.

"But even then, to the more reflective, another side was apparent. The same laws which produce growth also produce decay. Some day, the sun will grow cold, and life on earth will cease. The whole epoch of animals and plants is only an interlude between ages that will be too cold. There is no law of cosmic progress, but only an oscillation upward and downward, with a slow trend downward on the balance owing to the diffusion of energy. This, at least, is what science at present regards as most probable, and in our disillusioned generation, it is easy to believe. From evolution, so far as our present knowledge shows, no ultimately optimistic philosophy can be validly inferred.

"Was not our machinery the wonder of the world, and our parliamentary government a model for the imitation of enlightened foreigners?"

Sagan, Carl, *Cosmos* (New York: Random House, 1980), 365 pp.

p. 30 "The secrets of evolution are death and time—the deaths of enormous numbers of lifeforms that were imperfectly adapted to the environment; and time for a long succession of small mutations that were by *accident* adaptive, time for the slow accumulation of patterns of favorable mutations."

B. Communism and Nazism

Among the most bitter fruits of evolutionism are the unspeakably cruel systems fathered by Karl Marx (followed by Engels, Lenin, Stalin, Mao, etc.) and by Adolf Hitler (who was building on the ideas of Nietzsche and Haeckel and others). It is arguable whether communism (with its anarchist and socialist cousins) or Nazism (with Mussolini's fascism and similar dictatorships) have produced the greater amounts of death and suffering in the world, but both were and are vile and deadly.

It is very significant, therefore, that both Marx and Hitler, with all their respective forbears, associates and successors, were doctrinaire evolutionists, trying to build their respective societies on evolutionary premises. There is abundant documentation of this assessment and, in fact, few would even question it.

Evolutionism—especially in the form of Darwinism—has much to account for in these two evil fruits.

Barzun, Jacques, *Darwin, Marx, Wagner*, 2nd ed. (Garden City, New York: Doubleday, 958), 373 pp. Barzun was Dean of the Graduate Faculties at Columbia University and a prominent contemporary historian.

p. 8 "It is a commonplace that Marx felt his own work to be the exact parallel of Darwin's. He even wished to dedicate a portion of *Das Kapital* to the author of *The Origin of Species*."

p. 170 "It is that, like Darwin, Marx thought he had discovered the law of development. He saw history in stages, as the Darwinists saw geological strata and successive forms of life. . . .

"But there are even finer points of comparison. In keeping with the feelings of the age, both Marx and Darwin made struggle the means of development. Again, the measure of value in Darwin is survival with reproduction—an absolute fact occurring in time and which wholly disregards the moral or esthetic quality of the product. In Marx the measure of value is expended labor—an absolute fact occurring in time, which also disregards the utility of the product."

Bergman, Jerry, "Eugenics and the Development of Nazi Race Policy," *Perspectives on Science and Christian Faith*, vol. 44 (June 1992), pp. 109-123. Bergman is a Professor of Science at Northwest Technical College in Archbold, Ohio. He holds two doctorates in psychology and biology.

p. 109 "*Abstract.* A central government policy of the Hitler administration was the breeding of a 'superior race.' This required, at the very least, preventing the 'inferior races' from mixing with 'superior' ones in order to reduce contamination of the latter's gene pool. The 'superior race' belief is based on the theory of group inequality within each species, a major presumption and requirement of

Darwin's original 'survival of the fittest' theory. A review of the writings of Hitler and contemporary German biologists finds that Darwin's theory and writings had a major influence upon Nazi policies. Hitler believed that the human gene pool could be improved by selective breeding, using the same techniques that farmers used to breed a superior strain of cattle. In the formulation of his racial policies, he relied heavily upon the Darwinian evolution model, especially the elaborations by Spencer and Haeckel. They culminated in the 'final solution,' the extermination of approximately six million Jews and four million other people who belonged to what German scientists judged were 'inferior races.'"

Bethell, Tom, "Burning Darwin to Save Marx," *Harper's Magazine* (December 1978), pp. 31-38, 91-92.

p. 34   "Today the genetic classification of races is considered to be misguided at best. Richard C. Lewontin, a population geneticist and Alexander Agassiz, Professor of Zoology, at Harvard, . . . Like Gould, . . . has described himself as a Marxist."

pp. 36-7   "The foregoing exemplifies the problem of the classification of data in science—a problem that tends to be solved in a way that harmonizes with reigning political sentiment. . . . The natural world is, after all, filled with billions of 'facts,' only a tiny fraction in any given period are observed and described by scientists. And it seems that the facts that *are* picked out tend to recommend themselves precisely because they are to some degree aligned with political expectations.

                "A good example increasingly under discussion is Darwin's theory of evolution—the theory of natural selection (according to which plants and animals evolved because they left offspring that were 'fitter' than themselves). As with genetic theories of race, this has been found to have implications contrary to the egalitarian spirit of the times, hence in need of revision. As one would expect, the recent attack on Darwinism has come from the Left."

p. 37   "Marx admired [Darwin's] book not for economic reasons but for the more fundamental one that Darwin's universe was purely materialistic, and the explication of it no longer involved any reference to unobservable, nonmaterial causes outside or 'beyond' it. In that important respect, Darwin and Marx were truly comrades."

p. 38   "No longer is unrestrained competition, once perceived as beneficial to business production and animal production alike, considered acceptable. We now live in a time when lip service, at least, is paid to notions of collective effort and collective security. One can see why Darwinism would upset the Left. . . . Evolution was nature's eugenics program. How do you think our Marxist biologists like that idea? They don't like it at all."

p. 38   "Noam Chomsky is a devotee of Kropotkin, and so is Richard Lewontin."

p. 92   "[Natural selection] is accused of being an unfalisifiable theory which, according to the influential philosopher of science, Karl Popper, removes it from the realm of the scientific. Darwinian theory, Popper now says, is a 'metaphysical research program.'"

p. 92   "The left-wing critique of Darwinian theory has by no means prevailed, but if it should do so, let us also enjoy the fantastic irony that the fundamentalists, who have been trying for more than a hundred years to knock Darwin off his pedestal, without success, will be indebted not to the right-wingers, with whom they have always been aligned, but to biologists whose god is Marx."

Cartmill, Matt, David R. Pilbeam, and Glynn Isaac, "One Hundred Years of Paleoanthropology," *American Scientist*, vol. 74 (July/August 1986), pp. 410-420.

p. 418   "The nonscientific influence was the Holocaust. The military collapse of Germany and the unveiling of the death camps prompted a universal revulsion of the intelligentsia against the intellectual traditions that had contributed to Nazi ideology, foremost among them the notion of a hierarchical subordination of human populations. That notion, which had underlain most earlier thinking about human evolution, was extirpated from anthropological thought after World War II and replaced with a firm faith in the unity, continuity, and equality of the Family of Man."

Conner, Cliff, "Evolution vs. Creationism: In Defense of Scientific Thinking," *International Socialist Review (Monthly Magazine Supplement to the Militant)* (November 1980).

"Defending Darwin is nothing new for socialists. The socialist movement recognized Darwinism as an important element in its general world outlook right from the start. When Darwin published his *Origin of Species* in 1859, Karl Marx wrote a letter to Frederick Engels in which he said, '. . . this is the book which contains the basis in natural history for our view.'

"By defending Darwinism, working people strengthen their defenses against the attacks of these reactionary outfits, and prepare the way for the transformation of the social order.

"[We are] revolutionary socialists, . . [whose aim is] . . . as Marx said: not merely to interpret the world but to change it.

"And of all those eminent researchers of the nineteenth century who have left us such a rich heritage of knowledge, we are especially grateful to Charles Darwin for opening our way to an evolutionary dialectical understanding of nature."

Craige, Betty Jean, "The Pursuit of Truth is Inherently Disruptive and Anti-Authoritarian," *Chronicle of Higher Education* (January 6, 1993), p. A56.

p. A56   "The social and conceptual revolution that we are now witnessing, which is characterized by a call for the appreciation of diversity, can be traced back to Darwin."

p. A56   "The cultural holists' critiques of what has long been considered truth in the West are really not very different from the critiques of early 19th-century science made by the Darwinian evolutionists. Not only are the cultural holists, like the evolutionists, rejecting the conceptualization of reality bequeathed by Plato and Aristotle, but they also are using evolutionary and ecological concepts to explain social conflict and social change. As revolutionary as their work may appear to conservative scholars, it is grounded in the evolutionary model that scientists no longer question."

p. A56   "What right-wing critics of the academy did not understand in the late 19th century, and do not understand now, is that the pursuit of truth is inherently disruptive; it is anti-authoritarian. To seek truth is to disbelieve what others take on faith. It was to protect the pursuit of truth that late-19th-century American academics—responding to the effort to silence advocates of Darwin's theories—adopted the principle of academic freedom."

Eidelberg, Paul, "Karl Marx and the Declaration of Independence: the Meaning of Marxism," *Intercollegiate Review*, vol. 20 (Spring/Summer 1984), pp. 3-11. Eidelberg was Professor of Political Science, Bar Ilan University, Ramat-Gan, Israel.

p. 4   "What most distinguishes the Declaration of Independence from the *Communist Manifesto* is that the former affirms, while the latter denies . . . the power of reason to apprehend trans-historical truths or 'the laws of nature and of nature's God.'"

p. 5   "This freedom of the intellect is itself a part of the laws of nature and of nature's God, or say of creation; which means that these laws are constitutive of man's very being; they distinguish human from sub-human creation."

p. 5   "Hence each individual belongs to himself (ultimately to his Creator). He is a center of purposes and cannot be used as a mere means for a purpose. In other words, he cannot be used as if he were an inferior species. . . . He is the creature of God, not of society or of men."

p. 10   "Clearly, for Marx man has no 'nature.' Indeed it is the nature of man to have no nature, no permanent nature. . . . For man is his own maker and will consciously become his own maker in complete freedom from morality or from the laws of nature and of nature's God."

p. 10   "Here we see why Marxism justifies the ruthless sacrifice of men living today, men who, at this stage of history, are only partly human. . . . Indeed, Marx's eschatology, his materialistic philosophy of history is, for all practical purposes, a doctrine of *permanent* revolution, a doctrine which cannot but issue in periodic violence, terror, and tyranny."

p. 10   "In Marx we are at the opposite pole from the statesmen of the Declaration of Independence, nay, more, from the fundamental principles of western civilization."

Gasmann, Daniel, *The Scientific Origins of National Socialism: Social Darwinism in Ernst Haeckel and the German Monist League* (New York: American Elsevier, 1971), 208 pp.

pp. xvii   "Along with his social Darwinist followers, [Haeckel] set about to demonstrate the 'aristocratic' and non-democratic character of the laws of nature. . . . Up to his death in 1919, Haeckel contributed to that special variety of German thought which served as the seed-bed for National Socialism. He became one of Germany's major ideologists for racism, nationalism and imperialism."

p. 168   "[Hitler] stressed and singled out the idea of biological evolution as the most forceful weapon against traditional religion and he repeatedly condemned Christianity for its opposition to the teaching of evolution. . . . For Hitler, evolution was the hallmark of modern science and culture, and he defended its veracity as tenaciously as Haeckel."

Gould, Stephen Jay, and Niles Eldredge, "Punctuated Equilibria; the Tempo and Mode of Evolution Reconsidered," *Paleobiology*, vol. 3 (Spring 1977), pp. 115-151.

pp. 145-6   "Alternate conceptions of change have respectable pedigrees in philosophy. Hegel's dialectical laws, translated into a materialist context, have become the official 'state philosophy' of many socialist nations. These laws of change are explicitly punctuational, as befits a theory of revolutionary transformation in human society."

p. 146   "In the light of this official philosophy, it is not at all surprising that a punctuational view of speciation, much like our own, but devoid (so far as we can tell) of reference to synthetic evolutionary theory and the allopatric model, has long been favored by many Russian paleontologists. It may also not be irrelevant to our personal preferences that one of us learned his Marxism, literally at his daddy's knee."

Halstead, L. Beverly, "Museum of Errors," *Nature*, vol. 288 (November 20, 1980), p. 208. Halstead is Professor of Zoology and Geology, University of Reading, United Kingdom.

p. 208   "According to the stated assumptions of cladistics none of the fossil species can be ancestral by definition. This presents the public for the first time with the notion that there are no fossils directly antecedent to man. What the creationists have insisted on for years is now being openly advertised by the Natural History Museum."

p. 208   "The next question is why should the notion of gradualism arouse passions of such intensity? The answer to this is to be found in the political arena."

p. 208   "If it could be established that the pattern of evolution is a saltatory one after all, then at long last the Marxists would indeed be able to claim that the theoretical basis of their approach was supported by scientific evidence. Just as there are 'scientific' creationists seeking to falsify the concept of gradual change through time in favor of creationism, so too there are the Marxists who for different motives are equally concerned to discredit gradualism."

Halstead, L. Beverly, "Popper: Good Philosophy, Bad Science?" *New Scientist*, vol. 87 (July 17, 1980), pp. 215-217.

p. 215   "Karl Popper in his autobiography *Unended Quest* writes: 'I have come to the conclusion that Darwinism is not a testable scientific theory, but a metaphysical research program—a possible framework for testable scientific theories.'"

p. 215   "Peter Medawar: 'I think Popper is incomparably the greatest philosopher of science that has ever been.'"

p. 216   "Popper's definition of science is such that all disciplines with an historic or time component are automatically excluded."

pp. 216-7   "The theoretical basis of communism is dialectical materialism which was expounded with great clarity by Frederick Engels in *Anti-Duhrüng* and *The Dialectics of Nature*. He recognized the great value of the contributions made by geology in establishing that there was constant movement and change in nature and the significance of Darwin's demonstration that this applied also to the organic world. . . .The crux of the entire theoretical framework, however, is in the nature of qualitative changes. This is also spelt out by Engels in *The Dialectics of Nature*, 'a development in which the qualitative changes occur not gradually but rapidly and abruptly, taking the form of a leap from one state to another.' . . .

                "Here then is the recipe of revolution."

Hemstreet, Robert M., "Religious Humanism Meets Scientific Atheism," *The Humanist*, vol. 47 (January/February 1987), pp. 5-7, 34.

p. 6   "In spite of the disestablishment of the Russian Orthodox church in 1918, there is in fact an official state religion in the Soviet Union. Originally, it was called 'The Science of Marxism' or 'Dialectical Materialism,' the philosophy of Marxism. But since 1954, the year after the death of Stalin, by decree of the Central Committee of the CPSU, it has officially been dubbed 'Scientific Atheism.' This religion—or counter-religion—is spearheaded by a think-tank of some forty scholars comprising the Institute for Scientific Atheism, headquartered in Moscow, a division of the Academy of Social Sciences, founded in 1963."

p. 6   "One of the most important tasks of the parent institute is to design the curricula for the required university one-semester course on scientific atheism, which was introduced in 1964."

Hickey, David R., "Evolution, Environment, and the Collapse of Soviet Communism," *The Humanist*, vol. 52 (January/February 1992), pp. 33-35, 40.

p. 33   "And because environment, in turn, is by definition the sum product of biological evolution, I propose that the ultimate cause of Soviet communism's economic collapse lies in a state 'policy' on evolution upon which its economy—particularly its agricultural policy—was founded."

p. 34   "Politically tailored evolutionary theory is most evident and familiar in the Western world's adoption of Darwinian natural selection to justify its capitalist policies and rationalize its antagonism toward nature."

p. 34   "I propose that Stalin's unyielding support of Lamarckian evolutionary theory, which he deemed consistent with Marxist socioeconomic theory, was the final cause of Soviet communism's collapse."

p. 40   "We must accept the fact that the direction of evolution's change may well be antithetical to our notions of 'progress.'"

Himmelfarb, Gertrude, *Darwin and the Darwinian Revolution* (London: Chatto & Windus, 1959), 422 pp.

pp. 343-4   "From the 'Preservation of Favoured Races in the struggle for life' [i.e., Darwin's subtitle to *Origin of Species*], it was a short step to the preservation of favoured individuals, classes or nations—and from their preservation to their glorification. Social Darwinism has often been understood in this sense: as a philosophy, exalting competition, power and violence over convention, ethics and religion. Thus it has become a portmanteau of nationalism, imperialism, militarism, and dictatorship, of the cults of the hero, the superman, and the master race."

p. 344   "Recent expressions of this philosophy, such as [Hitler's] *Mein Kampf*, are, unhappily, too familiar to require exposition here. And it is by an obvious process of analogy and education that they are said to derive from Darwinism. Nietzsche predicted that this would be the consequence if the Darwinian theory gained general acceptance."

pp. 348-9   "There was truth in *Engels' eulogy on Marx*: 'Just as Darwin discovered the law of evolution in organic nature, so Marx discovered the law of evolution in human history.' What they both celebrated was the internal rhythm and course of life, the one the life of nature, the other of society, that proceeded by fixed laws, undistracted by the will of God or men. There were no catastrophes in history as there were none in nature. There were no inexplicable acts, no violations of the natural order. God was as powerless as individual men to interfere with the internal, self-adjusting dialectic of change and development."

Hoffman, Peter, *Hitler's Personal Security* (London: Macmillan Press, 1979), 321 pp.

p. 264   "Hitler believed in struggle as a Darwinian principle of human life that forced every people to try to dominate all others; without struggle they would rot and perish. . . . Even in his own defeat in April 1945 Hitler expressed his faith in the survival of the stronger and declared the Slavic peoples to have proven themselves the stronger."

Hofstadter, Richard, *Social Darwinism in American Thought* (New York: George Braziller, Inc., 1959), 248 pp.

p. 115   "Orthodox Marxian socialists in the early years of the 20th century felt quite at home in Darwinian surroundings. Karl Marx himself, with his belief in universal 'dialectical' principles, had been as much a monist as Comte or Spencer. Reading *The Origin of Species* in *1860*, he reported to Friedrich Engels, and later declared to Ferdinand LaSalle, that 'Darwin's book is very important, and serves me as a basis in natural science for the class struggle in history.' On the shelves of the socialist bookstores in Germany the words of Darwin and Marx stood side by side."

Hsü, Kenneth J., "Sedimentary Petrology and Biologic Evolution," *Journal of Sedimentary Petrology*, vol. 56 (September 1986), pp. 729-732.

p. 729   "Darwin all but ignored the fossil record, complaining about the imperfections of the geologic record. He and his followers wrote the history of life on the basis of what they thought the history should be. The Darwinistic dictum of variation/ adaption/natural selection/speciation has been supposed to be the rule in the history of life. This method of writing history is very much like attempting to develop a history of the antique by studying sociology, psychology, and political science of the present world."

p. 730   "Haeckelian Darwinism found its terroristic expression in national socialism. For Hitler, evolution was the hallmark of modern science and his 'views of history, politics, religion, Christianity, nature, eugenics, science, art, and evolution, . . . coincide for the most part with those of Haeckel.' In the biological theory of Darwin, Hitler found his most powerful weapon against traditional values.

              "The rising tides of modern creationism may have been inspired by a reaction against the philosophy of social Darwinism. But creationists are barking up the wrong tree. We have plenty of evidence in the geological record for the Darwinian theory of common descent. The root of the evil is not the postulate of evolution, but the Darwinian emphasis on natural selection as a consequence of biotic interactions."

Hull, David L., "Darwinism and Dialectics," review of *The Dialectical Biologist*, by Richard Levins and Richard Lewontin (Harvard University Press, 1985, 303 pp.), *Nature*, vol. 320 (March 6, 1985), pp. 23-24. Hull was Professor of Philosophy, Northwestern University.

p. 23   "Richard Levins and Richard Lewontin are two of the most knowledgeable and innovative evolutionary biologists working today. They also view themselves as Marxist revolutionaries. As Marxists, Levins and Lewontin insist that the economic substructure of a society strongly influences its ideational superstructure, including science."

p. 23   "Intellectuals are well aware that all sorts of half-articulated preferences and assumptions influence what they believe. For example, some of the resistance to Darwin's theory in the nineteenth century resulted from how messy and wasteful it was; whatever the God of the Galapagos might be, he certainly was not the Protestant God of Waste Not, Want Not."

p. 23   "As dialectical biologists, Levins and Lewontin share with Darwinians a commitment to materialism and the universality of change but reject the reductionism which they see as pervading present-day Darwinism."

Jorafsky, David, *Soviet Marxism and Natural Science* (New York: Columbia University Press, 1961), 433 pp.

p. 4   "However harshly a philosophy may judge this characterization of Marx's theory [i.e., that Marxism unifies science and revolution intrinsically and inseparably], an historian can hardly fail to agree that Marx's claim to give scientific guidance to those who would transform society has been one of the chief reasons for his doctrine's enormous influence."

p. 12   "More significantly, Marx and Engels were convinced that Darwin had 'delivered the mortal blow' to teleology in natural science by providing a rational explanation of functional adaptation in living things and by proving his explanation empirically. On the most general level, they welcomed Darwin's theory, and complementary theories of geological and cosmic evolution, as confirmation of their belief that throughout nature (the human variety included) present reality continually 'negates' itself, continually gives rise to a different reality in accordance with natural laws that can be established scientifically. These were presumably the reasons for their repeated statements to the effect that Darwin's work 'contains the basis of natural history for our view [of human history].' Indeed Marx wanted to dedicate parts of *Capital* to Darwin, but Darwin declined the honor because, he wrote Marx, he did not know the work, because he did not believe that direct attacks on religion advanced the cause of free thought, and finally because he did not want to upset 'some members of my family.'"

Keith, Sir Arthur, *Evolution and Ethics* (New York: G. P. Putnam's Sons, 1947), 246 pp.

p. 15   "Meantime let me say that the conclusion I have come to is this: the law of Christ is incompatible with the law of evolution . . . as far as the law of evolution has worked hitherto. Nay, the two laws are at war with each other; the law of Christ can never prevail until the law of evolution is destroyed."

p. 28   "To see evolutionary measures and tribal morality being applied rigorously to the affairs of a great modern nation we must turn again to Germany of 1942. We see Hitler devoutly convinced that evolution produces the only real basis for a national policy."

p. 72   "Christianity makes no distinction of race or of color; it seeks to break down all racial barriers. In this respect, the hand of Christianity is against that of Nature, for are not the races of mankind the evolutionary harvest which Nature has toiled through long ages to produce? May we not say, then, that Christianity is anti-evolutionary in its aim? This may be a merit, but if so it is one which has not been openly acknowledged by Christian philosophers."

p. 150   "The law of evolution, as formulated by Darwin, provides an explanation of wars between nations, the only reasonable explanation known to us. The law was in existence, and wars were waged, for aeons of time before Darwin was born; he did not invent the law, he only made it known to his fellow men."

p. 230   "The German Führer, as I have consistently maintained, is an evolutionist; he has consciously sought to make the practice of Germany conform to the theory of evolution. He has failed, not because the theory of evolution is false, but because he had made three fatal blunders in its application. . . . First . . . forcing the pace of evolution among his own people. . . . Second . . . his misconception of the evolutionary value of power. . . . Third . . . His third and greatest mistake was his failure to realize that such a monopoly of power meant insecurity for Britain, Russia, and America. His three great antagonists, although they do not preach the doctrine of evolution, are very consistent exponents of its tenets."

Lenczowski, John, "The Treason of the Intellectuals: Higher Education, the Culture War and the Threat to U.S. National Security," *Policy Counsel* (Fall 1996), pp. 35-52. Lenczowski is Former Director of European and Soviet Affairs, National Security Council, 1983-1987.

pp. 35-36   "Throughout that war, we were confronted with the phenomenon of the 'Treason of the Intellectuals,' where large segments of our intelligentsia collaborated intellectually and politically with our enemies. The treason took several forms, whose effects were to aid the political and ideological dimensions of the Soviet and international communist cold war against us."

p. 36   "Ultimately, it was not just a war between us here and them over there. It was a war between two visions of society, two philosophies of life. It was a moral conflict between truth and falsehood at two different levels."

pp. 41-42   "The question is: Where did these debilitating and dangerous policies come from? What is it that generates the treason of the intellectuals?

"The answer, I submit, is our educational system, and in particular, our elite universities, which are the most subversive institutions in American society today—more than the media, more than the movies, more than all the other influences.

"Because the rot starts in the head, and only then it spreads throughout the body.

"Parents can work hard to educate their children to be patriots and morally upright citizens. But four years of college of the kind I experienced—where I was surrounded by a culture of drugs, sexual libertinism, political radicalism and little homework—can destroy the efforts of the best parents in America. Add to that a few years of graduate school and the counter-cultural influence can prove to be irremediable."

p. 44   "In one fell swoop, through these various premises, the intellectuals deny the existence of God; they deny that God made human life a series of moral choices; and they assert that they, through the supremacy of their human reason, and not God, are the creative intelligence of this world."

p. 45   "But I would guess that 95 percent of the social scientists in America's elite universities—or could it be 99 percent?—would not sign the Declaration of Independence if they were honest about it. They simply do not believe in the first paragraph. They do not believe that rights come from any Creator. And thus, they cannot believe in the fundamental tenet of American democracy: majority rule with minority rights. Because unless rights come from a higher authority, one with the capability to endow rights unconditionally, the majority can always attach conditions to rights or deny them to whichever minority group it chooses to victimize."

Posner, G. L, and J. Ware, *Mengele: The Complete Story* (New York: McGraw-Hill, 1986), 364 pp.

p. 9   "In Munich, meanwhile, Joseph was taking courses in anthropology and paleontology, as well as medicine. . . . Probably it was a combination of the political climate and that his real interest in genetics and evolution happened to coincide with the developing concept that some human beings afflicted by disorders were unfit to reproduce, even to live. . . . His consummate ambition was to succeed in this fashionable new field of evolutionary research."

[Joseph Mengele, the "angel of death" at Auschwitz, noted for his gruesome experiments on humans at Auschwitz, was a respectable German medical student in the 1930's.—Editor]

Proctor, Robert N., "Science and Nazism," review of *Murderous Science*, by Benno Müller-Hill (New York: Oxford University Press, 1988, 208 pp.), *Science*, vol. 241 (August 5, 1988), pp. 730-731.

p. 730   "The thesis of the work is that 'human genetics played a crucial role in the atrocities committed by the Nazis.'

"Evidence for this claim is powerful, and disturbing. Eugene Fischer, for example, as head of the Kaiser Wilhelm Institute for Anthropology, Human Genetics and Eugenics (1927-1942), supervised the training of SS physicians and helped to administer the sterilization of German-Negro half-breeds in the Rhineland."

p. 730   "Much of this book reads as a catalog of horrors. We read how scholars at the Kaiser Wilhelm Institute for Brain Research scrambled to obtain the brains of murdered mentally ill (for purposes of dissection), and how the German Association for Scientific Research (DFG) provided support for Otmar von Verschuer, Fisher's successor at the Kaiser Wilhelm Institute for Anthropology, to have his assistant, Josef Mengele, prepare and ship eyes, blood, and other body parts back to Berlin for analysis."

p. 730   "Müller-Hill stresses that Nazi racial policy was the work of trained scholars, not ignorant fanatics: how else are we to interpret the fact that 7 out of 14 participants at the notorious Wannsee conference (outlining plans for the 'final solution') possessed doctorates or that leading German psychiatrists were mobilized with hardly a single protest to exterminate German's mentally ill? . . . That ideology, according to Müller-Hill, was that 'there is a biological basis for the diversity of Mankind.' Anthropologists and psychiatrists were able to give 'a scientific gloss and tidiness' to the Nazi regime and its activities."

pp. 730-1   "What is slowly becoming clear is that scientists and physicians played a much greater role in the construction of Nazi policy than has heretofore been recognized; new efforts will no doubt continue to shed light on this darker, hidden chapter in the history of science."

Reilly, Robert R., "Atheism and Arms Control," *Intercollegiate Review*, vol. 24 (Fall 1988), pp. 15-21. Reilly is President of Inter-Collegiate Studies Institute.

p. 19   "The problem is that, by denying the possibility of a relationship between God and man, atheism also denies the possibility of a just relationship between men. . . . Human life is sacred only if there is a God to sanctify it. Otherwise man is just another collection of atoms and can be treated as such."

p. 19   "The spiritual disorder within man's soul of which Saint James wrote has become, in the modern age, institutionalized. In other words the moral disorder of the individual soul has become the principle of a general public disorder first as it was articulated in the teachings of Nietzsche and Marx, and then incarnated in the Nazi regime and in the various Marxist-Leninist states today."

p. 20   "As Lenin said, 'Every religious idea of a god, even flirting with the idea of god, is unutterable vileness of the most dangerous kind, 'contagion' of the most abominable kind. Millions of sins, filthy deeds, acts of violence, and physical contagions are far less dangerous *than the subtle spiritual idea of a god.*'"

Rifkin, Jeremy, *Algeny* (New York: Viking Press, 1983), 298 pp.

p. 95   "Darwin's theory offered a resolution to humanity's perennial crisis of guilt. By proposing that each organism's drive for self-containment actually benefited the species as well as nature as a whole, Darwin found a convenient formula for expiating the accumulating guilt of an age when self-interest and personal aggrandizement ruled supreme."

p. 105   "As Geoffrey West notes: 'Darwinism has been seized upon by all parties as a strong bulwark in defence of their contradictory preconceptions. On the one hand Nietzche, on the other Marx, and between them most shades of Aristocracy, Democracy, Individualism, Socialism, Capitalism, Militarism, Materialism and even Religion.'" (*Charles Darwin: A Portrait*; New Haven, Yale University Press, 1938, p. 324)

p. 108   "Darwin's cosmology sanctioned an entire age of history. Convinced that their own behavior was in consort with the workings of nature, industrial man and woman were armed with the ultimate justification they needed to continue their relentless exploitation of the environment and their fellow human beings without ever having to stop for even a moment to reflect on the consequences of their actions."

Ruse, Michael, "The Ideology of Darwinism," in *Darwin Today*, edited by E. Geisler and W. Scheler (Berlin: Akademie-Verlag, 1983). Ruse is Professor of Philosophy, Guelph University.

p. 246   "Quite openly, one of the leading punctuated equilibrists, Stephen Jay Gould, admits to his Marxism, and lauds the way in which his science is informed by his beliefs, and how conversely his beliefs are bolstered by his science.

         "Specifically, Gould identifies three points where his paleontology and his Marxism interact, and where he feels drawn toward punctuated equilibrium because he is a Marxist—and where, no doubt, his Marxism guided his paleontological theorizing."

p. 246   "In short, what I argue is that through and through Gould produces and endorses a view of paleontology which is molded by, and conversely supports and proclaims a view of the world he holds dear. We are offered the fossil record as seen through the lens of Marxism."

Ruse, Michael, "Biology and Values: A Fresh Look," in *Logic, Methodology, and Philosophy of Science*, by Barcan Marcus *et al.* (Elsevier Science Publications B.V., 1986), pp. 453-466.

p. 456   "[Oparin] was quite open in his subscription to a Marxist-Leninist philosophy of nature, and consciously applied it to his work on the appearance of new life."

p. 460   "Much of Gould's justification for his paleontological perspective comes from Marxist philosophy. . . . Gould criticized Darwinian gradualism as being just as act of faith, reflecting Darwin's own 19th century liberal views about the virtues of gradual (as opposed to revolutionary) change. Gould, to the contrary endorses a philosophy which leads him to expect rapid, abrupt breaks with the past. His view of the fossil record is therefore simply his own world picture made, if not flesh, then stone."

Segerstrale, Ullica, "Colleagues in Conflict: An 'In Vivo' Analysis of the Sociobiology Controversy," *Biology and Philosophy*, vol. 1, no. 1 (1986), pp. 53-87.

p. 57 "Wilson's zeal in making sociobiology a truly predictive science, encompassing all social behavior, was intimately tied to an old desire of his: to prove the [Christian] theologians wrong."

p. 59 "Just as the key to understanding Wilson is his strong devotion to his view of evolutionary theory as a total explanatory scheme, so the key to understanding Lewontin is the latter's equally strong devotion to his version of Marxism."

p. 79 "For Wilson, the 'reductionist program' represented the tool which would help him combat metaphysical holism and irrational religious dogma, while Lewontin felt compelled by his more recent Marxist ambitions to criticize reductionism and especially reductionist claims about humans as both scientifically incorrect and politically suspect."

Simon, Edward, "Another Side to the Evolution Problem," *Jewish Press* (January 7, 1983), p. 24B. Simon is Professor of Biology, Purdue University, Association of Orthodox Jewish Scientists, 45 West 36th Street, New York, New York 10018.

"I don't claim that Darwin and his theory of evolution brought on the holocaust; but I cannot deny that the theory of evolution, and the atheism it engendered, led to the moral climate that made a holocaust possible.

"But there is another, equally sinister, side to this argument. *Consider*—if life has evolved, by chance alone, then no creature is qualitatively different from any other. If it is morally reprehensible to kill a man, then it is equally odious to kill our 'brother' the chimpanzee. By the same token, how can we kill cows for food, or dogs or mice for research? And mosquitoes? Well, let's not carry things too far.

"The Torah teaches us a different approach. . . . Man was also given dominion over all animals on land, sea, and air, as well as a moral code to live by. Therefore, he cannot be compared to animals and treated as such, nor can the animals be compared to man and accorded his rights."

Stein, George J., "Biological Science and the Roots of Nazism," *American Scientist*, vol. 76 (January/February 1988), pp. 50-58.

p. 52 "National socialism, whatever else it may have been (for example, a revolt of the petty bourgeoisie) was ultimately the first fully self-conscious attempt to organize a political community on a basis of an explicit biopolicy: a biopolicy fully congruent (or so it was claimed) with the scientific facts of the Darwinian revolution. What then were the roots of the biopolicy?

". . . All manner of liberal thinkers have appropriated Darwin to find, at last, a scientific foundation for the liberal belief in progress, democratic egalitarian socialism, and an altruistic ethic of human solidarity. Marx himself viewed Darwin's work as confirmation by the natural sciences of his own views, and even Mao Tse-Tung regarded Darwin, as presented by the German Darwinists, as the foundation of Chinese scientific socialism."

p. 53   "Darwin's insight was rather that 'success' or the 'preservation of favoured races' is the result of biological 'fitness' in the living conditions of a given time and place; there is no equation of survival and progress in Darwin. The Germans, who focused on selection and the 'struggle' or *Kampf* as it was translated, were closer to the radical insight of Darwin's efforts."

pp. 53-54   "Ernst Haeckel (1834-1919) was the man who brought *Darwinismus* into German intellectual life. Not only did he succeed in establishing his interpretation of the strictly scientific aspects of Darwin as the correct view for a generation of scholars, but he went far beyond science to establish a unique German form of social Darwinism. This social Darwinism combined an almost mystical, religious belief in the forces of nature (i.e., natural selection as the fundamental law of life) with a literal and not analogical, transfer of the laws of biology to the social and political arena. It was, in essence, a romantic folkism synthesized with scientific evolutionism. It included the standard Darwinian ideas of struggle (*Kampf*) and competition as the foundation for natural law, and therefore social law, with a curious 'religion' of nature, which implied a small place for rationalism, the lack of free will, and happiness as submission to the eternal laws of nature."

p. 56   "The basic outline of German social Darwinism as developed by Haeckel and his colleagues is clear. It was argued that, on scientific grounds, man was merely a part of nature with no special transcendent qualities or special humanness. On the other hand, the Germans were members of a biologically superior community. German social Darwinism, contrary to Anglo-American social Darwinism, rejected the liberal individualistic state in favor of a natural, organic, folkish state of blood and soil. It attacked the alienation and atomization of individualistic modern civilization in the name of a psychological fulfillment resulting from union with the natural processes of evolution seen as a collective struggle for existence. And, of course, it argued that politics was merely the straightforward application of the laws of biology. In essence, Haeckel and his fellow social Darwinists advanced the ideas that were to become the core assumptions of national socialism."

Turner, John, "Why We Need Evolution by Jerks," *New Scientist*, vol. 101 (February 9, 1984), pp. 34-35. Turner was a Reader in Evolutionary Genetics, University of Leeds.

p. 34   "Twentieth-century man was as upset by the new attempts to link him to the animal as his Victorian ancestors had been by Darwin. It was the turn of E. O. Wilson and Richard Dawkins to be denounced, not this time from the pulpit as atheists, but by radical movements as fascist sympathizers. A Harvard group denounced Wilson's work as being in the intellectual tradition of Adolph Hitler."

p. 35   "Stephen Gould, who has repeatedly urged the need to see man as essentially different from animals, and was one of the signatories of the 'Hitler' statement about E. O. Wilson, has found the answer in the punctuated equilibrium theory."

p. 35   "Of the essential jerk theory, one can say as Gould did of sociobiology, that it brings no new insights, and can cite on its behalf not a single unambiguous fact."

p.35   "The point is not that the punctuated equilibrium theory is wrong. It might be right. The point is that despite its very poor scientific foundations it is attracting an enormous amount of attention. And as the Harvard radicals so cogently argued in the case of race and IQ, when an essentially meretricious scientific theory causes such a fuss, we must look to non-scientific causes."

Wurmbrand, Richard, *Marx and Satan* (Westchester, Illinois: Crossway Books, 1987), 143 pp.

p. 12   "Shortly after Marx received this certificate, something mysterious happened in his life: he became profoundly and passionately antireligious. A new Marx began to emerge.

"He writes in a poem, 'I wish to avenge myself against the One who rules above.'"

p. 15   "'The hellish vapors rise and fill the brain,

Till I go mad and my heart is utterly changed.

See this sword?

The prince of darkness

Sold it to me. For me he beats the time and gives the signs.

Ever more boldly I play the dance of death.'"

Young, Robert M., "The Darwin Debate," *Marxism Today* (Theoretical and discussion journal of the Communist Party, London), vol. 26 (April 1982), pp. 20-22.

p. 21   "Aspects of evolutionism are perfectly consistent with Marxism. The explanation of the origins of humankind and of mind by purely natural forces was, and remains, as welcome to Marxists as to any other secularists. The sources of value and responsibility are not to be found in a separate mental realm or in an immortal soul, much less in the inspired words of the Bible."

p. 22   "The most eloquent defender of scientific evolutionism, Stephen Jay Gould, is an avowedly non-Marxist radical—on the left of the scientific/political consensus but working well and truly within it."

p. 22   "I would say, then, that no Marxist should want to look to biology for a guide to the formulation of social and political goals and strategies, i.e., to the limits of human nature. It seems no more fruitful to look to natural science than to the Bible for justification of ethical, social and political beliefs. The 'science' which is most relevant to Marxist approaches to these matters is the science of history. There are of course both natural and human aspects of history, but these must be seen as mutually conditioned, whatever the scientific creationists, the scientific evolutionists, or the scientific Marxists say."

Zirkle, Conway, *Evolution, Marxian Biology and the Social Scene* (University of Pennsylvania Press, 1959), 527 pp.

pp. 85-86   "Marx and Engels accepted evolution almost immediately after Darwin published *The Origin of Species*. Within a month, Engels wrote to Marx (Dec. 12, 1859): 'Darwin whom I am just now reading, is splendid.' Evolution, of course, was just what the founders of communism needed to explain how mankind could have come into being without the intervention of any supernatural force, and consequently it could be used to bolster the foundations of their materialistic philosophy. In addition, Darwin's interpretation of evolution—that evolution had come about through the operation of natural selection—gave them an alternative hypothesis to the prevailing teleological explanation of the observed fact that all forms of life are adapted to their conditions."

[Paraphrased from various places in the book: Quotations may be drawn which demonstrate clearly the following points:

(1) Marx and Engels accepted the fact of evolution.

(2) They rejected population pressure as a selection in part; they rejected Malthus' contribution to the theory of natural selection and they attacked him personally. . . .

(5) They were complete environmentalists.

(6) They accepted Lamarck's inheritance of acquired characters.

(7) They accepted the inherited effects of a meat diet on human beings, and held that eating meat made those that ate it stronger and wiser, and

(8) Because of their environmentalism and belief in the inheritance of acquired characters, they held that races that lived in poor environments were inferior.]

p. 335   "On hearing this remark, the present writer asked the administrator whether this doctrine would not imply that the colonial, minority, and primitive peoples, those who had had less chance for mental and physical development, were not also genetically less advanced than the dominant ones. 'Ah, yes,' he replied in confidential manner, and after some hesitation, 'yes, we must admit that this is, after all, true. They are in fact inferior to *us* biologically in every respect, including their heredity. And that,' he added, 'is in fact the *official* doctrine.' . . continued our authority, 'after two or three generations of living under conditions of Socialism, their *genes* would have so improved that *then* we would all be equal.'"

C. Social Darwinism and Racism

Western capitalists should not be overly smug in their condemnations of the totalitarian systems of Nazism and communism. Although lesser in degree of death and suffering caused, the system of *laissez-faire* capitalism also applies the philosophy of Darwinism in its Spencerian form (survival of the fittest among corporations and businesses, as well as in human societies). In fact this system, embodying such harsh practices as monopolism, child-labor, sweatshops, and the like—even slave labor in its earlier forms—has been known as Social Darwinism. It was practiced vigorously by such "robber barons" of the 19th century as Rockefeller, Carnegie, Rhodes, Vanderbilt, and many others.

This type of thing also generated the notion of the "white man's burden," leading to colonialism, militarism and imperialism. The subjugation of so-called "lower races" (even after slavery was abolished) was justified by most leading evolutionists (Darwin, Huxley, Haeckel *et al.*) on Darwinian principles until the middle of the twentieth century, when the genocidal policies of Hitler gave racism such a bad name that even evolutionary anthropologists finally abandoned it.

It is well to remember that Social Darwinism (which is still alive and well today, even among "conservative" industrialists and business men) and racism also have their supposedly scientific rationale in evolutionism.

Asma, Stephen T., "The New Social Darwinism: Deserving Your Destitution," *The Humanist*, vol. 53 (September/October 1993), pp. 10-12.

p. 11   "Spencer coined the phrase *survival of the fittest*, and Darwin adopted the parlance in later editions of his *Origin of Species*. Spencer used this principle—where competition for limited resources results in the survival of the inherently 'better' candidate—to explain past, present, and future social conditions. . . .

"What, then, is this idea? According to Spencer and his American disciples—business entrepreneurs like John D. Rockefeller and Andrew Carnegie—social hierarchy reflects the unwavering, universal laws of nature. Nature unfolds in such a way that the strong survive and the weak perish. Thus, the economic and social structures that survive are 'stronger' and better, and those structures that don't were obviously meant to founder. . . . How do we know that capitalism is better than communism and that the mammal is better than the dinosaur? Because they survived, of course.

"Andrew Carnegie, who practically worshipped Spencer, replaced his disenchanted Christian theology with the laissez faire motto 'All is well since all grows better.' And John D. Rockefeller pronounced: 'The growth of a large business is merely a survival of the fittest. . . . This is not an evil tendency in business. It is merely the working out of a law of nature.' These capitalist moguls eagerly embraced a metaphysics that provided the ultimate justification for their ruthless business tactics."

p. 11   "James G. Kennedy, in his book *Herbert Spencer*, informs us that in 1896 'three justices of the Supreme Court were avowed Spencerians and participated in decisions recognizing corporations as individuals, and disallowing government regulation of contracts with regard to hours of work, a minimum wage, or child labor.' Spencer himself adamantly opposed all state aid to the poor on the grounds that it would be an interference with the 'natural' developmental process."

p. 12   "The idea that whole populations—whether abroad or at home—are 'naturally unfit' is the ultimate license for social policies of domination. Indeed, domination is for us a virtue rather than a vice. If one pauses for a moment to reflect on whether or not the 'natural law of competition' is sound, then one is immediately suspected of impiety. The church of capitalism watches its flock carefully."

p. 12   "It goes without saying that social Darwinism has lent spurious credence to racism."

p. 12   "Social Darwinism, however, runs very deep in this country. Spencer was the only intellectual that this country wholly embraced, and that embrace is still strong. A whole series of subterfuges must be created in order to justify exploitation, the most powerful of which is to convince people that it is 'natural.'"

Barnes, Harry Elmer, *Historical Sociology* (New York: The Philosophical Library, 1948).

p. 13   "Unquestionably the most potent influences contributing to the rise and development of truly historical sociology were Spencer's theory of cosmic evolution and the Darwinian doctrine of organic evolution and their reactions upon social science."

Burnham, John C., "A Discarded Consensus," review of *Outcasts from Evolution: Scientific Attitudes of Racial Inferiority, 1859-1900,* by John S. Haller, Jr. (Urbana: University of Illinois Press, 1971, 228 pp.), *Science,* vol. 175 (February 4, 1972), pp. 506-507.

p. 506   "Before 1859 many scientists had questioned whether blacks were of the same species as whites. After 1859, the evolutionary schema raised additional questions, particularly whether or not Afro-Americans could survive competition with their white near-relatives. The momentous answer was a resounding no."

p. 506   "Some of the impact of Darwinism in buttressing racial suppression was of this theoretical kind. The African was inferior because he represented the 'missing link' between ape and Teuton (a satisfying resolution of the polygenist-monogenist debate about the origin of races)."

p. 506   "That generation of scientists believed that no artificial process of education or forced evolution would ever enable the blacks to catch up."

Carnegie, Andrew, *Autobiography* (Boston: 1920), cited in *Social Darwinism in American Thought,* by Richard Hofstadter (Boston: Beacon Press, 1955), p. 45.

p. 327   "I remember that light came in as a flood and all was clear. Not only had I got rid of theology and the supernatural but I found the truth of evolution."

Cartmill, Matt, "Misdeeds in Anthropology," review of *Bones, Bodies, Behavior: Essays on Biological Anthropology,* edited by George W. Stocking, Jr. (Madison: Wisconsin University Press, 1988, 272 pp.), *Science,* vol. 244 (May 19, 1989), pp. 858-859. Cartmill is in the Department of Biological Anthropology, Duke University).

p. 858   "In his lucid and disturbing chapter, 'From *Anthropologie* to *Rassenkunde,*' Robert Proctor traces the development of physical anthropology in Germany from a medical anatomists' hobby into the clinical specialty of *Rassenhygiene.* He shows how the major German societies of physical anthropologists collaborated with the SS program of race hygiene, helping to make racial policy, train SS physicians, and organize Gestapo sterilization programs. Eugen Fischer, the most distinguished of German physical anthropologists, regarded by many as the founder of human genetics, was particularly helpful in these efforts."

p. 858   "But surely American physical anthropologists spoke out clearly against the Nazi perversion of their science? They did not. Elazar Barkan's chapter relates their failure in depressing detail."

Cavalli-Sforza, L. L., "The Genetics of Human Populations," *Scientific American*, vol. 231 (September 1974), pp. 81-89. Cavalli-Sforza was Professor of Genetics, Stanford University.

p. 85   "When we look at the main divisions of mankind, we find many differences that are visible to the unaided eye. It is not hard to assess the origin of an individual with respect to the major racial subdivisions: the straight-haired, tan Orientals, the wiry-haired, dark Africans and the lank-haired, pale Caucasians. If we analyze our impressions in detail, we find that they come down to a few highly visible characteristics: the color of the skin, the color and form of the hair and the gross morphology of the face, the eye folds, the nose and the lips. It is highly likely that all these differences are determined genetically, but they are not determined in any simple way. For example, where skin color is concerned there are at least four gene differences that contribute to variations in pigmentation."

p. 89   "The simplest interpretation of these conclusions today would envision a relatively small group starting to spread not long after modern man appeared. With the spreading, groups became separated and isolated. Racial differentiation followed. Fifty thousand years or so is a short time in evolutionary terms, and this may help to explain why, genetically speaking, human races show relatively small differences."

Conklin, Edwin, *The Direction of Human Evolution* (New York: Charles Scribners' Sons, 1925, 247 pp.), cited in "Eugenics and the Development of Nazi Race Policy," by Jerry Bergman, *Perspectives on Science and Faith*, vol. 44 (June 1992), p. 115. Conklin was Professor of Biology at Princeton.

p. 34   "Comparison of any modern race with the Neanderthal or Heidelberg types shows that . . . Negroid races more closely resemble the original stock than the white or yellow races. Every consideration should lead those who believe in the superiority of the white race to strive to preserve its purity and to establish and maintain the segregation of the races."

Darwin, Charles, *The Descent of Man*, 2nd ed. (New York: A. L. Burt Co., 1874), 797 pp.

p. 178   "At some future period, not very distant as measured by centuries, the civilized races of man will almost certainly exterminate and replace the savage races throughout the world. At the same time the anthropomorphous apes . . . will no doubt be exterminated. The break between man and his nearest allies will then be wider, for it will intervene between man in a more civilized state, as we may hope, even than the Caucasian, and some ape as low as a baboon, instead of as now between the negro or Australian and the gorilla."

Darwin, Charles, *Life and Letters, I, Letter to W. Graham, July 3, 1881*, p. 316, cited in *Darwin and the Darwinian Revolution*, by Gertrude Himmelfarb (London: Chatto & Windus, 1959), p. 343.

"I could show fight on natural selection having done and doing more for the progress of civilization than you seem inclined to admit. . . . The more civilized so-called Caucasian races have beaten the Turkish hollow in the struggle for existence. Looking to the world at no very distant date, what an endless number of the lower races will have been eliminated by the higher civilized races throughout the world."

Ferguson, James, "The Laboratory of Racism," *New Scientist*, vol. 103 (September 27, 1984), pp. 18-20.

p. 18   "In nineteenth-century Europe the concept of race was a preoccupation for the growing human sciences. . . . These first physical anthropologists helped to develop the concept of Aryan supremacy, which later fueled the institutional racism of Germany in the 1930's, and of South Africa today."

p. 18   "The new anthropology soon became a theoretical battleground between two opposed schools of thought on the origin of humans. The older and more established of these was 'monogenism,' the belief that all humankind, irrespective of color or other characteristics, was directly descended from Adam and from the single and original act of God's creation. Monogenism was promulgated by the Church and universally accepted until the 18th century, when opposition to theological authority began to fuel the rival theory of 'polygenism,' which held that different racial communities had different origins."

p. 20   "Monogenists, polygenists and Darwinists alike, despite fundamental doctrinal differences, proposed the existence of a metaphorical ladder, each race representing a rung in its vertical construction with black people at the bottom and whites at the top."

p. 20   "The ideas of racial inequality and Aryan supremacy have had tragic consequences when put into practice. The ideology of Nazi Germany and South African apartheid have their roots in the work of the 19th century theorists of race, and it is significant that Hitler readily acknowledged Gobineau as a source of inspiration. The early application of science to race has created the preconditions for the various forms of racism which have marked the political climate of the modern world."

p. 20   "Count Arthur de Gobineau . . . claimed that the rise and fall of every civilization and the history of humanity itself was the direct consequence of racial chemistry and racial inequality."

Gould, Stephen Jay, "Human Equality is a Contingent Fact of History," *Natural History*, vol. 93 (November 1984), pp. 26-33.

p. 28   "We cannot understand much of the history of late nineteenth- and early twentieth-century anthropology, with its plethora of taxonomic names proposed for nearly every scrap of fossil bone, unless we appreciate its obsession with the identification and ranking of races."

p. 28   "This theory of ancient separation had its last prominent defense in 1962, when Carleton Coon published his *Origin of Races*. Coon divided humanity into five major races—caucasoids, mongoloids, australoids, and, among African blacks, congoids and capoids. He claimed that these five groups were already distinct subspecies during the reign of our ancestor, *Homo erectus*."

p. 30   "We recognize only one formal category for divisions within species—the subspecies, Races, if formally defined, are therefore subspecies. . . . Human variation exists; the formal designation of races is passé."

p. 31   "... the division of humans into modern 'racial' groups is a product of our recent history. It does not predate the origin of our own species, *Homo sapiens*, and probably occurred during the last few tens (or at most hundreds) or thousands of years."

Hsü, Kenneth J., "Darwin's Three Mistakes," *Geology*, vol. 14 (June 1986), pp. 532-534.

p. 534   "Few geologists today subscribe to the Lyellian substantive uniformitarianism."

p. 534   "Darwinism was also used in a defense of competitive individualism and its economic corollary of *laissez-faire* capitalism in England and in America. Andrew Carnegie wrote that the 'law of competition, be it benign or not, is here; we cannot evade it.' Rockefeller went a step further when he claimed that 'the growth of a large business is merely a survival of the fittest; it is merely the working out of a law of nature and a law of God.'

"Not only capitalists but also socialists welcomed Darwinism; Karl Marx thought Darwin's book important because it supported the class struggle in history from the point of view of natural science. Worst of all, Darwinism opened the door to racists who wanted to apply the principle of natural selection to better mankind. Darwin's theory in biology, transferred to Germany and nurtured by Ernst Haeckel, inspired an ideology that led eventually to the rise of the Nazis."

Hsü, Kenneth J., reply to comment on "Darwin's Three Mistakes," *Geology*, vol. 15 (April 1987), pp. 376-377.

p. 377   "My abhorrence of Darwinism is understandable, for what member of the 'lower races' could remain indifferent to the statement attributed to the great master (Darwin, 1881, in a letter to W. Graham) that 'at no very distant date, what an endless number of the races will have been eliminated by the higher civilized races throughout the world.' If Kellogg had been a victim of social Darwinism, she would not have been blinded by hero worship. Charles Darwin was not a prophet, not a messiah, not a demigod. He was a gentleman scientist of the Victorian Era, and an establishment member of a society that sent gunboats to forcibly import opium into China, all in the name of competition (in free trade) and survival of the fittest."

Huxley, Thomas, *Lay Sermons, Addresses and Reviews* (New York: Appleton, 1871), 384 pp.

pp. 20-1   "No rational man, cognizant of the facts, believes that the average negro is the equal, still less the superior, of the white man. And if this be true, it is simply incredible that, when all his disabilities are removed, and our prognathous relative has a fair field and no favour, as well as no oppressor, he will be able to compete successfully with his bigger-brained and smaller-jawed rival, in a contest which is to be carried on by thoughts and not by bites. The highest places in the hierarchy of civilization will assuredly not be within the reach of our dusky cousins, though it is by no means necessary that they should be restricted to the lowest. But whatever the position of stable equilibrium into which the laws of social gravitation may bring the negro, all responsibility for the result will henceforward lie between Nature and him. The white man may wash his hands of it, and the

Caucasian conscience be void of reproach for evermore. And this, if we look to the bottom of the matter, is the real justification for the abolition policy."

Lewin, Roger, *Bones of Contention* (New York: Simon and Schuster, 1987), 348 pp.

p. 307   "Racism, as we would characterize it today, was explicit in the writings of virtually all the major anthropologists of the first decades of this century, simply because it was the generally accepted world view. The language of the epic tale so often employed by Arthur Keith, Grafton Elliot Smith, Henry Fairfield Osborn, and their contemporaries fitted perfectly an imperialistic view of the world, in which Caucasians were the most revered product of a grand evolutionary march to nobility."

p. 308   "So it was that several threads of argument were woven together to form a theoretical fabric whose pattern matched closely the ethos of the Edwardian world. If the white races were economically and territorially dominant in the world, it was surely the natural outcome of natural processes. The slow pace of evolutionary change, the long separation between the races, the inimical environment of the tropics—all combined to produce a graded series of races, rising from the Australian aborigines at the bottom, through the black races and the Mongols, and reaching the Caucasians at the apex."

Mintz, Sidney W., review of *Outcasts from Evolution: Scientific Attitudes of Racial Inferiority, 1859-1900*, by John S. Haller, Jr. (University of Illinois Press, 1971, 228 pp.), *American Scientist*, vol. 60 (May/June 1972), p. 387. Mintz was in the Department of Anthropology, Yale University.

"This is an extremely important book, documenting as it does what has long been suspected: the ingrained, firm, and almost unanimous racism of North American men of science during the nineteenth (and into the twentieth) century. By 'racism,' a word not employed by Professor Haller, the reviewer means in this instance the unquestioning conviction that groups of differing physical type differ as well in their inherent abilities, capacities, and intelligences, along a scale going from inferior to superior, or from high to low, and that physical type and these capacities are genetically interlocked. In the case of North American scholars, many of them eminent, this racism was directed specifically and most intently against their fellow-citizens of African or part-African origin. *Ab initio*, Afro-Americans were viewed by these intellectuals as being in certain ways unredeemably, unchangeably, irrevocably inferior. North American society (far more than evolutionary theory) would have to take account of this 'fact' and adjust accordingly.

". . . It is significant that most North American intellectual leaders of the last century were racists; it is more significant that their racism made a concrete and specific contribution to the worsening of the material and civil condition of Afro-Americans after 1865."

Osborn, Henry Fairfield, "The Evolution of Human Races," *Natural History* (January/February 1926), reprinted in *Natural History*, vol. 89 (April 1980), p. 129.

"If an unbiased zoölogist were to descend upon the earth from Mars and study the races of man with the same impartiality as the races of fishes, birds and mammals, he would undoubtedly divide the existing races of man into several genera and into a very large number of species and subspecies.

". . . This is the recognition that the genus *Homo* is subdivided into three absolutely distinct stocks, which in zoölogy would be given the rank of species, if not of genera, stocks popularly known as the Caucasian, the Mongolian and the Negroid.

"The spiritual, intellectual, moral, and physical characters which separate these three great human stocks are far more profound and ancient than those which divide the Nordic, Alpine and Mediterranean races. In my opinion these three primary stocks diverged from each other before the beginning of the Pleistocene or Ice Age. The Negroid stock is even more ancient than the Caucasian and Mongolian, as may be proved by an examination not only of the brain, of the hair, of the bodily characters, such as the teeth, the genitalia, the sense organs, but of the instincts, the intelligence. The standard of intelligence of the average adult Negro is similar to that of the eleven-year-old youth of the species *Homo sapiens*."

Plochmann, George Kimball, "Darwin or Spencer?" *Science*, vol. 130 (November 27, 1959), pp. 1452-1456.

". . . in his own day, which was that of Darwin, too, Spencer was regarded as a giant, and his *Principles of Biology* was adduced as one of the chief evidences for this high estimation. Of course, this could not be on literary grounds. Spencer is no more a first-class stylist than Darwin. . . .

"Had Darwin and Spencer been more tendentious men, they would doubtless have become embroiled in Newton-Leibniz disputes regarding priorities. . . . It would be difficult to establish the interlocking priorities here: Spencer's preliminary essays were published some time before *The Origin of Species*."

Rachels, James, *Created from Animals* (New York: Oxford University Press, 1990), 245 pp. Rachels is Professor of Philosophy, University of Alabama.

pp. 63-64   "'The survival of the fittest' was quickly interpreted as an ethical precept that sanctioned cutthroat economic competition.

"Capitalist giants such as John D. Rockefeller and Andrew Carnegie regularly invoked what they took to be 'Darwinian' principles to explain the ethics of the American system. Rockefeller, in a talk to his Sunday School class, proclaimed that 'The growth of large business is merely a survival of the fittest. . . . The American Beauty rose can be produced in the splendor and fragrance which bring cheer to its beholder only by sacrificing the early buds which grew up around it. This is not an evil tendency in business. It is merely the working out of a law of nature and a law of God.' Carnegie, who became a close friend of Spencer's, was equally rhapsodic: in defending the concentration of wealth in the hands of a few big businessmen, he proclaimed that 'While the law may sometimes be hard for the individual, it is best for the race, because it ensures the survival of the fittest in every department.' Rockefeller's and Carnegie's understanding of natural selection was only a little better than that of the Manchester editorial."

Simpson, George Gaylord, "The Biological Nature of Man," *Science*, vol. 152 (April 22, 1966), pp. 472-478.

p. 474   "Moreover, races are evanescent in the course of evolution. A given race may change, disappear by fusion with others, or die out altogether while the species as a whole simply continues its evolutionary course.

"Races of man have or perhaps one should say 'had,' exactly the same biological significance as the subspecies of other species of mammals."

p. 475   "Evolution does not necessarily proceed at the same rate in different populations, so that among many groups of animals it is possible to find some species that have evolved more slowly, hence are now more primitive, as regards some particular trait or even over-all. It is natural to ask—as many have asked—whether among human races there may not similarly be some that are more primitive in one way or another or in general. It is indeed possible to find single characteristics that are probably more advanced or more primitive in one race than in another."

p. 476   "Human language is absolutely distinct from any system of communication in other animals. That is made most clear by comparison with other animal utterances, which most nearly resemble human speech and are most often called 'speech.' Non-human vocables are, in effect, interjections. . . . The difference between animal interjection and human language is the difference between saying 'Ouch!' and saying 'Fire is hot.'"

p. 477   "Darwin's study and many later studies sought to trace the evolutionary origin of language from a prehuman source. They have not been successful. As a recent expert in the field has said, 'The more that is known about it [that is, communication in monkeys and apes], the less these systems seem to help in the understanding of human language.'

". . . Moreover at the present time no languages are primitive in the sense of being significantly close to the origin of language. Even the peoples with least complex cultures have highly sophisticated languages, with complex grammar and large vocabularies, capable of naming and discussing anything that occurs in the sphere occupied by their speakers. . . .

". . . The oldest language that can reasonably be reconstructed is already modern, sophisticated, complete from an evolutionary point of view."

p. 477   "It is still possible but it is unlikely that we will ever know just when and how our ancestors began to speak."

Tuttle, Russell H., "Five Decades of Anthropology," review of *A History of American Physical Anthropology 1930-1980*, edited by Frank Spencer (New York: Academic Press, 1982, 496 pp.), *Science*, vol. 220 (May 20, 1983), pp. 832-834.

p. 832   "However, chapter 1, 'The roots of the race concept in American physical anthropology,' by Brace, merits a wide readership and high marks for erudition. Brace squarely confronts racist influences on the two chief founders of institutional physical anthropology in the United States—Hrdlicka, based at the American Museum of Natural History, and E. A. Hooton, with whom most of the second generation of physical anthropologists studied at Harvard."

p. 832   "Brace's closing comments are upbeat. He reiterates the modern view that we should abandon the concept of race altogether and instead record the gene frequencies and traits of populations that are identified simply by their geographic localities. This genotypic and phenotypic information is to be interpreted in terms of historical and proximate selective forces."

Valentine, Mrs., *The Victoria Geography* (Frederick Warne & Co., 1872), cited in "Darwinism and Indoctrination," *Harper*, p. 266.

p. 24   "The Caucasian race is the highest in intellect and energy, and occupies the most highly civilized part of the world. . . . It is found in every part of the world, and is always the dominant or ruling race."

p. 27   ". . . of an Oriental Negro, who is the lowest of all savages, living in trees, and more like an animal than a man; and above is an African Negro who has been civilized by slavery; for dreadful as slavery was, it did *some* good. . . . The Negroes who lived in America or West Indian slavery were . . . much higher (being Christians) in the scale of being than the free Negroes of Africa. . . . An American Indian, or Redman, a race inhabiting the wilds of America, and far superior to the Malay, Mongol, or Negro . . . unhappily, he is dying out before the advance of the European or Caucasian race."

Wiggam, Albert Edward, *The New Dialogue of Science* (Garden City, N.Y.: Garden Publishing Co., 1922), cited in *Perspectives on Science and Faith*, by Jerry Bergman (44, 1992, 116).

p. 102   "At one time man had scarcely more brains than his anthropoid cousins, the apes. But, by kicking, biting, fighting . . . and outwitting his enemies and by the fact that the ones who had not sense and strength . . . to do this were killed off, man's brain became enormous and he waxed both in wisdom and agility if not in size. . . ."

Wrangham, R. W., review of *Racial Adaptations*, by Carleton S. Coon, *The Biology of Race*, by James C. King, and *Human Variation*, by Stephen Molnar, *American Scientist*, vol. 72 (January/February 1984), pp. 75-76. Wrangham was at the Center for Advanced Study in the Behavioural Sciences, Stanford, California.

p. 75   "To many anthropologists there are no such things as human races. How can this be? . . . Even if particular individuals from different populations occasionally look alike, surely the distinctions between whole populations are big enough to justify calling them racial.

"This was the dominant view from the mid-18th century onward. . . . Authors varied in their opinion of the number of human races, from Cuvier's three to as many as thirty or more in the 20th century, but with few exceptions they agreed that the concept of race was sound.

". . . The dominant view today is that race is an outmoded concept."

Chapter 15

Evolution and Modern Issues

A. Problems in Human Behavior

Not only has the evolutionary tree produced corrupt fruits in great social and economic systems (communism, racism, etc.) but also a multitude of wicked and socially harmful practices in human behavior. If people are taught in school during their younger years that they are merely evolved animals, they sooner or later will come to live like animals, and to justify their animalistic behaviors in terms of their professedly scientific justification in evolution.

Many of these evil practices—abortionism, homosexuality, promiscuity, drugs, etc.—have always been present in human society, of course, but never on such a large scale. They are being excused—even promoted—by many modern psychologists, sociologists, lawyers, educators, etc.—on the ground of being "scientific," as based in evolution. The following quotes are illustrative of this deadly impact of evolutionism in human behavior.

Breggin, Peter R., "Mental Health versus Religion," *The Humanist*, vol. 47 (November/December 1987), pp. 12-13. Dr. Breggin was a practicing psychiatrist in Bethesda, Maryland.

p. 12　　　"Nowadays, many religions seem more like secular mental health associations than Judeo-Christian sects."

p. 12　　　"At annual and regional meetings of the Association for Humanistic Psychology, we are more likely to find yoga sessions and Sufi dancing than psychotherapy seminars. The latest fad is reducing the science of physics to metaphysics and spirituality."

p. 13　　　"The average psychiatrist has more power to do harm in the lives of individuals than most religious leaders on Earth."

p. 13　　　"Moreover, it would be hard to find a more unhappy lot than those clustered in the mental health field. Especially among psychiatrists, suicide, depression, drug addiction, and alcoholism are notoriously rife. Among nonmedical mental health professionals, the situation doesn't seem much better. Not only are many mental health professionals unhappy but they do not live ethically inspired lives. Too many, for example, prostrate themselves before the psychiatric establishment."

Burke, Barbara, "Infanticide," *Science–84* (May 1984), pp. 26-31.

p. 29　　　"Among some animal species, then, infant killing appears to be a natural practice. Could it be natural for humans too, a trait inherited from our primate ancestors. . . .

". . . Charles Darwin noted in *The Descent of Man* that infanticide has been 'probably the most important of all' checks on population growth throughout most of human history."

Cevasco, G. A., "Freud vs. God," review of *Sigmund Freud's Christian Unconscious*, by Paul C. Vitz (New York: Guildford Press, 1988), *Intercollegiate Review*, vol. 24 (Fall 1988), pp. 39-40.

p. 39   "[Vitz] develops the claim that Freud had a strong attraction to Christianity. A corollary emphasis treats of Freud's unconscious hostility toward the Faith, which, as Vitz details, was a consequence of a curious preoccupation with the Devil, Damnation, and the Anti-Christ."

p. 40   "At every point, Vitz turns introspective eyes back onto Freud in order to expose the psychological motives for his rejection of God. Vitz even questions if Freud made a Faustian pact with the Devil."

p. 40   "That Freud disproved religion, Vitz makes clear, is an overstated and oversimplified judgment bandied about by superficially educated and tragically uninformed individuals."

Darwin, Charles, *The Descent of Man*, as cited by Stephen Jay Gould, "The Moral State of Tahiti—and of Darwin," *Natural History* (October 1991), pp. 12-19.

p. 14   "It is generally admitted that with woman the powers of intuition, of rapid perception, and perhaps of imitation, are more strongly marked than in man; but some, at least, of these faculties are characteristic of the lower races, and therefore of a past and lower state of civilization. The chief distinction in the intellectual powers of the two sexes is shown by man attaining to a higher eminence in whatever he takes up, than woman can attain—whether requiring deep thought, reason, or imagination, or merely the use of the senses and hands."

p. 14   "It is, indeed, fortunate that the law of the equal transmission of characters to both sexes has commonly prevailed throughout the whole class of mammals; otherwise it is probable that man would have become as superior in mental endowment to woman as the peacock is in ornamental plumage to the peahen."

Drummey, James J., "Abortion: The Other Holocaust," *The New American*, vol. 2 (January 20, 1986), pp. 21-26.

p. 22   "One of the key elements in the abortion debate is the true nature of the victim. If the unborn child is a human being, then he or she deserves the full and equal protection of the law. Though it may still surprise some, there are few things more certain in January 1986 than that the unborn are human beings. It is a biological and scientific fact that human life begins at fertilization, when the sperm cell of the father penetrates the egg cell of the mother. That unique genetic package, something that each of us once was, contains everything that a person will become—the color of her eyes, the size of his feet, even whether he or she will contract diabetes at age fifty.

                "Thanks to the wonders of modern technology, we are able to study the unborn child from the earliest moments of its existence. We know that its heart begins to beat eighteen days after fertilization, that brain waves can be recorded by the fortieth day, and that all body systems are present at eight weeks and working by the eleventh week. Technological advances are such that more and more babies are surviving births after only 20 to 24 weeks of the normal forty-week pregnancy. and yet, the Minnesota Supreme Court ruled last month that an 8½ month-old unborn child was not a human being under Minnesota law."

Goleman, Daniel, "Lost Paper Shows Freud's Effort to Link Analysis and Evolution," *New York Times*, February 10, 1987, pp. C1, C4.

p. C1   "In a 1915 paper, Freud demonstrates his preoccupation with evolution. Immersed in the theories of Darwin, and of Lamarck, who believed acquired traits could be inherited, Freud concluded that mental disorders were the vestiges of behavior that had been appropriate in earlier stages of evolution."

p. C4   "The evolutionary idea that Freud relied on most heavily in the manuscript is the maxim that 'ontogeny recapitulates phylogeny,' that is, that the development of the individual recapitulates the evolution of the entire species."

Gould, Stephen Jay, "Dr. Down's Syndrome," *Natural History*, vol. 89 (April 1980), pp. 142-148.

p. 144   "In Down's day, the theory of recapitulation embodied a biologist's best guide for the organization of life into sequences of higher and lower forms. (Both the theory and 'ladder approach' to classification that it encouraged are, or should be, defunct today.) . . . This theory, often expressed by the mouthful 'ontogeny recapitulates phylogeny' held that higher animals, in their embryonic development, pass through a series of stages representing, in proper sequence, the adult forms of ancestral, lower creatures. Thus, the human embryo first develops gill slits, like a fish; later a three-chambered heart, like a reptile; still later a mammalian tail. Recapitulation provided a convenient focus for the pervasive racism of white scientists, they looked to the activities of their own children for comparison with normal, adult behavior in lower races."

Huxley, Aldous, "Confession of a Professed Atheist," *Report: Perspective on the News*, vol. 3 (June 1966), p. 19. From an article by Helming, "An Interview with God."

"I had motives for not wanting the world to have meaning; consequently assumed it had none, and was able without any difficulty to find satisfying reasons for this assumption. . . . The philosopher who finds no meaning in the world is not concerned exclusively with a problem in pure metaphysics; he is also concerned to prove there is no valid reason why he personally should not do as he wants to do. . . . For myself, as no doubt for most of my contemporaries, the philosophy of meaninglessness was essentially an instrument of liberation. The liberation we desired was simultaneously liberation from an certain political and economic system and liberation from a certain system of morality. We objected to the morality because it interfered with our sexual freedom.."

Huxley, Aldous, "History of Tension," *Scientific Monthly*, vol. 85 (July 1957), pp. 3-9.

p. 9   "But the pharmacologists will give us something that most human beings have never had before. If we want joy, peace, and loving kindness, they can give us loving kindness, peace, and joy. If we want beauty, they will transfigure the outside world for us and open the door to visions of unimaginable richness and significance. If our desire is for life everlasting, they will give us the next best thing—eons of blissful experience miraculously telescoped into a single hour. They will bestow these gifts without exacting the terrible price which, in the past, men had to pay for resorting too frequently to such consciousness-changing drugs as heroin or cocaine or even that good old stand-by alcohol."

p. 9   "Meanwhile, all that one can predict with any degree of certainty is that many of our traditional notions about ethics and religion and many of our current views about the nature of the mind will have to be reconsidered and reevaluated in the context of the pharmacological revolution. It will be extremely disturbing; but it will also be enormous fun."

Kidwell, Kirk, "Planned Parenthood has Plans," *The New American*, vol. 2 (January 20, 1986), pp. 7-9.

p. 7   "Originally known as the Birth Control League of America, it was founded in 1916 by the militant leftist Margaret Sanger. . . . Author Miriam Allen Defort, writing in the Spring 1965 issued of *The Humanist* describes Sanger and her early followers: 'It was the radicals—political, economic, and religious—among whom Margaret Sanger found her first supporters: and she herself was one of them. Her father, Matthew Higgins, was a Socialist and the "village Atheist" of Corning, New York.' As for her religious background, DeFord writes, 'The word "Humanism" in its present religio-scientific meaning was not then current. but call it Freethought or Rationalism or Secularism, it was and it remained Margaret Sanger's creed. The first paper she founded and edited was called *The Woman Rebel*, and its masthead bore the motto: "No gods, no masters."'

"For Sanger, the world was composed of three classes. The first class practices birth control and is wealthy and intelligent. The second would practice birth control but did not then have access to it. The third class 'are those irresponsible and reckless ones having little regard for the consequences of their acts, or whose religious scruples prevent their exercising control over their numbers.'"

p. 8   "'Through birth control Sanger saw a way to control the people whom she now labeled "human weeds" and to preserve the freedom of those whom she judged a superior stock, capable of ruling.'"

p. 9   "For the majority of medical authorities associated with Planned Parenthood actually seem to regard pregnancy as a disease or even a plague.

"For example, Dr. Warren Hern, writing in the January 1971 issue of Planned Parenthood's *Family Planning Perspectives*, describes pregnancy as 'an episodic, moderately extended, chronic condition . . . an illness [to be treated] by evacuation of the uterine contents.' That, of course, means abortion.

"Again, while Dr. Willard Cates, Jr., was addressing the Association of Planned Parenthood Physicians in November 1976, he stated, 'Unwanted pregnancy is transmitted sexually, is socially and emotionally pathologic . . . and has many other characteristics of conventional venereal diseases.'

"And, finally, Dr. Mary S. Calderone, former medical director for Planned Parenthood, wrote in the February-March 1968 issue of the *Medical Moral Newsletter*, 'We have yet to beat our public health drums for birth control in the way we beat them pro polio vaccine; we are still unable to put babies in the class of dangerous epidemics, even though that is the exact truth.'"

Money, John, "Agenda and Credenda of the Kinsey Scale," in *Homosexuality/Heterosexuality: Concepts of Sexual Orientation*, ed. David McWhirter, Stephanie A. Sanders, and June M. Reinisch (New York: Oxford University Press, 1990), pp. 41-60.

p. 43   "Culturally institutionalized bisexuality signifies either that bisexuality is a universal potential to which any member of the human species could be acculturated or that bisexuality is a unique potential of those cultures whose members have become selectively inbred for it. There are no data that give conclusive and absolute support to either alternative. However, genetically pure inbred strains are an ideal of animal husbandry, not of human social and sexual interaction. Therefore, it is likely that acculturation to bisexuality is less a concomitant of inbreeding than it is of the bisexual plasticity of all members of the human species."

p. 45   "Any theory of the genesis of either exclusive homosexuality or exclusive heterosexuality must address primarily the genesis of bisexuality. Monosexuality, whether homosexual or heterosexual, is secondary and a derivative of the primary bisexual or ambisexual potential. Ambisexuality has its origins in evolutionary biology and in the embryology of sexual differentiation."

Rachels, James, *Created from Animals* (New York: Oxford University Press, 1990), 245 pp. Rachels is Professor of Philosophy, University of Alabama.

p. 5   "Darwinism undermines both the idea that man is made in the image of God and the idea that man is a uniquely rational being. Furthermore, if Darwinism is correct, it is unlikely that any other support for the idea of human dignity will be found. The idea of human dignity turns out, therefore, to be the moral effluviam of a discredited metaphysics."

p. 125   "Suppose God *is* somehow involved in the process that evolutionary biologists since Darwin have been describing. This would mean that he has created a situation in which his own involvement is so totally hidden that the process gives every appearance of operating without any guiding hand at all. In other words, he has created a situation in which it is reasonable for us to believe that he is not involved. But if it is reasonable for us to believe that, then it is reasonable for us to reject the theistic interpretation."

Reilly, Robert R., "Atheism and Arms Control: How Spiritual Pathology Afflicts Public Policy," *Intercollegiate Review*, vol. 24 (Fall 1988), pp. 15-22.

p. 18   "The vertical harmony between man and God is also the prelude to and necessary condition for the horizontal peace between men. A man who is still at war within himself is not likely to make true peace with his neighbor. . . .

"There is no greater act of revolt than the denial of God's existence. Atheism is not only a disorder in the God-man relationship, but a denial of it."

p. 19   "The problem is that, by denying the possibility of a relationship between God and man, atheism also denies the possibility of a just relationship between men. In other words, atheism removes the grounds for the recognition of, and therefore respect for, another person as a fellow human being. . . . Human life is sacred only if there is a God to sanctify it. Otherwise, man is just another collection of atoms and can be treated as such."

p. 19   "Lenin followed Marx's ideas to their inevitable conclusion. 'We must hate,' Lenin counselled; 'hatred is the basis of communism.' It is extremely important to note that, for Lenin, hatred is not so much a passion as it is the theoretically correct solution to the philosophical problem arising out of a world without God."

p. 19   "The spiritual disorder within man's soul of which Saint James wrote has become, in the modern age, institutionalized. In other words, the moral disorder of the individual soul has become the principle of a general, public disorder: first as it was articulated in the teachings of Nietzsche and Marx, and then incarnated in the Nazi regime and in the various Marxist-Leninist states of today."

p. 20   "As Lenin said: 'Every religious idea of a god, even flirting with the idea of god, is unutterable vileness of the most dangerous kind, "contagion" of the most abominable kind. Millions of sins, filthy deeds, acts of violence, and physical contagions are far less dangerous than the subtle spiritual idea of a god.'"

p. 21   "While the casualties from war have been estimated at 45.7 million people, well over twice that number of innocent people have fallen victim to totalitarian state violence during the same period. . . . 'One traffic death, that is a tragedy; a million executions of counter-revolutionaries, that is a statistic.' . . . since the end of the Vietnam War in 1975, more people have lost their lives to the victorious communists than during the entire course of the war. In Cambodia, only several thousand of the 60,000 Bhuddist monks survived the religious extirpation efforts of the Khmer Rouge."

Richards, Eveleen, "Will the Real Charles Darwin Please Stand Up," *New Scientist*, vol. 100 (December 22/29, 1983), pp. 884-887.

p. 884   "[Emma] had little interest in his science, but she helped proofread *The Origin of Species* and dutifully watched over his experiments. Moreover, she was deeply religious and many of his opinions were painful to her."

p. 887   "Darwin's concept of sexual selection and his associated interpretations of human evolution were not directly based on biological phenomena, but were in some degree taken over from his socially derived perceptions of feminine characteristics and abilities."

p. 887   "Wilma George, in her recent book *Darwin*, is one of the few to have pointed out that the origin of man by natural law rather than divine creation was made more palatable for its Victorial audience by Darwinian concepts of male superiority. . . . In a period when women were beginning to demand the suffrage, higher education and entrance to middle-class professions, it was comforting to know that women could never outstrip men; the new Darwinism scientifically guaranteed it."

p. 887   "As a result, *The Descent of Man* is fast becoming notorious in feminist literature, and the sexist thus discerned is a far cry from the stereotyped 'great man' we have become accustomed to."

p. 887   "Social attitudes have changed somewhat since the Victorian era, and perhaps it would be more appropriate to reserve the label ['sexist'] for those who insist on perpetuating the Darwinian tradition of legitimating our current sexual inequalities on the basis of an evolutionary reconstruction that centres on the aggressive, territorial, hunting male and relegates the female to submissive domesticity and the periphery of the evolutionary process."

Schatzman, Morton, "Freud's Debt to Darwin," review of *Darwin's Influence on Freud: A Tale of Two Sciences*, by Lucille B. Ritvo (Yale University Press, 267 pp.), *New Scientist*, vol. 129 (February 9, 1991), p. 62.

p. 62   "Evidently influenced by Haeckel, Freud believed that each person's history from fetus to adult recapitulates in brief the entire development of the human race. Both libido and ego, Freud argued, 'are at bottom heritages, abbreviated recapitulations of the development which all mankind has passed through from its primeval days. . . .'"

p. 62   "Freud thought that individual libidinal development recapitulates stages of human civilization. He believed that he could reconstruct human prehistory from studying children, as well as from observing neurotics."

p. 62   "Freud did believe in the inheritance of acquired characteristics and explicitly espoused Lamarck."

Schneour, Elie A., "Life Doesn't Begin, It Continues: Abortion Foes Err in Setting Conception as the Starting Point," *Los Angeles Times*, Sunday, January 29, 1989, Part V. Schneour is Chairman of the Southern California Skeptics, a Pacific affiliate of AAAS, and Director of the Biosystems Research Institute in La Jolla.

p. 5   "Ontogeny recapitulates phylogeny. This is a fundamental tenet of modern biology that derives from evolutionary theory, and is thus anathema to creationism as well as to those opposed to freedom of choice. Ontogeny is the name for the process of development of a fertilized egg into a fully formed and mature living organism. Phylogeny, on the other hand, is the history of the evolution of a species, in this case the human being. During development, the fertilized egg progresses over 38 weeks through what is, in fact, a rapid passage through evolutionary history: From a single primordial cell, the conceptus progresses through being something of a protozoan, a fish, a reptile, a bird, a primate and ultimately a human being. There is a difference of opinion among scientists about the time during pregnancy when a human being can be said to emerge. But there is a general agreement that this does not happen until after the end of the first trimester."

Schwabenthan, Sabine, "Life Before Birth," *Parents* (October 1979), pp. 44-50.

p. 50   "Fetoscopy makes it possible to observe directly the unborn child through a tiny telescope inserted through the uterine wall. Finally, modern medicine's ability to keep premature babies alive and healthy has led to increased knowledge about the fetus six or seven months after conception.

     "The development of the child—from the union of the parents' cells to birth— has been studied exhaustively. As a result, long-held beliefs have been put to rest. We now know, for instance, that man, in his prenatal stages, does not go through the complete evolution of life—from a single cell to a fishlike water creature to man. Today it is known that every step in the fetal developmental process is specifically human."

Smit, Jacob, "In the Beginning: Homosexuality and Evolution," *International N.W. Guide Magazine*, issue 19 (August 1987), pp. 6-8.

p. 6   "Homosexuality is seldom discussed as a component in evolution, but it undoubtedly plays a role. Homosexual behavior has been observed in most animal species studied, and the higher we climb on the taxonomic tree toward mammals, the more apparent homosexual behavior we see."

p. 6   "In light of this sort of thing, researcher R. H. Dennison, professor of zoology at the University of Wyoming, has concluded that in evolution homosexuality may act as a tension-lowering device, satisfying the mating practices of more dominant males."

p. 6   "Whether the result of deprivation or a natural tendency for the organism, homosexuality also serves evolutionary processes by acting as a form of population control."

p. 7   "Unlike lower animals, we have the ability to influence our own evolution. Instead of merely mimicking the animal world around us, human beings can combine the positive aspects attributed at present to one sex or the other alone and jettison the negative aspects."

p. 8   "The removal of restrictive ranges of behavior and boundaries that interfere with the intimacy and learning of gay people [would assure] a better world for all mankind. Without question, this would represent a considerable evolutionary jump. It may well turn out to be that God does have room for an Adam and Steve."

Sobran, Joseph, "The Averted Gaze, Liberalism and Fetal Pain," *Human Life Review* (Spring, 1984), pp. 1-14.

p. 6   "I think that what [columnist Ellen Goodman] imagines is that the human embryo undergoes something like the whole process of evolution, as in the old adage that 'ontogeny recapitulates philogeny,' The adage has been discredited, of course, but this does not mean it has lost its power over the imagination of many modern people. They still suppose that the human fetus is in the early stages of development a 'lower' form of life, and this is probably what they mean when they say it isn't 'fully human.'"

p. 6   "So the abortion debate has its roots in two alternative ways of imaging the unborn. Our civilization, until recently, agreed in imagining the unborn child on the pattern of the Incarnation, which maximizes his dignity; but many people now imagine him on the pattern of evolution, as popularly understood, which minimizes his dignity."

p. 10   "My guess is that the popular theory of evolution appeals precisely as an alternative to the Christian view of man, which not only demands faith but imposes moral obligations. People who adopt Evolutionism are not driven to it by consideration of the evidence; they like it without respect to the evidence, because they are passionate creatures, and it offers no moral impediment to their passions."

Thomson, Keith Stewart, "Ontogeny and Phylogeny Recapitulated," *American Scientist*, vol. 76 (May/ June 1988), pp. 273-275.

p. 273   "Surely the biogenetic law is as dead as a doornail. It was finally exorcised from biology textbooks in the fifties. As a topic of serious theoretical inquiry it was extinct in the twenties. . . . They also noted that the sequence of acquisition of those specialized characteristics that typify given groups of organisms appeared *in general* to be the same order as that in which we hypothesize they must have been acquired in evolutionary history."

p. 274   "Another major factor keeping some sort of recapitulation alive was the need of comparative morphologists and especially paleontologists for a solid theoretical foundation for homology. They had long since come to rely on comparative ontogenetic information as a base."

p. 275   "In the end, all the versions of a biogenetic law have the same infuriating but fascinating quality. They reveal nothing beyond the generality that we already know. No one has yet succeeded in developing a greater range of hypothesis, and, given the opportunistic nature of evolutionary change, the chances are no one ever will."

Watters, Wendell W., "Christianity and Mental," *The Humanist*, vol. 47 (November/December 1987), pp. 5-11, 32. Dr. Watters was Clinical Professor of Psychiatry at McMaster University.

p. 5   "I want you to entertain the hypothesis that Christian doctrine, the existential soother par excellence, is incompatible with the principles of sound mental health and contributes more to the genesis of human suffering than to its alleviation."

p. 5   "In my view, all religions are inhuman anachronisms, but here I am only dealing with Christianity and, more specifically, with the noxious nature of Christian doctrine at the personal and interpersonal levels."

p. 10   "A true Christian must always be in a state of torment, since he or she can never really be certain that God has forgiven him or her for deeply felt negative feelings—in spite of the Catholic confessional and the fundamentalist trick of self-deception known as being saved or born again."

B. The New Age

Another strange and deadly fruit of evolutionism is the complex of social systems (environmentalism, multi-culturalism, world federalism, etc.), psychological cults (mental health movement, dianetics, self-awareness groups, etc.), pseudo-scientific concepts (anthropic principle, morphogenetic fields, Gaia hypothesis, etc.), occult practices (witchcraft, astrology, channeling, etc.), quasi-religious sects (Christian Science, prosperity gospelers, theosophy, etc.), and various others, all associated with the so-called New Age Movement.

As diversified as all these systems and concepts may be, they all postulate evolutionism as their scientific rationale. This is not atheistic evolution, however, but pantheistic evolution—the religion of the ancient nations (Greece, Rome, Babylonia, etc.)—as well as the modern ethnic religions of the Far East (Hinduism, Buddhism, Taoism, etc.). All deny a transcendent Creator and special creation, and all are opposed to Biblical Christianity.

Anonymous, "Music Composed in France Heals Body, Mind and Soul," *New Age Journal* (December 1991), p. 11.

p. 11   "In February of 1985, an automobile accident became the catalyst for changing the life of Marcey Hamm, and eventually her music."

p. 11   "Ms. Hamm continued her interest in this non-conventional medicine and began to practice meditation and a holistic approach to life. She attributes this to her present good health and state of mind, and to the spiritual awakening that inspired the music of her last three tapes."

p. 11   "'I remember very little of actually composing the music,' Ms. Hamm admits. 'I've never heard it, but I could feel it deep inside of me as if it were in my cells—I became the music.'"

p. 11   "'The first person to come by was an elderly gentleman,' explains Ms. Hamm. 'When he put on the head-phones, his face turned white as a sheet."

p. 11   "'He looked straight into my eyes and said, "Young lady, I want you to know that several years ago I had a heart attack in the hospital and was pronounced dead for 16 minutes. While I was dead I left my body and went through a tunnel of light. The music I heard towards the end of the tunnel was the same music you are playing on those headphones." ' "

Bak, Per, *How Nature Works* (New York: Springer, Verlag, 1996), 212 pp.

p. 113   "Life cannot have started with a chemical substance as complicated as DNA, composed of four different, complicated molecules called nucleotides, connected into a string, and wound up in a double helix. DNA must itself represent a very advanced state of evolution, formed by massively contingent events, in a process usually referred to as prebiotic evolution."

p. 131   "In self-organized critical systems most of the changes often concentrate within the largest events, so self-organized criticality can actually be thought of as the theoretical underpinning for catastrophism, the opposite philosophy to gradualism."

p. 155   "One might think of self-organized criticality as the general, underlying theory for the Gaia hypothesis. In the critical state the collection of species represents a single coherent organism following its own evolutionary dynamics. A single triggering event can cause an arbitrarily large fraction of the ecological network to collapse, and eventually be replaced by a new stable ecological network."

p. 156   "The vigorous opposition to the Gaia hypothesis, which represents a genuine holistic view of life, represents the frustration of a science seeking to maintain its reductionist view of biological evolution."

Beardsley, Tim, "Gaia," *Scientific American*, vol. 261 (December 1989), pp. 35-36.

p. 35   "Lovelock's musings have had two consequences. They inspired a quasi-political movement based in London, complete with a publishing arm, that now includes thousands of adherents throughout the U.S. and Western Europe. Indeed, Gaia has almost become the official ideology of "Green" parties in Europe: it appeals naturally to scientifically innocent individuals who worry about the environment."

p. 35   "Gaia seems to require that some organisms restrain their reproduction in order to benefit the larger community. Yet natural selection favors genes that increase their frequency."

Capra, Fritjof, "The Dance of Life," *Science Digest*, vol. 90 (April 1982), pp. 30-33.

p. 30   "A living organism is a self-organizing system, which means that its order in structure and function is not imposed by the environment but is established by the system itself."

p. 31   "The power of regenerating organic structures diminishes with the increasing complexity of the organism."

p. 31   "Most organisms are not only embedded in ecosystems but are complex ecosystems themselves, containing a host of smaller organisms that have considerable autonomy and yet integrate themselves harmoniously into the functioning of the whole."

p. 33   "The new systems biology shows that fluctuations are crucial in the dynamics of self-organization. They are the basis of order in the living world: ordered structures arise from rhythmic patterns."

p. 33   "The idea of fluctuations as the basis of order, which Nobel laureate Ilya Prigogine introduced into modern science, is one of the major themes in all Taoist texts. The mutual interdependence of all aspects of reality and the nonlinear nature of its interconnections are emphasized throughout Eastern mysticism."

Carlson, Shawn, "A Double-Blind Test of Astrology," *Nature*, vol. 318 (December 5, 1985), pp. 419-425. Dr. Carlson was in the Department of Physics, University of California, Berkeley.

p. 425   "We are now in a position to argue a surprisingly strong case against natal astrology as practiced by reputable astrologers. Great pains were taken to insure that the experiment was unbiased and to make sure that astrology was given every reasonable chance to succeed. It failed. Despite the fact that we worked with some of the best astrologers in the country, recommended by the advising astrologers for their expertise in astrology and in their ability to use the CPI, despite the fact that every reasonable suggestion made by the advising astrologers was worked into the experiment, despite the fact that the astrologers approved the design and predicted 50 percent as the 'minimum' effect they would expect to see, astrology failed to perform at a level better than chance. [Note: CPI = California Personality Inventory.] Tested using double-blind methods, the astrologer's predictions proved to be wrong. Their predicted connection between the positions of the planets and other astronomical objects at the time of birth and the personalities of test subjects did not exist. The experiment clearly refutes the astrological hypothesis."

Carr, B. J., and M. J. Rees, "The Anthropic Principle and the Structure of the Physical World," *Nature*, vol. 278 (April 12, 1979), pp. 605-612.

p. 605   "The structure of the physical world is manifested on many different scales, ranging from the Universe on the largest scale, down through galaxies, stars and planets, to living creatures, cells and atoms. . . .

"There are several amusing relationships between the different scales. For example, the size of a planet is the geometric mean of the size of the Universe and the size of an atom; the mass of man is the geometric mean of the mass of a planet and the mass of a proton."

p. 612   "The possibility of life as we know it evolving in the Universe depends on the values of a few basic physical constants—and is in some respects remarkably sensitive to their numerical values. . . . From a physical point of view, the anthropic 'explanation' of the various coincidences in nature is unsatisfactory, in three respects. First, it is entirely *post hoc*: it has not yet been used to predict any feature of the Universe (although some people have used it to rule out various cosmological models). Second, the principle is based on what may be an unduly anthropocentric concept of an observer. The arguments invoked here assume that life requires elements heavier than hydrogen and helium, water, galaxies, and special types of stars and planets. It is conceivable that some form of intelligence could exist without all of these features—thermodynamic disequilibrium is perhaps the only prerequisite that we can demand with real conviction. Third, the anthropic principle does not explain the exact values of the various coupling constants and mass-ratios, only their order of magnitudes. With enough anthropic conditions, one may be able to be more precise about the constants of nature, but the present situation is unsatisfactory."

Catalfo, Phil, "Glory Be to Gaia," *New Age Journal* (Janaury/February 1995), pp. 63-65, 130-131.

p. 63   "No, this wasn't a late-night rave party. It was the start of a 'Planetary Mass,' a form of multimedia worship spawned nearly a decade ago in Sheffield, England, by a passionate young band of Anglicans called the Nine O'Clock Service (NOS) community."

p. 63   "The ritual—also known as the 'rave Mass'—was inspired by the work of maverick priest Matthew Fox, as well as by the 'new creation story' propounded by the likes of theologian Thomas Berry and cosmologist Brian Swimme."

p. 65   "From among the worshipers seated on the floor, Matthew Fox himself arose to deliver the sermon, 'Where is this promise?' Fox began, referring to the promise of eternal salvation inherent in the Word. His answer: 'The Light of the Divine One is in each of us.'"

p. 65   "'With the advent of the printing press,' he continued, 'we anthropocentrized the Word. But "In the *beginning* was the Word"—that's 14 billion years ago! The Word of God is everywhere. . . . What we've longed for . . . is a language to express our mysticism. Perhaps now, in the postmodern age, it's emerging; the language of Light.'"

p. 130   "But for one moment I was able to see that, by taking Communion, I was partaking of the life force that fuels Creation; able to perceive of myself as a part of the divine Body of the universe receiving the energy of the 'cosmic Christ.'"

p. 131   "The Planetary Mass is a reformulation of traditional Christian worship, and more; It is the Mass reborn for a new millennium—looking not only back to the life of Jesus, or ahead to eternity, but also around, to the state of the world we have inherited, and within to the beings we can become."

Coleman, William Emmette, "Evolution of the Spiritual Universe," in *The Encyclopedia of Death—and Life—in the Spirit World*, edited by J. R. Francis (Chicago: Progressive Thinker Publishing House, 1900), pp. 143-150.

p. 143   "If the law of evolution is paramount in all departments of the material universe, including all manifestation of mind in that universe, which may be considered an established fact, then, carried to its legitimate sequence, this law should be alike operative in the spiritual universe."

p. 145   "Through the law of evolution, we have out-grown the horrible conception of divine vengeance (mistermed justice) so natural to our undeveloped forefathers; and the doctrines anent the spirit realm are rapidly becoming affected by the workings of this law in the earth's mental realm."

pp. 145-6   "If I am not mistaken, the first definite formulation of the doctrine that evolution was the law in all departments of the spiritual universe was in the earlier outcroppings of the philosophy of Spiritualism; and this idea has been continually advanced in all its more important subsequent literature. The fundamental or basic principle of Modern Spiritualism has ever been 'Eternal Progression' both of matter and spirit. Not only is the material universe a product of the law of evolution, but the spiritual realm as well. In *Nature's Divine Revelations*, by Andrew Jackson Davis, delivered in trance in 1845-47, the evolution of the material worlds by natural laws is taught, including the development of higher species from lower, and of man from the animal world; also that the spiritual worlds or spheres were evolved from the material world, and that in these spiritual worlds all human souls, by natural evolution, progress eternally nearer and nearer to the Deific Sensorium of the Univercoelum."

p. 146   "In 1859, a short time before Darwin's *Origin of Species* was published, volume one of Mr. Tuttle's *Arcana of Nature* was issued; and it sought to establish the evolution of the material world by natural law, upon an unteleological and seemingly atheistic basis."

p. 147   "Spiritual essences that once formed a part of the inner life of our planet now compose its spirit world,—its land and water, rocks and hills, plains and forests, fruits and flowers, and beasts and birds, as well as its men, women, and children; all are the flowering and fruitage of our old Mother Earth."

p. 150   "Each one of us will be a god or goddess and in unison with all others on the same plane of being, ever shall, when thus conjoined, exercise, in unity, the prerogative of the God of Universal Being.

                "In this teaching we find the climax of evolutionary doctrine, God himself, in a sense, being a product of evolution,—The Deific principle existing in nature unindividualized until embodied in man, and when thus personalized it evolves, by a long course of development into a personalized and individualized God."

p. 150   "It is certain that every form of belief, philosophic or theologic, that does not adjust itself to the great law of evolution in spiritual matters as well as in material, must die the death."

Davies, Paul C., "Chaos Frees the Universe," *New Scientist*, vol. 128 (October 6, 1990), pp. 48-51. Davies is Professor of Mathematical Physics, University of Adelaide.

p. 51   "What can we conclude about Laplace's image of a clockwork universe? The physical world contains a wide range of both chaotic and non-chaotic systems. Those that are chaotic have severely limited predictability, and even one such system would rapidly exhaust the entire Universe's capacity to compute its behavior."

p. 51   "This conclusion is surely profound. It means that, even accepting a strictly deterministic account of nature, the future states of the Universe are in some sense 'open.' Some people have seized on this openness to argue for the reality of human free will. Others claim that it bestows upon nature an element of creativity, an ability to bring forth that which is genuinely new, something not already implicit in earlier states of the Universe, save in the idealized fiction of the real numbers. Whatever the merits of such sweeping claims, it seems safe to conclude from the study of chaos that the future of the Universe is not irredeemably fixed."

Davies, Paul C., "Law and Order in the Universe," *New Scientist*, vol. 120 (October 15, 1988), pp.58-60.

p. 60   "John Wheeler, for example, has denied the independent existence of physical laws. He prefers to envisage what we call laws as trends that somehow emerge over time as the Universe evolves through its early states. Some philosophers and biologists have even favoured the idea of a sort of Darwinian evolution of competing laws."

p. 60   "I suspect that most physicists would regard as 'true' only those laws that have a timeless, transcendent existence, the rest being demoted as secondary or derivative. This still leaves the difficult question of where these eternal laws come from. Many physicists have remarked on the 'unreasonable' effectiveness of mathematics in describing the physical world. Why do the fundamental laws of the Universe always seem to be expressible in simple and elegant mathematical statements?"

p. 60   "Alternatively, there might be only one Universe, but a deeper level of reality beneath the laws, possibly a sort of 'metalaw,' or law of laws, a selection principle that happens to have brought into existence laws especially suited to producing life and consciousness. Whether the selection happened by accident or design must remain a matter for personal belief, for it is hard to see how science can ever answer this ultimate question."

Davies, Paul C., *The Cosmic Blueprint* (New York: Simon and Schuster, 1988), 224 pp.

p. 20   "There exists alongside the entropy arrow another arrow of time, equally fundamental and no less subtle in nature. Its origin lies shrouded in mystery, but its presence is undeniable. I refer to the fact that the universe is *progressing*— through the steady growth of structure, organization and complexity—to ever more developed and elaborate states of matter and energy. This unidirectional advance we might call the optimistic arrow, as opposed to the pessimistic arrow of the second law.

"There has been a tendency for scientists to simply deny the existence of the optimistic arrow. One wonders why. Perhaps it is because our understanding of complexity is still rudimentary, whereas the second law is firmly established. Partly also, perhaps it is because it smacks of anthropocentric sentimentality and has been espoused by many religious thinkers. Yet the progressive nature of the universe is an objective fact, and it somehow has to be reconciled with the second law, which is almost certainly inescapable. It is only in recent years that advances in the study of complexity, self-organization and cooperative phenomena has revealed how the two arrows can indeed co-exist."

p. 85   "The study of dissipative structures thus provides a vital clue to understanding the generative capabilities of nature. It has long seemed paradoxical that a universe apparently dying under the influence of the second law nevertheless continually increases its level of complexity and organization. We now see how it is possible for the universe to increase both organization and entropy at the same time. The optimistic and pessimistic arrows of time can co-exist: the universe can display creative unidirectional progress even in the face of the second law."

p. 119   "Prigogine's work on dissipative structures and Eigen's mathematical analysis of hypercycles both indicate that the primeval soup could have undergone successive leaps of self-organization along a very narrow pathway of chemical development. Our present understanding of chemical self-organization is still very fragmentary. It could perhaps be that there are as yet unknown organizing principles operating in prebiotic chemistry that greatly enhance the formation of complex organic molecules relevant to life."

p. 203   "The very fact that the universe *is* creative, and that the laws have permitted complex structures to emerge and develop to the point of consciousness—in other words, that the universe has organized its own self-awareness—is for me powerful evidence that there is 'something going on' behind it all. The impression of design is overwhelming. Science may explain all the processes whereby the universe evolves its own destiny, but that still leaves room for there to be a meaning behind existence."

Davies, Paul C., "The Creative Cosmos," *New Scientist*, vol. 116 (December 17, 1987), pp. 41-44.

p. 41   "It is fashionable to refer to the big bang which marked the origin of the Universe as the 'creation.' Yet it is quite wrong to suppose that in the beginning, the Universe already possessed the imprint of our intricately ordered world. The initial big bang may have served to bring a rudimentary Universe into existence, but the creative activity of nature is a continuous process. As the Universe evolves over billions of years, so new and ever more elaborate structures and systems arise."

pp. 41-2   "What is the origin of this creative power? For the past century, scientists have discussed the question of cosmological order in the context of the laws of thermodynamics. According to the second law, the Universe is inexorably degenerating, sliding irreversibly towards a state of maximum entropy, or chaos. Yet the facts flatly contradict this image of a dying Universe. Far from sliding *towards* a featureless state, the Universe is progressing *from* featurelessness to states of greater organization and complexity. This cosmic progress defines a global arrow of time that points in the opposite way to the thermodynamic arrow."

p. 42   "In recent years, more scientists have come to recognize that matter and energy possess an innate ability to self-organize. The study of self-organizing systems is now a multi-disciplinary subject, with many practical applications."

p. 42   "It is in biology that we find the most striking examples of self-organization. I need only cite the astonishing ability of an embryo to develop from a single strand of DNA, via an exquisitely well-orchestrated sequence of formative steps, into an exceedingly complex organism."

p. 44   "There is now a real hope that the age-old conceptual conflict between physics and biology is nearing an end. Biological processes such as morphogenesis and evolution, which seem miraculous to the physicist, are just one, albeit distinctive, example of general organizational principles. Orthodox Neo-Darwinism, while correctly identifying the basic mechanism of evolutionary change, fails to capture the organizational element that generates the progressive arrow of time. But Neo-Darwinism, combined with the mathematical principles emerging from network theory and related topics, will, I am convinced, explain the 'miracle' of life satisfactorily."

p. 44   "We are undoubtedly entering a new era of multidisciplinary scientific inquiry, in which concepts such as complexity and organization constitute the key feature. as we come to understand the properties of complex, organized systems in greater generality, so we will come to regard the principles governing their behavior as irreducible fundamental statements about the world.

"For centuries, mystics have attributed the existence of creativity in nature to vital, or occult, forces. This led to a strong reaction among scientists who ignored the creative, self-organizing processes going on all around us. Now, with the aid of new techniques, we are discovering that these creative processes represent a genuine, fundamental quality of physical systems that is amenable to proper scientific investigation."

Dubos, René, "Humanistic Biology," *American Scientist*, vol. 53 (March 1965), pp. 4-19.

p. 8   "What is almost certain, however, is that the various components of human culture are now required not only for the survival of man, but also for his existential realization. Man created himself even as he created his culture and thereby he became dependent upon it."

Durant, Will, "John Dewey," *Encyclopedia Brittannica*, vol. 7 (1949), p. 297.

"The starting point of his system of thought is biological: he sees man as an organism in an environment, remaking as well as made. Things are to be understood through their origins and their functions, without the intrusion of supernatural considerations."

Ferguson, Marilyn, *The Aquarian Conspiracy* (Los Angeles: J. P. Tarcher Co., 1980), 448 pp.

p. 159   "(1) It requires a mechanism for biological change more powerful than chance mutation, and (2) it opens us up to the possibility of rapid evolution in our own time, when the equilibrium of the species is punctuated by stress. Stress in modern society is experienced at the frontiers of our psychological rather than our geographical limits."

Gale, George, "The Anthropic Principle," *Scientific American*, vol. 245 (December 1981), pp. 154-170.

p. 154   "At the least the anthropic principle suggests connections between the existence of man and aspects of physics that one might have thought would have little bearing on biology. In its strongest form the principle might reveal that the universe we live in is the only conceivable universe in which intelligent life could exist."

Gliedman, John, "Scientists in Search of the Soul," *Science Digest*, vol. 90 (July 1982), pp. 77-79, 105.

p. 77   "At age 79, Sir John Eccles . . . has declared war on the past 300 years of scientific speculation about man's nature.

"Winner of the 1963 Nobel Prize in Physiology or Medicine for his pioneering research on the synapse—the point at which nerve cells communicate with each other—Eccles strongly defends the ancient religious belief that human beings consist of a mysterious compound of physical matter and intangible spirit.

". . . Boldly advancing what for most scientists is the greatest heresy of all, Eccles also asserts that our non-material self survives the death of the physical brain.

"Eccles is not the only world-famous scientist taking a controversial new look at the ancient mind-body conundrum. From Berkeley to Paris, and from London to Princeton, prominent scientists from fields as diverse as neurophysiology and quantum physics are coming out of the closet and admitting they believe in the possibility, at least, of such unscientific entities as the immortal human spirit and divine creation."

p. 77   "Eccles drives home his controversial conclusion: 'If I say that the uniqueness of the human self is not derived from the genetic code, not derived from experience, then what is it derived from? My answer is this: from a divine creation. Each self is a divine creation.'"

p. 77   "Eccles, however, points out that the more scientifically orthodox point of view that only what is material is real is equally beyond scientific disproof. In fact, Eccles notes, Popper's great doctrine—which Eccles supports—is itself unscientific. 'What experiments can you do to test Popper's theory of scientific theories?' asks Eccles."

Goodwin, Brian, and Gerry Webster, "Biological Fields?" *The Observer*, August 16, 1981.

> "The orthodox theory has simply stuffed the problem of the origins of animal forms into a back room and called it the common ancestor. Doing this explains nothing.
>
> "The genetic programme is no more the directing center of organismic structure than a dictionary is the directing centre of a text.
>
> "If Goodwin is right, and the fundamental forms of living organisms are expressions of biological fields, the 'adaptations' at the centre of orthodox neo-Darwinism must simply be superficial modifications of much more fundamental realities. Instead of seeing animals as collections of devices for survival, we may have to look at them as more like works of art. . . . In this sense a grasp of biological fields could lead us to see embryological development as more like the unfolding of a symphony than the generation of survival devices. The whole idea of evolution would then change profoundly."

Hooper, Judith, "Perfect Timing," *New Age Journal*, vol. 2 (December 1985), pp. 17-19.

p. 18   "The window of initial conditions necessary to produce our kind is very narrow, it turns out. . . . Given the facts, our existence seems quite improbable—more miraculous, perhaps, than the seven-day wonder of Genesis. As physicist Freeman Dyson of the Institute for Advanced Study in Princeton, New Jersey, once remarked, 'The universe in some sense must have known we were coming.'"

p. 18   "Since the question seems unanswerable at present, let us turn to the second grand cosmological question after Where do we come from?—namely, Where are we going? Well, in more than ten billion years, as our sun begins to die, the earth and all the other planets in this solar system will become cold. About a trillion (10^{12}) years hence, all the stars in the universe will have cooled, leaving dead planets detached from dead suns. After 10^{32} - 10^{44} years even the dead stars will evaporate. By 10^{128} years from now (assuming the universe is open, that is, infinitely expanding, as most cosmologists now believe), there will be only a void—cold, lifeless, and dark. The end thus will resemble the beginning according to Genesis, when 'the earth was without form and void, and darkness was upon the face of the deep.'"

p. 19   "The game is to get as much complexity as you can. One Nobel Prize Winner [Manfred Eigens] has speculated that with the human DNA molecule we have reached the limit of complexity that carbon can generate."

Lovelock, James, *The Ages of Gaia* (New York: W. W. Norton and Co., 1988), 252 pp.

p. xv   "Things have taken a strange turn in recent years; almost the full circle from Galileo's famous struggle with the theological establishment. It is the scientific establishment that makes itself esoteric and is the scourge of heresy."

p. 12   "But suppose that the Earth is alive. Then the evolution of the organisms and the evolution of the rocks need no longer be regarded as separate sciences to be studied in separate buildings of the university. Instead, a single evolutionary science describes the history of the whole planet. The evolution of the species and the evolution of their environment are tightly coupled together as a single and inseparable process."

p. 22   "The second law is the most fundamental and unchallenged law of the Universe; not surprisingly, no attempt to understand life can ignore it."

p. 23   "Schrodinger concluded that, metaphorically the most amazing property and characteristic of life is its ability to move upstream against the flow of time. Life is the paradoxical contradiction to the second law, which states that everything is, always has been, and always will be running down to equilibrium and death. Yet life evolves to ever-greater complexity and is characterized by an omnipresence of improbability that would make winning a sweepstake every day for a year seem trivial by comparison."

p. 24   "To describe the burgeoning life of our planet as improbable may seem odd. But imagine that some cosmic chef takes all the ingredients of the present Earth as atoms, mixes them and lets them stand. The probability that those atoms would combine into the molecules that make up our living Earth is zero. The mixture would always react chemically to form a dead planet like Mars or Venus."

p. 33   "Not seeing a mechanism for planetary control, they denied its existence as a phenomenon and branded the Gaia hypothesis as teleological. This was a final condemnation. Teleological explanations, in academe, are a sin against the holy spirit of scientific rationality. They deny the objectivity of Nature."

p. 206   "What if Mary is another name for Gaia? Then her capacity for virgin birth is no miracle or parthenogenetic aberration, it is a role of Gaia since life began."

p. 208   "How did we reach our present secular humanist world? In times that are ancient by human measure, as far back as the earliest artifacts that can be found, it seems that the Earth was worshipped as a goddess and believed to be alive. The myth of the great Mother is part of most early religions."

p. 209   "In ancient times, belief in a living Earth and in a living cosmos was the same thing. Heaven and Earth were close and part of the same body."

p. 218   "In no way do I see Gaia as a sentient being, a surrogate God. To me Gaia is alive and part of the ineffable Universe and I am a part of her."

p. 219   "Mathematicians and physicists are, without seeming aware of it, into demonology. They are found investigating 'catastrophe theory' or 'strange attractors.'"

p. 219   "It seems that the world of dissipating structures, threatened by catastrophe and parasitized by strange attractors, is the foreworld of life and of Gaia and the underworld that still exists."

p. 223   "The country folk, who are destroying their own forests, are often Christians and venerate the Holy Virgin Mary. If their hearts and minds could be moved to see in her the embodiment of Gaia, then they might become aware that the victim of their destruction was indeed the Mother of humankind and the source of everlasting life."

Morain, Lloyd, and Oliver Reiser, "Scientific Humanism: A Formulation," *The Humanist*, vol. 48 (September/October 1988), pp. 33-34 reprinted from Spring 1943 issue. Morain was editor of *The Humanist*; Reiser was Professor of Philosophy at University of Pittsburgh.

p. 33   "The scientific humanist holds that humans are natural creatures living in a natural universe. Evolved from stardust by cosmic processes, humans emerged from creatures that *adapt* themselves to nature into the self-directive agents who *re-create* that nature to serve the needs of their own progressive enlightenment. There are in this universe not gods and humans, masters and slaves, but human beings in various stages of development, all born of the Earth-womb."

p. 33   "Scientific humanists are not dogmatists who believe that they know all the answers to all the questions. They see, however, that there are some things in this universe we must accept as basic, brute fact. An uncreated universe—the space-time-matter trinity, or the cosmic movement-continuum—is one such brute fact."

p. 34   "Morality needs no supernatural sanctions or motivations. It is not heaven-sent; it is human-evolved."

p. 34   "In the coming planetary civilization of a world-embracing humanism, those 'religions' that obstruct social advance must be subordinated. In the world of scientific humanism, religion will be obsolete, but the religious spirit—the sense of awe and reverence in the presence of a majestic universe—will constitute a wholesome ingredient in the economic-political-reflective synthesis."

Motulsky, Arno G., "Brave New World?" *Science,* vol. 185, no. 4152 (August 23, 1974), pp. 653-663. Motulsky was Professor of Medicine, University of Washington, Seattle.

p. 653   "We no longer need be subject to blind external forces but can manipulate the environment and eventually may be able to manipulate our genes. Thus, unlike any other species, we may be able to interfere with our biologic evolution. It is most remarkable that the human brain had already reached this supreme position at the dawn of prehistory. The biological substrate that later created the philosophies of Plato and Spinoza, the religions of Jesus and Buddha, the poetry of Shakespeare, Molière, and Goethe, as well as modern science, may have been in existence about 50,000 years ago. There is little evidence that our brains have changed much during this period."

p. 654   "Thus, human 'goodness' and behavior considered ethical by many societies probably are evolutionary acquisitions of man and require fostering. . . .

               "An ethical system that bases its premises on absolute pronouncements will not usually be acceptable to those who view human nature by evolutionary criteria."

Muller, Robert, Cited in "United Nations' Robert Muller—A Vision of Global Spirituality," by Kristin Murphy, *The Movement Newspaper*, September 1983. Muller was Asst. Secretary-General, United Nations Organization.

p. 10   "I believe the most fundamental thing we can do today is to believe in evolution."

Oldroyd, D. R., *Darwinian Impacts* (Atlantic Highlands, New Jersey: Humanities Press, 1983), 398 pp.

p. 254   "So a metaphysical system, although naturalistic and secular, has been built up by modern humanists around the nucleus of biological evolutionism. Such a system may be seen to the best advantage in the writings of the well-known biologist, Julian Huxley (1887-1975), grandson of Darwin's 'bulldog,' Thomas Henry Huxley. Really Julian Huxley espoused a new religion, rather than a mere metaphysical system. Accepting with enthusiasm the doctrine of evolutionism, he maintained that the future evolutionary process on Earth is to be carried out almost exclusively by man. Thus man's destiny has become that of realizing his evolutionary potentialities and furthering the evolutionary process, which for Huxley is a notion that may be contemplated with a kind of religious enthusiasm."

p. 255   "The tenets of the humanist movement mesh well with the generality of beliefs in the contemporary liberal West even though the number of people specifically calling themselves humanists is quite small. In other words, in one direction at least, the evolutionary doctrines of Darwinism have emerged as a point of wide consensus in the secular world of the twentieth century."

Rifkin, Jeremy, *Algeny* (New York: Viking Press, 1983), 298 pp.

p. 188   "Evolution is no longer viewed as a mindless affair; quite the opposite. It is mind enlarging its domain up the chain of species."

p. 195   "In this way one eventually ends up with the idea of the universe as a mind that oversees, orchestrates, and gives order and structure to all things. If this idea of the universe as mind seems to bear an uncanny resemblance to the idea of fields, it is no accident. When scientists grope to define 'fields' in the universe, they are edging closer and closer to the concept of nature as mind."

p. 244   "We no longer feel ourselves to be guests in someone else's home and therefore obliged to make our behavior conform with a set of preexisting cosmic rules. It is our creation now. We make the rules. We establish the parameters of reality. We create the world, and because we do, we no longer feel beholden to outside forces. We no longer have to justify our behavior, for we are now the architects of the universe. We are responsible to nothing outside ourselves, for we are the kingdom, the power, and the glory for ever and ever."

p. 247   "The new temporal theory is not an accurate explanation of nature any more than Darwin's theory of natural selection was."

p. 255   "Our future is secured. The cosmos wails."

Sheldrake, Rupert, *The Rebirth of Nature: The Greening of Science and of God* (New York: Bantam Books, 1991), 260 pp. Sheldrake has a Ph.D. in Biochemistry, Cambridge, and is the Director of Studies in Cell Biology at Cambridge, and Studies in Philosophy at Harvard.

p. 10   "But today, with the rise of the green movement, Mother Nature is reasserting herself, whether we like it or not. In particular, the acknowledgment that our planet is a living organism, Gaia, Mother Earth, strikes a responsive chord in millions of people; it reconnects us both with our personal, intuitive experience of nature and with the traditional understanding of nature as alive."

pp. 26, 28   "There is no doubt that the spread of the cult of Mary involved the assimilation of various elements of pre-Christian goddess worship. Indeed the fifth-century council of the church at which she was proclaimed Mother of God took place at Ephesus, an ancient center of goddess worship, only a few decades after the temple of Artemis was suppressed. Mary is Queen of Heaven, a title inherited from Astarte-Ashtoreth, the aspect symbolized by her blue star-spangled cloak; she is lunar, like Artemis, and is often depicted standing on a crescent moon; she is the Star of the Sea, with many sanctuaries all around the shores of the Mediterranean; and as Virgin Mother of God, she is heir to the ancient tradition of the primal Mother. She also took on aspects of the Earth Mother, not least through her shrines in caves, grottos and crypts, and as the protectress of many holy wells."

p. 44   "Although there was much debate over the details, animism was central to Greek thinking. The great philosophers believed the world of nature was alive because of its ceaseless motion. Moreover, because these motions were regular and orderly they said that the world of nature was not only alive but intelligent, a vast animal with a soul and a rational mind of its own."

p. 71   "Thus through Darwin's theory, nature took on the creative powers of the Great Mother, powers quite unsuspected in the original mechanistic conception of nature. Evolutionary philosophers conceived of these creative powers in a variety of ways. In the dialectical materialism of Marx and Engels, the creative mother principle is matter, undergoing a continual spontaneous process of development, resolving conflicts and contradictions in successive syntheses. In the philosophy of Herbert Spenser, progressive evolution itself was the supreme principle of the entire universe. The vitalist philosophy Henri Bergson attributed the creativity of evolution to a vital impetus, the *élan vital*. In his view, the evolutionary process is not designed and planned in advance in the mind of a transcendent God but is spontaneous and creative."

p. 81   "That left only God, and [Newton] concluded that gravitational forces were a direct expression of God's will: 'There exists an infinite and omnipresent spirit in which matter is moved according to mathematical laws.'"

p. 95   "The magnitude of this mystery is staggering. The great majority of the matter in the universe is utterly unknown, except through its gravitational effects. Yet through the gravitational field, it has shaped the way in which the universe has developed. It is as if physics has discovered the unconscious. Just as the conscious mind floats, as it were, on the surface of the sea of unconscious mental processes, so the known physical world floats on a cosmic ocean of dark matter.

"This dark matter has the archetypal power of the dark, destructive Mother. It is like Kali, whose very name means 'black.' If there is more than a critical amount of dark matter, then the cosmic expansion will gradually come to an end, and the universe begin to contract again, pulled in by gravitation, until everything is ultimately devoured in a terminal implosion, the opposite of the Big Bang—the Big Crunch."

pp. 95-6   "For the modern conception of nature gives an even stronger sense of her spontaneous life and creativity than the stable, repetitive world of Greek, medieval, and Renaissance philosophy. All nature is evolutionary. The cosmos is like a great developing organism, and evolutionary creativity is inherent in nature herself."

p. 151   "The organismic or holistic philosophy of nature that has grown up over the last sixty years is a new form of animism. It implicitly or explicitly regards all nature as alive. The universe as a whole is a developing organism, and so are the galaxies, solar systems, biospheres within it, including the earth."

p. 209   "In the Soviet Union, a great deal of interest was aroused by the fact that the Ukrainian word for 'wormwood' is *chernobyl*."

Smith, Wolfgang, *Teilhardism and the New Religion* (Rockford, Illinois: Tan Books & Publishers, Inc., 1988), 248 pp.

p. 9   ". . . however, one cannot but agree with Ludwig von Bertalanffy (a distinguished biologist, let us add) when he writes: 'The fact that a theory so vague, so insufficiently verifiable, and so far from the criteria otherwise applied in "hard" science has become a dogma can only be explained on sociological grounds.'"

p. 242   "The point, however, is that the doctrine of evolution has swept the world, not on the strength of its scientific merits, but precisely in its capacity as a Gnostic myth. It affirms, in effect, that living beings create themselves, which is in essence a *metaphysical* claim. This in itself implies, however, that the theory is scientifically unverifiable (a fact, incidentally, which has often enough been pointed out by philosophers of science). Thus, in the final analysis, evolutionism is in truth a metaphysical doctrine decked out in scientific garb."

Teilhard de Chardin, Pierre, *The Phenomenon of Man* (New York: Harper and Row, 1965), 318 pp.

p. 2   "[Evolution] is above all verification, as well as being immune from any subsequent contradiction by experience."

p. 219   "Is evolution a theory, a system or a hypothesis? It is much more: it is a general condition to which all theories, all systems, all hypotheses must bow and which they must satisfy henceforward if they are to be thinkable and true. Evolution is a light illuminating all facts, a curve that all lines of thought must follow."

Teilhard de Chardin, Pierre, *Christianity and Evolution* (New York: Harcourt, Brace & Jovanovich, 1974), 255 pp.

p. 99   "The world (its value, its infallibility, and its goodness)—that, when all is said and done, is the first, the last, and the only thing in which I believe."

p. 179   "God cannot create, except evolutively."

Teilhard de Chardin, Pierre, *The Heart of the Matter* (New York: Harcourt, Brace & Jovanovich, 1979), 276 pp.

p. 92   "It is Christ, in very truth, who saves—but should we not immediately add that at the same time it is Christ who is saved by Evolution?"

Thomsen, Dietrick E., "A Knowing Universe Seeking to be Known," *Science News*, vol. 123 (February 19, 1983), p. 124.

p. 124   "'There are two major problems rooted in science, but unassimilable as science, consciousness and cosmology.' With that statement George Wald of Harvard University, winner of the 1967 Nobel Prize for Physiology or Medicine, began to tell his audience at the recent Orbis Scientiae meeting in Miami that we live in a very special universe indeed."

p. 124   "'Seeing' is related to self-consciousness. Consciousness seems to be characteristic of higher organisms, and a particular self-awareness connected with the ability to plan future actions on the basis of past experience of human beings.

                    "He concedes that nothing one can do as a scientist identifies the presence or absence of consciousness. . . . Consciousness lies outside the parameters of space and time."

p. 124   "Believing in the importance of consciousness, he now tries to put consciousness and cosmology together. Perhaps consciousness, rather than being a late evolutionary development, was there all the time. Consciousness formed the material universe and brought out life and overt forms of consciousness. 'The universe wants to be known,' Wald says. 'Did the universe come about to play its role to empty benches?'"

p. 124   "Objections will be raised by those who want to insist that the material universe is all the reality there is. Materialism of this kind is a doctrine that anyone may choose as a working hypothesis or as a religion, but I am unaware of a proof of it."

Trefil, James, "Was the Universe Designed for Life?" *Astronomy*, vol. 25 (June 1997), pp. 54-57.

p. 56   "So we live in a universe where the fundamental constants of nature seemed to be 'fine-tuned' to permit the existence of life and, perhaps, intelligence. Change any of the fundamental constants of nature and you could well have a universe in which no life exists at all."

p. 57   "The distinguishing feature of science—the thing that makes it different from fields like literary criticism—is its unrelenting demand that all ideas and claims about the universe by checked by experiment on or observation of the universe itself. No matter how clever, an idea can't survive unless it meets this test. I don't think it's going too far to say that if a statement can't be subjected to experimental or observational test, it simply isn't a part of science."

p. 57   "The anthropic principle will always be a fascinating subject for debate and philosophical discussion. If it remains untestable, however, it will also always rest outside the realm of science."

C. Evolutionary Miscellany

The quotes in this final section do not fit in well with the other chapters and sections of this book, and so are simply grouped together in this final section.

Some represent additional fruits of evolutionary thinking (e.g., inferior status of women). Some reflect modern educational developments, some refer to different aspects of scientific and religious thinking.

In concluding the book, it is obvious that evolutionism affects the whole spectrum of human life and thought. It is not merely a biological theory which one can take or leave as he chooses. And it does require a decision. "If the LORD be God, follow Him: but if Baal, then follow him" (I Kings 18:21).

Alfvén, Hannes, "Memoirs of a Dissident Scientist," *American Scientist*, vol. 76 (May/June 1988), pp. 249-251.

pp. 250-1   "This has been a great advantage because it gives me a possibility to approach the phenomena from another point than most astrophysicists do, and it is always fruitful to look at *any* phenomenon under two different points of view. On the other hand it has given me a serious disadvantage. When I describe the phenomena, according to this formalism most referees do not understand what I say and turn down my papers."

p. 251   "The mentioned conditions and quite a few other factors have led to a disagreement between a very strong establishment (E) and a small group of dissidents (D) to which the present author belongs. This is nothing remarkable. What is more remarkable and regrettable is that it seems to be almost impossible to start a serious discussion between E and D. As a dissident is in a very unpleasant situation, I am sure that D would be very glad to change their views as soon as E gives convincing arguments. But the argument 'all knowledgeable people agree that . . .' (with the tacit addition that by not agreeing you demonstrate that you are a crank) is not a valid argument in science. If scientific issues always were decided by Gallup polls and not by scientific arguments science will very soon be petrified forever."

Beck, Stanley D., "Natural Science and Creationist Theology," *Bioscience*, vol. 32 (October 1982), pp. 738-742. Beck was in the Department of Entomology, Wisconsin University; Sigmi Xi lecture at Virginia Tech, May 4, 1981.

p. 738   "Twentieth century biology rests on a foundation of evolutionary concepts. . . . The evolutionary basis is also apparent in peripheral independent fields such as chemistry, geology, physics and astronomy. No central scientific concept is more firmly established in our thinking, our methods, and our interpretations, than that of evolution."

p. 739   "The first of the unprovable premises on which science has been based is the belief that *the world is real and the human mind is capable of knowing its real nature*. . . .

"The second and best known postulate underlying the structure of scientific knowledge is that of cause and effect. . . .

"The third basic scientific premise is *that nature is unified*."

p. 739   "These scientific premises define and limit the scientific mode of thought. It should be pointed out, however, that each of these postulates had its origin in, or was consistent with, Christian theology. . . . Scientific thought soon parted from theology, because no assumption is made concerning any force outside of or beyond natural measurable forces."

p. 740   "Is scientific creationism scientific? Obviously, it is not. Creationism involves acceptance of a premise that lies outside of science."

p. 740   "If separated from its origin in a religious tradition, might not the creationist view of life on earth be offered as a scientific theory? . . . The answer is an unequivocal 'no,' because the creationist theory requires the belief that some force, some factor has created and, in so doing, has bypassed the natural forces and mechanisms by which the physical universe operates."

Bishop, Beth A., and Charles W. Anderson, "Student Conceptions of Natural Selection and its Role in Evolution," *Journal of Research in Science Teaching*, vol. 27 (May 1990), pp. 415-427. Bishop and Anderson are in the College of Education, Michigan State University. (Tests were given to 110 college juniors and seniors.)

p. 415   "*Abstract*. Although students had taken an average of 1.9 years of previous biology courses, performance on the pretest was uniformly low. There was no relationship between the amount of previous biology taken and either pretest or posttest performance. Belief in the truthfulness of evolutionary theory was also unrelated to either pretest or posttest performance."

p. 422   "We have found that difficulty in seeing how change can result from the combined effects of random mutation and nonrandom selection is an especially persistent problem."

p. 425   "Fifty-nine percent of students answering the question 'Do you believe the theory of evolution to be truthful?' on the pretest were classified as believers, 11% were classified as nonbelievers, and 30% were unsure ($n = 90$). Answers to the same question on the posttest gave similar results: 49% believers, 26% nonbelievers, and 27% unsure ($n = 57$)."

p. 425   "Student conceptions of the process of evolutionary change were not associated with their belief (or lack of belief) in the truthfulness of evolution. . . . In fact, a slightly higher percentage of the nonbelievers understood the scientific conceptions."

p. 426   "Most students who believed in the truth of evolution apparently based their beliefs more on acceptance of the power and prestige of science than on an understanding of the reasoning that had led scientists to their conclusions."

Born, Max, "Physics and Metaphysics," *Scientific Monthly*, vol. 82 (May 1956), pp. 229-235.

p. 235   "But a real enrichment to our thinking is the idea of complementarity. The fact that in an exact science like physics there are mutually exclusive and complementary situations which cannot be described by the same concepts, but need two kinds of expressions, must have an influence, and I think a welcome influence on other fields of human activity and thought. Here again, Niels Bohr has shown the way. In biology the concept of life itself leads to a complementary alternative: the physicochemical analysis of a living organism is incompatible with its free functioning and leads in its extreme application to death. In philosophy there is a similar alternative in the central problem of free will. Any decision can be considered on the one side as a process in the conscious mind, on the other as a product of motives, implanted in the past or present from the outside world. If one sees in this an example of complementarity the eternal conflict between freedom and necessity appears to be based on an epistemological error. . . . Has the lesson in epistemology which we learned from physics any bearing on this problem? I think it has, in showing that even in restricted fields a description of the whole of a system in one picture is impossible; there are complementary images which do not apply simultaneously but are nevertheless not contradictory and exhaust the whole only together."

Croft, L. R., *How Life Began* (Durham, England: Evangelical Press, 1988), 176 pp. Croft was a lecturer in Biological "Sciences," University of Salford.

pp. 20-21   "Darwin was well aware that a satisfactory explanation for the origin of life was of crucial importance to his theory. Undoubtedly he recognized that this was the weakest link in his theory. On the other hand, his early opponents, rather than accept defeat, found that here was a position whereby they might compromise with evolution. They argued that if God created the first living cell to contain the instructions for evolution, then the Christian need not surrender his faith. The Genesis account of creation could be believed by interpreting the days to be aeons of time. Darwin in fact had himself realized that this might be a subtle way of getting acceptance for his theory. Thus we find in the early editions of *Origin of Species* the concluding paragraph: 'There is grandeur in this view of life, with its several powers, having been originally breathed by the Creator into a few forms or into one. . . .'

"Darwin's dishonesty is apparent. He had long been an atheist and had inserted the above paragraph to lessen the tumult he knew his book would create. He no more believed in a Creator than he did in a flat earth."

Davis, Bernard D., "Social Determinism and Behavioral Genetics," *Science*, vol. 189 (September 26, 1975), p. 1049. Davis was at Harvard Medical School, Boston, Massachusetts.

"To be sure, in behavioral genetics premature conclusions are all too tempting, and they can be socially dangerous. Moreover, even sound knowledge in this field, as in any another, can be used badly. Accordingly, some would set up lines of defense against acquisition of the knowledge, rather than against its misuse. This suggestion has wide appeal, for the public is already suspicious of genetics. It recognizes that earlier, pseudoscientific extrapolations from genetics to society were used to rationalize racism, with tragic consequences; and it has developed much anxiety over the allegedly imminent prospect of genetic manipulation in man. Hence one can easily visualize an American Lysenkoism, prescribing an environmentalist dogma and proscribing or discouraging research on behavioral genetics. . . .

"In the continuing struggle to replace traditional myths by evolutionary knowledge, the conflict over human diversity may prove even more intense and prolonged than the earlier conflict over special creation: the critics are no less righteous, the issues are even closer to politics, and guilt over massive social inequities hinders objective discussion."

Denton, Michael, *Evolution: A Theory in Crisis* (London: Burnett Books, Ltd., 1985), 368 pp.

p. 62   "It was not only his general theory that was almost entirely lacking in any direct empirical support, but his special theory was also largely dependent on circumstantial evidence. A striking witness to this is the fact that nowhere was Darwin able to point to one *bona fide* case of natural selection having actually generated evolutionary change in nature, let alone having been responsible for the creation of a new species."

p. 66   "As far as Christianity was concerned, the advent of the theory of evolution and the elimination of traditional teleological thinking was catastrophic. The suggestion that life and man are the result of chance is incompatible with the biblical assertion of their being the direct result of intelligent creative activity. Despite the attempt by liberal theology to disguise the point, the fact is that no biblically derived religion can really be compromised with the fundamental assertion of Darwinian theory. Chance and design are antithetical concepts, and the decline in religious belief can probably be attributed more to the propagation and advocacy by the intellectual and scientific community of the Darwinian version of evolution than to any other single factor."

p. 144   "The phenomenon of homology has remained the mainstay of the argument for evolution right down to the present day."

Dewey, John, "Evolution and Ethics," *Scientific Monthly*, vol. 78 (February 1954), pp. 57-66.

p. 66   "There are no doubt sufficiently profound distinctions between the ethical process and the cosmic process as it existed prior to man and to the formation of human society. So far as I know, however, all of these differences are summed up in the fact that the process and the forces bound up with the cosmic have come to consciousness in man. That which was instinct in the animal is conscious impulse in man. That which was 'tendency to vary' in the animal is conscious foresight in man. That which was unconscious adaptation and survival in the animal, taking place by the 'cut and try' method until it worked itself out, is with man conscious deliberation and experimentation. That this transfer from unconsciousness to consciousness has immense importance, need hardly be argued. It is enough to say that it means the whole distinction of the moral from the unmoral."

Dickerson, Richard E., "The Game of Science," *Perspectives on Science and Faith*, vol. 44 (June 1992), pp. 137-138.

p. 137   "Science fundamentally, is a game. It is a game with one overriding and defining rule:

"Rule No. 1: Let us see how far and to what extent we can explain the behavior of the physical and material universe in terms of purely physical and material causes, without invoking the supernatural.

"Operational science takes no position about the existence or non-existence of the supernatural; only that this factor is not to be invoked in scientific explanations."

p. 138   "It is a reasonable prediction that the attitude of future generations toward twentieth-century 'scientific creationism' (an inherent oxymoron according to Rule No. 1, above) will be one of ridicule."

Dirac, P. A. M., "The Evolution of the Physicist's Picture of Nature," *Scientific American*, vol. 208 (May 1963), pp. 45-53.

p. 53   "There is one other line along which one can still proceed by theoretical means. It seems to be one of the fundamental features of nature that fundamental physical laws are described in terms of a mathematical theory of great beauty and power, needing quite a high standard of mathematics for one to understand it. You may wonder: Why is nature constructed along these lines? One can only answer that our present knowledge seems to show that nature is so constructed. We simply have to accept it. One could perhaps describe the situation by saying that God is a mathematician of a very high order, and He used very advanced mathematics in constructing the universe. Our feeble attempts at mathematics enable us to understand a bit of the universe, and as we proceed to develop higher and higher mathematics we can hope to understand the universe better."

Durant, Will, "We Are in the Last Stage of a Pagan Period," *Chicago Tribune*, April 1980.

"By offering evolution in place of God as a cause of history, Darwin removed the theological basis of the moral code of Christendom. And the moral code that has no fear of God is very shaky. That's the condition we are in. . . . I don't think man is capable yet of managing social order and individual decency without fear of some supernatural being overlooking him and able to punish him."

"I should say we are now in the last stage of the pagan period and that consequently I would expect there would be a resurrection of religious belief, and an aid to the moral life that is an aid to civilization."

"Chaos is the mother of dictatorship, and then the sequence goes all over again. Dictatorship is the mother of order, order is the mother of liberty, liberty is the mother of chaos, chaos is the mother of dictatorship, and then the cycle renews."

Gould, Stephen Jay, "Darwin at Sea," *Natural History*, vol. 92 (September 1983), pp. 14-20. Gould is
at the Museum of Comparative Zoology, Harvard University, Cambridge, Massachusetts.

p. 14   "Darwin, to begin, did not become an evolutionist until several months after
his return to London—probably not until March 1837 (the *Beagle* docked in
October, 1836). He did not appreciate the evolutionary significance of the
Galápagos while he was there, and he originally misunderstood the finches so
thoroughly that he was barely able to reconstruct the story later from his sadly
inadequate records."

p. 15   "All creationists admitted that species often differentiated into mildly distinct
forms in situations, as on island chains and archipelagoes, where populations
could become isolated in different circumstances of ecology and climate. These
local races were called varieties, and they did not threaten the created and
immutable character of a species 'essence.'"

p. 18   "Darwin's finches are not mentioned at all in the *Origin of Species* (1859);
the ornithological star of that great book is the domesticated pigeon."

Gould, Stephen Jay, "Darwin's 'Big Book,'" review of *Natural Selection*, by Charles Darwin, ed. by
R. C. Stauffer (New York: Cambridge University Press, 1975, 694 pp.), *Science*, vol. 188 (May 23,
1975), pp. 824-826.

p. 826   "Today, all scientists accept materialism (at least in their workplace), and
the philosophically astute realize that it poses no threat to our love for music,
subjective insight, and love itself! Yet, when I read the tracts of the Creation
Research Society and watch Arthur Koestler groping for inherent meaning, I
wonder if we are ready for Darwin yet."

Greenwell, J. Richard, "The Dinosaur Vote," *Science Digest*, vol. 90 (April 1992), p. 42.

p. 42   "Recently, two members of the American Geophysical Union proposed a
'democratic solution' to the question of the dinosaurs' extinction. Whatever
hypothesis received the most votes from the Union members should, the scientists
suggested, be declared the official reality!

               "This dinosaur 'solution' interest me because, with Dr. James King of the
University of Arizona, I recently polled 300 leading scientists—100 physical
anthropologists, 100 aquatic biologists and 100 chemists—about the reality of
Bigfoot and the Loch Ness monster."

p. 42   "We now are reasonably sure that scientists' notions of reality are influenced
not only by objective conditions but also by subjective considerations. It would
seem to follow that as beliefs change over time, so does reality.

               ". . . It is sobering to realize that with the change of a few percentage points
in a poll, whole menageries of new creatures could enter our textbooks almost
overnight."

p. 42   ". . . 23 percent of the anthropologists thought Nessie was a large animal
unknown to science, while a surprising 39 percent of the biologists did."

Himmelfarb, Gertrude, "Revolution in the Library," reprinted from Spring 1997 edition of *The American Scholar*, *Key Reporter*, vol. 62 (Spring 1997), pp. 1-5. Dr. Himmelfarb is Professor Emeritus of History at the Graduate School of the City University of New York.

p. 5   "The humanities, however, are about more than the retrieval of facts. They are also about appreciating a poem, understanding an idea, finding significance in a historical event, following the logic of an argument, reasoning about human nature, inquiring into ethical dilemmas, making rational and moral judgments— all of which require an exercise of mind that calls upon all the human faculties, and that no technology, however sophisticated, can satisfy. If we want, for example, a concordance to the Bible, we can find no better medium than the Internet. But if we want to read the Bible, to study it, think about it, reflect upon it, we should have it in our hands, for that is the only way of getting it into our minds and our hearts."

Hoagland, Hudson, "Science and the New Humanism," *Science*, vol. 143 (January 10, 1964), pp. 111-114.

p. 113   "But man himself and his behavior are an emergent product of purely fortuitous mutations and evolution by natural selection acting upon them. Nonpurposive natural selection has produced purposive human behavior."

Hughes, David W., "Draughtsmen of the Constellations," *Nature*, vol. 312 (December 20/27, 1984), p. 697.

p. 697   "This means that the originators of the constellations must have lived somewhere on the longitude line 36°N. And, allowing for precession, the centre of the zone corresponds to the south celestial pole of around 2,500 BC."

p. 697   "The Babylonians are stronger contenders: the Sumero-Akkadian people of the Euphrates region were great believers in astrology, and the movement of planets through the Zodiac was used for calendrical and religious purposes. The records left on their clay tablets leave us in no doubt that as far back as 2,100 BC they were using a system of constellations essentially similar to that given in Aratus's poem."

Hull, David L., "A Recent Huxley," reviews of *If I am to Be Remembered: the Life and Works of Julian Huxley*, by Krishm R. Dronarmraju (River Edge, New Jersey: World Scientific, 1993, 249 pp.), and *Julian Huxley*, ed. C. Kenneth Waters and Albert Van Helden (Houston, Rice University Press, 1993, 344 pp.), *Science*, vol. 262 (November 12, 1993), pp. 1079-1080.

p. 1079   "The proceedings of a conference held at Rice University, where Huxley taught from 1913 to 1916 and where his papers now reside, make up for the deficiencies of Dronamraju's book. In the introduction Kenneth Waters sets out a clear chronology of Huxley's life from his birth on 22 June 1887 during Queen Victoria's Jubilee, through his schooling and series of university positions, to an abortive engagement that landed him in a sanitorium. Soon he was joined by his younger brother, Trevenen, whose own depression led to suicide. Huxley eventually married a French-Swiss governess, Juliette Baillot, in 1919 and had two sons and a second nervous breakdown, this one caused apparently by his feelings of inadequacy as a teacher."

p. 1079   "A third nervous breakdown did not keep him from becoming the first Director-General of this agency.

                 "After his stint at UNESCO, Huxley never took on another regular position but spent the next 27 years traveling, writing, and lecturing as a part of the international intelligentsia."

p. 1079   "In 1958 he was knighted. He also had three more nervous breakdowns, in part brought on by anxieties over whether he actually deserved the honors that were being conferred on him."

p. 1080   "Huxley emphasized the importance of genetic diversity in evolution and was, for his time and station, politically left. Paul notes that his student H. J. Muller was even more radical in his political leanings but emphasized the culling effect of natural selection."

p. 1080   "Although Huxley was uncomfortable about it, he held during the course of his lifetime various racist beliefs and attitudes. For example, his fear of the population explosion was based not on numbers alone but on the composition of those peoples who were increasing most rapidly."

Huxley, Leonard, ed., *Life and Letters of Thomas Henry Huxley* (Macmillan, 19038, vol. 1, p. 241.

                 " . . . 'creation' in the ordinary sense of the word, is perfectly conceivable. I find no difficulty in conceiving that, at some former period, this universe was not in existence; and that it made its appearance in six days (or instantaneously, if that is preferred), in consequence of the volition of some pre-existing Being. Then, as now, the so-called *a priori* arguments against Theism, and, given a Deity, against the possibility of creative acts, appeared to me to be devoid of reasonable foundation."

Johnston, George Sim, "The Genesis Controversy," *Crisis* (May 1989), pp. 12-18.

p. 12   "Many scientists would rather cling to Darwin's theory, in whatever baroque form, than face the implications of its demise. Darwin's scientific detractors, moreover, are generally reticent about taking their objections public for fear of being labeled 'creationist.' So the newspaper-reading public has not been let in on what the British scientific journal *Nature* recently called 'the sharp dissent and frequently acrimonious debate' over evolutionary theory, while the armies of biology teachers, science writers, and public television wildlife hosts carry on as though there were no problem with Darwin at all.

                 "Charles Darwin (1809-82) was a dull, reticent Englishman whose large fortune allowed him to pursue a passion for studying nature. Although he claimed his work had no objectives other than scientific, it is clear from his private journals that his motives were no less metaphysical than those of the clergy who attacked him."

Judson, Horace F., "Century of the Sciences," *Science-84* (November 1984), pp. 41-43.

p. 41   "Yes, previous centuries had scientists and, yes, they made discoveries fundamental to our understanding. But how many lived in Galileo's Day or Newton's whom we would now call scientists? They could all have found seats in one lecture hall. . . . Even by the end of the 19th century, the practicing scientists could all still know one another.

"The exponential growth of the enterprise of science marks the modern era."

p. 42   "Still, even today certain major sciences offer scant prospect of practical application. Astronomy and cosmology are of little earthly use. Evolutionary theory has not bred a single new species of animal or vegetable, let alone improved the intensity of our pleasures or the intelligence or docility of our children."

p. 43   "More generally, even if we wanted to, we cannot turn the sciences back. Our salvation is ours alone to make. This is the profoundest transformation the sciences have made in our expectations."

Kitts, David B., "The Theory of Geology," in *Fabric of Geology*, ed. C. C. Albritton, Jr. (Stanford, Connecticut: Freemon, Cooper & Co., 1963), pp. 49-68.

p. 50   "Generalizations employing terms denoting probability or possibility, however, far outnumber generalizations of universal form in the geologic literature. A striking feature of geologic discourse is the frequency with which such words and phrases as 'probably,' 'frequently,' and 'tends to' occur in generalizations."

Krochmal, Arnold, "Olive Growing in Greece," *Economic Botany* (July/September 1955).

p. 228   "The adaptable nature of the trees permits them to be grown in soils of high lime content and on rocky hills unsuited for other crops."

Lewontin, Richard C., "The Inferiority Complex," review of *The Mismeasure of Man*, by Stephen J. Gould, *New York Review of Books* (October 22, 1981), in which Gould argued that the sociopolitical bias of a scientist might have an unconscious effect on his scientific results.

"Like Kamin, I am, myself rather more harsh in my view. Scientists, like others, sometimes tell deliberate lies because they believe that small lies can serve big truths."

Macbeth, Norman, "Darwinism: A Time for Funerals," interview in *Towards*, vol. 2, no. 2 (Spring 1982), pp. 18-31.

p. 18   "But a much deeper and more penetrating analysis of the problem was put together by Professor Ronald H. Brady of Ramapo College in the quarterly called *Systematic Zoology* for December 1979. . . . He seemed to me to utterly destroy the entire idea of natural selection as presently conceived."

p. 22   "So here we have another example, a living example of the basic theme in my book—that they are not revealing all the dirt under the rug in their approach to the public. There is a feeling that they ought to keep back the worst so that their public reputation would not suffer and the Creationists wouldn't get any ammunition."

p. 22   "A few minutes ago I mentioned Ron Brady's article on natural selection in *Systematic Zoology*. I will not name the man or the college in this case but it was an Ivy League college and a respectable man. . . . So they told [a student] to go on down to the library . . . and read it right there. He came back in half an hour and said, '. . . the article isn't there, it's been scissored out.' Next day, the assistant professor went into the office of the head of the department on some other business and on the head's table he saw the missing pages. . . . The head of the department said, 'Well, of course I don't believe in censorship in any form, but I just couldn't bear the idea of my students reading that article.' End of story."

Morre, Oliver S., III, "The Year's Top 100 Innovations," *Science Digest*, vol. 93 (December 1985), pp. 6, 27-61.

p. 6   "For this issue's special section, [Helen] Howard surveyed over 1,200 corporations, universities, colleges, scientific and engineering associations, non-profit institutions and agencies for their ideas of significant innovations and the people responsible. Receiving over 500 nominations from these varies sources, she then coordinated efforts . . . to narrow the field to 100." [Note: Not one of the 100 outstanding scientific innovations of 1985 was based on discoveries or advances in evolutionary "science."—Editor]

p. 27   "Science is a relatively recent endeavor in the course of human history. . . . The word *scientist* was coined only in 1840 by Cambridge historian and philosopher William Whewell.

              "Today, science impacts every corner of our culture."

Slobodkin, Lawrence B., "The Strategy of Evolution," *American Scientist*, vol. 52 (September 1964), pp. 342-357.

p. 342   "In the literature of biology, discussions of evolution consist of either historical statements, whether phylogenetic or genetic, and of physiological or morphological descriptions. Despite this reticence on the part of biologists, an enormous amount of bad philosophy, psychology, and, on occasion, political theory, has been initiated by a consideration of evolutionary phenomena. There is apparently an almost irresistible temptation to try to find some point, purpose, or goal in the evolutionary process. In some sense, the narrowly biological discussions of evolution are unsatisfying, so that para-biologists feel called upon to provide a theatrically acceptable finale."

Smith, Huston, "Evolution and Evolutionism," *The Christian Century*, vol. 99 (July 7-14, 1982), pp. 755-757. Smith was Professor of Religion, Syracuse University.

p. 755   "One reason education undoes belief is its teaching of evolution; Darwin's own drift from orthodoxy to agnosticism was symptomatic. Martin Lings is probably right in saying that 'more cases of loss of religious faith are to be traced to the theory of evolution . . . than to anything else.'"

p. 756   "Neo-Darwinism's proponents do not present it as a mere description of life's journey on this planet, they claim that it is a theory explaining that journey. Specifically, neo-Darwinists claim that natural selection working on chance mutations accounts for what has occurred. But 'natural selection' turns out to be a tautology, while the word 'chance' denotes an occurrence that it inexplicable. A theory that claims to explain while standing with one foot on a tautology and the other in an explanatory void is in trouble."

p. 757   "As Professor Pierre Grassé, who for 30 years held the chair in evolution at the Sorbonne, has written: 'The probability of dust carried by the wind reproducing Dürer's 'Melancholia' is less infinitesimal than the probability of copy errors in the DNA molecules leading to the formation of the eye.'"

Taylor, F. J., "California's Strangest Crop," *Saturday Evening Post*, October 2, 1954, pp. 32-33, 54-56.

p. 56   "So indestructible that it can survive in the poorest soil through drought, pests, grass fires, or years of neglect, it revives when fed and irrigated and pruned, and yields prodigious crops."

p. 56   "By pruning back the branches to blunt stubs, chopping off the roots and digging out the burl, an olive grower can lift and transplant a full-grown tree any time. After a year to recover from this shocking treatment, the burl sends out new roots for moisture, grows new branches, and bears crops anew."

Tudge, Colin, "Evolution and the End of Innocence," *New Scientist*, vol. 122 (April 15, 1989), pp. 58-59.

p. 59   "Perhaps, though, there is a reference to this change in attitude in the stories of *Genesis*: stories which some anthropologists feel are folk memories of pre-agricultural times. The Garden of Eden was the rich land of the Middle East, in the times when people were hunters and gatherers, and the fallow deer and gazelle practically gave themselves up: and the banishment from the garden into harsh realities of farming, are memories of the time when those animals had been overhunted (or perhaps the climate changed) and people became obligated to live in the relentless manner of Cain, the tiller of the ground, and of Abel, the keeper of sheep, and of their multitudinous descendants. But why were Adam and Eve banished from the Garden in the first place? Because, says *Genesis*, they had eaten the fruit of the tree 'of the knowledge of good and evil.'

"They had learnt, indeed, for the first time in human development, to think for themselves, learnt that anything they wanted to know could be found out by further thinking."

Vaughan, H. W., *Types and Market Classes of Live Stock* (College Book Co., 1945).

p. 85   "The number of animals per car varies greatly depending on the size and age of the animals. For example, a stock car 36 feet long will hold 55 calves weighing 400 pounds each, 35 yearlings weighing 700 pounds, 25 cattle averaging 1000 pounds, 21 cattle weighing 1200 pounds, or 19 cattle weighing 1400 pounds each.

"Reports of stock yards and railroads show that the average number of meat animals to the carload is for cattle about 25 hogs in single deck cars about 75, and sheep about 120 per deck."

Weber, Christian O., *Basic Philosophies of Education* (New York: 1960).

p. 252   "Dewey was the first philosopher of education to make systematic use of Darwin's ideas."

Index of Names